NARRATIVES OF THE MISSION OF GEORGE BOGLE TO TIBET, AND OF THE JOURNEY OF THOMAS MANNING TO LHASA.

NARRATIVES OF THE MISSION OF GEORGE BOGLE TO TIBET, AND OF THE JOURNEY OF THOMAS MANNING TO LHASA.

EDITED, WITH NOTES, AN INTRODUCTION, AND LIVES OF MR. BOGLE AND MR. MANNING

BY

CLEMENTS R. MARKHAM, C.B., F.R.S.
GEOGRAPHICAL DEPARTMENT, INDIA OFFICE.

GYAN

Published by

GYAN

Gyan Publishing House
5, Ansari Road
Daryaganj, New Delhi-110002
Phone: 011-47034999, 9811692060
E-mail: books@gyanbooks.com

Distribution Network
gyanbooks.com
India, USA, Canada, UK, Australia, France

ISBN : 978-81-212-3807-6 (PB)
First Published, 1876

2nd Impression 2020

Printed at: Gyan Press, Delhi.

Narratives of the
Mission of George Bogle to Tibet, and of the
Journey of Thomas Manning to Lhasa.
Author: Clements R. Markham

NARRATIVES

OF THE

MISSION OF GEORGE BOGLE

TO

TIBET,

AND OF THE

JOURNEY OF THOMAS MANNING

TO

LHASA.

EDITED, WITH NOTES, AN INTRODUCTION, AND LIVES OF MR. BOGLE AND MR. MANNING

BY

CLEMENTS R. MARKHAM, C.B., F.R.S.

GEOGRAPHICAL DEPARTMENT, INDIA OFFICE.

LONDON:
TRÜBNER AND CO., LUDGATE HILL.

1876.

THE RIGHT HON. WARREN HASTINGS.

FROM AN ORIGINAL MINIATURE BY OZIAS HUMPHRY, R.A.

DEDICATION.

To the Right Hon. the Lord Northbrook, G.M.S.I., *Viceroy and Governor-General of India.*

My dear Lord Northbrook,

I am glad to be allowed to inscribe to you, from whom, when I was your Private Secretary, in times past, I received so much kindness, my editorial labours in connection with a book which cannot, I venture to think, fail to have interest for the Viceroy of India.

The most important portion of the volume would, without doubt, have been dedicated to Warren Hastings, the first Governor-General, by his envoy Mr. George Bogle, if untoward circumstances had not intervened to prevent its publication. A century has since elapsed, and now that the intention of Warren Hastings that it should be given to the world is fulfilled, it is appropriate that the book should be dedicated to his successor, the present Viceroy and Governor-General of India.

In the long period that has intervened, since the first Governor-General retired, no greater advances have been made towards the establishment of friendly commercial intercourse between India and the countries on the northern side of the Himálaya than in the time of your Lordship's administration. A mission has visited Kashgar, the Pamír table-land has been explored, and Mr. Edgar has held friendly converse on the Jelep-la with the Tibetan officials of Pari-jong, the prelude of further steps towards acquiring the goodwill of the Lhasa Government.

The contents of the present volume will, I trust, prove to be useful contributions towards that knowledge which will be the means of some day re-establishing friendly intercourse between India and Tibet; and in the hope that my efforts towards that end will receive your approval,

I remain,

Dear Lord Northbrook,

Yours with much regard and respect,

CLEMENTS R. MARKHAM.

Geographical Department, India Office,
December, 1875.

PREFACE.

It has long been known that the first British mission to Tibet was sent by Warren Hastings in 1774 under Mr. George Bogle, B.C.S., that a great friendship was formed between Mr. Bogle and the Teshu Lama, and that intercourse was then established between the Governments of British India and Tibet. But up to the present time no full account of this important mission has been given to the world. All attempts to find adequate materials among the records at Calcutta, or at the India Office, have failed.

It is less generally known that the only Englishman who ever visited Lhasa, the capital of Tibet, and saw the Dalai Lama, was Mr. Thomas Manning, an adventurous traveller who performed that extraordinary feat in 1811. No account has hitherto been published of Mr. Manning's remarkable journey.

These two gaps in the history of intercourse between India and Tibet have now been filled up.

The whole of Mr. Bogle's journals, memoranda, official and private correspondence, have been carefully preserved by his family in Scotland. Through the kindness and public spirit of Miss Brown of Lanfine, in Ayrshire, the representative of the Bogle family, these valuable manuscripts, after having been judiciously arranged by Mr. Gairdner of Kilmarnock, were placed in the hands of the present editor. They were contained in a large box, and consisted of journals, memoranda of various kinds, and on many subjects; numerous bundles of private letters, including correspondence with Warren Hastings, Sir Elijah Impey, Sir Gilbert Elliot, Mrs. Morehead, Dr. Hamilton, and the members of Mr. Bogle's family; appointments, minutes of conversations, and official despatches. No commencement had been made of a work intended for publication. The whole of this voluminous mass of papers had to be carefully read through and annotated before any attempt could be made to arrange a consecutive narrative of the mission. My object has been to keep the author constantly in the foreground, and to avoid any sign of editorial intrusiveness, and, as the journal was fragmentary, and it was necessary to supplement it occasionally with extracts from letters and other materials, there were some difficulties in adhering to this plan. They have, however, been overcome, and a connected history of the Mission to Tibet is now presented to the world. It must, however, be remembered that Mr. Bogle had not prepared any of his materials for the press, that they are submitted in a more or less crude form a century after they were written, and that, therefore, it would be unfair to judge of them as of a work completed and revised by its author.

Mr. Manning appears to have hastily jotted down his first impressions, day by day, in a rough note-book, which was copied out fair by his sister, and has since remained in manuscript. He was a man of learning and great ability, and was well able to have written a good account of his remarkable journey. He never did so. But, through the kindness of his nephew, the Rev. C. R. Manning, Rector of Diss, in Norfolk, I have had the rough journal placed in my hands. Thus an account of the visit to Lhasa of the only Englishman who ever entered that famous city, is presented to the world. It must be remembered that Manning's narrative is from the hasty and desultory jottings of a note-book. We are fortunate to have obtained this relic, and must make the most of it. Good or bad, it stands alone. No other countryman of ours has ever followed in Manning's footsteps. And; for those who know how to find it, there is much wheat to be gathered from amongst Mr. Manning's chaff.

In my introduction, I have attempted, in a narrative form

with foot-note references, to enumerate all the sources of information respecting Great Tibet, and the region between it and British India; and especially to furnish particulars as to the visits of Europeans to those countries. My first object is thus to show the exact positions, in history, which are occupied by the mission sent by Warren Hastings and conducted by Mr. Bogle, and by the journey of Mr. Manning to Lhasa. My second object is to supply facilities for the exhaustive study of an important subject, and one which ought to be thoroughly understood by all public men connected with British India, and by all who interest themselves in the progress and welfare of our Eastern Empire.

The introduction is followed by two biographical sketches, one of Mr. George Bogle, B.C.S., and the other of Mr. Thomas Manning.

The narratives of Grueber, Desideri, and Horace della Penna, Catholic priests who visited Lhasa in the fifteenth and sixteenth centuries, are given in an Appendix.

I should not have been able to complete my task if I had not received much kind assistance from many quarters. In the first place, the proof sheets of Bogle's narrative have had the inestimable advantage of revision from Mr. Brian Hodgson, who, in addition, has supplied me with many hints from his vast storehouse of information. I have also to thank Sir John Davis, Colonel Yule, Colonel Haughton, Dr. Hooker, Commodore Jansen of the Hague, Professor Veth of Leyden, the learned President of the Dutch Geographical Society, Mr. Major of the British Museum, Mr. Charles B. Phillimore, and Colonel Montgomerie, for valuable assistance.

The staff of the Geographical Department of the India Office have zealously made the aid they have given in the production of this volume a part of their extra work. Mr. Trelawney Saunders, besides preparing the maps, has been indefatigable in identifying names of places, and in conducting difficult bits of research. It must be remembered that a single identification, represented perhaps by a sentence or a word, may have occupied many hours and even days of weary searching and close study. Mr. Charles E. D. Black, whose aptitude for orderly and lucid exposition, and whose accomplishments as a linguist render his co-operation most acceptable, has given a helping hand, which is only very partially represented by the translations in the Appendix. Last, but not least, Mr. W. Ronson has been a most valuable assistant in the labour of passing the sheets through the press, and in attending to their methodical arrangement.

TABLE OF CONTENTS.

INTRODUCTION.

NOTE ON THE MAPS OF TIBET, NEPAL, SIKKIM, AND BHUTAN.

BIOGRAPHICAL SKETCH OF GEORGE BOGLE.

BIOGRAPHICAL SKETCH OF THOMAS MANNING.

NARRATIVE

OF THE

MISSION OF MR. GEORGE BOGLE TO TIBET

(1774).

CHAPTER I.

MISSION TO TIBET.

LETTER FROM THE TESHU LAMA — MISSION TO TIBET — APPOINTMENT OF MR. BOGLE — HIS INSTRUCTIONS.

CHAPTER II.

FROM KUCH BAHAR TO TASSISUDON.

CHAPTER III.

TASSISUDON, THE CAPITAL OF BHUTAN.

CHAPTER IV.

HISTORY AND GOVERNMENT OF BHUTAN.

CHAPTER V.

BHUTAN: NEGOTIATIONS.

CHAPTER VI.

SUGGESTIONS RESPECTING BHUTAN AND ASSAM.

CHAPTER VII.

THE JOURNEY TO TIBET.

CHAPTER VIII.

AT DESHERIPGAY.

CHAPTER IX.

RIDE FROM DESHERIPGAY TO TESHU LUMBO.

CHAPTER X.

TESHU LUMBO.

CHAPTER XI.

A VISIT TO A TIBETAN COUNTRY SEAT.

CHAPTER XII.

AN ACCOUNT OF TIBET.

FACE OF THE COUNTRY — PRODUCE — FOOD — DRESS OF THE PEOPLE — PRIESTS AND NUNS — HORSES AND OTHER ANIMALS — HOUSES — DISPOSAL OF DEAD BODIES — POLYANDRY.

CHAPTER XIII.

TRADE OF TIBET.

CHAPTER XIV.

NEGOTIATIONS.

CHAPTER XV.

CONVERSATIONS WITH THE TESHU LAMA AT TESHU LUMBO.

CHAPTER XVI.

THE EPISODE WITH THE CHAUDURI.

CHAPTER XVII.

RETURN FROM TIBET TO BENGAL. NEGOTIATIONS IN BHUTAN.

CHAPTER XVIII.

GENERAL REPORT BY MR. BOGLE ON HIS RETURN FROM TIBET.

CHAPTER XIX.

JOURNEY OF THE TESHU LAMA TO PEKING, AND HIS DEATH. PROJECT OF MR. BOGLE FOR MEETING THE LAMA AT PEKING.

JOURNEY OF MR. THOMAS MANNING TO LHASA

(1811–12).

CHAPTER I.

JOURNEY FROM CANTALBARY TO PARI-JONG.

CHAPTER II.

FROM PARI-JONG TO GIANSU.

CHAPTER III.

RESIDENCE AT GIANSU.

CHAPTER IV.

JOURNEY FROM GIANSU TO LHASA.

CHAPTER V.

LHASA.

CHAPTER VI.

VISIT TO THE GRAND LAMA.

CHAPTER VII.

STORY OF THE RIOT—EXECUTION OF A GOOD MANDARIN.

CHAPTER VIII.

RESIDENCE AT LHASA.

CHAPTER IX.

FRAGMENTARY NOTES—RETURN JOURNEY.

APPENDIX.

LIST OF ILLUSTRATIONS.

MAPS.

ERRATA.

Page .lix, line 24, *for* 1780 *read* 1680.

" lxiii, " 2, " Gauvil *read* Gaubil.

" " " 10, " Bicin (Bi-tsion) *read* Biciu (Bi-t[illegible]).

" lxvi, line 2 from bottom; page lxvii, line 2 of note [1]; and page 126, line 14 of note [3], *for* Guiseppe *read* Giuseppe.

" xciv, line 8 of note [1], *for* Tubeto riental *read* Tubet oriental.

" cxxv, line 5, *for* Purbe tou *read* Purbet ou.

" 135, line 6 of note, *for* desert of Gobi *read* Kirghiz Steppe.

INTRODUCTION.

THE first Governor-General of India conceived the plan of opening friendly commercial intercourse between the people over whom he ruled and the natives of the lofty table-land behind the snowy peaks to the north. On this grand object Warren Hastings bestowed much thought, and he gradually developed a policy which was continuous while his influence lasted. He took a broad and enlightened view of the requirements of the case, and he appears to have seen from the first that the end could only be gained by persistent efforts extending over a long period.

It is owing to the absence of a continuous policy that this and many other great measures which were once full of promise have produced no permanent results. Warren Hastings opened a correspondence with the rulers of Tibet and Bhutan; he succeeded in establishing most friendly relations by the despatch of an embassy; his liberal encouragement of trade brought down crowds of mountaineers to his fair at Rangpúr; he followed up his first mission by a second and third to Bhutan, with the object of cementing the recently formed friendship; and finally, he sent a fourth embassy to Bhutan, which extended its operations into Tibet. Yet, when the master-mind was removed, the work so admirably commenced was abandoned. No English official has since held personal intercourse with the rulers of Tibet, and when, a quarter of a century after the retirement of Warren Hastings, a solitary Englishman did once force his way to Lhasa, no use was made of his brave and successful enterprise, and he was left to perish or to return, as chance would have it.

So completely was the policy of opening commercial intercourse between India and the Trans-Himálayan region abandoned, that the very history of the Hastings negotiations was forgotten,[1] and most of the valuable records of the Tibet and Bhutan missions were lost. Thus the knowledge that was then acquired with so much care, the lessons of experience that were taught, instead of being carefully stored up and made available as a point of departure for future efforts, have been totally disregarded. It is by a series of mere accidents that copies of records long since lost or destroyed, owing to official neglect, have been preserved through the more patriotic and discriminating care of private families.

The account of the important mission of George Bogle to Bhutan and Tibet has been gathered partly from journals, partly from official despatches, and partly from private correspondence; and it is now presented for the first time in a connected form. That of Mr. Manning's extraordinary journey to Lhasa is from a fragmentary series of notes and jottings which alone remain to bear testimony to a feat which still remains unparalleled.

As an introduction to the perusal of these narratives, I propose to give an account of the region to which they refer; to furnish some information respecting what is known of the inhabitants, their history and religion; and to pass in review the several steps by which our existing knowledge has been acquired, and the events, so far as we can learn them, which have formed the more recent history of Tibet, Nepal, Sikkim, and Bhutan. To perform such a task with any approach to completeness would require a separate volume, and the possession of local knowledge. My aim in this introduction will therefore

[1] See Hamilton's 'East India Gazetteer.' This writer, with access to official records, was so ignorant, that he did not know the difference between the Deb Rajah of Bhutan and the Dalai Lama.

be confined to such a general glance at the subject as will suffice to place the narratives in their due relative positions, and to explain all circumstances relating to them directly or indirectly. Another object will be to furnish references, in their proper order, through which this important subject may be more thoroughly studied and understood; and thus, in some measure, to assist in replacing and restoring those foundations of a great policy which the genius of Warren Hastings had laid, but which subsequent neglect has destroyed.

The Himálayan system is composed of three great culminating chains, running more or less parallel to each other for their whole length, from the gorge of the Indus to that of the Dihong; and the lofty region of Great Tibet lies mainly between the inner and outer range, with the Central Chain, whence most of the rivers of northern India take their rise, running through its length. It is with the portion of the Himálayan region which includes Great Tibet and the countries between it and the plains of India, that the narratives composing this volume have to do; and, therefore, the introductory remarks will be mainly confined to that portion.

The inner and most northern of the three ranges is naturally divided into a western and an eastern section. The western is known as the Karakorum Range, separating the valley of the Indus from that of the Yarkand River and other streams belonging to the inland system of Lob-nor. It has vast glaciers and lofty peaks, including that called K 2, which is 28,000 feet above the sea,[1] while it is traversed by passes of great height, such as the Chang-chenmo, 19,000 feet,[2] and the Karakorum, 18,000 feet above the sea. The sources of three great rivers are on the southern slopes of the northern range, and forcing their way through the central and southern chains, they reach the plains of India: namely, the Indus, Sutlej, and Brahmaputra.

[1] K 2 stands between the parts of this range called Mustang and Karakorum, referring to the Mustang and Karakorum passes.

[2] There are two Chang-chenmo passes: that of Pangtung-la, 18,900, and of Changlung-barma la, 19,280 feet above the sea. (Trotter's Map.)

The eastern section of the Northern Range forms the natural northern boundary of Great Tibet; for although an extensive region farther north is included on the maps as part of Tibet, it is really inhabited by wandering, independent tribes, called Hor. and Sok.[1] Tibetan influence, so far as we yet know, is here confined to the route to Rudok and the Thok Jalung gold fields,[2] and to a few monasteries in the mountains and on the banks of Lake Tengri-nor, although Tibetan sovereignty must be considered as extending to the Kuen-lun Mountains. This lofty region is almost entirely unknown to Europeans, except through the Lama surveys.[3] It is drained by streams flowing into a system of inland lakes, and its elevation above the sea has only been ascertained at three points. Mr. Johnson, in his journey to Khotan, entered the region of inland drainage by the Chang-chenmo pass, and found the height of the Lingtsi plain to be 17,000 feet. The Pundit of 1867 found the gold mines of Thok Jalung, which are on this lofty plateau, to be 16,330 feet; and Colonel Montgomerie's explorer of 1872 reached the shores of Lake Tengri-nor, and ascertained its height to be 15,000 feet above the sea. The great Northern Chain of the Himálayan system, called the Karakorum Range in its western section, is here known as the *Ninjinthangla* or *Nyenchhen-tang-la* Mountains, and separates the inland system of lakes from the basin of the Brahmaputra. To the westward it commences at the famous central peak or knot called Kailas[4] by the Hindus, and Gangri by the Tibetans, which is 22,000 feet above the sea.

[1] Horsok is the name given by the Tibetans to the whole region between the Northern Himálayan Range (Nyenchhén-thanglá) and the Kuen-lun. It is inhabited by two distinct races, called Hor and Sok: Horpa is the western half of this region, and Sokpa the eastern half, as well as part of Sokyeul, round the Kokonor Lake. They are all styled Kháchhén (Muhammadans) by the Tibetans. Sokyeul is the same as Tangut. The Hor are Turks, and the Sok are of Mongol race. *Yeul* means an encampment, so that Sokyeul is the encampment of the Soks or Mongols.

[2] The northern slopes of the range are reported to contain a whole string of gold fields, extending from the meridian of Lhasa to that of Rudok.

[3] See p. lxi for some account of this survey.

[4] On the map of D'Anville, in Du Halde, it is called *Kentaisse*.

The chain then continues in an easterly and north-easterly direction, forming the northern watershed of the Brahmaputra, throwing up lofty peaks, one of which is reported by the explorer of 1872 to be at least 25,000 feet high; while the pass by which he crossed the range to the inland plateau was 17,200 feet above the sea. The name given to the eastern section of this most northern of the ranges by Mr. Brian Hodgson is *Nyenchhen-tang-la*;[1] and the same name is referred by the explorer of 1872 to one of the peaks. Mr. Trelawney Saunders has proposed as the name of this range, Gang-ri,[2] the Tibetan for "snowy mountain," by which the Kailas Peak is known in Tibet. But perhaps the most convenient way of distinguishing this important but almost unknown mountain chain will be by referring to it as the inner or northern chain of the Himálayan system.

Parallel to the Northern Range runs the Central Range of the Himálaya, which is also little known, and but very partially explored. The section of this range with which we have to deal commences at the Mariam-la pass, near the Kailas or Gangri Peak. Here a comparatively low saddle connects the Northern and Central ranges, and separates the valley of the Sutlej from that of the Brahmaputra. To the eastward this Central Chain, on its northern side, forms the southern watershed of the Brahmaputra, while on its southern slopes are the sources of many important rivers, which, forcing their way through the Southern Chain of the Himálaya, eventually join the Ganges or the Brahmaputra. Such are the rivers Kali, Karnali, Narayani, Buria Gandak, Tirsuli Gandak, Bhotia Kosi, and Arun, in Nepal; possibly some of the feeders of the Monass, in Bhutan, and the Lopra-cachu, or Subanshiri, farther east. Only three Englishmen have ever crossed the Central Chain to the eastward of the Mariam-la pass (all at the same point), namely, Bogle, Turner,

[1] See 'Selections' (Government of Bengal), No. xxvii. p. 93; and 'J. A. S. B.,' ii., of 1853.

[2] Klaproth has Gang-dis-ri. *Gang* is snow, in Tibetan; *dis*, colour, in Sanscrit; and *Ri*, a mountain, in Tibetan. ('Magasin Asiatique,' p. 233. Paris, 1825.)

CHAPTER XV.

CONVERSATIONS WITH THE TESHU LAMA AT TESHU LUMBO.

CHAPTER XVI.

THE EPISODE WITH THE CHAUDURI.

CHAPTER XVII.

RETURN FROM TIBET TO BENGAL. NEGOTIATIONS IN BHUTAN.

CHAPTER XVIII.

GENERAL REPORT BY MR. BOGLE ON HIS RETURN FROM TIBET.

CHAPTER XIX.

JOURNEY OF THE TESHU LAMA TO PEKING, AND HIS DEATH. PROJECT OF MR. BOGLE FOR MEETING THE LAMA AT PEKING.

JOURNEY OF MR. THOMAS MANNING TO LHASA

(1811–12).

CHAPTER I.

JOURNEY FROM CANTALBARY TO PARI-JONG.

Teshu Lumbo was visited by Bogle and Turner, and is fully described by the former envoy, in the following pages.

Between Janglaché and Shigatzé two rivers fall into the Tsanpu on the south bank, called the Shakiadong-chu and the Shiábgi-chu. At a distance of 30 miles up the valley of the former river, 13,860 feet above the sea, on one of the slopes of the Central Chain, is the great monastery of Sakia-jong (Sankia of D'Anville), the head-quarters of the Red Cap sect of Buddhists. It is 30 miles from Janglaché, and 48 from Shigatzé. In the lower part of the Shakiadong-chu there are many villages, with cornfields, and a considerable town nestles at the foot of the "Red Cap" monastery.

Near Shigatzé two rivers, one from the north and the other from the south, enter the Brahmaputra. They have been traced from their sources, so that here we first get a knowledge of the whole width of the valley, from the Southern and Central to the Northern Chain of the Himálaya. The southern river is the Penanang-chu or Painam.[1] It rises from two lakes, discovered by Mr. Bogle, at the foot of the Chumalhari Peak, on the Southern Range, forces its way through a gorge in the Central Range,[2] where there are hot springs,[3] waters the fertile valleys of Giansu[4] (Giangze-jong) and Painam (Pena-jong), and falls into the Brahmaputra near Shigatzé. This river was first followed by Bogle along its whole course in 1774, then by Captain Turner in 1782, and as far as Giansu by Manning in 1811.

The river flowing from the north is the Shiang-chu. It rises near the Khalamba-la pass, over the Northern Range, which is 17,200 feet above the level of the sea, and after a lateral course in the mountains of about 30 miles, it flows south-

[1] Monotchou of D'Anville.

[2] In crossing the Central Range, Bogle describes the route as "passing through valleys bounded by bleak and barren hills, through whose openings we saw distant mountains covered with snow" (p. 74). Turner says: "The river has a considerable fall, and hurried with violence over a rocky bed. High rocks, perpendicular and bare, and vast impending crags" (p. 221).

[3] See p. 182; and Turner, p. 220.

[4] Tchiantse of D'Anville; and Gialdze-dzoung of Klaproth.

wards down a valley for 50 miles into the Brahmaputra. In this valley of the Shiang-chu is situated the town and monastery of Chamnamring[1] (Namling), 12,220 feet above the sea, the small palace of Desheripgay, and other religious establishments. The only Englishman who has ever visited this valley is Mr. Bogle. He was followed, at an interval of nearly a century, by Colonel Montgomerie's explorer of 1872.

From the mouth of the Shiang-chu to the point where the road to Lhasa crosses the river, a distance of 85 miles, the course of the Brahmaputra is entirely unknown, except from the Lama Survey;[2] but at that point it has been crossed by Mr. Manning, by the Pundit of 1866, and the explorer of 1872. The river of Lhasa, called the Ki-chu[3] by the explorer of 1872, falls into the Brahmaputra, in longitude 90° 30′ E., 2 miles to the eastward of Chusul-jong, where the river is 11,334 feet above the sea. The city of Lhasa, the capital of the U province, and the residence of the Dalai Lama and of the Chinese political agents, is in the valley of the Ki-chu, and about 25 miles from its junction with the Brahmaputra, in latitude 29° 39′ 17″ N., and 11,700 feet above the sea. Lhasa stands in a level plain, surrounded by mountains, and dotted over with populous monasteries. This upper valley of the Brahmaputra, though 11,000 to 15,000 feet above the sea, yields harvests of barley and millet, has abundant pastures, and there are clumps of trees, and even gardens, round the towns and monasteries.

Beyond the point where the Lhasa route crosses the river, in longitude 90° 40′ E., the course of the Brahmaputra within the mountains is entirely unknown (except from the Lama Survey)[4] for a distance of about 400 miles, when, under the name of Dihong, the mighty stream emerges into the valley of Assam

[1] Chámnamrim of D'Anville.

[2] See p. lxi.

[3] Kaltiou of D'Anville; and Galdjao-mouren ("la rivière furibonde") of Klaproth, who gives a long account of the Lhasa river. ('Magasin Asiatique,' ii. p. 263. Paris, 1826.)

[4] See p. lxi. The Lama Survey appears to extend only to the Central Range, the latitudes being carried much too far south.

and becomes the Brahmaputra of the plains. Yet there can be no reasonable doubt that the Tsanpu of Great Tibet and the Brahmaputra of the plains are one and the same river. The question has occupied the attention of geographers for upwards of a century. In his instructions, dated 1774, Warren Hastings specially enjoined Mr. Bogle to inform himself respecting the course of the Brahmaputra.[1] D'Anville, and afterwards Klaproth, believed that the Tibet river was the upper course of the Irrawaddy. But there never appears to have been any doubt, among English geographers, that Rennell was correct in his identification of the Tsanpu with the Brahmaputra. In 1825 Captains Burlton and Wilcox were sent to explore its course. Burlton followed up the course of the Dihong, until he was stopped by wild tribes, while Wilcox crossed the water parting towards Burma, and reached the banks of the Irrawaddy.[2] From the point reached by Burlton on the Dihong, to the place where Manning crossed the Tsanpu, there is an interval of about 400 miles, and a difference of level of 11,000 feet, which is entirely unknown.

On the south the Great Tibetan valley of the Tsanpu is bounded by the Central Range of the Himálaya, the culminating peaks of which are covered with eternal snow, while the sides bear the weight of enormous glaciers. But the snow line on the Central Chain is much higher than that on the Southern Himálaya. As the snow is deposited by southerly winds it falls mainly on the culminating ridge which faces the south, and screens the central ridge behind it. Thus the snow line is 5000 feet lower down on the Southern Himálaya than on the Central Chain. From this latter Range many lofty saddles branch in several directions, in some places forming inland lakes, in

[1] See p. 9.

[2] See 'Asiatic Researches,' xviii. p. 314, for the work of Wilcox and his colleague. In this paper Wilcox replied to Klaproth, and maintained that the Dihong was the Tsanpu. He was never answered by Klaproth, who died in 1835. Subsequently, both Pemberton and Hodgson received native information identifying the Brahmaputra and Dihong with the Tsanpu.

others directing the course of rivers, either to the Tsanpu or through the gorges of the Southern Range. Most of the region between the Central and Southern Ranges is within the territory of Tibet. Much of our knowledge of this part of the country is still dependent on the map compiled by D'Anville in 1733, from the survey of the Lamas, and the rest is mainly derived from native explorers.

To the eastward, in an entirely unknown country, the Central Range is drained by numerous tributaries of a great river, called the Lopra-cachu, which appear to break through the Southern Range and reach the plains of Assam, under the name of the Subanshiri, or Lohit. In this eastern part of the Central Range is also situated that remarkable lake of Palti, Peiti, or Yamdok-chu, which is delineated by D'Anville as surrounding a large central island, like a moat encircling a castle. But the western shore alone has been described, and Mr. Manning is the only Englishman who has ever seen it. Both he and the Pundit of 1866 describe it as being separated from the valley of the Tsanpu by a range of mountains, called the Khamba-la,[1] a spur from the Central Range; and the Pundit adds; that the lake has no outlet. Our information respecting Lake Palti will be found condensed in a note to Mr. Manning's narrative at page 244.

To the westward of the Lopra-cachu basin there appears to be a high saddle, connecting the Central and Southern Ranges, for the river of Painam, already referred to, flows north from the Chumalhari Peak to the Tsanpu, forcing its way through the Central Range.

Farther westward our principal informant respecting the Central Range, and the region between it and the Southern Himálayas, is Colonel Montgomerie's explorer of 1871, known as No. 9.

West of the Painam basin various lofty spurs from the

[1] The Chinese geographers, quoted by Klaproth, name the Khamba-la as on the boundary between the provinces of U and Tsang.

Central Chain lead the drainage, for a distance of 150 miles, into the Arun river, which breaks through the Southern Himálaya into Nepal. North of the Arun basin, and, like the Palti lake, encircled by spurs from the Central Range, is the Chomto-dong lake, about 20 miles in length and 16 broad, and without an outlet. It is not shown on the map of D'Anville, and was, therefore, discovered by No. 9 in 1871. This lake is 14,700 feet above the sea. The main chain of the Central Range towers over the Chomto-dong lake on its northern side, and is crossed by the Lagulung-la pass 16,000 feet above the sea, where the glacier ice is seen close to the road taken by travellers. According to No. 9 this part of the region between the Central and Southern Ranges belongs to Sikkim, and the boundary between Sikkim and Tibet is on the Lagulung-la of the Central Range. The Central Range has also been crossed (by No. 9) by the Dango-la pass above the great Sakia monastery, and 28 miles east of the Lagalung-la. The western branch of the Arun flows from west to east through an extensive plain, between the Central and Southern Ranges, called the Dingri[1] Maidan, 13,900 feet above the sea, where there is a town of two hundred and fifty houses. The Dingri river is believed to rise in a large lake, which is shown but not named on D'Anville's map, but which was heard of as the Dalgu-chu, 15,000 feet above the sea, by Colonel Montgomerie's explorers. It has never been visited. Still farther to the west the Central Chain is crossed by the Taku-la pass,[2] which has never been explored; the No-la pass, at a height 16,623 feet above the sea; and the Photu-la, at a height of 15,080 feet. The latter is just above the town of Loh-Mantang,[3] a place of very considerable trade, and thousands of wild ponies find pasture on the slopes along the pass.

In Eastern Nepal, farther west, the only pass with which

[1] Tinkia of D'Anville.

[2] To the north of the Chinese post of Jonka-jong.

[3] Mustang (?).

we have become acquainted is that of Taklakhar, in the gorge of the Karnali. But the range in Kumaon and Bussahir has been examined, and four passes have been explored.[1]

Thus the Central Range of the Himálaya has been crossed at six different points from east to west, within the region of which we are treating. First, at the gorge of the Painam river, by Bogle, Turner, and Manning; next, at the Lagulung-la and Dong-la passes, by No. 9; next, at the No-la pass, by the Pundit of 1866; and lastly, at the Photu-la pass. Very magnificent views of its long line of glaciers and snowy peaks, forming a continuous chain, have been enjoyed by Dr. Hooker from the Donkia pass, by Bogle and Turner from the foot of Chumalhari, by Manning looking back from the Khamba-la, and by Colonel Montgomerie's explorers from many other points. From its northern face the ravines, opening into valleys, slope pretty regularly to the Tsanpu. But to the south, the region between the Central and Southern ranges is broken by long parallel spurs and saddles of great height, in two instances completely encircling large lakes, in others leading the rivers for considerable distances in courses parallel to the axes of the chains, before they burst through one or other of them, and flow down the meridional slopes.

Such is the topographical aspect of Great Tibet, or the provinces of U and Tsang, comprised in the valley of the Tsanpu, or upper Brahmaputra, and in the broken region parallel to it, and at a greater elevation, between the Central and Southern ranges.

We next come to the consideration of the Southern Himálaya[2] and its chain of stupendous peaks, of the hydrography of its southern slope, and of the routes leading from India over its dangerous and little-known passes.

[1] Two from Milun to Gartuk; one from Badrinath, on the Ganges, to Gartuk; and one from Nilung to Gugé; besides the Dalhousie route, which leads to where the Sutlej breaks out of Tibetan territory at Shipki.

[2] The Rimola Mountains of D'Anville and the Chinese geographers. Perhaps a misprint for Himola.

The portion of the Southern Himálaya between Great Tibet and India consists of a stupendous chain of snow-clad mountains, with a line of culminating peaks, and slopes deeply furrowed into alternate ravines and ridges, which gradually sink down into the valleys of the Ganges and Brahmaputra. The distance from the culminating ridge to the plain averages about ninety miles; a breadth which Mr. Brian Hodgson describes by dividing it into three equal longitudinal zones: the lower comprising the Dhúns, or Maris of Nepal, and the Dúars of Bhutan, as well as the *bhabur* or sal forest, and the *terai*;[1] the middle, between the Dhúns and the snow line; and the upper or alpine zone. The first ranges from the plains to 4000 feet; the central, from 4000 feet to 10,000 feet; and the upper, from 10,000 feet to 29,000 feet above the sea level. The amount of heat and cold in these several zones depends almost entirely on the elevation, there being a diminution of temperature equal to 3° or 3½° Fahr. for every thousand feet of height. But, as regards moisture, every movement to the west or north-west brings the traveller into a drier climate, and takes him farther and farther from the line of the rainy monsoon. The ridges also, being in the direct line of the monsoon, check its progress, and their height has an effect on the amount of moisture in adjacent valleys. Thus there are great differences of climate in places of equal elevation. The character of the Himálayan slope is a perpetual succession of vast ridges with narrow intervening glens; and open valleys, such as that of Nepal, are very rare.[2]

In ascending the gorges from the *terai* to the alpine ridges, the traveller passes through three zones of vegetation. In the lower region he finds splendid timber trees, such as the *sal* and *sissu*, banyans and peepuls, bamboos and palms. The central slopes are clothed with oaks, chestnuts, magnolias,

[1] *Terai*, or *Tarai*, lowlands or swampy tracts at the base of the hills. See, for the derivation of the word, Hodgson's 'Geography of the Himálaya,' p. 3, note.

[2] See Mr. Brian Hodgson's 'Physical Geography of the Himálaya.'

laurels, rhododendrons, cherry and pear trees, thorns, ashes, and elms; and the upper region is that of junipers, larches, yews, poplars, dwarf rhododendrons, hollies, birches, and willows. The fauna is also divided into zones of altitude; and Mr. Hodgson[1] has given us an interesting account of the zoological distribution.

In the direction of its length the Indian slope of that part of the Himálaya of which we now have to treat is properly divided according to its river basins. Commencing from the east, Nepal embraces the Karnali (or Ghagra), Gandak, and Kosi river systems, all affluents of the Ganges. Sikkim has the Tísta and Am-machu, or Tursa, rivers; and Bhutan is traversed by the feeders of the Minagaon, Sankos, Monass, and Lopra-cachu, or Subanshiri.[2]

In the west of Nepal, the Karnali system consists of the rivers Kali (or Sarda), Sweti-ganga, Karnali, Bhei, Sarju, and Rapti. Their sources lie between the Nanda-deri (25,693 feet) and the Dawala-giri Peak (27,693 feet); and in this part of the main ridge one pass is known, leading from Nepal to Tibet, along the gorge of the Karnali river, by Taklakhar, in the Tibetan province of Ari. Both the Kali and Karnali rise in the Central Himálaya, and force their way through the Southern Chain. The upper zone of the Karnali basin (Ghagra) is occupied by the district of Jumla or Yumilla. Lower down is the country of the former Baisi (or twenty-two) Rajahs, and the streams unite in the plain to form the Ghagra (Gogra).

Central Nepal embraces the river system of the "Sapt Gandaki," or seven Gandak rivers, called the Narayani, Seti-Gandak, Marsyanghi, Buria Gandak, Tirsuli Gandak, and two others of less importance. Their sources lie between the peaks of Dawala-giri (27,600 feet) and Dayabung (23,762 feet), and they converge to one pointn ear Lora Ghat, within the hills, and flow down to the Ganges as the Gandak river. Four of these rivers, namely, the Kali Gandak, Karnali Gandak, Buria

[1] 'Geography of the Himálaya,' p. 16.

[2] Or Lohit.

Gandak, and Tirsuli Gandak, have their sources in the Central Range, while the others drain the slopes of the Southern Himálaya only. There are three passes over the Central Chain into Tibet by the gorges of the Gandak rivers, namely, the Muktinath pass, by the river Narayani to Mantang (Mustang?); the No-la, by the Buria Gandak; and the Taku-la pass, by the Tirsuli Gandak. The country of the Gandaks is that of the former Chaubisi (twenty-four) Rajahs.

Eastern Nepal is drained by the Kosi river system, consisting, like the Gandak, of seven main streams: the Milamchi, the Bhotia Kosi, the Tamba Kosi, the Likhu, the Dúd Kosi, the Arun, and the Tambur or Tamor. Their sources are included between the Dayabung (23,762 feet) and the Kangchan (28,158 feet), while Mount Everest (29,002 feet) towers above the left bank of the Arun. The Kosi rivers, after draining the Kiranti country in Eastern Nepal, including the districts of Khatang and Chayanpur, unite within the hills into one stream, which flows through the Murung, or Terai region, and past Bijapúr, places often mentioned in Bogle's narrative. The Bhotia Kosi and Arun rise in the Central Chain, and the Arun has a long Tibetan course before it bursts through the Southern Himálaya, and flows down to the Ganges. There are four passes from Nepal to Tibet by the Kosi rivers: one up the Bhotia Kosi, and by the Nilam pass and Kuti, a place mentioned several times by Mr. Bogle; a second up the Arun river and by the Hatia pass; a third up the ravine of the Tambor river by Wallanchún, and over the Tipta-la; and a fourth leads up the gorge of the Yangma, an alpine tributary of the Tambur, over the Kanglachan pass.

The three Nepal basins drain the Indian slopes of the Himálaya for a distance of 800 miles. But the rivers which unite to form the Gogra, Gandak, and Kosi, must necessarily converge to three separate centres, leaving intervals on the lower slopes. In that between the Gandak and Kosi is the beautiful valley of Nepal, with the city of Kathmandu, watered by the Bagmatti river. This famous valley, surrounded by mountains, is 16 miles long and broad, and from 4200 feet to 4700 feet above the sea.

Sikkim, called Demo-jong in Mr. Bogle's narrative, is drained by the river Tísta, and its affluents, the Lachen and Lachung, the Buri Rangit, the Moing, the Rangri, and Rangchu; and the Am-machu rises near Pari-jong, at the foot of the Chumalhari Peak (23,929 feet), and flows through the Chumbi valley, which separates Sikkim from Bhutan. It continues its course through the plains of Julpigori as the Tursa. Two passes, the Kongra-lama and Donkia, besides others at the heads of the Lachen and Lachung tributaries of the Tísta, lead from Sikkim to Tibet; while Pari-jong, at the head of the Chumbi valley, is the pass used by Bogle, Turner, and Manning. The Chumbi valley belongs to Tibet, and not to Sikkim; though the Sikkim Rajah has a house at Chumbi, and resides there during part of the year. The lofty spur dividing the Chumbi and Tísta valleys, called the Chumbi Range, is traversed by several passes, the Yak-la, Cho-la, and Jelep-la. From the eastern boundary of Chumbi, the states of Bhutan and Tawang extend nearly to the Lopra-cachu, a distance of about 200 miles, with an average width of 90 miles from the alpine passes of the Southern Himálaya to the plains of India.

The *dúars* of Bhutan—literally *doors* or approaches—embrace the strip of land extending along the foot of the Bhutan mountains in Bengal and Assam, like the *terai* or *murung* of Sikkim and Nepal. There are eighteen of these dúars or passes: eleven on the frontier of Bengal, and seven on that of Assam; the breadth of this dúar tract being from ten to twenty miles, and the length 220 miles. The more southern frontiers are all partially under rice cultivation, but the intervening space to the foot of the mountains is occupied by dense and lofty forest, and heavy grass jungle. Several streams and rivers flow over pebbly beds from the gorges of the different defiles to the Brahmaputra. The most northern portion of the dúars presents a rugged, irregular surface, occasioned by the spurs which project into the plain, and it is very malarious. The eleven Bengal dúars are Dalim-kotta, Zamar-kotta, Chamurchi, Lakhi, Buxa, Bhulka, Bara, Gumar, Ripu, Cherrung or Sidli, and Bagh or Bijni. The names of the seven Assam dúars are Buri Gumah and Kalling, bordering on the Durrung district; and Ghurkola, Baksha, Chapaguri, Chapaklamar, and Bijni, bordering on Kamrup. East of Durrung is the Kureahparah Dúar held by the Tawang Rajah, a dependent of Tibet; and still farther east are the wild tribes of Abors, Daflas, and Mishmis, extending to and beyond the Dihong, whose mountains, generally inaccessible, have recently been entered by our troops.[1]

Above the dúars, up to the snowy ridge of the Southern Himálaya, all Bhutan is a succession of lofty and rugged mountains separated by gorges, and a few valleys somewhat wider than the generality of the ravines. The streams are numerous and rapid, in beds filled with huge boulders.

There are three river systems in Bhutan besides that of the Am-machu or Chumbi, which flows through a portion of that State on its way to the Brahmaputra. The first, from the west, is the Pachu-Chinchu, which is formed by several rivers. The Pachu flows from a saddle near Pari-jong, waters the Paro valley, and joins the Chinchu. It was by the Pachu valley that Bogle, Turner, and Manning made their way into Tibet. The Chinchu, receiving the Wangchu, flows through the valley of Tassisudon, and joins the Pachu. The united streams, in flowing down into Assam, are at first called the Pachu-Chinchu, and then the Raidak and Minagaon. The next river system of Bhutan is the Machu, which flows past the winter palace of Punakha, and enters the plain as the Sankos. Lastly, by far the largest river of Bhutan, and the one whose tributaries

[1] Under the command of Brigadier Stafford, C.B. See a paper on the "Geology of the Dafla Hills," by Major Godwin Austen, of the Topographical Survey of India, who accompanied this expedition. ('J. A. S. B.,' xliv. part ii.)

drain the widest extent of country, is the Monass. Its basin occupies the eastern half of Bhutan. There are four principal Monass affluents: the Matichu, which flows past Tongsu; the Tongchu, Korichu, and Monass. Several passes into Tibet are said to lead up the gorges of these rivers into the basin of the Lopra-cachu. The region of the Monass is unexplored, except by Pemberton, and nothing is known beyond his route. Some of the peaks of the Bhutan Himálaya, eastward of Chumalhari, have, however, been measured from the Assam plain by Mr. Lane. One at the head of the Matichu is 24,737 feet; and two twin peaks, at the head of branches of the Monass, are respectively 20,965 feet and 20,576 feet above the sea.

The above topographical sketch is intended to embrace the regions with which the narratives in the present volume have to do; and to describe cursorily the orography and hydrography of Great Tibet, Nepal, Sikkim, and Bhutan.

Travellers and systematic geographers have devoted a large share of attention to the structure of the great Himálayan mass, and, in my 'Memoir on the Indian Surveys,'[1] I have given some account of the views of the physical character of the Himálaya formed by Herbert, Henry Strachey, Forbes Royle, Cunningham, Thomson, Brian Hodgson, and Hooker. Mr. Hodgson has stated his view of the question with remarkable clearness, and his explanation of the hydrography of Nepal is a masterpiece of lucid description. Mr. Trelawney Saunders has also treated of the whole subject in his 'Memoir of the Mountains and River Basins of India,' and has illustrated his view of Himálayan geography by means of a large diagram which has not been published. But the Himálayan portion of the beautiful and very clear maps of India which illustrate my 'Moral and Material Progress Reports for 1871–72 and 1872–73,' are based upon the large diagram, the first attempt, of which I am aware, to give clear expression to the whole Himálayan system by means of cartographic illustration. Mr. Saunders

[1] Page 247.

shows that the Himálaya culminates in two parallel ranges running through their entire length, which I have called the Southern and Central Himálayan Chains, separated by a series of valleys. This view is in opposition to those very ably stated by Mr. Brian Hodgson, Dr. Thomson, Dr. Hooker, and others, who consider that the Southern Himálaya, with its line of snowy peaks, is not a true chain or *cordillera,* because it is broken by the defiles through which rivers force their way, whose sources are on what I have called the Central Chain. They consider the Southern Himálaya to be not a chain, but a series of spurs from the Central Chain. It will at once be seen that this is not a question of fact, but of nomenclature, which would scarcely have arisen if the similar facts relating to other great mountain masses, such as the chains or cordilleras of the Andes, had been considered. When this is done it will be seen that a great chain of mountains, with a continuous series of culminating ridges and a continuous slope, is a chain, whether rivers force their way through its gorges or not, and that these phenomena of the Himálaya occur also in the Andes, which are nevertheless properly called cordilleras.[1]

Warren Hastings was the first to notice the striking analogy between the Andes and the Himálaya,[2] after perusing the work

[1] Mr. Wilfred Heeley, in an otherwise admirable article on Tibet, in the 'Calcutta Review' (July, 1874, p. 139), carries this theory of the broken chain to an extreme. He tells us that the Himálaya "is not one continuous *sierra* [probably meaning *cordillera*], but rather a series of short parallel ranges running south from the *watershed* [presumably meaning *water parting*], and each having its highest peak near its southern termination. The ridges may be joined by spurs, and the passes into Tibet cross these, not the main mountain crest." Again, he quotes Dr. Hooker, who says ('R. G. S. J.,' xx. p. 52), "In Sikkim the Himálayas consist of *meridional* ridges separated by water flowing southward. They are not a continuous snowy chain."

[2] All really efficient administrators of the first order are geographers by instinct, and Warren Hastings was no exception to the rule. Under his auspices surveying operations were carefully fostered and encouraged. Major Rennell, the father of Indian geographers, made his famous survey of Bengal, and constructed his maps of the Ganges and Brahmaputra, in the days of the first Governor-General. Sir John Call, the Surveyor-General, compiled a general map of India. Colonel Pearse, the friend of Hastings, and his second in the duel with Francis, and Colonel Colebrooke, took a series of

of M. de la Condamine.[1] The analogy between the two great mountain masses of the old and new world is indeed most remarkable. Both consist of three parallel chains. In both great rivers have their sources in the inner chain, and force their way through the other two. The cuesta of La Raya, separating the valley of the Vilcamayu from the basin of Titicaca, is the counterpart of the Mariam-la saddle dividing the basin of the Sutlej from the valley of the Brahmaputra. In both systems numerous rivers rise in the central cordillera, and after lateral courses between the two, eventually force a way through the outer chain. The Southern Himálaya bears an exact analogy to the outer Andes which rise from the valley of the Amazon. Both have a low range at their feet, enclosing valleys or dhuns; both have deep gorges, separated by lofty ridges, which are spurs from a main chain of culminating snowy peaks; and in both several rivers rise in an inner central range, and force their way through profound ravines between the culminating summits. The rivers Mapiri and Chuqui-apu pierce the cordillera, flowing through chasms in beds 18,000 feet below the snowy peak of Illimani which almost overhangs one of them. Yet no one maintains that the "Cordillera Real de los Andes" is not a chain of mountains! The analogy between the land of the Yncas and the plateau of Tibet may be carried still farther. In both the staple produce is wool, yielded by llamas, alpacas, and vicuñas in Peru, and by sheep and shawl-goats in Tibet. In both the beasts of burden are llamas or sheep needing a wide area of pasturage, and consequently numerous passes on their journeys, in order that a profitable trade may be carried on with the low country. Both abound in the precious metals. In both the people cultivate hardy cereals, and species of chenopodium, called *quinua* in Peru, and *battu* in Tibet. The people, too, have many beliefs and customs in common, down to that of heaping

astronomical observations, and mapped the country along the coast from Calcutta to Madras. Nor were marine surveys neglected; and Ritchie, Hudart, and Blair were actively employed in preparing charts.

[1] See p. 12.

up huge piles of stones on the crests of mountain passes; and the Tibetan is actuated by the same feeling when he mutters his *Om mani padmi hum,*[1] as the Peruvian when, on passing a heap of stones, he bows and reverentially exclaims, *Apachicta muchhani!*[2]

The analogy pointed out by Warren Hastings, and which I have ventured to carry a little farther, strikingly suggests the importance of taking a comprehensive view of such questions as those of the physical structure of a great mountain range, or of the best means of establishing commercial intercourse between inhabitants of a lofty plateau difficult of access, and those of tropical valleys separated by snowy mountains. If the frightful gorges of the Andes did not prevent the Yncas from exchanging the products of the *sierras* for the coca of the *montañas,* there is nothing that a wise policy may not overcome to hinder the Lamas of Tibet and the Rulers of India from establishing a friendly interchange of commodities between the lofty plateaux of the one, and the fertile tropical valleys of the other.

The inhabitants of Tibet belong to the great Mongolian family, and they are described by Huc[3] as a people with small, contracted, black eyes, thin beard, high cheek bones, flat noses, wide mouths, and thin lips. The skins of the upper classes are as white as those of Europeans, but the ordinary complexion is tawny. They are of middle height, and combine agility and suppleness with force and vigour. They are said to be generous and frank, brave in war, religious, and fond of display. They must be hardy mountaineers, and have developed most of the natural resources of their country. They have domesticated the yak, breed ponies in large numbers, sheep and goats, cultivate such cereals as will ripen in their climate, work the

[1] "*Oh! the jewel in the lotus. Amen!*" equivalent to our "*Pater noster qui es in cœlo.*"

[2] Quichua words, meaning literally, "*I offer thanks that this has been carried;*" or, as the Ynca explains it, "I give thanks and make an offering to Him who enables me to raise this burden, and who grants me strength to ascend such rugged heights as these." (See my translation of the 'Commentarios Reales de los Yncas, por el Ynca Garcilasso la Vega,' i. p. 117.)

[3] ii. p. 141.

precious metals, and are skilful weavers and potters. Their language is said to be more nearly allied to that of Burma than to any other of the same group;[1] but it has not yet been exhaustively studied.[2] It is now confined to the valleys of the Tsanpu, Upper Indus, Sutlej, and Chenab. The early history of the Tibetans, before the introduction of Buddhism, is probably quite fabulous; although there is some trace of the old religion of Tibet lingering in the eastern province of Kam. It is called the *Bon* or *Pon* religion, and appears to have been a worship of the powers of nature, with a creed identical with the Chinese doctrine of Taossé.[3] The people still have deities of the hills, the trees, the dales, and lakes.

It was centuries after the death of Sakya Muni in India, in 543 B.C., that the light of his doctrine spread over the Tibetan plateau. The disciples of Buddha long had to contend against opposition in their own country; their religion of peace and goodwill, not to man only, but to all the animated creation, was very gradually accepted, and it was more than three centuries before the famous King Priyadarsi, or Asoka, made Buddhism the religion of the State in India. Then a new era dawned upon the world. Former inscriptions of ancient kings that have been

[1] The Jesuit and Capuchin fathers who were in Lhasa in the last century studied the Tibetan language, and their records enabled Giorgi to publish his 'Alphabetum Thibetanum' at Rome, in 1759. In 1826, P. Schröter brought out a Tibetan-English dictionary, edited by John Marshman, which was published at the Serampore Press, and followed by the grammar and dictionary of J. J. Schmidt, in 1839. Meanwhile, that learned and indefatigable scholar, Csoma de Körös, produced a grammar and dictionary of Tibetan, at Calcutta, in 1834. There are also the grammar of Ph. Ed. Foucaux, and the 'Tibetische Studien' of A. Schiefner. In 1866, the Moravian missionary, H. A. Jäschke, published his grammar and small dictionary, lithographed in British Lahoul; and he commenced the publication of a more complete Tibetan lexicon in 1871.

[2] General Cunningham says that it resembles English in the similarity in sound of many words, and in that words are not spelt as they are pronounced. In Tibetan, to bring is *brang;* can is *kyan;* dull is *dal;* thick is *tuk;* wool is *wal;* lump is *lhumpo* (*lumbo*); there is *der;* here is *dir;* rogue is *rog.* ('Ladak,' p. 388.)

[3] The question of the *Pon* religion of Tibet is discussed by Colonel Yule in his edition of 'Marco Polo,' i. pp. 315–319. (See also Cunningham's 'Ladak,' p. 358.)

laboriously deciphered, record bloody victories and ruthless conquests. But the rock and pillar edicts of the Rajah Priyadarsi[1] inculcate goodness, virtue, piety, and kindness to animals; and they ordain the introduction of a general system of instruction in moral conduct, and the establishment of medical dispensaries throughout the empire. It was Asoka or Priyadarsi who first sent missionaries beyond his frontiers to spread the glad tidings of *Dharma*, or religion, among distant peoples. His son Makinda brought the sacred canon to Ceylon,[2] together with the Pali language of Magadha, in which it was first taught; and in that island Buddhism has been preserved in its purest and most primitive form.[3] At about the same time the new religion was introduced into Ladak, Khotan, Afghanistan, and the countries of the Oxus valley; and it reached China at about the commencement of the Christian era. But it seems clear that Great Tibet remained in darkness for some centuries later, though almost surrounded by the peace-giving light of Dharma.

The routes taken by the Chinese pilgrims to India show that Tibet was at that time still in outside darkness. When, in the beginning of the fifth century,[4] Fa-Hian, the heroic Buddhist monk, and his four companions, set out from China to visit the sacred sites in India, and to obtain copies of the Scriptures, they took the circuitous road to the north of Tibet, and reached Khotan, then a stronghold of Buddhist culture. The farther route of Fa-Hian was over the Pamír and Hindu Kush, and across the Swat valley—that region which has lately been found to be so rich in Buddhist sculptures—to the Punjab. Two centuries later, the route of the other pilgrim, whose narrative has been preserved, Hiuen Thsang, also avoided Great Tibet[5] by a still wider circuit. He travelled over Tsun-

[1] See my 'Memoir on the Indian Surveys,' p. 177, for some account of the labours of James Prinsep and his fellow-workers, in deciphering the Priyadarsi edicts, and for references to more complete sources of information.

[2] B.C. 316.

[3] See the introduction to Mr. Childers's Pali Dictionary.

[4] A.D. 399–414.

[5] A.D. 629–645.

garia to the valley of the Jaxartes, crossed the Oxus into Balkh, and entered Kabul by the Bamian pass, finding the religion of Buddha in a flourishing state along the whole of his route.

It was, indeed, at about the period of Hiuen Thsang's journey that Buddhism first began to find its way into Tibet, both from the direction of China and that of India; but it came in a very different form from that in which it reached Ceylon several centuries earlier. Traditions, metaphysical speculations, and new dogmas had overlaid the original Scriptures with an enormous collection of more recent revelation. Thus Tibet received a vast body of truth, and could only assimilate a portion for the establishment of a popular belief. Since the original Scriptures had been conveyed into Ceylon by the son of Asoka, it had been revealed to the devout Buddhists of India that their Lord had created the five Dhyani or celestial Buddhas, and that each of these had created five Buddhisatwas, or beings in the course of attaining Buddha-hood. The Tibetans took firm hold of this phase of the Buddhistic creed, and their distinctive belief is that the Buddhisatwas continue to remain in existence for the good of mankind by passing through a succession of human beings from the cradle to the grave. This characteristic of their faith was gradually developed, and it was long before it received its present form; but the succession of incarnate Buddhisatwas was the idea towards which the Tibetan mind tended from the first. At the same time, as Max Müller says: "The most important element of the Buddhist reform has always been its social and moral code, not its metaphysical theories. That moral code, taken by itself, is one of the most perfect which the world has ever known;" and it was this blessing that the introduction of Buddhism brought into Tibet.

It is said that a native king established the seat of government at Lhasa in 617 A.D.; that he married a Chinese princess of the Buddhist persuasion, and that he sent his minister to India, who returned with the great body of truth contained in the Buddhist canonical Scriptures, framed the Tibetan alphabet from the Devanagari of India, and commenced the translation of the canon from Sanscrit into the language of the country.[1] For a long time there was a struggle for supremacy between the old nobility and the new hierarchy, in which, after several vicissitudes, the Buddhist monks gained the ascendancy.

It was during this early period of Buddhist rule in Tibet that the first European visited the country. We are indebted to Colonel Yule[2] for a complete knowledge of the adventurous journey of Friar Odoric of Pordenone, between A.D. 1316 and 1330. It was on his return from Cathay that, after travelling many days through Kansan, the modern Shensi and Szechuen, he came to the chief and royal city of Tibet, obviously Lhasa, all built with walls black and white. He tells us that, in this city, no one dare to shed the blood of any, whether man or beast, and that there dwells the *Abassi*,[3] which in their tongue is the Pope. More than three centuries elapsed before another European visited Lhasa, and momentous events took place in the interval.

In the middle of the fourteenth century a great reforming Lama arose in Tibet, named Tsong-khapa, who proved to be an incarnation of one of the Dhyani Buddhas, named Amitabha. He was born near Lake Kokonor in 1358, and died in 1419. Tsong-khapa built and took up his abode in the Galdan monastery, near Lhasa, of which he was the first khanpo or abbot, and where his body lies. He forbade clerical marriages, prohibited necromancy, and introduced the custom of frequent conferences among the Lamas. His reforms led to a schism in the Tibetan church. The old sect, which resisted all change, adhered to their dress, and are called Shammars, or Dukpas, and Red Caps. Their chief monastery is at Sakia-jong, and they retain supremacy in Nepal and Bhutan. The reformers adopted a

[1] It had previously been translated from Pali, the old language of Magadha, into Sanscrit.

[2] 'Cathay, and the Road Thither,' i. p. 146.

[3] Colonel Yule, after putting aside the ponderous erudition of Giorgi ('Alphabetum Tibetanum,' p.688), discusses the probable meaning and derivation of this word *Abassi*, used by Odoric (ubi sup. p. 149, note).

yellow dress, and are distinguished as the Yellow Cap, or Gelupka sect; since the days of Tsong-khapa they have been in the ascendant in Tibet.

Gedun-tubpa, another great reformer, was contemporary with Tsong-khapa, having been born in 1339, and dying in 1474. He built the monastery at Teshu Lumbo in 1445, and it was in the person of this perfect Lama, as he was called, that the system of perpetual incarnation commenced. He was himself the incarnation of the Buddhisatwa Padma Pani, and on his death he relinquished the attainment of Buddha-hood that he might be born again and again for the benefit of mankind. When he died, his successor was found as an infant, by the possession of certain divine marks.

Thus arose the two powerful Abbots of Galdan and Teshu Lumbo, both of the Gelupka or Yellow sect; but the former were soon eclipsed by the superior piety and learning of the incarnations at Teshu Lumbo; and the sixth in succession of those incarnations made himself master of all Tibet, and founded the successions of the Dalai and Teshu Lamas as they now exist. This was Navang Lobsang. He rebuilt the palace or monastery of Potala, at Lhasa, in 1643, and in 1650 he visited the Emperor of China, and accepted the designation of Dalai (or ocean) Lama. After a long reign he went away to reappear as two infants, if not three; for, although he was the fifth Teshu Lama, he was the first Dalai; and since his time there have been two great incarnations of equal rank: the Dalai Lama at Potala, who is an incarnation of the Buddhisatwa Avalokiteswara; and the Teshu Lama at Teshu Lumbo, the incarnation of the Buddhisatwa Amitabha, and also of Tsong-khapa, who was himself the incarnation of Amitabha. The Dalai Lama also has the title of Gyalba Rimboché, or "the Gem of Majesty;" and the Teshu Lama that of Panchen Rimboché, or "the Gem of Learning." When the Lamas assume political functions they are also Gyalpo or king; but the regency at Lhasa is generally held by a vicegerent or temporal sovereign, called the Gesub Rimbochè, or Nomen-khan. The death of the first Dalai Lama was concealed at Lhasa for no less than sixteen years, by an ambitious Nomen-khan, and two false Lamas were set up afterwards. In 1717 an army of Dsungarians, or Eleuths, stormed Lhasa,[1] and the Nomen-khan was murdered; but at length, in 1720, Kang-hi, the Emperor of China, exerted his power to restore order, and the true Dalai Lama, named Lobsang Kalsang, was duly installed. Two Chinese Political Residents, or Ambas, with an adequate force, were, however, permanently established at Lhasa, at the same time.

There is another incarnate Buddhisatwa, in the person of a Grand Lama, whose influence extends over Mongolia, but whose existence has generally been ignored in English histories of Tibetan Buddhism. This is the Taranath Lama,[2] whose succession commenced in the middle of the sixteenth century certainly, if not earlier; for a Taranath Lama, who was born in 1575, completed a work on Buddhism, in the Tibetan language, in 1608. The Taranath Lama was also known as the Je-tsun-tampa,[3] or, according to the Abbé Huc, Guison-tamba.[4] Huc tells us that the Guison-tamba formerly had his seat at a place called Koukou-Khotou, or "Blue Town," beyond the Great Wall of China, and near the northern bend of the Yellow River. When the Emperor Kang-hi (1662–1723) was engaged in his campaign against the Kalmuks, or Eleuths, he paid a visit to the Guison-tamba, and owing to some fancied want of respect on the part of the holy man, one of the Emperor's officers drew

[1] An account of the extraordinary march of the Dsungarians is given by Father Palladius of the Russian Peking Mission, in one of his articles on China in 1848.

[2] I am indebted for the research respecting the Taranath Lama to Mr. Trelawney Saunders. The text of the work, referred to in the text, was printed in Tibetan, from four manuscripts, for the Imperial Academy of St. Petersburg, in 1868, with a Russian translation and notes by Professor Wassiljew, and also with a German translation by Professor Schiefner.—"Târanâthæ de Doct. Buddh. in India propagatione narratio. Contextum Tibeticum e codd. Petropol. Ed. Ant. Schiefner. Petropoli, 1868."

[3] Schiefner's German translation of Wassiljew's Russian translation of 'Taranath,' pp. 26–28.

[4] Huc, i. pp. 83, 87, 113; ii. p. 15.

his sword and killed him. This violence caused a tumult, and soon afterwards it was announced that the Guison-tamba had reappeared among the Khalkas,[1] who threatened to avenge his former death. The Emperor engaged the diplomatic interposition of the Dalai Lama, who succeeded in pacifying the Khalkas. But it was arranged that the future births of the Guison-tamba should be found in Tibet, so that the Khalkas might not again have a sympathizing fellow-countryman as their high-priest.

The present seat of the Taranath Lama, in the Khalka country, is an immense monastery, with more than ten thousand monks, at Urga Kuren, on the Tula river, a description of which is given by the Abbé Huc,[2] who visited the place. There is now a Russian Consul permanently resident at Urga.

Thus there are three great and influential incarnations of the Yellow sect: the Dalai Lama, the Teshu Lama, and the Taranath Lama. The latter is alluded to several times by Mr. Bogle,[3] and also by Captain Turner.[4] A fourth may probably be added, in the person of the Changay Lama or High Priest of Peking, mentioned by Bogle.[5]

[1] This name is derived from the river Khalka. It came into use when the Mongol or Yuen dynasty of China was driven from the throne in 1368, and found a new home on the banks of the Khalka (De Guigne's 'Hist. des Huns,' iii. p. 234). These princes, descended from Jingis Khan, through Kublai Khan, who founded the Yuen dynasty in 1279, are now represented by the Khans of Tuchetu, Sannoin, Tsetsen, and Sassaktu, who rule over the four Khalka Khanates in outer Mongolia, near the Russian frontier, under the Emperor of China.

[2] The Abbé Huc met one of the new births of the Guison-tamba (Taranath) journeying from Urga to Lhasa, in 1844. In the 'Geographical Magazine' for April, 1874, there is a notice of an itinerary from Lhasa to Urga, giving the route taken by the Urga Khutuktu, or Taranath Lama, collected by M. Shishmaroff, the Russian Consul at Urga. Again, in the 'Geographical Magazine' for March, 1875, an account is quoted from the 'Journal de St. Petersburg' of the journey of another new birth of the Taranath Lama (or Urga Khutuktu) from Lhasa to Urga. See, for the journey of the eighth Guison-tamba from Lhasa to Urga, the 'Peking Gazette' for 1874, pp. 68, 74, and 124 (Shanghai, 1875).

[3] See pp. 98, 110, and 134.

[4] See Turner, p. 273, where he mentions the intercourse between the Taranath and the Russian Government; and pp. 279 and 314.

[5] See p. 130.

Under the incarnate Lamas there is an order of Buddhist ecclesiastics in Tibet, China, and Mongolia, called *Khutuktus*, who also have divine incarnation; and indeed Mr. Brian Hodgson considers that the term is a Tatar equivalent for the divine Lama of the Tibetan tongue.[1] There also appears to be at least one female incarnation, in the person of the abbess of a convent on the island in Lake Palti, whose acquaintance was made by Mr. Bogle. The professed monks or clergy, subordinate to the holy and sacred lamas, are also called lamas, and are very numerous in Tibet. All who have taken vows of celibacy are called gedun. A professed monk is gylong; a neophyte, getshul; a nun is anní. They are bareheaded, though those of high rank wear caps; their hair is cut short, and they are dressed in a yellow robe and high leathern boots, with the mendicant's food bowl and the prayer wheel in their hands. They are collected in vast monasteries scattered over the country, the largest and most numerous being round the city of Lhasa. The Galdan[2] and Potala monasteries have already been mentioned. The valley of Lhasa also contains the Sara monastery, with 5500 lamas; the Muru[3] and Ramoché monasteries, at the north end of Lhasa; the Chumuling, at the north-west corner; the Tankyaling, at the west end; the Kontyaling monastery, about a mile to the west of the city; the Chochuling, and the Debang monastery, which is the most important. These monasteries contain many thousands of lamas, and similar establishments are scattered not only in the inhabited valleys, but over the wildest parts of Great Tibet.

The monasteries are called *Gonpas;* the Lama's house, *Labrang;* and the temple, consisting of a room full of images and pictures, *Lha-khang*. The *Dung-ten* is a relic repository, (the *Stupa* of India,) and the votive piles of stones or dykes, from a few feet to half a mile in length, covered with slabs, and stuck over with banners inscribed with the Tibetan prayer, *Om mani padmi hum*, are called *Mani*. The images of Buddha are always

[1] See p. 11, and compare Giorgi, 'Alphabetum Tibetanum.'
[2] Huc, ii. p. 219. [3] *Ibid.*

seated, with the right hand resting on the knee, the left on the lap and holding the alms dish, the body painted yellow, or gilt, and the hair short and curly, and painted blue. They are of all sizes, and there are other images of beings connected with Buddhistic ideas.

The services consist of recitations and chanting of the *Sutras* or precepts, and rules of discipline, to the sound of musical instruments, trumpets, drums, cymbals, and *chank* shells. The tunes are impressive and solemn, incense is burnt during the services, and there are offerings of fruits and grain to Buddha and to the Buddhisatwas, especially to Avalokiteswara, who is incarnate in the Dalai Lama. Mystical sentences and titles of Buddha are also recited. The bell is used during the performance of service; and the prayer wheels—metal cylinders, containing printed prayers in rolls with the axes prolonged to form handles—are in constant use, not only during the service, but on every occasion, being fixed in rows on the walls of temples, near villages, and in streams to be turned by water. The prayer wheels have been in use for more than a thousand years, for they are mentioned by the pilgrim Fa-Hian.[1]

The Tibetans possess a vast literature, including all the Buddhist canon of Scripture translated from the Sanscrit, the 'Tripitaka,' or three baskets of precepts, and other works, one list of which has been given by Csoma de Körös. For many centuries they have known the art of printing, by means of engraved stereotyped wooden blocks, which last for a century. Thus not only prayers and invocations are printed on sheets of Tibetan paper made from the *Daphne cannabina*,[2] and on

[1] A good deal that is curious respecting the religion of Tibet will be found in 'Tibetan Buddhism, illustrated by Literary Documents and Objects of Religious Worship,' by Emil Schlagintweit, LL.D. (Trübner, 1863.) See also 'Die Religion des Buddha und ihre Entstehung'; and 'Die lamaische Hierarchie und Kirche,' C. F. Köppen. (Berlin, 1857, 1859.) Mr. Brian Hodgson's 'Essays' should of course be consulted (Trübner, 1874), and Cunningham's 'Ladak,' p. 356.

[2] Colonel Sykes exhibited some large sheets of Nepal paper at the Great Exhibition of 1851, made from the inner bark of the *Daphne Bholua*, or *cannabina*. Mr. Hodgson has given an account of the uses of this plant, which is abundant in the Himálaya, in the 'Journal of the Asiatic Society of Bengal' for 1832 (i. p. 8). He also

banners for display on the *Manis*, but voluminous works, so that each monastery possesses a library of Buddhistic lore. The lamas of Tibet also excel as workers in metal and modellers in clay, designing leaves and flowers of exquisitely delicate workmanship.

While the Gelupka, or Yellow sect, is in the ascendant in Tibet, the adherents of the older, but now heretical Red sect, still have a large monastery at Sakia-jong,[1] and have retained supremacy among the Buddhists in Nepal and Bhutan, on the slopes of the Southern Himálaya. In the well-wooded and moist gorges of the Cis-nivean Himálaya, the country was occupied, in very ancient times, by people of Tibetan descent, especially in the upper and middle zones; while lower down, and bordering on the plains of India, the tribes are of more mixed race.

Mr. Brian Hodgson, who is unrivalled in his knowledge of the Cis-nivean Himálayan races, divides the inhabitants of the region between the Kali and the Monass into ten tribes, the Cis-Himálayan Bhotias or Tibetans in the upper zone, the Sienwar, Gurung, Magar, Murmi, Newar, Kirati, and Limbu, in Nepal; the Lepcha in Sikkim, and Lhopa or Dukpa[2] (Bhutanese) in Bhutan.

The aborigines of Nepal survive in two wild forest tribes, called Chepang and Kusunda, dwelling in the dense jungle of the central region, of which Mr. Hodgson has given a very interesting account.[3] But the people of Tibetan or Mongolian race made their way over the numerous passes, and established themselves in the deep gorges and forest-covered slopes of Nepal, Sikkim, and Bhutan not later than in the fifth century,

describes the method of making the paper, which is remarkable for its toughness as well as for its smoothness. Among Mr. Bogle's papers there are several long letters from the Teshu Lama, written on this paper, in the cursive Tibetan character. (See also Boyle's 'Fibrous Plants of India,' p. 312.)

[1] The Abbot of the Red Cap monastery at Sakia, in Tibet, has the title of Gongso Rimboché. (Turner, p. 315.)

[2] Lho is the native name of Bhutan. Lhopa is therefore a territorial designation, while Dukpa refers to their belonging to the Red Cap sect.

[3] "On the Chepang and Kusunda Tribes of Nepal." ('J. A. S. B.,' 1857.)

for the occupation certainly took place before the introduction of Buddhism into Tibet. The Magars people the lower part of the hills in Western Nepal, and are men of great bodily vigour and mental activity, but cruel and treacherous. The Gurungs are a pastoral people, addicted to arms, frequenting the alpine regions in summer. The Newars inhabit the valley of Nepal. They are peaceful agriculturists and traders, and are more advanced in the arts than the other tribes: their chiefs, of a family called Mal, having been the rulers of the country before the Gorkha conquest. The Murmis are a low caste tribe in the mountainous parts of Nepal proper. The Kirats were a warlike and enterprising people, but very rude, occupying Eastern Nepal; and the Limbus form a tribe settled in the country of the Kirats.

When the successive Muhammadan invasions spread terror over the plains of India, and caused the destruction of many native dynasties, numerous princes and their followers took refuge, with attendant Brahmans, in the Nepal hills, and received the name of *Parbatiya*, or Mountain Hindus. The wild native tribes were gradually converted to Hinduism, and the chief warrior families were admitted as belonging to the Kshatriya, or Rajput caste. From them, and from the offspring of Brahmans and native women, sprang the numerous and now predominant Khas tribe of Nepal, and in the course of centuries the Khas language became a corrupt form of Hindi. The Khas were spread over the Chaubisya region, and, with the Gurungs and Magars, form the military race of Nepal, now known, from the small State which led them to conquest, as Gorkhas.[1] In Mr. Hodgson's opinion they are by far the best soldiers in Asia, possessing love of enterprise, and confirmed military habits, combined with susceptibility to discipline.

The Newars were a more peaceful and civilized people,

[1] The town of Gorkha is about 60 miles W.N.W. of Kathmandu. The name is derived from that of the deity of the royal family, Gorkhanath, who also gave his name to our district of Gorakpúr.

among whom Buddhism of the Red sect continued to prevail, who inhabit the valley of Nepal, which is about 16 miles long and broad, and 4200 to 4700 feet above the sea. The Mal dynasty of Newar encouraged the arts, agriculture, and commerce, and in their time a flourishing trade was carried on between Tibet and the plains of India, through the passes of Nepal. The sixth king of the Mal dynasty, at his death, divided his dominions into three principalities with capitals within the valley, Kathmandu, Lalita Patan, and Bhatgaon. In these towns there were mints for coining money, and they seem to have formed centres of trading enterprise in the seventeenth and first half of the eighteenth century. The Kashmiri merchants carried their goods by Ladak to Kuti, at the head of the pass, to procure wool; and their manufactures went thence partly for use in Tibet, partly to China by Sining, and partly to Patna by the valley of Nepal. Tibet merchants brought woollen cloths, ponies, shawl goats, yaks, sheep, musk, salt, borax, gold, silver, and paper to Kathmandu, and the lamas sent much bullion to the Nepal mints. From India came cotton cloth, cutlery, glassware, coral, pearls, spices, camphor, betel, and hardware, which were passed on, from Nepal, over the passes to Tibet.[1]

As long ago as in 1583, Ralph Fitch, a traveller who visited India at that time, had evidently heard of the trade which then flourished between Tibet and Bengal.[2] His quaint account of this trade leaves no doubt as to the region and the people he has in his mind. The trade in musk, *cambals* (evidently the blankets still imported), silk, and agates; the use of the cow-tails; the names of *Bootanter* and *Booteah;* the mention of lofty mountains; the merchants coming from China, Tatary, and Persia, all prove that Ralph Fitch had heard an account, and a correct account, of the intercourse which then prevailed between India and Tibet, through the passes of Bhutan and Nepal.

[1] Buchanan Hamilton, p. 212. [2] 'Hakluyt's Voyages,' ii. p. 257.

The Lepchas of Sikkim are ruled by a chief of their own, have retained the Buddhist religion, and have generally been subject to Tibet. But the fiercer mountaineers of Bhutan have long maintained virtual independence. Savage and illiterate, they have preserved but vague traditions of their history, and the account given by Mr. Bogle is probably as historical as any other.[1] Mr. Eden received a somewhat different account; according to which the present Bhutanese only overran the country about three centuries ago, when they found it occupied by a people from Kuch Bahar, whom they conquered. The invaders were Tibetan soldiers, over whom a lama of the Red sect, named Dupgain Sheptún, acquired paramount influence, as Lama Rimboché, or Dharma Rajah. On his death, the spirit of Sheptún became incarnate in a little child at Lhasa, who was conveyed to Bhutan. When this child grew up, he confined himself to spiritual concerns, and appointed a regent, called the Deb Rajah, to perform all administrative functions. But the real power has long been in the hands of the military governors or Penlos of East and West Bhutan, whose capitals are respectively at Tongso and Paro.

The Muhammadan conquests in Hindustan tended to check the formerly unfettered intercourse between Tibet and the valley of the Ganges, through the passes of the Southern Himálayas, as Mr. Bogle was told by the Teshu Lama; but this obstacle was by no means permanent, and the commercial enterprise of the Newars and Kashmiris brought the land of the peace-loving Lamas into friendly intercourse with peoples whose countries extend from the frontiers of Siberia to the shores of the Bay of Bengal.

Yet an interval of three centuries elapsed, from the time of Father Odoric of Pordenone, before another European set his foot on the soil of Great Tibet.

The present Manchu dynasty (Ta-Tsing) of China, founded by Shun-che in 1651, has produced two emperors of great

[1] Pages 33 and 191.

ability, who enjoyed unusually long lives. Kang-hi reigned from 1662 to 1723, and had the wisdom to admit Catholic priests into China, and to utilize their scientific knowledge. Kien-lung, who ruled over the Chinese empire from 1736 to 1796, was also a prince of great capacity; and the ascendency of China over Tibet was fully established during these reigns. Yet it was from the side not of China, but of India that Europeans first penetrated into Tibet, in the guise of missionaries. The Jesuit, Antonio Andrada, in 1624, set out from Agra to scale the appalling mountains, the snowy pinnacles of which were visible from the plains of India. He climbed the terrific passes to the source of the Ganges, and eventually, after fearful sufferings, reached the shores of the sacred lake of Mansarowar, the source of the Sutlej. Thence the undaunted missionary found his way over the lofty passes to Rudok, and eventually, by way of Tangut, to China. He was the first European to enter Tibet after Friar Odoric of Pordenone, in 1325, just three centuries earlier.[1]

The next journey, that of Fathers Grueber and Dorville, was still more remarkable, for these enterprising missionaries succeeded in passing from China, through Lhasa, into India. John Grueber was born at Lintz, in Austria, in 1620, and becoming a Jesuit, was sent from Rome to Macao in 1657, proceeding thence to Peking. He was ordered to return to Europe, to receive instructions from the general of the order at Rome, but all the ports were closed by a Dutch fleet. He therefore resolved to attempt the journey by land. Setting out, with Father Dorville as a companion, in June, 1661, he travelled by way of Sining, crossed the Tangut desert, and reached Lhasa in six months from Peking. There he remained two months, and in his letters he describes the worship of the Dalai Lama, and

[1] The Jesuit Antonio Andrada was born in 1580, and went to India as a missionary. After his memorable journey to China he returned to Goa, and died there in 1634. His narrative appeared at Lisbon in 1626. It was translated into French in 1628, and a new edition appeared at Paris in 1796, in the 'Recueil de Voyages du Thibet,' MM. Péron et Billecocq.

the religious system of the Buddhists. Thence he made his way along a route, by tremendous precipices, into Nepal; crossing the Kuti pass, which is several times mentioned by Mr. Bogle, the intrepid travellers reached Kathmandu, and eventually arrived at Agra, 214 days after they had left Peking. Dorville died, but Grueber continued his journey on foot through India and Persia, and embarked at Smyrna for Rome. Father Grueber died, in 1665, on his way back to China; and the only record of his wonderful journey is contained in a few meagre letters which have been preserved in a small volume.[1] An abstract of those addressed to Kircher[2] was originally published by him in the 'China Illustrata,' and all were reproduced in the collection of Thevenot.[3] Indeed, it would appear that Grueber was not

[1] 'Notizie varie dell' Imperio della China' (Florence, 1687), edited by Jacopo Carlieri, 12mo. This volume contains an account of China gathered from a discourse held with Father Grueber (80 pages), as well as letters in Latin, addressed by Grueber to various fathers, giving accounts of China and Tibet (42 pages). One of the letters is apparently a sort of abstract or compilation, headed "ex literis Grueberi Kirchero inscripto," and is written in the third person. The other three are written in the first person, and seem not to have been altered from the manuscripts of Grueber.

[2] Grueber's 'Iter e Chinâ in Mogor' forms the second chapter of the second part of the 'China Illustrata' of P. Kircher.

Athanasius Kircher was born at Geysen, a small town near Fulda, in Germany, in 1602. He was a Jesuit, and was one of the most laborious and learned men that the Company has produced. He studied all branches of learning with ardour, but his chief object was the acquisition of a complete knowledge of the Oriental languages, of which he was professor at Wurtzburg. On the breaking out of the Thirty Years' war he retired to Avignon, and went thence to Rome, where he died in 1680. His erudition was something stupendous, but he was devoid of the critical faculty, and thus much of his indefatigable industry and marvellous power of acquiring knowledge were wasted. His work relating to Tibet is one out of about forty that he produced on various subjects. The title is 'China monumentis quà sacris, quà profanis, necnon variis naturæ et artis spectaculis illustrata' (Amsterdam, folio, 1667). It was translated into French by d'Alquié in 1670; and partly into English by John Ogilby in 1669, but merely as an appendix to a folio volume containing a translation of an account of a Dutch Embassy to China. The 'China Illustrata' gives an account of the arrival of the missionaries in China: it is the first work in which the characters of the Devanagari alphabet were ever engraved, and it contains the account of Grueber's visit to Lhasa.

[3] Melchisedek Thevenot, uncle of Jean Thevenot, the famous traveller, was born in 1620, and died in 1690. He published Grueber's letters in 'Relations de divers Voyages curieux qui

very communicative; had not the gift of narration; but the essential portion of what has been preserved of his account of the journey will be found in the Appendix at the end of this volume. The only genuine sketch of the palace of Potala is, I believe, that given in the 'China Illustrata' of Kircher, from Father Grueber.

Grueber was followed by two other Jesuits, named Desideri and Freyre. Hippolito Desideri was born at Pistoia in 1684, became a Jesuit, and was sent to Goa in 1712. In 1714 he went by way of Surat to Delhi, where he was joined by Father Manoel Freyre as a companion. Crossing the Pir Panjal Range the two Jesuits came to Kashmir on the 10th of May, and travelled thence by Leh and over the Mariam-la pass to Lhasa, the journey occupying them from August, 1715, to March, 1716. Desideri remained at Lhasa until 1729, when he was recalled by the Pope, and not allowed to return, owing to complaints against him from the Capuchin friars, who had found their way into Tibet. We have one letter of Desideri, which describes his journey through Ladak and as far as the Mariam-la pass, but there the narrative breaks off abruptly. A translation of this letter, from the 'Lettres Édifiantes,'[1] will be found

n'ont point été publiées' (Paris, 1663–72, 4 parties en 2 tom. folio).

A good abstract of Grueber's letters, taken from Kircher and Thevenot, is given in 'Astley's Collection of Voyages and Travels,' vol. iv. (London, 1745–47), which is copied into Pinkerton's 'Collection,' vol. vii. (London, 1808–14). A briefer abstract is given in Hugh Murray's 'Historical Account of Travels in Asia,' i. p. 425 (London, 1820).

[1] The 'Lettres Édifiantes' were brought out by Legobien and Du Halde.

Charles Legobien was a Jesuit, who was born at St. Malo in 1653, and died in 1708. He published 'Lettre sur les Progres de la Religion à la Chine' (Paris, 1697). After the Emperor Kang-hi ordered the persecution of the Christians to cease, by an edict, dated March 22, 1692, Legobien published 'Histoire de l'Edit de l'Empereur de la Chine en Faveur de la Religion Chretienne' (Paris, 1698). In 1702 he published, 'Lettres de quelques Missionaires de la Compagnie de Jesus écrites de la Chine et des Indes Orientales' (1 vol. 12mo). The second issue was called 'Lettres édifiantes et curieuses,' and made two volumes, and Legobien brought out six more, making nine in all.

Jean Baptiste Du Halde, also a Jesuit, was born at Paris in 1674, and succeeded Legobien in the work of collecting and arranging the letters written from various countries by the fathers of the Company. His 'Lettres édifiantes et curieuses écrites des Missions Étrangères' continue the Legobien series from

in the Appendix to this volume. Another letter from Desideri is inserted in the 'Bibliotheca Pistoiensis' (p. 185), by Zaccaria. But there is much valuable material from the pen of Desideri still in manuscript which will soon be given to the world, and will be most useful to students of Tibetan history and geography. The manuscript containing the narrative of his journey to and residence in Tibet has recently been examined by Signor Carlo Puini. That learned scholar reports that it is in the library of a private gentleman at Pistoia, and consists of a large folio volume, dated 1727, of about 500 pages closely but very clearly and legibly written. It contains a great abundance of notices respecting the geography of Tibet, and the manners and customs, and religion of the Tibetans. There are two other documents of Desideri in the library of the Congregation of the Propaganda at Rome. The first is another narrative, dated February 17, 1717, soon after his arrival at Lhasa, and addressed to the Pope, and the second is a letter written in autograph by Desideri to the Pope.[1]

Father Desideri also translated the 'Kangiar' of the great reforming Lama, Tsong-khapa, into Latin.

The Capuchin friars had already found their way to Lhasa in the time of Desideri; and we have several letters from their leader. This was Francisco Orazio della Penna, or Pinnabillensis. He was born at Macerata, in Italy, in 1780, became a Capuchin, and was sent to Tibet with twelve of his brethren as missionaries. They reached Lhasa by way of Nepal in 1719, and established a mission which flourished for nearly a quarter

vol. ix. to vol. xxvi. The letter of Desideri is in vol. xv. In 1781 a new edition appeared in twenty-six volumes (bound in twelve), and edited by M. de Querbœuf. Du Halde died in 1743. Mention will be made of his great work on China in another note, at p. lxii.

[1] Signor Carlo Puini examined the manuscript at Pistoia on November 19, 1875, and he will be furnished with copies both of it and of the documents at Rome. He will then write an exhaustive paper on Father Desideri and his travels, and eventually he hopes to publish the manuscript itself, with the necessary elucidations. I am indebted to Colonel Yule for this important news respecting the Desideri manuscripts, and their contemplated publication, which ought to be promptly followed by an English edition.

of a century. Horace della Penna studied Tibetan at Lhasa for twenty-two years. During that time nine of the Capuchin friars died, and Horace returned to Rome in 1735, representing that the three survivors were worn out with age and hard work, and expressing a wish for reinforcements, and for the establishment of annual communication between Rome and Lhasa. The Pope nominated nine more Capuchins, who set out from Rome, with Horace della Penna, in 1738, bearing letters from his Holiness to the Dalai Lama. In 1741 Horace wrote that the mission had arrived at Lhasa during the previous year. The affairs of the mission afterwards took him to Nepal, and he died at Patan, in the Nepal valley, on the 20th of July, 1747. A monument was erected over his grave, with an inscription, which is given by Giorgi. The letters of this enterprising missionary were carefully edited and published by Klaproth, in the 'Journal Asiatique,'[1] and a translation of them will be found in the Appendix to this volume. Much information collected by Della Penna is embodied in the ponderous 'Alphabetum Tibetanum' of Giorgi.[2] The way in which Horace della Penna passed to and fro between Tibet and India proves that the intercourse was free and unrestrained between the two countries, and that the traffic was protected by the enlightened policy of the Lamas of Tibet and the Newar Kings of Nepal.

[1] 'Journal Asiatique,' second series, xiv. p. 177.

[2] Antonio Augustin Giorgi was born at Santa Maura, near Rimini, in 1711. He became an Augustin friar, and was a great linguist, and altogether a most erudite person. His work, 'Alphabetum Tibetanum' (Rome, 1762, 1 vol. 4to), was compiled from materials sent from Tibet by the Capuchin friars, especially Horace della Penna (or Pinnabillensis?) and Cassien de Macerata. He obtained the Tibetan characters from Della Penna, which were engraved in 1738 by Anton Fontarita. The huge work contains a chronology of Tibetan kings and lamas, itineraries, and other information, which is overlaid by a confusing and superfluous mass of erudition and puerile etymologies. Giorgi died on the 4th of May, 1797.

For an account of the Capuchin Mission to Lhasa, see also 'Alla sagra congregazione de propaganda fide deputata sopra la missione del Gran Thibet, rappresentanza de Padri Cappuccini Missionaj, dello stato presente della medesima, e de' provvedimenti per manteneola ed accrescerla,' 1738, pp. 55, in the India Office library, bound up with other tracts.

Just before the Capuchin missionaries reached Lhasa the famous native survey of Tibet had been completed, which still forms the basis of our geographical knowledge of that country. The Emperor Kang-hi, having been satisfied of the accuracy of the European method of surveying, from the examination of a map which the Jesuit missionaries had executed of the country round Peking, resolved to have a survey made of the whole empire on the same principles. This great work was commenced in July, 1708, and the completed maps were presented to the Emperor in 1718. The records preserved in each city were examined, topographical information was diligently collected, and the Jesuit Fathers checked their triangulation by meridian altitudes of the sun and pole star, and by a system of re-measurements. The result was a more accurate map of China than existed, at that time, of any country in Europe.

As regards Tibet, an embassy had been sent to Lhasa by the Emperor Kang-hi, to reconcile the Yellow and Red Cap factions, and during the stay of the envoys, of two years, a map of Tibet was prepared, and placed in the hands of Father Regis, one of the leading surveyors of China, on their return.[1] But it was found that their positions had not been fixed by astronomical observations, and that the distances had not been systematically measured. Regis declined to use this map as material for a part of the general map of the empire. Kang-hi, therefore, resolved to have another map constructed, and accordingly two lamas were carefully trained as surveyors by the Jesuit Fathers at Peking, and sent to Tibet with orders to include the country from Sining to Lhasa, and thence to the sources of the Ganges, in their survey. The result was a map of Tibet, which was submitted to the Fathers, in 1717, and though not without faults, it was found to be a great improvement on the former attempt. From it the Jesuits prepared the well-known maps which were forwarded to Du Halde, and from which D'Anville constructed his atlas. The Lama Survey of Tibet

[1] The account of Tibet, by Regis, is given in Du Halde, ii. pp. 384-388.

still continues to be the basis of our geographical knowledge of that country,[1] although it is rapidly being superseded by the efforts of Colonel Montgomerie and his native explorers.

During the reign of the Emperor Yung-ching, son and successor of Kang-hi, who caused the surveys to be executed, or between 1723 and 1736, the most remarkable journeys ever made by a European in Tibet were achieved by a Dutchman, who went from India, by Lhasa, to Peking, and returned by the same route.

This traveller was Samuel Van de Putte. His family is well known in Zeeland, and the illustrious statesman Frausen Van de Putte, recently Minister of the Colonies in Holland, is descended from the traveller's father in direct line. Carel Van de Putte, the traveller's father, was Vice-Admiral of Zeeland, and, by his wife Johanna Constantia Biscop, he had a son Samuel, born at Flushing in 1690. The Admiral died in 1725, and Samuel studied jurisprudence at Leyden, taking his Doctor's degree in 1714. In 1715 he was chosen Alderman of Flushing. In 1718 he left the Netherlands, in company with another gentleman of good family, named Egmond Van der Nyenburg, of Alkmaar. They started with the intention of being absent for about three years, but a thirst for knowledge and adventure led them to exceed this period by many years. Van de Putte travelled with a caravan from Aleppo to Isfahan, and went thence to India, arriving at the port of Cochin in August, 1724. After travelling for several years through the territories of the

[1] The Lama Survey came to the knowledge of the Europeans through the great work of Du Halde: 'Description géographique, historique, chronologique, politique, et physique de l'Empire de la Chine et de la Tartarie Chinoise' (Paris, 1735, 4 vols. folio). It was accompanied by an atlas of forty-two maps by D'Anville. A second edition appeared at the Hague in the following year, in quarto, with important additions. An English translation was published in 1742 in London, in 2 vols. folio; and a German translation in 1747. But the English translator has made several abridgments. Du Halde's work is based on information contained in letters and other communications from numerous Jesuit missionaries in China. The maps, including that of Tibet, were constructed by D'Anville from materials supplied by Regis and the other surveyors employed by the Emperor of China.

Great Moghul, in the dress of a native, he eventually made his way to Lhasa; and Father Gauvil[1] assures us that he acquired the Tibetan language, and became intimate with some of the Lamas. After a long residence at Lhasa, he set out, in the dress of a Chinese mandarin, accompanying a deputation of Lamas to Peking. He went by the route afterwards traversed by Huc, and entered China by the Great Wall. Father Horace della Penna, in one of his letters,[2] quotes a passage from the journal of Van de Putte, in which he describes the passage of the river Biciu (Bi-tsion), the upper course of the Yang-tsze. The river was traversed in boats made of hides. Embarking in the morning, the travellers passed the night on a little island in the middle of the stream, and only reached the opposite shore at about noon on the following day.

Van de Putte is the only European who has ever completed the journey from India, through Lhasa, to China. He returned to India, also passing through Lhasa, and was an eye-witness of the sack of Delhi by Nadir Shah in 1737. In 1743 he finally left India, sailing from Bengal to Batavia, and in September of the same year he was at Malacca, and made a trip to the famous Mount Ophir. He went back to Batavia, intending to return home, and took up his residence in the house of Mr. P. W. Lammens, where he died on the 27th of September, 1745, aged fifty-five.

The premature death of this illustrious traveller is the more to be lamented because his vast knowledge died with him; for he desired, in his will, that all his papers should be burnt, fearing that, owing to the imperfect state in which they were left, some fraudulent use might be made of them, and erroneous accounts be published under the sanction of his name. The dangers to which he had been exposed obliged him to write the greater part of the notes on small strips of paper, and

[1] In a letter from Peking, dated August 13, 1752, published in the 'Journal Asiatique,' x. p. 223.

[2] Published in the 'Journal Asiatique,' xiv. p. 191, and edited, with notes, by Klaproth.

in a character which it was impossible for anyone but himself to decipher. Mr. Lammens, on his return to Holland, presented some of the collections made by Van de Putte to the Zeeland Society of Science at Middelburg, and they are still preserved in its museum, with a few specimens of his notes. There is also a map of part of Tibet by Van de Putte in the museum at Middelburg. On this map, which includes the region between the Ganges and the Tsanpu (Brahmaputra) in Tibet, Van de Putte uses the Italian language, but his Dutch occasionally comes out, as, for example, in spelling Purneah, he uses *oe*, the Dutch equivalent for the English *oo* and Italian *u*. It appears from the notes upon it that the map was drawn at Lhasa, after receiving topographical information from the son of the Khalon, or minister of the ruler of Bramascjon (Sikkim[1]), with the intention of asking him some further questions, but that the Khalon's son left Lhasa before Van de Putte found an opportunity of resuming his inquiries. On this map we have the Tibetan course of the Arun from Tinkri (Tingry) Maidan more correctly laid down than on any other, until the journey of Colonel Montgomerie's explorer No. 9 in 1871. The places between Pary (Pari-jong) and Shigatze (Gigatzé) are also given, and Bhutan is called "*Broukpa*" ("Dukpa," the Red Cap sect). Professor Veth, of Leyden, has also kindly examined the manuscript notes of Van de Putte, which have been sent to him by the Secretary of the Zeeland Scientific Society. They are on little scraps of paper, and contain descriptions of mineral, vegetable, and animal products of which the traveller had collected specimens, which are now in the museum at Middelburg. There are also a few geographical notes, with slight sketches of the form of several lakes. On the notes there are frequent references to the journal, which has most unfortunately been destroyed. The great Dutch traveller is said to have been considered almost as a saint by his acquaintances in Tibet, and

[1] Horace della Penna also uses this name for Sikkim. Bogle calls it Demojong.

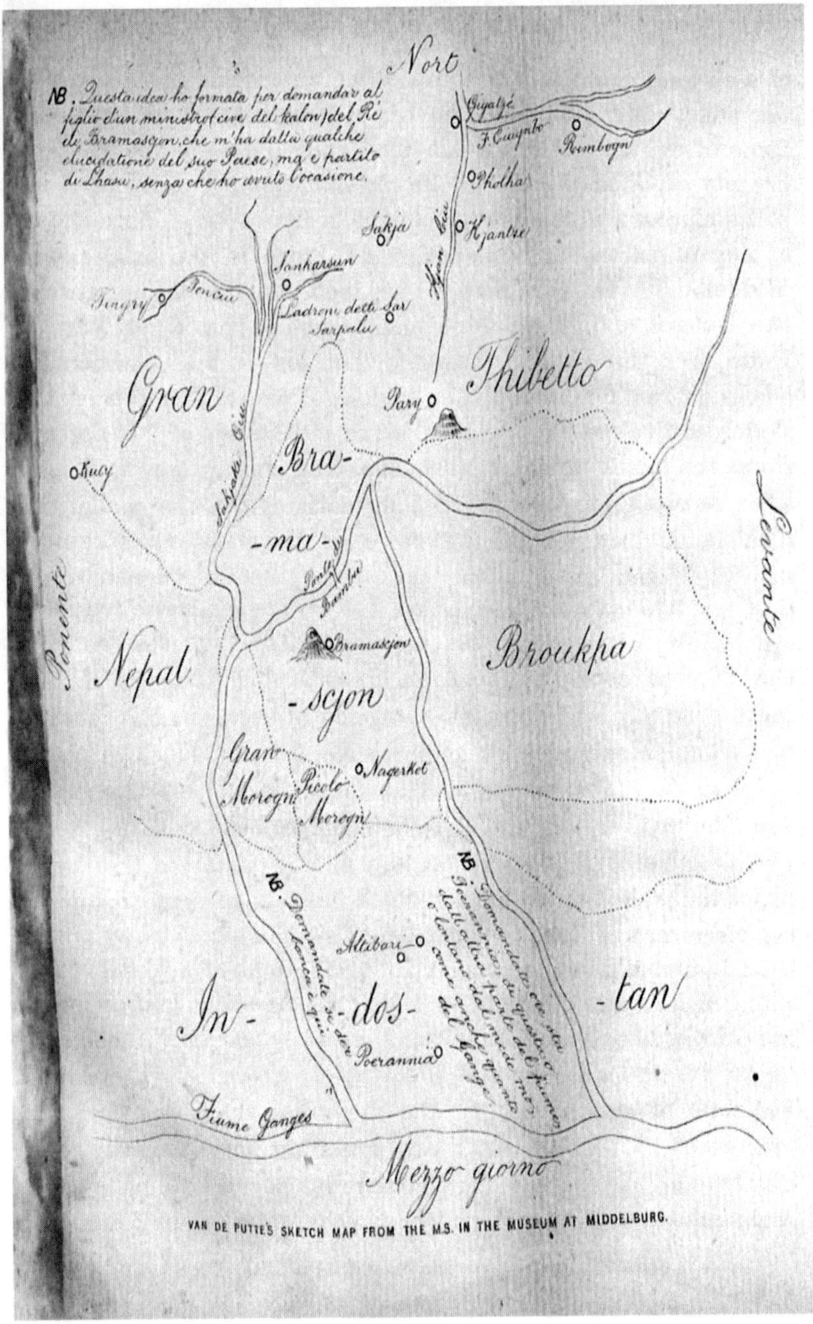

VAN DE PUTTE'S SKETCH MAP FROM THE M.S. IN THE MUSEUM AT MIDDELBURG.

in the East generally, on account of the purity of his life; and he is praised for his great proficiency in several Oriental languages.[1]

The period of the residence of Capuchin friars in Lhasa, when the Lama Survey of Tibet was executed, and Van de Putte made his remarkable journey, was by no means one of internal tranquillity in the capital of the Dalai Lama. The sixth incarnate Buddhisatwa was Lobsang Kalsang, already mentioned, who reigned from 1706 to 1758, when he was succeeded by Lobsang Champal. In 1749, the Chinese Ambas, or political agents, put the Tibetan Gyalpo, or Regent, to death, and the people flew to arms. The tumult led to a massacre of the Chinese, and the leader of the expedition sent by the Emperor to restore order was prudently instructed to make concessions, so that the ascendency of China was maintained while the wrath of the Lamas and the people was appeased. The succeeding Gyalpos, or Gesub Rimbochés, were completely under the influence of the Chinese,

[1] I am indebted to the courtesy of Professor Veth, the learned President of the Dutch Geographical Society, for the above particulars of the life of Samuel Van de Putte, one of the most successful travellers who ever crossed the Himálaya mountains.

The references to his remains at Middelburg are as follows: 'S. de Wind, Mededeeling omtrent den landreizeger S. van de Putte in Archief. vroegere en latere mededeelingen uitgegeven door het Zeeuwsch Genootschap der Wetenschappen' (Middelburg, 1856–63), i. p. 21; 'Inventaris der Handschriften van het Zeeuwsch Genootschap,' bl. 36; 'De Navorscher,' ii. 58; v. 38; vi. 113, 175; vii. 141; viii. 328; ix. 40. In 1871 Mr. J. P. Bodèl Nyenhuis read a paper on the travels of Van de Putte at Leyden, and exhibited his map of part of Tibet. (See 'Handelingen en mededeelingen van de Maatschappy der Nederlandsche letterkunde to Leiden' voor 1871, p. 51; also 'Vd. Aa. Biographisch Woordenboek,' art. Van de Putte; and 'Reizen van Egmond van der Nyenburg, en Johannes Heyman' (Leyden, 1758), ii. p. 396.

He is mentioned in two letters: one from Father Gaubil, the other from Horace della Penna, in the 'Journal Asiatique,' x. p. 323, and xiv. p. 191; and in a note to the latter, Klaproth, the editor, says, "He is the only European who has ever made the interesting journey from the capital of Tibet to that of China." Klaproth adds that the traveller's journal was lost. He erroneously calls him Van der Put. Colonel Yule was the first English geographer to notice the travels of Van de Putte, in his 'Cathay, and the Road Thither,' i. p. 49 (note). Mr. D'Israeli, in one of the editions of his 'Curiosities of Literature,' has an article on Van de Putte, entitled, "A Mandarine from Middelburgh." It calls him *Hudde*, and contains almost as many mistakes as lines.

as is shown by their expulsion of the Catholic priests, and by their jealous conduct at the time of the missions of Bogle and Turner.

The Capuchin missionaries were expelled from Lhasa in about 1760, and took refuge at Lalita Patan, in the valley of Nepal. Here they were witnesses of a revolution which has had a fatal influence on the commercial prosperity and progress of Tibet, by blocking up the passes into India through Nepal. This event was the destruction of the Newar dynasty by the military tribes led by the chief of the petty State of Gorkha. The Mal rulers of Nepal, who encouraged commerce and the arts of peace, consisted of the three Kings of Kathmandu, Patan, and Bhatgaon, in the Nepal valley. Their own dissensions appear to have been the immediate cause of their fall. The King of Bhatgaon applied to the Chief of Gorkha, named Prithi Narayan, to help him against the other two kings; but he soon saw the danger he had invited, and took measures of defence, making common cause with his brethren of Patan and Kathmandu. It was too late. The Gorkhas, under Prithi Narayan, had occupied all the mountains that surround the valley of Nepal, which they blockaded. Their leader then broke into the valley, and after three sieges captured the town of Sirtipúr, committing atrocious acts of cruelty on the inhabitants. The Newar Rajahs entreated aid from the English in India, in 1769, and a small force was sent under Captain Kinloch, whose approach created a diversion, but he eventually retreated, and Prithi Narayan captured the three Nepal capitals, one after the other, in 1769. The King of Bhatgaon was allowed to retire to Benares; the King of Kathmandu fell in the field, and he of Patan died in chains. Thus, in four years, the Nepal valley was subdued, and Prithi Narayan, with his warlike tribes, founded the present Gorkha dynasty by much hard fighting, followed by the most hideous atrocities on the vanquished.

The Fathers Guiseppe (who was Prefect of the Roman Mission) and Michael Angelo were eye-witnesses of this conquest and of the horrible cruelties which disgraced it.[1] The missionaries afterwards obtained permission to retire with their flock into British territory, and they settled at Bettiah, near Patna. Prithi Narayan died in 1771, three years after the conquest of Nepal, leaving two sons named Sing Pertab and Bahadar Sah. The former succeeded, and died in 1775, leaving an infant son, and Bahadar Sah became regent. In the time of the regency, the Gorkhas conquered the whole of Nepal, and so persecuted the merchants by their enormous tolls and other exactions, that the once flourishing trade between Tibet and India, by the Nepal passes, was almost annihilated. The misconduct of the Gorkha Rajah was a constant subject of complaint in the conversations of the Teshu Lama with Mr. Bogle.

While Prithi Narayan was conquering Nepal, an equally ambitious though less fortunate disturber of the peace arose in Bhutan in the person of Deb Judhur,[2] who overran Sikkim and held possession of it for several years. He then invaded Kuch Bahar in 1772, an aggression which brought him into collision with the British, and led to his overthrow.[3] The family of the Kuch Bahar Rajah solicited the aid of the Government of India, and Warren Hastings organized a small field force, under Captain John Jones, which speedily drove the Bhutanese back into their hills, seized some of their strongholds, and forced them to sue for peace. The Teshu Lama of Tibet also wrote a letter interceding for them, and sent it to Calcutta.[4] Deb Judhur strove to form a coalition against the English, and the Rajahs of Nepal, Assam, and Sylhet promised to join him, and would certainly have done so if any success had attended his arms.

Warren Hastings had assumed the government of Bengal in April, 1772; and in the following cool season of 1772–73 the

[1] See "An Account of the Kingdom of Nepal," by Father Guiseppe, Prefect of the Roman Mission, in 'Asiatic Researches,' ii. pp. 307–322.

[2] Called Deb Jeedah by Mr. Eden (p. 111).

[3] An account of the career of Deb Judhur will be found at p. 37; and he is frequently mentioned throughout Mr. Bogle's narrative.

[4] See note at p. 1.

operations against the Bhutanese were undertaken.[1] At their successful close he received the dignified letter of intercession from the Teshu Lama which is printed at page 1; and he then conceived and matured that enlightened policy which was continuous during his tenure of office, and which had for its object the reopening of commercial and friendly intercourse between the lofty plateau of Great Tibet and the plains of India. Much leniency and forbearance were shown in dealing with the defeated Bhutanese, both to conciliate the goodwill of the mountaineers themselves, and out of deference to the wishes of the Teshu Lama.

Warren Hastings also resolved to send an embassy to the Deb Rajah of Bhutan, and to the Teshu Lama of Tibet. He took this step after very mature consideration, and his preliminary memorandum[2] shows that he had carefully studied all the works bearing on the subject to which he had access, including De Guignes, Du Halde, Bell, and Astley's voyages. He selected Mr. George Bogle, of the Bengal Civil Service, as envoy, whose instructions are dated on the 13th of May, 1774. The narrative of this mission is now published for the first time, and will, I believe, be read with much interest. Mr. Bogle was the first Englishman—except his companion Dr. Hamilton and Mr. Manning—who ever crossed the Tsanpu in its upper course, and the only European who ever had the advantage of close and friendly intercourse with one of the Grand Lamas of Tibetan Buddhism, and who left a record of his impressions and conversations. Besides the valuable information he collected, Bogle's mission was very successful in other respects. It laid the foundation of a policy which, had it been steadily and cautiously, but continuously, carried out, would long ere this have secured permanent results. Bogle formed a close friendship with the Teshu Lama and all his kindred. He

[1] See Gleig's 'Memoirs of Warren Hastings,' vol. i. pp. 279 and 295.

[2] See p. 9.

secured their hearty co-operation and support in the encouragement of trade, and even succeeded after tedious negotiations in inducing the Bhutan Government to allow the passage of merchants through their territory to and from Tibet and Bengal. These successes were confirmed by the great reduction of duties on the frontier,[1] and the establishment of a fair at Rangpúr, under conditions which were extremely advantageous to the Bhutanese. Their expenses were paid by government, stables were erected for their horses, and houses for themselves.[2] But Mr. Bogle found that the Gesub Rimboché, or Regent, at Lhasa, under the influence of the Chinese agents, opposed the more liberal and enlightened views of the Teshu Lama, as regards the admission of foreigners into Tibet, with fatal effect. It seemed clear that the only way to counteract this was to obtain, through the Teshu Lama, a hearing at Peking. Mr. Bogle returned from Tibet in June, 1775, and Warren Hastings determined to continue an intercourse which had been inaugurated with such excellent judgment and tact.

In November, 1775, Dr. Hamilton, who accompanied Mr. Bogle to Tibet, was appointed to a second mission to Bhutan; and in January, 1776, he reached the frontier, and received a friendly letter from the Deb Rajah inviting him to proceed to Punakha. He endeavoured to enter Bhutan by an easier and better route, leading by the Lakhi Dúar to Paro; but obstacles appear to have been raised, and he eventually took the old and difficult route, by the Buxa-Dúar, which he had formerly traversed with Mr. Bogle. Dr. Hamilton reached Punakha on April 6, and was at Tassisudon in May, 1776. One of his duties was to examine into the claims of the Deb Rajah on

[1] Followed by their total abolition.

[2] This wise encouragement of Bhutan trade, by a fair at Rangpúr, was continued until 1831–32, at an annual cost of about 20*l*. But in 1832, at the recommendation of Mr. Nesbit, an economical Commissioner of the Revenue at the time, it was ordered to be discontinued. The consequence was the falling off in the trade, and it has dwindled ever since. (Pemberton, p. 175.)

the districts of Ambari Fala-kottah and Jalpaish, and he came to the conclusion, after taking evidence, that equity demanded their restoration to Bhutan. He reported that if restitution was made, he would probably be able to induce the Deb Rajah to fulfil his agreement with Mr. Bogle, and only to levy moderate transit duties on merchandise. Dr. Hamilton returned, after insisting upon the agreement between the Deb Rajah and Mr. Bogle being faithfully observed.

In July, 1777, Dr. Hamilton was sent on a third mission to Bhutan, to congratulate a new Deb Rajah on his accession, returning in September.[1] Thus Warren Hastings prevented the opening made by Mr. Bogle from again being closed, by keeping up regular intercourse with the Bhutan rulers, by maintaining a correspondence with the Teshu Lama, and by means of the annual fair at Rangpúr.

In April, 1779, Mr. Bogle was appointed as envoy to Tibet a second time, but the arrival of news that the Teshu Lama was about to undertake a journey to Peking caused the postponement of the mission. What followed is detailed in chapter XIX.[2] The Teshu Lama, at one of his first interviews with the Emperor of China, took an opportunity of speaking in favour of Warren Hastings and the English in India. Mr. Bogle, it had been arranged, was to have met his friend the Lama at Peking, and would probably have returned with him to Tibet. But two great calamities frustrated these admirable plans. The Teshu Lama died of smallpox at Peking, on November 12, 1780, and Mr. Bogle died at Calcutta on the 3rd of April, 1781.

Looking to the success which had attended Mr. Bogle's negotiations, and to his special aptitude for the work, the death of that distinguished public servant was a national calamity. But Warren Hastings was not to be turned aside from his wise and statesmanlike aim. He carefully watched the course of events for an opportunity to make another move. At length,

[1] Dr. Hamilton died in 1780.

[2] See p. 207.

on February 12, 1782, the news arrived at Calcutta that the Teshu Lama had reappeared in the person of an infant;[1] and the Governor-General resolved to send a fourth mission to Bhutan, which was also to continue its functions as far as Tibet, with a view to congratulating the Regency on the renewed incarnation of the good Teshu Lama, and to continuing friendly relations with the Tibetan government.

For this duty he selected Captain Samuel Turner,[2] a young kinsman of his own, who was accompanied by Lieut. Samuel Davis,[3] and Dr. Robert Saunders[4] as medical officer to the mission.

[1] The expectation of the event was communicated to the Governor-General by the Regent Chanzu Cusho, brother of the Teshu Lama, and by Sopon Chumbo, his cupbearer, in letters announcing the death of the Teshu Lama; translations of which are given in Turner's 'Embassy,' pp. 449 and 454.

[2] Samuel Turner was born in Gloucestershire in 1749, and entered the army of the East India Company. He was a kinsman of Warren Hastings, who, having assured himself of the young officer's ability, appointed him to conduct the second embassy to Tibet, and he was absent from January, 1783, to March, 1784. In 1792 Turner distinguished himself at the siege of Seringapatam, and he afterwards, as envoy to Tipú Sultan, conducted some negotiations to the satisfaction of the Government. Having amassed a considerable fortune, he returned to England, and published his narrative of the Tibet Mission in 1800. He died suddenly, in London, on January 2, 1802. His work was translated into French by Castera. (Paris, 2 vols. 8vo.)

[3] Lieut. Samuel Davis, of the Bengal Engineer Corps, was born in 1760, his father having also been in the army, his military commission having been signed by George II. in the last year of his reign, and countersigned by William Pitt. Lieut. S. Davis was an excellent artist, and the Bhutan illustrations in Turner's work are from his pencil. The original drawings are still preserved by his son, Sir John Davis, at Hollywood. But his scientific profession was regarded with so much jealousy, that the Tibetan Government (or more probably the Chinese Residents) insisted upon his remaining in Bhutan until the return of the embassy. Hence his drawings are confined to Bhutan, and do not extend to Tibet. Mr. Davis afterwards received the appointment of judge and magistrate at Benares. A very interesting narrative of the disturbance excited at Benares by the dethroned Vizier Ali Khan, of Oudh, in January, 1799, when Mr. Davis defended his family, single-handed, with a long spear, against a host of assailants, was printed in 1844 by his son, and there was a second edition in 1871 ('Vizier Ali Khan, or the Massacre of Benares: a Chapter of Indian History'). Mr. Davis was called from Benares to fill higher offices of trust at Calcutta. He returned to England in 1806, and became a Director of the East India Company in 1809. At the time of the renewal of the Charter in 1814, the Committee of the House of Commons intrusted him with the task of drawing up, in their

Turner's mission proceeded to Tassisudon, by the Buxa-Dúar, exactly following Mr. Bogle's route, and reaching the summer palace of the Deb Rajah early in June, 1783. Captain Turner ceded, by order of his Government, the districts of Ambari Fala-kottah and Jalpaish to Bhutan, in accordance with the advice of Dr. Hamilton. They had previously been held by the Baikantpúr Zamindar.[5] During Captain Turner's stay at Tassisudon a rebellion broke out against the ruler, who was the successor of the Deb with whom Mr. Bogle negotiated, headed by the Zumpan or Governor of Wandipore,[6] an important castle in the valley in which Punakha is situated, the winter palace of the Bhutan rulers, but some miles below that place, and 24 miles east of Tassisudon. After some desultory fighting, the Deb Rajah's troops blockaded and eventually captured Wandipore, and soon afterwards the members of the mission were permitted to visit both Wandipore and Punakha. On the 8th of September, after a stay of three months, Captain Turner and his companions left Tassisudon on their way to Tibet, attended by Purungir Gosain, who had also accompanied Mr. Bogle, and who wrote the interesting account of the Teshu Lama's journey to Peking, and death.[7] They still travelled over exactly the same route as had been

name, the memorable "Fifth Report on the Revenues of Bengal," which remains a monument of his intimate acquaintance with the internal administration of India. He died prematurely, at the age of fifty-nine, in the year 1819. His son, Sir John Davis, Bart., K.C.B., was three years old when his life was saved through his father's intrepidity and presence of mind at Benares, having been born in 1795. He was attached to Lord Amherst's Embassy to Peking, in 1816; was joint Commissioner with Lord Napier for arranging commercial matters with China, in 1836; and from 1843 to 1848 was Plenipotentiary in China and Governor of Hong Kong. He is the author of numerous valuable works and essays on subjects relating to China.

[4] Dr. Robert Saunders, some years after his return from Tibet, retired from the service, and resided in London, where he practised as a physician for many years.

[5] Mr. Eden considered this cession to be unjust.

[6] The Angdaphorang of modern maps.

[7] See note at p. 207

taken by Mr. Bogle, and arrived at Teshu Lumbo on the 22nd of September. In passing through the valley of Painám, Captain Turner notices having seen, just visible, peeping through the midst of some tall trees, a large white house, memorable for the birth of the new Teshu Lama, whose father, an uncle of the Dalai Lama, and mother were residing with him there. The place was called Kisu, or Kyli.[1]

At the time of Turner's visit the late Teshu Lama's brother, Chanzu Cusho, who is often mentioned by Mr. Bogle, was regent, and the Sopon Chumbo or cupbearer of the late Lama was his chief adviser. Soon after the arrival of the English mission the infant Lama was removed from the place of his birth, in great pomp, and attended by the Regent and a guard of Chinese soldiers, to a monastery prepared for his reception, called Terpaling, about two days' journey south of Teshu Lumbo. During his stay Captain Turner visited and described the country round Teshu Lumbo, the interior of the monastery, the devotional ceremonies, and the tomb dedicated to the memory of the late Teshu Lama. He also gives an interesting account of his conversations with the Chanzu Cusho and the Sopon Chumbo, and some valuable notes respecting the religion and government of Tibet.

On the 2nd of December, 1783, the mission set out on its return to Bengal, but Captain Turner was allowed to make a slight detour from his previous route, in order to pay his respects to the infant Teshu Lama at the monastery of Terpaling. On the morning of the 4th of December the British envoy had his audience, and found the princely child, then aged eighteen months, seated on a throne, with his father and mother standing on the left hand. Having been informed that, although unable to speak, he could understand, Captain Turner said "that the Governor-General, on receiving news of his decease in China, was overwhelmed with grief and sorrow, and continued to

[1] See Turner, pp. 230 and 249.

lament his absence from the world until the cloud that had overcast the happiness of this nation was dispelled by his re-appearance, and then, if possible, a greater degree of joy had taken place than he had experienced of grief on receiving the first mournful news. The Governor anxiously wished that he might long continue to illumine the world by his presence, and was hopeful that the friendship which had formerly subsisted between them would not be diminished, but rather that it might become still greater than before; and that by his continuing to show kindness to my countrymen there might be an extensive communication between his votaries and the dependents of the British nation." The infant looked stedfastly at the British envoy, with the appearance of much attention, and nodded with repeated but slow motions of the head, as though he understood every word. He was silent and sedate, his whole attention was directed to the envoy, and he conducted himself with astonishing dignity and decorum. He was one of the handsomest children Captain Turner had ever seen, and he grew up to be an able and devout ruler, delighting the Tibetans with his presence for many years, and dying at a good old age.

Captain Turner took his leave, and after a short stay with the Deb Rajah at Punakha, he rejoined the Governor-General at Patna, in March, 1784.[1]

In the following year, 1785, India lost the services of her

[1] See 'An Account of an Embassy to the Court of the Teshu Lama, in Tibet; containing a Narrative of a Journey through Bhutan and Part of Tibet, by Captain Samuel Turner; to which are added views taken on the spot by Lieutenant Samuel Davis; and observations botanical, mineralogical, and medical, by Mr. Robert Saunders.' (London, 1800, 4to, pp. xxviii and 473, including appendices.) It is illustrated by thirteen engravings, and a route map engraved by John Walker.

Captain Turner gives an interesting account of his intercourse with the officials in Bhutan and Tibet; of the manners, customs, and religion of the people, and pleasantly describes the scenery and incidents along his line of march. This work has hitherto been the only one on Great Tibet, written by an Englishman who had himself visited the country.

In a letter to Lord Mansfield, Warren Hastings gives an account of Turner's mission, and speaks highly of his journal, to which great interest was attached.

first English Governor-General, and with his retirement all direct diplomatic intercourse between Tibet and India ceased, and has never been renewed. Warren Hastings had a policy which was alike wise and consistent. Each separate step was not a long one, but each was a step in advance, and what was once gained was never lost. The knowledge once acquired was preserved, in order to furnish guidance for future action; and a policy was established which was persistent and continuous, and at the same time cautious and conciliatory. With the retirement of the great statesman all this came to an end; and even now it will be long before the Government of India regains the ground, as regards friendly intercourse with Tibet, that it had actually reached when its measures were guided by the genius of Warren Hastings.

When Warren Hastings left India he actually had a diplomatic agent at the Tibetan Court. This was Purungir Gosain, the faithful companion of Bogle and Turner, and of the Teshu Lama in his journey to Peking. Purungir witnessed the removal of the infant Teshu Lama from the Terpaling monastery to Teshu Lumbo, amidst imposing pomp and general rejoicings; and his solemn installation in presence of the Dalai Lama, the Chinese political agent or Amba, the Gesub Rimboché, and the heads of all the monasteries in Tibet, in October, 1784. Purungir Gosain was dismissed by the Regent Chanzu Cusho with the most cordial assurances of his desire to continue the friendly relations established by Mr. Bogle, and to encourage trade with Bengal.[1]

This Mission to Tibet should be remembered, as it was the last. Matters were allowed, a few years afterwards, to drift until they reached a crisis, the result of which was permanently to seal up the passes into Tibet, and they continue closed to English officials to this day. The turbulent Gorkhas, under the

[1] Captain Turner translated Purungir Gosain's report, and presented it to Mr. Macpherson, who succeeded Warren Hastings as Governor-General (pending the arrival of Lord Cornwallis), on February 6, 1786. (Turner, p. 423.)

Regent Bahadar Sah, had conquered all Nepal, and during a course of years had committed lawless aggressions on the frontiers. In 1788 they invaded Sikkim, led by the Subah of Murung, and only retired after the Tibet Government had ceded a piece of territory at the head of the Kuti pass. At the same time the Regency appears to have been willing to enter into arrangements with the Government of Lord Cornwallis to protect the trade of the two countries, and in 1792 a commercial treaty was negotiated with Nepal, by Mr. Jonathan Duncan, the Resident at Benares.[1]

But, in the same year, the Nepal Regency suddenly determined to invade Tibet, tempted by stories of the great riches in the Teshu Lama's palace, brought by a refugee Tibetan monk named Sumhur Lama. The pretext of war was that the Tibetans insisted upon circulating base coin, and refused either to withdraw it or to establish a fair rate of exchange.[2] The distance of Kathmandu to Kuti is 141 miles, over one of the most difficult roads in the world, and thence to Teshu Lumbo 257 miles. The Gorkha army, 18,000 strong, marched over the whole distance of 398 miles with extreme rapidity, arrived before Teshu Lumbo, and took and plundered the palace without meeting with any resistance. The Tibetans were panic-stricken. The Regent fled across the Tsanpu with the infant Teshu Lama, and conveyed him to Lhasa, whence entreaties for help were despatched to Peking. The Chinese Government at once prepared an expeditionary force, and sent an envoy in advance to the Nepal army, demanding the restitution of all the plunder taken at Teshu Lumbo, and the surrender of Sumhur Lama. The reply was an insolent defiance: on the receipt of which the army, under the command of a general named Sund Fô,

[1] By the Treaty of Commerce with Nepal, in 1792, it was agreed that 2½ per cent. shall reciprocally be taken as duty on the imports from both countries. The treaty was signed on the 1st of March, 1792, but was repudiated by the Nepal Durbar a few years afterwards.

[2] 'Kirkpatrick's Nepal,' Appendix No. 1, p. 339: "Memorial of the Court of Kathmandu, relative to the origin of the War with Tibet."

commenced its march. His force consisted of 70,000 men, with the necessary stores, which he divided into two columns, of 40,000 and 30,000. Meanwhile the Gorkhas had evacuated Teshu Lumbo, and retreated to the plain of Tengri Maidan, where they awaited the approach of the Chinese army. In the battle which followed the Gorkhas were entirely defeated, and Sund Fô overtook them, in their retreat, at the head of the pass into Nepal, and again routed them with great loss. He laid siege to Kuti, which post was evacuated, and then marched down into Nepal, by way of Kirong. He had a large army, far superior in numbers to that of the Nepalese, and was provided with very light artillery, the guns being made of leather, which served their purpose well for five or six rounds, and then burst. The loss of men in the Chinese army, while crossing the snowy passes, was immense; but still the numerical strength of the invaders was far beyond that of the Gorkhas. The latter made a final stand in a strong position, on the banks of the river Tâdi, just above Nayakot, and only 20 miles from Kathmandu.

At this point the two armies faced each other for some time until the Chinese general, in a fury, turned his own guns on his own men from the rear, and drove them forward in a mass upon the Gorkhas, sweeping great numbers, and still more of the Gorkhas, into the roaring torrent. Thus a decisive victory was gained within one march of the enemy's capital, in September, 1792.[1] The Nepal Regency then sued for peace, which was granted on very humiliating conditions. The Gorkhas agreed to restore all their plunder; to pay an annual tribute to the Emperor of China; and to send an embassy to Peking once in every five years. The Chinese army returned partly by the Kirong pass, and partly by that of the Arun river.

The conduct of the British Government, under Lord Cornwallis, during the course of these events was unfortunate in its

[1] Mr. Brian Hodgson's recollection of conversations with Bhim Sên Thappa, the sage old minister at Nepal, who was murdered in 1838.

results. It would seem that the wisest policy would have been to prevent or check the invasion of Tibet by the Gorkhas, even by using force, if necessary. Such a course would have ensured the gratitude of the Lamas, curbed the restless aggression and secured the respect of the Gorkha Regency, obviated the march of the Chinese army, and prevented the final sealing up of the passes. The actual policy adopted was one of waiting and drifting.

In August, 1792, Lord Cornwallis received a letter from the Dalai Lama, informing him that the Chinese army had defeated the Gorkhas, and warning him not to interfere on their behalf. The Gorkha Regent had besought the military aid of the British, and Lord Cornwallis wrote to him, on the 15th of September, 1792, declining to give him assistance, and assigning for a reason that the English Company carry on extensive commercial concerns with the Chinese, and have a factory at Canton, and that therefore it is necessary to preserve a good understanding with the Emperor. But he offered to depute a gentleman in his confidence to mediate between China and Nepal. Lord Cornwallis also replied to the Dalai Lama proposing mediation after the rains, and saying that Colonel Kirkpatrick had been commissioned to proceed to Kathmandu with that object.

But Colonel Kirkpatrick was too late, and long before he could arrive on the scene, the Chinese general had settled the question in his own way. The British envoy was accompanied by Lieutenant Scott, Lieutenant Knox, Lieutenant Gerard, and Dr. Freer, with an escort of sepoys. The mission was allowed to advance as far as the Court of Bahadar Sah, but it was then coolly bowed out of the country, and Colonel Kirkpatrick returned to Patna, in March, 1793.[1] In 1795 Run

[1] See 'An Account of Nepal; being the Substance of Observations made during a Mission to that Country in the Year 1793, by Colonel Kirkpatrick.' (London, 1811.) This work was published without the concurrence of the writer, who never corrected the proofs, and it contains many misprints and other errors. The map is by Colonel Gerard. The book contains chapters

Bahadar, the son of Pertab Sing, murdered his uncle, the Regent Bahadar Sah, and entered upon a career of intolerable tyranny, until, in 1800, he was forced to abdicate in favour of his son, and he retired to Benares, where Captain Knox, who had accompanied Colonel Kirkpatrick's mission, was appointed to attend upon him.

In October, 1802, a treaty was negotiated with Nepal, by Captain Knox, to renew the provisions of that of 1792, which had become a dead letter; and in the same year that officer proceeded to Kathmandu as Resident. But he also was bowed out, and the only result of his mission was the valuable work of Dr. Buchanan Hamilton, the father of Indian statistics, who accompanied it.[1] In March, 1803, Captain Knox withdrew from Nepal, and on the 24th of January, 1804, Lord Wellesley formally dissolved the alliance with the Durbar.[2]

The Chinese general who invaded Nepal gave a very unfavourable report of the conduct of the English, and is even believed to have suspected that British troops were in the Gorkha army. We lost all the good results of the policy of Warren Hastings and the friendship of the Lamas, excited the jealous suspicion of the Chinese Government, and the scorn of the Nepal Durbar, and were despised by all. The immediate consequence was that the Chinese closed all the passes into Tibet to the natives of India. Pari-jong and the other frontier stations were occupied, and the Chinese also established a strong post at Jonka-jong,[3] commanding the Kirong pass, the use of which has ever since been forbidden to any one but officials.

on the routes, on the valley of Nepal, the climate, population, arts, learning, trade, and history; with appendices giving the text of Lord Cornwallis's correspondence with the Dalai Lama and Gorkha Regent.

[1] See 'An Account of the Kingdom of Nepal,' by Francis Hamilton (formerly Buchanan), M.D., F.R.S., F.S.A., F.L.S. (Edin., 1819.) Dr. Hamilton enumerates the different tribes of Nepal; describes the various zones of climate, including the valley of Nepal, with their productions; gives an account of the history of the country, its government, and trade.

[2] 'Aitchison's Treaties,' ii. p. 189.

[3] Probably the Ari-jong of D'Anville's map.

Yet, even subsequent to these stringent measures of exclusion, a solitary English traveller succeeded in making his way from India to Lhasa, and is the only Englishman who ever entered the holy city. It is this that gives importance to Mr. Manning's brief journal, which is printed for the first time in this volume. Without any recognized position or official credentials, he entered Bhutan by the Lakhi Dúar in 1811, and reached Parijong, on the frontier of Tibet, in the guise of a medical practitioner. There he found a Chinese general with troops, some of whom he cured, and the general permitted him to accompany his escort back to Lhasa. He remained in the capital of Tibet for several months, but orders eventually came from Peking to send him back by the way he came, and he returned to Calcutta in May, 1812. His narrative is to a great extent filled with accounts of personal troubles and difficulties, but it is valuable by reason of the insight it gives into the social habits of the people, and the relative positions of the Chinese and Tibetans at that time. It also proves that, in spite of the exclusive system of the paramount power, the natives gladly welcome strangers, and that a persistent and energetic traveller, even when so quick-tempered and imprudent as Mr. Manning shows himself to have been, may still make his way to Lhasa, and, like Manning, enjoy the ineffable delight of gazing upon the divine features of the Dalai Lama.

But for officials the way to Tibet was permanently closed; while the countries on the southern slopes of the Himálaya were alienated by the change of policy from that of Warren Hastings to that which has prevailed since. The former was a policy of constant and watchful vigilance; of firmness combined with conciliation; and of persistent resolution to keep open friendly relations and to encourage trade. The latter is one of indifference and neglect, varied by occasional small but disastrous wars, which are waged not for any broad imperial end, but on account of some petty squabble about boundaries. The course taken at the time of the Chinese invasion resulted in the Nepal war.

In 1804, Run Bahadar returned to Nepal, and was murdered soon afterwards. One of his followers, named Bhim Sen Thappa, then became regent, the Rajah, a grandson of Pertab Sing, being only two years old. He was regent until 1838, and represented a martial and turbulent policy. Under him the Gorkha Durbar commenced a system of encroachment and menace along the frontier; and on the 1st of November, 1814, the Government of India, under Lord Hastings, declared war. General Ochterlony, with 6000 men, was to attack the west frontier; General Gillespie, with 3500, was to occupy the Dehra Dún; Generals Wood and Marley, with 4500 and 8000 men respectively, were to advance from the plains on Palpa and Kathmandu; and Major Latter, with a local force, was to operate to the eastward of the Kosi, and in the direction of Sikkim. Gillespie's force occupied Dehra, but through gross mismanagement was repulsed at the siege of Kalunga with great slaughter, and the general was killed. Ochterlony's operations near the Sutlej were more successful. But Wood, in his advance towards Palpa, got disheartened, and fell back on Gorakpúr; and Marley also retreated after advancing a short distance. Major Latter, however, occupied Murung, and formed an alliance with the Rajah of Sikkim.

The general result was that the Gorkhas were driven beyond the Kali, and agreed to make peace, abandoning all territory west of the Kali, ceding all the Teraï country and all territory taken from Sikkim, and allowing a British agent to reside at Kathmandu. But the Nepal Durbar refused to ratify the treaty, and in February, 1816, Sir David Ochterlony again took the field with 17,000 men, and steadily advanced from the plains towards the Nepal capital. The Nepalese then yielded, and the treaty was finally signed on March 3, 1816.

The permanent results of the war were good. The Gorkhas were confined to the country east of the Kali on one side, and on the other their encroachments on the side of Sikkim were stopped, while that little State, under British protection was interposed between the turbulent Gorkhas and Bhutanese. The Lepchas of Sikkim are ruled over by a dynasty of Rajahs originally from Lhasa, who have always been under the dominion of Tibet, and of the Buddhist religion and Dukpa (Red Cap) sect. The Tísta valley thus formed a barrier to Gorkha encroachments on the east, and in Sikkim alone English travellers are able to advance as far as the passes over the Southern Himálaya leading into Tibet.

The new policy led to the same results as regards Bhutan. Instead of friendly intercourse, the history of the relations between the British and the Bhutanese has been one of local disputes about frontiers, and raids. In 1815, Mr. David Scott, the Judge at Rangpúr, sent a native officer, named Kishen Kant Bose, to settle some frontier disputes with the Deb Rajah, and his report has been printed for official information.[1] But it was owing to the annexation of Assam, and the consequent great extension of the frontier between Bhutan and British territory, that frontier disputes became more frequent, and assumed a more important aspect. The Government of India had to take up the relations which had previously existed between the sovereigns of Assam and the Deb Rajah. In former times, owing to the inability of the Assam rulers to expel the invaders, the Bhutanese aggressions in the frontier Dúars had been allowed by them. In 1828, the British occupied the Buri Gumah Dúar, because a raid had been made from it into Assam, and held it until 1834, when it was restored, owing to a letter from the Deb Rajah soliciting its restitution. Other raids into Assam took place in 1835 and 1836; and in 1837 it was resolved to despatch a mission into Bhutan, as it was suspected that letters to the Deb Rajah had frequently been withheld by the Subahs, or subordinate officers, in command of the Dúars. The Deb Rajah showed great reluctance to receive

[1] 'Account of Bootan,' by Baboo Kishen Kant Bose, translated by D. Scott, Esq., pp. 187–206 of the volume containing "Political Missions to Bootan." (Calcutta, 1865.) Also in the 'Asiatic Researches,' xv. p. 128.

an envoy, but the Government of India adhered to its intention, and Captain Pemberton was appointed, with a staff consisting of Dr. Griffith, Ensign Blake, and an escort of twenty-five Assam police.

Captain Pemberton resolved to enter Bhutan by the Banska Dúar, to the east, so as to traverse the country diagonally, and see as much of it as possible, before reaching the capital. In 1838 the mission marched through Kamrúp to Dewangiri, on the range of mountains overlooking the valley of Assam. Thence they proceeded to Punakha by a very circuitous route: first north, nearly to the confines of Tibet; and then over many lofty spurs from east to west; the journey occupying twenty-six travelling days from Dewangiri to Punakha, which place they reached on the 1st of April, 1838. Pemberton returned by Buxa-Dúar, the same route that was taken by Mr. Bogle, and the mission reached Goalpara in May, 1838. Pemberton received a very much less favourable impression of the rulers and people of Bhutan than Bogle or Turner. The country is in a state of continual anarchy. Nominally, while the Dharma Rajah, or Lama Rimboché, is a perpetual incarnation of the Deity, and the Deb Rajah is elected by a council of six for three years, in reality there is an incessant struggle between the governors of East and West Bhutan, called the Paro Penlo and Tongso Penlo, and the Deb is a puppet of the one which happens to have the upper hand. The executive council, according to Pemberton, consists of the Lama Zimpé, who represents the interests of the Dharma Rajah; the Donnai Zimpé; the Tipu Zimpé, who is governor of Tassisudon; the Puna Zimpé, or governor of Punakha; the Deb Zimpé, who represents the Deb Rajah; and the Kalling Zimpé. Captain Pemberton's valuable report, besides the narrative of his journey, contains a *resumé* of previous relations with Bhutan; an account of the Dúars; a general description of Bhutan; its rivers, roads, geology, government, priesthood, revenue, military resources, agriculture, manufactures, trade, population, and civil and social state. It is accompanied by the journal of Dr. Griffith, containing remarks on the nature of the country, especially its vegetation, boundaries, divisions, and population.[1]

Pemberton's mission was followed by no satisfactory results. The Bhutanese really do appear to be a barbarous and irreclaimable race, without records or organization; and, in 1838, all memory of the visits of Bogle and Turner was entirely obliterated. The raids into Assam continued from year to year, followed by fruitless remonstrances, and a barrier was permanently formed in this direction between India and Tibet.

In Nepal, on the other hand, although the passes were equally closed, and no European was or is allowed to travel in the country, yet the residence of an English officer at Kathmandu led to the acquisition of priceless treasures of information respecting the early history, ethnology, religion, and literature of Nepal and Tibet. The honoured name of Brian Hodgson is indissolubly connected with these discoveries.

After the conclusion of peace with Nepal, the first Resident at Kathmandu was the Hon. Edward Gardner, who held the appointment from 1816 to 1829, Mr. Brian Hodgson being his secretary from 1820. From 1829 to 1830, for two years, Mr. Hodgson was in charge; Sir Herbert Maddock was Resident in 1830; and Mr. Brian Hodgson succeeded him, and was Resident at Kathmandu from 1831 to 1843. But he had been in Nepal since 1820, a continuous residence of twenty-three years. Yet

[1] 'Report on Bootan,' by Captain Boileau Pemberton, dated Calcutta, Nov. 30, 1838; and 'Journal of the Mission to Bootan in 1837–38,' by William Griffith, M.D.; 186 pp. of the volume on "Political Missions to Bootan" (printed at Calcutta in 1865).

Captain Pemberton was a distinguished geographer. Between 1825 and 1830 he surveyed Munipúr and portions of Cachar; and his exceedingly valuable large map, compiled from his own work, and that of Bedford and Wilcox, was lithographed at Calcutta in 1838. Dr. Griffith was equally distinguished as a botanist. He accompanied Dr. Wallich to Assam, and Captain Pemberton to Bhutan; joined the army of the Indus in 1839; and made his way from Kabul to Khurasan. He died in 1845. The great object of his life was the preparation of a general scientific Flora of India.

Dr. Griffith's 'Bhutan Journal' was published in 1847 (Calcutta). He made extensive collections of plants in Bhutan, which have been since arranged by Mr. Oliver.

even a quarter of a century seems but a short time for the achievement of the immense results for which, independent of his great public services, his country is indebted to Mr. Hodgson.

He devoted himself to the study of every branch of knowledge relating to Nepal and Tibet. In 1824, Mr. Hodgson announced the fact that the original documents of the Buddhist canon had been preserved in Sanscrit in the monasteries of Nepal. "Before that time our information on Buddhism had been derived at random from China and other countries far from India, and no hope was entertained that the originals of the various translations existing in those countries could ever be recovered."[1] He procured copies of these works, and sent complete collections to the Asiatic Society in London, and to the Société Asiatique of Paris; while he himself threw a flood of light on the history of the Buddhist religion, in several essays written on the spot.[2] The news of Mr. Hodgson's literary

[1] Max Müller's 'Chips from a German Workshop,' i. p. 189. (See also Mrs. Speir's 'Life in Ancient India,' p. 251.)

[2] "Notices on the Languages, Literature, and Religion of the Bauddhas of Nepaul and Bhot, by B. H. Hodgson" ('Asiatic Researches,' xvi. p. 409).

"Sketch of Buddhism, derived from the Bauddha Scriptures of Nepal" ('J. A. S. B.,' ii. p. 222, and v. p. 28).

These essays were reprinted in one volume, 'Illustrations of the Literature and Religion of the Buddhists' (Serampore, 1841).

Eugene Burnouf studied the manuscripts sent by Mr. Hodgson to Paris, and, after seven years, he published, in 1844, 'Introduction à l'Histoire du Buddhisme:' "a work," says Max Müller, "which laid the foundation for a systematic study of the religion of Buddha." Burnouf's death, in 1851, prevented the completion of his work. His last book, 'Le Lotus de la bonne Loi,' published in 1852, after his death, is dedicated to Mr. Hodgson.

Mr. Hodgson also received a complete copy of the Tibetan Cyclopædia (Ghah-gyur and Stan-gyur), in 334 large volumes, as a present from the Dalai Lama, which he gave to the East India Company. In 1864 he presented a vast mass of valuable manuscripts to the India Office library, consisting of chronicles of the Newari and Gorkhali dynasties of Nepal, and numerous documents relating to Nepal administration.

Mr. Trübner has done very good service by the publication, in a single volume, in 1874, of 'Essays on the Language, Literature, and Religion of Nepal and Tibet, with further Papers on the Geography, Ethnology, and Commerce of those Countries, by B. H. Hodgson, Esq.'

The book contains the article on the religion and literature of Nepal and Tibet, from vol. xvi. of the 'Asiatic Researches;' the "Sketch of Buddhism,"

labours in Nepal eventually reached as far as Lhasa, and the Dalai Lama opened a friendly correspondence with him. As a proof of his appreciation of Mr. Hodgson's right feeling, his Holiness sent the English envoy the whole of the existing literary remains of the once flourishing Christian mission at Lhasa. These Mr. Hodgson presented to the Pope.

Besides his marvellous literary industry, Mr. Hodgson, while at Kathmandu, drew up two memoirs on the military system of Nepal, recommending the expediency of procuring the services of a considerable body of Gorkha soldiers, whereby we should diminish the chances of collision with Nepal caused by the pressure on its Government of an excessive soldiery. The Gorkhas have neither arts, literature, nor commerce to draw off their attention from arms. They have that lusty hardihood of character, love of enterprise, and contempt of drudgery, which make war especially congenial.

Mr. Hodgson next turned his attention to promoting the revival and extension of that commerce which flourished in Nepal before the Gorkha conquest, and submitted to his Government lists of imports and exports, routes, and every kind of information calculated to incite natives of India and Nepal to take up the matter in a spirit suited to the times. Mr. Hodgson, himself, made a trip to the Kosi river and the Nayakot valley, and is the only Englishman, except Dr. Hooker, who has ever been allowed to travel in Nepal beyond a circuit of twenty miles round Kathmandu. His essay on the fitness of the Himálaya for the settlement of Europeans marked an epoch in the history of British India, for from its publication dates the movement for the establishment of hill stations, and the enterprises of tea and chinchona planters.

from the 'Transactions of the Royal Asiatic Society,' vol. ii.; papers from the 'J. A. S. B.,' vol. iv. p. 211; iii. p. 215; vi. p. 682. The essays on the "Physical Geography of the Himálaya," from the volume of 'Selections from the Records of the Bengal Government,' xxvii. (1857); on the "Aborigines of the Himálaya" ('J. A. S. B.,' xvi. and xvii.); on the "Military Tribes of Nepal;" on the "Tribes of Northern Tibet;" on the "Commerce of Nepal," &c.

The eminent political services of Mr. Hodgson are a matter of history; how, by his tact and intimate knowledge of Nepalese politics, he succeeded in substituting a friendly for a hostile administration; how he prevented a rupture with Nepal throughout the trying period of the Afghan war; and how his personal influence converted a concealed and dangerous enemy into a friend. Before his retirement, the Nepal Durbar placed the whole military force of the country at the disposal of the Governor-General.

Since our first relations with Nepal, in 1792, the English have had to deal exclusively with military *Maires du Palais.* The ablest, and he who had the longest tenure of power, was Bhim Sen Thappa. But he at last was overthrown and forced to commit suicide, in July 1838, after having been at the head of affairs for thirty years. Kala Panday, the new minister, commenced a series of hostile intrigues with native states in India, until Mr. Hodgson obtained a formal promise that these intrigues should cease.[1] A nephew of the old minister Bhim Sen Thappa, named Mataber Sing, became Prime Minister in 1843, when Sir Henry Lawrence succeeded Mr. Hodgson as Resident. The supersession of Mr. Hodgson, in 1843, was a great blunder. His long experience, and the respect and friendship that were felt for him by the governing class in Nepal, rendered his continued tenure of office most important; while his abrupt and unwise recall put a stop to many valuable literary investigations, and has abridged the knowledge we should otherwise have had with more completeness respecting Nepal and Tibet. The minister, Mataber Sing, was murdered in 1845, the same year in which Sir Henry was succeeded by Mr. J. R. Colvin. The latter was followed by Major Thorsby, in 1847, and Major Ramsay was Resident from 1849 to 1868.[2] Guggun Sing became Minister in 1845, and his murder, together with the massacre of

[1] See Aitchison's 'Treaties,' ii. pp. 212 and 220.

[2] When he was succeeded by Mr. Girdlestone, the present Resident at Kathmandu.

thirty-one of the most influential chiefs in Nepal, paved the way to the rise of Jang Bahadar, a nephew of Mataber Sing, to the office of Prime Minister in 1846, with Surundra Bikram Sah as Maharajah of Nepal.

Except for a few months in 1856, Jang Bahadar has retained power ever since, and the bearing of the Nepal Durbar has been more friendly to the British Government, especially since the visit of the powerful minister to Europe in 1850.[1] But the passes remain closed, and Europeans are not allowed to visit any part of Nepal, except the valley round Kathmandu.

Alexander Csoma de Körös, the eminent Tibetan scholar, worked in the same field of research as Mr. Hodgson, and at the same time. A Siculo-Hungarian of Transylvania, and without means, this devoted student made his way to India by land, with the object of investigating Eastern languages and literature, and of ascertaining their relation to his own Magyar tongue. It is much to the credit of the Government and officials of British India that Csoma de Körös should have been cordially welcomed and liberally assisted. He first went to Ladak and Zanskar, and studied the Tibetan language and literature in the Buddhist monastery of Pugdal, from 1827 to 1830; and he then proceeded to Calcutta, for the purpose of giving some of the results of his labours to the world, where he was very kindly received by Mr. Wilson and Mr. James Prinsep.

Csoma de Körös ascertained that the literature of Tibet was entirely of Indian origin, the immense volumes being translations from Sanscrit. His teacher in the Tibetan language was a learned Lama of Zanskar, named Bandé Sangs-rgyas Phuntshogs; and when his grammar and dictionary were completed, the Government of India very properly sanctioned its being brought out at the public expense. He also published several

[1] See 'Narrative of a Five Years' Residence at Nepál, from 1841 to 1845,' by T. Smith (1852). This book is very untrustworthy, and is full of inaccurate statements. See also, 'A Journal to Katmandu with the Camp of Jung Bahadoor' (Murray, 1852), by Mr. Laurence Oliphant, who accompanied the Nepalese Minister, on his return, from Ceylon to the capital of Nepal.

valuable papers in the 'Asiatic Researches,' and in the 'Journal of the Asiatic Society of Bengal.'

In 1842, M. Csoma de Körös set out on an adventurous journey in the footsteps of Mr. Manning, with the intention of making his way to Lhasa, in order to gain access to the stores of Tibetan literature which he believed, from his reading in Ladak, were still extant there. But this indefatigable scholar died, of fever, in 1842, in Dr. Campbell's house at Darjíling.[1]

Next to Mr. Hodgson and Csoma de Körös, the most distinguished contributor to our knowledge of the region lying between India and Tibet, during the present century, is undoubtedly Dr. Campbell. Archibald Campbell was born in 1805, and was appointed an assistant surgeon in the East India Company's service in 1828. He first came to Nepal in 1830, as surgeon to the residency at Kathmandu, and left in 1838, having been sent by Mr. Hodgson to settle a boundary dispute with Sikkim. This service was so well performed that it led to Dr. Campbell receiving charge of the hill station at Darjíling. While under Mr. Hodgson he wrote a narrative of our political relations with Nepal, and an excellent paper on the agriculture of the Nepal valley.[2]

The hill station of Darjíling, 370 miles to the north of Calcutta, is on a ridge of the Sikkim Himálaya, at a height varying from 6500 feet to 7500 feet above the sea. In 1828

[1] See 'J. A. S. B.,' xi. p. 303 (1842). The works of Csoma de Körös were: 'Essay towards a Dictionary, Tibetan and English.' (Calcutta, 1834.) 'A Grammar of the Tibetan Language in English.' (Calcutta, 1834.) "Notices on the Life of Sakya," and of some Tibetan works, in the 'Asiatic Researches,' vol. xx. pp. 285, 393, and 553.

In the 'Journal of the Asiatic Society of Bengal' there are "Geographical Notice of Tibet," i. p. 121; "Note on the Origin of the Käla-Chakra and the Adi-Buddha Systems," ii. p. 57; "Translation of a Tibetan Passport," ii. p. 201; "Origin of the Shakya Race," ii. p. 385; "Extracts from Tibetan Works," iii. p. 57; "Analysis of a Tibetan Medical Work," iv. p. 1; "Different Systems of Buddhism, from Tibetan Authorities," vii. part i. p. 142; "Enumeration of Tibetan Works," vii. p. 147; also ix. part ii. p. 905; v. pp. 264 and 384.

[2] "Notes on the Agriculture and Rural Economy of the Valley of Nepal," in vol. iv. of the 'Transactions of the Agricultural and Horticultural Society of India.'

Mr. J. W. Grant and Major Herbert, the Surveyor-General of India, reported on the eligibility of Darjíling as a sanitarium, and the Sikkim Rajah was induced to sign a deed, in February, 1835, ceding the territory in exchange for a pension of 300*l.* a year.[1] Dr. Campbell was appointed superintendent of the new station in 1840, and was entrusted with the charge of political relations with Sikkim.

Dr. Campbell described Sikkim—called *Dinjing* by the inhabitants—as covering an area of about 1550 square miles, with a population of 7000, of whom 3000 are Lepchas, 2000 Bhutanese, and 2000 Limbus. There is no money revenue, and the contributions in kind from agricultural produce and transit duties would not exceed Rs. 7000 a year. The country is to a great extent covered with forest and thick underwood. The Rajah is tributary to China through Lhasa, and resides from November until May at Tumlúng, and the rest of the year at Chumbi, within Tibetan territory. The Rajah of Sikkim had desired to secure an exchange of runaway slaves, which was refused, and in the preposterous hope of securing compliance, his officers suddenly seized and imprisoned Dr. Campbell and Dr. Hooker, while travelling, in 1849, and detained them for six weeks. As a punishment for this outrage the allowance was stopped, and a piece of territory, including the lower course of the Tísta and the Sikkim Terai, was annexed.

The settlement of Darjíling, meanwhile, advanced rapidly under Dr. Campbell's able management. In 1839 it did not contain more than 100 souls; in 1849 there were 10,000, chiefly by immigration from Nepal, Sikkim, and Bhutan, in all of which States slavery is prevalent. Allotments of land were bought by Europeans, barracks and houses were built, and Dr. Campbell established an annual fair at the foot of the hills, which was most successful. A considerable trade in musk, salt, gold dust, borax, ponies, and woollen cloths soon sprang up.

Dr. Hooker thus wrote in 1854: "He [Dr. Campbell] raised

[1] Increased, in 1846, to 600*l.* a year.

British Sikkim from its pristine condition of an impenetrable jungle, tenanted by half savage and mutually hostile races, to that of a flourishing European hill station, and a rich agricultural province." It has since become a centre of tea and chinchona cultivation.

The misunderstandings with the Sikkim Rajah arose from his kidnapping propensities. Two specially gross cases, in 1860, caused an order that his territory north of the Rumam river, and west of the Great Runjít, should be occupied until restitution was made. The occupying force was, however, attacked and driven back, and in February, 1861, a larger detachment, under Lieutenant-Colonel Gawler, with the Hon. Ashley Eden as envoy, crossed the Great Runjít into Sikkim, proceeded to Tumlúng, and enforced the Rajah's agreement to another treaty, dated March 28, 1861. Nurugay Dewan, who had imprisoned Dr. Campbell, and had been incessantly hostile, was expelled from Sikkim for ever, and Chíbu Lama, a friend to the English, was appointed Dewan in his place. The other articles secured free trade, and the right of travelling and making roads in Sikkim.[1]

Dr. Campbell presided over the destinies of the hill station of Darjíling for twenty-two years, from 1840 to February 1862, when he retired. He returned to England, but he continued to take an active part in furthering projects for the good of Darjíling, especially the cultivation of tea, the establishment of chinchona plantations, and the construction of the Darjíling railway. He was a very active member of the Society of Arts, and also of the Anthropological Institute. When Dr. Campbell died, on November 8, 1874, his great experience and wide knowledge of these subjects were missed, and his loss will long be felt by those who are interested in the progress of Indian

[1] See 'Sikkim; with Hints on Mountain and Jungle Warfare, exhibiting also the Facilities for Opening Commercial Relations through the State of Sikkim with Central Asia, Thibet, and Western China,' by Colonel J. C. Gawler, F.R.G.S. (Stanford, 1873.) This little book gives an interesting account of the military operations in Sikkim in 1861.

trade, and in the opening of friendly intercourse along our Himálayan frontier.[1]

In November, 1847, Dr. Hooker left England on his memorable expedition to Sikkim, where he resided for two years, and his exploring journeys throw much new light on the geography of the Himálaya, and furnish the only information we have respecting some of the passes into Tibet. He, with Dr. Campbell, was the first European to visit the passes at the head waters of the Tísta, and he is still the only European who has explored those on the Tambur river, in Eastern Nepal.

In November, 1848, Dr. Hooker entered the valley of the Tambur, a tributary of the Kosi, in Eastern Nepal, ascending it, and its affluent the Yangma, until he reached the passes of Wallanchún (10,385 feet), Yangmachen, and Kambachen or Nango, obtaining a view into Tibet. From some of the points on this adventurous journey the scenery was superb, and its grandeur is brought home to us by a master hand. From the Tonglo hill, above the Tambur valley, "Kanchan-junga was nearly due north—a dazzling mass of snowy peaks intersected by blue glaciers which gleamed in the slanting rays of the rising sun, like aquamarines set in frosted silver. To the east was a billowy mass of forest-clad mountains, on the north-east horizon rose Donkia and Chumalhari, to the west Mount Everest."

Afterwards, in the autumn of 1849, accompanied by Dr. Campbell, he went up the valley of the Tísta in Sikkim, and

[1] Besides his 'Memoirs on the Political Relations with Nepal,' and 'On the Agriculture of the Nepal Valley,' already referred to, Dr. Campbell was the author of many articles in the 'Journal of the Asiatic Society of Bengal,' and other periodicals.

Among these were ethnological papers on the Lepchas, Limbus, Murmis, and Lushais, which have also been printed in the 'Journal of the Anthropological Institute;' a paper "On the Valley of Chumbi," in the 'Journal of the Royal Asiatic Society' for September, 1873; "On the Commerce of India," in the 'Journal of the Society of Arts' for 17th of March, 1871; and "On the Relations with Sikkim and Nepal," in the 'Oriental' of January, 1874. He also wrote a valuable paper, "On the Government, Literature, Officers, and Agriculture of Eastern Tibet," in the 'Journal of the Asiatic Society of Bengal' for 1855, p. 219, reprinted in the 'Phœnix,' pp. 83, 107 (edited by Rev. James Summers).

of its feeders the Lachen and Lachung, to the Kongra-lama (15,745 feet) and Donkia passes (18,466 feet), and even succeeded in going some distance into Tibet beyond the pass, as far as the small lake of Cholamú, the actual source of the Lachen, 17,000 feet above the sea. Here they obtained a magnificent view of the Central Range of the Himálaya, and ascertained that the nearest Tibetan village was Kamba-jong. Dr. Hooker also visited the Cho-la pass leading from Sikkim into the Chumbi valley, and explored all the valleys of Sikkim, making a very magnificent botanical collection, including the glorious Sikkim rhododendrons. Dr. Hooker returned to England in 1851.

The 'Himálayan Journals' form a fascinating book of travels, in which the reader may obtain a vivid impression of the scenery, and the nature of the country from the *terai* fringing the plains, to the passes into Tibet and the snowy peaks; and the work is quite indispensable to a student of Himálayan geography.[1] Dr. Hooker also made a topographical survey of Independent Sikkim, resulting in what is still the only map of that country. This is the most valuable contribution that any private traveller ever made to the geography of the Himálayan region.

Dr. Hooker was the first European who reached the passes leading into Great Tibet since the return of Mr. Manning in 1812. But, in the interval, students of Chinese literature had collected much accurate information respecting that interesting country. Heinrich Julius Klaproth is the most eminent of these scholars. Born in 1783, the son of a professor of chemistry at Berlin, he early devoted himself to the study of Oriental languages, and in 1805 he accompanied a Russian Ambassador to Peking. He afterwards visited the Caucasus, and on his return he settled at Paris, where he organized the Asiatic

[1] 'Himálayan Journals; or, Notes of a Naturalist in Bengal, the Sikkim and Nepal Mountains, &c.,' by Joseph Dalton Hooker, M.D., R.N., F.R.S. (2 vols. Murray, 1854.)

Society, and edited the 'Journal Asiatique,' and where he died in 1835. His most valuable service to those who are interested in Tibet consists in the translation of a detailed description of that country from the great geographical dictionary of China, published at Peking in 1775. It contains a short history and descriptive lists of the towns, rivers, lakes, mountains, and passes in the four provinces of U, Tsang, Kâm, and Ari.[1]

Another scholar who has thrown some light on Tibetan history and geography from Chinese sources is Dr. Gutzlaff, a native of Stettin, born in 1803, who went to China as a missionary in 1830, and was afterwards appointed Secretary to Government at Hong Kong, where he died in 1851. In chapter IX. of his valuable work, 'China Opened,' he gives some account of the geography and history of Tibet, and he has collected more information on the same subject in his 'History of China,' and other writings.[2]

The only Europeans who have visited Lhasa since the time of Mr. Manning are MM. Huc and Gabet, the adventurous French missionaries who, in 1844, when residing near the Great Wall, were appointed by their ecclesiastical superiors to make their way to the city of the Dalai Lama. After eighteen months of long marches and terrible hardships, the missionaries arrived at Lhasa, weary and exhausted. They were only allowed to reside about a month in the capital of Tibet; but, besides giving much very interesting information respecting the Buddhist hierarchy and the people, they happened to arrive at the time of a crisis in Tibetan history.

[1] See 'Magasin Asiatique; ou, Revue, géographique et historique, de la Asie centrale et septentrionale,' publiée par M. J. Klaproth (i. and ii., 1825 and 1826, Paris); 'Description du Si Dzang ou Tibet' (pp. 209–307); and 'Route de Tckhing-tou-fou en Chine à travers le Tubeto riêntal, jusqu'à H'lassa ou Lassa.' (Pekin, 1792, pp. 97–132.) See also 'Nouv. Journal Asiatique,' iv. p. 81; vi. p. 161; vii. pp. 161, 185. Klaproth edited the letters of Orazio della Penna, and other missionaries, in the 'Journal Asiatique.'

[2] 'China Opened,' by the Rev. C. Gutzlaff (2 vols., 1838); 'History of China;' "Remarks on the Present State of Buddhism in China" ('Journal of the Royal Asiatic Society,' xvi. p. 73); "Tibet and Sefau" ('R.G.S.J.,' xx. p. 191).

The Chinese military supremacy had recently been practically tested by a repetition of such an expedition to repel invasion as was undertaken against Nepal in 1792. Gulab Sing, of Jammu, afterwards Maharajah of Kashmir, had, in 1834, sent an army of Dogras, commanded by his General Zorawar Sing, to invade Ladak, which mountainous region was overrun and conquered. In May, 1841, this chief, with 5000 men, advanced up the valley of the Indus, and occupied Gugé and the country round the sacred Mansarowar lake. The news of this invasion reached Lhasa in November, and a Chinese army advanced over the Mariam-la pass, near which the hostile forces met on the 12th of December, 1841. The battle-field was 15,000 feet above the sea. There was a desultory fight for two days, when Zorawar Sing was killed, the Dogras entirely defeated, and only one-sixth escaped from the field.[1] Some fled by the Nepalese pass of Taklakhar to the British province of Kumaon, others laid down their arms. The Chinese troops advanced as far as Leh, but eventually peace was made in 1842, and the old boundary was re-established.

This campaign was followed by important events at Lhasa. Lobsang Champal, the seventh Dalai Lama, died in 1805, and since then a Gesub Rimboché, or Nomen-khan, named Si-Fan, a native of Kansu, had been regent for many years, while no less than three Dalai Lamas had died suddenly and under suspicious circumstances. Gradually dark rumours of assassination began to circulate. The four ministers, called Kahlons, entertained no doubt of the Regent's guilt, but the Gesub had a large and powerful party in some of the monasteries. They therefore sought aid from the Teshu Lama, the same sacred personage who, in his infancy, had honoured Captain Turner with an interview fifty-seven years before. His Holiness, as soon as the new Dalai Lama was discovered and enthroned, appealed to the Emperor of China to save him from the fate of his predecessors.

[1] In the same month of the same year the British army was destroyed at Kabul. (Cunningham's 'Ladak,' p. 353.)

Compliance with the request of the Teshu Lama was at once resolved upon, and a statesman named Keshen (Ki-chan), who had been disgraced for making peace with the English at Canton, was sent as special envoy to Lhasa, in 1844, to settle the matter respecting the Nomen-khan. In concert with the Teshu Lama, the Chinese envoy arrested the suspected assassin, obtained confessions by the use of torture on his followers, and the Nomen-khan confessed his crimes to escape a similar ordeal. He was condemned to perpetual banishment, and an insurrection of 15,000 lamas of his faction, from the monastery of Sera, was suppressed owing to the pusillanimity of their patron, "who had the cowardly energy of an assassin, but not the audacity of a revolutionist."[1]

A young lama of the Bripung or Debang monastery (named Rating Lama[2]) was chosen as Nomen-khan by the Chinese, and as both he and the Dalai Lama were minors, the senior Kahlon, named Pe-chi,[3] became regent. The Pundit of 1866 relates that formerly the regent was chosen from the monasteries of Kontyaling, Tankyaling, Chumuling, and Chochuling; but that when the assassinating Regent was removed, the Chinese were aided by the 7700 monks of the Debang monastery, and that consequently it will supply the regents in future.

The new Regent was extremely kind to Huc and Gabet. The former describes him as a man of fifty, whose large features, mild and remarkably pallid, breathed a truly royal majesty, while his dark eyes, shaded by long lashes, were intelligent and gentle. M. Huc gives a very interesting account of his interviews with this great man. It is clear that the Tibetan authorities were willing to receive the strangers cordially; that they were true to the enlightened and tolerant spirit of their religion, and that Mr. Bogle's impression of the friendly feeling in his time held good in the succeeding generation. But

[1] Huc, ii. p. 165.

[2] Gyalbo Riting of the Pundit, p. xxiv.

[3] The *Shete Shaffee* of Edgar; and *Sata Safadé* of the Pundit.

Chinese jealousy and exclusiveness intervened, and it was Keshen who expelled Huc and Gabet from Lhasa, and sent them back by way of Szechuen.[1]

When Rating Lama attained his majority there was a struggle for power between him and Pe-chi, the Regent who won the hearts of Huc and Gabet. At first Pe-chi was banished; but the great body of the lamas was in his favour, and eventually Rating Lama retired to Peking, where he died, and Pe-chi was installed as Gesub Rimboché. He led a national party, and was strongly opposed to Chinese interference.

During the regency of Pe-chi the influence of the Chinese was at a very low ebb, and if the policy of Warren Hastings had been understood at Calcutta, a great step might then have been taken towards retrieving lost ground. In 1854 hostilities broke out with Nepal, and it is said that the Tibetan troops repulsed the Gorkhas, taking several guns. The Gorkhas advanced as far as Sakar-jong, a fort on the Sakar-chu, between the Central and Southern Himálayan Chains, a tributary of the Arun.[2] But in March, 1856, a treaty, disadvantageous to Tibet, was concluded between the Tibetan and Nepal Governments, in which both acknowledged the suzerainty of China. The Tibetan Government agreed to pay an annual tribute of Rs. 10,000 to the Gorkhas; another article stipulated for an exchange of arms and prisoners; and the Gorkha Government was to be allowed to establish an agent and a trading factory at Lhasa.[3]

The Regent Pe-chi died before 1869, and was succeeded by

[1] 'Souvenirs d'un Voyage dans la Tartarie le Tibet et la Chine, pendant les Années 1844, 1845, 1846' (2 vols., 1853), Huc et Gabet.

'Le Christianisme en Chine, en Tartariè, et en Thibet' (4 vols.).

My quotations are from the English translation (2 vols., 3rd edition).

Sir John Davis wrote the article on the travels of Huc and Gabet, in the 'Edinburgh Review,' reprinted in his 'Chinese Miscellanies' (Murray, 1865).

Colonel Yule is the author of the article on Huc's work in 'Blackwood's Magazine' for March, 1852.

Mr. H. T. Prinsep reviewed the work of M. Huc in his 'Tibet, Tartary, and Mongolia' (2nd ed., Allen, 1852).

[2] G. T. S. Report for 1871–2.

[3] Aitchison's 'Treaties,' ii. p. 193, note.

the aged Abbot of Galdan, who held office until the Dalai Lama came of age. The old Abbot died quite recently. The Dalai Lama then became gyalpo or king, as well as pontiff. The explorer No. 9 heard, when at Shigatzé in September, 1872, that there had been a serious rebellion at Lhasa in April, 1871, during which hundreds of people were killed.[1] The Teshu Lama, the next in succession to the friend of Mr. Bogle, and the one who, as an infant, graciously received Captain Turner, became as good and holy a pontiff as he was in his former transmigration. Huc describes him[2] as of a fine majestic frame, and astonishing vigour for his advanced age, which was then sixty. His influence was very great, not only in Tibet, but throughout Mongolia, and crowds came to worship him from far and near. Huc also relates some curious prophecies of the Teshu Lama. The venerable saint died in 1854, for when Colonel Montgomerie's Pundit was at Teshu Lumbo, in 1865, another incarnation was eleven years of age.

At present the new Teshu Lama must be of age, and his colleague the Dalai Lama would also be Gyalpo or sovereign;[3] but a rumour has lately arrived that he is dead. It is to be hoped

[1] G. T. S. Report for 1871–2. [2] Huc, ii. p. 157.

[3] The succession of the Dalai Lamas, according to various authorities, is as follows:

Klaproth.	*Desgodins.*	*Schlagintweit.*
1. Ghendoun-djoub-ba (nephew of Tson-khapa).	1391. Gue-dun-tchsan.	1388–1473. Gedun Grab.
2. Ghendoun-ghian-dzo.	1475. Bué-dun-guia-tso.	
3. Sotnam-ghian-dzo.	1543. Sou-nam-guia-tso.	
4. Yondam-ghian-dzo (a Mongol).	1588. Yeun-ten-guia-tso.	
5. Ngawang Lobdzang-ghian-dzo.	1617. Ga-ouang-lo-zong-guia-tso.	Ngagvang Lobzang Gyamtso.
6. Lobdzang Galdzong-ghian-dzo (?)	1682. Tsong-yong-guia-tso (?)	
7. Lobdzang-dambaü-wangt-siouk-azimbal-ghian-dzo.	1708. Le-tsong-kel-zong-guia-tso.	Lobsang Kalsang.
	1758. Guiam-pel-guia-tso.	Lobsang Champal.
	1805. Long-tsong-guia-tso.	
	1815. Tseal-tchian-guia-tso.	
	1837. Kar-djou-guia-tso.	
	1856. (*Name not known.*)	

that this may be false news; for it seems to be clearly for the good both of Tibet and India that the holy Buddhisatwas should personally rule, and make the tolerant precepts of their creed and their goodwill for all mankind prevail over the narrow exclusiveness of the Chinese political agents. It appears that there are now about 4000 Chinese troops in Tibet, under Tonglings, or colonels, and that the Ambas at Lhasa still arrogate to themselves the control of traffic over the frontiers.

This concludes our meagre knowledge of the recent history of Great Tibet; and it only remains to refer briefly to recent events in the hill countries leading from India to Tibet, and to pass in review the journeys of recent explorers employed under the superintendence of the Great Trigonometrical Survey of India.

In Nepal there has been no change since the accession to power of Jang Bahadar, as regards the opening of commercial intercourse between India and Tibet. The passes are still closed to Europeans, who are also excluded from all parts of Nepal except the valley in which Kathmandu is situated. Nepal is still tributary to the Chinese Empire, and the restoration of the flourishing trade which existed in the days of the Newar dynasty seems as far off as ever. In February, 1855, a treaty was signed for the surrender of heinous offenders, and the assistance afforded during the mutinies by Jang Bahadar was rewarded by the cession of the Oudh Terai, in a treaty dated November 1, 1860.[1] Jang Bahadar has been created a K.C.B. and G.C.S.I., but ruinous export and import duties are levied on his frontiers, from 17 to 20 per cent.; a large army is kept up for which there is no use whatever in the administration of the country; a policy of worse than Chinese exclusiveness and obstruction is maintained; and Nepal is, in fact, the vassal not of the British, but of the Celestial Empire.

The history of our intercourse with Bhutan since Pemberton's mission has been one of complaints against petty raids

[1] Aitchison's 'Treaties,' ii. pp. 220 and 223.

and aggressions, and controversies about boundaries, ending in a small war. "The whole history of our connection with Bhutan," says Dr. Campbell,[1] "is a continuous record of injuries to our subjects all along the frontier of 250 miles, of denials of justice, and of acts of insult to our Government." In 1839, the Bhutanese carried off twelve British subjects, which showed that Pemberton's mission had had no effect upon them. In 1841 they seized five British villages, when Colonel Jenkins, the Commissioner in Assam, proposed the despatch of a mission, but this measure was not approved. The Assam dúars were then occupied.[2] In 1842, outrages were commenced on the side of the Bengal dúars, and continued at intervals until 1856. Sir Frederick Halliday, the Lieutenant-Governor of Bengal, then proposed that the districts of Ambari Fala-kottah and Jalpaish, which had been given to Bhutan in 1784 and 1787, but which had formerly belonged to the province of Julpigori, should be occupied; but the measure was prevented by the mutinies. Further outrages followed; and in 1863, the Honourable Ashley Eden was appointed envoy to Bhutan, to obtain a treaty. He was accompanied by Major Godwin Austen, of the Topographical Survey Department, Captain Lance, and Dr. Simpson.

The time selected for this mission was unfortunate. Bhutan was in a state of anarchy owing to a rebellion. The Jungpen of Punakha had closed its gates against the Deb Rajah. The Paro Penlo, or Governor of Western Bhutan, had taken part with the Deb; while the Tongso Penlo took the other side, and besieged the Deb in Tassisudon, who surrendered and was sent into retirement at Shiptoka. At the same time, the Paro Penlo and his subordinate, the Jungpen of Dalim-kotta, were carrying on a private war on their own account.

Mr. Eden's mission left Darjíling in 1864, crossed the Tísta,

[1] 'Oriental,' Jan. 1874, p. 25.

[2] Seven in number, namely, Buri Gumah and Kalling, bordering on the Durrung district; and Shurkolla, Banska, Chapaguri, Chapkahama, and Bijni, bordering on Kamrúp.

and proceeded to Dalim-kotta. From this place the route was over quite new ground, by the Tulalah pass, 10,000 feet above the sea, where the snow was deep, and then across the Am-machu, the river which rises near Pari-jong, and flows through the valley of Chumbi. Thence the mission proceeded, by way of Paro, to Punakha, which place was reached on the 18th of March.

The Bhutan Durbar treated Mr. Eden with audacious insolence, asked for the restitution of the Assam dúars, and enforced their demands by stopping supplies of provisions, and even by personal outrages. Mr. Eden complied with the demands under protest, and escaped by forced marches by way of Paro. In his report, dated July 20, 1864, Mr. Eden reviewed the whole of our political relations with Bhutan from first to last, described his route, and gave an account of the Government and people, of whom he naturally formed a very unfavourable opinion, strikingly in contrast with those expressed by Mr. Bogle and Captain Turner in the last century.[1]

It became necessary to punish the outrage on Mr. Eden's mission, and this led to a war with Bhutan during the year 1865. Hostilities were confined to the Dúars. There was a reverse at Dewangiri, where the Tongso Penlo captured two guns, but afterwards severe loss was inflicted on the enemy at Dewangiri and Bala on one side; while Dalim-kotta, Chamurchi, and Buxa were seized and occupied on the other.[2] In January, 1866, the Bhutan Government agreed to a treaty surrendering the document to which Mr. Eden's signature was placed under protest, apologizing for the insults, agreeing to give up two British guns which the Tongso Penlo had succeeded in cap-

[1] Mr. Eden's report is printed first in the volume of 'Political Missions to Bootan' (Calcutta, 1865), pp. 1 to 137; with an Appendix containing the routes known in Bhutan. An excellent précis of Mr. Eden's report is given by Dr. Rennie, 'Bootan, or the Story of the Dooar War,' chapters iv., v., and vi.

[2] See 'A Military Report on the Country of Bhutan; containing all the Information of Military Importance which has been collected up to July 12, 1866,' by Lieut. C. M. MacGregor. (Calcutta, 1873.)

turing at Dewangiri, and ceding the whole of the eleven Bengal dúars,[1] as well as the tract between the rivers Tísta and Jhaldakha. This brings British territory into direct contact with that of Tibet in the Chumbi valley. The English Government agreed to pay the Deb Rajah a yearly sum of Rs. 50,000, provided that his conduct continued to be satisfactory. These arrangements were negotiated by Colonel Bruce.

The Bhutanese are, however, in all probability incorrigible, and, in the opinion of Dr. Campbell, it will in the end be necessary to annex their territory, in order to secure the continuance of peace and the free passage of merchandise.[2]

On the eastern frontier of Bhutan there is a small State occupied by a tribe called the Tawang Bhuteas, which is independent of Bhutan, but tributary to Tibet. The Tawang Rajah has always been peaceable and friendly; and in 1844 he relinquished all claim on the Dúar leading from his territory into the Assam plain, in exchange for a payment of 500*l.* a year. The Tawang frontier lies between the rivers Deosham and Rowta. A very considerable trade is carried on between Tibet and Assam through Tawang, and this may hereafter become a route of great importance.

British Sikkim, at first under a Superintendent, and since 1866 under a Deputy Commissioner, was, until 1874, included in the

[1] Namely, Dalim-kotta, Mynaguri or Zamir-kotta, Chamurchi, Lakhi, Buxa (Passaka), Bhulka, Bara, Gumar, Ripu, Chirrung, and Bagh or Chota Bijni.

[2] See 'Bhutan, and the Story of the Dooar War,' by Surgeon Rennie, M.D. (Murray, 1866). Also 'Papers relating to Bootan;' and 'Further Papers relating to Bootan,' presented to Parliament Feb. 15, 1865, No. 47; and Feb. 8, 1865, No. 13.

Dr. Rennie's book is carefully written, after much research, and is comprehensive. It describes the geographical position and extent of Bhutan, the nature of the country, and the government and religion, as well as its military resources. Dr. Rennie then reviews the history of British intercourse with Bhutan; and in the last chapters he gives an account of the war in the Dúars, in 1865, of which he was an eye-witness. The experience of the war showed that the Central Government, consisting of Deb and Dharma Rajahs, was a mere fiction, as far as all real power is concerned; and that in future it will be futile to negotiate with any officials in Bhutan, except the Paro and Tongso Penlos, the actual governors of West and East Bhutan.

Commissionership of Kuch Bahar, which had existed since 1788. Among the Commissioners, Mr. Richard Ahmuty, from 1797 to 1802, was a man of great ability, and administered the State during the minority of the Rajah. Mr. David Scott was Commissioner from 1816 to 1831, and also joint-magistrate of Rangpúr, and afterwards Governor-General's agent in Assam and on the north-east frontier, retaining charge of Kuch Bahar, which, until January, 1864, continued under political charge of the Commissioners of Assam. It was Mr. Scott who sent the mission to Bhutan under Kishen Kant Bose. In 1866 Kuch Bahar was made the nucleus of a new commissionership, and Colonel Haughton, C.S.I., was Commissioner of the Kuch Bahar division from December, 1866, to February, 1873. This officer has taken great interest in the questions relating to Sikkim and Bhutan, and to the establishment of friendly intercourse with Tibet; and has collected much valuable information on the subject.

Dr. Campbell was succeeded at Darjíling, in 1862, by Mr. Wake, V.C.; and in 1866, Major B. W. D. Morton, who had long served in Assam, and had distinguished himself in suppressing the rebellion in Jaintea, was appointed Deputy Commissioner of British Sikkim, under the Commissioner of Kuch Bahar. When he went on leave, Mr. J. Ware Edgar, C.S.I., who had written a valuable report on the cultivation of tea in India, was appointed to officiate during his absence.

Since the signature of the treaty of 1861, the relations with Sikkim have been satisfactory; and some exploring work has been done in the direction of the Tibet passes. During the autumn of 1871, Mr. W. T. Blanford, of the Geological Survey of India, accompanied by Captain Elwes, explored the upper valley of the Tísta, in Dr. Hooker's footsteps, their main object being to collect birds and study the zoology of the upper branches of the Tísta valley. They reached the Donkia pass; ascertained the position of another pass, never before laid down on any map; met with three unmapped lakes, and made a good collection of birds. Mr. Blanford also explored the passes leading into the Chumbi valley. Since Dr. Campbell and Dr. Hooker explored this region, in 1849, only one European had penetrated to the Donkia pass previous to Mr. Blanford's visit.[1]

In June, 1873, the Rajah of Sikkim, accompanied by his brother and minister, Changzed Rabu, a man of great natural powers and predominating influence over his countrymen, entered British territory for the first time, and paid a visit to Sir George Campbell, the Lieutenant-Governor of Bengal, at Darjíling. Sieingputti, the Rajah's sister, who was free from affectation and any ideas of seclusion, and was delighted with every novelty; and a younger brother, called the Chota Rajah, were also of the party.

Changzed Rabu is now the leading man in Sikkim, and is favourable to freedom of trade, and to the spread of British influence. He assured Sir George Campbell that the prohibition of trade with Tibet was solely due to orders from Peking, and that the Tibetans would gladly facilitate direct trade. Even now there is considerable local traffic carried on across the passes.

In 1873, Mr. Edgar, C.S.I., proceeded to return the Sikkim Rajah's visit, and was received in a most friendly manner. He also visited the passes, already explored by Mr. Blanford, which lead from Sikkim into Chumbi. The most southerly of these passes is that of Jelep-la, about 50 miles from Tumlúng, the capital of Sikkim, and 13,000 feet above the sea. The two next, to the north, are those of Guatiula and Yak-la, the latter 14,000 feet high. These are rarely interrupted by snow for many days, and form the easiest way into the Chumbi valley. Next, to the north, is the Cho-la pass, 15,000 feet high, which is the direct route from Tumlúng to Chumbi. Then comes the

[1] This was Captain Chamer, who made a rapid journey in search of sport in the spring of 1870. For an account of Mr. Blanford's expedition, see 'J. A. S. B.,' vol. x. part ii., p. 367. See also papers by Major J. L. and Captain W. S. Sherwill, 'J. A. S. B.,' xxii. pp. 540, 611; and xxxi. p. 457.

Tankra-la, 16,083 feet high, the most snowy pass in Sikkim, difficult of access, and unsuited for traffic.

Mr. Edgar left Darjiling on the 23rd of October, 1873, and encamped at the foot of the Jelep-la pass on the 30th, where he was met by the Dewan Changzed, the ex-Dewan Nurugay,[1] who had imprisoned Dr. Campbell, and was expelled by the treaty of 1861, and the Tibetan Governor or *Jongpen* of Pari-jong. Mr. Edgar consented to receive the ex-Dewan unofficially, and he supplied him with much valuable information. He has great influence both at Sikkim and Lhasa, but has no recognized official position; and Mr. Edgar thinks that much use might be made of him in our dealings with Tibet. The Jongpen of Pari-jong was a young man, tall and stout, with a courteous and dignified manner, and a pleasant voice. He is said to be the son of a highly-placed Tibetan official.

Mr. Edgar proposed that he should be invited to proceed to Chumbi, in order that the Rajah might be saved the trouble of meeting him on the pass. The Jongpen said that no European had ever visited Tibet, to which Mr. Edgar replied by relating to him the missions of Mr. Bogle and Captain Turner. The Jongpen answered that the present arrangement had been made by the Chinese envoy, Keshen, about thirty years ago. This official, the same who expelled Huc and Gabet from Lhasa, arranged with the Tibetan authorities that direct management of frontier affairs should be committed to the Ambas, or Chinese political agents, and that there should be no intercourse between Tibet and British India. The Jongpen explained this arrangement, and said that all he could do was to obey orders, whether he approved of them or not; but he offered to report the matter to his immediate superior, the Chechap Depen of Giansu.[2]

Both the Dewan Changzed and the ex-Dewan strongly urged upon Mr. Edgar the advisability of getting a declaration from the Government of Peking that the obstacles now put in the way of free intercourse are unauthorized, which would strengthen

[1] Namguay (?)

[2] Edgar has *Giantzi*.

the hands of the Tibetans. Mr. Edgar also gathered that much uneasiness was felt in Tibet at the threatening attitude of the Nepalese, which obliged the Dalai Lama and his advisers to make up their disputes with the Ambas, in order to be secure of help from China.

Mr. Edgar took the opportunity of fully explaining to the Tibetan officials the policy and wishes of the British Government, and that their object was the encouragement of trade, and the maintenance of strong, friendly States along our frontier. He also appears to have excited their fears by saying that he could not see how his Government could interfere between a friendly State and one that refuses to have any relations with us, his object being to impress upon them the advisability of seeking the alliance of the British Government. The ex-Dewan was very anxious to obtain forgiveness for his misconduct towards Dr. Campbell and Dr. Hooker, and promised to repeat to the Tibetan officials, and to the Dalai Lama himself, the arguments which Mr. Edgar had used against the policy of isolation.

In the morning of the 4th of November, 1873, the Rajah himself arrived, in deep distress, owing to the hopeless state of his sister. Mr. Edgar informed him that the Government had increased his pension to 1200*l*. a year. Mr. Edgar was much touched by his intense sorrow, and urged him to return at once to his poor sister at Chumbi, accompanying him to the head of the Jelep-la. The Jelep-la and the Chumbi valley are localities of very great importance, because it is probable that the first great commercial road from India to Tibet will take this direction. The conference between the English official and the Tibetan Governor of Pari-joug, on the Jelep pass, is therefore a very significant event; and the important and interesting report of Mr. Edgar,[1] in which he records the information

[1] 'Report on a Visit to Sikkim and the Thibetan Frontier, in October, November, and December, 1873,' G. J. Ware Edgar, C.S.I., Officiating Deputy Commissioner of Darjeeling. (Calcutta, 1874.) With photographs, pp. 103.

In the 'Calcutta Review,' of July, 1874 (No. 117), there is a very able article on Tibet, by Mr. Wilfred L.

he collected respecting recent political events in Tibet, and describes the pass and the nature of the country leading to it, deserves very careful attention.

From Western Tibet it is also probable that much will be done to restore the old friendly intercourse between India and the central region. Something indeed has already been effected, on the one hand, by the Moravian missionaries in Lahaul, headed by Mr. Jäschke and Mr. Heyde, who have learned the Tibetan language, and will be able to convey intelligence of the policy of the British Government, through the heads of Buddhist monasteries in Ladak; on the other hand, by the explorers, who are instructed and sent forth on long journeys of discovery from the head-quarters of the Great Trigonometrical Survey of India.

For upwards of a century the attention of the Moravian missionaries has been turned towards the Kalmuk and Mongol tribes, and in 1765 a Moravian settlement was formed near Czarizin on the Volga, affording opportunities of communicating with the nomad tribes of the steppes. In the beginning of the present century some slight progress was made among the Kirghis tribes, but the mission terminated in 1821, owing to the interference of the Russian Government. Having been refused permission to pass through Russian territory, two Moravian missionaries set out, in 1853, with the intention of penetrating into Mongolia, by way of India. They were stopped on the borders by the Chinese officials, and then received orders from Herrnhuth to settle down where they best could among the Tibetans. A place called Kaelang, in British Lahaul, was selected, and a few years afterwards the mission was placed on

Heeley, of the Bengal Civil Service. It was originally intended to be a review of Mr. Edgar's Report, but Mr. Heeley was led away by the interest of his subject, and it is actually an admirable essay on the religion and history of Tibet, and on the trade between Tibet and India. Besides Mr. Edgar's Report, Mr. Heeley heads his article with the 'Alphabetum Tibetanum' of Giorgi, and the works of Turner, Huc, Köppen, Schlagintweit, Cooper, and Desgodins.

a more regular footing, under Brothers Jäschke, Rechler, and Heyde. In 1873, the staff consisted of Brothers Heyde and Redslob, with their wives and twenty converts. The mission house is 10,000 feet above the sea, and has fields and carefully tended gardens and orchards attached to it.[1]

Brother H. A. Jäschke, after eleven years' residence in Lahaul, returned to Germany in the end of 1868. He is the highest authority in Europe on the modern Tibetan language and its dialects, and is the author of more than one valuable work on the subject.[2] The Moravian Brethren will continue to occupy their present important station in North-Western India, as a basis of operations, until they are permitted to cross the Chinese frontier into Tibet. Their knowledge of the Tibetan language, and their intercourse with the Lamas, will be one influential means of preparing the way for future unrestricted intercourse between India and Tibet.

Meanwhile the efforts of our surveying officers in promoting the exploration of Tibet is another powerful means of gaining the same object. It is now fourteen years since Colonel Montgomerie inaugurated the system, under Colonel Walker, of completing our geographical information respecting the unknown parts of Asia by means of native explorers. These explorers are very carefully selected, instructed in the use of the compass, sextant, and boiling-point thermometer, and in the method of working out a route by traverse or dead reckoning, and then despatched in various directions. By means of this agency

[1] See 'The Abode of Snow,' by Andrew Wilson, chapter xxx. (Blackwood, 1875.) Dr. Cleghorn also visited the Lahaul mission. See his 'Report upon the Forests of the Punjaub and the Western Himalayas' (Roorkee, 1864), p. 150.

[2] Mr. Jäschke has written 'A Short Practical Grammar of the Tibetan Language, with Reference to the Spoken Dialects' (Kyelang, 1865); a Romanized Tibetan and English Dictionary (Kyelang, 1866); and a Tibetan and German Dictionary, just completed. These works are all auto-lithographed. In 1866, he submitted to the Berlin Academy a treatise on the phonetic laws of the Tibetan language. Since 1873 he has been engaged, for the India Office, on a comprehensive modern Tibetan and English Dictionary, which is now nearly ready for the press.

very important additions have quite recently been made to our knowledge of Nepal and of Great Tibet.

Colonel Walker engaged two Pundits (A and B), who were British subjects, from one of the upper valleys of the Himálaya, and, under Colonel Montgomerie, they were trained to the use of the sextant and compass. They were then directed to make a route survey from Lake Mansarowar to Lhasa, a distance of about 800 miles. They made a first attempt to advance direct from Kumaon, but did not find this route practicable. They, however, met some Bisahiris, British subjects, who had been robbed whilst trading in Chinese territory, near Gartokh, and who asked the Pundits to be their *vakils*, in order to obtain redress from the Lhasa Government. This furnished a plausible reason for the journey, and it was then decided that the best chance of reaching Lhasa would be through Nepal. They accordingly set out,[1] and reached Kathmandu on the 7th of March, 1865.

The Pundits heard that the route by the Kirong pass was clear of snow earlier than that by Kuti (Nilam), and they, therefore, selected that route, leaving Kathmandu on the 20th of March; but the Chinese Governor of Kirong refused to allow them to pass, and they returned to Kathmandu on the 10th of April.

One of the Pundits, B, then gave up the attempt, and contented himself with making a long journey in the upper parts of Western Nepal, including an examination of the Muktinath pass.[2] The other, A, set out, disguised as a native of Ladak, as a companion of a Tibetan merchant, named Dawa Nangul, on the 20th of June, and made his way to Kirong.

The post of Kirong is very important in connection with the question of intercourse between India and Tibet. It com-

[1] They had a large sextant, two box sextants, prismatic and pocket compasses, pocket chronometer, boiling-point thermometers, and a common watch.

[2] No account has ever been published of the journey of this Pundit in Western Nepal, and of his visit to the Muktinath pass.

mands what is probably the best of the Nepalese passes. The Pundit describes it as a place with a fort, a good-sized temple, about twenty shops, and a population of 3000 to 4000. Wheat and barley are raised round the town, and there is a trade in salt from Tibet and in rice from Nepal.

The road through Kirong leads past the important Chinese post of Jonka-jong, on the Central Chain, which is probably the Ari-jong of D'Anville's map. But the Pundit was again refused leave to proceed, and with very great difficulty he eventually got permission to take another route, to the westward, over the No-la pass of the Central Chain, 16,600 feet above the sea. His route was through forest on the outer slopes of the Southern Chain as far as a village called Lue, where the mountain sides become bare and rocky, and then across the Southern Chain by the Ga-la pass, which is the boundary between Tibet and Nepal, and 16,700 feet high. The No-la pass was crossed next day, so that here the two chains approach very closely, the intermediate plain sinking to 14,000 feet.

On the 2nd of September the Pundit reached the banks of the Tsanpu, and crossed to the Tadum monastery, on the north shore, 14,200 feet above the sea. Here he learnt that once in two years the Maharajah of Kashmir sent a merchant to Lhasa with a great quantity of goods, who is called "Lopchak;" and that once a year the Government of Lhasa sent a merchant, called "Jang Chongpon," to Ladak. The Pundit joined the Kashmiri merchant's head man, named Chiring Nurpal, who passed through Tadum with seventy laden yaks, and they set out together for Lhasa on the 3rd of October.

The party travelled along the northern side of the Tsanpu, crossing a large tributary called the Charta-Tsanpu, flowing from the Northern Chain; and then passing over a range into the valley of the Raka-Tsanpu, a river which has a long course parallel to the Tsanpu, into which it falls below Janglaché. From Tadum to a place called Ralung there were no signs of cultivation, and the population was very scanty; but from Ralung onwards there were clumps of willow trees and cultivated patches. Ralung is just below the Ka-la pass, over a spur from the range between the rivers Raka-Tsanpu and Tsanpu, which separates the Tsang province from those of Western or Little Tibet.

On the 22nd of October the party crossed the Tsanpu by a ferry, 190 miles below Tadum, and arrived at the town of Janglaché, where there is a strongly-built fort on the top of a hill, a fine monastery, and a number of shops kept by Nepalese. From Janglaché to the town of Shigatzé goods and men are transported on the river, which is wide and navigable, in boats covered with hides. Here they were joined by the second part of the Kashmiri merchant's caravan, consisting of 105 laden yaks; and on the 29th they reached Shigatzé,[1] 11,800 feet above the sea. At a place called Phuncholing, between Janglaché and Shigatzé, the river is spanned by an iron chain bridge.

On the 1st of November, 1865, the Pundit went from Shigatzé to Teshu Lumbo, to do homage to the Teshu Lama or Panchen Rimboché,[2] a boy eleven years old, who was seated on a high throne covered with rich silk. The Pundit reports that there are 3300 monks in the monastery of Teshu Lumbo, and that the town of Shigatzé has a population of 9000, exclusive of the monks, but including a garrison of 100 Chinese soldiers, and 400 Tibetan militia. A market is daily held on the space between Shigatzé and Teshu Lumbo, and good crops are raised in the neighbourhood.

At Shigatzé the caravan was joined by the Kashmiri merchant himself; and setting out again on the 22nd of December, they passed through Painám,[3] and reached Giansu[4] on the 25th, a distance of 46 miles.[5]

Giansu was visited by Bogle and Turner, and Mr. Manning resided there for some time. The Pundit describes it as a city

[1] The Pundit calls it Digarcha. Here he took a number of observations for latitude.

[2] He calls him the "Panjan Ringbo Che."

[3] Penájong.

[4] Gyangze.

[5] According to the Pundit; 39 according to Turner.

about the size of Shigatzé, with a fort on a low hill in the centre of the town, and a large gilded temple. It is ruled by a *Depon*,[1] assisted by two Jongpens, and has a garrison of fifty Chinese soldiers and 200 Tibetan militia. The surrounding plain produces wheat, barley, radishes, peas, and ghee, while rice is imported from Bhutan. Woollen cloths are manufactured in the town, and also small bells with which horses are adorned in Tibet.

From Giansu the Pundit followed the route taken by Mr. Manning to the Palti or Yamdok-cho lake, crossing a spur of the Central Chain by the pass of Khoro-la, 17,000 feet above the sea. He describes the lake as 45 miles in circumference, 2 to 3 miles broad, with a hilly island in the centre, the water very deep and good to drink, though the lake has no outlet.[2] He found the lake to be 13,700 feet above the sea.

On the 4th of January, 1866, the Pundit left the shores of this famous ring-shaped lake, crossed the Khamba-la Mountain separating the provinces of U and Tsang, and reached the left bank of the Tsanpu, at the village of Khamba-barchi, where it is 11,400 feet above the sea level. Here the party took a boat, and rowed down the stream to Chusul-jong. Crossing the river at Chusul, they followed Mr. Manning's route up the valley of the Ki-chu, and arrived at Lhasa on the 10th.

The Pundit describes the Lhasa valley as full of large and populous monasteries. He visited that of Sara (Sera of Huc), three miles from the city, where there are 5500 monks, and the famous monastery of Galdan, founded by Tsong-khapa, which is three quarters of a mile in circumference, and peopled by 3300 monks. The city of Lhasa has a circumference of 2½ miles, and in the centre stands a large temple containing images richly inlaid with gold and precious stones, and surrounded by bazaars with shops kept by Tibetan, Kashmiri, Ladaki, and Nepalese merchants, many of whom are Muhammadans. Chinese tradesmen are also numerous. The plain of Lhasa is about 12

[1] The *Chechep Depen* of Edgar.

[2] See note at p. 244.

miles long by 7 broad, and is surrounded by mountains. Around the town are the monasteries of Muru, Ramoché, Chumuling, Tankyaling, Kontyaling, and the palace-monastery of Potala, the residence of the Dalai Lama, or Goor (Gewan) Rimboché, called also the Lama Guru. It is a mile and a half in circumference, and stands on an eminence 300 feet above the plain. Four miles west of it is the Debang monastery, with 7700 monks; and to the south, on the other side of the Ki-chu, is the Chochuling monastery.[1]

The Pundit went with the Kashmiri merchant (Lopchak), to pay his respects to the Dalai Lama, who was a fair and handsome boy about thirteen years old, seated on a throne six feet high, with the Gesub Rimboché,[2] or Regent Minister, on his right hand. The Pundit relates the popular belief to be that the Dalai Lama will transmigrate thirteen times, and that he is now in his thirteenth transmigration. But he is only in the twelfth according to the list of Desgodins. Below the Regent there are four ministers, called Khalons,[3] who conduct all public business; and the Amba, or Chinese political agent, has special, but apparently undefined powers. As a rule, he does not interfere in the internal affairs of Tibet. The Pundit also heard that 36 miles east of Lhasa, on the north shore of the Tsanpu, there is a town called Sáwe, where the Tibetan treasury is kept; that 40 miles farther east there is a town, on the south bank, called Shotang, as large as Shigatzé; that the river flows thence eastward for 120 miles, and then turns due south.

The hills round Lhasa are barren, except for one thorny

[1] According to another authority, the principal *Gonpas* or monasteries round Lhasa, with the numbers of monks in each, are as follows:

Gandan Monastery	3,500	Kontyaling Monastery ..	200
Lía "	5,500	Tankyaling "	200
Depong "	7,500	Chochuling "	300
Gentu "	500	Chumuling "	1,000
Grume "	500		
Chenamgé "	1,000		20,400
Chemchung "	200		

[2] Nomen-khan of Huc, ii. p. 156. The Pundit calls him Gyalpo-Khuro-Gyago.

[3] *Kaskaks*, of the Pundit.

bush called *sia*, but there are trees of two kinds in the gardens, though not indigenous, called *changma* and *jawar*. The crops of the Lhasa plains consist of barley, wheat, peas, mustard, radishes, carrots, onions, potatoes,[1] beans, and other garden produce. There are cows, sheep, goats, yaks, ponies, asses, and pigs; and fowls, pigeons, and ducks are plentiful. The manufactures at Lhasa are chiefly woollen cloths and felt.

The population of Lhasa, according to a census taken in 1854, was 15,000, and owing to the number of celibates there is a large preponderance of women: 9000 women to 6000 men. The garrison consists of 500 Chinese soldiers, and 1000 Tibetans, armed with flint guns, and seven small pieces of ordnance.

The Pundit left Lhasa on the 21st of April, 1866, and, returning by the same route, reached Tadum on the 1st of June. Journeying up the Tsanpu valley, he crossed the Mariam-la pass, and returned to India, reporting himself to Colonel Montgomerie at the head-quarters of the Great Trigonometrical Survey.[2]

In May, 1867, the same Pundit who was at Lhasa, A, with a third man who had been trained in the interval, C, as B had proved to be somewhat wanting in nerve, set out to explore the gold mines of Thok-jalung, on the lofty plateau in rear of the great Northern Range. After a most trying journey, these hardy and persevering explorers crossed the Chomorang-la pass, 18,760 feet above the sea, and after a long march through snow, reached the chief gold-field,[3] on a large desolate plain, 16,330 feet above the sea, where the camp of the Tibetan gold diggers was pitched. The master of the gold diggings was a native of Lhasa, a shrewd and well-informed man. The Pundit describes the method of working the gold, and the habits of the

[1] Probably due to the benevolent forethought of Warren Hastings, and introduced through Bhutan. (See p. 19, and note.)

[2] See 'General Report on the Operations of the Great Trigonometrical Survey of India during 1866–7,' by Colonel J. T. Walker, R.E., F.R.S., ix. pp. i to xxix.

[3] In 32° 24′ 26″ N.; 81° 37′ 38″ E.

diggers. The explorers left Thok-jalung in August, and returned to head-quarters in November, 1867.[1]

Some very important journeys were made by an explorer whom Colonel Montgomerie calls No. 9, and whose results he reported upon in 1872. No. 9 went up the valley of the Tambur, in Eastern Nepal, in the footsteps of Dr. Hooker, as far as the Wallanchún pass, which No. 9 calls Tipta-la; and then succeeded in gaining permission to enter Tibet by his successful medical treatment of the wife of a chief official, at Tashirak, a large standing camp on a feeder of the Arun, 15,000 feet above the sea. He then crossed a mountain spur by the Ni-la pass, and entered the district of Tinki-jong. Advancing southward, he first came to patches of cultivation at a place called Lamadong, on the banks of the Khantongíri, another tributary of the Arun. Crossing over another spur, by the pass of Tinki-la, he reached the banks of the Chomto-dong lake, 20 miles long by 16 miles wide, and 14,700 feet above the sea. He then crossed the Central Range by the Lagulung-la pass, 16,200 feet above the sea, with glacier ice close down to it, which forms the boundary between Sikkim and Tibet. The explorer journeyed thence to Shigatzé, and duly paid his respects to the Teshu Lama.

No. 9 returned by the Sakia monastery of the Red Cap sect, crossed the Central Chain by the Dong-la pass, on the 3rd of October, 1871, and proceeded, by Sakar-jong, Tingri, and Nilam, to the gorge of the Bhotia Kosi into Nepal. Nilam, or Kuti, is the last Tibetan town in this direction, and the pass thence into Nepal, according to the account given by No. 9, is one of the most dangerous in the whole Himálayan range.[2]

In 1871, Colonel Montgomerie organized a party to explore some portion of the unknown region north of the Tibetan watershed of the Upper Brahmaputra, or Tsanpu, led by a young

[1] 'General Report on the Operations of the Great Trigonometrical Survey of India, 1867–8,' by Lieut.-Colonel J. T. Walker, R.E., F.R.S., xi. pp. i to x.

[2] See note at p. 155. 'General Report on the Operations of the Great Trigonometrical Survey of India during 1871–2,' by Major T. G. Montgomerie, R.E., F.R.S.

semi-Tibetan, who is neither distinguished by name nor number, so we will call him D. He had with him four assistants from the border districts. Crossing the Mariam-la, they arrived at Shigatzé on the 24th of November, where D prepared for a journey across the great Northern Chain to the unvisited lake of Tengri-nor, which was only known from the Lama's survey of 1716. Sheep were the only animals that could stand the journey, as the road was too stony for yaks and the climate too cold for donkeys. D therefore purchased fifty sheep to carry the baggage, and, setting out on the 6th of December, the party crossed the Tsanpu, and travelled up the valley of the Shiang-chu, in the footsteps of Mr. Bogle.[1] The villages the explorers passed through were Peting, on the Tsanpu; Chua Dongdot-la, and Chom; and on the 14th they reached Namling, the Chamnamring of Mr. Bogle,[2] where there are a monastery with five hundred monks, a fort, and about two hundred houses surrounded by gardens, with an iron bridge over the river. This route is frequented by traders in salt and borax.

Following up the valley they next came to Kholam, and then to Gonkiang, where there is a monastery. On the 20th they halted at another monastery, called Rabdan Chuling Gonpa, the residence of a high Lama, called the Shaptung Rimboché, who was said to be about a hundred years old, and who had built the monastery eighty years before. Beyond this point the cold became very intense; and at the village of Gunje the explorers were told that white bears, called *tik-dumba*, abound, which commit great havoc amongst the cattle. They next came to some very remarkable hot springs and geysers in the mountains;[3] and on the 8th of January, 1872, they crossed the Khalamba-la pass over the great Northern Range, in a heavy snowstorm, which is 17,200 feet above the sea. On the other side they came to an encampment of Dokpa shepherds, and a little farther on the first view was obtained of the great Tengri-nor lake, called on the spot Jang-Namcho[4] Chidmo,

[1] See p. 80. [2] See p. 80. [3] See note at p. 182. [4] *Nam*, sky; and *cho*, lake.

and they crossed the large river Ghaika-chu, flowing into it from the west. They reached the monastery, on the banks of the lake, called Dorkia-lugu-dong,[1] whence there is a magnificent view of the wide expanse of water. D resolved to execute a complete survey of the lake, making this monastery his head-quarters; but there were constant heavy falls of snow, which impeded his work. The principal peak in this part of the Northern Range is called *Ninjinthangla,* 25,000 feet high, and the lamas say it is a god surrounded by three hundred and sixty smaller snowy peaks as its servants. The range was traced for 150 miles, running in a north-easterly direction.

The lake is quite frozen over in November, though the water is too salt to be used for drinking. The level is 15,200 feet above the sea. It is 60 miles long by from 16 to 25 miles broad, and has some large islands. To the north there is another smaller lake, called Bul-cho, about 6 miles long by 5 miles wide, whence a kind of borax is obtained.

On their return, D and his companions were attacked by robbers, and stripped of nearly all they possessed, with difficulty making their way round the east side of the lake, and across the Central Chain, by the Damniargan-la pass, to Lhasa. On the 2nd of March the weary travellers arrived at the Jang-talung monastery, where there are a thousand monks; and on the 9th they reached Lhasa; whence, after a long and difficult return journey, they made their way to the head-quarters of the Great Trigonometrical Survey in safety.[2]

A second explorer, whose journey is described in the same report, made his way through the upper part of Western Nepal, from Kumaon, across the Kali and Karnali, to Muktinath, and then, by Mantang, over the Photu-la pass of the Central Chain, 15,080 feet above the sea, to Tadum, in Tibet.

Another most important exploring achievement has been

[1] *Dor*, a rock; *lugu*, a sheep; and *dong*, face.

[2] 'General Report on the Operations of the Great Trigonometrical Survey of India during 1873–4,' by Colonel J. T. Walker, R.E., F.R.S., pp. i to x.

done by a Pundit this year, the full account of which has not yet reached England. He was detached from Mr. Forsyth's mission at Yarkand; made his way across the lofty unknown plateau of the inland lakes, and over the Northern Chain to Lhasa; went some distance farther down the Tsanpu than any of his predecessors, and finally reached Assam by the Tawang route, east of Bhutan, which, though unknown to us, appears to be much frequented by Tibetans, and may hereafter become a great commercial highway. The report of this Pundit will be extremely interesting and important.

The training and despatch of these native explorers have added very materially to our knowledge, not only of the geography, but also of the condition of the people, and the state of trade in Nepal and Tibet. Colonel Walker and Colonel Montgomerie have rendered most important service in having conceived and ably carried out so useful a project; and the Pundits themselves deserve the highest praise for their painstaking accuracy, perseverance, and gallant adventurous spirit.

Pundit A has given us an excellent sketch of the commerce of Tibet, which, combined with the valuable chapter[1] on trade in the work of the Abbé Desgodins, enables us to acquire a clear idea of its character, and of the extent of the mercantile operations that have Lhasa and Shigatzé as their centres.

The Pundit says that traders bring their merchandise to Lhasa in December from far and near: from China and Mongolia, Kam and Szechuen, up the passes from Bhutan and Sikkim and Nepal, and from Kashmir and Ladak.[2] From China come silks of all varieties, carpets, and hardware; from Mongolia come leather, saddlery, sheep, and horses; from Kam

[1] Chap. vii. p. 278.

[2] The current coin is a silver piece called *Naktang*, 2½ being equal to a rupee. The silver pieces are cut into halves, called *Chikyahs*; or thirds, *Karima*. Two thirds of a *Naktang* is called *Shokang* or *Miscal*. There is also a large lump of silver bearing the seal of the Emperor of China, worth 333 *Naktangs*, called *Dojah* or *Kuras*. Desgodins says that there are many Indian rupees in the country. (See also p. 120 and note.)

comes much perfume; from Szechuen, tea; from Tawang, Bhutan, and Sikkim, rice and tobacco; from Nepal, broadcloth, silk, indigo, coral, pearls, sugar, spices, and Indian manufactures; from Ladak and Kashmir, saffron and Indian commodities.

English woollen cloths are much prized; and the Abbé Desgodins saw a vast number of bales of cloth, marked "Halifax," on their way to Pa-mou-tang,[1] a place S.W. of Bhatang. The Tibetans are used to the sizes of English cloth, the price being 20 to 40 francs a square piece of the whole breadth. Scarlet is the favourite colour, and a good yellow would fetch a high price. Flowered calicoes are also much used for lining walls.

Brick tea, for Tibet, is made mostly in Szechuen from a hedgerow tree, 15 feet high, with large coarse leaves. The packet of four bricks of 5 French lb. each (25 centimetres long) is bought for 8 francs where it is grown, and sells at Lhasa at from 30 to 35 francs. The annual supply for Tibet is 6,000,000 French lb., worth about 2,400,000 francs.[2]

The merchants who come in December, leave in March, before the rivers become flooded. Silver and gold are the most important articles of export; then follow salt, wool, woollen manufactures, furs, drugs, and musk. The people in the direction of Szechuen are clothed in Tibetan blankets, which are also much worn in Sikkim and Nepal. There is a great demand for musk in China; and Szechuen, Yunnan, all the wild tribes north of Burma, Nepal, Sikkim, and Bhutan are supplied with salt from Tibet. By the Nepal and Ladak routes, Tibet exports large quantities of yaks' tails, borax, gold, silver, and ponies.

In Assam, the centres of Tibetan trade are at Dewangiri, and at Udelgiri, where there is a great fair twice a year in connection with the Tawang route. Darjiling is the central mart for the Chumbi valley trade; Patna, for that passing through Nepal; and Kashmir, for the long route by the Mariam-la pass.

The great and inexhaustible staple of Tibet is its wool, which

[1] Desgodins, p. 308. [2] Desgodins, p. 299.

can be produced on its vast plains and mountain slopes in any quantity and of the finest quality. Mr. Edgar believes that if a good frontier road were opened through Sikkim, from the Jelep-la pass into Chumbi to Darjiling, large quantities of cows and sheep, *ghi*, and wool, the real wealth of Tibet, would find their way into India. But this would only be a small beginning. For the real development of its vast resources, Tibet must have the same advantages as are enjoyed by the *sierra* of Peru, a country which it resembles in so many respects.[1] It is essential for her growth in prosperity that all the passes into India should be freely opened to her commerce. This is a necessity when the staple of a mountain plateau is live stock. In Peru, the droves of llamas are brought down with produce for the markets by numerous passes, because there must be a vast area of pasturage by the way. There is the same need for Tibet.

The great future measure which may hereafter reward the adoption of a broadly conceived and continuous policy will be the establishment of unfettered intercourse through all the Himálayan passes from the Kali to the Dihong. And the first essential for the initiation of such a policy is a comprehension of the physical and political geography of the region, and a thorough knowledge of its history. If this is conceded, it will follow that the publication, for the first time, of a full account of Mr. Bogle's mission to the Teshu Lama, and of Mr. Manning's journey to Lhasa, will usefully fill up two gaps in a history which would otherwise be incomplete.

Moreover, the study of Bogle's negotiation with the Lama is specially important. For the great statesman who despatched the mission reached a point in his policy, as regards the maintenance of friendly intercourse with Tibet, which was afterwards

[1] Both are lofty table-lands, from 9000 to 12,000 feet above the sea, intersected by mountain ranges. The wealth of both consists in wool and the precious metals; in both the people are religious, peaceful, and industrious; and the Buddhistic Lamas, in their moral code and system of government, have much in common with the Yncas, the priest-kings of Peru.

lost and has never been regained. It will be useful to examine the curiously close points of resemblance, as regards Tibet, between the period when Warren Hastings was at the helm and the present time. Then, as now, the Tibetans were most friendly and cordial, from the sacred Lama of Teshu Lumbo downwards. Then, as now, all obstruction came from the Chinese agents. Then, as now, the chief dread of the Tibetans was the aggressive policy of the warlike Gorkha Rajahs. The Lama made constant complaints of Nepalese misconduct to Mr. Bogle. A century afterwards, when Mr. Edgar met a Tibetán official on the Jelep-la, the conversation about the Gorkha bugbear may be said to have been renewed in 1873 just where it was broken off in 1775.

Warren Hastings applied himself to the adoption of the wisest measures for solving these questions. As regards the first, he maintained continuous interchanges of good offices by correspondence, and by despatching missions under Bogle, Hamilton, Turner, and Purungir Gosain. As regards the second, Mr. Bogle early saw that it would be necessary to bring influence to bear directly on the Government at Peking. He succeeded in inducing the Teshu Lama to exert such influence with the Emperor; while Mr. Bogle himself intended, with the sanction of the Governor-General, to have proceeded to Peking.

It may be gathered from a perusal of Mr. Edgar's report that his instructions, when employed to meet the Sikkim Rajah and Tibetan officials, were conceived in the spirit of that enlightened policy which was adopted with such success by Warren Hastings. There can be no doubt that a conciliatory but firm and persistent series of representations at Peking would lead to the removal of Chinese obstructions, and to the reception of English envoys, as in times past, by the sacred Lamas. The latter point may be insisted upon, because it has already been conceded to Russia. For some time there has been a resident Russian Consul at Urga, near the Court of the Taranath Lama.[1] England has a right to the same privilege, as regards the Teshu or Dalai Lamas. But so much is not needed at present; though a smaller concession, namely, the occasional reception of a friendly mission at Lhasa and Shigatzé may be demanded as a right.[2]

The danger from Gorkhali aggression is more serious and more difficult to deal with. This danger has been a cause of alarm to the peaceful Tibetans ever since the deplorable overthrow of the Newar dynasty of Nepal, more than a century ago. The warlike state founded by Prithi Narayan is still a source of alarm. Jang Bahadar has long been minister, and has kept the peace with England, but not with Tibet. He has not, however, been so long in power as was his relation, old Bhim Sen Thappa, whose fall was sudden and violent. He has been equally obstructive, equally an enemy to free trade and civilizing progress.

If the Tibetan Government could be made to understand that, in exchange for active co-operation in the removal of Chinese obstruction, the whole influence and power of the Government of India would be exerted to check aggressive designs on the part of the dreaded Gorkhas, there is every reason to believe that such co-operation would be heartily given.

The first step towards the achievement of objects so fraught with good, both for Tibet and India, will doubtless be in the direction of the Chumbi valley, a step for which Sir George Campbell and Mr. Edgar have been diligently preparing. We

[1] See page xlix.

[2] The first resident Russian Consul at Urga was appointed under the provisions of a Supplementary Treaty negotiated at Peking by Ignatief on $\frac{2}{14}$ November, 1860, and ratified at St. Petersburgh in January, 1861. The Consul is entitled also to a Russian escort. M. Shishmaroff was the first Consul at Urga, and in 1868 he made a rapid journey of thirteen days from Urga to Uliasutai, to conclude a trade convention with the Chinese Amba. See, for the provisions of the Treaty of 1861, 'The Russians on the Amur,' by E. G. Ravenstein (Trübner, 1861), p. 182.

may hope that before long a good road will be made from the central mart at Darjîling to the Jelep-la pass, which will be contemporaneous with an exploration of the Chumbi valley, and with a visit of English officers to Pari-jong. The second step will be a mission to Lhasa and Shigatzé, to renew friendly intercourse with the Lamas, and place the arrangements with regard to trade on a satisfactory footing. But no progress can be made until negotiations have been opened at Peking, to secure for the English Government the same privilege, as regards the Teshu Lama (in accordance with the "most friendly nation" clause), as Russia has acquired at Urga, as regards the Taranath Lama.

It is believed that the present volume, by filling up two wide gaps in the history of intercourse between India and Tibet, will be useful to those who are officially entrusted with the conduct of these grave and important measures. It is also hoped that it may help to enable a large circle of readers, who are interested in the welfare and progress of India, to form a sound judgment on momentous questions which may not improbably be under discussion in the near future.

NOTE

ON THE

MAPS OF TIBET, NEPAL, SIKKIM, AND BHUTAN.

I PROPOSE in this note to give an account of the principal maps that exist of the above countries, and to enumerate all that are in the collection of the Geographical Department of the India Office.

The early Dutch compilers of maps, Ortelius, Mercator, Hondius, and Plancius had no information to enable them to insert any details of interest relating to Tibet. But with the rise of the French geographers, began the arrival of the news from the Jesuit missionaries.

Nicolas Sanson, the pioneer of geography in France, was born at Abbeville in 1600, and died in 1667; his son Guillaume survived until 1733, and Adrian died in 1718. The Sansons represent the transition from the crude ideas of the middle ages to the more precise notions represented by Delisle and D'Anville. They published atlases, which were reproduced at Amsterdam from 1690 to 1696, and several contained details respecting Central Asia.

But Guillaume Delisle, the principal creator of the modern system of geography, was the first to publish a map of Tibet. He was born at Paris in 1675, and in 1700 he produced his map of the continents of the old world, continuing to bring out maps of various countries up to the time of his death in 1726. His map of Central Asia of 1706[1] contains many details, pub-

[1] 'Carte des Inde et de la Chine, dressée sur plusieurs relations particulières rectifiées par quelques observationes,' par Guillaume De L'Isle.

lished for the first time, which must have been obtained from the Jesuit missionaries. Here appears "Le Royaume de Utsang," "Lassa ou Baratola," "Zekatche," "Tassoo Loomboo," "Couti" (Kuti); and the Himálaya mountains are called "M. de Purbe tou de Naugracut."[1] "Tassoo Loomboo" is omitted in the edition of 1720. Delisle obtained much information, but he had no precise knowledge respecting relative positions, so that his map is very confused. For instance, Thibet and Utsang are inserted at a distance from each other, as if they were different places. This blunder has been repeated on very recent maps in Germany; and there is evidence of confused ideas in Spruner's Historical Atlas.

Several English map makers used the materials of Delisle, two of which are referred to at p. cxli.

It was Jean Baptiste Bourguignon D'Anville, however, who produced the first map of Tibet with any pretension to accuracy. D'Anville was born at Paris in 1697, and died in 1782. His maps of China, including Tibet, based on the surveys of the Jesuits and the Lamas,[2] were published in the work of Du Halde,[3] and at the Hague in 1737.[4] A part of his general map of Tibet is reproduced in the present volume in *fac simile.* It is still the basis of our knowledge of Tibet, and has been but slightly altered or modified up to the present time. The maps of Tibet by D'Anville are specially interesting, because a set of them, which has been preserved, were the companions of Mr. Bogle during his mission to the Teshu Lama.

After the death of D'Anville, Englishmen began to take the lead as geographers and map makers. Major Rennell, the father of Indian geography, returned to England in the year that D'Anville died, and published his atlas of Bengal. In his

[1] Mr. Bogle uses the same word. (See p. 15.)

[2] See Introduction, p. lxi.

[3] See p. lxiv, note.

[4] 'Nouvelle Atlas de la Chine, de la Tartarie Chinoise, et du Thibet,' par M. D'Anville, Geographie Ordinaire de sa Majesté Chretienne (La Haye, 1737); No. 32, 'Carte Générale du Thibet et 9 feuilles particulières du Thibet.'

memoir he discussed the question of the course of the Brahmaputra, and the positions of Tassisudon and Lhasa, but he was unable to add much to the map of D'Anville as regards Tibet.

After Rennell's time there succeeded a period when explorers were at work in the field collecting materials for the map makers. Turner prepared a map of his route through Bhutan into Tibet, which was published in 1800 in his book, and a great deal of information was collected in Nepal.

In the Geographical Department of the India Office there is a manuscript map of part of Nepal drawn in 1793, and showing Colonel Kirkpatrick's routes (4′ to an inch); and a manuscript "Memoir for Illustrating a Geographical Sketch of Nepal and the adjacent Countries," by Captain William Kirkpatrick (400 *pages foolscap*). On these materials the map in Kirkpatrick's work on Nepal is based.

Major Crawford also contributed much geographical information at the same time. We have from him an elaborate manuscript map of the valley of Nepal (¾′ to an inch); a manuscript map of the route to Nepal, including the valley; a map of the Nepal territories, and other portions of the Himálaya mountains, in manuscript, with the sources of the Ganges delineated from the reports of pilgrims; and a manuscript map of the Nepal territories, on a scale of 7⅓ miles to an inch, dated 1811, with many snowy peaks laid down.

It was from these materials that Aaron Arrowsmith compiled this portion of his "Map of India from all the latest and most authentic materials, 1816." He copies Tibet from D'Anville, adding Turner's route, while his Nepal is derived from Major Crawford's observations and compilations.

The Nepal war of 1816 led to the production of additional materials. We have a manuscript map, by Lieut. G. Lindesay, of the routes by which Sir David Ochterlony's army advanced in three divisions towards Mukwanpúr in February, 1816, and a sketch of the stockades covering the pass on the route to Mukwanpúr. There is also a series of boundary maps between

Nepal and British territory, by Lieuts. Garden, Boileau, J. A. Hodgson, and Pickersgill; and a more recent one, dated 1861, by Lieut. F. C. Anderson.

Dr. Buchanan Hamilton, during his residence at Kathmandu, obtained five native maps of parts of Nepal and Sikkim, which he deposited in the library of the East India Company. They have since unfortunately been lost, previous to the organization of the Geographical Department of the India Office. Dr. Hamilton's work on Nepal is illustrated by a "Map of the Dominions of the House of Gorkha," constructed by himself from all existing materials, in 1819, on a scale of 35 miles to an inch.

Mr. Brian Hodgson's physical map of Nepal, showing the river systems, appeared in the 'Selections from the Records of the Government of Bengal,' No. 27 (1857); together with routes obtained by Mr. Hodgson from Kathmandu to Peking, from Kathmandu to Darjíling, and a measurement of the great military road through Nepal, from Kumaon to Sikkim.

In the Geographical Department of the India Office there is a manuscript sketch map of the frontier districts of Nepal between the rivers Gandak and Kosi, dated 1840, compiled from official records (scale 4′ to 1 inch).

The latest map of Nepal is a "Preliminary Sketch of Nepal and the Countries adjoining to the South, West, and East, October, 1855; compiled in the Office of the Surveyor-General of India from actual Surveys, other available Materials, Itineraries of Travellers, and from Information" (1856, 16 miles to an inch).

Nepal is, however, included in the trans-frontier maps of the Great Trigonometrical Survey (*Sheet* 9). In this map the hills are not delineated, and it is confined to the results of observations made by actual exploration. Consequently it shows the various gaps which are still unmapped, and practically unknown. This sheet has the advantage of including the Tibetan territory up to the Tsanpu, so far as it has been explored by Colonel Montgomerie's assistants. The map is dated at Dehra Dún, in 1873.

The only map of the native state of Sikkim is that by Dr. Hooker. The original manuscript is in the Geographical Department of the India Office: "Map of Sikkim and Eastern Nepal, by J. D. Hooker, Esq., M.D., R.N., F.R.S., exhibiting the Routes of that Traveller, 1850" (4 miles to an inch). This map is a very able piece of work, and is certainly the most striking contribution to the geography of the Himálaya that has ever been made by a private traveller. It is also lithographed with this title: "Independent Sikkim, from a Sketch by J. D. Hooker, Esq., M.D., R.N., F.R.S., based on the Operations of the Great Trigonometrical Survey, 1850" (same scale as the MS.).

There are several maps of British Sikkim. The first is a manuscript map comprising the Darjíling hill territory and two Murung Parganas, from surveys by Captain W. S. Sherwill, in 1852, and reduced in 1853 to a scale of 4 miles to an inch. It includes a list of the principal tribes, and of trees and plants, with approximate elevations at which they grow. Captain Sherwill's map was published in 1852, at Calcutta. Next followed a map of the hill territory of British Sikkim and the Darjíling district, by E. T. S. Johnson, Assistant Revenue Surveyor, in 1861 to 1867, one on a scale of 2 inches to 1 mile, on five sheets; published also on a scale of 1 mile to 1 inch. Another map of the Darjíling district was brought out by the Surveyor-General in 1874, on a scale 4 miles to an inch, showing also the route to Tumlong. There are also maps of the subdivisions of the Darjíling district, published on a large scale.

The first general map of Bhutan was drawn by Captain Pemberton. It is included in two sheets of his large map of the Eastern Frontier of British India, in twelve sheets (Calcutta, 1838). The next was compiled in the office of the Surveyor-General, on a scale of 8 miles to the inch, including the Bengal dúars, to illustrate the route of the Mission of 1864. It illustrates the volume published at Calcutta in 1864, containing

"Reports of Missions to Bhutan." The first edition of this map was published in October, 1864, and the second in July, 1865.

"A Sketch Map of Bhutan and of the Dooars" was inserted in the Bhutan 'Blue Book,' presented to Parliament in 1865, and is also used to illustrate Dr. Rennie's work on Bhutan. The chief object of this sketch was to define the extent of the Dúar districts.

In 1874, a new preliminary map of Bhutan was published by the Surveyor-General, on a scale of 8 miles to the inch: it includes, with previous work, the topographical surveys executed by Captain Godwin Austen, R.E., and Lieuts. Strahan, R.E., and Holdich, R.E., in 1864–65, 1865–66; and information collected by Colonel MacGregor. This map illustrates Colonel MacGregor's Military Report on the country of Bhutan.

In the collection of the Geographical Department of the India Office there is an original plane table-sketch of Western Bhutan, on a larger scale, surveyed by Captain Godwin Austen in 1864, which illustrates the route of Mr. Eden's mission.

The most important general maps including Tibet have been those of Klaproth[1] and Berghaus; followed by the maps of Kiepert and others, to illustrate Ritter's 'Erdkunde.' But no real additions were made to our knowledge of Great Tibet, supplied by M. D'Anville's maps, until Colonel Montgomerie's explorers penetrated into that country, and brought back valuable geographical results. The map of the Pundit of 1865, including the upper part of the valley of the Brahmaputra, the city of Lhasa, and the route from Kathmandu into Tibet by the No-la, is in the report of the operations of the Great Trigonometrical Survey for 1866–67. The report for 1871–72 contains another important map, compiled by Colonel Montgomerie from a route survey made by an Asiatic explorer (No. 9) of the Dingri

[1] 'Carte de l'Asie Centrale dressée d'après les cartes levées par ordre de l'Empereur Khian Loung, par les missionnaires de Peking, et d'après un grand nombre de notions extraites et traduites de livres Chinoises,' par M. J. Klaproth. (Paris. 4 sheets.)

Maidan, the upper Arun river, and part of Great Tibet (16 miles to an inch). It supplies important rectifications of the last general map of Nepal, published in 1855, and embraces all Eastern Nepal from Kathmandu to the Sikkim frontier. The report for 1872–73 has a map from the route survey of an explorer who reached Shigatzé, and went thence across the northern range, round the great lake Tengri-nòr, to Lhasa. It also contains a map from a route survey of another explorer who traversed Western Nepal.

These four maps, obtained from the work of native explorers who have entered Great Tibet within the last ten years, represent the first accurate geographical information, with the exception of Turner's route, that has been obtained respecting the territories of the Dalai and Teshu Lamas since the publication of D'Anville's map, more than a hundred years ago.

The routes of these explorers, as well as of Captain Turner, Dr. Hooker, and the missions of Pemberton and Eden in Bhutan, are shown on the general map prepared for my "Report on the Moral and Material Progress of India for 1872–73," by Mr. Trelawney Saunders, entitled, "A Map of Trade Routes to Tibet from the Lower Provinces of Bengal and Assam" (scale 30 miles to an inch).

A GENERAL MAP OF THE TABLE-LAND OF TIBET

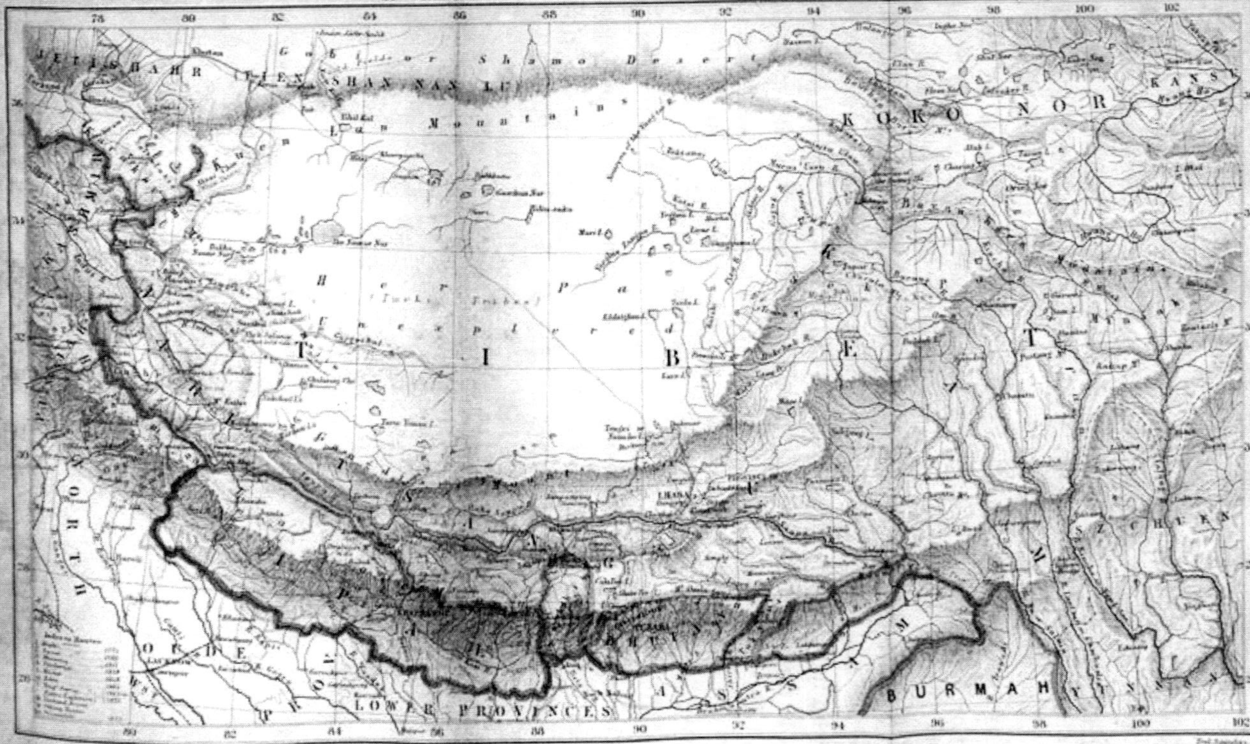

BIOGRAPHICAL SKETCH

OF

GEORGE BOGLE,

BENGAL CIVIL SERVICE.

THE genius of Warren Hastings is shown in nothing more than in his rare insight in the selection of subordinates. He surrounded himself with young men of great ability and talent for administration, who worked for him with a zeal which was stimulated by warm personal attachment. Among those who were trained by and won distinction under the eye of the first and greatest of the Governors-General of India may be mentioned young Alexander Elliot,[1] who was cut off in his prime; William Markham,[2] the Resident of Benares, who assisted his revered chief during the trial; Jonathan Duncan,[3] the Governor of Bombay; Claud Alexander, of Ballochmyle; David Anderson; Augustus Clevland,[4] the civilizer of the Santhal tribes; and

[1] Brother of Sir Gilbert Elliot, first Earl of Minto, of whom more hereafter.

[2] Son of Dr. Markham, Archbishop of York; brother of Colonel David Markham, who led the forlorn hope at the siege of Bangalore; uncle of General Frederick Markham, who commanded a brigade at the siege of Moultan; and grandfather of the present editor. Of him also more presently.

[3] Jonathan Duncan entered the East India Company's service in 1772. He was the friend of George Bogle, and his value was cordially appreciated by Warren Hastings. He was Resident of Benares from 1787 to 1795, where he introduced the permanent settlement, and negotiated an important commercial treaty with Nepal in 1792. He became Governor of Bombay in 1795, and continued to administer the affairs of that important Presidency until his death on August 11, 1811. Two volumes of 'Selections from the Duncan Records' were published at Benares, by authority, in 1873.

[4] Sir Cecil Beadon tells me that the name of Augustus Clevland is still remembered and revered in Bengal. He was a younger son of John Clevland, Esq., of Tapely Hall, near Bideford, by Sarah, daughter of Charles Shuckburgh, Esq., of Longborow, in Gloucestershire, and was born in 1751. Warren Hastings thus describes the nature of

George Bogle, the subject of the present short memoir, whom Warren Hastings selected as his envoy to Tibet.

George Bogle was the son of George Bogle of Daldowle, a beautiful place near Bothwell, on the right bank of the Clyde.[1] George, the elder, was born in 1700, was educated at Leyden, and became a merchant in Glasgow, where he was six times elected Lord Rector of the University between the years 1737 and 1748. He married Anne, daughter of Sir John Sinclair of Stevenson, by Martha Lockhart,[2] heiress of Sir John Lockhart of Castlehill, in Lanarkshire, brother of Sir William Lockhart of Lee. Sir John "was a man of great parts and knowledge of our laws, and was appointed by Charles II. one of the Senators of the College of Justice, and a Lord of Justiciary, as Lord Castlehill."[3] Mr. and Mrs. Bogle, of Daldowie, had nine children, of whom two died in infancy.

Mr. Clevland's services, in the luminous memorandum on his administration of India, which he wrote during his voyage home in 1785 (page 131):

"I have often with pleasure expatiated on the peculiar talents of the late Mr. Clevland, in civilizing the inhabitants of the mountainous districts of Rajmehal, by a system of conciliation which will long endear his memory to those who have felt the benefits of it; and I cannot deny myself the gratification arising from the reflection that the exertion of those talents was in a great measure owing to the public support and private encouragement which he received from me. In the honours bestowed upon his memory, the Board has consulted the interests of the Company, by holding forth for imitation a character so worthy of it. The immediate advantages of his labours are seen in the security which the inhabitants of the adjacent lands possess; no longer apprehensive of being plundered of the produce of their labour by a lawless banditti, they have extended their cultivation over large tracts of land till lately impassable; and the country at the bottom of the Rajmehal Hills, which I myself have seen in a state of nature, has assumed an appearance of universal fertility. The remote advantages will be more considerable should the continuance of the same plan of civilization increase the intercourse which has so lately been established between the inhabitants of the hills and those of the lowlands. At all events, the Company has acquired a large accession of new subjects, who are not only peaceable in themselves, but have been successfully employed in maintaining the peace of the country, and who, being warmly attached to us by the superior benefits they have received from their civilization, may, in case of public exigency, be usefully employed in the defence of our territories against foreign invasion."

[1] Now the property of Mr. M'Call.

[2] This lady was the widow of Cromwell Lockhart of Lee, eldest son of the great ambassador Sir William Lockhart, who married Robina, daughter of John Sewster, Esq., by Anna, sister of Oliver Cromwell, the Lord Protector.

[3] Baronage of Scotland.

The rest were Martha, Robert, Mary, Elizabeth, John, Anne, and George the youngest, who was born on the 26th of November, 1746. They were brought up together at Daldowie, and in one of his early letters from Calcutta to his sister Anne, whose pet name was Chuffles, George Bogle recalls the happy days of their childhood. "Throwing myself back in my great chair, I am transported to the nursery at Daldowie. The picture of Julius Cæsar recalls to my mind the shows which you remember we used to make. You two stools, how often have I ate bread and milk upon you, or played at catch honours or comet! Need I ask you if you remember one night that the beds were to be filled with fresh chaff and afterwards lay upon the floor, what diversion we had in tumbling one another from the top of the drawers? Do you remember how we broke open the window, at the bottom of one of the beds, to get at some shells? Never shall I wish for anything so much as I did to get at those shells, which we could always see and never get at. All was one continued scene of health and pleasure. This gave way to the life of a schoolboy, and away I was hurried to Haddington, where I passed happy years; but my pleasures, although very great, were different from those in the nursery. The last were perhaps the most unmixed of the two, but a boy learns to despise them and affects more manly diversions. During this Latin and Greek period, I from time to time paid annual visits to the nursery, and was generally there when it was adorned with the brown maiden and her scarlet girdle. After this I lived in Glasgow, and generally passed the Saturday nights in the nursery. Away I was whirled up to London. What expectation and curiosity! It was so great that I hardly felt grief at parting with my friends. And I quitted the nursery for many years, and I had just time to hurry down to Scotland to take farewell. I was only there three weeks, but let me not pass them over like the other weeks of my existence. Every hour of them was marked with joy at meeting with so many friends whom I so tenderly loved, and who returned my fondness, and they ended with heartfelt regret at parting with such friends, with so distant a prospect of meeting them again."

He was never to see them again. He decided upon adopting the career of a merchant, and it was settled that he should, after completing his education, either go into his brother Robert's counting-house, in London, or to his brother John, who was established as a merchant at Falmouth, on the Rappahannock river, in Virginia. After leaving Glasgow, he attended Edinburgh University, studying logic and other branches of education, from November, 1760, to April, 1761. He was then sent to Mr. Kinross's school, at Enfield, and in December, 1764, he accompanied a sick friend to the south of France, who died at Toulouse, in January, 1765. Young Bogle travelled in France until the following June, when he was summoned to London by his eldest brother Robert, of the firm of Bogle and Scott, whose counting-house he entered as a clerk. Here he remained for the next four years, acquiring much experience in business, and in 1769 his friends obtained for him an appointment in the service of the East India Company.

George Bogle at the age of twenty-three found himself on board the 'Vansittart,' Indiaman, commanded by Captain Lewin, with letters of credit to a considerable amount, and introductions to the principal people in Bengal. He embarked on the 25th of January, 1770, but did not get clear of the Channel until the 24th of February. After touching at the Cape, at Johanna, one of the Comoro Islands, and at Madras, the 'Vansittart' arrived in the Hugli, and on the 19th of August George Bogle landed at Calcutta.

The young civilian arrived in Bengal at the time of the great famine of 1770, and the misery he witnessed left a deep impression on his mind. Writing to his father, in September, he says: "Last year the crops failed to an extent never known before in the memory of man, which has reduced the inhabitants to the utmost distress. This town was better provided than most others, and yet it has suffered amazingly. The Governor[1] and Council had a magazine of grain with which they fed fifteen thousand every day for some months, and yet this could not prevent many thousands from dying of want, and the streets from being crowded with the most miserable objects. There were sometimes 150 dead bodies picked up in a day, and thrown into the river. In the country the distress was greater, as it was farther removed from the sea and not so easily supplied from distant countries. Whole families perished of hunger, or fed upon leaves of trees, or, contrary to their religion, ate animal food; some even subsisted on the dead carcasses. Their distress is unparalleled, and it shocks one to think of it. A million and a half of people are said to have famished in the provinces that belong to the English. There is one thing that must amaze everyone that has been used to a free country. There is an indolence and indifference about them that is astonishing, and despair rather increases it. They have died without a single effort to obtain grain either by force or even by toil and labour. What mobs and commotions there would be with us were grain to increase to three times its price! and in many places it was a hundred times what it usually is." In a subsequent letter, written on October 24, 1770, he reverts to the subject of the famine again: "The distress has put a stop in some manner to trade, for grain was one of the best articles to export from this country, and was the means of bringing money in return; and the death and ruin of such a number of inhabitants must necessarily hurt the manufactures of cotton, which Bengal is famous for all over the world. I hope, however, that things will soon begin to revive, and that the inhabitants, as soon as they are relieved from their distress, will return with spirit to their industry and manufactures." In December he wrote that "the price of grain is very much fallen, and the people are again living in plenty, and contented."

Writers, on their arrival at Calcutta, were appointed as

[1] Mr. Cartier.

assistants in the different offices, and Bogle was placed in that of the Select Committee which transacted all political business, so that he early got an insight into the situation of the Company's possessions, and into its foreign relations. Meanwhile he diligently studied Persian, and within the first year he was able to read and converse in that language.

In February, 1772, when young Bogle had been eighteen months in Calcutta, Warren Hastings arrived from Madras to succeed Mr. Cartier as Governor of Bengal; but he did not take his seat as President of the Council until the following April, having carefully investigated the state of affairs in the interval, and found all the departments in a deplorable state of confusion. The new Governor at once began to inaugurate a more efficient system of administration. Among other appointments, Mr. George Bogle received the post of Assistant-Secretary to the Board of Revenue, under Mr. Higginson, on the 10th of October, 1772; and in the same month he accompanied the Governor and some of the Members of Council on a tour of inspection to Cossimbazar, with a view to making a settlement of the land on leases of five years. They went first to Kishangarh, where they remained about a month, and thence to Cossimbazar, where the revenue business detained them for nearly three months. This employment was very advantageous to young Bogle, as it furnished an opportunity for him to become better known to Warren Hastings, and at the same time gave him a practical insight into revenue business. He described his appointment as "attended with much trouble and small advantages, but it is highly agreeable to me from placing me immediately under the eye of the Governor and Council."

His letters at this time to his father and sisters are full of the warmest expressions of affection, and betoken a strong home feeling, which, however, in no way lessened his official zeal and efficiency. This is especially shown in the letters to his favourite sister Anne, whom he calls by the old pet name: "Your letters, my dear Chuffles, are the very nutmeg of delight, so long, so particular about everything my friends are doing. I have read them over again and again, and find new beauties in them every day. They are just as if you were chattering, with this advantage, that they cannot give me a headache and I can stop them if I chose, which, you know, is not always an easy matter with your ladyship. They want, however, the snap of the fingers and the hearty laugh. The good news of all my friends gives me the most sincere delight. God grant I may long continue to receive such comfortable news! My heart overflows with gratitude to Heaven, but it is not unmixed with regret." He then writes of the projected improvements at Daldowie, dwelling fondly on all the details and on all the well-remembered places round his home on the Clyde.

In 1773, his brother Robert suffered great commercial losses, his father's estate became encumbered, and George Bogle generously resolved to save money, year by year, so as to aid in freeing his relations from their embarrassments, and in paying off the debt on his beloved home at Daldowie. On the 9th of March, 1773, he was appointed to the office of Registrar to the Sadr Diwáni Adálat, the Court of Appeals for the natives; and soon afterwards Secretary to the Select Committee. At this time he thus writes of the Governor:

"Mr. Hastings is a man who is every way fitted for the station which he holds. He possesses a steadiness, and at the same time a moderation of character; he is quick and assiduous in business, and has a fine style of language, a knowledge of the customs and dispositions of the natives, whose tongue he understands, and, although not affable, yet of the most ready access to all the world. During his administration many abuses have been reformed, and many useful regulations have been established in every department of government. The natives are possessed of a code of laws far more ancient than Justinian, which have been handed down through a succession of ages, are interwoven with the system of their religion, and are framed to suit the manners of the people for whom they are intended. To revive these laws is at present a principal object with Mr. Hastings, and some progress has been made in translating them into English. This work, when finished, will do great credit to Mr. Hastings, and will furnish an excellent guide to the decisions of the Courts, while it pleases the people, who are attached to their own laws and usages."

George Bogle was now very high in the favour of Warren Hastings, who had not only a good opinion of his abilities and official aptitude, but a warm personal friendship for himself. The latter feeling was fully reciprocated by the young Scot, as it was by most of the youthful administrators who were honoured by the confidence and friendship of the Governor. Among them all, however, none were more devotedly loyal to their chief than George Bogle and his bosom friend Alexander Elliot, the younger brother of Sir Gilbert.[1]

When George Bogle was appointed as Envoy to the Lama of Tibet, on the 13th of May, 1774, Alexander Elliot officiated for him as Secretary to the Select Committee, and Registrar to the Sadr Diwáni Adálat; and the most affectionate letters passed between them during this separation. The Envoy also wrote home constantly in the course of his journey to the unknown table-land, and his warm heart was full of recollections of his distant home. Writing from Tassisudon, the capital of Bhutan, in August, 1774, to his sister Elizabeth, he says: "It is true, Bess, what you say; the country people who live among their friends and relations are strangers to the

[1] Alexander Kynynmond Elliot was the third son of Sir Gilbert Elliot, Bart., by Agnes Murray Kynynmond, heiress of Melgund and Kynynmond. His eldest brother, Gilbert, became first Earl of Minto, and was Governor-General of India. The second brother, Hugh, was Governor of Madras. Sir Gilbert Elliot, the eldest, was born in 1751. He was Viceroy of Corsica in 1795, created Baron Minto in 1797, President of the Board of Control in 1806, and Governor-General from 1807 to 1812. In 1813 he was created Earl of Minto and Viscount Melgund, and he died in 1814. Alexander, the third son, entered the East India Company, and became a dear friend of George Bogle, and a favourite of Warren Hastings.

pangs of parting, and to the solicitude of absence. But they never feel the joy which your letters give me, and the tear which now starts from my eye is worth an age of their vegetable affection. Yet I would have wished to have passed the two months with Robin at Daldowie. If the three little weeks I spent there[1] gave me so much pleasure, what must I have enjoyed with the addition of his company! But, alas! our destinies have wove for us a different web. We are scattered over the face of the earth, and are united only by hope and a tender remembrance. While you are passing your cheerful evenings with friends and relations at Daldowie; while Robin, with his negroes (and happy are they that are under him), is planting the sugar cane;[2] while I am climbing these rugged mountains, there is a secret virtue, like the magnet, which attracts us together, and cheers and solaces us. Beyond this hangs a cloud which we cannot penetrate." His letters from Tibet are also full of amusing stories, and they repeat the contents of his journal in a somewhat different style for each of his sisters.

When Bogle left Tibet, and the moment of separation came, the Teshu Lama took from his own neck three charmed strings of beads forming one necklace, and presented them to his friend, telling him that the ladies upon whom he bestowed them would be protected from all evil. Bogle gave the lower string, with the pendant ornaments, to his sister, Mrs. Brown, and it is now in the possession of her granddaughter, Miss Brown of Lanfine. The upper string he gave to his cousin, Mrs. Morehead, who bequeathed it to the eldest daughter of her son Robert, now Lady Lowther.[3]

[1] Before starting for India.

[2] Robert Bogle had settled in the island of Grenada as a sugar planter.

[3] See 'Memorials of the Life and Writings of the Rev. Robert Morehead,' edited by his son, Charles Morehead, M.D. (Edinburgh, 1875), p. 48, note. Mrs. Morehead was a first cousin of George Bogle, being a daughter of John Sinclair Lockhart, of Castlehill, whose sister Ann was George Bogle's mother. At p. 392 of the 'Memorials,' quoted above, there is a notice of George Bogle, followed by several letters to him from Mrs. Morehead. Her son, the Rev. Robert Morehead, was born in

A wood engraving of the Teshu Lama's charmed necklace is here presented. The centre string was of bright blue and green glass beads, and it is now lost. The upper and lower strings are formed of highly-polished beads of Tibetan carnelian, red, with an orange tint, and nearly opaque. To the lower one

a variety of ornaments are attached. One of these consists of three beads strung together, the colour and size of green peas, terminating with a carnelian drop set in gold. Two strings are of dull pink glass beads. At one end, suspended by flat silk braid, are two ornaments of transparent blue glass; one flat

1777, and died in 1842. He married a sister-in-law of Lord Jeffrey, and had, with other children (one of whom was twice Acting Governor of Madras), a daughter Isabella, married, in 1834, to Sir Charles Lowther, Bart., of Swillington, near Leeds. It is to her that the upper string of beads of the necklace of the Teshu Lama was bequeathed by her grandmother.

My dear Bogle

I have just rec'd yours of the 6th — Your other Letters have come safe to Hand. I have not answered them, expecting so soon to see you. But as you express an Anxiety on this Account, I wish to remove it as early as I can by telling you that I am perfectly satisfied, & pleased with every Circ. of your Conduct, & equally so with the Issue of your Commission. I wanted an open Communication of Trade between Tibbet & Bengal, but I do not wish for Leave to establish English Residents. Whatever I might have thought of this Point, I am now better pleased to have failed in it. — I have hired Two Houses for your Embassadors. I have many Thanks to make for your Journal,

which

wth y World must have. Its Merit shall not be lost where I can make it known. — I have not yet read y last section, having had it only half an Hour.

I am with the tenderest Affection

Dear Bogle

Yrs WHastings

PS. Since writing the above ~~the~~ I have read through your last Chapter of yr Journal. I am pleased exceedingly pleased with all y preceding, but most with this, & have had y satisfaction of discovering while I read it the place of your late Residence Teshoolumbo in an old Map of Tartary.

oval, set in gold, the other pear-shaped and unset; two clouded chalcedony beads the size of marbles, and two long vase-shaped beads of carnelian. At the other end, also suspended by flat silk braid, are one oval-shaped flat bead, and three beads the size of marbles, all of dull red glass, and one carnelian vase-shaped bead. A number of small gold chased rings, some having stars in the centre, form connecting links here and there. A large white chalcedony was the centre bead of the upper string.

On his return Mr. Bogle received a letter from the Governor-General, of which the following is an extract:

"I am perfectly satisfied and pleased with every circumstance of your conduct, and equally so with the issue of your commission. . . . . I have many thanks to make for your journal, which the world must have. Its merit shall not be lost where I can make it known. I have not yet read your last section, having had it only half an hour.

"I am, with the heartiest affection,

"Dear Bogle, yours,

"W. HASTINGS.

"P.S.—Since writing the above I have read through the last chapter of your journal. I am pleased, exceedingly pleased, with all your proceedings; and have had the satisfaction of discovering, while I read it, the place of your late residence, Teshoo Loombo, in an old map of Tartary."[1]

[1] It is an interesting question in what old map of Tatary Warren Hastings found the name Teshoo Loombo. It does not occur on the map of D'Anville in Du Halde. But the word *Tache Limbou* (in the right place for Teshu Lumbo) was found in two maps in the British Museum by Mr. Major, who kindly made a search for me. One is by Hermann Moll, with this title: "To the Right Honourable William Cowper, Lord High Chancellor of Great Britain, this Map of Asia, according to the newest and most exact observations, is most humbly dedicated, by your Lordship's most humble servant, Hermann

When George Bogle returned from Tibet, in 1775, he found a sad change in the state of affairs. Warren Hastings had, it is true, become the first Governor-General; but in October, 1774, the new Council, consisting of Philip Francis, General Clavering, and Colonel Monson, had arrived at Calcutta, and their factious conduct had deprived the great statesman of all power and authority, and reduced him to a cipher. The two others were mere tools in the hands of Francis, who, with complete ignorance of Indian affairs and overweening self-conceit, combined a malignant pleasure in using his power to inflict petty annoyances on the Governor-General, especially by injuring those whom he had trusted. The country, at a very critical period, was thus thrown into a state of dangerous anarchy, in which it remained for nearly two years, until the opportune death of Colonel Monson, in September, 1776, once more gave Warren Hastings a majority at the Council Board.

During this period young Bogle was placed in a most difficult position. In July, 1775, Alexander Elliot went home,[1] partly to advocate the cause of his beloved chief, and to take care that the truth was known respecting the trial of Nuncomar; for Francis was busily disseminating the most unscrupulous misrepresentations, and truth had little chance of being heard

Moll, geographer." Lord Cowper was Chancellor from 1714 to 1718, and died in 1724. The other map is entitled: "Asia Corrected from the Observations communicated to the Royal Society at London, and the Royal Academy at Paris, by John Senex, F.R.S., London. To Sir George Markham, Baronet, this map is dedicated, by his humble servant, John Senex." Sir George Markham died in 1736. Both Moll and Senex probably copied from the map of China of 1705, by Delisle, on which the name *Tassoo Loomboo* occurs in the right place. But, curiously, it does not appear on Delisle's map of Asia of twenty years later. Any one of the above three maps may have been before Warren Hastings, when he read Bogle's journal.

[1] In the summer of 1776 Alexander had returned, and for a short time all the children of Sir Gilbert and Lady Elliot were reunited under their roof at Twickenham. Gilbert had just entered Parliament with every prospect of obtaining a position there; Hugh and Alexander were already high in the confidence of the governments they served. Alexander wrote: "I have visited the mill, and the rivulet, and the Thames, the spots where we first learned to love each other, and now only you (Hugh) are wanted to make us perfectly happy." Alexander returned to India in 1777.

where falsehood and slander enjoyed such powerful patronage. Writing to his sister, Mrs. Brown, at this time, Bogle says: "A particular, I may say a bosom friend of mine, a son of Sir Gilbert Elliot, is going home, and as we are warmly attached to the same interest, we are employed from morning to night in going to one place or another, or in conjuring over what is past and what is to come. This scene altogether forms a strange contrast to my peaceful existence in Tibet."

Francis and his clique had deprived George Bogle of all his appointments. Writing to his brother Robert, in 1775, he says: "The other day Mr. Hastings proposed me for a high office. He was seconded by Mr. Barwell, but it was carried against me by the other three members. So that at present, when I expected to reap the fruit of all my labours, I am disappointed. The particular favours with which Mr. Hastings has honoured me, leave me, however, in these times, in no suspense as to the line I am to take. There is only one honourable course. Yet I do not despair. I have got myself some credit. I have, I think, no enemies; and I must hope for the best. These disputes, I trust, will soon be settled by an order from England, and that Mr. Hastings, whose able and spirited administration has raised the Company's affairs to the most flourishing situation they were ever in, will meet with that support which his services deserve. As I am not called at present to act in any public employment, I propose to dedicate my time entirely to the service of Mr. Hastings, and to improving myself in the Persian. The factions in Calcutta render society, beyond the circle of one's intimate friends, very unpleasant, and I intend, therefore, to lead a quiet life, and see what turn things will take."

On 20th of January, 1776, George Bogle thus writes to his father: "As Mr. Hastings has always patronized me, my success in this country depends in a great measure upon his fate. His colleagues, who came out last year, have taken every means in their power to ruin him. However, his merit is so great, and he has done so much for the Company, and put their affairs in Bengal in so flourishing a state, that I hope he will be supported. Should things turn out otherwise it will be a severe stroke upon me. My Tibet journey has turned out as well as I could wish, and although my connection with the Governor-General renders me not very acceptable to the new members, they have given me all credit for it. I am at present, however, without any office, except my employment about Mr. Hastings, and have no near prospect of getting any post." The factious majority, however, so far acknowledged the value of Mr. Bogle's work in Tibet, as to grant him a sum of 15,000 rupees, besides his expenses. By almost every ship, in spite of his want of employment, he contrived to send home small remittances to his father, towards paying off the debt on Daldowie.

On March 26, 1776, he writes: "Mr. Hastings bears this attack [of the Francis clique] with a calmness and equanimity which raises his character in the eyes of everybody; and although to pay court to him is the sure way to give umbrage to his opponents, who are possessed of all power, yet the respect that is felt for his character preserves his levées, now when he is stripped of power, as crowded as ever. As regards myself, fidelity is, in my opinion, a virtue of all others the most indispensable, and there is only one *beau chemin* to take. Thus you will observe that my fortune depends on Mr. Hastings. If he succeeds I have everything to hope for. If he falls I must betake myself to some other line, more independent of the Supreme Council."

At length the death of Colonel Monson, on September 25, 1776, deprived Francis of his majority, and put an end to his factious misrule. The Governor-General was restored to power, and on the 12th of November George Bogle was appointed, in conjunction with Mr. David Anderson, to superintend an office for the preparation and arrangement of the necessary materials for forming a new settlement of the Company's provinces, at the expiration of the existing leases. He entered upon this important work with zeal and assiduity. "It is a work," he writes to his father, "which will engross my whole time, and require my greatest exertions to execute my part of it." The information collected by Mr. Anderson and Mr. Bogle was invaluable; and there were not two gentlemen better qualified at the disposal of Government, both on account of their talents and their business-like habits.[1] Bogle also managed the Company's law business, as Commissioner of Lawsuits, during about fifteen months, a very difficult and harassing service.

Meanwhile an attempted revolution by the Francis clique was thwarted. On the 24th of November, 1777, Bogle writes to his father: "You will have learnt the consequences which the unexpected accounts of Mr. Hastings' resignation produced in this settlement; the assumption of the government by General Clavering; the refusal of Mr. Hastings to relinquish it; the appeal of both parties to the Judges; their opinion in favour of Mr. Hastings; the General's suspension of his claim; the apparent quiet that succeeded, and, finally, the death of General Clavering, on the 30th of August. This event has relieved Mr. Hastings from a great part of the opposition to which he had been so long exposed. How far it will give stability to his government must depend on the supreme power in England. Independent of partiality, if I can divest myself of it, I hope, for the sake of the British nation, that Mr. Hastings will be confirmed and his hand strengthened. He is possessed of talents which it may be difficult to equal, and of a mind more just and disinterested than is commonly to be found in a man who has passed so many years in public business. The remaining member of the majority, Mr. Francis, is of a more pliant disposition than General Clavering, and regulates his conduct more from policy and less from passion."

Alexander Elliot returned to India in 1777, and was warmly welcomed by the Governor-General and by his friend Bogle. But his early promise was cut off by an untimely end. He was

[1] Gleig's 'Memoirs of Warren Hastings,' ii. p. 12.

on his way to Nagpore, charged with an important mission, when he died of fever, in 1778, in Orissa, where he was buried, and Warren Hastings caused a monument to be erected over his grave.[1] He touchingly alluded to his young friend in a fine paraphrase of Horace's Ode xvi. lib. 2 (*Otium Divos*), which he wrote on his way home from Bengal in 1785:

> "An early death was Elliot's doom.
> I saw his opening virtues bloom,
> And manly sense unfold:
> Too soon to fade! I bade the stone
> Record his name midst hordes unknown,
> Unknowing what it told."[2]

Bogle wrote: "I cannot pass over the name of poor Elliot without a heavy heart. I never had, I never can have, so strong an esteem—I should say veneration—for anyone as I had for him, and I was happy beyond everybody in his friendship. I had not a thought that I concealed from him. He had none that he concealed from me. But, alas! he is gone for ever." In three short years the friend who wrote these lines was to follow young Elliot to the grave.[3]

[1] Sir Gilbert Elliot wrote, in 1781: "The honour paid by the Government to my brother's memory is extremely affecting to us, and gives us the highest satisfaction of which this subject is capable; and the share which the friendship of Mr. Hastings has taken in it, at the same time that it adds so much to the honour intended to my brother, reflects some part of it on the warmth and sincerity of his own character, and demands the affection and gratitude of all those who knew my brother." It is melancholy to reflect that all this was insincere, and that Sir Gilbert, in five short years, became, in conjunction with Burke and Sheridan, one of the most virulent traducers of his brother's best and truest friends, for whom, in this letter, he expresses so much gratitude and affection.

[2] It is addressed to Mr. Shore, afterwards Lord Teignmouth, and was published in the 'Asiatic Journal' (First Series), vi. p. 619.

[3] Bogle was one of Alexander Elliot's executors; the other was Mr. Claud Alexander. This led to a correspondence with Sir Gilbert Elliot, commenced by Bogle in a letter dated December 7, 1778, announcing his friend's death. On February 10, 1781, Sir Gilbert writes: "Give me leave to entreat some portion of that affection and confidence which my poor brother possessed, and which I have occasion to know he valued so highly. On my part I can freely offer you my heart. Our poor Alick had prepared us all for such a union, and it is now become both a duty in some degree to our common friend, and a consolation in our common loss." Bogle did not live to receive this letter.

Warren Hastings had no intention of losing the results to be derived from Bogle's first mission to Tibet, and the friendship he had formed for the Teshu Lama. He resolved to continue the same policy, with a view to establishing free commercial intercourse between Tibet and Bengal. On the 19th of April, 1779, George Bogle was "appointed to proceed again to Bhutan and Tibet, for the purpose of cultivating and improving the good understanding subsisting between the chiefs of those countries and the Government, and to endeavour to establish a free and lasting intercourse of trade with the kingdom of Tibet, and the other states to the northward of Bengal."[1] In the course of the summer news arrived that the Teshu Lama had undertaken a journey to Peking, and the mission was consequently postponed. Mr. Bogle then wrote the important memorandum, proposing to meet the Lama at Peking, which is printed at p. 207. In September, 1779, Mr. Bogle was appointed to succeed Mr. Purling as Collector of Rangpúr, where he was on the high road to Bhutan, and in a position to encourage commercial intercourse, and to superintend the annual fair. He writes to his sister Anne: "I am at length fairly out of Calcutta again, and although not in my Bhutan hills, I am within sight of them. Yet I felt a pang at leaving Mr. Hastings, for whose character and abilities I have a respect bordering on veneration." To his brother Robert, who by this time had returned home to Daldowie, he writes, on 18th of January, 1780: "I have schemes and projects for introducing new articles of commerce through Bhutan, and of perfecting what has already cost me so much trouble. The narrow-minded jealousy of the Bhutanese opposes obstacles, but my

[1] His monthly allowances during this service were to have been:

	Sikka Rs.
Lieut.-Colonel's pay and double batta	1488
Fixed salary	1000
Contingencies, including servants, interpreters, &c. ..	500
	2988

situation here leads me at least to make an attempt. It is probable, when I have settled the business of Rangpúr, that I may take a month's trip into the hills. But I shall regret the absence of my friend the Teshu Lama, for whom I have a hearty liking, and should be happy again to have his fat hand on my head." He had already transmitted 2500*l.* of his savings towards paying off the debt on Daldowie, and in this letter he expresses a hope of being able to send home 1500*l.* a year in future.[1] This generous conduct could not have been adopted without much self-denial; and was a practical proof of his affectionate disposition and love for his relations and his old home.

During his residence at Rangpúr, George Bogle received many letters from Warren Hastings, Mrs. Hastings, Sir Elijah and Lady Impey, which show the intimate terms of friendship he was on with them. The Governor-General, especially, discussed all the public news with his young friend, and in one letter says how much he is missed at Calcutta, especially in draughting despatches to the Directors. On the 27th of January, 1780, the Governor-General writes: "I have missed you much, for I am a very bad law casuist,[2] and our letters home, though they contain abundance of good matter, and are well expressed, yet want that method and entireness which fix the subjects on the memory." Hastings frequently sent him packets of seeds: on one occasion some seeds of hyson tea, "to aid your benevolent plan of introducing the luxuries and elegances of our world into that of Bhutan." On the 1st of March, 1780, Warren Hastings wrote a letter to Bogle, in which he enters very fully upon the properties of Bhutan cinnamon, which he correctly suspects to be a cassia, and asks

[1] He sent home altogether 4500*l.*

[2] He was in the thick of his battle with the Judges. He calls it "a serious and decided war, which gives me much uneasiness." A true account of the misunderstanding between the Government and the Judges will be found in chap. vii. of the 'Memoirs of Sir Elijah Impey,' by his son. An account which cannot be so designated is given in Macaulay's 'Essay on Warren Hastings.'

him to procure samples of the branches and roots for analysis. He adds, "You would wonder that I could write to you on such trifles, if you knew what mighty concerns pressed upon my mind. But I do not think this altogether a trifle; and if it was, trifles are a relief to me."

On the 14th of March, 1780, Boglē wrote to his father that Mr. Barwell, the second in Council, who uniformly supported the Governor-General, had sailed for England.[1] In that year Bogle held a fair at Rangpúr. "There was a great concourse of Bhutan merchants, who, having been excused all duties and left to the freedom of their own will in buying and selling, went away very well satisfied." This measure had a most satisfactory effect, and the Rangpúr fair was continued for many years.

The last letter written by Mr. Bogle, that has been preserved, is dated at Rangpúr, on the 28th of October, 1780, and is addressed to his father. The old man wrote to his son on the 5th of December of the same year, from Daldowie, saying, "Accept of these few lines from your affectionate parent, now running his eightieth year in good health, and who, with the highest gratitude, very often reflects on the substantial great favour you laid him under in clearing off the debt on Daldowie, by which it may be continued in the family."

On the 16th of January, 1781, the Collector of Rangpúr received the following letter from the Governor-General:

"Dear Bogle,—It is determined to dissolve the Provincial Councils, and to appoint a Committee of Revenue at Calcutta, which will have the immediate charge of all the collections in the provinces. This Committee will consist of Anderson, Croftes, and yourself. Perhaps a fourth will be added. If you are pleased with your appointment to it, come immediately to

[1] On the following 17th of August, Warren Hastings fought his duel with Francis, and soon afterwards Francis went home, leaving the Governor-General in full possession of the field.

Calcutta. If you are not, stay where you are, and I will nominate another; but I should be sorry to lose you.

"Yours affectionately,

"WARREN HASTINGS."

On the receipt of this letter George Bogle proceeded to Calcutta without delay, to enter upon his new duties. There he was attacked by a fatal illness, and died on the 3rd of April, 1781, at the early age of thirty-four.

The character of George Bogle is shown by the facts of his life here briefly stated, by his letters, and by the journal and other documents relating to the Tibet mission. His selection to fill post after post of responsibility and difficulty, by so sagacious an administrator as Warren Hastings, is a sufficient proof that Bogle was an able, zealous, and hard-working public servant. His letters show that he was an affectionate, warm-hearted, and generous man; and his journal in Tibet is that of a singularly calm and cautious diplomatist, possessed of an inexhaustible fund of patience and good humour. The friendship he formed for the Teshu Lama and his family, which was evidently much more than a mere passing feeling, is an interesting trait in his character.[1]

Robert Bogle eventually succeeded his father at Daldowie, but all the brothers and sisters died unmarried except the eldest, Martha, who married Mr. Thomas Brown of Langside.[2]

[1] The following notice of the death of George Bogle appeared in one of the Glasgow papers at the time:

"We hear from Bengal that George Bogle, Esq., Chief and Resident of Rungpoor, son of George Bogle, Esq., of Daldowie, N.B., died at Calcutta, on the 3rd of April, 1781. In him the East India Company has lost a disinterested, intelligent, and upright servant. His relations have reason long to lament his amiable, kind, and affectionate disposition, and the world a generous, friendly, and valuable member of society. His courage and extensive knowledge of the science of commerce, and of the affairs of the Honourable Company in the East is an incontestable proof of the first, as his account of Tibet and of his journey as envoy to that undescribed country presented to the Royal Society will be a permanent and honourable monument of the last."

[2] Mr. Robert Bogle of Daldowie, died on the 10th of August, 1808. Miss Anne, George's favourite sister, died at Daldowie, on the 18th of September, 1824; and Martha (Mrs. Brown), on the 23rd of August, 1820.

Dr. Thomas Brown, the eldest son by this marriage (a physician in Glasgow), was of Langside in Renfrewshire, where Mary Queen of Scots was defeated, and of Lanfine in Ayrshire. He married Marion, sister of Lord Jeffrey. Their son, Thomas Brown of Waterhaughs and Lanfine, was the author of 'Borgia, a Tragedy,' and other poems, and was a man of ability and literary attainments. At one time he contemplated the preparation of the Bogle manuscripts for publication, and consulted his uncle, Lord Jeffrey, on the subject. But he never found time to carry out his intention. He died in 1873, and was succeeded by his sister, Miss Martha Brown, now of Lanfine.

George Bogle, if he had been spared, had fully intended to publish the journal of his mission to Tibet; and the letter from Warren Hastings, already quoted,[1] shows that the Governor-General considered that this interesting narrative should be given to the world. In another letter, to Dr. Samuel Johnson, dated the 7th of August, 1775, Mr. Hastings referred to the same subject, and enclosed a copy of Bogle's journal. "When I read the account of your visit to the Hebrides," he continues, "I could not help wishing that a portion of that spirit which could draw so much entertainment and instruction from a region so little befriended by nature, or improved by the arts of society, could have animated Mr. Bogle, the author of this journal, but I flatter myself that you will find it not unworthy of perusal. I confess I received great pleasure from it, and I assure myself, that whatever originality you may discover in the description of the countries and inhabitants of which it treats, you will at least be pleased with the amiable character of the Lama. I am afraid it may look like an ill compliment, after having desired your acceptance of this production, to tell you that I have endeavoured to prevail on the writer to put it into a more connected form, and to send it, with some additional materials, to England for publication. If it would not be assuming too

[1] See p. cxli.

great a liberty, I should request to be favoured with your opinion upon the propriety of this intention."[1]

In 1777, Mr. Stewart, F.R.S., returned from India, and in a letter to Sir John Pringle, dated March 20, 1777, he gave an interesting account of Bogle's mission to Tibet, saying that he had reason to believe that the Envoy would himself give a relation of his journey to the world, but that in the meanwhile he presented a few particulars such as his recollection of Mr. Bogle's letters and papers enabled him to draw up. Mr. Stewart's letter was read at a meeting of the Royal Society, on the 17th of April, 1777.[2] This is the first and, until now, the only account of Bogle's mission that has seen the light.

The untimely death of George Bogle, the weighty affairs which fully occupied the time of the Governor-General during the next four years, and the long persecution to which he was subjected after his return home, prevented the project of publishing the narrative of the Tibet mission from being carried into effect. But copies of the documents relating to it remained in the possession of Warren Hastings until his death.[3] Mr. William Markham, the eldest son of the Archbishop of York, arrived in India in 1778, and was Private Secretary to Warren Hastings during the time that the measures connected with an intended second mission to Tibet were under consideration, in 1779. He took great pains to collect information on the subject, and preserved copies of por-

[1] Gleig's 'Memoirs of Warren Hastings,' ii. p. 19. Dr. Johnson died in 1784, before the return of Warren Hastings to England.

[2] Printed in the 'Philosophical Transactions' for 1777, vol. lxvii. part ii. pp. 465–488, with the title, "An Account of the Kingdom of Thibet, in a Letter from John Stewart, Esq., F.R.S., to Sir John Pringle, Bart., F.R.S." The letter is followed by a translation of the Teshu Lama's letter, at p. 1.

The letter of Mr. Stewart was translated into French, and published with three other short narratives of travels, by "Bryltophend," in a small volume. (Pekin, 1789, et se trouve à Paris.)

[3] Mr. Gleig published an extract from the Letter of Instructions to Mr. Bogle (p. 7 of this volume), and the Memorandum of Private Commissions (p. 8). But it would appear that Mr. Gleig had had a copy of the whole journal in his possession, for he speaks of not being justified in giving a detailed account of the mission, as if he could have done so had he seen fit. ('Memoirs of Warren Hastings,' i. p. 40.)

tions of Mr. Bogle's journal during the first mission, especially those in which the conversations with the Teshu Lama are recorded.[1] Mr. Markham's copy was deposited in the library at Becca, his seat in Yorkshire, and its discovery originated the investigations which led to the preparation of the present volume.[2]

Among George Bogle's papers there is a short memorandum, probably the last thing he ever wrote, desiring that all his letters may be sealed up and sent to Mr. Anderson. It ends: "The letters directed to Anderson and Alexander I request may be sent in the securest manner. Farewell." These two civilians were probably Bogle's executors, and the whole of the papers appear to have been transmitted to Daldowie. Mr. Robert Bogle always intended to publish them, but he put it off from year to year owing to the difficulty in meeting with anyone qualified to correct and arrange them properly for the press. At last he became acquainted with Mr. Alexander Dalrymple,[3] the well-known geographer to the East India

[1] Forming chapter xiv. of the present volume, p. 130.

[2] William Markham was born in 1760; was sent to Westminster School, and, like Warren Hastings before him, got head into college. He went out to India in 1777, as Private Secretary to the Governor-General, a post which he held for three years, and early in 1781 he was appointed Resident at Benares, during a most critical period, including the revolt of Cheyt Sing. There are three interesting letters from Warren Hastings to Mr. Markham, at Benares, in Gleig's 'Memoirs,' ii. pp. 434, 591. In 1783 Mr. Markham returned to England, and rendered the most efficient assistance to his revered chief during the whole of his tedious trial. There is a letter from Warren Hastings, preserved at Becca, expressing the warmest gratitude for this loyal aid. Mr. Markham died at Becca Hall, his seat in Yorkshire, in January, 1815, leaving eight children.

[3] Alexander Dalrymple, the seventh out of sixteen children of Sir James Dalrymple, was born at New Hailes, on the 24th of July, 1737. He went out to Madras as a writer in 1752, and acquired much nautical experience during a voyage to the Eastern Archipelago in 1759. In 1776 he was appointed a Member of Council at Madras, and finally returned home in 1777. In 1779 he was appointed Hydrographer to the East India Company, and was a most untiring and industrious workman. He translated and published a valuable collection of voyages in the Pacific, gave innumerable tracts to the world, and produced many hundreds of useful charts and plans of harbours. He also brought out the 'Oriental Repertory,' in two vols. In 1795 he was appointed Hydrographer to the Admiralty, but was dismissed in 1808. This unjust treatment broke the old man's heart, and he died the same year.

Company of that day, who voluntarily offered his assistance. In a letter from Robert Bogle to Dalrymple, dated at Daldowie, the 28th of January, 1792, an arrangement for handing over the manuscripts was made; and it seems that a volume, containing a copy of the reports of George Bogle's conversations with the Deb Rajah and the Teshu Lama, was actually entrusted to Dalyrmple. But no publication ever took place, and at the sale of Dalrymple's library this Bogle manuscript was bought by Lord Valentia. At the Arley Castle sale it was purchased by Messrs. Boone, of whom the Trustees of the British Museum bought it in 1833. It is now in the British Museum. It would appear from the notice in the Glasgow paper,[1] that another copy was presented to the Royal Society. The only document relating to Bogle's mission, which has been preserved among the records at Calcutta and in the India Office, is the report on the trade of Tibet.[2]

Searches have frequently been made for the complete journal of George Bogle, and for other papers relating to his mission to Tibet, both in India and in this country, but without success. At length, thanks to the liberal kindness of Miss Martha Brown of Lanfine, the representative of the family, and to the care of Mr. Gairdner of Kilmarnock, who judiciously sorted and arranged the great accumulation of papers, the complete narrative of George Bogle's important mission to Tibet is now presented to the world.

[1] Note at p. cl.

[2] Comprised in chapter xiii. of this volume.

BIOGRAPHICAL SKETCH

OF

THOMAS MANNING.

THOMAS MANNING is the only Englishman who has ever visited Lhasa and seen the Dalai Lama. He was the second son of the Reverend William Manning, Rector of Diss, in Norfolk, and was born at his father's first living of Broome, in the same county, on the 8th of November, 1772. Owing to ill health in early life, he was obliged to forego the advantages of a public school; but under his father's roof he was a close student of both classics and mathematics, and became an eager disciple of the philosophy of Plato. On his recovery he went to Caius College, Cambridge, and studied intensely, especially mathematics. While at Cambridge he published a work on algebra, in 1796 (two vols. 8vo), and a smaller book on arithmetic. He passed the final examination, and was expected to be at least second wrangler, but his strong repugnance to oaths and tests debarred him from academic honours and preferments, and he left the University without a degree. At Cambridge Manning was the friend of Porson. He also made the acquaintance of Charles Lamb, with whom he regularly corresponded.

After he had lived at Cambridge for some years, he began to brood over the mysterious empire of China, and devoted his time to an investigation of the language and arts of the Chinese, and the state of their country. He resolved to enter the Celestial Empire at all hazards, and to prosecute his researches till death stopped him, or until he should return with success. To enable him to undertake this hazardous enterprise, he studied the Chinese language under the tuition of Dr. Hagar, in France, and afterwards, with the aid of a Chinese, in London. When the English travellers were seized by Napoleon on the breaking out of war in 1803, Manning obtained leave to quit France, entirely owing to the respect in which his undertaking was held by the learned men at Paris. His passport was the only one that Napoleon ever signed for an Englishman to go to England after war began.[1]

In the collection of Charles Lamb's letters there are thirty-three to Thomas Manning,[2] and those attempting to dissuade him from undertaking his Chinese enterprise are very humorous. On the 19th of February, 1803, Lamb wrote to his friend, begging him to get the idea of visiting Independent Tatary out of his head. He tells Manning that the reading of Chaucer has misled him, with his foolish stories about Cambuscan and the ring, and the horse of brass. "Believe me," he continues, "there are no such things. 'Tis all the poet's invention. A horse of brass never flew, and a king's daughter never talked with birds. These are all tales. Pray try and cure yourself. Take hellebore. Pray to avoid the fiend. Read no more books of voyages; they are nothing but lies."

But Manning was quite resolved. On the 31st of March, 1806, Sir Joseph Banks, the President of the Royal Society, addressed a letter to the chairman of the Court of Directors, explaining the objects of Manning's undertaking, and his conviction that unless he could assume the manners and dress of the Chinese with the utmost exactness, and speak their language with purity and a proper accent, he could never succeed. He desired, therefore, to proceed to Canton, in the first instance, to acquire these difficult accomplishments; and Sir Joseph Banks, believing that Mr. Manning was likely to succeed, requested the Directors to assist his earnest endeavours to accomplish this great purpose. Sir Joseph concluded his letter thus:

[1] 'Notes and Queries,' Second Series, x. 143.

[2] There are a few more in Talfourd. 'Final Memorials.'

"For my part I take a deep interest in the fate of this very amiable young man, both on account of his mild character and the energies of his mind, and I shall feel infinite obligation to you, Sir, and to the Court, if my application has any effect in deciding them to grant the favour he solicits."[1]

Thus strongly recommended, Thomas Manning went out to China in one of the Company's ships, in 1806, and took up his abode in the English factory at Canton. Auber mentions that, in February, 1808, Manning made a trip from Canton to Cochin China. Charles Lamb continued to correspond with his "old adventuring friend, who had gone to wander among the Tartars," during the time of Manning's residence at Canton, which lasted from 1807 to 1810.

The Select Committee at Canton addressed a letter to Lord Minto, the Governor-General of India, dated 19th February, 1810, in which they introduced Mr. Manning, who was about to proceed to Calcutta, and who had been permitted to reside in the Company's factory, at Canton, during the previous three years. "The object of this gentleman's visit to China," they said, "has been to qualify himself, by studying the Chinese language and customs, to explore the country. In these pursuits he has made considerable progress, but finding his ultimate views impracticable from this quarter, he proceeds to Calcutta, and will personally explain his future plans. As we consider Mr. Manning eminently qualified for the task he has undertaken, we anxiously hope your lordship will not consider it improper to afford Mr. Manning every practicable assistance in the prosecution of his plans, and this we beg to solicit in his behalf."

Accordingly, Mr. Manning proceeded to Calcutta, and the

[1] This letter is preserved among the records of the India Office. It is printed in full, together with the reply of the Court of Directors granting the permission sought for, in 'China: an Outline of its Government, Laws, &c.,' by Peter Auber. (London, 1834.) Mr. Auber mentions Manning as one of many doctors who applied to go to China in 1806, through Sir Joseph Banks, with a view to exploring the interior.

Governor-General in Council replied, on the 16th of June, 1810, "We shall not fail to pay due attention to your recommendation of Mr. Manning by affording him every practicable assistance in the prosecution of his scientific pursuits." But the great statesman who opened up friendly intercourse between Bengal and Tibet, in the days of Bogle and Turner, was shelved at Daylesford. In his place was one of the managers of his prosecution, and the days of small half measures had arrived. Mr. H. T. Prinsep remembered Manning at Calcutta, as wearing a fancy dress, which he said was that of a Tatar gentleman; but with his broad English face and full flowing beard, as looking as little like a Tatar as any son of Adam one might meet in London. He was fêted and lionized at Calcutta, and, after a few months, set out with his Chinese servant to Rangpúr, and thence started on his expedition.[1] He appears to have received little or no aid from the Government; to have been left entirely to his own resources without official recognition of any kind, and all the credit of his extraordinary journey is solely due to himself. Whether his disguise was effectual or not, he succeeded in reaching Lhasa, a feat which no official has ever yet achieved. He resided there for several months, had interviews with the Dalai Lama, and returned to India safely in 1811. He wrote from thence a long and interesting account of his expedition to Dr. Marshman, which unfortunately does not appear to have been preserved. It concluded by saying that, having lived for some time on terms of good fellowship with the Lamas, and made arrangements for penetrating farther into those unknown regions, the Emperor of China had sent for his head; but as he preferred to retain it on his shoulders, he had made the best of his way back. He had hoped to have been able to proceed by Sining to China; but what he actually did was sufficient to place him in the first rank of English travellers. His journal, fragmentary though it be, tells the

[1] Manning's journey to Lhasa is mentioned in 'Tibet, Tartary, and Mongolia,' by H. T. Prinsep (London, 1852, 2nd edition), pp. 17 and 94. Manning is also mentioned in the correspondence of Mr. David Scott, among the Kuch Bahar records.

story in sufficient detail; though it consists merely of hasty jottings, sorely needing the revision of the author.

He appears to have been disgusted with the official treatment he received; and when he returned to Calcutta, he would give no one any particulars of his journey. After a short stay, he went back to Canton by sea, and again took up his residence in the factory. Charles Lamb continued to correspond with him, often urging him to come home. On the 25th December, 1815, he writes: "Still in China! Down with idols—Ching-chang-fo and all his foolish priesthood. Come out of Babylon, O my friend!"

In 1817, Thomas Manning joined Lord Amherst's Embassy as Chinese interpreter, and proceeded to Peking.[1] The Ambassador objected at first to his beard, as incongruous in a British Embassy, but consented to his joining the mission on his agreeing to change his Chinese dress for an English one. On the voyage home, H.M.S. 'Alceste,' carrying the Embassy, was wrecked in the Straits of Gaspar, and its members, reaching Batavia, were taken home in the 'Cæsar,' of London. In July, 1817, Manning had an interview with Napoleon, at St. Helena, reminding the Emperor that he was the only Englishman to whom he had granted a passport in 1803. Sir John Davis, who was a member of Lord Amherst's mission, thus writes of Mr. Manning:

"I knew Manning well, and liked him much. His eccentricities were quite harmless, and concerned only himself personally. His beard was merely continued from his first adoption of it previous to his journey to Lhasa, and gratified his natural indolence. He was not liable to the ridicule of the great epigrammatist:

'Εἰ τὸ τρέφειν πώγωνα δοκεῖ σοφίαν περιποιεῖν,
Καὶ τράγος ευπώγων εὔστοχος ἐστι Πλάτων.'

'If a beard of dimensions true wisdom declare,
Then Plato his claims with a he-goat must share.'

[1] See 'Journal of Lord Amherst's Embassy to China,' by Henry Ellis. (London, 1817.) At p. 58 Mr. Manning is mentioned as having joined the Embassy at Macao; and at p. 61 his name occurs as one of the Chinese Secretaries, in a list of members of the Embassy.

He was seldom serious, and did not often argue any matter gravely, but in a tone of banter in which he humorously maintained the most monstrous paradoxes, his illustrations being often highly laughable. I found him, in 1813, on my arrival in China, established as a guest of the East India Company's establishment, where the table and library were excellent, and quite to his taste. He was a very pleasant companion during the Embassy to Peking, but did not keep a journal, or at least never published one. He did everything in his own odd and eccentric way. Being one day roused by a strange shouting, I went out and discovered it was Manning, who, wishing to cross the water, and finding nobody who would attend to him, commenced a series of howls like a dog, supplemented by execrations derived from the Chinese vernacular. This led our attendant mandarins very naturally to infer that he was mad, and they lost no time in conveying him over the river to the other side, which was all he wanted. I was sorry to part with him in 1817, at the termination of the Embassy, when he returned home, but have never seen him since, nor read anything of his concerning China. His great friend and companion, Samuel Ball, a member of the Athenæum Club, died lately, at an age bordering on one hundred."

Thomas Manning returned to England, after an absence of nearly twelve years, apparently a disappointed man. He was in Italy from 1827 to 1829, and then went to live in strict retirement at Bexley, whence he removed to a cottage near Dartford, called Orange Grove. He led a very eccentric life. It is said that he never furnished his cottage, but only had a few chairs, one carpet, and a large library of Chinese books. He wore a milky white beard down to his waist. Mr. Manning revised the proof-sheets of the 'Reports on the Poor Laws,' published by order of the House of Commons, and did other work of the same kind, but he never published any of the results of his Chinese labours. Auber, however, says that he drew up a paper of observations on the consumption of tea in

Bhutan, Tibet, and Tatary. In 1838 he had a paralytic stroke, and in the same year he removed to Bath, where he died on the 2nd of May, 1840, aged sixty-eight. He was buried in the Abbey Church, at Bath, on the 8th of the same month.[1]

Manning left behind him a collection of letters, and numerous writings in Chinese, but no manuscripts of his own sufficiently advanced for publication. His brother presented his Chinese library to the Royal Asiatic Society.[2]

Through the kindness of the Rev. C. R. Manning, Mr. Thomas Manning's nephew, who is now Rector of Diss, the rough notes of the remarkable journey to Lhasa have been placed at my disposal, and are now printed for the first time.

[1] Most of the above details of Mr. Manning's life, after his return from China, are from the 'Gentleman's Magazine,' xiv. N. S. p. 97. This article was written by Mr. A. J. Dunkin, of Dartford.

[2] It is still there, in a separate case, and called the "Manning Collection."

NARRATIVE

OF THE

MISSION OF MR. GEORGE BOGLE TO TIBET

(1774).

NARRATIVE

OF THE

MISSION OF MR. GEORGE BOGLE TO TIBET

(1774).

CHAPTER I.

MISSION TO TIBET.

LETTER FROM THE TESHU LAMA—MISSION TO TIBET—APPOINTMENT OF MR. BOGLE —HIS INSTRUCTIONS.

1.

LETTER FROM THE TESHU LAMA[1] TO WARREN HASTINGS.

(*Received March* 29, 1774.)

THE affairs of this quarter in every respect flourish. I am night and day employed in prayers for the increase of your happiness and

[1] This was a letter of mediation, sent at the request of the Government of Bhutan. In 1772 the Bhutanese, under Deb Judhur, descended into the plains, and overran Kuch Bahar. This aggression threatened the peace of Rangpúr and adjacent parts of Bengal. Warren Hastings, therefore, resolved to drive the mountaineers back into their fastnesses. A battalion of native infantry was employed on this service. But the invaders made a desperate resistance. They defended the fort of Bahar, which was stormed and taken by Captain John Jones, at the head of his troops, nearly one-fourth of the detachment being killed or wounded. Captain Jones himself was wounded. Soon afterwards a night attack was made, at Chichakotta, on a small detachment under Lieutenant Dickinson and Mr. Purling, of 226 rank and file, by 3000 Bhutanese, who were beaten off with great loss. (See Letters from Warren Hastings to Sir George Colebrooke and to Mr. Purling. 'Memoirs,' i. pp. 279 and 295.) Eventually the invaders retreated into their own mountainous country, followed by our troops. Captain Jones occupied the Dalim-kotta Dúar (Daling) at the foot of the hills, and took the fortress of Dalim-kotta by assault in April, 1773. Our troops also defeated the Bhutanese at Chichakotta, and drove them up to Buxa-Dúar. But the troops were decimated by disease. The malaria proved fatal to Captain Jones and many other officers. The Bhutan Government was however thoroughly alarmed, and entreated the Teshu Lama of Tibet to interpose in their favour. The Lama sent a deputation to Calcutta, consisting of a Tibetan named Paima, and a Hindu pilgrim named Purungir Gosain, who were entrusted with this letter from the Teshu Lama. It is given in the introduction of 'Turner's Embassy,' p. ix. Captain Turner speaks of it "as an authentic and curious specimen of the Lama's good sense, humility, simplicity of heart, and, above all, of that delicacy of sentiment and expression which could convey a threat in terms of meekness and supplication."

prosperity. Having been informed by travellers from your quarter[1] of your exalted fame and reputation, my heart, like the blossom of spring, abounds with gaiety,[2] gladness, and joy; praise[3] that the star of your fortune is in its ascension; praise[4] that happiness and ease are the surrounding attendants of myself and family. Neither to molest nor persecute is my aim; it is even the characteristic of my[5] sect to deprive ourselves of the necessary refreshment of sleep, should an injury be done to a single individual. But in justice and humanity I am informed you far surpass us. May you ever adorn the seat of justice and power, that mankind may, under the shadow of your bosom, enjoy the blessings of happiness and ease.[6] By your favour, I am the Rajah and Lama of this country, and rule over numbers[7] of subjects, a particular[8] with which you have no doubt been made acquainted by travellers from these parts. I have been repeatedly informed that you have been[9] engaged in hostilities against the Deb Judhur,[10] to which, it is said, the Deb's own criminal conduct, in committing ravages and other outrages on your frontiers, has given[11] rise. As he is of a rude and ignorant race (past times are not destitute of instances of the like misconduct,[12] which his own[13] avarice tempted him to commit), it is not unlikely that he has now renewed those instances; and the ravages and plunder which he may have committed on the skirts of the Bengal and Bahar provinces have given you provocation to send your vindictive[14] army against him. However,[15] his party has been defeated, many of his people have been killed, three forts[16] have been taken from him, and he has met with the punishment he deserved; and it is as evident as the sun your army has been victorious, and that, if you had been desirous of it, you might, in the space of two days, have entirely extirpated him, for he had not power to resist your efforts. But I now take upon

[1] Turner's version has *country*.
[2] Turner has *satisfaction*.
[3] Turner has *praise be to God*.
[4] Turner has *praise be to Him*.
[5] Turner has *our*.
[6] Turner has *peace and affluence*.
[7] Turner has *a number*.
[8] Turner has *circumstance*.
[9] Turner omits *been*.
[10] Turner has *Dêh Terria* throughout, and *Dêh*.
[11] Turner has *gave*.
[12] Turner has *faults*.
[13] Turner omits *own*.
[14] Turner has *avenging*.
[15] Turner has *nevertheless*.
[16] Dalim-kotta, Chichakotta, and Buxa. The last was taken by Lieutenant Dickinson and "young Purling," of the Warren Hastings correspondence, who lost some men in the retreat, owing to the indiscretion of a native officer. This man would fight the Bhutanese, who rolled down stones on the rear-guard.

me to be his mediator, and to represent to you that, as the said Deb Rajah is dependent upon the Dalai Lama, who rules in this country with unlimited sway (but on account of his being in his minority, the charge of the government and administration for the present is committed to me), should you persist in offering further molestation to the Deb's country, it will irritate both the Lama and all his subjects against you. Therefore, from a regard to our religion and customs, I request you will cease[1] all hostilities against him, and in doing this you will confer the greatest favour and friendship upon me. I have reprimanded the Deb for his past conduct, and I have admonished him to desist from his evil practices in future, and to be submissive to you in all matters.[2] I am persuaded that he will conform to the advice which I have given him, and it will be necessary that you treat him with compassion and clemency. As to my part, I am but a Fakir, and it is the custom of my sect, with the rosary in our hands, to pray for the welfare of[3] mankind, and for the peace and happiness of the inhabitants of this country; and I do now, with my head uncovered, entreat that you may cease all hostilities against the Deb in future. It would be needless to add to the length of this letter, as the bearer of it, who is a Gosain, will represent to you all particulars, and it is hoped that you will comply therewith. In this country[4] worship of the Almighty is the profession of all. We poor creatures are in nothing equal to you. Having a few things in hand, I send them to you by way[5] of remembrance, and hope for your acceptance of them.

2.

MINUTE BY WARREN HASTINGS.

May 4, 1774.

The President acquaints the Board that, since he laid before them the letter from the Teshu Lama of Tibet, he has written an answer to it, and, among other things, has proposed a general treaty of amity and commerce between the two states of Bengal and Bhutan.[6] He begs leave to observe that such a treaty has ever been

[1] Turner has *cease from.*
[2] Turner has *things.*
[3] Turner has *all mankind.*
[4] Turner has *the worship.*
[5] Turner has *as token.*
[6] *Bhot*, the native name of Tibet.

a favourite object with our Honourable Masters, and that they have repeatedly recommended the establishment of an intercourse with that country. The present juncture appeared to him the most favourable which has yet occurred for pursuing these views.

The letter from the Lama invites us to friendship, and the late final arrangement of the disputes on the frontier renders the country accessible without danger either to the persons or effects of travellers. Therefore, no sooner was the treaty for the affairs of Kuch Bahar[1] signed and ratified than he thought seriously of carrying this project into execution; and conceiving it to be most proper that a European, and servant of the Company, should be entrusted with the negotiation in preference to any native, he wrote immediately for the necessary passports for such a person, which he informs the Board he has now obtained. The person he has made choice of for this trust is Mr. George Bogle, a servant of the Company, well known to this Board for his intelligence, assiduity and exactness in affairs; and the President further expects to draw much advantage in the conduct of the business from the coolness and moderation of temper which he seems to possess in an eminent degree. He proposes that Mr. Bogle should set out without loss of time, and will charge himself with furnishing him proper instructions and despatches. He hopes the Board will approve of his choice, and as Mr. Bogle undertakes this difficult and hazardous commission without any immediate prospect of advantage, and with great uncertainty as to its success, he would recommend to the Board that he be continued in possession of the appointments which he now holds at the Presidency, and permitted to act by deputy till his return, or till it shall be thought proper to dispose of him another way. The President

[1] He alludes to the treaty between the East India Company and the Deb Rajah of Bhutan, signed on April 25, 1774. The English agreed to relinquish all the lands which belonged to the Deb Rajah before the commencement of his war with the Rajah of Kuch Bahar; but for the possession of Chichakotta the Deb Rajah was to pay an annual tribute of five Tangun ponies. The Deb Rajah agreed to deliver up the Rajah of Kuch Bahar and his brother, whom he had made prisoners. The Bhutan merchants were allowed to go with their caravans to Rangpúr every year without paying duties. The Deb Rajah promised never to cause incursions to be made, and to give up any inhabitants of the Company's territories on application. (See 'Aitchison's Treaties,' i. p. 143.)

further acquaints the Board that he has nominated Mr. Alexander Hamilton, assistant-surgeon on the establishment, to accompany Mr. Bogle on this expedition.

The President has only further to observe that he is far from being sanguine in his hopes of success, but the present occasion appears too favourable for the attempt to be neglected. He also can assure the Board that the information which he has been able to procure of the people, the country, and government of Tibet, gives considerable encouragement to it. They are represented as a simple, well-disposed people, numerous and industrious, living under a well-regulated government, having considerable intercourse with other nations, particularly with the Chinese and northern Tatars, and possessing at home the principal means of commerce, gold and silver in great abundance. For the more particular satisfaction of the Board he subjoins to this minute the substance of this information, which, being on record, will also exhibit to our Honourable Masters the grounds of the present undertaking, whatever may be its success, and enable them to judge how far it may be advisable to prosecute it on any future occasion.

He also annexes to this an account of such goods as he has ordered Mr. Bogle to provide for presents to the Lama, or as samples of the commodities which this country is capable of supplying, and he moves that the Board should order the amount to be paid out of the treasury.

3.

LETTER FROM WARREN HASTINGS TO THE COURT OF DIRECTORS.

The President, having received a letter from Teshu Lama, who is the guardian and minister of the Dalai Lama, the sovereign and high-priest of all Tibet, thinks it a proper opportunity to open intercourse between these countries and Bengal, through Mr. G. Bogle, whose merits and abilities we have frequently noticed to you, and who by his patience, exactitude, and intelligence seemed peculiarly fitted for the duty. Accordingly, Mr. G. Bogle will be sent to the Lama, with a letter and presents and different samples of goods, to see which would sell best there. Mr. Hamilton, assistant-surgeon, is to accompany him, but the great length of the journey and the natural difficulties which Mr. Bogle has to encounter from the severity of the climate and the rudeness of the country will make it a long while before we shall hear from him.

4.

APPOINTMENT OF MR. BOGLE.

FORT WILLIAM, 13*th May*, 1774.

SIR,—Having appointed you my deputy to the Teshu Lama, the sovereign of Bhutan,[1] I desire you will proceed to Lhasa, his capital, and deliver to him the letter and presents which I have given you in charge.

The design of your mission is to open a mutual and equal communication of trade between the inhabitants of Bhutan and Bengal, and you will be guided by your own judgment in using such means of negotiation as may be most likely to effect this purpose.

You will take with you samples for a trial of such articles of commerce as may be sent from this country according to the accompanying list, marking as accurately as possible the charge of transporting them.

You will inquire what other commodities may be successfully employed in that trade. And you will diligently inform yourself of the manufactures, productions, goods, introduced by the intercourse with other countries, which are to be procured in Bhutan, especially such as are of great value and easy transportation, such as gold, silver, precious stones, musk, rhubarb,[2] munjít,[3] &c.

The following will be also proper objects of your inquiry —the nature of the road between the borders of Bengal and Lhasa, and of the countries lying between; the communi-

[1] The word *Bhutan* is here, and in other places, used by Warren Hastings for *Bhot*, the native name of Tibet.

[2] Râwend.

[3] *Rubia mungista*. A madder used as a dye, and also for medicinal purposes.

cations between Lhasa and the neighbouring countries, their government, revenue, and manners.

Whatever observations you may make on these or any other subjects, whether of useful knowledge or curiosity, I desire you will communicate to me from time to time, reporting the success of your negotiations.

The period of your stay must be left to your discretion. I wish you to remain a sufficient time to fulfil the purposes of your deputation, and obtain a complete knowledge of the country and the points referred to your inquiry. If you shall judge that a residence may be usefully established at Lhasa without putting the Company to any expense, but such as may be repaid by the advantages which may be hereafter derived from it, you will take the earliest opportunity to advise me of it; and if you should find it necessary to come away before you receive my orders upon it, you may leave such persons as you shall think fit to remain as your agents till a proper resident can be appointed, and you will apply to the Lama for his permission and the necessary passports for the person who may be hereafter deputed in this character.

You will draw on me for your charges, and your drafts shall be regularly answered. To these I can fix no limitation, but empower you to act according to your discretion, knowing that I need not recommend to you to observe a strict frugality and economy where the good of the service on which you are commissioned shall not require a deviation from these rules.

I am, Sir,

Your most obedient servant,

Mr. GEORGE BOGLE. WARREN HASTINGS.

P.S.—I have appointed Mr. Alexander Hamilton, assistant-surgeon, to attend you on this deputation.

5.

PRIVATE COMMISSIONS TO MR. BOGLE.

FORT WILLIAM, 16*th May*, 1774.

1. To send one or more pair of the animals called tús,[1] which produce the shawl wool. If by a dooley, chairs, or any other contrivance they can be secured from the fatigues and hazards of the way, the expense is to be no objection.

2. To send one or more pair of the cattle which bear what are called cowtails.[2]

3. To send me carefully packed some fresh ripe walnuts for seed, or an entire plant, if it can be transported; and any other curious or valuable seeds or plants, the rhubarb and ginseng[3] especially.

4. Any curiosities, whether natural productions, manufactures, paintings, or what else may be acceptable to persons of taste in England. Animals only that may be useful, unless any that may be remarkably curious.

5. In your inquiries concerning the people, the form of their government, and the mode of collecting their revenue, are points principally meriting your attention.

6. To keep a diary, inserting whatever passes before your observation which shall be characteristic of the people, the country, the climate, or the road, their manners, customs, buildings, cookery, &c., or interesting to the trade of this country, carrying with you a pencil and a pocket-book for the purpose of minuting short notes of every fact or remark as it occurs, and putting them in order at your leisure while they are fresh in your memory.

7. To inquire what countries lie between Lhasa and Siberia, and what communication there is between them. The same with regard to China and Kashmir.

[1] *Tús* is the wool of the shawl goat.

[2] Yaks.

[3] A drug, the root of an araliaceous plant (*Panax ginseng*), much used in China for fevers. Properly, *Jin-san*. There is also an American ginseng (*Panax quinquefolium*).

8. To ascertain the value of their trade with Bengal by their gold and silver coins, and to send me samples of both.

9. Every nation excels others in some particular art or science. To find out this excellence of the Bhutanese.

WARREN HASTINGS.

10. To inform yourself of the course and navigation of the Brahmaputra, and of the state of the countries through which it runs. W. H.

6.

MEMORANDUM ON TIBET, BY WARREN HASTINGS.

[*Accompanying the Instructions to Mr. Bogle.*]

Tibet is a cold, high, mountainous country. The inhabitants approach more in figure to the Persians and other inhabitants of Western Asia, than to any of their neighbours, Chinese, Hindus, or Tatars.

It should seem that Tibet consisted of a great variety of tribes more or less addicted to the pastoral life. At times they appear to have united into powerful confederacies, and become formidable to their neighbours. At other times, when divided, they fell a prey to irruptions of Tatars, or to the policy and power of the Chinese. The Caucasus formed a barrier on the south that protected reciprocally both Hindustan and Tibet from any dangerous hostilities in that quarter.

In the fourth century, the Tatar confederacy of the Typa subdued the north and east of Tibet. In the eighth and ninth centuries, when the Tatar confederacy of the Turks became feeble, the power of those nations, which now acknowledge the supremacy of the Dalai Lama, was very great. Sometimes they penetrated into the heart of China, but at other times the Chinese took advantage of their divisions to recover what had been lost.

In 1102, the chief of Great Tibet seems to have resided at Lhasa. He at that period found it necessary to become lama, in order to strengthen his authority over the different tribes that had raised him to be their leader, and for the same reason, it is said, that he submitted to become a vassal of the Chinese empire in 1125.

In the thirteenth century, the Tatar confederacy of the Moghuls under Mangu Khan overran Tibet, and soon after Kublai Khan, who was Emperor of China as well as chief of the Moghuls, divided it into provinces, and gave the title of King to the Lama of Lhasa. The Moghul princes being expelled from China, the Emperor Yonglo, of the dynasty of Ming, which succeeded them, gave the title of King, in 1373, to eight more lamas in Tibet. In 1426, these took the title of Grand Lamas; and then, or some time afterwards, the Lama of Lhasa took the distinguishing title of Dalai Lama. At least, we find the Chinese Emperor Kang-hi appointing, in 1705, a Dalai Lama, who is said to be the sixth in succession who had borne that title.

It was in the middle of the fifteenth century that the Dalai Lama of Bhutan,[1] or Greater Tibet, first named a Typa[2] Lama for the administration of civil affairs. The late intercourse opened between the Presidency of Bengal and Bhutan shows that the office of Typa remains and actually engrosses the authority of the state. It is not likely that the Dalai Lama retains the power of nominating to this office.

Although the Chinese historians ascribe to their emperors the power of nominating the Dalai Lama, it does not follow that this nomination is more than a bare acknowledgment or confirmation of his appointment by the lamas or Tibetan tribes. It may likewise not be improbable that the Typa Lama is chosen by the priests. It is, at least, generally said that the chiefs of the Tibetan tribes that acknowledge a sort of supremacy in the Dalai Lama are all elected by the priests, or lamas, the nobility at the same time having some influence in the transaction.

A curious enough precaution against hereditary succession in the chiefship is ascribed to these tribes. No sooner, it is said, is a new chief chosen, than his wife and children are for ever separated from him. I have never heard what is done with *them*, nor whether

[1] Or Bhot. (See note at page 6.)

[2] The Typa Lama is the *guru* or teacher of the young Dalai Lama.

the chief is, after his elevation, debarred the use of women. If the institution is true, it seems to indicate a very high advance in political establishments. Rude men have no apprehension of losing their independence; people only become jealous of their liberty when they grow doubtful of their resolution to retain it.

The religion and hierarchy established in Tibet is, however, a matter of much greater curiosity. We are told that the Dalai Lama is held to be an incarnation of the legislator prophet, or god Buddha or Fo, who over all Hindustan gives his name (like Thauth or Mercury, the prophet legislator and god of the Egyptians) to the planet Mercury, and to the fourth day of the week. When the Dalai Lama dies, a child is said to be pitched on as possessing certain marks which show that the soul of the deceased has been transmigrated into him; and the divinity and identity of the new manifestation of the god is of course acknowledged.

Among the different Tatar tribes which are of this religion, there are persons called Ku-tchuck-tus,[1] who are likewise esteemed living Fos. It is, however, said that though each tribe pays a particular respect to its own Ku-tchuck-tu, the divinity of those of other tribes is not the less acknowledged, and it is even pretended that the Ku-tchuck-tus admit a superiority in the Dalai Lama, so that his excrements are sold as charms at a great price among all the Tatar tribes of this religion. I have already mentioned that no less than eight Lamas in Tibet, besides the Lama of Lhasa, have the title of King, and are called Grand Lamas.[2] But I do not know whether these, too, are esteemed incarnations of the divinity, or what subjection, if any, they pay to the Dalai Lama.

[1] The *Kutuktus* are the highest order of Buddhist ecclesiastics next to the Dalai, having divine incarnation of the second class. Mr. Brian Hodgson apprehends that *Kutuktu* is the Tatar equivalent for the divine Lama of the Tibetan tongue. A *Kutuktu* is the high-priest of Mongolia, residing at Urgu. The office is elective within certain Tibetan families residing near Lhasa. (See 'Geographical Magazine,' for March, 1875, p. 87; also, 'Nouveau Journal Asiatique,' iv. p. 120.)

[2] Of the eight personages referred to by Warren Hastings, Mr. Hodgson thinks that four belong to Tibet and four to the Tatar regions beyond Tibet. There have always been two divine incarnations in Tibet, the Dalai and Teshu Lamas; and since the Mongols became supreme in China and the regions around it, their policy has been to increase this plurality of divinities. Thus they have sanctioned the claims of several Kutuktus, in addition to the divine Lamas already existing.

Any information with regard to the antiquity and to the creed of this religion, as well as to the authority, civil and ecclesiastical, of the lamas, could not fail to be extremely interesting.

It would also be desirable to have any facts relative to the state of Tibet with respect to China and Tatary. I have been told that a large river forms a boundary between China and Tibet, which was carefully guarded by the troops of both countries; and that Tibet received European commodities by the valley of Kashmir. But I have learned nothing satisfactory on these subjects, not so much as whether Kashmir and Lesser Tibet are at present dependent on Bhutan[1] or Greater Tibet, or whether the Dalai Lama is still a vassal to China.

It is said that in Tibet it is very common for one lady to have several husbands.[2] I should wish much to know if this practice obtains in all the ranks of society, and whether those husbands who all have intercourse with one woman have not likewise other women that are their wives, with whom likewise they hold an intercourse in common. We have instances in other countries where, though each man in a family had a wife that was properly his own, all the men in the family had likewise an intercourse with all the women in it. Perhaps this may be the case also in Tibet; and if we knew anything of the laws of succession in Tibet, or to whom the children of a wife with several husbands were understood to belong, one might be able to discover how the fact stood, though we had no direct information with regard to it.

The history, government, and religion of Tibet are no doubt more interesting objects of inquiry than its climate or topographical and physical characters; yet these, too, are highly curious. The great rivers of the south and east of Asia appear to issue from its mountains. It is probably, therefore, the highest land in the old continent, and this circumstance, together with the difficulty of access to it, give it a striking analogy to the valley of Quito, in South America, which is the highest land in the new continent, and whose climate and situation M. de la Condamine has exhibited in so interesting a point of view. Though Lhasa is situated in a more southern latitude than Alexandria, in Egypt, we are told that

[1] Or *Bhot*. (See note at page 6.) [2] See page 74, and note.

people sent by Colonel Cumming had to travel to it through snow so late as the month of April. Any observations made in such a country by a thermometer would, therefore, be valuable.

I have preferred stating what I know of the subject to putting mere interrogatories. By this means I flatter myself it will be better perceived what information I want, and what information is desirable.

CHAPTER II.

FROM KUCH BAHAR TO TASSISUDON.[1]

THE Governor having occasion to send a person[2] with some despatches to the Lama of Tibet, thought proper to pitch upon me, and I readily accepted of the commission. I was glad of the opportunity which this journey through a country hitherto unfrequented by Europeans would give me of showing my zeal for the Governor's service, at the same time that it gratified a fondness I always had for travelling, and would afford me some respite from that close and sedentary business in which I had for some years been engaged. I was to be continued in my offices at the Presidency, and allowed to act by deputy during my absence; and Mr. Hastings was also pleased to assure me that whatever might be the issue of this commission, I might depend on the continuance of his favour.

I was detained in Calcutta till the middle of May, 1774, when I set out with Mr. Hamilton, the surgeon, who was appointed to attend me. It was then the hottest season of the year; the thermometer was often above the degree of blood heat, and the sun being almost vertical, it was necessary to travel chiefly during the night time. I passed through Murshidabad and the provinces of Dinajpúr and Rangpúr, and reached Bahar, the north-east boundary of Bengal, on the last of May. As the rains were ready to set in, I stayed there only a few days; and having made the necessary preparations, I hastened to proceed on the journey.

The country about Bahar is low. Two kos[3] beyond Bahar we entered a thicket formed of reeds, brushwood, and long grass closely

[1] Or Tasi-cho-jong. Eden has *Tassisshujung*. Schlagintweit makes it *Chra-shis-chhos-jong*—"the holy town of the doctrine." It is probable that Tassisudon, as given by Bogle, is correct. MacGregor has Tasichozong.

[2] Here Mr. Bogle's own narrative commences.

[3] A kos is about two miles.

interwoven; frogs, watery insects, and dank air: one can hardly breathe. This continues five kos; towards the end there are sal[1] and large forest trees. Two miles farther on we crossed the river which separates the Kuch Bahar country from that of the Deb Rajah, in sal canoes fastened together. I was now arrived at the foot of that chain of hills which stretches along the northern frontier of Bengal and separates it from Tibet. In old maps, I believe, they are called the Nagracut,[2] in late ones the Tibet or Bod-la[3] mountains. As none of the Company's servants, and I might almost say no European, had ever visited the country which I was about to enter, I was equally in the dark as to the road, the climate, or the people; and the imperfect account of some religious mendicants, who had travelled through it, however unsatisfactory, was the only information I could collect. We passed the forts of Bowani-ganj, and Chichakotta,[4] lately destroyed, and arrived at some new houses, in one of which we were accommodated.

The house was thatched, the floor of lath of bamboo, and raised four feet from the ground; the walls of reeds, tied together with slips of bamboo; and the stair a stump of a tree, with notches cut in it. It had much the look of a birdcage, and the space below being turned into a hogstye contributed little to its pleasantness. There was not a bit of iron or rope about it. The houses for the three next stages were in the same style. The head man of the village and some of the neighbours got tipsy with a bottle of rum. A female pedlar sojourned with him; good features and shape, fine teeth, and Rubens' wife's eyes; whole dress one blanket wrapped round her, and fastened over the shoulders with a silver skewer. She drank rum too. Men, women, and children sleep higgledy-piggledy together. The country at the foot of the hills, subject to

[1] *Shorea robusta*, a valuable timber tree.

[2] *Nagorkote* Pass, north of Purneah, is shown on Rennell's Bengal Atlas of 1781. In his Memoir he mentions a place called by Giorgi *Nogliocot*, and by the Bengalis *Nogarcot*, as a pass leading from Bhutan to Kathmandu (p. 224). In the itineraries collected by Mr. Hodgson ('Bengal Selections,' xxvii. p. 121, 1857), Nagri Kot is mentioned as an old fort in ruins on the road from Purneah to Nepal. In the present maps of British Sikkim the name appears as *Nagri*.

[3] *Bod* is the native name of Tibet, and *la* means a pass. "The Pass into Tibet."

[4] Captain Turner followed on the same route, by the Buxa-Dúar, in 1783. Chichakotta was at the Bhutan frontier. He describes it as an oblong square encompassed by a high bank and thick stockade. The latter was obliterated in 1864-65.

the Deb Rajah, is in general inhabited by a people who, although they associate and intermix with the natives of Bhutan, are plainly of a different race, and resemble the Bengalis in colour, in shape, and features.[1]

Set out early. The chain of mountains which stretches along the northern frontier of Bengal, 18 miles distant, seemed over our heads. As we approached the hills there were strong marks of a change in the climate and face of the country; forests crowded with sals, pines,[2] and trees different from and more robust than those in Bengal; rivulets clear, and running on sand, pebbles, and stones. The road became uneven; and we reached the foot of the hills at about two o'clock; walk; ascent at first easy; way through a wood; some fine groves of first-rate trees; grows steep; narrow path zigzag up the hill; what a road for troops! about four miles to climb; many little springs to drink at; from the bottom of the hills to their summit covered with wood; variety of well-grown trees of the largest size; some grand natural amphitheatres, with the noise of waterfalls. We arrived at Buxa-Dúar[3] towards evening; situated on a hill, with much higher ones above it, glens under it, and a 3-feet wall of loose stones about it; a fine old banian tree;[4] that's all.[5]

The commander (Pasang Katam,[6] *vulgo* Buxa Subah) being at Bahar, I was visited by his dewan with presents, a white Pelong[7] handkerchief (the general nazir throughout Bhutan), butter, rice,

[1] The Dúars are chiefly inhabited by Rajbangsis, an agricultural caste in Rangpúr, of the Koch tribe.

[2] The pine no longer exists here, if it ever did.

[3] Dúar is simply the English word *Door*. The door or entrance to the mountains. Buxa-Dúar is 1809 feet above the sea.

[4] This tree still exists. On the morning of the 20th of March, 1865, Colonel Haughton found a party of artillery-men cutting it down, and his intervention saved it.

[5] Turner makes the distance from Chichakotta to Buxa-Dúar as 20 miles. He here gives an account of the method of making a spirit from rice or wheat, called *chong*. Facing p. 39 he has an engraving of Buxa-Dúar, from a drawing by his companion, Captain Davis.

[6] *Katam* is the title of office, and *Pasang* is the name we render *Buxa*. But it should be *Pas-aka*. Turner gives a curious account of the origin of the word *Buxa*, at p. 41. The *Katam* of Bogle is the *Gcatong* of Turner, p. 41. The correct form is *Jadu*, as given in the narrative of Kishen Kant Bose, at p. 193.

[7] The Tibetans call the English in India *Peling* (*Pelong*), a word signifying stranger (Huc's 'Tibet,' p. 270). A *Pelong* handkerchief is one from India, or from Europe coming through India. *P* is used by the Chinese for *F*, and *l* for *r*. So that *Peling* may be nothing more than *Fringy*, or *Feringhi* (*Frank*).

BUXA DUAR.

(FROM A DRAWING BY LIEUT DAVIS IN TURNER'S EMBASSY TO TIBET.)

milk, and some coarse tea. We were detained a day for want of coolies.

On the 9th of June I entered the hills, and being now out of Bengal and beyond the Company's jurisdiction, I was furnished with a passport from the Deb Rajah, who is the chief of the country. The following part of the journey was a perfect contrast to the former.

The only way of transporting goods in this hilly country is by coolies. The roads are too narrow, steep, and rugged for any other conveyance, and the rivers too stony and rapid for boats. There is no particular class of people who follow this profession. The carriers are pressed from among the inhabitants, receive an allowance for victuals at the pleasure of the person on whose service they are employed, and are relieved by others procured in the same manner at the next village by order of the head man, without which not a coolie is to be had. This is a service so well established that the people submit to it without murmuring. Neither sex, nor youth, nor age exempt them from it. The burden is fastened under the arms upon their backs, with a short stick to support it while they rest themselves. Naturally strong, and accustomed to this kind of labour, it is astonishing what loads they will carry. A girl of eighteen travelled one day 15 or 18 miles, with a burden of 70 or 75 pounds weight. We could hardly do it without any weight at all.

We were provided with two tangun ponies[1] of a mean appearance, and were prejudiced against them unjustly. On better acquaintance they turned out patient, sure-footed, and could climb the monument. Many a time afterwards, when, on the edge of a precipice, I was mounted on a skittish young horse, with a man holding him by the head and another steering him by the tail, have I thought of them. We had to cross the mountain Pichakonum,[2] which hangs over Buxa-Dúar; the way a narrow path, extremely steep, which went winding round the side of it; the

[1] Tanghan or Tangun, a strong little pony of Tibet and Bhutan. They are called Tangun, vulgarly Tannian, from Tangastan, the general appellation of the mountainous region of Bhutan. (See 'Hooker's Himalayan Journal.')

[2] This is the Peachokum mountain of Turner (p. 44). He describes it as an ascent of two hours, whence there is a glorious view. MacGregor has Peachakam.

upper part paved with stones of bastard marble, put together like ill-formed steps. Midday, cold and chilly; very high precipices, but not frightful, because covered with trees. Indulged in the pleasure of tumbling down stones.

The road led almost to the top of the mountain, and before we crossed it I turned to take another look at Bengal. It is impossible to conceive any change of country more abrupt, or any contrast more striking. To the southward the atmosphere was clear. The eye stretched over a vast tract of land, and the view was bounded only by the circular horizon. This part of the view, however, is striking only because it is extensive. There are no hills, spires, or other objects to distinguish it. The country—one continued flat—is marked only by its being cleared or woody, by the course of the rivers, or by some smoking villages. Whether it be that I am partial to hills or not, I beheld the opposite part of the prospect with much greater pleasure. The rapid descent, the deep glens, the hills covered with trees the most lofty and luxuriant, the town of Buxa-Dúar immediately below at a great distance, and behind nothing but mountains with their tops hid in the clouds. It was lucky for them, as I fancied them much higher than they really are. We were then on the top of one of the highest. What fine, baseless fabrics might not a cosmographer build on this situation, who, from a peat or an oyster-shell, can determine the different changes which volcanoes, inundations, and earthquakes have produced on the face of this globe. He would discover that the sea must once have covered Bengal, and washed the bottom of these mountains, which were placed as a barrier against its encroachments. But instead of following out these antediluvian reveries, which make the head giddy, one had better see to what uses nature now puts them, and how she fits the inhabitants for their respective situations. The natives of Bengal, weak and thin-skinned, are ill suited to bear fatigue or cold. Their country is cut through with rivers and creeks to carry their goods for them. The earth produces its fruits with an ease almost spontaneous, and every puddle is full of fish. The Bhutanese, of a constitution more robust and hardy, inhabit a country where strength is required. They have everything to transport on their backs; they are obliged to make terraces, and conduct little streams of water into them, in order to cover their rice fields, and to build houses with thick stone walls, to secure themselves from the cold. The one cannot endure heat, the other cannot suffer cold; and so these mountains are set up as a screen between them. They shelter Bengal from the northerly winds which blow over Tatary, all the way from Novaya Zemlya, and give them moderate winters; and they serve to keep off the hot southerly monsoon from the Bhutanese, and preserve them cool when the sun is within six degrees of them. The climate accordingly changes in the most rapid manner, and Muri-jong, which is not above two days' journey from the entrance into the hills, produces apricots, peaches, apples, pears, mulberries, and even oaks. But I am getting into the clouds.

At the place where the road crosses the mountain, standards or banners are set up, of white cloth, with sentences written upon them. They denote something religious, and are common at the tops of hills. The prospect within the hills is confined—not above 25 miles; country all equally clad with wood. There were not above six or eight villages to be seen on the brow of the mountain, with little patches of wheat, barley, or Indian corn; the road all down hill. We went down much against the grain, for we must climb it all up again; first place we came to Jaigugu.

Only three birdcage houses, and two Nepal dogs. I planted ten potatoes.[1] Through these hills, and about a mile below Jaigugu,[2] runs Pachu-Chinchu[3] to the south-east. From all the laws of hydrostatics it seems a plain deduction that a more level road might be made by following the course of this river than by going over the mountains. If the last is done to render the entrance into the country difficult it is very politic. A branch of this river was near us all the way to Tassisudon: it runs so fast, and dashes so over stones, that it is half a cascade. The road to Muri-jong consists of steep descents and ascents the whole way; a few distant villages. There had been a heavy shower of rain. Three or four fine waterfalls were passed; one fell perpendicular about 40 feet from the top of a rock; another a stream foaming and

[1] Warren Hastings desired Mr. Bogle to plant some potatoes at every halting place, in order that a valuable new product might be introduced into Bhutan.

[2] According to Turner, the distance from Buxa-Dúar to Jaigugu (or *Gygoogoo*) is 12 miles.

[3] Formed by the union of the two rivers Pachu and Chinchu, the latter flowing past Tassisudon, the former by Paro.

tumbling over large stones; another embosomed in a fine grove, with arches formed by the trees and rocks. There were wooden bridges over all the rivulets which ran from them.

We arrived at Muri-jong[1] as they were beating the evening tom-tom. It consists of twenty houses, some of them stone; many inscribed banners;[2] and a good deal of arable land and cattle. I planted fifteen potatoes.

To Chúka a long stage, and difficult road; a good deal of rain —it does not fall from the clouds, but comes upwards. The villages increase in number. There is a grand cascade on the opposite side of the river. We climbed a rock that hangs over Pachu-Chinchu[3] by steps, almost perpendicular; the horses scrambled up too. We passed through a passage cut in a small rock near the top, and came in sight of Chúka,[4] with its iron bridge, situated in a valley—the first we had seen. This village is in a different district from Buxa-Dúar.

From Chúka for the rest of the way to Tassisudon the country opens gradually. The mountains are still very high, but being more sloped have more arable land, and being at a greater distance from one another, leave room for villages in the hollows between them. On the former part of the journey there were nothing but glens, now there are valleys. But the sides of the mountains are more bare; there are few large trees, mostly fir;[5] the road is more level, except at two or three places; and we can ride the greatest part. The country seems populous, and well cultivated; houses, stone and clay, two and three stories high; temples; and on the two last stages rice fields.

It would be tedious to mention every stage. A list of them is subjoined. There are about ten, fifteen, or twenty large houses at each.

It grew colder every stage till we reached Kepta.[6] There the

[1] Murichom of Turner. Rather more than 4000 feet above the sea. (Griffith, p. 151.) MacGregor says 3788 feet.

[2] At the present day these banners are texts of Buddhist scriptures, printed on calico from wooden blocks.

[3] Turner calls it the river Tchintchieu. He gives an engraving (p. 53) of a beautiful waterfall.

[4] *Chuka*, or *Suka*, the passage or crossing of the river. 4449 feet.

[5] *Pinus excelsa*, *P. Smithiana*, and rhododendrons are mentioned by Griffith, p. 150.

[6] *Chupka* of Turner, and *Chupcha* of Pemberton. 7984 feet.

THE BRIDGE AT CHUKA.

(FROM A DRAWING BY LIEUT DAVIS IN TURNER'S EMBASSY TO TIBET.)

thermometer was at 58° morning and evening, and would creep to 64° in the heat of the day. Thus it was during the three days we stayed there. At Tassisudon it was about 61° in the morning, and 68° to 70° at midday.

Most of the trees and plants are unknown to me. Bengal trees are chiefly met with on the other side of Chúka—plantain, jack, bamboo, thick and crabbed blackwood. European trees and plants are mostly on this side; some I have already mentioned, others are walnut, elderberry, holly, willow, ash, aspen-leaf, sweet brier, roses, brambles, juniper, wormwood, sage, thistles, southernwood, strawberries, primroses, ground ivy. The people cultivate turnips,[1] leeks, shallots, water melons, musk melons, cucumbers, and brinjals.

After the variety of uses to which the bamboo is applied in Bengal, one would hardly think it possible to discover any other; but the people in that part of the country where it grows have discovered two more. It answers as a vessel to hold anything in, and as a pot to boil anything. This last operation is performed by covering the bottom with clay, and then putting on the fire.

The bridges are either entirely of wood or entirely of iron.[2] The wooden bridges are very common, and are from 30 to 70 feet long. On each side of the river four or six piles are built slopingly into piers of bare stones, so as each to project about a third of the way over. The centre beams rest upon the tops of these, which are first joined together with a cross beam dovetailed, and this forms the support of the planks. When it is necessary to make a bridge very strong, short piles are placed under the others, like the spring of a chaise. All the parts are fastened together with wooden pins, so that there is not a bit of iron about them. At Chúka the river is very rapid and broad, and an iron bridge is hung over it.[3] Five chains are stretched from one side to the other, and covered with laths and mats of bamboo, which form the floor. Two other chains are extended across the river at about seven feet perpendicular above the outermost of those on each side, and joined to

[1] Bhutan produces probably the best turnips in the world.

[2] That is, chain bridges. (See Turner, p. 54.)

[3] Turner gives an engraving of this bridge, facing p. 55.

them with twisted rattans. It is 147 feet long, and 6 feet broad. As soon as one steps upon it, it moves from one end to the other. Near Lumbolong there is a bridge formed with two chains.

There is another way of passing rivers, by means of two ropes stretched across, with two hoops hung upon them, which serve to support the feet or knees, while the hands hauling on the ropes slide the hoops along. The hoops are of one piece of rattan, and are often 60 or 70 feet in length.

LIST OF STAGES.

Bogle.	Kos.	*Pemberton and Turner.*	Miles.
1. Bahar to Chichakotta, about	10	Bahar to Chichacotta	20
2. Chichakotta to Buxa-Dúar ..	13	Chichacotta to Buxa	18
3. Buxa-Dúar to Jaigugu	8	Buxa } to Murichom	19
4. Jaigugu to Muri-jong	10	Gygoogoo }	
5. Muri-jong to Chúka	10	Murichom to Chúka	18
6. Chúka to Kepta	9	Chúka to Chupcha (Kepta)	17
7. Kepta to Paku	5	Chupcha to Panga	11
8. Paku to Lumbolong	4	Panga to Nomnoo	8
9. Lumbolong to Wangoka ..	4	Nomnoo to Wangoka	10
10. Wangoka to Tassisudon	3	Wangoka to Tassisudon	8
Computed	76	Miles	129

MacGregor.

Buxa to Tchinchu-la (4869 feet)	6
Tapsee (3003 feet)	9
Murichom (3788 feet)	6½
Choonkar	9
Chúka (4449 feet)	9
Pinaka	8
Chupcha (7984 feet)	9
Panga (7511 feet)	11
Somloo	8
Oolaka (7120 feet)	10
Tasi-cho-zong (7271 feet)	8
	93½

CHAPTER III.

TASSISUDON, THE CAPITAL OF BHUTAN.

WE were accommodated in a good house near the palace; and soon found it so cold that I was glad to hang my room, which was a wooden balcony, with Bhutan blankets. The window looked to the river, and commanded the best prospect.

The palace of Tassisudon[1] is situated in a valley about five miles long and one broad, entirely surrounded with high mountains. The river Chinchu gallops by; the low grounds near it being covered with rice, and well peopled. Villages are scattered on the brow of the hills. The least steep places produce wheat. Immediately behind Tassisudon there is a very high mountain, rising into two turrets, which are clad with wood almost to the top; and some solitary cottages, the retreat of dervises, are here and there dropped as from the clouds. In these airy abodes they pass their days in counting their beads, and look down with indifference on all the business and bustle of the world, from which they are entirely excluded.

The character of a fakir is held in great estimation in this country. It is not confined, however, to these self-denying sons of abstinence. The statesmen and the provincial governors, when weary of power or dismissed from office, assume the name and garb of a fakir.[2] They retire to their houses, or to a castle they have built on the top of some mountain; but instead of that poverty and those acts of mortification which are the proper characteristics of the hermit's life, they are surrounded by their families and servants; they indulge themselves in the daintiest victuals under the salvo of killing no living creature, and eating no animal food

[1] 7271 feet above the sea, according to Pemberton.

[2] The Government being hierarchical, the officials are nominally of the orders of Buddhist priesthood. Bogle here confounds the Buddhist monk with the Hindu mendicant, amongst Europeans known as a fakir. The term is properly only applicable to Muhammadans.

on the day on which it was slain, and being generally allowed to carry their effects along with them, may be considered among the most opulent class of inhabitants. Deb Seklu, after a prosperous reign of eighteen years, named his successor, and spent the rest of his days in this peaceful retirement.

One day we ascended the high mountain. We set out early in the morning, and reached the summit at about three o'clock. The palace of Tassisudon with its gilded turrets, the windings of the Chinchu with its wooden bridges, the fields below covered with rice and with villages, the tops of distant mountains, and the lofty castles of fakirs[1] formed the prospect. We met with some wild cherries and one currant bush, and got down after it was dark.

The Deb Rajah was absent on our arrival. His return to Tassisudon was in this wise. At about ten o'clock the balconies of the palace were covered with priests, who are all clad in red cloth,[2] the manufacture of Bhutan; and 4 long brass trumpets, 6 castanets, 4 tabors, and 4 fifes were sounded at intervals. At eleven, 30 matchlocks were fired on the road he was to pass, and the salute was repeated when he came up to them. The procession consisted of 12 led horses; 120 men dressed in red, with blue solitaires; 30 matchlock men; 30 archers; 30 horses laden with cloths and other furniture; 40 men on horseback, some of them with bushy caps; the chief dewan, with a bushy party-coloured standard; 6 musicians; the Deb Rajah on horseback, covered with a scarlet cloak, a large yellow hat like a cardinal's, a choura burdar[3] on each side of him, and behind a man carrying a small white silk umbrella with different coloured fringes. As they came near the palace everybody except the Rajah alighted; the men with bushy caps pulled them off, and walked up to the gate. At different parts of the road which he had to pass, fires were lighted, and the people prostrated themselves before him. In the whole cavalcade there were about 400 persons.

Two days afterwards the Deb Rajah sent for me. If there is any satisfaction in being gazed at, I had enough of it. I dare to

[1] No doubt Buddhist monks are referred to.

[2] This colour denotes the older or Nyanginapa sect. The more recent or Gelukpa sect, which is now dominant in Tibet, uses the yellow colour.

[3] That is, one who carries a flyflap formed of the tail of the yak.

say there were 3000 spectators. I was led through three courts, and after climbing two iron-plated ladders, which serve for stairs in this part of the world, arrived in an antechamber hung round with arms. Here I waited some time before I was conducted into the presence chamber, through a dark entry and down two steps. The Rajah was seated on his throne or pulpit (for that is what it is like), raised about two feet above the floor. He was dressed in the festival habit of a gylong or priest, being covered with a scarlet satin cloak, and a gilded mitre on his head. A man kept twirling the umbrella over him. The pulpit was gilded, and surrounded with silver ewers and vases, and the floor was covered with carpets. His officers to the number of twelve were seated on cushions close to the wall. After making my bows, which, according to the ceremonial of this country, ought to have been prostrations, and laying my presents before him, I was conducted to a cushion prepared for me in the middle of the apartment. Several copper platters with rice, butter, treacle, tea, walnuts, Kashmirian dates, apricots, cucumbers, and other fruits were set before me, together with a little wooden stool. All this passed in silence. Then a man entered with a silver kettle full of buttered tea, and having poured a little into his palm and drunk it off, filled a dish for the Rajah, and went round to all his officers. Now every Bhutanese carries a little wooden cup for such occasions, black glazed in the inside, wrapped in a bit of cloth, and lodged within the tunic, opposite to the heart and next the skin; but not being so well provided, I got a china cup. After all the dishes were filled, the Deb Rajah said a grace, in which he was joined by all the company; and then he opened his mouth and spoke to me. When we had finished our tea, and every man had well licked his cup and deposited it in his bosom, a flowered satin gown was brought me. I was dressed in it as a *khilat;* a red handkerchief was tied round me for a girdle, and I was carried to the Rajah, who bound my head with another, and squeezing my temples, put something on my head, which I afterwards found to be the image of the god Sakya,[1] and muttered some prayers over

[1] Sakya was the name of Buddha most used in the north, and Gotama in Ceylon. Muni (Saint, or Holy Man) is often added; and the usual form is Sakyamuni.

me. He then tied two silk handkerchiefs together, and threw them over my shoulders. I was conducted to my cushion; we had two or three more dishes of tea, as many graces, a cup or two of whisky, and betel-nut. I then retired. The walls of the presence chamber were hung round with Chinese landscapes mixed with their deities painted on satin. The ceiling and pillars were covered with the same devices, and at the lower end of the room, behind where I sat, there were three or four images placed in niches. Before them were censers burning with incense, and lamps with butter; little silver pagodas and urns, elephants' teeth, flowers, &c., the whole ornamented with silks, ribbons, and other gewgaws. Among these I must not omit to mention a solitary print of Lady Waldegrave,[1] whom I was the means of rescuing out of the hands of these idols; for it happening to strike some of the household that she would make a pretty companion to a looking-glass I had given the Deb Rajah, she was hung up on one of the pillars next the throne, and the mirror on the other.

The palace is a very large building, and contains near 3000 men, and not a woman. Of these about 1000 may be gylongs, some of the former chief's adherents, who are kept in a kind of imprisonment, and the rest the Rajah and Lama's officers, and all their train of servants. A tower, about five or six stories high, rises in the middle, and is appropriated to Lama-Rimboché.[2] He dwells near the top. His apartments are furnished in the style of the Rajah's, but better. In the former chief's days nobody could see him, but times are altered. His reception was like the Rajah's, only no *khilat* or whisky. On our arrival he lived in a castle on a little mount behind the palace. His apartments were finished while we were there, and a large image of Sakya was gilded and set up in his presence chamber. When he came down the Rajah went out to meet him. After the first visit he used to receive us without any ceremony, and appeared to have more curiosity than any man I have seen in the country. One day Mr. Hamilton was

[1] This was Maria, illegitimate daughter of the Hon. Sir Edward Walpole, K.B. As Dowager Countess Waldegrave she was married, in 1766, to the Duke of Gloucester, brother of George III., and was mother of the Duke of Gloucester who died in 1834; and of the Princess Sophia of Gloucester, who was born in 1773, and died in 1844.

[2] Schlagintweit has *Rimpoché*; but Bogle is right. This is the Dharma Rajah of the Hindus.

THE PALACE AT TASSISUDON.

(FROM A SKETCH BY LIEUT DAVIS IN TURNER'S EMBASSY TO TIBET.)

showing him a microscope, and went to catch a fly; the whole room was in confusion, and the Lama frightened out of his wits lest he should have killed it. We used to get dinners at the Lama's—boiled rice, with sugar and butter, and a stew of bits of kid, with slices of cucumbers, and well seasoned with red pepper—it is called *giagu.* He partook of the dessert, which consisted of fruits and sour curds cut like pieces of leather, and fried with butter and honey. He has got a little lap-dog and a mungoos, which he is very fond of. He is a thin sickly-looking man of about thirty-five years of age.

The palace is divided into courts, flanked with galleries, supported on wooden pillars running round them, like the inns in England. The different officers have each their apartments. The gylongs live in a large church,[1] besides which there is a smaller one where they officiate, and where the larger images are kept. These images are mostly decent and well-proportioned figures, sitting cross-legged. There is a large gallery above the church, painted with festoons of death's-head and bones, where folks go to see the ceremonies. I went once or twice myself; and the Rajah, thinking I was fond of it, used to send for me to church by break of day and at all hours, and congratulated me greatly on my good fortune in happening to be at Tassisudon during the grand festival. All the governors of provinces repaired there to the presence, and there were dances every day in one of the courts of the palace. About twenty gylongs, dressed in various coloured satin cloaks and gilded mitres, were seated on a bench, with each a large tabor or drum, resting on a stick which they held in one hand, and in the other a crooked rod of iron, with a knob at the end of it, with which they beat time to a priest, who was placed in the midst of them, with two silver cups which he struck against each other. A yellow satin curtain was drawn before the door of the lesser church, from behind which run out six, eight, ten, and sometimes a score of priests in masquerade dresses, with visors like horses' heads, like beaks of birds, or other grotesque figures. They danced and capered with whimsical gestures, the burden of which was to throw down their heads till the red tuft of hair touched the ground, and then suddenly toss it up again. Between the acts we

[1] *Vihar*, or monastery. The lesser building is the *chaitya* or church.

had singing by the peasants, and abundance of antic tricks by two or three merry Andrews.

The walls of the palace[1] are between two and three stories high, and built, as all walls in this country are, inclining inwards. What with stairs, pillars, galleries, and roofs, there is an immense quantity of timber about it. The building of it stripped naked several mountains. The roofs are of planks two or three deep, and kept down by stones; and the load of beams and open wooden work which is used to support them gives the upper parts of the palace the look of the centres of Blackfriars Bridge.[2] The roof of the Lama's tower is entirely gilt, is ornamented with dragons, &c., and rises like the top of a Chinese temple.

The palace gates are shut in the dusk of the evening, after which nobody is allowed to go out or in. The inhabitants seldom stir out, except once in eight or ten days, in a string of 500 or 600, to bathe in the Chinchu.[3] They seem to lead a joyless, and, I think, an idle life; for so much authority is given into the hands of the provincial governors that very little is done at the Sadar.[4] They have little connection with foreign states, Teshu Lama excepted, and less intercourse with strangers.

Among a people where there is no pre-eminence of birth, and no finery in dress, there cannot well be much pride. The Bhutanese seem to have none of it, and live among their servants and dependents on the most familiar footing. One day the Governor (Jong-pen)[5] of Tassisudon asked me to a match at quoits.[6] All his own people were of the party. They are very dexterous at it, and I soon gave over a diversion where I could get no credit, and betook myself to shooting wild pigeons. After it was over we sat down upon the ground to dinner. When we had drunk a dish of tea, and eaten three hard-boiled eggs a-piece, a basket full of boiled rice was brought, and distributed in handfuls, together with boiled pork cut into steaks,

[1] See the plate in 'Turner.' This palace is said to have been built by Deb Judhur, and was burnt down during a civil war, a few years ago. It is now rebuilt.

[2] Begun in 1760, and opened in 1769. Bogle would have seen the centerings in the arches before he left England.

[3] Turner gives an engraving of this bathing procession.

[4] That is the court or chief place.

[5] *Jong*, a castle. *Pen*, head or chief.

[6] See Pemberton, p. 86, where he describes the game as played in Bhutan.

hogs' hearts, and *giagu.* We ate off cloths, and with our fingers, and when the repast was finished had a cup of whisky and some fruit.

They say there is little ceremony at the Bhutanese marriages. The parties satisfied with each other have no occasion for the sacerdotal benediction, and the priests, condemned to celibacy themselves, will not be instrumental in breaking it in others. Polygamy is not allowed; divorces are, where there are no children.

The Bhutanese, like their neighbours in Bengal, burn their dead. One of the priests in the palace happening to die, I went to see the ceremony. It was the third day after his death. I found about forty priests assembled in a tent on the side of a rivulet which runs by the palace, and employed in chanting their prayers, while some workmen were cutting timber and forming the funeral pile. As they objected to my remaining near the tent, I crossed the brook, and ascended a little bank which overlooked the place where the obsequies were to be performed. At about 20 yards from the pile a temporary booth was erected, from which tea was occasionally distributed to the clergy, and some large pots that were boiling on the fire seemed to promise a more solid repast. The priests continued at different intervals to recite their offices in a low voice, accompanying them with the tinkling of bells and the sound of tabors and trumpets, and some old women, placed at a distance, were counting their beads and repeating their *Om mani padmi hums!* [1] When night came on, the body, wrapped in a linen sheet, was silently brought, and at the same instant that it was laid on the pile a shrill pipe, like a cat-call, was sounded. All this passed in the dark. Then a relation of the deceased came with a lighted brand in his hand, and set fire to the pile. Two of the priests fed it with fresh wood; another, dressed in white, threw in from time to time spices, salt, butter, oil, betel leaf, and twenty other articles, and the rest joined in a flourish with trumpets, bells, and tabors, while each of these different rites were performing. The fire burned slowly, a heavy shower of rain came on, and I returned home without waiting till the conclusion of the ceremony. It is

[1] The favourite prayer of the Tibetan Buddhists. It means "Oh the jewel in the lotus! Amen." It is an invocation to Padmapani, who is incarnate in the Dalai Lama. The lotus is the symbol of highest perfection, and the invocation is an allusion to Padmapani's genesis from that flower.

usual, I am told, to collect the ashes on the third day after the funeral, and carrying them in solemn procession to throw them into the river Chinchu.

The barbarous Hindu custom of women burning themselves with their husbands is unknown in this country. The Bhutanese wives never give such heroic proofs of their fortitude and affection, and this difference in their conduct naturally arises from the manners peculiar to each country.

The practice of burning has been considered by some as a political institution to deter women from poisoning their husbands, and by others as proceeding solely from excessive love. The first opinion seems as groundless as it is ungenerous, and the last is, perhaps, too refined for this iron age. Mankind are neither so good nor so bad as they are generally represented. Human life is a stream formed and impelled by a variety of passions, and its actions seldom flow from single and unmixed sources.

A Hindu woman, married at an early age, and immured within the walls of a zenana, is unacquainted with all those pleasures and avocations to which a liberal education or the free intercourse of society gives birth. A fondness for dress and the management of her family occupy her whole attention, and the solaces of conjugal and maternal affection are the only source of her enjoyments. She lives but for her husband and her children, and every passion of her soul, heightened by the force of the climate, is centered in them. On the death of her husband, by devoting herself to the flames she performs an action meritorious in the highest degree, and which reflects the greatest honour on herself and her family. If she survives him she is confined to her room, condemned to perpetual widowhood, obliged to lay aside all gaudy apparel, and to feed on the most abstemious diet. "Alas!" says she, "a life so gloomy and joyless is not worth preserving—is not to be supported." Her heart sinks in despair, and is overwhelmed with grief and affection for her husband. Now zeal for the honour of her children and the desire of distinguishing herself combine with this indifference for life. She forms the fatal resolution while under the first impression of these different passions, and mounts the funeral pile before they have had time to spend their force.

But the institution of castes and every other hereditary distinction being unknown in Bhutan, the elevated sentiments which spring from a consciousness of superiority are never felt. The women in particular are degraded by this levelling system. As the Rajah, the priests, and all the officers of government lead a life of celibacy, they are married only to landholders or husbandmen. They are employed in the most laborious offices, they are dirty in their persons, they use strong liquors, they are bred up in the greatest liberty, they mix with the lowest class of people; they are allowed to enter into a second marriage, and the death of a husband opens to them no such dismal prospect.

At Tassisudon a peasant came to visit me who had been taken prisoner in Bahar Fort, and after being kept some months had been sent back safe and sound to his own country. He had come two days' journey to tell me the story, and to present me with a goat, a roll of butter, and some rice as a mark of his gratitude. He paid me several visits afterwards, and gave me a bow and arrows. It would be a pity to omit his name, it was Uchong; nor the officer's, who released him, it was Captain Jones.[1]

Servants are so much used to usurp a degree of authority in Bengal that it was difficult to restrain them from assuming it towards the Bhutanese.[2] But what threatenings and even punishments could not do was brought about by an old woman. On some difference with one of my people, she took up a stone and offered to knock a servant down. After this there were no more complaints.

Some stages from Tassisudon we were joined by a servant sent by the Deb Rajah to facilitate our journey. He was like a jemidar of harkáras. Having a dispute about my horse with the head man of a small village, he wanted to strike him, and in endeavouring to wrest a bow from one of the bystanders he hit him a blow in the scuffle. In a moment half-a-dozen arrows were pointed at his breast, and he escaped the fate of St. Sebastian only by getting out of the way.

Whenever a Bhutanese offers anything to eat or drink he first

[1] See *ante*, note at p. 1.

[2] In 1863, in Jyntea, Colonel Haughton tells me that, having with great difficulty induced the people of a very large village to submit and return to their homes, his labour was nearly frustrated by the conduct of the only servant he had.

tastes it himself, or makes one of his people do so, to remove mistrust. This suggests a bad idea. But forms and customs often outlive the state of society which gave birth to them.

Every man in the palace is dressed in a darkish red woollen cloth.[1] They are remarkably dirty in their persons, even to the Rajah's dewans. He himself is an exception.

The horses are unshod tanguns,[2] with hoofs as hard as iron; all stallions, extremely vicious when young, and ill broke in. The saddle is of wood, with a peak 8 or 9 inches high, which the rider holds on by, and which keeps him from slipping off in descents. The stirrups are remarkably short. The bridle is generally tied round the nose, and the horses led. They use mules for very steep or difficult paths. They are brought from Teshu Lama's country.

In about the middle of August droves of cow-tailed cattle[3] were brought to Tassisudon. During the hot months they are kept among the coldest mountains. All the butter is made of their milk, and is very rich and good. Their beef is lean and coarse. The Bhutanese hang it up to dry, and often eat it when one would think the smell sufficient. Their principal food, however, is pork and dried fish from Bengal mixed with their rice. Their bread is made of unsifted flour. They use a great deal of butter, and I got as much in presents as would have set me up for a tallow-chandler.

There are numbers of temples on all the roads. One kind is a long wall, with stones inscribed *Om mani padmi hum!* all round, and small basso-relievo figures, with gilt faces cut in black marble, and placed in the middle and at each end. Sometimes they have *Om mani padmi hum* written on a barrel and turned round by water.[4] Another kind of temple is a house about 15 feet square, and they take a most effectual way to preserve it unpolluted by giving it no doors or windows.[5] In every house there is a small altar for the household gods, which they set out with chanks[6] and flowers, and daily offer up their devotions to them.

[1] Sign of belonging to the Nyangi-napa sect. (See note at p. 24.)

[2] Only ponies. There are no horses in Bhutan. (See note at p. 17.)

[3] Yaks.

[4] Praying wheels.

[5] This is the real temple or *chaitya*, which is solid.

[6] Large shells (*Buccinum*) from the Gulf of Manar and Bay of Bengal, used by the Hindus for sounding in worship, and by their women, cut into bracelets.

CHAPTER IV.

HISTORY AND GOVERNMENT OF BHUTAN.

In ancient times this hilly country was parcelled out among a number of independent chieftains. A lama from the north united them, under one government, and introduced his religion among them. His death gave birth to three lamas. His body fell to the share of one; his heart to another; and his mouth or word to a third. Upon the death of these holy men, their souls pass into the bodies of children, who, after a strict examination into their identity, are recognized; and thus a succession of saints under various forms, but animated by the same spirit, have continued, at different intervals, to enlighten this corner of the world. The periodical return of the lamas to the earth is undeterminate. At present there are only two, viz. the body and the heart. The word died about twelve years ago, and having never since appeared, it is uncertain whether his soul may not be swallowed up in that ineffable spirit, of which it is only an emanation.

The lamas are first in rank, and nominally first in power. They enjoy a joint and coequal authority; and in all their deliberations are assisted by the clergy.

The apparent wisdom of this system is evident. In other governments, to qualify a person for the supreme administration requires a course of study and observation too long for human life; and after all, the waywardness of subjects will dispute his commands; but in Bhutan the chief magistrate is instructed by the experience of ages, and his orders carry with them all the weight which on this account they deserve.

But the time and attention of these holy men being engaged in the duties of religion, the executive part of government is entrusted to a person styled Kushu Dêbu.[1]

[1] The Government of Bhutan, as of Tibet, and of Japan, is a theocracy, assigning the first place to the spiritual chief. That chief being by profession a recluse, the active duties are discharged ordinarily by a deputy.

The various occupations to which the wants of a refined and luxurious people give rise, are little known in this country. The number of mechanics is inconsiderable; there is hardly any distinction of professions. The same arm which at one time is employed in tilling the ground, at another is lifted up in its defence; and the arrow which has killed the wild goat or the musk deer, is now pointed against the breast of an enemy. Every family is acquainted with most of the useful arts, and contains within itself almost all the necessaries of life. Even clothes, which is a considerable article in so rude a climate, are generally the produce of the husbandman's industry. At one season he and his sons carry the fruits of their ground, and barter them for the wool of Teshu Lama's country. This is spun, dyed, and wove into cloth, by his wife and daughters; the family are clad; and what remains is either disposed of to his neighbours, or transported, at a different season, with his musk and horses, to Rangpúr, and exchanged for hogs, salt fish, coarse linen; or for dyes, spices, broadcloth, and other articles which may enable him to carry on his trade to Tibet with greater advantage.

The inhabitants, therefore, may properly be divided into three classes: the priests, the servants or officers of government, and the landholders and husbandmen. The priests are formed from among the body of the people. They are received at an early age; instructed in the arts, and initiated in the mysteries of the profession for which they are destined. When admitted into orders, they take a vow to live chaste, to kill no living creature, and to abstain from eating animal food on the day on which it is killed. The second class comprehends ministers, governors of provinces, collectors, and all their train of dependents. These, though not absolutely prohibited from marriage, yet, finding it a bar to their preferment, seldom enter into that state. They are taken, like the priests, from families in the country; are bred up in the palaces under the patronage of some man in office, by whom they are fed and clothed, but receive no wages; they seldom arrive at

But the subordinates of the one or of the other will in fact govern according to their relative energy and ability, and often according as the weight of foreign influence is thrown into the one scale or the other, which it always is nowadays by China, and all the more easily because of the plurality of the *soi-disant* divinities.

places of trust or consequence till far advanced in life; and having passed through all the different gradations of service, it is no uncommon thing to see a minister as expert in mending a shoe or making a tunic, as in settling the business of the nation. The landholders and husbandmen, although by far the most numerous class, and that which gives birth to the other two, are entirely excluded from any share in the administration. They live at home, cultivate their lands, pay taxes, serve in the wars, and beget children who succeed to honours to which they themselves could never aspire.

Among these different classes, the priests, in point of political importance, hold the first place; and independent of that influence which their holy character and superior learning give them over the minds of a superstitious people, enjoy privileges so extensive that the chief power appears in fact to reside in their order. The lamas, though nominally supreme in the government, yet, as they owe their appointment to the priests, are tutored by them from their earliest infancy, and, deriving all their knowledge of public affairs from them, are entirely under their management. The right of electing the Deb Rajah is vested in the superiors of their order, jointly with the lamas. He is bound to consult with them as to peace or war, and in general to take no measure of consequence without their advice and approbation. He is accountable to them for the exercise of his power, and holds it only during their pleasure. Their sacred profession, so far from disqualifying them from the conduct of civil affairs, is the means of advancing them to it. They are often appointed to the government of provinces, employed as ministers, or entrusted with other offices of the first consideration in the state. The chief is frequently chosen from the sacerdotal order, or if from among the lay officers is immediately received into it.[1] As the priests are taken from among the subjects at large, and keep up an intercourse with their respective families, they naturally retain an influence in every part of the country, and in all their measures are sure to be supported by the people. The late revolution in the government affords a

[1] The above is not clear. It may help to make it so to compare the passages in Mr. Hodgson's book, which are cited at p. 37 *infra*, quoad the social aspect of the case, for, in a political view, the Nepal example holds not.

striking proof of their authority; and by accustoming the people to look up to them for the redress of their grievances, serves also to confirm it. The institution of castes and every other hereditary distinction being unknown in this country, offices of power are the only source of pre-eminence; and this system of equality, while it prevents the violent commotions to which the rivalship of pride and ambition gives rise, leaves no competitor to dispute the dominion of the priests. Thus the power of the clergy, founded on deep-rooted prejudices and pretensions of divine origin, interwoven in the nature of the constitution, and supported by the uniform spirit of an order that never dies, is likely to be as permanent as it is considerable.

But although the Deb Rajah is liable to be deposed by the clergy, instances of this seldom occur; and his authority in the internal government of the country appears to be very complete. The appointment to offices, the collection and management of the revenue, the command and direction of the military force, and the power of life and death, are vested in him. The scantiness, however, of his revenue, which it is difficult to increase, the want of mercenary troops, the nature of the country, the free spirit of the people, and his own advanced age when he is raised to the government, are strong obstacles to his becoming independent.

The provincial governors are entrusted with a very ample jurisdiction. The police of the country, the levying of taxes, and the administration of justice, are committed to them. Complaints against them are seldom preferred or attended to; and their judgments are revised by the chief only in capital cases, or others of great consequence. They are not continued long at one station. They live in a large palace, are surrounded by priests and officers, and their durbar is an epitome of the court of the chief.

The taxes, moderate in themselves, are rendered still less oppressive by the simple manner of gathering them. Every family, according to its substance, is rated at a particular sum, which is often received in produce; and this mode of collection, however repugnant to the refined ideas of European policy, leaves them unencumbered with a heavy expense for tax-gatherers, and precludes the necessity of employing a numerous body of subjects in a vocation so useless to the state and so vexatious to the people.

As the public revenue is small, the expenses of government are proportionally moderate. The officers receive no salaries; the troops, composed of the inhabitants trained to the use of the bow, and bound to follow the standard of their chief, are supported at a trifling charge; and pomp and luxury being unknown, the expenses of the court are inconsiderable. The principal drains, then, upon the public treasury, are an annual payment to Teshu Lama, and the establishment of a numerous body of priests, whom it is much the interest of the chief to gratify.

The simplicity of their manners, their slight intercourse with strangers, and a strong sense of religion, preserve the Bhutanese from many vices to which more polished nations are addicted. They are strangers to falsehood and ingratitude. Theft, and every other species of dishonesty to which the lust of money gives birth, are little known. Murder is uncommon, and in general is the effect of anger, not of covetousness. The celibacy of a large part of the people,[1] however, is naturally productive of many irregularities, and the coldness of the climate inclines them to an excessive use of spirituous liquors.

Deb Judhur[2] was raised to the government about seven years ago.[3] Having been employed in different enterprises against the neighbouring chiefs, and having filled the highest offices in the country, he acquired a considerable degree of wealth and importance before his succession to the chiefship, and owed his election more to intrigue and a dread of his power than to the free choice of the clergy. A rooted enmity, founded on a natural opposition of interest, took place between him and Lama-Rimboché. The executive power was in his hands; the supreme authority and control were claimed by the other. His bold and restless spirit was unable to brook the cautious maxims of priests, and he endeavoured by every means to render himself independent of their authority. With this view he strengthened his connection with Teshu Lama and the Rajah of Nepal; he endeavoured to secure

[1] The extent and nature of this celibacy, and more generally the nature of the classification of the people in a Buddhist country, will be better understood by reference to Mr. Hodgson's book 'On Nepal and Tibet,' pp. 51, 52, 63, 64, and 139 *et seq.*

[2] The ruler who invaded Kuch Bahar, and came into collision with the British. (See note at p. 1.)

[3] That is, in about 1767.

the friendship and protection of the Emperor of China, by circulating his seal in the country; he kept the Lama in a state almost of imprisonment; he transacted the most important business without the advice of the priests; he seldom employed them in any of the departments of government, and he engaged in wars with his neighbours, and filled his coffers with the booty which he thereby procured. But his administration, although more spirited than that of most of his predecessors, was far from being popular. The inhabitants, obliged by the custom of the country to serve without pay, were harassed with his military enterprises, from which he alone reaped advantage; the law by which upon the death of an officer of government his money and effects escheat to the Rajah was by him carried rigidly into execution; and the clergy, excluded from all share in public affairs, and treated with neglect, encouraged the general discontent, which was kept from breaking out only by the boldness and activity of his measures.

At length he attempted the conquest of Kuch Bahar. His undisciplined militia was unable to cope with regular troops; but being unaccustomed to ill fortune, he continued the war in opposition to the remonstrances of the clergy and his most experienced counsellors, and exerted every effort to render it more successful. The burdens which these extraordinary services imposed upon the inhabitants were rendered still more insupportable by an unforeseen accident. The palace of Tassisudon was burned to ashes; and Deb Judhur, in order to render himself famous by rebuilding it in one year, pushed on the work with a severity little suited to the distressed situation of the country. The people everywhere gave vent to their complaints; and the Lama's party, seizing the opportunity of his being absent with the army, deprived him of the government, issued orders to seize his person, and elected the present chief in his stead. He received the news of this revolution while at Buxa-Dúar with Teshu Lama's messengers, and immediately betaking himself to flight, escaped by a bye road to the neighbourhood of Lhasa. One or two of his principal officers were taken and put to death. The rest of those who were most obnoxious followed their master's fortunes.

By this revolution Lama-Rimboché and his party regained that influence in the government to which, by the constitution, they consider themselves entitled. The chief, whom they had raised and supported, submitted implicitly to their pleasure; the Emperor of China's seal was suppressed, and the war in Bahar immediately discontinued. Many of the priests, however, continued attached to Deb Judhur, who, though jealous of the power of their order, was often liberal to individuals; and they were dissatisfied with an administration that was parsimonious as well from the genius of the persons who conducted it as the situation of their affairs. For the wealth and effects of Deb Judhur, either from the fear of driving him to extremity, or of giving offence to Teshu Lama, under whose protection he had taken refuge, remained untouched; the public treasury has been exhausted by the war, and the country from the same cause was little able to replenish it. Such as had held offices under the former government were equally disaffected. At first several of them had been continued in their employments by the Lama; but afterwards, either from a suspicion of their fidelity, or in order to provide for his own friends, they were dismissed, and allowed to retire to their houses. There they carried on a secret correspondence with the exiled chief and the priests in his interest, and concerted the plan of an insurrection.

The Lama, though ignorant of the circumstances of this conspiracy, was no stranger to Deb Judhur's pretensions to the government. He had received letters from him asserting his claim, warning him upon no account to touch his property, and desiring him to quit the house which he had built, as he intended to return to take possession of it, and to cut down his corn as soon as the harvest was ready. The Rajah of Nepal had refused to acknowledge the present chief; and Lama Shabdong,[1] a child of seven years old, who had been revived by Teshu Lama about twelve months before as a check upon Lama-Rimboché, was tutored to declare for Deb Judhur's restoration, and to refuse all sustenance unless it was agreed to. Everything, however, was still quiet in the country, when the Rajah set out for a castle about a day's journey from Tassisudon, accompanied by Lama Shabdong, whom he was afraid to leave in the palace surrounded by the malcontent priests.

[1] Pemberton gives *Lam Suddoon* as one of the titles of the Dharma Rajah or Lama-Rimboché, p. 114. Dupgain Sheptun was the first Lama-Rimboché, and this child was probably intended as an avatar of some portion of him.

The night after his departure was pitched upon by the conspirators for executing their designs, and they hoped, by surprising the palace and getting possession of the Lama and the superiors of the clergy, to strike at once a decisive blow. The former governors of Tassisudon and Targa,[1] with about 250 men, were to have made the attack from without, while their associates within set open the gates, and otherwise facilitated the attempt. But their scheme being discovered, and several of the priests immediately put to death, they hastened to Simptoka,[2] a castle about five miles from Tassisudon, and made themselves masters of it without resistance. Here they found arms, ammunition, provisions, and some treasure; and being next day joined by about sixty priests, who found means to escape from Tassisudon, they had the boldness to advance almost to the gates of the palace.

As soon as the Deb Rajah was informed of these particulars he returned to Tassisudon and prepared to oppose the insurgents. He has assembled men from every part of the country; he has collected in the palace a large magazine of stores; he has burnt some villages which were favourable to the enemy; and his principal officers, with a considerable body of troops, are now endeavouring to reduce Simptoka. This enterprise, however, may cost him some trouble; for the place, although not fortified, is strong by its situation, and may stand out for some time against an attack carried on with swords, bows and arrows, and a few matchlocks.

But while each party thus has recourse to arms in support of their cause, they neglect not to urge their respective titles by dint of argument. The friends of Deb Judhur, after expatiating on his great abilities, contend that the government of this country is held for life; that the instances of a chief being deposed are so few, and attended with such peculiar circumstances, that they cannot be construed into a precedent; that besides, supposing such a power is really vested in the clergy, it is in the whole body, but that Deb Judhur was expelled by only one of the lamas and a junto of the priests, without being heard in his defence, while he was absent,

[1] The Targa Penlo was governor of Central Bhutan.

[2] Symtoka of Turner (see p. 125). Eden spells it Simtoka, and describes it as a little fort.

and upon unjust pretences; that the rebuilding of the palace is a service which the subjects are undoubtedly bound to perform; and its being expeditiously finished was equally convenient to the Lama and the priests as to the chief; that so far from his persisting in the war, he had applied to Teshu Lama for his mediation to bring about a peace, and was actually employed for that purpose at the time of the revolution.

Lama-Rimboché's party, on the contrary, insist that as the privilege of electing the chief resides in the Lama and the clergy, they certainly have a right to control his conduct and to remove him for maladministration; and that the history of this country furnishes examples of their having opposed and even put the chief to death. They enlarge upon the severity and oppression of Deb Judhur's government, his disregard of their advice, and, to crown all, they urge that he endeavoured, by introducing a foreign seal into the country, to render this state, naturally free and independent, a province of the Chinese empire.

CHAPTER V.

BHUTAN: NEGOTIATIONS.

1.

INTERVIEW WITH THE DEB RAJAH.[1]

ON the day fixed to receive me I walked to the palace of the Deb Rajah. If there is any pleasure in being gazed at, I had enough of it. Being the first European they had ever seen in these parts, the windows of the palace and the road that led to it were crowded with spectators. I dare say there were 3000. After passing through three courts, and climbing two iron-plated ladders, I was carried into an antechamber hung round with bows and arrows, swords, matchlocks, cane-coiled targets, and other implements of war, and filled with a number of priests, servants, &c., squatted down in different places. Having waited here about half an hour, I was conducted to the Rajah. He was seated upon a throne, or pulpit, if you please (for that is what it is like), raised about two feet from the ground. At entering I made him three low bows, instead of as many prostrations, with which, according to the etiquette of this court, I ought to have approached him. I then walked up and gave him a white satin handkerchief, while my servants laid my presents of spices, cloths, cutlery, &c., before him; after which I was conducted to a cushion prepared for me at the opposite end of the room. As all this passed in a profound silence, I had now time to get over a kind of flurry which it had occasioned. In the meantime several copper trays, with rice, butter, treacle, tea, walnuts, apricots, cucumbers, and other fruits, were set before me, together with a little stool and a china cup. But it is time I should make you acquainted with the company, and let you know where you are.

[1] This account of the interview is from a letter of Mr. Bogle to his sister. The interview is described in the Journal (see p. 24). I, however, insert the second account which Mr. Bogle gave to his sister, as being fuller and more graphic.

The Deb Rajah was dressed in his sacerdotal habit of scarlet cotton, with gilded mitre on his head, and an umbrella with fringes twirling over him. He is a pleasant-looking old man with a smirking countenance. On each side of him his principal officers and ministers to the number of a dozen[1] were seated upon cushions close to the wall, and the rest of the company stood in the area or among the pillars. The panels of the room and also the ceiling were covered with Chinese sewed landscapes and different coloured satins; the pulpit was gilded, and many silver and gilt vases about it; and the floor all around was laid with carpets. At the opposite end of the apartment, and behind where I sat, several large Chinese images were placed in a kind of niche or alcove, with lamps of butter burning before them, and ornamented with elephants' teeth, little silver temples, china-ware, silks, ribbons, and other gewgaws. Among these I must not forget a solitary print of Lady Waldegrave,[2] whom I had afterwards the good fortune to be the means of rescuing out of the hands of these idols; for it happening to strike some of the courtiers—whether the upholsterer, the chamberlain, or a page, I cannot pretend to say—that Lady Waldegrave would make a pretty companion to a looking-glass I had given the Rajah, she was hung up on one of the pillars next the throne, and the mirror on the other; and as I would wish to give you the best and latest accounts, you may depend upon it that things continue still in that posture, agreeable to the arrangement I found at my second visit.

In came a man carrying a large silver kettle, with tea made with butter and spices, and having poured a little into his hand and drank it, he filled the Deb Rajah a cup, then went round to all the ministers, who, as well as every other *Boot*, are always provided

[1] The council of permanent ministers, in Bhutan, is called *Lenchen*, and consists of ten members:

1. Lampa Zimpen (Chief Secretary to the Lama-Rimboché).
2. Donai Zimpen (the Dewan).
3. Timpu Jongpen (Governor of Tassisudon).
4. Punakh Jongpen (Governor of Punakh).
5. Angdu Forung Jongpen (Governor of Angdu Forung).
6. Deb Zimpen (Chief Secretary to the Deb).
7. Jum Kaling (Chief Judge).
8. Paro Penlo (Governor of West Bhutan).
9. Tongso Penlo (Governor of East Bhutan).
10. Targa Penlo (Governor of Central Bhutan).

[2] See note at p. 26.

with a little wooden cup, black glazed in the inside, wrapped in a bit of cloth, and lodged within their tunic, opposite to their heart and next their skin, which keeps it warm and comfortable; and last of all the cup-bearer filled my dish. The Rajah then said a grace, in which he was joined by all the company. When we had finished our tea, and every man had well licked his cup, and deposited it in his bosom, a water tabby gown, like what Aunt Katty used to wear, with well-plated haunches, was brought and put on me; a red satin handkerchief was tied round me for a girdle. I was conducted to the throne, where the Deb Rajah bound my temples with another satin handkerchief, and squeezing them hard betwixt his hands, muttered some prayers over me, after which I was led back to my cushion. We had next a cup of whisky fresh and hot out of the still, which was served round in the same manner as the tea, of which we had also two more dishes, and as many graces; and last of all betel nut.

During these different refreshments a great deal of complimentary conversation passed between me and the Deb through the means of an interpreter, which, however brilliant and witty, I will not here set down. At taking leave the Rajah tied two handkerchiefs together, and threw them over my shoulders by way of a sash. Thus attired, I paid two or three visits to some of the officers in the palace, and walked home, like Mordecai, in great state to my lodgings.

2.

REPORTS TO WARREN HASTINGS.

TASSISUDON, *July* 16, 1774.

Some days before I reached Tassisudon a messenger from Teshu Lama arrived, and delivering a Persian letter, informed me that he had charge of another from his master to you, and of some presents which would arrive in the evening.

Being without a munshi, and little accustomed to the character in which it was written, the Lama's letter cost me some pains to decipher. He begins with his "having heard of my arrival at

Kuch Bahar on my way to him, and, after some formal expressions of satisfaction, informs me that his country being subject to the Emperor of China, whose order it is that he shall admit no Moghul, Hindustani, Patan, or Fringy, he is without remedy, and China being at the distance of a year's journey prevents his writing to the Emperor for permission; desires me therefore to return to Calcutta, and if I have any effects (mâl) to carry them with me, but to retain the letter in my hands, and that he will afterwards send a person to Calcutta." As I cannot make out some of the words at the end of the letter, I beg leave to refer you to the original, which I have now the honour to enclose.

The Gosain, who was down in Calcutta, received also a letter from the Lama, in which the reason assigned for delaying my journey was, as he told me, the great distress his country was in on account of the smallpox, which had obliged him to quit his usual place of residence and retire to the northward.

These two objections, however different, admitted of the same interpretation. Teshu Lama was averse to my visit, and the violence of the smallpox, or an order of the Emperor of China, served for a pretence as well as any other. But from what cause this proceeded I could not then discover. The messenger could give me no information. He was one of the people who had been sent by the Lama to Kuch Bahar. He had gone from thence to Patna and Gaya, and as he was returning home said he was met by some of the Lama's people, who delivered to him the despatches to convey to me. The account he gave of the remainder of his journey was equally unsatisfactory, and he reported the place of the Lama's residence to be at a much greater distance than was consistent with the receipt of his letter, written after the news of my arrival at Kuch Bahar had reached him. I determined to come to no resolution before I had seen the Deb Rajah.

In the evening the Lama's people pressed me much to receive the silks, &c., which he had sent as presents, and to take charge of his letter to you. But as this would have been giving up the point, and would have left me little room to combat those difficulties which I must endeavour to overcome, I excused myself, and begged they would accompany me to Tassisudon.

The Deb Rajah was then about 15 miles from this place,

employed in the performance of some religious duties. I wrote to him with the news of my arrival, and waited two days for his answer. He mentioned "the occasion of his absence; that he would be glad to see me, and had given orders for my accommodation." I entered Tassisudon next day, but his confidential people being with him, all business was suspended until his return, which was not before the 4th instant.

When I considered the situation in which the Deb Rajah stood with respect to the Company, I built great hopes on his ready assistance to remove the objections to my journey, and that his connection with Teshu Lama would render it effectual. But I was soon undeceived; for the Rajah, at my second visit, adopted and even magnified the affair of China; advised me to lay aside all thoughts of prosecuting my journey; and seconded Teshu Lama's desire that I would return to Calcutta. This produced many remonstrances on my part. I had frequent conversations with him and his officers, and left nothing undone to interest him in my behalf; but I could succeed no further than to obtain a letter from him to the Lama, which was given with so much reluctance that I am not sanguine about its good effects.

In this situation my hopes of seeing Teshu Lama were chiefly founded on the Gosain. As my journey had been undertaken upon his assurances, he was engaged in honour to see it accomplished, and I endeavoured to strengthen this principle by more powerful motives. While he remained at Tassisudon he could be of no service, and I readily consented to his proceeding to the Lama.

The messenger renewed his solicitations that I would take charge of his master's despatches, and I advised him to proceed to Calcutta. He could not, he said, without orders. I excused myself from receiving them on the same grounds, and they are to remain with the Deb Rajah until I am favoured with your commands. The Lama's letter to you, from a Bhutan copy which was read to me, contains nothing more than the prohibition of the Court of China with respect to Fringies. By declining to receive it I preserve a stronger hold upon the Lama, keep the negotiation open, and leave you at liberty to act as you may think proper.

The Gosain set out yesterday, in company with the messenger and the Bhutanese, who was down in Calcutta, and carried the Rajah's letter, with a few lines from me to the Lama. They are obliged, they say, to travel by an indirect road on account of the smallpox, and may be twenty days before they arrive with the Lama; but they assure me of an answer in less than two months.

The Rajah urged my return to Bengal as strongly as he decently could, but the expectation of answers from the Lama and from Calcutta afforded me reasons to prolong my stay.

I beg therefore to be informed of your pleasure in the event of the Lama persisting to refuse me admittance into his country, as well as in regard to his letter and presents.

TASSISUDON, *August* 20, 1774.

I wish it was in my power to explain with more certainty the Lama's motives for refusing me admittance into his country. I am persuaded it proceeds from a suspicion of Europeans. I can perceive this disposition in the Deb Rajah. On the journey I was sometimes led over rocks and mountains, with a plain road running parallel on the side of the river. The Gosain and his baggage were once carried the one way, I the other. My servants are not suffered to purchase the smallest article but through the Rajah's people. Some persons who visited me before his arrival have been forbidden since. His extreme solicitude about my departure, besides other circumstances too trifling to mention, are all strong symptoms of this jealousy. Now, as Teshu Lama's country and this are contiguous, the language and faith the same, the Rajah acknowledges the Lama to be his religious superior, and sends him annually money and produce, which the one styles a donative, the other a tribute. In accounting for the conduct of two persons so intimately connected, one may almost venture to decide from analogy. One day in conversing with the interpreter he said to me, I believe unwittingly, "that he did not imagine Teshu Lama would allow me to enter his country, as the neighbouring Rajahs would advise him against it."

I have been obliged, on account of this jealous eye with which all my actions are viewed, to pursue a conduct very inconsistent with the purposes of my mission, and to appear little inquisitive, particularly about the country or its trade, lest it should have raised up fresh obstacles to my journey to the Lama. His servants, however, being now gone, and my continuance here for two months certain, I am no longer under the necessity of following the same plan. But this place is very little favourable to my commercial inquiries. It is monkish to the greatest degree. The Rajah, his priests, his officers, and his servants, are all immured like state prisoners in an immense large palace, and there are not above a dozen other houses in the town.

Upon my leaving Dinajpúr, Mr. Lambert gave me a letter to Muhammad Taki, the Dewan at Rangpúr, who came to visit me. In speaking about Bhutan, he sent for a merchant who had been all over the country as far as Lhasa, spoke the language, and who, he said, would go with me if I chose it. I put a good many questions to him, and he seemed an intelligent man; but afraid of hampering myself with the Gosain, I did not ask him to accompany me. It has since occurred to me that this person may be a useful agent. His residence in Bengal will serve to secure his fidelity, and in any scheme for extending the communication and intercourse between that country and Bhutan, it would be easy to give him such encouragement as would make it his interest to promote it. The trade between Lhasa and the low country is, as I am informed, principally carried on by the way of Patna and Nepal through the means of Moghuls and Kashmiris, in which, as he can have no concern, he would have no scruples in endeavouring to discover new sources; and the narrow traffic in which he himself is now engaged must lie very wide of those distant and extensive channels which you wish to open.

Should this proposal meet with your approbation, might I request you would be pleased to issue your orders to Muhammad Taki to encourage this person to proceed to me, and to despatch him without delay. I have taken the liberty to write to Taki on the subject, but have no reason to think that either he or the merchant will enter heartily into it unless they know that it is your pleasure.

In my former advices I did myself the honour to acquaint you with the obstacles which Teshu Lama raised to my journey, on pretence of an order from the Emperor of China forbidding the admittance of Fringies into his country. I am now happy to inform you that he has at length consented to my proceeding, and I propose to continue my journey as soon as I have the pleasure of hearing from you. On this occasion I have no letters from the Lama myself, but the Deb Rajah informs me that the Gosain and the Bhutanese who were down in Calcutta are sent by the Lama to wait my arrival on the borders of his country. Having received no letters from Calcutta except immediately upon my arrival, I am afraid of some miscarriage, and therefore forward these few lines by a barkára.

Tassisudon, *September* 18, 1774.

A few days before the receipt of your orders the Deb Rajah read to me a letter from the Teshu Lama, informing him that he had written to Lhasa, the residence of the Dalai Lama, on the subject of my passports, and had obtained their consent to my proceeding on the journey, provided I came with only a few attendants; and that he (the Lama) had therefore sent back the Gosain, who had been down in Calcutta, to wait for me on the borders of his country.

From several circumstances I am persuaded the former objections to my journey took their rise, or at least were cherished by the Deb. Even after the Lama's permission he endeavoured to dissuade me from proceeding. I believe there is no great cordiality between the two. The Lama's mediation in regard to the peace was procured during the government of his predecessor, who, upon his expulsion in February last, fled to him, and is now in his country. The present chief is jealous of this, as well as apprehensive of the Nepal Rajah taking him by the hand, and would be glad if the Teshu Lama would give him up, when I imagine there would be little scruple of throwing him into the Pachu-Chinchu, as was done with a chief who was deposed about forty or fifty years ago.

Tassisudon, *October* 8, 1774.

I have been honoured with the receipt of your commands of the 9th August by the merchant from Rangpúr.

In several conversations with the Deb Rajah and his officers I represented to them your wish to extend the intercourse between

Bengal and the northern nations, and the advantages which would thence arise to this state; that Bhutan, being the channel of communication, would naturally share in the benefits of an extensive commerce; that on your part you would be ready to afford all encouragement and protection to the trade from this; and that a mutual intercourse between the two countries would serve to strengthen and cement that amity and good understanding which is now happily established. In answer, I received assurances of the Rajah's wish to cultivate your friendship; that I was now on my way to the Teshu Lama, and that on my return he would listen favourably to any proposal from you.

From the information I have been able to gather concerning the trade between these countries and Bengal, I am led to think that Teshu Lama will be more disposed to promote its extension than the Deb Rajah, and that if I can succeed in gaining the former's consent, he may be brought to exert his influence, which is very considerable, with the latter; that as my deputation is immediately to the Lama, who is undoubtedly the religious superior and pretends to a paramount authority also in the temporal affairs of this state, he will naturally expect that he should be considered as the principal in these negotiations; and the present unsettled state of this country is abundantly unfavourable for concluding them here. For these reasons I intend to try my success at the Lama's court before I push the Deb Rajah any further.

The adherents of Deb Judhur, the former chief, have made an insurrection in his favour, which, although at present not formidable, occupies fully the attention of the Rajah and his officers. I have therefore taken leave, and propose to continue my journey northwards to-morrow.

I have been solicited here to request that you would be pleased to issue your order that the annual caravan from this country to Rangpúr may meet with every assistance and protection, and have free liberty to trade according to ancient custom. As the peace has been so lately concluded, it would be a satisfaction to the Rajah to receive your *parwana*[1] to this purpose before the departure of the caravan.

[1] A permit or custom-house pass.

TASSISUDON, *October* 11, 1774.

The merchant from Rangpúr arrived here a few days after my address of the 18th. I hope to benefit considerably by his knowledge of the language and commerce of these countries.

The annual caravan from this to Rangpúr is principally an adventure of the Deb Rajah, his ministers, and provincial governors. Each of them sends an agent, with his tanyans,[1] musk, cowtails, coarse red blankets, or striped woollen cloth half-yard wide. The other Bhutanese go under their protection. The returns from thence, consisting chiefly of broadcloth, spices, dyes, Malda cloths, go almost wholly into Teshu Lama's country either as tribute or in trade. In the last case they are converted into Pelong[2] handkerchiefs, flowered satins, tea, salt, wool, &c.

This traffic is very beneficial to the Rajah and his people, and they are jealous of it. One can show them the advantages their country may receive from an extension of commerce; but it is more difficult to make their own interest appear in it. But Teshu Lama, I believe, has no such warp. His territories, being the heart, ought to benefit by a large circulation of trade and the resort of strangers; and unless his dependence upon China should stand in the way, I would fain hope for some success with him. As to what you were pleased to propose about making Tassisudon the central point of communication with Lhasa, I consider it only as a *dernier ressort*, and as my way is now open, I have not mentioned it until I can see what is to be done otherwise.

The more I see of the Bhutanese, the more I am pleased with them. The common people are good-humoured, downright, and, I think, thoroughly trusty. The statesmen have some of the art which belongs to their profession. They are the best-built race of men I ever saw; many of them very handsome, with complexions as fair as the French. I have sometimes been tempted to wish I could substitute their portrait in the place of my friend Paima's.

The Deb Rajah, with all his court and the inhabitants of the neighbouring villages, in imitation, I suppose, of their Scythian ancestors, migrate from this place in about two months hence. Their winter quarters are at Punakha, two days' journey to the

[1] Tangun ponies. (See note at p. 17.) [2] See note at p. 16.

south-east, and the climate there is so much hotter that it produces mangos, pine-apples, &c., and they say cassia. The palace, I am told, is larger than the one here, and well finished. I am to see it on my return.

There are few trees in this part of the country; but I have abundance of promises from the great men of getting me seeds, and have employed a Bhutanese on purpose. As to plants, I leave them till my return, when the sap will be down, except a slip of sweet brier which goes by this opportunity. There are plenty of cow-tailed cows, but the weather is too hot for them to go into Bengal. I have not been able to get a live musk goat, but have sent a skin, likewise a sentimental cup, or the skull of a Lama guru.

The weather is growing very cold; the thermometer under 50° in the mornings. I have had great benefit from the shawl cloth you were so good as to give me. Lama-Rimboché has now presented me with his yellow satin gown, lined with lambskins, and the Deb Rajah with about a dozen of blankets, so that I am well fortified.

I took the liberty of recommending the Deb Rajah's desire to have your *parwana* for the caravan proceeding to Rangpúr, and I have been applied to here by the Paro Penlo[1] that his agent may go to Dinajpúr, according to ancient custom. I am aware that some of the Bhutanese would wish to proceed farther, and even to Calcutta. The late war has enlarged their minds. They hope to purchase many articles of trade on better terms there, and I believe also they would be glad to get some firearms. As it is my duty to lay before you whatever occurs to me on the business upon which I am deputed, I beg leave to submit to you that, although you allow their caravan to proceed to Rangpúr and Dinajpúr as formerly, as a proof of your inclination to protect their trade, that any new concessions ought to be on stipulation; and I confess the privilege of sending their agents into the interior parts of Bengal is one engine I hope to avail myself of with some advantage. I shall have need of them all to bring me to a point in which their own particular interest is concerned.

The trade between Rangpúr and Bhutan may extend to about two or two and a half lakhs a year; that through Nepal amounts,

[1] The Governor of Western Bhutan.

I am told, to three or four times that sum.[1] Such husbandmen as join the caravan for Rangpúr pay for this permission. There are two or three houses at Rangpúr which carry on a trade through this country to Lhasa—the merchant who has joined me is one of them. They are restricted from broadcloth and some other articles. Their dealings may yearly amount to about a lakh of the above sum.

3.

FROM WARREN HASTINGS TO THE RAJAH OF BHUTAN, DATED 28TH NOVEMBER, 1774.

I have repeatedly heard from Mr. Bogle the news of your welfare, which gave me the greatest pleasure. That gentleman also informs me in the strongest terms of gratitude of the many kindnesses and civilities you have shown to him. This also calls on me for my acknowledgments, as I consider every assistance you have given to Mr. Bogle as an obligation conferred on myself. Accept, therefore, of my sincerest thanks. Agreeably to your desire communicated to me through Mr. Bogle, I enclose you a *parwana* for the encouragement of any of your subjects who may wish to travel with caravans to Rangpúr and other districts under the Company's authority for the purposes of trade. It is my earnest desire that the friendship between you and the Company may be strengthened daily. I have directed Mr. Bogle to settle on his return such articles between your subjects and the Company's as may be most agreeable to you and for your benefit. I shall write you more fully on all these subjects by the return of the caravan.

I send you a piece of cloth as a token of friendship, and request that you will frequently make me happy by the news of your welfare.

Parwana enclosed in the foregoing.

Notice is hereby given to all the merchants of Bhutan, that the strictest orders have been issued to the officers at Rangpúr and

[1] It reached a total of 33 lakhs in 1831, according to Mr. Hodgson's report to Government. It was in the hands of Newars, Kashmiris, and merchants of Benares and Patna, and is so still.

Ghoraghat[1] dependent on the Subah of Bengal (the paradise of nations), that they do not obstruct the passage of the Bhutan merchants to those places for the purpose of carrying on their trade as formerly, but that they afford every assistance to their caravans. They are therefore required not to entertain the least apprehension, but with the greatest security and confidence to come into Bengal and carry on their traffic as formerly. Placing an entire reliance on this, let them act agreeably thereto.

4.

FROM WARREN HASTINGS TO THE RAJAH OF BHUTAN, WRITTEN THE 6TH OF JANUARY, 1775.

I have received your letter and understand the contents. It is my most earnest desire to increase and establish the friendship between you and this government on the firmest footing. Nothing shall be wanting on my part to promote this end. I am particularly desirous that your subjects should be encouraged to come into Bengal for the purposes of trade, in consequence of which, at Mr. Bogle's desire, I sent you a *parwana* for their encouragement. I have lately heard, from report only, that some obstructions have been made to the trade in cotton between your subjects and those of this government, in consequence of which I have written the strongest injunctions to have them removed: by this you will be convinced of my desire to promote your advantage to the utmost, not only on this but on every other occasion. With respect to the accounts, I will take another opportunity of writing to you concerning them. As the distance between us is so great that many obstructions to the trade of your subjects, and causes of complaint may arise, of which I may be wholly ignorant, and as I wish to prevent any such, it would be proper that a vackil should reside here on your part to deliver your letters to me, and to lay before me any representations you may have to make to me.

I send you a pair of shawls, as a token of friendship, of which I beg your acceptance.

[1] Or the horse-ferry; a town, once of great importance, on the Kuratia, a tributary of the Tista, in the Dinajpúr district of Bengal.

CHAPTER VI.

SUGGESTIONS RESPECTING BHUTAN AND ASSAM.

THE country that has been the scene of our military operations[1] against the Bhutanese extends over a distance, as troops march, of about 85 miles.[2] A great part of this tract consists of almost impenetrable jungles and immense forests of sal trees, and, taken at the rate of 9 kos from the mountains, forms that strip that by the treaty is ceded to the Bhutanese. This country is intersected by numerous nullahs and small rivers, deep and rapid. The great rivers are the Tístà, Manshi, Tursa, and Baidak. All these rivers, the Tísta excepted,[3] run in a south-eastern direction into the Brahmaputra, and are navigable for six months of the year as high as within 10 kos of the foot of the mountains; but their not communicating with the Ganges renders the fine timber on their banks but of little value. The produce of this strip, where cultivated, consists of rice, mustard seed, tobacco, some opium, and about 40,000 maunds of fine cotton annually; to the eastward it yields some black pepper and *munga* silk.[4] The country, however, is extremely populous. The trade carried on with the Bhutanese is by way of barter. They pay little or no revenue to the Deb Rajah, and living easy under his government, are much attached to the Bhutan interest; and, indeed, from the nature of their situation, they can never be independent of it.

Our troops having acted in this tract[5] of country was the reason of their having suffered so much, as it is low and unhealthy through the whole year. The water, however, is in general very good; but the great moisture of the air, and the great and sudden changes of the weather, occasion the frequency of intermittent fevers of the

[1] See note at p. 1.

[2] The Bengal Dúárs.

[3] But see Memoir on 'Indian Surveys,' p. 260.

[4] *Anthera Assama.* See a full account of the cultivation of *munga* silk in Assam, at p. 112 of Mr. Geoghegan's 'Report on Silk in India.'

[5] The tract here described is comprised in the western portion of the Bengal Dúárs.

most obstinate kind. It is to be remarked that the Bhutanese[1] are as subject to them as our troops, and never, if they can avoid it, remain in the low country during the rains.

I would beg leave to recommend, should there ever be occasion again to employ troops against the Bhutanese, a different mode of carrying on the service to that which was followed. Acting on the defensive serves only to protract the service, and from the number of small detachments necessary to form the chain of posts for covering so extensive a frontier, such a course occasions great expense to Government, extreme fatigue to the troops, and gives the enemy every advantage they could wish, especially as they can depend on ample supplies from the country between their posts and the hills, and have always a secure retreat in them.

For these reasons acting offensively is to be preferred. There are two ways in which this may be done; either by penetrating into their country at once, or else by seizing and garrisoning the passes of Chichakotta, Buxa-Dúar, and Repu-Dúar; for though they reckon eighteen passes, these are the principal ones. Three companies would be sufficient to garrison each of them, and a flying detachment of five companies would answer the purpose of supplying provisions or exchanging the garrisons if necessary. The passes of the Chamurchi and Repu-Dúars are the most practicable, although that of the Buxa-Dúar is the most frequented, owing to its central situation, and being opposite to Bulrampúr and the nearest to Rangpúr. The troops should be ready early in November to take possession of these posts; and I am firmly of opinion the Bhutanese would submit to any measures we should think proper to dictate to them; but in case they proved obstinate, there would be time to follow the other alternative, by entering their country and finishing the expedition before the rains set in. If there were two complete battalions employed on this service, I think it would be best to act separately, entering the two passes I have mentioned above. There would be no occasion for troops in Bahar whilst they were in Bhutan, as they would draw the whole force and attention of the Bhutanese. The Bhutanese have only six hundred men in pay as soldiers; but though their government is elective, they hold their

[1] Hindi Bhōt makes Bhōtia, equal the native Bod and Bodpa, for our Tibet and Tibetan. Bhutan and Bhutaner, or Bhutanese, are distinct, and equal the native Lho and Lhopa. The two should not be confounded.

lands by military service, and every man in their country is a soldier when called on. In short, the feudal system prevails amongst them in its full force. One custom amongst them is remarkable, and, I believe, peculiar to them. When they rise to any post of honour and trust in their country they are separated from their families, and never after permitted to hold any intercourse with them, lest their attachment to their children should induce them to attempt rendering the government hereditary in their families.

Should an expedition against them ever take place, everything necessary should be provided before the troops enter the jungles, that they might not contract those diseases incidental to that climate, and which they would not fail to do if they remained any time in it.

The greatest difficulty that would attend an expedition of this nature would be the carriage of provisions and ammunition. Twenty-five or thirty days is as little as they could think of entering the hills with, and from the nature of the service a larger supply of ammunition would be required than the same number of troops would require for any other service. If guns could be carried they would be of great use. This would be difficult, and if at all done must be by elephants.

But supposing all the success that could be expected should attend an expedition into Bhutan, I can see no great advantage that could redound from it to the Company further than what they now enjoy—possession of Bahar and quiet from the Bhutanese. The trade carried on is scarce an object to the Company; as for keeping possession of any part of it if conquered, or forming a settlement there, I consider it as impracticable unless done with the consent of the Bhutanese, which I believe will never be obtained. Attempting it by force will never answer. The difficulties are insurmountable, at least without a force and expense much greater than the object is worth. This does not arise from the power of the Bhutanese. Two battalions, I think, would reduce their country, but two brigades would not keep the communication open, and if that is cut off the conquest could be of no use. In all the schemes that I have heard of for an expedition to Nepal this has been overlooked, on a supposition that if a conquest was effected, all the rest would follow, of course; but that, I am convinced, would not be the case, and when the natural strength of the country is considered this will appear still more forcibly. For those reasons I am no advocate for an expedition into these countries unless the people should commence hostilities, and then it should be done only with a view to reduce them to peace on such terms as should appear honourable and advantageous to the Company; and this would be easily effected by acting vigorously for one season.

The objections I have made against an expedition into Bhutan hold good with respect to Nepal and Lhasa, for this sole reason, that a communication cannot be kept open; and should our troops march into these countries, they must consider all communication with the low country out of the question till they return.

With regard to our treaty with the Bhutanese, I am of opinion they will adhere firmly to it, as they are, I believe, fully convinced of their inability to carry on a war against the Company; and I am of opinion the battalions in Bahar may be withdrawn if wanted for other service, because while the Bhutanese continue quiet they are not wanted. Should they recommence hostilities, our battalions would not be sufficient to reduce them. It would not, however, be amiss to keep two subalterns with two companies in Bahar fort for another season, when, if the Bhutanese strictly observe the treaty, they may be recalled.

An open trade with Bhutan, Nepal, and Lhasa has been considered as an object worthy the attention of Government, but the jealousy of the nation prevents this being obtained on pacific terms,[1] and the natural strength and situation of these countries render it extremely difficult, if not impracticable, to do it by force. An open and unrestrained trade and intercourse with Assam, considered separately, is an object of much greater consequence; but when it is known that it will include all the advantages attending the other, it must of course become a much more desirable object. The Bhutanese, the inhabitants of the Gorkha Rajah's country, the natives of Lhasa, and of many other countries lying north-west of the Brahmaputra, carry on a constant trade to Assam. A settlement formed on the banks of the Brahmaputra, near the capital, would become the mart for supplying all the countries lying north-west of

[1] By arms and diplomacy we strove to uphold the old trade with Nepal prior to the Gorkha conquest, but were foiled by the malaria, and, since the conquest, by the jealousy adverted to.

the Brahmaputra as well as those countries to the eastward of that river; it would open an ample field for commerce in general, and, considering its northern situation, would greatly increase the demand for European commodities, and particularly for broad-cloths. Assam produces numerous and valuable articles for exportation; the jealousy of the government has, however, restricted the trade in such a manner that it is of little advantage to Bengal, the whole amount not exceeding six or seven lakhs per annum, and this mostly by way of barter; and when a balance arises we pay it in silver. By this means the trade is rather disadvantageous to the countries under the government of the Company, especially as most of what we receive of them is for home consumption. The natives of Assam are permitted to trade in the Company's territories without let or molestation; the same liberty may therefore be demanded in return from their government, and, if refused, insisted on with justice. Their jealousy of foreigners, however, would probably induce them either to refuse or evade this request; but it might be easily enforced, without the risk of failure that would attend the hill expeditions.

Assam itself is an open country of great extent, and by all accounts well cultivated and inhabited; the road into it either by land or the Brahmaputra lies open. The communication can always be preserved. The advantages of a river navigable the whole year, whether considered with regard to commerce or war, are obvious, as the great objection against entering Nepal, &c., arises from the difficulty of keeping open the communications; so, on the other hand, the easy access to Assam, whether by land or water, invites us to the attempt.[1] The distance of a settlement near the capital would not be more, or but very little more, from the Presidency than it is from there to Patna; the trade would be carried on entirely by water, and as the banks of the Brahmaputra are covered with fine timber, all the boats and vessels necessary for carrying on the trade might be built on the spot, by what I learnt from the people who had been permitted to trade to that country. The river known to us by the name of Brahmaputra is but a branch of that great river. It divides above the

[1] In Mr. Hodgson's report stress is laid on the advantages of the Assam routes into Tibet; and the success of the tea cultivation in and around Assam gives additional weight to all that is urged in that report.

capital of Assam. The body of the river runs in an eastern direction; and it is said the banks of it are well furnished with teak timber of great size. This would prove highly advantageous, whether for importation, building of vessels either for trade or for pursuing our discoveries down that great river; and if pursued would open a trade and intercourse with countries unexplored by Europeans. I think there is little reason to apprehend a failure if the attempt is made, for should unforeseen difficulties arise with regard to supply of provisions on our first entering the country, this might easily be remedied by drawing them from Bengal for a short time; and I have not a doubt but our troops would meet with ample supplies after they had once passed the frontiers of Assam. The stores necessary for the expedition would be conveyed by water, and the boats so employed would be sufficient to procure any provisions that might be wanted on our setting out. Assam, as I have already observed, yields many valuable articles for exportation. Gold is a considerable article of inland trade; Bhutan, Lhasa, and Nepal supply them both with gold and silver, and when the restrictions against exportation are taken off, it must give the balance of trade greatly in our favour.[1] Supposing it should not turn out so great an object as I have represented, still it cannot with reason be doubted that it would more than reimburse the Company, by the advantageous terms they would be glad to give us in point of trade, setting all acquisition of territory out of the question; and I make no doubt but that, a few months after our entering Assam, the troops might be paid and provisioned without making any demands on the Company's treasury. It may be objected that a great part of what I have advanced is unsupported by proofs; but it ought to be remembered that in all the valuable discoveries and acquisitions that have been made these have always at first been wanting. We have, however, the reports of those that have visited that country, and that is more than is usual in cases of this nature. Probable conjecture has been found sufficient to stimulate enterprising spirits, and success has generally justified their undertakings of this kind when conducted with spirit, resolution, and prudence.

[1] There were large receipts of gold from Tibet through Nepal up to the Gorkha conquest of Nepal. The last order received by Mr. Hodgson, as Resident, directed him to report to the Government the causes of the cessation of the import of gold from Tibet.

CHAPTER VII.

THE JOURNEY TO TIBET.

1.

FROM TASSISUDON TO PARI-JONG.

WHILE I was at Tassisudon an insurrection broke out in favour of Deb Judhur,[1] the former chief; and the disturbances which this occasioned protracted my stay. The malcontents, after a fruitless attempt on the palace of Tassisudon, seized Simptoka, a castle in its neighbourhood, in which they found arms and ammunition.

There are no cannon in this country. The castles are built on eminences, with lofty and thick walls which have loopholes; the windows are high, project out, and are provided with heaps of stones to throw upon assailants. The doors are strong and secured by bars of iron; the entrance to some of them is by a covered way, defended by towers; and they want but the mote and the bridge to resemble the Gothic castles of our ancestors. There are only two ways of reducing them—by fire or by famine. The first appears easy enough, for as there are no arches, the roofs and floors are all of wood. But Simptoka having been built by Deb Seklu, a very popular Rajah, and being full of furniture and effects belonging to the government, it was resolved to blockade it. Troops were accordingly collected from the distant provinces, and three of the roads were stopped up. The fourth, however, was still open. The Deb Rajah's force increased every day. Deb Judhur's party saw no prospect of assistance; and after a siege of ten days they abandoned Simptoka, and being favoured by moonlight, escaped over the mountains into Teshu Lama's country.

I left Tassisudon on the 13th of October, 1774, the day of their retreat, in company with Mr. Hamilton; Mirza Settar, a native of Kashmir, who had joined me from Rangpúr, and spoke

[1] See *ante*, p. 37.

the language of this country; the Tibetan Paima, a messenger of Teshu Lama, who had been sent for me; and a servant of the Deb Rajah, who was to attend me to the borders of his country.

Our way was by Rinjipu, commonly called Paro-gaund.[1] The direct road is over the mountains, and we were to have travelled over it, escorted by a guard. This, however, was now unnecessary, and we took the low road along the banks of the Chinchu. It was the same by which we had come from Buxa-Dúar. We passed Simptoka, and came up with a party of the Deb Rajah's men. They halted at a little village, and their leader sent for us. He had formerly been Kalling,[2] or secretary, to the Deb Rajah, and had been lately promoted to the office of Donnai,[3] or Head Dewan. He enjoys the first place in the chief's favour, and his sagacity and superior abilities entitle him to it. In anything that relates to the government of his own country, he might be pitted against many a politic minister. As a philosopher, he would twist him round his finger. Of a truth, an ounce of mother-wit is worth a pound of clergy.

The Donnai was sitting on the ground surrounded by his men. He gave me part of his carpet. We had a dram of whisky. He told me of the escape of the insurgents from Simptoka; that he was in pursuit of them by the foot of the mountains, while another detachment had taken the upper road. As soon as we left him, I saw a village on the top of the mountain in flames: it was a punishment for its attachment to the Deb Judhur.

A soldier in Bhutan has not a distinct profession. Every man is girt with a sword, and trained to the use of the bow. The hall of every public officer is hung round with matchlocks, with swords and shields. In times of war or danger, his servants and retainers are armed with these; the inhabitants, assembled from the different villages, are put under his command, and he marches in person against the enemy. The common weapons are a broadsword of a good temper, with shagreen handle; a cane-coiled target, painted

[1] Paro. Turner also gives the names of Parogong, and Rinjipo, p. 177.

[2] The Joom Kalling, in Eden's List (p. 113), is the chief judge. Pemberton calls him Kalling Zimpé (p 54). Turner has Cullum.

[3] According to Eden (p. 112), the Donnai Zimpen is the Dewan; Pemberton has Donnay Zimpe. He holds the second seat in the Council.

with streaks of red; a bow formed of a piece of bamboo; a quiver of a junk of the same tree, the arrows of reeds, barbed, and often covered with a poison said to be so subtile that the slightest wound becomes mortal in a few hours. Some few are armed with a pike. They put great confidence in firearms; but are not so cunning in the use of the matchlock, as of their ancient weapons, the sword and the bow. Their warlike garb is various and not uniform. Some wear a cap quilted, or of cane and sugar-loaf shape, with a tuft of horse-hair stained; others, an iron-netted hood, or a helmet with the like ornament; under these they often put false locks to supply the want of their own hair, which among this tribe of Bhutanese is worn short. Sometimes a coat of mail is to be seen. In peace as well as in war, they are dressed in short trousers, like the Highland philabeg; woollen hose, soled with leather and gartered under the knee; a jacket or tunic, and over all two or three striped blankets. Their leaders only are on horseback, and are covered with a cap, rough with red-dyed cowtails. They sleep in the open air, and keep themselves warm with their plaids and their whisky. When they go to war or to an engagement, they whoop and howl, to encourage each other and intimidate the enemy. They are fond of attacking in the night time. As to their courage in battle, those can best speak who have tried it. I saw only some skirmishes.

We arrived at Lumbolong towards night, the 14th of October. Our room was like a large warehouse, supported by posts. A fire was lighted upon a stone in the middle, and as there are no vents, we suffered as much from its smoke as we benefited by its heat. For want of a more polite entertainment, I sent for some women who had come with the baggage, and had a Bhutan song. There is no giving a description of it; and as I know nothing of music, I could not take it down. It is more like church chimes than anything else. Some of the notes are lengthened out as long as the breath will last, and people used to climbing mountains are far from being short-winded. A battle with fists between our guide and the landlord—the second I have seen here. What a contentious place is Lumbolong!

We left it the next morning, and continued to descend the Chinchu, till it is joined by the Pachu,[1] near Paku. Here we

[1] The Parchoo of Eden, p. 91.

crossed it, and entered the narrow valley through which this last runs rapidly. The mountains along which we passed are bare and rocky, and there are no houses to be seen except the dwellings of some fakirs. On the opposite side is a village, and some wheat fields.

A heavy shower of snow had fallen two days before we left Tassisudon, and the tops of all the mountains were white with it. The Bengalis, when they got up in the morning, were much surprised at the sight of it. They inquired of the Bhutanese, who told them it was white cloths, which God Almighty sent down to cover the mountains and keep them warm. This solution required, to be sure, some faith; but it was to them just as probable as that it was rain, or that they were afterwards to meet with water hard as glass, and be able to walk across a river. When different climes exhibit such incredible phenomena to the inhabitants of other countries, why should not the accounts of travellers be treated with indulgence, and even the adventures of Sinbad the Sailor be read with some grains of allowance?

We arrived at Essana after midday on the 15th of October. This is a village situated in a small but fruitful valley. Everybody was busy with the harvest. As soon as a field of rice is ripe the water is drained off, and the stream that supplied it diverted into a different channel. It is then cut down with teethless sickles, and is either placed against the narrow ridges which surround the fields and separate them from each other, or it is laid flat upon the stubble-ground. In a few days it is built up in little ricks, regularly, but without being bound. From these it is taken down; a beam is raised breast high, and supported upon two posts; under it a large mat is spread, and the men and women, leaning upon it, tread out the rice with their feet. A different method is used with the wheat, which is bearded. It is tied up in small sheaves. In some places (Kepta) they separate the grain from the straw by burning it; in others (Tassisudon) they thrash it out with flails. The wheat is reaped in the beginning of June.

In all these different occupations of husbandry the heavy burden lies upon the fair sex: they have a hard lot of it. Besides all this, the economy of the family falls to their share. They have to dress the victuals and feed the swine. They are not much troubled indeed with washing or scrubbing: the fashion of the country renders this quite unnecessary. But not unfrequently one sees them with a child at the breast, staggering up a hill with a heavy load, or knocking corn, a labour scarcely less arduous. And with all this bitter draught they appear to have few of those sweetenings which might render it more palatable. They have none of the markets, fairs, churches, and weddings of England; they have none of the skipping and dancing of France; they have none of the devotion of the lower people in other Roman Catholic countries; they have none of the bathings, bracelets, &c., of the Bengali; and yet I know not how it comes to pass, but they seem to bear it all without murmuring; and, having nothing else to deck themselves with, they plait their hair with garlands of leaves or twigs of trees. The resources of a light heart and a sound constitution are infinite.

Proceeding up the Pachu, we arrived at Rinjipu, the capital of the province, on the 16th of October. I was lodged in a long hall adjoining the temple. The palace is a miniature of Tassisudon. The valley is large, well cultivated, and filled with detached villages. In one of these there is a bazaar, the only one I believe in the country, and two Kashmiri houses; but there is no calling it a town.

The government of Paro-gaund is the most important under the Deb Rajah. The person who now holds it is a cousin of Lama-Rimboché, who, upon the late revolution, laid aside the habit of a fakir, which he had assumed under the former administration, and returned to worldly affairs. His jurisdiction is very extensive. Besides the districts from which he takes his title of Paro Penlo, the governments of Dalim-kotta, Lukhi-Dúar, Chamurchi-Dúar, and all the districts towards the Murungs[1] are under him. He has the power of life and death in his hands. He repairs once a year to Tassisudon, and pays a fixed annual revenue to the Deb Rajah; but delivers in no account of his administration. He retains, however, his office only during pleasure, and a mandate from the presence reduces him to the level of other subjects.

The revenue of Paro-gaund, as well as of most of the interior

[1] The Murungs are forests at the foot of the Sikkim and Nepal mountains. This is, in fact, the local Nepalese name for the *Terai*.—'Hooker's Himalayan Journal,' i. p. 378.

districts, is paid chiefly in grain, horses, blankets, &c., and the money comes principally from Lukhi-Dúar, Buxa-Dúar, and other Dúars or outlets into the low country. But I must not here pretend to give particulars.

I was waked in the morning with the firing of guns and the war whoop. I thought we had not yet done with our fighting; but it turned out to be only the head of a rebel, which they were carrying into the palace in procession, with a white handkerchief as a flag before it.

I stayed two or three days at Paro-gaund; visited the Penlo; received a reinforcement of blankets from him, and continued my journey on the 19th October. I also received a visit from the Donnai.

We were obliged to make short journeys on account of the coolies. We stopped at Duko-jong[1] on the night of the 20th, and were lodged in the castle, romantically enough situated on the top of a mount. Under most of the windows are hives of bees in the open air. They have cold quarters of it.

Our next stage was Chanon,[2] which we reached on the 21st. It consists of four or five houses on the banks of the Pachu, surrounded with turnip fields, for which alone it is famous.

The road from Tassisudon had been pretty level; we could ride most part of the way. Our next stage was extremely steep; keeping close to the Pachu, which dashes over rocks, wet with its spray. One place was very picturesque. High perpendicular rocks were overhead. The Pachu, now reduced to a large stream, running rapidly by: on the other side a high round mountain, covered with silver firs and pines, intermixed with other trees, red, yellow, and all those colours with which a natural wood is variegated towards the close of autumn. The summits of the hills were white with snow. When we got up to the highest part of the road, we found the sides of the mountains entirely bare, owing, I suppose, to their being exposed to the north wind. We met a flock of sheep, the first we had seen;[3] small, with good wool.

[1] Apparently the Dukka-jung of Turner, p. 182; and Dakya-jung of Eden, p. 91. In the Bhutan map of 1874 it is Domgit Zong.

[2] The last Bhutan village on this road. Turner calls it Sana, p. 184.

[3] Tibetan sheep. They are as numerous and fine in Tibet as they are rare and poor in Himalaya or the Cis-nivean countries.

We met also droves of cow-tailed cattle; they are used as beasts of burden, and were then carrying skins, with the wool upon them, to Paro-gaund, where the coarse blankets are mostly manufactured. They were almost all black, very rough, uncouth make, a large hump, short legs, and the large bushy tail for which they are noted.[1]

There are no inhabitants at Gaissar,[2] a place we arrived at on the 22nd of October. There is only a low house, like a stable without doors. We were obliged to bring our provisions and fuel from the last stage. We required it all to keep us warm. The hills all about were covered with snow; and to mend the matter, a heavy shower of it came on in the night time.

This was all frozen in the morning, and most of our road to Pari-jong was covered with snow. When we got down the hill to the Pachu, we found the stones and bridges hanging with icicles. There were no houses to be seen, and only some herds of cattle feeding on the sides of the valley, which was bounded on the north-west by a hill between two moderate mountains. On reaching the top we found six heaps of stones with banners. They serve to mark the boundary between the Deb Rajah's country and that of the Lama, which now lay before us; plain and open to the north; hilly to the west; behind, to the east and south, mountains. I arrived at Pari-jong on October 23.

I found the Bhutanese, who was down in Calcutta, waiting for me. I have dismissed the Deb Rajah's servant, and am to proceed towards Shigatzé in a day or two.

2.

FROM PARI-JONG[3] TO DESHERIPGAY.

The first object that strikes you, as you go down the hill into Tibet, is a mount in the middle of the plain. It is where the

[1] See Turner's account of the yak, p. 186. See also 'Hooker's Himalayan Journal,' i. pp. 212–214. The engraving given by Turner is from a painting by Stubbs, the famous animal painter, formerly in the possession of Warren Hastings. This picture is now in the Museum of the College of Surgeons.

[2] Turner has Gassa, p. 193.

[3] Turner calls it Phari or Paridsong. On the Bhutan Map of 1865 it is spelt Phak-rhi or Phari, and is placed at the head of the Chumbi Valley, between Sikkim and Bhutan. Klaproth has Phari-dzoung (Phari

people of Pari-jong expose their dead. It happened, I hope not ominously, that they were carrying a body thither as we came down. Eagles, hawks, ravens, and other carnivorous birds were soaring about in expectation of their prey. Every village has a place set apart for this purpose. There are only two exceptions to it. The Lamas are burnt with sandal-wood, and such as die of the smallpox are buried, to smother the infection; so that three of the five kinds of funerals (and I know no more) which the inhabitants of this world use are known to the people of Tibet.

As we advanced a little farther, we came in sight of the castle of Pari-jong, which cuts a good figure from without. It rises into several towers with the balconies, and having few windows, has the look of strength; it is surrounded by the town. The houses are of two low stories, flat-roofed, covered with bundles of straw, and so huddled together that one may chance to overlook them. There is little to be said for them. The ceilings are so low, that I have more than once been indebted to the thickness of my skull; and the beams being very short, are supported by a number of posts, which are little favourable to chamber-walking. In the middle of the roof is a hole to let out the smoke, which, however, departs not without making the whole room as black as a chimney. This opening serves also to let in the light; the doors are full of holes and crevices, through which the women and children keep peeping. I used to give them sugar-candy, and sometimes ribbons; but I brought all the children of the parish upon my back by it. The straw upon the top keeps the house warm. The same style of architecture prevails in the villages upon the road. It has a mean look after the lofty buildings in the Deb Rajah's country; but having neither wood nor arches, how can they help it?

There is no walking out after it is dark, on account of the number of dogs which are then let loose; they are of the shepherd breed, the same kind with those called Nepal dogs, large size, often shagged like a lion, and extremely fierce.[1]

The two Lhasa officers who have the government of Pari-jong sent me some butter, tea, &c., the day after my arrival; and, letting me know that they expected a visit from me, I went. The inside of the castle did not answer the notion I had formed of it. The stairs

[1] The Tibetan mastiff, a noble animal.

are ladders worn to the bone, and the rooms are little better than garrets. The governor was dressed in a russet coloured tunic of coarse woollen, and a linen cloth folded and laid upon his bare head. The other, who I understand is a sort of judge, was clad in coarse black cloth. They were seated beside one another upon carpets. The etiquette is much the same as with the Dewans at Tassisudon.

Four score of Deb Judhur's people had taken refuge in this fort. The Deb Rajah sent to demand them, but they were not given up. The conversation which passed on that occasion was, I am told, as full of the principles of government and the law of nations, as if it had been conducted by Grotius and Puffendorf.

Pari-jong stands in a confined plain, entirely surrounded by hills and mountains, except to the north-east, which allows that ruffian wind free entrance. It is on every account abundantly bleak, and bare and uncomfortable.

My friend Paima was considered here as a great man, and all Teshu Lama's vassals endeavoured by their presents and attention to secure his interest at court. His levées were crowded with suitors; and the night before our departure he invited all his friends, and gave them a grand entertainment. I knew nothing of this, and sent for him to play a game at chess. My servant found him dressed out in the governor's *khilat,* seated under a piece of green silk for a canopy, surrounded by all the peasants and peasants' wives, singing, dancing, and drinking, and as great as a prince.

It was, therefore, the morning of October 27, 1774, before we set out. Our party was now considerably increased by the accession of Paima and six other of Teshu Lama's servants. Everybody was mounted on horseback; the horses being all geldings, low sized, and quiet, hardy, ill-dressed, unshod. Having got clear of all the dogs and of all the beggars at Pari-jong, we journeyed slowly over the plain.

One of Paima's servants carried a branch of a tree with a white handkerchief tied to it. Imagining it to be a mark of respect to me and my embassy, I set myself upright in my saddle; but I was soon undeceived, for after stopping at a tent to drink tea with the abbot of a monastery in the neighbourhood of Pari-jong, subject to Teshu Lama, we rode over the plain till we came to a heap of stones opposite to a high rock covered with snow. Here we halted, and the servants gathering together a parcel of dried cow-dung, one of them struck fire with his tinder-box, and lighted it. We sat down about it, and the day being cold, I found it very comfortable. When the fire was well kindled, Paima took out a book of prayers; one brought a copper cup, another filled it with a kind of fermented liquor out of a new-killed sheep's paunch, mixing in some rice and flour, and after throwing some dried herbs and flour into the flame, they began their rites. Paima acted as chaplain. He chanted the prayers in a loud voice, the others accompanying him, and every now and then the little cup was emptied towards the rock. About eight or ten of these libations being poured forth, the ceremony was finished by placing upon the heap of stones the little ensign, which my fond imagination had before offered up to my own vanity. The mountain to which this sacrifice was made is named Chumalhari.[1] It stands between Tibet and Bhutan, and is generally white with snow. It rises almost perpendicular like a wall, and is attended with a string of smaller rocks, which obtain the name of Chumalhari's sons and daughters.

As the water of the Ganges, or of some refreshing brook, is considered holy among the sun-scorched Hindus, so rocks and mountains are the objects of veneration among the Lama's votaries. They erect written standards upon the tops of them, they cover the sides of them with prayers formed of pebbles, in characters so large "that those that run may read," and like the Jews of old, when they went a whoring after strange gods of the heathen, they get themselves up into high places.

The plain over which we had to ride is covered with gravelly sand. It produced nothing but some tufts of withered grass, which afforded a scanty subsistence to the herds of cattle. The sides of the hills to the westward are perfectly bare; they appear like rocks over which the sand and stones had been heaped, leaving here and

[1] Turner has Chumularee, p. 203. This lofty peak is 23,944 feet above the sea. Chumalhari, with many other Himalayan peaks, was included in the triangulation of the North-East Himalayan series, which was completed, under the superintendence of Sir Andrew Waugh, in 1850. On the Surveyor-General's Bhutan Map of 1865, it is spelt Chumala Rhi. Chumalha-ri means holy mountain of Chuma; and Chuma may be Chu (water), ma (mother), "Holy Mountain of the Mother of Waters." (See note at p. 166 of 'Hooker's Himalayan Journal,' vol. ii.)

there the sharp points jutting out; beyond these you see the high mountains in the Demo Jong[1] country, among which, I imagine, is the snowy hill seen from Dinajpúr[2] and other plains in Bengal. For several days the country bore the same bleak and barren aspect, answering to Churchill's[3] description:

> "Far as the eye can reach no tree is seen,
> Earth clad in russet scorns the lively green."

The plain cause of this poverty of soil is that God Almighty has so ordered it; but a much more ingenious reason may be drawn from the following circumstances.

The coldness of the climate renders fuel a very essential article, and as no wood is to be had, the Tibetans are obliged to use cow-dung, which is carefully gathered from the fields. This is built up in a circular form, or put into a pot with a hole in the bottom. It makes a cheerful and ardent fire when well kindled, and the people are abundantly skilful in the art of managing it, which my own ill success has often shown me to be a very difficult science.

We arrived at Tunno,[4] our next stage, about three o'clock. Some of my servants who walked were so tired that they were brought home on peasants' backs, as I had not been able to find horses for them all. I next day got cow-tailed bullocks, but the Hindus would not ride on them, because if any accident should happen to the beast while they were on him, they would be obliged, they said, according to the tenets of the Shaster, to beg their bread during twelve years, as an expiation for the crime. *Memo.*—Inconvenient carrying Hindu servants into foreign parts.

Our road next day (October 28) led us along the banks of the lake called Sham-chu Pelling.[5] It is fed by a large mineral

[1] Demo-jong (or Damoo-jung) is the Tibetan name for Sikkim. (See Gutzlaff, 'China Opened,' i. p. 273.) Hence Deunjong Maro for Sikkimites. But their own proper name is Roug. The Gorkhas, and we after them, call them Lepchas.

[2] This will be the peak of Kangchan jeunga (Kang chan, abounding in snow), 28,156 feet above the sea.

[3] Charles Churchill, the poet and satirist, was an old schoolfellow of Warren Hastings, Mr. Bogle's patron, at Westminster. The poets Cowper, Cumberland, Churchill, Colman, and Thornton, Lord Shelburne (Prime Minister), Warren Hastings, and Elijah Impey, were all at Westminster together. Churchill died in 1764, at the early age of thirty-three. See also note at p. 95.

[4] Turner has Teuna, 14 miles from Phari, p. 207.

[5] Ramtchieu of Turner, p. 211. *Chu* means a lake.

stream, which issues out of the side of a mountain, and extends about eighteen miles from the north to south. It was half frozen over, and well stocked with wild ducks and geese. We also met with some hares, and a flock of antelopes,[1] besides a herd of wild animals called kyangs,[2] resembling an ass, and which I shall afterwards have occasion to describe more particularly.

We should have had excellent sport, but for my friend Paima's scruples. He strongly opposed our shooting, insisting that it was a great crime, would give much scandal to the inhabitants, and was particularly unlawful within the liberties of Chumalhari. We had many long debates upon the subject, which were supported on his side by plain common-sense reasons drawn from his religion and customs; on mine, by those fine-spun European arguments, which serve rather to perplex than convince. I gained nothing by them, and at length we compromised the matter. I engaged not to shoot till we were fairly out of sight of the holy mountain, and Paima agreed to suspend the authority of the game laws, in solitary and sequestered places.[3]

The religion of the Lamas is somehow connected with that of the Hindus, though I will not pretend to say how. Many of their deities are the same; the Shaster is translated into their language, and they hold in veneration the holy places of Hindustan. In short, if the religion of Tibet is not the offspring of the Gentoos,[4] it is at least influenced by them. The humane maxims of the Hindu faith are taught in Tibet. To deprive any living creature of life is regarded as a crime, and one of the vows taken by the clergy is to that effect. But mankind in every part of the world too easily accommodate their consciences to their passions, and the Tibetans find no difficulty in yielding obedience to this doctrine. They employ a low and wicked class of people to kill their cattle, and thus evade the commandment. The severe prohibition of the Hindus in regard to eating beef is likewise easily got over. The

[1] Probably the Chiru, or *Antelope Hodgsoni* of Abel. Huc calls it the unicorn of Scripture.

[2] Equus (*asinus*) Kyang, the wild ass of Tibet.

[3] In a letter to his family, Mr. Bogle says: "There were plenty of wild ducks and geese in the lakes and rivers, and we had good shooting when we were away from any house. I killed three wild geese at one shot. But I was afraid of giving offence, and, so gave it up." (See paper on the migration of the wading and swimming birds in 'B. A. S. Journal.')

[4] See note at p. 88.

cows of Tibet are mostly of the bushy-tailed kind, and having therefore set them down as animals of a species different from the cow of the Shaster, they "eat, asking no questions for conscience' sake." The general principle by which they determine the degree of culpability in depriving an animal of life is very ingenious. According to the doctrine of transmigration, there is a perpetual fluctuation of life among the different animals of this world, and the spirit which now animates a man may pass after his death into a fly or an elephant. They reckon, therefore, the life of every creature upon an equal footing, and to take it away is considered as a greater or smaller crime, in proportion to the benefit which thereby accrues to mankind. According to this doctrine, "the ox who clothes the ground in all the pomp of harvest, the sheep who lends them his own coat, and yields them milk in luscious streams," are slaughtered without mercy; while the partridge and wild duck enjoy the protection of government, and the trout lives secure and unmolested to a goodly old age. The musk goat [1] is condemned, on account of its perfume. The deer [2] and the hare [3] are tried on a double charge, and suffer for their skin as well as their flesh. But I am following out disquisitions foreign from my journey.

A stream of water falls from the Sham-chu into the Calo-chu Lake, which extends about ten miles east and west. A large village, named Caloashur,[4] stands upon the bank of it, and another stream runs from it northwards. We kept close to this stream for several days: it falls into the Tsanpu Shigatzé,[5] turning many mills on its way. These are constructed on the simplest plan: a duct is cut in the same manner as in Europe; but the wheel, instead of being perpendicular, is horizontal, and turns the upper millstone, which is fixed to its axle, without any other machinery. There are also several bridges on this river, but very different from the wooden ones we met with among the mountains. They are walls, with breaks or openings to let the water through, which are covered with planks or large flags. In the Deb Rajah's country they choose the narrowest

[1] The musk goat is *Moschus Moscifer Auct.*

[2] The *Shou* of the Bhutanese. *Cervus Affinis Hodg.*

[3] *Lepus Oiostolus Hodg.*

[4] Calo of Bogle is probably the *Chaloo* of Turner, a village placed on his map between the two lakes. Calo-chu is the lake of Calo.

[5] That is the Tsanpu, or great river, which flows past Shigatzé.

part of the river to throw over a bridge: here they take the broadest.

Our route continued almost due north through valleys little cultivated and bounded by bleak and barren hills, between whose openings we saw distant mountains covered with snow. Here and there we saw a few houses, with some spots of rushy ground, or of brown pasture, but not a tree or a plant was to be seen, and the number of ruinous houses and deserted villages rendered the prospect more uncomfortable. At Kanmur[1] a few willows were planted round the village. We were lodged in the temple at the top of the house, which is generally the best apartment. Towards evening we had a visit from a priest who resides at Giansu, on the part of Teshu Lama, and began an acquaintance which we had afterwards abundance of opportunity to improve. He was dressed in a lay habit, consisting of a red broadcloth tunic, with a cap turned up with furs. He sat about an hour with us, and applied to Mr. Hamilton about medicines.

This village is subject to Lhasa. The house in which we lodged had lately changed its inhabitants. Of fifteen persons who formerly lived in it every one had died last year of the small-pox.

As we generally set out by sunrise, we arrived early at our stages. Dudukpai, the next village, which belongs to Teshu Lama, had also a good many willows about it. The people were all busy building and stacking their straw, and were singing at their work. Our landlords' family seemed to be one of the happiest in Tibet. The house belongs to two brothers, who are married to a very handsome wife,[2] and have three of the prettiest children I ever saw. They all came to drink tea and eat sugar-candy. After night came on, the whole family assembled in a room to dance to their own singing, and spent two hours in this manner with abundance of mirth and glee. I would stop to describe, but I shall have an opportunity afterwards, and am now going to discuss a philosophical and much more important subject.

[1] Gangamaar of Turner, p. 219.

[2] Polyandry is common in Tibet. (See Turner, p. 349.) See Warren Hastings' remarks, at p. 12. Several brothers marry one woman, but more than one is seldom at home. The effect of the huge number of persons bound to celibacy and the poverty of the land, rather complicate than explain this custom. (See pp. 37 and 57.)

The inhabitants of Tibet seem to be of a distinct race from those in the Deb Rajah's country. It struck me on my arrival at Parijong, and every day's journey has served to confirm it. The latter were the most robust and well-built race I ever saw. I cannot say so much for the former. Their strength, too, is in the same proportion; any burden with which the one will climb the steepest mountains, must be diminished fully a third to be carried by the other on level ground. One might seek for the cause of this in the difference of soil and climate. I will endeavour to account for it on another principle, because it may throw some light on the way of life among each people.

Labour certainly renders a man strong: *cæteris paribus,* a blacksmith or a carpenter will be stronger than a tailor or a barber. I have already mentioned the toilsome life of the Deb Rajah's subjects. The nature of this country exposes its inhabitants to no such hardships. The hills, although in many places abundantly steep and high, are so bare and sterile that they are left in a state of nature. The valleys only are cultivated, and the roads lead through them, which cuts off all climbing of mountains. Goods are chiefly carried on bullocks and asses; the corn is trod out by cattle, and ground by water-mills, and the country producing no forests, the inhabitants are freed from the hard labour of hewing down trees, and transporting them from the tops of mountains.

But however this easy life may contribute to render the men less robust, it has evidently a very favourable effect upon the women, who are certainly more delicate and joyous than their neighbours; and this freedom from intense labour gives likewise to the whole body of the people more time for gossiping and other sociable amusements, which soften the heart and cheer the temper. This also, together with other causes which it is needless to mention, renders the Tibetans much better bred and more affable than their southern neighbours, and the women are treated with greater attention. In the Deb Rajah's country, whatever a countryman saves from his labour is laid out in adorning his sword with silver filigree work, or buying a square box which contains a little gilt image, and is buckled to his back. Here it is bestowed on purchasing coral and amber beads, to adorn the head of his wife. The head-dress of the women is extremely neat and becoming. I have elsewhere described it. But the dirtiness of their hands and faces (many of which deserve a better fate) is a point which, as I cannot attempt to excuse, my partiality to the Tibetans will not allow me to enlarge upon.

I must except, however, our landlady, who kept herself and her family as neat as a Dutch woman, and, saving her black eyes, she had something the look of one.

The first part of our ride next day, the 2nd of November, was through the same bleak country we had hitherto met with; but the valley in which Giansu[1] stands is extensive, well cultivated, and full of whitened villages. The hills on each side draw close towards the north; between them rises a high and almost perpendicular rock, upon the top of which stands Giansu Castle. It is formed of many walls and turrets. The tower is built at the foot of the rock on the east side; on the west, it is washed by the river, beyond which a monastery and village are built on the declivity of a mountain. Altogether it makes a fine prospect.

Towards evening we arrived at our quarters, about three miles short of Giansu.[2] They belong to the priest who paid us a visit on the road. The house is surrounded with willows and other trees. It has a number of small windows, and the roof is adorned with little ensigns and written banners. We were lodged in the temple, which was full of painted chests, matchlocks, bows, cushions, and other lumber. One corner was hung with mythological paintings, and below a parcel of little gilt cross-legged images, with a lamp burning before them, from which, as all the family are gone to bed, I have taken the liberty to steal some oil in order to finish this account, hoping that it will not be imputed to me as a sacrilege.

This evening the Gosain, who was down in Calcutta, arrived with three of the Lama's servants. Our host arrived in the morning. He had applied to Mr. Hamilton about an inveterate complaint, and I tarried a day on purpose. He is an elderly man, of gentle and modest manners. He sat with me most of the afternoon, and I am sure I drank above twenty cups of tea. As I had waited upon the Lhasa officers at Pari-jong, I offered a visit to those

[1] Jhansu-jeung of Turner. Giangze of the Pundit of 1865; 12,895 feet above the sea. Klaproth has Gialdzé dzoung.

[2] The same place that Turner stopped at, which he calls Tehukku, p. 225.

at Giansu, but it was declined on the pretence of one of them being absent.

On our journey next day we passed through the town of Gainsu, and under the castle. The streets are narrow, and the houses as I have before described them. Crowds of people assembled to look at us. These exhibitions were very irksome at first, but I have grown to be accustomed to them. I have remarked that we are much more stared at and run after in towns than in villages, and in villages than in solitary houses. Curiosity, perhaps, although natural to mankind, and however the seeds of it may be implanted in them, requires, like music, to be cultivated. It gathers strength from being exercised; it languishes and lies asleep when there are no objects to engage its attention.

We met with no more ruinous houses. The villages came now to be more numerous; and the low lands in the valleys, though light and sandy, were covered with barley stubble. We arrived at our stage in good time; and having nothing else to fill up my paper with, will beg leave to give a description of a Tibetan churn. I have often admired the construction of the Bengal ones. I think in this country, however, they have improved on them. The barrel which contains the milk is put on the ground; the strap has two cross boards at bottom. It is put into the barrel, and the lid, with a hole for it to pass through, is fastened on; a thong of leather is then put twice round the staff, and the ends being brought over a small roller (which is supported horizontally by, and turns round between, two posts) are tied to two foot-boards, one end of them raised about six or eight inches from the ground, the other resting upon it. On this a man stands, and moving his feet alternately up and down, twists about the staff in the churn with great velocity and much satisfaction. If I could draw I would give a plan of it, but I cannot.

I met here also with a machine for cutting straw for cattle, but it is not worthy of description. As I remember what a great discovery the cutting of straw was considered in England, I mention it only to show that nations undervalued by Europeans can, without the assistance of Royal Societies, find out the useful arts of life, and for the rest, whether they be of advantage to mankind or otherwise is a question above my reach.

We proceeded next morning, November 5, along the banks of the river, now considerably increased. We saw a good many villages at a distance, and at length came in sight of Painám,[1] a castle built on a rock. The situation is a good deal similar to that of Giansu, but I think finer; the towers are more regular. Under the rock there is only a village. Deb Judhur passed the night in our neighbourhood, on his way to Giansu, where he was afterwards confined.

The valley to the north of Painám was by far the most populous I had yet seen. The villages stand very thick. A small town called Ghattong is built on the side of one of the hills, and the houses being all whitened make a good appearance. We had hitherto kept in the road towards Shigatzé,[2] but we now turned to the east, and took that of Chamnamring, in the neighbourhood of which Teshu Lama has for some years resided, on account of the small-pox which lately raged in Tibet. After passing the valley we had to ascend some hills by a difficult and stony path, then to descend, and then ascend again, after which we had a view of the Tsanpu, running eastwards. When we had got half-way down the hill we stopped at a single house, where we took up our quarters for the night.

On our way over these hills we met with a flock of sheep, which had come from the Dospa country (Tushkhind)[3] with a cargo of salt, and were then returning from Giansu, loaded with barley and wheat. They were of a large breed, with horns extended horizontally. There were about twelve hundred of them, and each sheep carried two bags of grain, which might be about twenty or twenty-five pounds. They were very obedient to their drivers' whistles, and if any of

[1] Painom of Turner, p. 229; or Pena Jong of the Pundit of 1865. Klaproth has Banam zoung, or the "town of cows." The river is called Penanang, or Painom.

[2] Here the routes of Bogle and Turner diverged. Bogle crossed the Tsanpu, while Turner took the direct road to Teshu Lumbo.

[3] The *Dospa* is simply the "salt country." *Thus*, (*dos*) being Turki for salt, and (*pa*) country.

Tushkhind has the same sound as Taishkhan valley mentioned in Wood's 'Oxus'(Yule's ed., p.161), in Badakshan; the stream flowing through it being an effluent of the Kokcha. The Taican of 'Marco Polo,' between Kunduz and Badakshan, is described as being near the mountains of salt. (See Colonel Yule's note in his edition of 'Marco Polo,' i. p. 146.) In his Report on the trade of Nepal, Mr. Hodgson says that all Nepal is supplied with rock-salt by way of Tibet.

them happened to get out of the road were easily brought back by the shepherds' dogs.

There are a great many rushy fields in the neighbourhood of the place where we stopped. Mr. Hamilton had good shots at four hares, but his fowling-piece was bent and he missed them.

On the 7th of November, after descending an easy hill, we arrived on the banks of the Tsanpu. It is here about the breadth of the Thames at Putney. The channel is not fordable. Having drank some of its water, washed my hands and face, and thrown a rupee into it, we embarked in the ferry-boat, of which there are several in this place. They are in the shape of an oblong square, about twenty-five feet long and broad. The bottom is a float of thick planks, closed in by perpendicular walls to the height of about four feet, with an opening on each side, cut down to about two feet, which serves for the entrance. The whole is bound together with bars of iron, and painted white. At each end of the boat is a white ensign about a foot square. This large hulk is moved by an oar on each side, which are pulled by two men, pushed by another standing opposite to them, and drawn by a woman, who holds a rope fastened to the end of the oar which is in the water. It is managed at the stern by one man with a large headed oar. In our boat there were twenty-three persons, seven horses, one cow-tailed bullock, and fourteen asses, besides baggage. As the river is far from being rapid, we crossed it without losing much ground. Large herds of bullocks and flocks of sheep were waiting on each side for a passage. There is another kind of boat used in the summer time for transporting goods. It is made of hides, about eight feet long, four broad, and two deep, the ribs of willow poles. There were none afloat, but we saw many of them upon the bank keel up, and one end being raised a little they thus serve for a habitation.

After crossing the river, we rode northwards over a large sandy bank, which is overflowed in the rainy season, and entered a valley which opens upon the Tsanpu. We had fine sandy roads here, and I ran some races with Purungir. The Tibet ponies are much swifter and better blood than I expected. We took up our quarters at a monastery in a small village. The abbot was a short, sickly-looking man, but courteous and hospitable. His dinner was just ready, and he sent us a couple of joints of most excellent mutton.

In the afternoon we walked out, and sat down on the banks of the rivulet which runs through the valley, and while we were looking at some dromedaries, a gylong[1] or priest came up to us, and sat down beside us. The few words of the language which I was master of were little able to support a varied and entertaining conversation. I understood, however, the priest's caution against sitting on the ground and in the sun. He was dressed in the habit peculiar to his order, which I have already described; but it had seen many years' service, and was now threadbare. He had thrown off his hose to wade the river, when our snuff-box attracted his notice. Upon this, he loosened a wallet which hung at his back, and after turning over some books of prayers, a yellow cloth coat lined with lambskin, a small parcel of tobacco, and another of tea, he came to a bundle of incense papers, and having presented four of them to Mr. Hamilton, claimed some snuff in return. This exchange being made, and having taken leave by a salutation of thumbs, which is the sign of the superlative degree of comparison, he laid his bundle and hose upon his back, and, wading the river, continued his journey.

The lower gylongs here are not so well off as in the Deb Rajah's country; they are a much more numerous body, and the lamas having engrossed all authority into their own hands, the priests, particularly the inferior ones, are without the political consequence enjoyed by the clergy in the neighbouring kingdom.

We set out early in the morning, and travelled northwards along the banks of the rivulet.[2] We passed opposite to Teshu-tzay, where the Lama received his birth, and at length came in sight of Chamnamring,[3] a castle belonging to Lhasa, situated upon the top

[1] Gylong, a monk, or ordained priest. Schlagintweit spells it Gelong; or, exactly transliterated, *d*Ge-slong. It is equivalent to the Hindustani *Bhikshu*, a mendicant.

[2] The young Tibetan explorer, sent by Colonel Montgomerie, in 1871, from Kumaon, crossed the Tsanpu (Sangpo) at about the same place, and ascended the same valley as that traversed by Mr. Bogle, along the banks of a river, tributary to the Tsanpu, which he calls the Shiang-chu. He mentions villages in this valley called Chua, Dongdot-lo, and Chom. At the latter place there is a nunnery.

[3] Namling of the explorer of 1871, on the banks of the Shiang-chu. He describes it as a large monastery on a high hill. The name is from *Nam* (sky) and *ling* (garden), the monastery being on a lofty eminence, with gardens at its base. Klaproth has *Dziang amring dzoung*, which he interprets as "The town to the north of the mountains of Amring."

of a hill, with a small town under it, built in the form of a square, and enclosed within walls. Having forded the river, we entered a little cross valley, where we stopped to drink tea at some tents prepared for us, and having received white handkerchiefs from a Gosain sent with inquiries by Teshu Lama, we proceeded to Desheripgay, a small palace in which the Lama resided.

CHAPTER VIII.

AT DESHERIPGAY.

On the 8th of November, 1774, we rode up to the gate of the palace, and walking into the court, went up the ladders to our apartments.

Desheripgay[1] is situated in a narrow valley, and at the foot of an abrupt and rocky hill. The palace is small; it is only two stories high, and is surrounded on three sides by rows of small apartments with a wooden gallery running round them, which altogether form a small court, flagged with stone. All the stairs are broad ladders. The roofs are adorned with copper-gilt ornaments; and on the front of the house there are three round brass plates, emblems of Om, Han, Hoong.[2] The Lama's apartment is at the top; it is small, and hung round with different coloured silks, views of Potalla,[3] Teshu Lumbo, &c. About two miles from Desheripgay is the castle of Chamnamring.

Immediately after our arrival, the Lama sent us a pot of ready-made tea, boiled rice, four or five sacks of flour and of rice, three or four dried sheep's carcasses, and some whisky. I had also compliments of tea from several of his officers, and many visitors whom curiosity brought to see me.

My room was small, but neatly furnished; it was immediately above the church, and I was entertained with the never-ceasing noise of "cymballines and timballines" from morning to night. But as soon as it grows dark everything is still as death, and the gates are shut about an hour after sunset. The night of my arrival they were kept open on account of my supper, as my servants were

[1] This place is not mentioned by the explorer of 1871.

[2] This is the invocation of the triad, common to Brahmanism and Buddhism. But with the latter it refers to *Buddha* (mind); *Dharma* (matter); *Sangha* (the union of both in the sensible world).

[3] The monastery near Lhasa, the residence of the Dalai Lama.

lodged without; but I took care there should be no occasion for this afterwards.

A number of Kampas,[1] who are natives of a country about a month's journey to the north-east of Lhasa, came to pay their devotions to the Lama. They were clad in yellow cloth gowns, and their heads shaven. On these occasions nobody goes empty-handed. Some of them carried bundles of tea, some parcels of gold dust, others china, and silver talents. They are a hard-featured race, and I cannot help fancying they have some of the Malay features.

In the afternoon, I had my first audience of the Lama. I have elsewhere put down the conversation that passed, and will here only mention the ceremonies.

The Lama was upon his throne, formed of wood, carved and gilt, with some cushions above it, upon which he sat cross-legged. He was dressed in a mitre-shaped cap of yellow broadcloth, with long bars lined with red satin; a yellow cloth jacket without sleeves, and a satin mantle of the same colour thrown over his shoulders. On one side of him stood his physician with a bundle of perfumed sandal-wood rods burning in his hand; on the other stood his *Sopon Chumbo*,[2] or cup-bearer. I laid the Governor's presents before him, delivering the letter and pearl necklace into his own hands, together with a white Pelong[3] handkerchief on my own part, according to the custom of the country. He received me in the most engaging manner. I was seated on a high stool covered with a carpet. Plates of boiled mutton, boiled rice, dried fruits, sweetmeats, sugar, bundles of tea, sheep's carcasses dried, &c., were set before me and my companion, Mr. Hamilton. The Lama drank two or three dishes of tea along with us, but without saying any grace; asked us once or twice to eat, and threw white Pelong handkerchiefs over our necks at retiring. After two or three visits, the Lama used (except on holidays) to receive me without any

[1] Kam is the eastern division of Tibet, bordering on the Szechuen province of China. But the people referred to were probably of Sokyeul or Sifan, for whom see Hodgson 'On the Tribes of North Tibet,' pp. 65, 82.

[2] Turner has Sopoon Choomboo, p. 232. He held, according to Turner, the second rank in the court of the Teshu Lama, was by birth a Manchu Tatar, and acquired the complete confidence of his master. Turner speaks very highly of him, p. 246. At the time of Bogle's visit he was not more than twenty-two years of age.

[3] See note at p. 16.

ceremony, his head uncovered, dressed only in the large red petticoat which is worn by all the gylongs, red Bulgar hide boots, a yellow cloth vest, with his arms bare, and a piece of coarse yellow cloth thrown across his shoulders. He sat sometimes in a chair, sometimes on a bench covered with tiger skins, and nobody but the *Sopon Chumbo* present. Sometimes he would walk with me about the room, explain to me the pictures, make remarks upon the colour of my eyes, &c. For, although venerated as God's vicegerent through all the eastern countries of Asia, endowed with a portion of omniscience, and with many other divine attributes, he throws aside, in conversation, all the awful part of his character, accommodates himself to the weakness of mortals, endeavours to make himself loved rather than feared, and behaves with the greatest affability to everybody, particularly to strangers.

Teshu Lama is about forty years of age, of low stature, and though not corpulent, rather inclining to be fat. His complexion is fairer than that of most of the Tibetans, and his arms are as white as those of a European; his hair, which is jet black, is cut very short; his beard and whiskers never above a month long; his eyes are small and black. The expression of his countenance is smiling and good-humoured. His father was a Tibetan; his mother a near relation of the Rajahs of Ladak. From her he learned the Hindustani language, of which he has a moderate knowledge, and is fond of speaking it. His disposition is open, candid, and generous. He is extremely merry and entertaining in conversation, and tells a pleasant story with a great deal of humour and action. I endeavoured to find out, in his character, those defects which are inseparable from humanity, but he is so universally beloved that I had no success, and not a man could find in his heart to speak ill of him.[1]

Being the first European they had ever seen, I had crowds of Tibetans coming to look at me, as people go to look at the lions in the Tower. My room was always full of them from morning

[1] Turner also tells us of the veneration in which the memory of the Teshu Lama was held in his time (1783), and quotes the above sentence from Mr. Bogle's Journal, p. 338. Through correspondence with him Mr. Hodgson derived a like impression of the Dalai Lama, from whom he obtained the perfect copy of the Tibetan cyclopædia, now deposited in the India Office, and also the relics of the old Christian establishments in Central Asia.

till night. The Lama, afraid that I might be incommoded, sent me word, if I chose, not to admit them; but when I could gratify the curiosity of others at so easy a rate, why should I have refused it? I always received them, sometimes exchanging a pinch of snuff, at others picking up a word or two of the language.

On the 12th of November a vast crowd of people came to pay their respects, and to be blessed by the Lama. He was seated under a canopy in the court of the palace. They were all ranged in a circle. First came the lay folks. Every one, according to his circumstances, brought some offering. One gave a horse, another a cow; some gave dried sheep's carcasses, sacks of flour, pieces of cloth, &c.; and those who had nothing else presented a white Pelong handkerchief. All these offerings were received by the Lama's servants, who put a bit of silk with a knot upon it, tied, or supposed to be tied, with the Lama's own hands, about the necks of the votaries. After this they advanced up to the Lama, who sat cross-legged upon a throne formed with seven cushions, and he touched their heads with his hands, or with a tassel hung from a stick, according to their rank and character. The ceremonial is this: upon the gylongs or laymen of very high rank he lays his palm; the nuns (*anní*) and inferior laymen have a cloth interposed between his hand and their heads; and the lower class of people are touched, as they pass by, with the tassel which he holds in his hand. I have often admired his dexterity in distinguishing the different orders of people, particularly in knowing the young priests from the nuns, both being dressed in the same habit, and it sometimes happening that they were crowded and jumbled together. There might be about three thousand people—men, women, and children—at this ceremony. Such as had children upon their backs were particularly solicitous that the child's head should also be touched with the tassel. There were a good many boys, and some girls devoted to the monastic order, by having a lock of hair on the crown of the head cropped by the Lama with a knife.[1] This knife came down from heaven in a flash of lightning.[2] The age at which these children are thus consecrated

[1] See Pravrajya-vrata, or initiatory rites, p. 139 *et seq.* of Hodgson's 'Language and Religion of Nepal and Tibet.'

[2] In other words, it was made from meteoric iron.

to religion and chastity is usually about seven or eight years. After the Lama retired, many people stayed behind that they might kiss the cushions upon which he had sat. We had two or three of these exhibitions while I was at Desheripgay; but having given a description of one, I will forbear mentioning the rest.

Among all offerings, dried sheep's carcasses always form a principal article. They are as stiff as a poker, are set up on end, and make, to a stranger, a very droll appearance. I was at some pains to inquire about the method of preserving them, as it is a practice common to Tatary as well as Tibet; but I could discover no mystery in it. The sheep is killed, is beheaded, is skinned, is cleaned; the four feet are then put together in such a manner as may keep the carcass most open. During a fortnight it is every night exposed on the top of the house, or in some other airy situation, and in the heat of the day it is kept in a cool room. After it is fully dried it may be kept anywhere. In this way they preserve mutton all the year round.[1] The end of autumn, when the sheep are fattened with the summer's grass, is the usual time for killing them; and the difficulty of supporting the flocks in the winter time is, I believe, the reason for adopting this method. In the hot and rainy season it is necessary to use a small quantity of salt; but few carcasses are then dried. I found the dried mutton generally more tender than that fresh killed, but not so juicy and high flavoured. The Tibetans often eat it raw, and I once followed their example; it had much the taste of dried fish. The facility with which meat is preserved from putrefaction in this country may be owing partly to the coldness of the climate, partly to the uncommon dryness of a gravelly and sandy soil, and partly to the scarcity of flies and other maggot-breeding insects.

Mirza Settar, the Kashmiri who accompanied me, was lodged outside the palace. A fakir had arrived from Lhasa, and having brought him tidings of his brother, the Kashmiri could not do less than give him a share of his quarters. This morning (November 19), before I got up, Mirza came into my room, and fell a skipping and dancing in a manner very unbecoming his years and gravity. He then lay down and rolled himself on the floor, and at length, falling upon me, overwhelmed me with embraces. I

[1] Like the *charqui* of South America, the "jerked" beef of the buccaneers.

concluded him mad, and starting up, called for my servants to carry him downstairs. His solicitude to get rid of an intermittent fever had, it seems, induced him to take a nostrum from his guest, which had operated in this extraordinary way. However, what by means of a vomit, which Mr. Hamilton gave him, and what from some charmed water which the Lama sent him, he soon recovered. But the fakir was thrown into prison, and it cost me some entreaties to procure his release. I think he will be cautious of acting again in a medical capacity.

The palace was illuminated on account of its being the Dalai Lama's birthday. Lamps were placed all around the balustrades of the terrace. The illuminations at the houses of some nuns, who live at the top of the hill which hangs over the palace, had a good effect. We had music and kettledrums, but no fireworks. They have them at Lhasa.

Among the other good qualities which Teshu Lama possesses is that of charity, and he has plenty of opportunities of exercising it. The country swarms with beggars who follow this profession from generation to generation, and the Lama entertains besides a number of fakirs who resort hither from India. As he speaks their language tolerably well, he every day converses with them from his windows, and picks up by this means a knowledge of the different countries and governments of Hindustan. Many of them come on commercial schemes; but although very opulent, they continue to wear a homely dress, and to receive charity from the Lama. Others come on pretence of pilgrimages to the Lama; their real object, however, being to share his bounty. He gives them a monthly allowance of tea, butter, and flour, besides money, and often bestows something considerable upon them at their departure. The Gosains, who are thus supported at the Lama's expense, may be in number about one hundred and fifty, besides about thirty Mussulman fakirs. For, although the genius of the religion of Muhammad is hostile to that of the Lama, yet he is possessed of much Christian charity, and is free from those narrow prejudices which, next to ambition and avarice, have opened the most copious source of human misery. This charity to the pilgrims flows, I imagine, partly from the generosity of the Lama's temper, partly from the desire of acquiring information, and satisfying his curiosity about Hindustan, the school of the religion of Tibet. But the fakirs, in their return to their own country, or in their rambles through other kingdoms of Asia, naturally extol the bounty of their benefactor, and thus serve to spread wide the fame of his character.

The Gentoo[1] fakirs, as far as I can judge, are in general a very worthless set of people, devoid of principle, and being separated by their profession from all those ties of kindred and family which serve to bind the rest of mankind, they have no object but their own interest, and, covered with the cloak of religion, are regardless of their caste, of their character, and of everything else which is held sacred among the Hindus. Their victuals are dressed by Tibet servants; there is no kind of meat, beef excepted, which they do not eat. They drink plentifully of spirituous liquors, and although directly contrary to their vows and to the rules of their order, above one half of them keep women. In their deportment they mix, by a strange combination, the most fawning and flattering servility with the most clamorous insolence. They intrude into every company, give their opinion in every conversation, and convey what they have to say in a voice like thunder. They are universally disliked by the Tibetans, have no protector but the Lama, and if he were to die to-morrow they would next day be driven from the palace. It may appear strange, after giving them this character, that I should have bestowed a good deal of money among the fakirs. But I will confess I did it from worldly motives, and am far from expecting that it will draw down the favour of heaven upon my constituents, or serve "to cover the multitude of my sins."

The Lama used to send a priest to me early every morning with some bread and tea, or some boiled rice and chopped mutton; of which last, as I always like to do at Rome as they do at Rome, I used to eat very heartily. This practice was continued till my departure for Bengal.

The weather was very cold; the water in my room used to freeze even in the day time; and I seldom stirred out of the house, where nothing was to be seen but bare hills, a few leafless trees, and a bleak and comfortless country. Some days after my arrival the Lama had given me a Tibetan dress, consisting of a purple satin tunic,

[1] A Hindu. A corrupt word derived from the Portuguese *Gentio*, a gentile or heathen. (Wilson.)

lined with Siberian fox skins; a yellow satin cap, faced round with sable and crowned with a red silk tassel, and a pair of red silk Bulgar hide boots. In this I equipped myself, glad to abandon my European habit, which was both uncomfortable and exposed me to abundance of that troublesome curiosity which the Tibetans possess in a degree inferior to no other people.

The Lama now prepared to return to his palace at Teshu Lumbo, which he had been obliged, about three years ago, to quit on account of the smallpox.

CHAPTER IX.

RIDE FROM DESHERIPGAY TO TESHU LUMBO.

AT length the 7th of December, the day of our departure from Desheripgay, arrived. The Lama sent to me to know whether I chose to accompany him, or to go on before, as he had heard we were fond of riding fast, and it might be irksome travelling in his slow way. This question arose, I believe, from the race I had run with Purungir upon the road.[1] There was nothing ill-natured in it. I returned him for answer that I wished to attend his stirrup.

We were wakened long before day, and before sunrise the Lama set out on his journey. The road was covered with cloth from his apartments to the steps by which he was to get on horseback. He was dressed, as usual, in a yellow broad cloth jacket without sleeves. When he came to the steps he pulled off his cap, and his *sopon*[2] put on him one lined with fur, together with a black silk flap with fringes to keep off the sun's rays. He then got upon horseback, and a yellow satin cloak lined with fur was thrown over him. Two men held his horse's head and two others his saddle. The Lama once got a fall, and is a very timorous rider.

The sun was not yet up and the cold was excessive. I thought I should have lost my fingers. When we had gone about half a mile the people gave three hurrahs, at each of which we turned our horses' heads towards the palace. Crowds of people were assembled to see and pay their adorations to the Lama. The horsemen, however, kept them off, and they were obliged to perform their three prostrations at a great distance. Only such as had erected little altars with fires were allowed to remain, and the smoke of these, however disagreeable, served to render the cold less intense. In this way we proceeded along the western banks of the Chamnamring rivulet.[3]

[1] See p. 79, and note at p. 1.

[2] Cup-bearer. (See p. 83.)

[3] The river Shiang-chu, according to Colonel Montgomerie's explorer of 1871.

Our line of march was as follows:

A Yellow Silk Standard, bound up in two or three places with white handkerchiefs, carried by a man on horseback.
Eight Kettledrums on horseback.
Four Trumpeters on horseback.
A Set of Bells in a frame on horseback.
About Fifty Horsemen, some with large yellow sheepskin bonnets and red broadcloth coats, others with fur caps and satin gowns.
Four Lamas, or High Priests, in yellow tunics, with brown serge thrown over, and yellow picked caps.
Sopon Chumbo, the Cup-bearer, or Favourite.
THE TESHU LAMA.
A Yellow Satin Umbrella, with strings of coral, carried on horseback.
The Chanzo[1] Cusho.
His Cup-bearer. The Treasurer.
Mr. Bogle.
Mr. Hamilton.
Cheyt Sing's[2] and other Hindu vakíls.
The Pyn Cushos, nephews of the Lama.
About a Hundred Horsemen of different ranks and in various dresses.

At sunrise we stopped at some tents and drank tea. That of the Lama was about the size of a captain's, and shut in with walls. The Chanzo Cusho's was rather less. The form of the tents was the same as in Europe. They were of white Assam canvas, with blue flowers and fringes. I was not in them, a separate tent being provided for me. Having halted about an hour, we continued our journey in the same order as before, and with the same crowds of people. After passing the different cross valleys which open into that of Chamnamring, we entered that of Teshu-tzay,[3] and arrived at the road which leads up to a monastery built on the top of a hill. Everybody alighted except the Lama, who rode up the hill, and then walked into the house upon cloths which were spread for him. I was carried into a tent as before, and besides tea had some cold mutton, rice broth, and fruits. The nuns[4] who live here went in procession to pay

[1] Turner has *Chanjoo Cooshoo*. He was brother of the Teshu Lama, and, in Turner's time, after the Lama's untimely death, regent of the country during the minority of the child Lama. Cusho is perhaps *Kushog*, a title of rank, religious and civil. Chanzo, or Chanjoo, may be *Thango-pa*, a word meaning "pure," "holy."

[2] The Rajah of Benares, who was afterwards deposed by Warren Hastings.

[3] On the west side of the Shiang-chu.

[4] The explorer of 1872 mentions a monastery inhabited by nuns in about this position, but he calls it *Chom*.

their respects to the Lama. Many of them were young and well-looking; but their dress, which is the same as the gylongs, is very unbecoming, and the loss of their hair is a great want. Two of the Lama's nieces are placed in this convent. We stayed about two hours, and halted again at an encampment two miles farther up the valley, to drink tea. About a mile farther on we arrived at Teshu-tzay, the Lama's birth-place.

I was lodged in a low room in a sorry house, at the foot of the mount upon which it stands. It was the worst quarters I had met with in the country. However, it was only for a day or two, so I did not mind. But the Lama sent a gylong overnight with some fruits, &c., and he having given a report of my accommodation, the Lama sent to me next day, and I was removed into a good room in the castle, which looked into a small court, where the dancers, &c., were to exhibit. The Lama's nephews came and passed the whole day with me, and I here began an acquaintance and connection with them, which turned out the most pleasurable of any I made in the country. I had also a visit from his nieces, the nuns, and the Teshu-tzay Dêbu, or Killadar,[1] likewise paid me a visit, and brought me a present of a handkerchief, two or three small purses of gold dust, some fruit, &c. I returned the compliment in the evening.

I passed the time in looking at the dancers, or playing at chess with some of the Tibetans. The court held about thirty dancers, half of them men, half of them women. The men were dressed in different and party-coloured clothes, with their large sheep's-wool bonnets, a bit of coloured silk in one hand, and a leather machine, something in shape of, but rather less than, a fiddle at their side. The women had their faces washed, and clean clothes, abundance of rings upon their fingers, and of coral, amber beads, bugles, &c., on their heads and necks, and each wore a small round hat, covered with circles of white beads. They formed a ring, the men being altogether, the women altogether, and five men were in the middle of it. They danced to their own singing, moving slowly round in a sort of half-hop step, keeping time with their hands, while the five in the centre twisted round and cut capers, with many strange

[1] Killadar, the governor of a fort in Hindustani. Dêbu is the equivalent in Tibetan.

and indescribable motions. The second part of the entertainment was performed by four or five men, with winged rainbow-coloured caps, who jumped and twisted about, to the lashing of cymbals and the beating of tabors. Among the rest was a merry Andrew with a mask stuck over with cowries, and a clown with a large stick in his hand. These two were more agile than the others, and between whiles carried on a dialogue, and the grimace and conversation gave great entertainment to those who understood it. As I was not so fortunate, I was obliged, as I have often been in more polite assemblies, to seek for amusement in the dress and physiognomies of the spectators.

In this manner did I spend two days. Towards the close of the last the Lama seated himself under a canopy and blessed the people, a ceremony which I have already described.

The house where the Lama was born is built on the top of a high bank. It is very large, the windows regular, flat-roofed, and of goodly appearance from without; within, irregular and smoked. I was not in many of the rooms. All the adjacent villages, together with the valley, which is pretty extensive, were granted to the Teshu Lama by the Dulai Lama, to whom they formerly belonged.

We got up before daybreak, continued our journey as soon as it was light; stopped at the tents to drink tea; got out of the valley of Teshu-tzay by the same road that we had entered it, and proceeded towards the great river. About eleven o'clock we reached some tents where refreshments of tea, cold mutton, &c., were prepared for us, and arrived towards evening at our quarters, which formed a little encampment. The Lama's tent was a large Kalmuk one enclosed within walls, and as he sent for me soon after our arrival, I had an opportunity of seeing it more narrowly. It was round, about sixty feet in circumference, and formed of a number of rods stuck into the ground, and gathered at the top into a hoop, which was covered with oiled paper to let in the light. On the outside it was covered with white cloth, except the top, over which some very beautiful panther skins were spread. The entrance was by a small door. All the inside was hung with crimson satin, and the floor covered with carpet. It was very warm and commodious. The Chanzo Cusho was lodged at a little distance in a small tent of a like construction, but I was not in it.

My habitation would have done better for a milder climate. The tent had walls round it, and was of double canvas, and in European form. However, I got a large fire, and covered myself well up at night with all my furs and sheep's clothing. In the morning before we set out I looked at the thermometer, which was kept in a basket among linen, and found it within two degrees of the bottom of the scale.

We did not stop till we arrived on the bank of the Tsanpu. Here we halted till our horses were ferried over, and had the same refreshments as usual. About two thousand people were assembled to see and prostrate themselves before his Holiness. The Lama walked upon cloths to the river side. His nephews, who had accompanied him, here took leave. He made me go in the boat with him, in which were only the Chanzo and the two *sopons*. The boat I have elsewhere described. The river was covered with shoals of floating ice. On the opposite bank the Kashmiri merchants and great crowds of Tibetans waited. They made their obeisance at a distance. We arrived at our quarters towards evening. They were like the former. The Lama sent for me, and observing that my saddle, however well calculated for travelling or hunting, was not suited to the fashion of this country, presented me with a Tibet one, which had a very deep peak of iron, all stuffed, so that it makes one look very lofty. All the ironwork of the saddle and also of the bridle was gilt. He also gave me a yellow satin tunic, faced with black fur; for, says he, "you are to go into my capital to-morrow." These little civilities gained a high value from the manner in which they were done.

We stopped about three miles from Teshu Lumbo, the crowds increasing as we advanced. The Lama had a large tent pitched for him, where everybody came to pay their respects and receive his blessing. He was dressed in his sacerdotal habit, and seated on his high-raised cushions. I was placed the second from the Chanzo Cusho, and next under the Dalai Lama's vakíl. We had some tea, boiled roots, and rice with sugar at the top, while numbers of people passed before him and received the *chawa* or imposition of hands. The Shigatzé Killadars[1] cut the most remarkable figure. They were dressed like women, but their whiskers and overgrown carcasses left

[1] See note at p. 92.

no room to mistake their sex. Their heads were bound with white turbans rolled into a square form; round turquoise earrings, about the size of a watch, hung from their ears, and fell upon their shoulders. They wore slippers, and the rest of their dress was of blue satin, with their arms bare to the elbows. This habit is worn by all the lay officers subject to Lhasa, on holidays and grand occasions. We had much singing and dancing without the Lama's tent, by gylongs dressed in party-coloured habits,[1] and also by the peasants. The castle of Shigatzé,[2] which stands to the eastward of Teshu Lumbo, was now above us. It is built on a hill with towers and battlements, and is subject to Lhasa.

From the resting place till we arrived at the Lama's palace the road was lined on both sides with ranks of spectators. They were all dressed in their holiday clothes. The peasants were singing and dancing. About three thousand gylongs, some with large pieces of chequered cloth hung upon their breasts, others with their cymbals and tabors, were ranked next the palace. As the Lama passed they bent half forwards, and followed him with their eyes. But there was a look of veneration mixed with joy in their countenances which pleased me beyond anything, and was a surer testimony of satisfaction than all the guns in the Tower, and all the odes of Whitehead[3] could have given. One catches affection by sympathy, and I could not help, in some measure, feeling the same emotions with the Lama's votaries.

The Lama rode as far as he could, and then walked slowly through the purlieus of the palace, stopping now and then, and casting a cheerful look among his people.

[1] This irresistibly recalls the doings of the "Monk of Misrule" of Christendom in the middle ages.

[2] Or Digárchi. Klaproth has Jikadze, meaning a fortress situated on a mountain.

[3] Here, again, Mr. Bogle's reading of Churchill crops up (see *ante*, p. 71). That satirist, in his 'Prophecy of Famine,' thus writes of Whitehead, the Laureate:—

"Thus spake a form, by silken smile and tone,
Dull and unvaried, for the Laureate known,
Folly's chief friend, Decorum's eldest son,
In every party found, and yet of none."

William Whitehead became Poet Laureate on the death of Colley Cibber, in 1757, and held the post until his death in 1785. Then followed Thomas Wharton, Pye, Southey, Wordsworth, Tennyson.

CHAPTER X.

TESHU LUMBO.[1]

WE passed by the foot of Teshu Lumbo, which is built on the lower declivity of a steep hill. The roof of the palace, which is large, is all of copper gilt. The building is of dark-coloured brick. The houses of the town rise one above another; four churches with gilt ornaments are mixed with them, and altogether it presents a princely appearance. Many of the courts are spacious, flagged with stone, and with galleries running round them. The alleys, which are likewise paved, are narrow. The palace is appropriated to the Lama and his officers, to temples, granaries, warehouses, &c. The rest of the town is entirely inhabited by priests, who are in number about four thousand.[2] The views of it, which the Lama afterwards gave to me, will convey a better idea of it than any account I can write. For there is no describing a place so as to give others a just notion of it.

I attended the Lama to his apartments, and as soon as I retired I was conducted to my own. They are new, having been built and finished by Chanzo Cusho during the Lama's absence at Desheripgay. There was one room for me, and another for Mr. Hamilton. I do not think the apartment allotted to me inferior to any at Teshu Lumbo; and although I have little success at these sorts of descriptions, I must attempt to give some account of it. You enter by a door formed of one piece of wood, painted red; the

[1] Turner gives the latitude of Teshu Lumbo at 29° 4′ 20″ N., from six meridian altitudes of the sun, and the longitude 89° 7′ E. (p. 293.) The 'Pundit' of 1865 gives the latitude of Shigatzé, which is a short distance from Teshu Lumbo, at 29° 16′ 32″ N., and the height above the sea at 11,822 feet. Schlagintweit spells the word Tashilhúnpo, but gives the exact transliteration as "*b*khra shis lhun po" (the Mountain of Grace). Mr. Bogle, in a vocabulary, gives the meaning of *Lumbo* as "country." It should be "hill," or "lump."

[2] In the small valley of Nepal, Mr. Hodgson tells us that, some years ago, there were 5000 Bandyas, which term seems to be the equivalent of Bogle's priest.

RELIGIOUS BUILDINGS IN THE TESHU LUMBO MONASTERY.

(FROM A DRAWING IN TURNER'S EMBASSY TO TIBET. p.314.)

hinges of iron, cunningly gilt, having a large ring of the same workmanship in the middle, with a white satin handkerchief tied to it, so that you may not wear off the gilding in pulling the door after you. The door turns upon two pegs cut out of the planks, and received into two holes top and bottom. It is fastened by an iron latch and staple, with a lock of the construction of Chinese ones, and about a foot long. The room is about fifty feet long and thirty broad, interrupted by nine square wooden pillars, painted red with white streaks, which make them look fluted. There are two small windows with wooden shutters at the west end, but I never opened them, having enough light from above, for in the ceiling of the room there is an opening about thirty feet long and fifteen wide; and the south side being covered only with loose planks, laid slopingly over, you remove as many of them as you please in the day time, and shut them up again at night. They rest upon a beam, supported by the two middlemost of the nine pillars, which are much longer than the others. The walls, which are of plaster, are painted green, broken with a few bands of blue and yellow. The capitals of the pillars, and the beams which form the four sides of the opening I have mentioned, are curiously carved, gilt and ornamented with festoons of dragons and flowers. The floor is of chalky clay, mixed with small pebbles, and formed into a smooth and very beautiful terrace, which, by the labours of a young gylong, who every morning gets his feet upon two woollen cloths, and exercises himself for three or four hours in skating about the room, will, in the course of fifteen or twenty years, acquire a polish equal to the other floors in the palace, which are not inferior to the finest variegated marble. Mr. Hamilton's room was much smaller and warmer than mine.

From the day of our arrival at Teshu Lumbo till the 18th of January, 1775, the Lama was engaged in receiving visits and presents. Among the rest of his votaries were a large caravan of Kalmuks, who offered up to his shrine talents of silver, furs, pieces of silk, and dromedaries. They remained about a month at Teshu Lumbo, and then proceeded to Lhasa, where, having spent about ten days, they returned to their own country, which was about three months' journey to the northward.

I was not present on any of these occasions, but remained at home, where I had enough visitors of my own; for crowds of gylongs used to come into my room to see me at all hours, or get upon the leads and look down upon me. Among these last came the Shigatzé Killadars, dressed in their feminine attire. I never forbade anybody; and after giving them a pinch of snuff and indulging them with a look at the chairs, &c., which always produced an exclamation of "Pah-pah-pah, tze-tze-tze!" they used to retire and make way for others. This continued, more or less, all the time I was at Teshu Lumbo.

The Lama went down to the large hall which adjoins my apartments, in order to bless the people. It is about sixty feet long and fifty broad; the ceiling supported by a number of high pillars, and the walls adorned with mythological paintings. The Lama was seated upon a lofty throne, raised with cushions, under an alcove at one end of the room. There was another, not so high, on his right hand, which belongs to Chanzo Cusho, who sat, however, on a low cushion at the foot of the Lama's throne, the *Sopon Chumbo* standing beside it. Immediately without the alcove were placed the four inferior Lamas. I was seated upon a cushion next to them, and opposite to me sat a Kalmuk Lama, lately arrived from the Khalka Lama, called by the Hindus Taranath,[1] and close to him the Dalai Lama's vakíl. Cheyt Sing's vakíl was placed below me and Mr. Hamilton, towards the door, and after him a vakíl from Kashmiri Mull, and other Hindus. I came in soon after the Lama was seated, and having made three profound bows, presented to him my handkerchief, which he always receives with his own hands. He spoke to me for about two minutes, inquiring about my health, what I thought of Teshu Lumbo, and how I liked my accommodation. After this crowds of people, gylongs, annís, Kampas, Kalmuks, governors of all the neighbouring castles, men, women, and children came to make their offerings and obeisances to the Lama, bringing purses of gold, talents of silver, pieces of Chinese satin, bundles of tea or of fruits, dried sheep's carcasses, bags of flour or of rice, small images with a bit of yellow satin wrapped mantle-wise over them, books of religion,

[1] The Taranath Lama is the third Pontiff of the Yellow Cap (Geluckpa sect); the Dalai and Teshu being the other two. The Taranath resides north of Tibet, among the Khalka tribes of outer Mongolia, near Urga.

bundles of incense, rods called *pyes*, bells, and a variety of different articles. Those of low degree gave only a white satin handkerchief. They went up in their turn to the Lama's throne, who touched their heads in the manner I have before described. The young gylongs immediately after the imposition of hands retired; but I could not help observing with pleasure the attention which the Lama paid to some of the old gylongs, speaking to them for a minute or two with that affable and engaging look which "wins the hearts of men." Between whiles the Lama, and everybody that was seated, drank a dish of tea. I had mine out of the Lama's golden teapot, an honour bestowed only upon Chanzo Cusho, the inferior Lamas, and the vakíls of the Dalai Lama and Taranath. There was a company of fifteen young boys, from seven to twelve years old, dressed in different coloured chintzes and kincobs, with white turbans, and small axes in their right hands, who at intervals danced before the Lama, to the music of hautboys, flutes, kettledrums, and bells, keeping time with their axes, with their hoppings, their twirlings, and many other motions which I attempt not to describe. I am told it was an imitation of a Sadak[1] dance. Another part of the entertainment consisted of public disputes, which were conducted by two and two gylongs. Religion was the subject of their debates; perhaps the immortality of the soul, or the unchangeable nature of right and wrong; but my ignorance of the language rendered them quite unintelligible to me. They were carried on with much vociferation and feigned warmth, and embellished with great powers of action, such as clapping hands, shaking the head, &c. These gestures are no doubt very improper and ridiculous, because they are quite different from those used by European orators, who are the true standards of what is just and what is graceful. Dinner was afterwards brought in. Six large, low tables, covered with wooden painted platters, filled with Chinese and Kashmiri dried fruits, sugar, treacle cakes, and sweetmeats, piles of platted biscuits, dried sheep's carcasses, &c., were set before the Lama. Two tables garnished in the like manner before the Chanzo Cusho; and some bread, pieces of dried mutton, plates of fruits and sweetmeats, before me and each of the other guests.

[1] Turner says that Sadík was a title of the Sopon Chumbo. It is synonymous with *Zempi* in Bhutan, and means cup-bearer (p. 246).

After drinking a dish of tea, cups of mutton hashed and of pounded rice and mutton boiled to a jelly were set before us, of which I ate heartily. Then a joint of mutton boiled and another roasted, upon the same wooden plate, were served up to each. The meat was tough and sinewy, but the Lama presently sent me a leg of most excellent boiled mutton off his own plate, and smilingly beckoned to me to eat of it. When we had finished our repast, the *Sopon Chumbo* distributed the fruits, sweetmeats, &c., according to a list which he held in his hand, sending some of them to people without the palace, and the rest to the guests. Mine were all upon silver dishes. Then everybody retired.

The Lama went up by a back stair to visit the new apartments, and carried me along with him. He went first into the gallery,[1] which is on the same floor with my room, and walking up to the image of the god Sakya, which is in the middle, fell down three times before it. I may as well describe this temple while I am here.

It contains thirteen gigantic figures, which would be about eight feet high standing; but they are all, except the image of the god of war and another, sitting cross-legged. They are of copper gilt, holding a pot with flowers or fruit in their lap. They are represented covered with mantles, and crowns or mitres on their heads; and altogether, particularly the drapery, are far from being badly executed. The thrones upon which they sit are also of copper gilt, adorned with turquoises, cornelians, and other stones not of inestimable value. The mouldings and ornaments of the thrones are in a good style. Behind each figure the wall is covered with a piece of carved work, like unto the heavy gilt frames of our forefathers' portraits, or looking-glasses. Behind them are china vases, some of them very handsome, loads of china and glass ware, the last partly Chinese, partly European, filled with grain, fruit, or gum flowers; a variety of shells, large chanks set in silver, some ostrich eggs, cocoanuts, cymbals, and a variety of other articles, making a most heterogeneous figure. Round the necks of the images are strings of coral, ill-shaped pearls, cornelian, agate, and other stones, and their crowns are set with the like ornaments. The ceiling of the gallery is covered with satins of a variety of patterns,

[1] This gallery is described by Turner at p. 274.

some Chinese, some Kalmuk, some European brought through Russia and overland. The gallery is lighted on the south side by five windows, and the walls between are hung with paintings of the different deities and views of heaven. The opposite side, where the images are, is shut in all the length of the gallery with a net of ironwork. The Lama went within, and as he went along sprinkled rice upon the images. It was a kind of consecration. When he came out we sat down to tea, and the Lama explained to me some of the paintings, and marked the different countries from which the silks overhead had come. At each end of the gallery was a large collection of books deposited in small niches, or rather pigeon-holes. Having finished our tea, we went by a back stair into my room, which the Lama also bespattered with rice. After examining the furniture, with a set of chessmen in battle array upon the table, he passed into Mr. Hamilton's room, and having there performed the same rites of dedication, I took my leave and the Lama proceeded to his own end of the palace.

Next morning, the Lama repaired again to the hall, whither we all attended him. But why should I repeat over the ceremonies of which I have already given so minute and so tiresome a description?

I had a visit from Debo Patza, who is one of the four Tibetan generals, and I took care to receive him in all due form. He said he came by the Lama's orders, who told him that as I had come from so far a country, and from the sovereigns of Hindustan, it was proper he should wait upon me. He is a very cheerful, pleasant man, and after some conversation, and drinking a dish or two of tea, we sat down to chess. Although my pieces were entirely new to him, he fought a tough battle, and I believe, if we had played another game, the general would have gained the victory. But he was next day to set out for Lhasa, and was afterwards ordered upon service into Demo Jong's country [1] to oppose the troops with which the Gorkha Rajah had invaded it.

On the 25th, Debo Dinjí came also to take leave of me. He is the governor of a castle belonging to the Teshu Lama, about six days' journey higher up the Tsanpu; and as nobody under the Lama's jurisdiction is put to death, all great criminals are sent

[1] Sikkim.

to him, where, by confining them without meat or drink, he soon puts an end to their existence. He had paid me frequent and unceremonious visits in my tents upon the road. His looks and his manners are exactly those of an overgrown country farmer, smelling strongly of tobacco. I could not help sometimes thinking him a little crack-brained. He discovered that the dress of the English was exactly that of the Russians; for indeed the tunic which I wore, and also my cap, the cut of which was four-square instead of being round, had been made a present of to the Lama by some Turki Tatars.[1] I had no business to undeceive him, especially as I got so much into his good graces on this account. He said he liked the Russians for their enmity to the Chinese, who were a base, treacherous, and scoundrelly people. I confess I was a good deal surprised at the warmth with which he always revived this treasonable subject, till I discovered that he had been in the service of Wang Cusho, the last of the Tibet Rajahs, who about twenty-five years ago was treacherously put to death by the Chinese at Lhasa.[2]

I had a visit from the Chauduri,[3] a native of Palpa,[4] whom I have elsewhere mentioned, accompanied by other Hindustanis. The vakils of Cheyt Sing and of Kashmiri Mull also came to see me, and afterwards frequently repeated their visits. Their discourse has no business to come in here. But I may be allowed to remark that the fulsome compliments and cringing humility with which it was mixed were to me little grateful, in comparison with the plain and honest manners of the Tibetans. For what is conversation, what is society, without sincerity?

The Lama was to receive the vakils sent by the Dalai Lama and Gesub Rimboché[5] at Lhasa, to congratulate him on his return. He asked me to be present. The ceremony was in the large church to the south of the palace. I was up in the balcony

[1] This is an instance of the confusion caused by the indiscriminate use of the word Tatar or Tartar.

[2] He was invited to the house of the *Ambas*, or Chinese residents at Lhasa, and there strangled, in 1749. This led to a massacre of the Chinese, and to concessions from the Peking Government.

[3] See p. 172.

[4] Palpa is a town in Nepal, on the right bank of the Gandak River, 112 miles from Kathmandu.

[5] Gesub Rimboché is the President of the Council of Five, and head of the executive during the minority of the Dalai Lama. *Rimbochay*, *Rimboché*, or *Rimpoche*, means "precious," or "jewel."

which looks into it. The church was full of gylongs, dressed in yellow caps and mantles, and seated as close to one another as possible. When the Lama came in, he made three prostrations towards the altar and the image of God; after which he ascended his throne, raised very lofty by steps. We had a great deal of praying, and some dishes of tea between whiles. Then came in the Dalai Lama's vakíl, with a large silver platter curiously embossed, and covered with rice divided into five heaps; and he, together with three others, stood with it before the Lama, while he made an harangue of a quarter of an hour long. I was in pain for him, as I thought once or twice he would have broken down. During all this time the Lama nor anybody else spoke not a word. When he had ended, the Lama answered him in a short speech, and taking up a little of the rice, threw it towards the altar. He then received the Dalai Lama's letter, together with four or five small images, as many books, and some chanks set in silver, all which he placed before him on his throne. Next came in a string of people carrying gifts; each man a talent of silver, a piece of silk, or a bundle of tea. When all the Dalai Lama's presents were finished, Gesub's were brought, in the same style, but of less value. Altogether there were about a hundred talents of silver, a hundred and twenty pieces of silk, and sixty bundles of tea. There were also about six talents of silver, ten pieces of silk, and four bundles of tea given to the Chanzo Cusho. While all this was passing, a great number of petitions were, according to the custom, thrown into the church, each being tied to a white satin handkerchief. The gylongs afterwards handed them from one to another till they reached the foot of the throne, where they were collected, and then handed up to the Lama. I am told they are principally desiring prayers for sick people, or for the souls of those lately dead. The Lama read over one or two of them, after which he said a short prayer by himself, and was followed by another by the gylongs. Then everyone departed.

What can I do to break the thread of these tiresome ceremonies? and how can I render the account of the tedious and uniform life I spent at Teshu Lumbo agreeable? It was monastic to the greatest degree. Nothing but priests; nothing from morning to night but the chanting of prayers, and the sound of cymbals and tabors.

Every attention was paid to me by the Lama. I enjoyed good health, and a mind free from care and anxiety. Yet the employment I found in attempting to acquire the language, in listening to the stories of fakirs and Kashmiris, or in carrying on a broken conversation with the crowds of Tibetans who used to frequent my apartment, yielded an entertainment listless and insipid when compared with the pleasures of society; and my life at Teshu Lumbo, when stripped of the little unmarked circumstances which amuse, one knows not why, and seen through the dull medium of description, must appear joyless and uninteresting.

I must confess the pleasantest hours I spent, before the arrival of the Pyn Cushos, were either in my audiences with the Lama, or in playing at chess. The arrival of a large party of Kalmuks furnished me with enough of combatants. Their method of playing differs from ours, in the privilege of moving two steps being confined to the first pawn played by each party; in castling and stalemate being unknown; and in the game being reckoned equal when the king is left solus without a piece or a pawn on the board. It is a generous principle. In my first trials of skill with the Tatars, I used often to come off loser. For when a Siberian sits down to chess, he gets two or three of his countrymen to assist him; they lay all their great bare heads together canvassing and consulting about every move. At length I found out the way of managing them, and encountered them with their own weapons. If I could not get a Siberian to enter the lists with me in single combat, I engaged an equal number of Tatars on my side, and we used to beat them hollow.[1]

Soon after their arrival at Teshu Lumbo, the Lama went to visit the different churches, and I was always invited to be present. A small tent was pitched for me on the leads, and I used to pass the first service, which generally lasted a couple of hours, in drinking tea, eating boiled mutton and sweetmeats, and playing at chess with the Kalmuks. After this, I was called to prayers, and sat another hour or two on a cushion next to the Chanzo Cusho in a balcony which looked into the church. The gylongs are all seated, as I have already described; the prayers are mostly chanted in

[1] See Turner, p. 235, who says that the rules of chess in Tibet are the same as ours.

different, and often not unmelodious, voices; and the service, except on particular holidays, is conducted with great decency. The priests here are much better taught than in the Deb Rajah's country, and in repeating their offices have no occasion for the books which are used at Tassisudon. On some festivals, however, a man, dressed in party-coloured clothes, and a cardinal's cap adorned with death's-heads, used to come in, and with many strange gestures hop and twist about, pouring out oblations of oil, brandy, rice, &c., and holding a human skull, a bell, a dagger, or an axe in his hand. Between the services, the Lama sometimes sent for me into a small room upon the leads. During my stay at Teshu Lumbo, I suppose I spent fifteen or twenty days in this manner at church, for I never failed to go when I was asked.

I had this day a visit from the vakíls who lately came from the Dalai Lama and Gesub Rimboché. One of them was a priest, and dressed in the habit of his order. The other was clad in feminine attire. They brought me some small barrels and boxes containing presents from Gesub Rimboché. Upon opening them, they were found to consist of Chinese distilled whisky, a variety of small cakes made by the same people, a kind of fish less than a minnow, dried, and some dried mushrooms, which they said came from Peking. The whisky was stronger and better than that of Tibet; the bread of very fine flour, but not half baked nor even kneaded; the fish we could never find out how to dress, but the mushrooms served greatly to improve the simple and unsavoury economy of our table. I received the vakíls in all due form; they stayed with me about an hour, and left me little satisfied with their manners or conversation.

The holidays at the new year drew nigh, and the Lama's relations came from different parts of the country to pay their respects to him. His cousin the Teshu-tzay Debo, with his wife and family; his nieces, the two annís whom I saw at Teshu-tzay; their mother Chum Cusho; their two brothers, the Pyn Cushos; and a half-sister named Durjay Paumo, a female lama, who is abbess of a monastery near the Piate Lake,[1] and is animated by the spirit of a holy lady who died many hundred years ago. All the ladies, together with the Debo and his wife, were lodged in a house

[1] The Piate, also called Palti Lake, and Yamdok-cho.

situated in a grove of old trees under the palace, and the Pyn Cushos in a Kalmuk tent adjoining to it. They stayed about two months at Teshu Lumbo, during which time Mr. Hamilton cured Durjay Paumo and Chum Cusho of complaints which they had long been subject to, and I improved my connection with the Pyn Cushos. They used often to come and pass two or three hours with me. I sometimes went down to their tent, where we spent the time in singing, smoking, drinking *chang*,[1] and playing upon the flute or the guitar, at which the eldest brother is a great adept. We made little excursions into the country; and I afterwards accompanied them to their estate at Rinjaitzay, and spent five or six cheery days at their castle. The eldest brother is about twenty-seven, the youngest about twenty-two.

There is another brother, who is bred up to the church. He is a lama or high-priest,[2] but is not yet allowed to officiate on account of his youth. He used also to come often to see me, and being very lively and of great curiosity, I had much pleasure in showing him anything; but the decorum of his character would not permit him to be of any of our parties with his brothers. Lama Allî is about sixteen: short for his age, but very fair and ruddy, and blessed with that fine temper which distinguishes all Teshu Lama's family.

On the first day of the Tibetan year, everybody, except the Lama, assembled in the large court which is under the palace. All the galleries which ran round it were crowded with spectators. I was placed, as usual, next the Chanzo Cusho in the highest balcony. The exhibitions began with dancing by merry Andrews in masks. Then a number of banners were set up, and a crowd of gylongs, dressed in various coloured habits, with their cymbals and tabors, and with trumpets, hautboys, and drums, marched in procession round the court. Next, about twenty gylongs, in visors representing the heads of different, mostly wild, animals, and in masquerade dresses, danced with antic motions, in the same manner (but better performed) as I had seen at Tassisudon. After this, the figure of a man, chalked upon paper, was laid upon the ground. Many strange ceremonies, which to me who did not understand

[1] *Chang*, or *Chhung*, any fermented liquor. (See 'Jaeschke's Dictionary.')

[2] Probably *Khunpo* or Abbot, head of a monastery or *Vihar*.

them appeared whimsical, were performed about it; and a great fire being kindled in a corner of the court, it was at length held over it, and being formed of combustibles, vanished with much smoke and explosion. I was told it was a figure of the devil, but am not sufficiently skilled in the Tibetan mythology to enter into particulars. One thing is certain, it was painted white with regular features; and whether or no it was intended to represent that being who "goes to and from upon the face of the earth, seeking whom he may devour," I could not help sometimes fancying that it much resembled a European.

I was visited by the vakil of Prithi Narayan,[1] the Rajah of Nepal, who presented me with two sheep, some rupees, rice, spices, &c. The conversation that passed I have elsewhere put down.

A good many Kalmuks visited Mr. Hamilton. He thought they were come to apply for some medicines. Every one presented him with a handkerchief, according to the custom of the country. They told him, that having heard of his great skill in the occult sciences, they were come to have their fortunes told, and at the same time stretched out their hands for that purpose. While he was hesitating whether to carry on the joke a little farther, they desired him first to tell what had happened to them last year, and then to proceed to unfold their future destiny. This would go far to prove skill in fortune-telling, and was a test Mr. Hamilton was unable to undergo. I have often myself been taken for a conjurer, and had applications of the same kind made to me, but it was only by my particular acquaintances. I dare say a man skilled in palmistry or a company of gipsies would have a world of business in these parts; for although I could not discover any Shamans in the country, the Tibetans have great faith in fortune-telling, which indeed seems to be common to all mankind, except our European philosophers, who are too wise to believe in anything.

The Teshu-tzay Debo paid me a visit, bringing two tables covered with dried fruits and sweetmeats. I offered to repay the compliment, but he never sent to me, and I did not wish to appear overzealous in cultivating his friendship, as it would have hurt my

[1] Pertab Singh Sah Deva, of the Gorkhali dynasty, succeeded in 1771 and reigned in Nepal until 1775. Prithi Narayan was his father.

connection with the Pyn Cushos, who are on but indifferent terms with him on account of his wife, who belongs also to them. It is a strange story, but I have no business to mention it.

We spent the 15th of February with the Pyn Cushos, at some tents prepared for us on the side of a hill, a few miles from Teshu Lumbo. Shooting at a mark, running races, and seeing some of the peasants dance and sing, formed our entertainment, for there is no hunting or killing animals so near the palace. Our friends had prepared a great feast for us, and not knowing what we would like, took care to have every kind of flesh and fowl they could think of. After dinner, tables covered with fruits were brought in, and they insisted on presenting us with dresses and horses. Having drank plenty of tea and *chang*, we returned to the palace. I rode the horse the Pyn Cushos gave me, which was a Kalmuk, but I did not find it so tractable as these horses are said to be. I had enough ado to keep it from running away with me.

I waited upon the ladies. The Chum Cusho is a cheerful widow of about five-and-forty, with a ruddy complexion, and the remains of having once been handsome. In her younger days she was a nun, and her husband, the Lama's brother, a gylong; but they happened somehow to form such a connection together as put an end to their state of celibacy. The Lama was much displeased with his brother, and would not admit him into his presence for many years. After his death, Chum Cusho, being passed the hey-day of life, resumed her religious character; and having taken up her vows of chastity, laid aside all her ornaments, dressed herself in a homely garb, and set out on pilgrimages to visit the temples in Nepal, Palpa, &c.[1] The Lama has since behaved to her and her children with much kindness. Her sons, the Pyn Cushos, and her daughters, the annís, were present. We had plenty of tea, mutton, broth, fruits, &c., and the old woman was as merry as a cricket.

The mother went with me into the apartment of Durjay Paumo, who was attired in a gylong's dress, her arms bare from the shoulders,

[1] See, in Mr. Hodgson's account of the Pravrajya-vrata, the statement of the full renunciation, and of the process by which it is modified. ('Languages and Religion of Nepal and Tibet,' pp. 139–145.) The red-vested and oldest sect tolerated marriage. The yellow-vested, and now dominant sect in Tibet, does not tolerate it.

and sitting cross-legged upon a low cushion. She is also the daughter of the Lama's brother, but by a different wife. She is about seven-and-twenty, with small Chinese features, delicate, though not regular, fine eyes and teeth; her complexion fair, but wan and sickly; and an expression of languor and melancholy in her countenance, which I believe is occasioned by the joyless life that she leads. She wears her hair, a privilege granted to no other vestal I have seen; it is combed back without any ornaments, and falls in tresses upon her shoulders. Her *chawa*, like the Lama's, is supposed to convey a blessing, and I did not fail to receive it. After making my presents and obeisances, I kneeled down, and stretching out her arm, which is equal to "the finest lady in the land," she laid her hand upon my head. The entertainment was the same as at the mother's. Durjay Paumo spoke little, and but for the old woman, who was present, the conversation would have been full of breaks. I never visited her but this time. Mr. Hamilton used to be there almost every day.

The two nuns are as merry and good-humoured as their mother. The eldest, who is about seven or eight and twenty, is dark complexioned and hard featured. The youngest is about nineteen; remarkably fair and ruddy. Their dress is the same as that of the gylongs. The head shaven, the arms bare, a red frieze jacket, reaching a little below the waist, a piece of coarse red woollen cloth thrown over their shoulders, a petticoat of red serge falling a little below the knee, and red woollen hose soled with leather, and gartered under the knee. They, as well as the priests, are not allowed to wear any kind of ornament, except it be a few beads of coral strung with their rosaries.

I may be excused, perhaps, in mentioning a circumstance, which, although it does not properly belong to these memoranda, I cannot, in justice to my Tibetan friends, omit. From the civilities which Teshu Lama and everybody about him had shown me, as well as from my desire of conciliating the good-will of the Tibetans, whose country I believe no Englishman had ever visited before, I resolved to make some presents to the Lama's relations; and accordingly purchased coral beads, which are much valued in this part of the world. I carried them with me on my visit to the Chum Cusho and her daughters, and had much ado to procure their acceptance of them. The Pyn Cushos were still more difficult, and I believe I spent an hour in their tent before I could get them to agree to take my beads. "You," said they, "are come from a far country; it is our business to render your stay agreeable; why should you make us presents?" This circumstance serves to set the character of the Tibetans in a stronger and more favourable light than if I were to write volumes upon the subject.

The Sokpo[1] (Kalmuk) Lama came to visit me. He is one of Taranath's[2] priests, and receives the title of Lama, I believe, only by courtesy. He is a native of Ladak, but has resided long in Siberia; is a very pleasant and entertaining man, and brought me a pot full of tea, and a handkerchief. I wanted to return his visit, but he excused himself on account of his attendance on Teshu Lama. He remained some time after the Kalmuk's departure for Lhasa, and paid me another visit before he set out.

About this time I undertook a work for the Lama which gave me a good deal of employment and a good deal of trouble. It was an account of Europe, and I confess I found it a very difficult task, for I had to fancy myself a Tibetan, and then put down the things which I imagined would strike him. I had abundance of difficulty also in translating it into the Tibet language, being obliged to use an interpreter, a kind of being who is generally more apt to follow out roundly his own ideas than to keep strictly to yours. I got through France, England, and such other countries as I have seen; but having no books to assist me, I was obliged to leave it unfinished. As it was, it afforded a great feast to the Lama's insatiable curiosity.[3]

As Mr. Hamilton was returning from Durjay Paumo's, he saw a crowd of people, in the midst of which a young gylong was being

[1] The Sokpo occupy the eastern half of Northern Tibet. The Horpo, who are Turks, the western half. (See pp. 65–82, of Hodgson's 'Languages of Nepal and Tibet.')

[2] There are three lamas over the *gelupka*, or yellow sect, of Tibetan Buddhists, called Dalai, Teshu, and Taranath. The Taranath Lama resides in the Khalka country of Mongolia. Turner has Kharka, p. 315.

[3] A copy of this curious and interesting document has been preserved. Mr. Bogle describes Europe as it was in 1770: the inns and stage-coaches, the highwaymen, the duels, the parliaments of France, and other Old World institutions. Doubtless this document is still studied in Tibet, and is the source whence the statesmen of that isolated region obtain their ideas of England and Europe.

chastised for neglecting his lesson. He was extended upon the ground and held down by four people, while a fifth was bastinading him. Let no one who has been at a public school in Europe cry out against the Tibetans for cruelty.

The Pyn Cushos used often to come and see me. To-day their sisters, the nuns, came along with them. They asked me to show them my Fringy dress,[1] and we prevailed on the youngest sister to put on my coat. We had a great deal of laughing and merriment. But who can repeat the little unimportant trifles which gladden conversation and serve to while away the time?

The priest, who every morning came to me with boiled rice and tea from the Lama, was called Debo Dinji Sampu. He was about fifty, marked with the smallpox, his eye mild and candid, and himself of great singleness of mind and simplicity. He came to understand my imperfect attempts to speak the Tibet language tolerably well, and we used to have long chats together. I grew very fond of him, and he, which showed his sagacity, took a great liking to me. He always kept a box of excellent snuff, and was not niggardly in offering a pinch of it. But with all Debo Dinji's good qualities, he was as averse to washing his hands and face as the rest of his countrymen. He happened one morning to come in while I was shaving, and I prevailed upon him for once to scrub himself with the help of soap and water. I gave him a new complexion, and he seemed to view himself in my shaving glass with some satisfaction. But he was exposed to so much ridicule from his acquaintances, that I never could get him to repeat the experiment.[2]

[1] Fringy and Feringhi (Frank) is the common Asiatic equivalent for European.

[2] Mr. Hodgson, in Nepal, once bribed a Tibetan mother to let him wash her child in order to judge of his complexion, which seemed singularly clear and white. The child struggled so violently as nearly to have a fit.

CHAPTER XI.

A VISIT TO A TIBETAN COUNTRY SEAT.

On the 11th of March, 1775,[1] the Pyn Cushos were to set out for their country seat, about two days' journey from Teshu Lumbo, and asked me to accompany them. I was glad of an opportunity of varying the insipid scene, and applied for the Lama's permission, which he readily granted me. We set out about midday. I carried with me only one Hindustani servant, resolving to live like a Tibetan. The Pyn Cushos had about a dozen servants. We arrived towards evening at a village, in the valley through which runs the Tsanpu, and took up our quarters in the head man's house. After drinking tea, dinner was brought in. A cup of hashed mutton, not unlike a greasy curry, another of boiled rice, a third of raw beef beat into a jelly, and highly seasoned with salt, turmeric, and other spices. It is far from unsavoury, when one can get the better of European prejudices. There were also a joint of mutton well boiled, and another just scorched on the outside but raw within. It requires no conjuring to find out on which I made my dinner. There is no such thing as two people cutting from the same joint of meat, or helping themselves from the same plate, so that a separate set of the above dishes was served up to each. After this we had fruits and sweetmeats, and, the Pyn Cushos having lent me a pipe, we sat down to smoke. We then adjourned to a small garden, to shoot arrows. A tent was pitched with a black cloth at some distance. Such as hit the bull's-eye had a handkerchief given them. I also received one, though unmeritedly. Night came on. We returned and sat down about a goodly fire, new kindled in the middle of the room, spending a couple of hours in singing, drinking *chang*, playing upon the guitar, or at chess. Mr. Hamilton and I then retired to another apartment, where a supper was prepared for us, as if we had not tasted meat that day; but afraid that we

[1] The day Nuncomar brought his accusations against the Governor-General.

would not relish Tibetan victuals, the Pyn Cushos had ordered their servants to ask our people about our usual food, and had prepared some eggs, fish, and roasted fowls.

Next morning we got up before day, and found the Pyn Cushos ready to sit down to breakfast, upon tea and cold mutton. As I can always eat at any hour of the day or night, I did not fail to partake with them. After this we had the ceremony of the master of the house presenting us with fruits, sweetmeats, and carcasses, and having settled all this in due form, we set out on our journey. Having ridden about an hour we reached the bank of the Tsanpu. The boats were all on the other side, and the river covered with shoals of snow-mixed ice. We had to wait here a couple of hours. There was a tent with tea prepared for us, and I spent part of the time in sliding on the ice, with which a neighbouring pool of water was covered. As soon as we were ferried over, we mounted our horses and rode cheerily up the sandy bank of the Tsanpu, stopping twice at tents prepared for us, to refresh ourselves with tea and mutton. In the afternoon we came to the foot of a mountain covered with red ochre, and dedicated to some wrathful deity. Here the Pyn Cushos set up the branch of a tree, with a white handkerchief fastened to it. The Tsanpu at this place forms a large sheet of water immediately below the road. You have a view of its windings for a great way up and down, and the prospect would be very fine if there was anything besides bleak bare hills to look at. The winds in this valley are very strong, often carrying up the dust in columns to a great height, or forming it into hills of sand. Turning to the right we entered the valley where the Pyn Cushos' estate is situated, and stopped at some tents set up by a servant of Gesub Rimboché, who has the care of a house belonging to that minister.[1] Among the rest of our entertainment were excellent mutton puffs, a dish which I had not before seen. Ascending the valley we arrived at Rinjaitzay Castle about an hour after it was dark, having, by our stoppings and tea drinkings, taken a complete day to perform a journey which might easily be done in six hours.

[1] Gesub Rimboché is the vicegerent of the divine Dalai Lama, who theoretically does not meddle with temporal matters. The Deb Rajah and Dharma Rajah (or Lama Rimboché) represent the same two offices in Bhutan.

I was lodged in the room of the church, which is generally the best in the house. As the Pyn Cushos, particularly the youngest, are keen sportsmen, it was hung round with matchlocks, bows and arrows, swords, shot-bags, &c., and one part of the wall was covered with Chinese paper-hangings. After presenting me with loads of fruit, they brought in supper, which made the sixth time that I had seen meat that day.

During the five or six days we spent at Rinjaitzay, the Pyn Cushos entertained us in the most hospitable manner, omitting nothing that could contribute to our amusement. They made parties on horseback, shooting matches with bows and matchlocks; they caught and bagged hares, for us to see them retaken by the greyhounds; partridges and other game for us to eat, and one day we went out with the nets to catch musk goats.[1] This requires a more particular description.

After riding about three miles from Rinjaitzay, we stopped at a tent and sat there two hours while the servants went up the hills to reconnoitre. I confess I did not much conceit this method of hunting in a tent, and formed no favourable presage of our sport. At length I prevailed on the younger brother to set out, and letting loose the dogs we rode along the sides of the hills, but without seeing anything except a covey of partridges; and although the Pyn Cushos make no bones of shooting when by themselves, they were afraid that some of the Lama's people who accompanied me might mention it at Teshu Lumbo, and so get them into a scrape.

At length, when we were about to return, one of the servants came with the news of having found a musk goat asleep in a quarry. The dogs were immediately tied up. The people with the toils went along the side of the mountain, and above the place where the game lay, while we followed slowly after. The toils are made of cords, formed into a number of nooses hung close to one another, on a rope which is extended at about three feet from the ground, and supported by rods stuck in the earth at intervals of about ten or twelve feet. There is another row of nooses similar to this placed parallel to it, and at the distance of about five feet. When these double toils were set all round one side of the quarry, and at about a gunshot from it, we spread ourselves, encircled the other

[1] *Moschus moschiferus.* The musk deer of Europeans, but more like an antelope.

side, and with shouts and stones at length awakened the musk from his profound sleep. As soon as he got upon the brow of the hill, he boundingly made towards the toils, and having twice attempted to leap over them, thrust his head into one of the nooses.[1] When we came up to him he was quite breathless with struggling, and all the skin, which is very tender, was torn off his neck with the cord. We carried him home and put him into a closet adjoining to my room; but he died before morning.

The musk is about the size of an antelope, but without any horns. The bag of perfume for which it is famous is produced only in the male, who is also of a colour more dark than the female, and distinguished by two tusks which fall perpendicularly from his upper jaw. The hair is speckled yellow and brown at the point, and resembles the fledges of a quill almost as much as hair. It has an amazing strong attractive quality, like amber, and sticks to your fingers so that it is difficult to shake it off. The skins of the musks which I have seen in the Deb Rajah's country are much darker than those in Tibet; they approach almost to black. The common way of killing the musk is by matchlocks and bows and arrows. It is sadly persecuted by the peasants about the beginning of winter, and numbers of them seek protection on the privileged mountains behind Teshu Lumbo.[2]

[1] Colonel Markham (p. 95) says that snaring is by far the most common method practised for the capture of musk deer in Ladak. A fence, about 3 feet high, is made, generally along some ridge, and often upwards of a mile in length. Openings for the deer to pass through are left every 10 or 15 yards, and in each a strong hempen snare is placed, tied to a long stick.

[2] There is an excellent account of the musk deer in Colonel Fred. Markham's 'Journal of Sporting Adventures in Ladak, Tibet, and Kashmir' (Bentley, 1854), p. 84. The musk deer is rather more than 3 feet long, and stands nearly 2 feet high at the shoulders. The head is small, the ears long and erect. The male has a tusk depending from each upper jaw about 3 inches long. The general colour is a dark speckled brownish-grey, deepening to nearly black on the hind quarters. The legs are long and slender, toes long and pointed. The fur is composed of thick spiral hairs, not unlike miniature porcupine quills, brittle, and very thickly set. The musk is only found in adult males. The pod is near the navel, between the flesh and skin, and is composed of several layers of thin skin in which the musk is confined. The musk itself is in grains, or powder, of a dark reddish-brown colour; and an ounce is the average yield of a full-grown animal. The musk deer is found all over the Himalayan chains, but generally at elevations at or above 8000 feet—generally in forests, and is of solitary and retired habits. In many respects they are not unlike hares in habits and economy; and they make forms in the same manner.

The partridges are considerably smaller than those in England. Regarding their taste I cannot say anything, for the cook allowed three, which Mr. Hamilton one day shot, to fly away some hours after they were dead; and those which the Pyn Cushos now caught for me were so tame, it would have been a sin to kill them; so I set them at liberty, which was considered by the Lama's servants to be a very pious action. As to the Pyn Cushos, they are little scrupulous about this or any venial sin, and, as long as it comes not to the knowledge of the Lama, will do anything you like.

The Pyn Cushos keep a large parcel of all kinds of dogs at Rinjaitzay, and some of them, particularly Shâmo, are great favourites. There is also a wolf[1] chained at the foot of the stair, a tiger cat fastened to a stone on the leads, besides other animals.

After supper everyone retired to his room and went to bed, thinking no evil. But about the middle of the night we were alarmed with a dreadful barking and howling among the dogs, which soon brought all the family together upon the leads; Mr. Hamilton and I in our shirts, the rest with only a blanket wrapped round them, it being the custom for the Tibetans, both men and women, to sleep naked. There was no light but starlight; the noises still continued. Some said it was thieves; but as I could not think anybody would be so wicked as attempt to rob the Lama's family, I had nothing for it but to conclude it was the devil. In the meantime a most extraordinary yelling began just under our nose, which being totally different from anything I had ever heard, would certainly have served to confirm my notion, had not the whole family, to my utter astonishment, burst out into a fit of laughing; and, Paima having managed to light a lamp with his tinder-box, we had the satisfaction to see Mr. Wolf, whose breaking loose had occasioned all this disturbance, pinned down by the tiger cat, with her claws fixed in his cheeks. And so, having remanded him into confinement, each of our motley group, after looking a little at one another, returned laughing to bed.

Early in the morning we took leave of our hosts, set out from Rinjaitzay, and reached Teshu Lumbo at night, by excusing myself from stopping to drink tea at various places, and pushing through a great whirlwind of dust towards the end of our journey. At

[1] *Lupus laniger* (Hodgson).

night the palace and all the town were illuminated, in honour of the last Teshu Lama. It is reckoned very unlucky if the lamps should be blown out, and yet they were blown out upon this occasion. However, the sons of men can easily find salvos for anything. A few extraordinary prayers, or one or two solemnities, avert the evil.

In the morning my friend Debo Dinji Sampu came to see me. He looked more thoughtful than usual; and after we had drank a dish of tea and exchanged a pinch of snuff, he told me the cause of it—that he was appointed Governor of Janglaché,[1] a castle of some consequence, about three days higher up the Tsanpu. I congratulated him on his good fortune; but it would not do. He said to me: "I know that many people would solicit this office, the obtaining of which gives me so much uneasiness; but I have from my youth continued with the Lama. I have never been employed on any public business; I am not used to writing, and have had no practice in accounts. I shall have a vast deal to do in my new employment; I know not well how to set about it, and am afraid of getting into a scrape." As the Christian virtue of humblemindedness is so rare, I could not help being pleased to meet with it in a Pagan. What I said to encourage Debo Dinji produced, as often happens, no effect; and he wanted me to apply to the Lama that he might accompany me, at least to Tassisudon; but he would not allow me to mention it as his desire, and I could not do it else. Soon after he set out for his government, having first taken leave of me, and presented me with some purses of gold dust and a white handkerchief at parting. I felt not the same heart's liking for the priest who succeeded to the honour of bringing me rice and tea in the morning, as I had for Debo Dinji. He afterwards was sent by the Lama to attend me to Tassisudon, and fell a sacrifice to a strange climate.

Some Chinese merchants came to Teshu Lumbo to buy lamb skins, and a Kashmiri brought one of them to see me. From his manners I thought he must be a little man. His cap was faced with black lamb skins; but as I understood the Lama did not wish

[1] Tchanglase, on D'Anville's map. Dziang-lodzé of Klaproth. It is on the south side of the Tsanpu, about 70 miles west of Teshu Lumbo. It was visited by Colonel Montgomerie's Pundit in 1865.

me to have any connection with him, I sent him away. I did not find him near so white as I expected.

I was invited to pass the afternoon at the Sopon Chumbo's, where I was treated with all the things I have so often repeated, set off with the most easy and entertaining conversation. The manners of the Tibetans are in general very engaging; but Sopon Chumbo, by travelling through Tatary and China, and by a long residence at the Court of Peking, has improved upon them.

I now seldom stirred out of my room, being employed from morning to night in translating some papers which the Lama gave me about Tibet.

The severity of the winter was now passed; the ice melted faster than it froze; the weather in the heat of the day was very comfortable, and I began to turn my views towards Bengal.

The Teshu-tzay Killadar's family had left us, and Durjay Paumo had set out for her convent. The Pyn Cushos were returned to Teshu Lumbo, but it was only to escort their mother and sisters to Teshu-tzay. I this day took leave of Chum Cusho and the two nuns, not without many blessings and much advice from the old woman, and many promises to the nuns of writing to them and sending them lories and looking-glasses. My parting with the Pyn Cushos was a harder task. I never could reconcile myself to the thoughts of a last farewell, and however anxious I was to return to Bengal and to the world, I could not take leave of my Tibetan friends with indifference, and would now find little satisfaction in repeating the circumstances of it.[1]

The last days of my stay at Teshu Lumbo were taken up with these ceremonies; all my acquaintances in the palace coming to me with pots of tea, little presents, kind looks, and kind expressions.

[1] Dr. Hamilton, in a letter to Mr. Bogle, dated at Tassisudon on May 30, 1776, announced the melancholy news that his young hosts the Pyn (or Pung) Cushos had recently died, within a few days of each other, just after having finished a long letter to their former guest.

CHAPTER XII.

AN ACCOUNT OF TIBET.

FACE OF THE COUNTRY — PRODUCE — FOOD — DRESS OF THE PEOPLE — PRIESTS AND NUNS — HORSES AND OTHER ANIMALS — HOUSES — DISPOSAL OF DEAD BODIES — POLYANDRY.

THIS country, from Ladak to the frontier of China, is called by the natives Pu,[1] pronounced as the French do *Dominus*, or as the Scotch do the Greek *upsilon*. It is full of hills: they might be called mountains if they were not so near to those in the Deb Rajah's kingdom; however, one has few of them to climb, the road leading through the valleys. Save here and there a monastery or a nunnery, they are left to the musk goats and other wild animals. The country is bare, stony, and unsheltered; hardly a tree is to be seen, except in the neighbourhood of villages, and even there in no great numbers. On the road from Pari-jong there are a great many ruinous houses, occasioned by a war with the Bhutanese about sixty years ago.

The valleys produce wheat and barley, and peas. The first are ground by water-mills of a very simple construction; the last is food only for cattle. The peasants and the bulk of the inhabitants live on flour made into dough, or baked with oil produced in the country; on mutton or the flesh of the cow-tailed cattle. The higher class of people eat rice brought from the Deb Rajah's country, unleavened bread made into twisted rolls with butter, mutton soup thickened with pounded rice, mutton boiled in joints or cut in pieces; beef, not much; sweetmeats and fruits brought from China and Kashmir. As to pork, so much used for food in the neighbouring kingdom, there are few swine in the country. All the world drink tea made in the same manner as in Tatary.[2]

[1] *Peu*, and the people *Peu-pa*; but more commonly *Bod* and *Bod-pa*.

[2] That is, the brick tea of commerce, so made up for transport. The supply is scanty, dear, and bad, and hence the certainty of a fine market for India tea, could the trade prohibition be annulled.

Among the great people there is a drinking of tea from morning till night. The lower class of people and the laymen will smoke eighty or a hundred pipes of tobacco in a day:[1] and they hold this but a small quantity indeed. They also drink brandy distilled from wheat, though seldom to excess. The priests are forbidden the use of both. They often trespass, however, in smoking, not in drinking.

The servants and peasants wear horizontal caps made of locks of sheep's wool dyed yellow. They are like the Scotch bonnets, but much larger. I never saw one above three feet in diameter. The women, in the winter time, cover their heads with small rough caps of the same materials. Sometimes they dye them a deep blood red. It has a droll appearance. Paima's dress may serve as a specimen of that of the inferior class of men. The higher laymen wear tunics of satin, brocaded or plain, lined with sheep and lamb skins, or Siberian furs; a round cap faced with fur, and crowned with a silk tassel, and Bulgar hide boots. Red broadcloth tunics are also far from uncommon. The women wear a jacket, and petticoat reaching a little below the knee, of coarse blanket, of serge striped or plain, or of Chinese satin, according to their condition; Tatar stockings soled with leather, and gartered under the knee. When dressed they have a piece of cloth thrown cloak-like over their shoulders. All ranks of them are at great pains in adorning their heads; plaiting their hair neatly enough with coral and amber beads, bugles, or pearls; they wear also necklaces of them, where the pieces of amber are sometimes as large as a hen's egg. The quantity of the two first kinds of beads that is on the head, even of a peasant's wife or daughter, is amazing. The two last sorts fall to the share only of the ladies.

It is not only uncomportable in this cold climate of Tibet, but directly contrary to the custom of the country for the inhabitants, whether male or female, high or low, ever to wash their hands or face. It is, therefore, difficult to determine with precision the complexion of the Tibetans. They are in general, I think, much darker than the Deb Rajah's subjects. Paima's hue, however, is among the blackest I have seen. They are also far from being so

[1] Of tobacco also the supply is scanty and dear; and for this commodity, too, a great outlet might be found in Tibet, were the artificial obstacles removed.

handsome or well made as their neighbour Bhutanese.[1] Here they are seldom above the middle size; in the Deb Rajah's country they are seldom under it. Many causes might be given for this difference; but they are perhaps only theoretical, and, at any rate, this is not the place for them.

The gylongs, or priests,[2] are a separate class of people. Their vows and their dress are the same as in the Deb Rajah's kingdom, but they are much more numerous; they have less political power, and the inferior ones are therefore worse clad, and fare worse. Besides the four thousand at Teshu Lumbo, and near three times that number at Lhasa, the gylongs are scattered over the country in monasteries with land annexed for their support. The annís, or nuns, have their heads shaven, and are dressed in red woollen; they take the same vows of chastity as the priests, and live in nunneries. Their number is not great. The gylongs and the annís, owing to a custom which I shall afterwards mention, contribute little towards increasing the population of the state.

The people in general are downright and good-humoured, not addicted to fawning, as in Bengal; but fond of laughing, dancing, singing, and taking snuff. In the Lama's palace, however, women and, of course, merriment are excluded.

The horses seldom rise above fourteen or fourteen and a half hands. They are mostly white; seldom piebald; strong, hardy, and not vicious, but ill treated. They run into the opposite extreme from the Bengalis. One man will feed, I cannot say take care of, twenty or five-and-twenty horses. The goats, sheep,[3] dogs, and cattle, which go down to Bengal, will give an account of themselves.

There are plenty of wild ducks and geese, which, being unmolested, are very tame, and numbers of hares; but I have seen only one covey of partridges.

[1] That is, the people of Bhutan, or the Lhopas. Mr. Hodgson observes that it may be questioned whether they are handsomer or fairer than the Bodpas, though the Sokpas of north-east Tibet are no doubt less handsome.

[2] Or rather monks.

[3] The wool of the Tibetan sheep is very fine. Mr. Hodgson sent a sample for examination, the value of which was placed at 9*d*. per lb. The following is a quotation from the prices current in October, 1875:

	Per lb.				
	s.	*d*		*s.*	*d.*
White East India wool	0	7	to	1	5½
Yellow and tinged ditto	0	5	„	1	3
Grey, black, and fawn, ditto	0	2½	„	0	11½

Some of the houses are of stone; others of brick, whitewashed or painted. The stairs are ladders; from the difficulty of getting long beams, the rooms are full of posts. They have no vents, but let out the smoke of their cow-dung fires by a hole in the roof, which answers also to give light. The whole room is abundantly dirty. The Lama's present habitation is small. His palace at Teshu Lumbo is, I am told, princely.[1] The ascent to the apartments here is also by ladders; but the apartments themselves are well painted, gilded, and finished: they want but windows and stoves. The first are only boards like the frames of a greenhouse; the last are unknown, and pots with charcoal are used in their stead.

I will mention only the two customs that appear most singular.

As there is little wood in the country, they cannot afford to burn their dead; but they take an equally effectual way of destroying them. The body is carried to a neighbouring mountain, and being cut and beat in pieces, is left to be devoured by the wild beasts. I went to visit one of these sepulchral mounts, and expected to find it like a charnel-house. Eagles, ravens, and hawks hovered over us; but not a vestige of mortality could I see. At length I was shown the spot where the body is laid, and could observe some fresh splinters. On the top of this gloomy hill, an aged virgin had fixed her solitary abode. I wanted much to see the inside of it. At last, after much rhetoric, I got her to open the only window of her hovel, and show her wrinkled face and dismal habitation. Having given us a kind of liquor made of wheat to drink, and muttered over many prayers for our safety, we took our leave. This female hermit subsists entirely on alms, and is held in general veneration throughout the country.

I am at a loss for a name to the other custom, unless I call it polyandry. In most Eastern countries polygamy is allowed. The advocates for it compare mankind to the deer; its enemies liken them to turtle-doves. Montesquieu and other political writers insist that it is destructive of population; and the women cry out that it is unjust and unreasonable that so many of their sex should be subjected to the pleasure of one man. But in this country they

[1] Mr. Bogle must have written this chapter at Deshcripgay, previous to his visit to Teshu Lumbo.

have their revenge. The elder brother marries a woman, and she becomes the wife of the whole family. They club together in matrimony as merchants do in trade. Nor is this joint concern often productive of jealousy among the partners. They are little addicted to jealousy. Disputes, indeed, sometimes arise about the children of the marriage; but they are settled either by a comparison of the features of the child with those of its several fathers, or left to the determination of the mother.

CHAPTER XIII.

TRADE OF TIBET.[1]

THE foreign trade of Tibet is very considerable. Being mountainous, naturally barren, and but thinly peopled, it requires large supplies from other countries, and its valuable productions furnish it with the means of procuring them. It yields gold, musk, cowtails, wool, and salt. Coarse woollen cloth and narrow serge are almost its only manufactures. It produces no iron, nor fruit, nor spices. The nature of the soil and of the climate prevents the culture of silk, rice, and tobacco, of all which articles there is a great consumption. But the wants of the country will best appear from an account of its trade. In this sketch, however, I propose only to give the outlines, which I will beg leave afterwards to fill up and correct.

The genius of this Government, like that of most of the ancient kingdoms in Hindustan, is favourable to commerce. No duties are levied on goods, and trade is protected and free from exactions. Many foreign merchants, encouraged by these indulgences, or allured by the prospect of gain, have settled in Tibet. The natives of Kashmir, who, like the Jews in Europe, or the Armenians in the Turkish empire, scatter themselves over the eastern kingdoms of Asia, and carry on an extensive traffic between the distant parts of it, have formed establishments at Lhasa and all the principal towns in this country. Their agents, stationed on the coast of Coromandel, in Bengal, Benares, Nepal, and Kashmir, furnish them with the commodities of these different countries, which they dispose of in Tibet, or forward to their associates at Seling,[2] a town on the borders of China. The Gosains, the trading pilgrims of India, resort hither in great numbers. Their humble deportment and

[1] A copy of the document, comprising this chapter, is in the archives at Calcutta, and it appears to be the only one that has been preserved there relating to Mr. Bogle's mission. Another copy has been preserved in the India Office.

[2] Sining.

holy character, heightened by the merit of distant pilgrimages, their accounts of unknown countries and remote regions, and, above all, their professions of high veneration for the Lama, procure them not only a ready admittance, but great favour. Though clad in the garb of poverty, there are many of them possessed of considerable wealth. Their trade is confined chiefly to articles of great value and small bulk. It is carried on without noise or ostentation, and often by paths unfrequented by other merchants. The Kalmuks,[1] who, with their wives and families, annually repair in numerous tribes to pay their devotions at the Lama's shrines, bring their camels loaded with furs and other Siberian goods. The Bhutanese and the other inhabitants of the mountains, which form the southern frontier of Tibet, are enabled by their situation to supply it as well with the commodities of Bengal as with the productions of their own states. The people of Assam furnish it with the coarse manufactures of their kingdom. The Chinese, to whose empire the country is subject, have established themselves in great numbers at the capital; and by introducing the curious manufactures and merchandise of China, are engaged in an extended and lucrative commerce. And thus Lhasa, being at the same time the seat of government and the place of the Dalai Lama's residence, is the resort of strangers, and the centre of communication between distant parts of the world.

The most considerable branch of commerce is with China. It is carried on by the natives of that kingdom, by Kashmiris, and by the Lama's agents, who proceed to Seling,[2] and sometimes even to Peking. The imports are coarse tea, of which the consumption is immense; flowered and brocaded satins of various kinds, Pelong[3] handkerchiefs, silk, thread, furs, porcelain cups, glass, snuff-boxes, knives and other cutlery, talents of silver, and some tobacco. The returns are made in gold, pearls, coral, chanks,[4] broadcloth, and a trifling quantity of Bengal cloths. The productions of Siberia are imported chiefly by the Kalmuks, or by the way of Seling. They consist of furs, red and black Bulgar hides, cowtails, some

[1] Kalmuk is here used as the equivalent for Manchurians. They and the Mongolians resort annually, in large numbers, to Lhasa and Teshu Lumbo, for trade.

[2] Sining.

[3] See note at p. 16.

[4] Shells.

dromedaries, bastard pearls, and silver, and are bartered for broadcloth, coral and amber beads, spices, and gold. The Kashmiris naturally engross the trade with their country. It is not considerable. The imports are chiefly sugar, dried raisins, and other fruits. The exports are goat's wool and gold. The imports from Assam are spices and timber, munga[1] doties, and other coarse manufactures of silk and linen. The native productions of the Deb Rajah's country brought into Tibet are rice, wrought iron, coarse woollen cloth, and some munjít,[2] which are exchanged for tea and other Chinese commodities, rock salt, wool, sheep's skins, and narrow friezes for their home consumption. The productions imported from Nepal are chiefly iron and rice. But as these two countries have been the principal channels of communication between Bengal and Tibet, it is necessary to give a more particular account of them.

While Nepal was divided among the different states of Kathmandu, Patan, Bhatgaon, and Gorkha, and remained under the government of rajahs, independent of each other's authority, every encouragement was given to trade.[3] A very moderate duty was levied on goods; the country, populous and well cultivated, easily furnished the means of transporting them, and the merchants, free from spoil or exactions, settled in Nepal, and contributed to enrich it at the same time that they improved their own fortunes. Some dispute arose among these petty chiefs; they went to war, and Prithi Narayan,[4] the Gorkhali Rajah, was called in to take part in the quarrel. Having subdued the enemy, he turned his arms against his ally; and partly by treachery, partly by the exertion of superior abilities, has, after a war of twenty-five years, made himself master of the whole of the country, and united it under one government.

[1] The silk of Assam. (See note at p. 55.)

[2] See note at p. 7.

[3] The valley of Kathmandu, in Nepal, was divided into three sovereignties called Patan, Bhatgaon, and Kathmandu, each governed by a rajah. But in 1768 Nepal was conquered by the Gorkhas. Gorkha is the name of a little state about 70 miles W.N.W. of the valley of Nepal. Gorkhali is the name of the people, who are chiefly of the Khas tribe. The conquered people of Nepal are the Newars. The former are addicted to arms, the latter to the arts of peace. (See the account of the Gorkhali conquest, by Father Guiseppe, in the 'Transactions of the Asiatic Society of Bengal,' ii. p. 307.)

[4] Of the Gorkhali Kings of Nepal, the first, Prithi Narayan Sah, reigned from 1768 to 1771; the second, Pertab Singh Sah Deva, from 1771 to 1775.

But although the wealth of Nepal furnished the Gorkha Rajah with the means by which he rose, he neglected to cherish the source from whence it flowed. Mistrustful of subjects disaffected to his government, he entertained a number of troops on regular pay. He disciplined them, he furnished them with firearms, he formed an artillery, and left nothing undone to render himself formidable. The ordinary revenue of countries where a standing army had hitherto been unknown, was unequal to these extraordinary expenses; and the Gorkha Rajah, among other expedients, had recourse to imposing high duties on trade in order to defray them. The merchants, subject to heavy and arbitrary fines upon the most frivolous pretences, and obliged to purchase the protection of a tyrannical government by presents scarcely less oppressive, quitted a country where they could no longer enjoy that freedom and security which are the life of commerce. The Gosains, who had formerly very extensive establishments in Nepal, having incurred the Gorkha Rajah's resentment by the assistance which they afforded his adversaries, were driven out of the kingdom; and many of the most wealthy inhabitants being stripped of their possessions, or exposed to the exactions of a conqueror, likewise deserted it. Only two Kashmiri houses remain, and the Rajah, afraid of their also abandoning him, obliges them to give security for the return of such agents as they have occasion to send beyond the boundaries of his dominions.[1]

The trade between Bengal and Tibet, through the Deb Rajah's country, used formerly to be engrossed wholly by the Bhutanese. Two of the Kashmiri houses, however, who fled from Nepal, being unwilling to forego the gainful commerce in which they had hitherto been concerned, settled at Lhasa, and having obtained permission from the Deb Rajah to transport their goods through his territories, established agents in Bengal. But as they are prohibited from trading in broadcloth and some other considerable articles, and as their traffic is carried on to no great extent, and all other merchants are excluded, it by no means compensates the loss

[1] Under the government of Jung Bahadur an essentially similar policy prevails at Kathmandu, where, according to Dr. Wright's semi-official sketch of Nepal, our trade is cramped by heavy duties (17 to 20 per cent.), and by endless monopolies. Yet the exports and imports of Nepal, in 1831, reached 33 lakhs.

which Bengal has sustained by the interruption of its commerce through Nepal.

The commodities of Bengal used also to be conveyed into Tibet through the Murung,[1] and a province adjoining to it which is subject to Lhasa, and governed by a chief styled Demo Jong.[2] The fakirs, when expelled from Nepal, generally frequented this road; but being esteemed unhealthy, it was not adopted by any creditable merchants. The Gorkha Rajah, however, having extended his conquests over the first of these countries, and having lately invaded the other, all intercourse is at present interrupted.

Besides these different communications, there is a road leading from Benares and Mirzapúr through the Mustang[3] country, and the hills to the northward of Bulwant Sing's territories,[4] which are subject to rajahs who still preserve their independence. The more valuable sorts of Bengal goods are sometimes imported into Tibet by this channel. But although the merchants travel in perfect security, and receive every assistance from these petty chiefs, the length of the way, the difficulty of the road, through a mountainous and, in several places, uninhabited country, and the many intermediate tolls upon the goods, render it far from eligible. Of late years it has become more frequented, on account of its being almost the only means of communication.

The principal articles of merchandise between Bengal and Tibet are broadcloth, otter skins, nil (indigo), pearls; coral, amber, and other beads; chank shells, spices, tobacco, sugar, Malta striped satins, and a few white cloths, chiefly coarse. The returns are made in gold dust, musk, and cowtails.[5]

A knowledge of the current specie, and of the proportionate value of money in a country, is of capital importance towards understanding the nature of its trade. But the intricacy of the subject, and the variety of circumstances requisite in forming a just notion of it, oblige me at present to mention it only briefly. There are no mints in Tibet. Payments are made in talents of China and Tatary, in small bulses of gold dust, or in the coin of the former

[1] See note at p. 65.

[2] Or Deunjong. Sikkim.

[3] Mustang is on the borders of Tibet, by the Muktinath Pass of the Nepalese Himalaya.

[4] Benares, of which Bulwant Sing, father of Cheyt Sing, was rajah.

[5] See a full list of exports and imports in Mr. Hodgson's Report, pp. 91, 121. (Trübner, 1875.)

rajahs of Kathmandu and Patan, which is the established specie of the kingdom.[1] The circulation of their rupees, which were of a base standard, proved very beneficial to these chiefs, and Gorkha, as soon as he had firmly established his authority in Nepal, endeavoured to introduce his coin into Tibet. For this purpose, he sent a deputation to Lhasa with a large sum in rupees struck in his name, and desired the sanction of government to circulate them through the country. The merchants, aware of the Gorkha Rajah's ill faith, refused to accept them, and the government returned him this artful answer: "We are willing to receive your coin, provided that you take back all the money of Nepal which is now in circulation." This condition was neither for the Gorkha Rajah's interest nor in his power to comply with. Nothing has since been done in this important affair. The old specie continues to pass; but the channel by which it was introduced having been long stopped up, it has risen greatly above its former value, as well in proportion to the talents of silver as to the gold dust.

[1] The valley of Nepal, before its conquest by the Gorkhas in 1768, was governed by three dynasties of rajahs, who all coined money. The coins of the Bhatgaon rajahs are distinguished by a shell; those of Patan by a *tirsúl* (trident); and those of Kathmandu by a sword. All money used in Tibet was coined by these rajahs, which was a source of considerable profit to them. The last reigning Rajah of Bhatgaon sent the Bhutanese such base coins as to cause a decrease of nearly one-half of their intrinsic value. This led to a desertion of the Nepalese mints for a time. But there is no other currency, and silver *mohurs* of Nepal are used in Tibet and Bhutan, either whole, or cut into halves, quarters, and eighths. The *mohur* is an 8-anna piece, weighing 87 grains, identical with the Muhammadan half rupee. The silver for coining is procured from China in stamped lumps. There are, however, a few specimens of silver coinage struck at Lhasa, with the inscription, "*Tsang pahu*," or Tsang money, and the date of the Tibetan year. Chinese brass money, with a square hole in the centre, is also current in Tibet. (See 'Prinsep's Tables.')

The following memorandum of weights used in Tibet is among Mr. Bogle's papers:

$6\frac{2}{3}$ *mahendra-malli** equal to 1 *tank*.

5 *tanks* make 1 *nega*.

20 *neyas* equal to 1 *call*, nearly equivalent to $30\frac{1}{8}$ seers of 80 sicca rupees.

Gold weights of Tibet:

$1\frac{1}{8}$ *mahendra-malli* equal to a *mascal*.

8 *mascals* equal to a *gaiton*, equivalent to $1\frac{1}{4}$ oz.

* Called after the Newar dynasty of the Malls.

CHAPTER XIV.

NEGOTIATIONS.

1.

POLITICS OF TIBET AND NEIGHBOURING COUNTRIES.

ABOUT seventy years ago, the Emperor of China acquired the sovereignty of Tibet, in the way that sovereignties are generally acquired, by interfering in the quarrels between two contending parties.[1] In consequence of a revolution, which happened about twenty-five years ago, the government of Tibet was committed to the former Dalai Lama.[2] Upon his death, Gesub Rimboché,[3] his cup-bearer or confidant, procured the supreme administration of affairs, partly through his own interest at the Court of Peking, and partly by the recommendation of Teshu Lama, who came now to be considered as the first man in the country. After two years, Teshu Lama discovered the child into whose body the Dalai Lama's spirit had passed, and gave notice to the Court of China. He was immediately recognized by the Emperor.[4] Changay Lama, the high-priest who resided at Peking, came to visit him,

[1] Chinese power was established in Lhasa in 1720, resident Political Agents being appointed. A certain supremacy, however, existed long before that date.

[2] An insurrection against the Chinese broke out in 1749, which ended in Lobsang Kalsang, the sixth Dalai Lama, being established at Lhasa, with two Chinese *Ambas* or Residents. The sixth Lama died in 1758.

[3] From time immemorial the oldest among the occupants of the four chairs of the Chemiling, Tengiling, Chechuling, and Kenduling monasteries had the title of Gesub (or Geshub) Rimboché, and was Regent during the Dalai Lama's minority. But now the Gesub Rimboché, or temporal ruler, is chosen from the Dibong monastery. He is also called the Nomen Khan. See also p. 2 3, and *note*.

[4] This was Lobsang Champal, the seventh Dalai Lama. It was with his sanction that the great emigration of the Kalmuks settled in Russian territory took place, in 1771, which is described by De Quincey. Lobsang Champal died in 1805. The eighth, ninth, and tenth Dalai Lamas were murdered by the Regent in 1815 and 1837. The eleventh died in 1855. The present Dalai Lama is the twelfth. He was born in 1856. His death has lately been reported, but not confirmed.

and after passing some months at Teshu Lumbo, returned to court. For many years after Gesub's promotion, Teshu Lama continued to have great influence in the government; but for some time past Gesub has endeavoured by his own interest to maintain himself in office, and although he appears to pay great deference to the Lama's opinion, he consults him as seldom as possible. The grand object of Gesub's politics is to secure the administration to himself, and afterwards to his nephews; while Teshu Lama, on the contrary, is exerting all his interest at the Court of Peking to procure the government for the Dalai Lama, who is now nearly of age, and to obtain the appointment of a minister devoted to himself. If he can carry his point, his influence will immediately revive; for, independent of the good understanding which subsists between all the Eastern pontiffs, the Dalai Lama owing his promotion to Teshu Lama, and having been tutored by his people, will naturally pay great attention to his advice and opinion.

The obstacles to my journey arose chiefly from Gesub Rimboché.[1] Soon after my arrival at Desheripgay, Teshu Lama gave me one of his letters, where he mentions "that he had heard of two Fringies being arrived in the Deb Rajah's dominions, with a great retinue of servants; that the Fringies were fond of war; and after insinuating themselves into a country, raised disturbances, and made themselves masters of it; that as no Fringies had ever been admitted into Tibet, he advised the Lama to find some method of sending me back, either on account of the violence of the smallpox, or on any other pretence." It was upon this letter that the Lama wrote to me to return to Calcutta. After the arrival of the Gosain, and the receipt of the letter I sent him from Tassisudon, he wrote to Gesub, "that he had from the beginning dissuaded Deb Judhur from going to war; that the government at Lhasa had encouraged him to it; that Deb Judhur had been defeated, and a great part of his country conquered; that he, the Lama, had written to the Governor, who had not only given over hostilities, but restored all the Deb Rajah's country; that as I was sent by the Governor, he thought it was proper to receive me; but if they, contrary to his opinion, persisted in refusing their permission, and any calamity should afterwards come upon the country, they had them-

[1] He also obstructed the journey of Captain Turner.

selves to blame for it." This letter procured me admittance; but Gesub, at the same time, wrote to Teshu Lama to prevent my coming to Lhasa, and repeated this in several letters after my arrival. The truth is, he is naturally of a jealous and suspicious temper, and was besides afraid of giving umbrage to the Chinese, as jealous and suspicious as himself. Gesub, however, sent me some Chinese brandy, biscuits, and fish; and his servants, who came to congratulate the Lama on his return to Teshu Lumbo, paid me two visits. By the return of his people, I sent him some trifling presents, for I had no other to send, and wrote him, or rather the Lama wrote for me, a letter; but I never received any answer.

In this situation I was obliged to confine my negotiations, for extending the trade between Bengal and Tibet, entirely to Teshu Lama. I could not think of going to Lhasa without such presents to the Dalai Lama, to Gesub, and to the four ministers, as were suitable to your character; and, at any rate, Gesub's jealousy put it out of my power. As to the Lama, I had every reason to think, both from his attention and civilities to me, and the manner in which he expressed his sense of the favour you had done him by concluding peace with the Bhutanese, that he entertained the most friendly dispositions towards you; and it was my business to cherish them as well as I could.

Teshu Lama is about forty years of age. He is of a cheerful and affable temper, of great curiosity, and very intelligent. He is entirely master of his own affairs; his views are liberal and enlarged, and he wishes, as every great man wishes, to extend his consequence. From his pacific character, and from the turn of his mind, naturally gentle and humane, he is averse to war and bloodshed, and in all quarrels endeavours by his mediation to bring about a reconciliation. In conversation he is plain and candid, using no flattery or compliments himself, and receiving them but badly if made to him. He is generous and charitable, and is universally beloved and venerated by the Tibetans, by the Kalmuks, and by a great part of the Chinese. The character I give of him may appear partial; but I received it in much stronger colours from his own subjects, from the Kashmiris, and from the fakirs; and I will confess, I never knew a man whose manners pleased me so much, or for whom upon so short an acquaintance I had half the heart's liking.

In consequence of my representing to him your wish to open a free communication of trade between the inhabitants of Bengal and Tibet, he wrote to Gesub Rimboché on the subject. He wrote also to the principal merchants, Kashmiris as well as natives. Many of them, either in person or by their agents, came afterwards to visit me. The Tibetans excused themselves from sending *gumashtas* into Bengal, on account of the heat and unhealthiness of that country. Several of the principal Kashmiri houses, who had been forced by the Gorkha Rajah's oppressions to abandon this trade, assured me that they would send their agents to Calcutta as soon as the rains are over, and the Lama engaged to procure them a passage through the Deb Rajah's territories. As the Gorkha Rajah had invaded the country of a chief subject to Lhasa, the Lama could make no application to him; but immediately on his death, he wrote to the new Rajah of Nepal, desiring him to favour and protect commerce, and to allow all merchants, Hindus, and Mussulmans, to trade freely through his dominions, "for," says he, "everybody is now afraid to enter your country, and it will become poor and desolate." He wrote also recommending the same thing to the Deb Rajah, and has sent one of his gylongs to co-operate with me at Tassisudon, in my applications on this subject. In regard to allowing Europeans to go unto Tibet, it was a point, although not particularly mentioned in your instructions, which I wished to have carried, as I was sensible it would have reflected great credit on my commission. But the jealousy of the hill people, of the administration at Lhasa, and the circumstances I have already mentioned, will, I imagine, serve to show that it was a thing simply impossible. If the government of Tibet is entrusted to the Lamas, I should think this point may then be urged with some prospect of success; but at present I consider it as out of the question. As the returns, however, for the commodities of Bengal carried into Tibet are made principally in gold, any extension of this commerce is so much clear gain to Bengal; and the channel through which the trade is carried on, although of consequence to individuals, is, I humbly apprehend, of very little to the country. If any Englishmen choose to embark in this traffic, I do not see why it may not be conducted by Asiatic agents as well as by European ones, without running any risk of disturbing that friendship and good understanding which I know you wish to cultivate with the Northern powers.

In my address of the 5th of December, I mentioned the Lama's desire of founding a religious house on the banks of the Ganges. About seven or eight hundred years ago, the Tibetan pontiffs had many monasteries in Bengal, and their priests used to travel to that country in order to study the religion and language of the Brahmans, and to visit the holy places in Hindustan. The Mussulmans, upon conquering Bengal, plundered and destroyed their temples, and drove them out of the country. Since that time there has been little intercourse between the two kingdoms. The Lama is sensible that it will throw great lustre on his pontificate, and serve to extend his fame and character, if he can, after so long an interval, obtain a religious establishment in Bengal, and he is very solicitous about this point. He proposes, also, to send some of his gylongs, during the cold season, to wait upon you at Calcutta, and afterwards to go on pilgrimages to Gaya and other places, and has written to Chidzun Tamba,[1] at Peking, who has great interest with the Emperor, informing him "that the English are now masters of Bengal; that you, their chief, have shown him great favour; that the English allow everyone to follow his own religion unmolested; and advising him to send some persons to wait upon you, and to visit the principal temples in Bengal." I own I encouraged all this, in the view of strengthening the intercourse and connection with Tibet, and thinking it would be of advantage to the Company to open any channel of communication with the Court of China; and although I am not so sanguine as the Lama about the success of his endeavours, however sincere, to obtain leave for you to send a person to the Emperor, I do not altogether despair, by your favour, of one day or other getting a sight of Peking.

The present Emperor is of a violent and imperious temper.[2] He

[1] The Guison Tamba of Huc; identical with the Taranath Lama (see note at p. 98). He resides at Urga, but several visits of the Taranath Lama to Peking are recorded. (See Huc, i. p. 98.) See, however, p. 146. It may be that Mr. Bogle confuses the Guison Tamba with the Changay Lama.

[2] This was the Emperor Kien-lung, who succeeded to the throne in 1736 His army subdued Eastern Turkistan, including Kashgar, Yarkand, and Kho-

has conquered Yarkand by dint of numbers. He has, partly by arts unworthy of a great monarch, reduced the Kalmuks to strict subjection. But a petty Kambu prince,[1] between Yunnan and Tibet, defended by his mountains, and assisted, I believe, by the King of Pegu, has kept his numerous armies at bay for several years past; and the quarrels about the boundaries and the migration of subjects, between him and the Court of St. Petersburg, are likely to come to a rupture, when, I imagine, he will get himself heartily drubbed. The Lama is endeavouring to prevent it; but the Chinese seem to be in the wrong, and the Emperor's haughty mind cannot stoop to make concessions.

2.

CONVERSATIONS WITH THE TESHU LAMA AT DESHERIPGAY.

The day after my arrival I waited upon the Lama with the Governor's despatches, having previously and without difficulty settled that I should be allowed to give the letter into his own hands. I delivered it, together with the pearl necklace, while my servants spread out the other presents before him. He received me with a very courteous and smiling countenance, and I was seated near him on a high stool covered with carpet. He spoke to me in Hindustani, of which language he has a moderate knowledge. After inquiries about the Governor's health and my journey from Tassisudon, he introduced the subject of the war in Bahar. He blamed Deb Judhur as the occasion of it. "I always," said he, "disapproved greatly of his seizing the Bahar Rajah, and going to

tan, and annexed it to the Chinese Empire. In 1771 the famous flight of the Kalmuks settled on the banks of the Volga, from Russian tyranny, took place. After suffering fearful hardships, they crossed the desert of Gobi, and reached Chinese territory with their numbers reduced from 600,000 to 250,000. Kien-lung provided for them with princely munificence, and they settled on the banks of the Ily. Kien-ung also made an unsuccessful attempt to subdue Burmah. He was more successful in Tibet, where, in 1796, his troops defeated an invading Nepalese army, and his forces advanced to within twenty miles of Kathmandu. Kien-lung abdicated in 1796, after a long and glorious reign of sixty years, and died in 1800. His son, Kea-King, reigned from 1796 to 1821, and was succeeded by Taou Kwang.

[1] Probably a Prince of Kam or Eastern Tibet.

war with the Fringies; but the Deb considered himself as powerful in arms, and would not listen to my advice. After he was defeated I wrote to the Governor, who, in ceasing hostilities against the Bhutanese, in consequence of my application, and restoring to them their country, has made me very happy, and has done a very pious (dürm) action. My servants who went to Calcutta were only little men, and the kind reception they had from the Governor I consider as another mark of his friendship."

I told him that Bahar is separated from Rangpúr, one of the provinces of Bengal, only by a rivulet; that the Bhutanese from time immemorial had confined themselves to their mountains, and when they visited the low countries it was in an amicable manner, and in order to trade; that when many thousand armed men issued at once from their forests, seized and carried off prisoner the Rajah of Bahar, a petty prince, who could be no object of their jealousy, possessed themselves of his country, and settled in it, the Company had just cause to be alarmed, and to conclude that, encouraged by their success in Bahar to-day, they would hardly be confined by an ideal boundary, but attempt the conquest of Rangpúr to-morrow, and even extend their views to the interior and more fertile provinces of Bengal; that the Governor, although he had heard much of the Lama's name and holy character, yet being totally unacquainted with the Bhutan nation, and having then had no connection with their chief, had the more reason for these apprehensions, and immediately upon an application from the Bahar people for assistance, despatched a battalion of the Company's Sepoys to repel the invaders; that he, the Lama, was well acquainted with what followed; that the Governor was extremely rejoiced on the receipt of his letters, immediately suspended the war against the Bhutanese,[1] and afterwards concluded a peace between them and the Company, by which the whole of their country was restored to them; being happy to cultivate the friendship of a man whose fame is known throughout the world, and whose character is held in veneration

[1] *Tibet* is a Persian word. The Indian name for the country is *Bhot*, whence *Bhotia* for a native of *Bhot*. *Bod* and *Bodpa* are the native terms. *Bhutanta*, or "the end of *Bhot*," is the Indian name for the Cis-Himálayan State which we call *Bhutan*. To prevent confusion it is, therefore, better to have a separate name for the people of Bhutan, and not to call them Bhuteas. I have adopted Bhutanese.

among so many nations; that he had therefore sent me to his, the Lama's, presence with the letter and tokens of friendship which I had then the honour to lay before him, and which I hoped would find favour in his eyes. He made no answer to what I said. Indeed, I doubt whether he understood it well, for I spoke in a language which he had not been used to, and the guttural R, which I inherit from my mother, probably increased the difficulty. After this I endeavoured to confine myself within the compass and to imitate the phraseology of his language, and so we made it out very well.

"You have no doubt heard," said the Lama, "that Deb Judhur has been turned out of his government, and has fled to me: he did not manage the country properly, and the Fringies were not pleased with him." I replied, that the English had no concern at Deb Judhur's expulsion; it was brought about by his own people; and that the Company only wished the Bhutanese to continue in their own country, and not to encroach upon Bengal, or raise disturbances upon its frontier. "The Governor," said he, "had reason for going to war, but, as I am averse from bloodshed and the Bhutanese are my vassals, I am glad it is brought to a conclusion." He then opened the Governor's letter, but it was not at that time explained to him.

Next day the Lama was engaged in receiving the visits and presents of some Kalmuks,[1] and I had an opportunity of waiting upon him. He sent for me the next morning. He was without his mitre cap, and nobody was with him besides the Sopon Chumbo, his confidant and favourite.

He resumed the story of Bahar, and repeated the reasons for the war on the same principle. He again expressed much satisfaction at the reception the Governor had given his servants; he said he had sent another person with them who was of a higher station, but he had been prevented from proceeding to Calcutta by sickness. "I will plainly confess," said he, "that my reason for then refusing you admittance was that many people advised me against it. I had heard also much of the power of the Fringies; that the Company was like a great king, and fond of war and conquest; and as my business and that of my people is to pray to God, I was

[1] Sokpas, of North-east Tibet.

afraid to admit any Fringies into the country. But I have since learned that the Fringies are a fair and a just people. I never before saw any Fringies, but am very happy at your arrival, and you will not think anything of my former refusal." I replied that I always attributed his refusal to the representations of some ill-minded people, which had made an unfavourable impression on his mind, as clouds for a time will darken the sun. "The Governor is above all things desirous of obtaining your friendship and favour. As your opinion is so generally and so justly regarded in this part of the world, he is sensible how much the character of the English is in your hands, and that their good or bad name depends greatly upon your judgment. I have therefore represented these things in your presence, the truth of which is known to all the world."

In return, the Lama assured me his heart was open and well disposed towards the English, and that he gave no credit to the representations which had been made to their disadvantage. "I wish," he said, "to have a place on the banks of the Ganges, to which I might send my people to pray. I intend to write to the Governor on this subject,[1] and wish you would second my application." I replied that as I knew how desirous the Governor was to cultivate his friendship, I was persuaded on this or any other occasion he would find him very ready to gratify him as far as in his power.

He inquired if we worshipped the Criss, making a cross with his fingers, and adding that there were formerly some Fringy padres at Lhasa who worshipped the Criss, but they bred disturbances, and were turned out of the country.[2] I said, I had heard of the priests who had been at Lhasa; that they were not of my country, spoke another language, and that their religion differed from mine; that the clergy of England remained at home, and travelled not into other countries; that we allowed everyone to

[1] "This he did after Mr. Bogle's return. A piece of land was purchased and given to him, on the banks of the Ganges, opposite to Calcutta; a house and a temple were constructed upon the spot by the Lama, under the direction of Mr. Bogle, and people from Tibet and Bhutan constantly resorted to it during the time for which my knowledge reaches; I conclude the same to this hour." [*This is a note on the manuscript, in another hand; I think that of A. Dalrymple.*]

[2] What remained of this Christian establishment, and of others (mostly books), was presented to Mr. Hodgson, when he was Resident in Nepal, by the Dalai Lama.

worship God in his own way, to which the Gosain or any of his people who had been in Bengal could bear witness; and that we esteemed a good and pious man, of whatever religion he might be. He changed the subject, and I was not sorry for it.

In the afternoon I visited the Chanzu Cusho,[1] who is brother to the Lama by the same mother, but by a different father, but has little of his engaging manners or abilities. The conversation was short, formal, and uninteresting.

I had been told that Cheyt Sing's vakíl had described the English as a people designing and ambitious; who, insinuating themselves into a country on pretence of trade, became acquainted with its situation and inhabitants, and afterwards endeavoured to become masters of it; and that his representations, in concurrence with other circumstances, had contributed to raise up obstacles to my journey.

He came to visit me; and as I think it best and most becoming the character of the English to deal openly with every man, I resolved to mention this to him. I accordingly told him what I had heard. I said that the English had always been befriended by Bulwunt Sing, his master's father; and if their transactions in Bengal were unjustifiable, Bulwunt Sing was equally to blame in assisting them; that, however, it was known to the whole world that the English were obliged by necessity and in self-defence to go to war. I briefly mentioned their rise in Bengal, enlarged upon the assistance Bulwunt Sing had afforded them; the friendship that had always subsisted between him and the Company, and which was still continued with Cheyt Sing. I added that as I knew how displeased the Governor would be were I to say anything unfavourable of his master, I was convinced Cheyt Sing would disown him in anything he might say to the disadvantage of the Company.

He declared he had not spoken anything against the English; that he believed a vakíl of Kashmiri Mull, who was lately gone to Lhasa, might; that he only told Teshu Lama what he knew of

[1] Chanzu Cusho was Regent for the infant Lama at the time of Captain Turner's visit to Teshu Lumbo, in 1783. Captain Turner describes him as of middle size, rather of a broad make, but not inclined to corpulency, short, wide face with nose a little turned up, small black eyes, and high cheek bones. There was an agreeable symmetry in his features, and a sweetness of expression in his countenance which was highly prepossessing. (Turner, p. 242.)

the affairs of Hindustan, and concluded with the rote of Hindustanis, that I was his master, a great man, &c. I replied, that as he was sent to the Lama by the Rajah of Benares, I in the same manner was deputed by the Governor on the part of the Company; that it was my duty to attend to the character of my constituents, and it was the custom of the English to deal openly; that I had only reported to him what I had heard, and was glad to find from him that I was misinformed.

After this altercation he and I became great friends. He used to come frequently to see me, and having been a great traveller, his conversation sometimes helped me to beguile a few tedious hours.

On the 15th of November, the Lama sent for me, and desired me to bring all my people with me. He repeated the assurances of his good opinion of the English, and expressed himself with respect to the Governor in very friendly terms, accompanied with that frank and candid look which ought to be the pledge of sincerity. After some observations on the coldness of the climate, he caused me to be dressed in a purple satin gown, lined with fox skins, and trimmed at the neck and cuffs with a scolloped gold lace, which he said had come from Russia; cap of European flowered silk brocade, turned up with sable, and crowned with a red silk tassel; and a pair of large red leather jack-boots. He equipped Mr. Hamilton also in Tatar costume, but his tunic was of blue satin; and all our servants, either this day or a few days afterwards, received tunics lined with sheep skins, and boots.

I next day went to the Sopon Chumbo,[1] who is a great favourite. He has been at Peking, through a great part of Tatary, and even as far as the borders of Russia, and has a knowledge of the languages of these different countries. I made a short visit;

[1] Captain Turner says that, at the time of his visit, in 1783, this Sopon Chumbo was treated by the Regent, Chanzu Cusho, more as a colleague than a subordinate officer. "The singular power he enjoyed seemed to be no more than what was justly due to his integrity and talents. His countenance was open and ingenuous. He had small eyes, thin eyebrows, high cheek bones, and was without even the rudiment of a beard. His duties under the Lama, as *Sadik*, were to receive and communicate his master's commands, to arrange the celebration of festivals, to take charge of the wardrobe, the treasury, and to act as cup-bearer. He had travelled much, into China, to Khalka, and even to the shores of Lake Baikal." (Turner, p. 248.)

for the Lama seemed fully master of his own affairs, and had before told me, though I recollect not at which conversation, that as I could speak to him without an interpreter, he wished me to apply only to him about any business I might have, and not to trouble myself with representing it through the channel of his officers.

The Lama began enumerating some causes of the decline of the trade between Bengal and Tibet. He mentioned, first, the war with Deb Judhur, during which nothing was allowed to pass through his country to or from Bengal, and, said he, "if I would allow him he would again go to war with his own people, but I will not suffer him to quit Giansu, where he now is." He next mentioned Prithi Narayan, the Rajah of Gorkha, who, he said, had conquered all the countries in Nepal, and by his exactions and oppressions had obliged all merchants to quit his country, as he seizes upon their money and goods whenever he has occasion. "He has now," said he, "taken possession of Bijapúr, on the borders of Bengal, and, I am told, threatens to invade the Deb Rajah's country. As to me, I give encouragement to merchants, and in this country they are free and secure."

I said that as he was so well acquainted with the causes of this stagnation of trade, and as he and the Company coincided in their treatment of merchants, I assured myself that he would apply an effectual remedy. He replied that the people of his country carried their goods only to Pari-jong, where they were received and purchased by the inhabitants of the Deb Rajah's country, and by them carried into Bengal; and that the goods of Bengal were conveyed into Tibet in the same manner. I told him that the people of the Deb Rajah's country always carried on some trade to Rungpúr, and were this year to send their horses, &c., as usual, and I was convinced would have no reason to be dissatisfied with their reception; that this, however, was only to a small extent, was nothing equal to the consumption of the two countries, and bore no proportion to what the trade was in former times. To this he fully assented, and finished his conversation with informing me that he expected one of the ministers from Lhasa in a few days, and that he would introduce me to him, as he wished me to be known to all the principal people in that country. From this I understood that something depended on this man.

Several holidays and much praying prevented me from seeing the Lama for some days. He introduced the subject of trade; he enumerated the different articles sent from this country to Bengal: gold, musk, cowtails, and coarse woollen cloths. He said that the Tibet people were afraid to go to Bengal on account of the heat; that he had last year sent four people to worship at Benares, of whom three had died, besides the person he intended should have gone to Calcutta; that the journey was also uncommon, and they were frightened at it; that in former times great numbers of the people of this country used to resort to Hindustan; that the Lamas had temples in Benares, Gaya, somewhere in Purneah, and at several other places, the names of which I did not know; that their priests used to travel thither to study the Shaster and the religion of the Brahmans; and after remaining there ten, twenty, or thirty years, returned to Tibet, communicating their knowledge to their countrymen, and thereby gaining great reputation; that about eight hundred years ago Bengal was invaded and conquered by the Mussulmans, who destroyed and pillaged the temples and plundered the people, so that such as escaped returned to their mountains along with some Brahmans who fled from the persecutions; since which time the inhabitants of Tibet have had little connection with Bengal or the southern countries.

I told him that times were much altered; that in Bengal and under the Company every person's property was secure, and everyone was at liberty to follow his own religion. He said he was informed that the country under the Fringies was very quiet; that as I had come so far a journey, and had been sent by the Governor, he would be ashamed if I were to return with a fruitless errand; that as soon, therefore, as he arrived at Teshu Lumbo, where he would have his officers about him, and likewise some of the people from Lhasa, he would consult with them, and also send for some considerable merchants, after informing them of the Governor's desire, and of the encouragement and protection which the Company afforded to traders in Bengal, discuss the most proper method of carrying it on and extending it. "You," said he, "will also speak with them, and we will see what can be done." I could have nothing to say against a proposal so reasonable, and I saw plainly he chose not to take any step before he had communicated this to his own officers and to the people at Lhasa.

On the 18th of November I had another audience of the Lama. He talked of religion and of the connection between his faith and that of the Brahmans; that they worshipped three of the Hindu gods, Vishnu, Brahma, and another,[1] but not their inferior deities. He then asked me how many gods there were in my religion. I told him one. He replied that he had heard that in my religion God was born three times. I had no mind to attempt an explanation of the mysteries of the Trinity. I felt myself unequal to it. I told him, therefore, that according to my faith God had always existed. He observed, charitably, that we all worshipped the same God, but under different names, and all aimed at the same object, though we pursued different ways. The answer I gave him was in the same tolerant spirit; for I am not sent as a missionary, and after so many able and ingenious Jesuits, dressed in the habits of apostles and armed with beads and crucifixes, have tried in vain to convert unbelieving nations, I am not so arrogant as to believe that my labours would be successful.

The Lama told me that he had written to Lhasa on the subject of opening a free commercial communication between this country and Bengal. "I have told them," said he, "that as you are come so far, and from the King of Hindustan, they must attend to your business."

Although he spoke this with all the zeal in the world, I confess I did not much like the thoughts of referring my business to Lhasa, where I was not present, where I was unacquainted, and where I had reason to think the ministers had entertained no favourable idea of me and my commission. I represented to him, therefore, that I considered him as the principal; that during the minority of the Dalai Lama the government of the country was in his hands; and that I trusted solely to him for removing the obstacles to the trade between this country and Bengal. He said he had also written to encourage the merchants to trade to Bengal. I replied that the merchants, if they found their advantage in this traffic, would no doubt be ready to follow it; but as he had informed me of the difficulties they were exposed to in passing

[1] Siva.

through Nepal, and as he knew that the Deb Rajah did not allow a free trade through his dominions, I begged to know by what road they could go. He said that formerly Deb Judhur would not suffer the Tibet people to trade into his country; that the Bhutanese as well as the inhabitants of Demo Jong's country [1] lying between Pari-jong and Murung,[2] were oppressive and lawless, so that merchants lay at their mercy. I begged leave to represent to him that I had found them very honest and peaceable; as I knew his influence over the Bhutanese I made no doubt but he could procure their permission for a free trade. He observed that the present Deb Rajah was an old man, and spoke not very respectfully of him, but added that he would write to him on the subject, and I might be assured of his exerting himself in the business I was sent upon. It was late and I took my leave.

The Lama sent for me on the 6th December, and delivered me some letters from Calcutta and Bahar. At his desire I opened them in his presence. He inquired what news, and particularly if there was anything said about the Gorkha Rajah. I told him there was not. "Because," said he, "his forces are employed in attacking Demo Jong, whose country is in the neighbourhood of Bengal. They have surrounded it; the Gorkha Rajah has trained Sepoys after the English manner, and given them muskets; but I am told they are not good marksmen, and do not hit above once in a hundred times." I said I had been told in the Deb Rajah's country that the Gorkha Rajah was somewhere on the borders of Tibet. Says he, "They must have meant Demo Jong's dominions, which are subject to Lhasa. O," says he, "I have just now a letter from the Deb Rajah. He is in a sad plight about Deb Judhur, having heard that he was about to return to invade the country, and he writes me by all means to detain him." After this he inquired about lightning in Bengal. He said in Tibet the thunderbolts are sometimes of stone or iron, and then showed me a knife, with an open-worked handle of steel and gold, with several heads carved upon it, and some Chinese characters on the blade, which he said had fallen from the clouds. It was almost the only part of all his conversations that was marvellous. He asked me many questions, but it is endless putting them down. As he had

[1] Sikkim. [2] See note at p. 65.

deferred my business till his arrival at his capital, I said nothing on the subject.

On the 7th of December I had a short interview with the Lama. He was to set out from Desheripgay next morning, in order to return to Teshu Lumbo, his palace, from which he had been three years absent.

CHAPTER XV.

CONVERSATIONS WITH THE TESHU LAMA AT TESHU LUMBO.

AT the first meeting after his return to Teshu Lumbo, the Teshu Lama spoke to me of what he had before mentioned as to forming a religious house somewhere on the Ganges,[1] and I repeated my belief of the readiness with which his desire would be complied with. He said he had also written or proposed to write to Changay Lama,[2] the high-priest at Peking, with whom he was upon the most friendly and intimate terms, mentioning that the Fringies were masters of Bengal, and had shown him great favour; and, says he, "I think it probable he will send some of his people to visit the principal religious places. I," added he, "am but a little man in comparison of the Changay Lama, for he is always in the Emperor's presence, and has great influence over him. The favour which the Emperor shows to me and the Dalai Lama is in a good measure owing to Changay Lama's good offices at court. I hope, therefore, in case he sends any persons, that the Governor will give them a good reception." I encouraged him very much in all this. "At present," said he, "I cannot say whether they will come or not. If they do, I will send them to the Deb Rajah, and from thence they will proceed to Bengal." I said the Governor, I imagined, would be glad to know some little time beforehand, that he might give orders for their journey. Nothing else of consequence passed, and I went to receive the Lhasa deputies.

[1] On hearing of the Lama's wish, Warren Hastings immediately gave the necessary orders about building a Buddhist temple on the banks of the Hugli, and as soon as it was completed he wrote and informed the Lama, who had previously sent images to be deposited in it. Referring to the temple, Warren Hastings says, in a letter to Teshu Lama: "By the blessing of God, it will be the means of making your name known in this country, and of strengthening the friendship which is between us, and you will consider it as a mark of the confidence and regard which I bear to you." Turner mentions this Buddhist temple as being opposite Calcutta, on the banks of the river (p. 269).

[2] He is called by Huc the Tchang-Kia-Fo, a sort of Grand Almoner of the Imperial Court (ii. p. 197).

There were two of them. The one was a gylong, the other a layman dressed in a feminine garb, and they came with about twenty attendants. They brought with them many boxes, full of small dried fish, cakes, flour, mushrooms, &c., and some bamboos filled with distilled spirits. The layman spoke. He said they were come from Lhasa to wait upon the Lama, and brought these China meats from Gesub to me, of which they desired my acceptance; that, although it was not the custom, the Lama had ordered them to wait upon me, as I had come from such a distance, and from the chief of the Fringies. In return, I made acknowledgments for the favour which Gesub had shown me; that I was sent by the Governor to pay his respects to the Lama, and that I was extremely happy and honoured by their visit.

They said the Fringies had shown great favour to the Lama and to them, by making peace with the Bhutanese and restoring their country. I replied, that the name and character of Dalai Lama and of Teshu Lama were well known to my constituents, and that the Governor was very ready to cultivate their and Gesub Rimbochè's friendship and good opinion; that the English were far from that quarrelsome people which some evil-minded persons represented them to be, and wished not for extent of territories; that as they were entrusted with the management of Bengal they only wished that it should remain in tranquillity; that the war with the Bhutanese was of their seeking; that they, the deputies, being well acquainted with government, could judge whether the Company had not cause to be alarmed when 8000 or 10,000 Bhutanese, who had formerly always confined themselves to their mountains, poured at once into the low country, seized the Rajah of Bahar, took possession of his territories, and carried their arms to the borders of Bengal; and whether they were not in the right to oppose them; that in the course of the war some of the Bhutan country was taken from them, which, however, was immediately restored at the Lama's request; that so far from desiring conquest, the boundaries of Bengal remained the same as formerly; and although the English kept up a large army, the war with the Deb Rajah was the first they had been engaged in for many years. The layman gave a nod with his head. He then said, the Lama had written to Lhasa about merchants; that the people of this country were afraid of the heat, and proceeded, therefore, only to Pari-jong, where the Deb Rajah's subjects brought the commodities of Bengal and exchanged them for those of this country; that this was the ancient custom, and would certainly be observed. I replied, that this trade had always been carried on by the Deb Rajah's people, who were this year gone to Bengal, as usual; but, besides this, there was formerly a very extensive trade carried on between this country and Bengal, which my constituents were sorry to see had declined very much of late years; that it was needless for me to represent to them, who were acquainted with the state of affairs, the causes from which this proceeded; that the Governor was desirous of removing these obstacles, and had ordered me to represent them to the Lama, who had, in consequence, written to Lhasa on the subject, and I trusted that Gesub Rimboché and the government there would readily comply with so reasonable a proposal. They answered, that Gesub Rimboché would do everything in his power, but that he and all the country were subject to the Emperor of China. This is a stumbling-block which crosses me in all my paths. The Lhasa people took their leave. I offered to return their visit. They seemed not to wish it, but said they would come to see me again.

On the 23rd of December, before the Lama went to church he sent for me. At his desire I repeated to him what had passed between me and the deputies from Lhasa. I told him that they said the ancient custom would certainly be observed; that according to the ancient custom Nepal was governed by its own rajahs, and merchants were at liberty to trade through that country between Bengal and Tibet; that unless the government at Lhasa could restore Nepal to its former state, or order the Gorkha Rajah to treat the merchants with indulgence, I confessed I did not see how the ancient custom could be preserved. He said he was very sensible that the trade with Bengal had declined very much of late years; that formerly the merchants used to bring coral, pearls, and broadcloth in abundance into the country, which was not the case nowadays; that as to the Gorkha Rajah, there was no trusting him; that a few years ago he encouraged some merchants to settle in Nepal, treated them well at first, but afterwards cut off their ears and turned them out of the country; that he had also promised again and again to him, the Lama, and to the government at Lhasa, that he would never encroach a finger's breadth on their territories, but now he had attacked Demo Jong's country,[1] which was subject to Lhasa; that he was convinced of the reasonableness of my proposals in regard to trade, and had accordingly written to Lhasa on the subject, and had received an answer from thence, in which Gesub Rimboché mentioned his apprehensions of giving umbrage to the Chinese; and that besides the disturbances which the Gorkha Rajah was making in Demo Jong's country, and on the borders of that of the Deb Rajah, rendered this an improper time to settle anything of the kind, but that in a year or two he hoped to bring it about; that the Debo, who had visited me and played at chess, with two others, was gone with forces to oblige the Gorkha Rajah either to quit Demo Jong's country, or fight with him. I replied that as to the Gorkha Rajah, I did not imagine from all I could judge that he was likely to be a smaller man, but, on the contrary, a greater; that so far from being satisfied with the conquests he had made, and the extensive country of which he had got possession, he was meditating new schemes of ambition; that he had subdued Murung, Bijapúr, and had now attacked Demo Jong's country, which gained, he would make himself master of the Deb Rajah's dominions, or perhaps extend his views towards Pari-jong; that, in short, the Gorkha Rajah's views aimed plainly at conquests. The Lama was obliged to go to church, but as I was taking leave he desired me not to mention what he had said at my last visit about the persons from China, which was a great affair (*Burrah Kaum*). I assured him of my silence in general, and as to this in particular.

On the 28th December I had an audience of the Lama, where nobody but his confidant was present. He expatiated largely on the Gorkha Rajah's war with Demo Jong, his treachery and breach of promise to him and to the government at Lhasa. I repeated to him my opinion of the Gorkha Rajah; that his ambition and his abilities made him aspire at conquests; that if he succeeded in the conquest of Demo Jong's country, he would attempt Pari-jong or the Deb Rajah's country, and that having assumed the title of King of the Hills (*Parbat-kai-Padshah*), he wished to be so in

[1] Sikkim.

reality; that in judging of the intentions of men their actions ought to be the criterion; and that I could not help being concerned that the Gorkha Rajah, after having from a petty rajah made himself master of all Nepal, after having subdued Bijapúr[1] and Murung,[2] and after having at length attacked the territories of Demo Jong, a vassal of Lhasa, should be considered by Gesub and the government of this country as more to be trusted than the English, who during twelve or fifteen years had never attempted to extend the boundaries of Bengal, who had restored the Deb Rajah's country, and who were known to adhere religiously to their engagements. The Lama replied that the government at Lhasa's eyes were opened, and that they viewed the Gorkha Rajah's designs in a very different light; that as to the English, Gesub had received such accounts of them as raised his suspicions; "and," added he, "his heart is confined, and he does not see things in the same view as I do." I said I had heard a great deal of Gesub's abilities, but I confessed in the present case I thought he was blind to his own interest; that I knew the Gorkha Rajah was afraid of the English; that he was sensible also how firmly they adhered to their treaties and to their friends; that he had seen Shujâu-'d-Daulah's[3] country enjoy a state of perfect tranquillity during twelve years, merely from the Mahrattas and the other powers of Hindustan knowing that the English would be ready to assist him; that Shujâu-d'-Daulah, when apprehensive of an invasion, had even sometimes called in the assistance of the Company's troops, which had marched to the extreme boundaries of his dominions, and had afterwards, when there was no further occasion for their presence, returned to Bengal; that I confessed I saw nothing more likely to make the Gorkha Rajah desist from his war with Demo Jong[4] and confine himself to his own country, than the knowledge of a connection between the government of this country

[1] The Vijapur of Buchanan Hamilton. This place was the residence of the Subah of the Murung, and of a former dynasty of princes. It is on the high part of the low hills, overlooking the Murung, east of the Kosi river.

[2] Buchanan Hamilton describes the Murung as extending, in the low country, from the Kosi to the Tísta, about 87 miles from east to west, and 48 miles across. The inhabitants are chiefly of the Koch or Rajbangsi tribe (p. 156). See also note at p. 65.

[3] The Nawab of Oudh.

[4] Sikkim.

and that of Bengal. He seemed to be much pleased with what I had said, and asked me if he might write this to Gesub. I told him he might, and that I had no doubt that the Governor would be ready to employ his mediation to make the Gorkha Rajah desist from his attempts on the territories subject to Lhasa, and that I had reason to think, from the Gorkha Rajah's dread of the English, that it would be effectual; but I added that if Gesub, contrary to reason, and what he had seen of the fidelity and moderation of the English, continued to entertain suspicions of them, I was helpless, and my constituents were helpless. He said that Gesub's apprehensions of the English arose not only from himself, but also from his dread of giving offence to the Chinese, to whose empire this country was subject, and that he wished to receive an answer from the court at Peking. I replied that whenever he mentioned the name of the Emperor of China I was struck dumb; that from his letter to the Governor, as well as from every account, my constituents considered him (the Lama) as the chief of the country during the Dalai Lama's minority, and that although the Emperor was paramount sovereign, everything was left to his management; that Gesub owed his promotion to him, and followed his advice; that the Governor, in his proposals about trade, was promoting the advantage of Tibet, as well as of Bengal; that in former times merchants used to come freely into this country, that the Gorkha Rajah's wars and oppressions had prevented them for some years past, and only prayed him to remove the obstacles which these had occasioned. He replied that he had no doubt of carrying the point I wished, but that it might require a year or two to do it effectually; that besides the obstruction to trade which the Gorkha Rajah's conduct in Nepal had occasioned, his present war with Demo Jong[1] prevented the importation of sugar, spices, tobacco, &c., and that the people of this country complained loudly of it. After thanking him for his intentions of opening trade in the course of two years, I told him that, being sent by the Governor upon this business, I could not help being zealous for its success; that it depended on him whether I should return to Bengal happy and crowned with reputation, or covered with shame, which would certainly be my portion if I failed in the point which, by the Governor's orders, I had represented to him.

[1] Sikkim.

On the 30th of December, Gesub Rimboché's people came to take leave of me. I mentioned to them that I wished to have waited upon them; but they had declined my visit; that, however, I proposed to write to Gesub Rimboché by them, and begged they would be so good as to take care of my letter. They said if I mentioned simply in my letter the receipt of the Chinese brandy, &c., they would carry it, but that if I said anything of business, or anything about the Kalmuks that might bring troubles on the country or on Gesub, they would not carry it. I confess I was much struck with this answer. I replied that being sent to Teshu Lama and living under his roof, I had asked his opinion about writing to Gesub, that he had advised me to it (through the Gosain), and that I should write nothing without showing it to him and receiving his approbation; that I was concerned at their expressing an apprehension of my writing anything that could embroil Gesub; that I was come into the country with a pure heart and wished its happiness and Gesub Rimboché happiness. They desired I would give them a copy of the letter I intended to write to Gesub. I replied that I would give the letter and copy to the Teshu Lama, and if he thought proper he would show it to them. I added that I wished to know the ground of Gesub's suspicions, and as I knew the uprightness of my constituents' intentions as well as my own, I was ready to give him every satisfaction. Their answer was that they were come to take leave of me, that much conversation was not the custom of this country, and so wished me a good journey to Bengal. I endeavoured to get them to listen to me. I wished to introduce the subject of trade, but it was to no purpose; so we parted.

This conversation gave me more concern than any I had in Tibet. I immediately applied for an audience of the Lama, and was admitted. I repeated to him what had passed. He said the people from Lhasa were little men and knew no better. I replied that had I thought their conversation proceeded only from themselves I would feel little uneasiness at it; but I had reason to consider their sentiments as those of Gesub's, and could not help being concerned that he should suspect me of coming into this country to raise disturbances; that God was my witness that I wished him well, that I wished the Lama well and the country well, and that a suspicion of treachery and falsehood was what I could not bear. I was a good deal affected, and said this with some warmth. The Lama endeavoured to remove my concern. He said that Gesub was unacquainted with the character of the English; "but," said he, "at any rate the Dalai Lama will be of age in a year or two, and then Gesub's management will be at an end." I told him that I had before sent to ask his opinion as to the propriety of my writing to Gesub, and having now represented to him what had passed between me and Gesub's vakíls, I was come to ask his advice and opinion. Upon this I took out the draft of a letter I intended to have sent to Gesub, and read it to him. "Every country," quoth the Lama, "has its particular manner of writing. If you please I will write a letter for you." I accepted his offer. He immediately called in one of his people, and making him sit down, dictated a letter in the Tibet language in my name to Gesub Rimboché, explaining it to me at the same time in the Hindustani language. To the best of my remembrance it was to the following purpose:

To Gesub Rimboché.

[After some compliments.]

"I have received the Chinese wine, fish, mushrooms, biscuit, &c., that you were so good as to send me in great abundance, and all very good of their kinds. May your country enjoy tranquillity and yourself happiness. I request, in the name of the Governor my master, that you will allow merchants to trade between this country and Bengal. I have sent you a gun, a piece of broadcloth, and a handkerchief, which you will please accept of."

After the letter was written I took leave of the Lama.

Next day I sent the letter with the broadcloth, &c., to Gesub's servants by one of Teshu Lama's people, and begged him to tell them how concerned I was for what had passed; that if Gesub in spite of everything would entertain suspicions of me, and if they would not listen to what I had to say in order to remove them, I was helpless; that I had sent a letter, &c., for Gesub, which I requested them to deliver to him, and in case they wished to know the contents, they would apply to the Lama, who had seen and approved of it. They returned me an answer that they were sorry and ashamed at what passed at our last meeting; that they would deliver the letter to Gesub, and would faithfully mention to him what I had said. From this I found that the Lama had spoken to them.

It may appear extraordinary that, though I was exposed to so many inconveniences from the seat of government being at Lhasa, I should never have proposed my going thither to the Lama, and it is necessary that I should give my reasons for it. I had every cause to think, from Gesub Rimboché's letter to the Lama, from the Lama's conversation, and from other accounts which I had received, that Gesub Rimboché was extremely jealous of me; that he considered me as come to spy "the nakedness of the land," and that the English had designs upon this country. I was suspicious therefore that he would refuse my visit while he continued in this way of thinking, and I entertained some hopes that the Lama's letters and the representations of the Chauduri[1] (a man whose connection with me I shall afterwards mention) would bring him to entertain a more favourable idea of me and of my business. Another thing, I could not (in the character I bore as being sent on the part of the Company) go to Lhasa without suitable presents to Gesub, to the Dalai Lama, and, perhaps, to the Chinese officers, and these presents I had it not in my power to make.

I visited the Lama on the 13th January, and he introduced this subject himself. He said that as I had come so far he would be very glad that I should see Lhasa also; that Gesub, however, was averse from it, and had written to him to keep me with him, and that I should not go to Lhasa; that he was afraid of my seeing the city; that, however, if I chose to send any of my servants to Lhasa he would give them passports, and they could afterwards give me an account of it and of anything I wished to know. It became now necessary that I should give an answer either one way or the other. I replied that I was exceedingly concerned to find that Gesub still continued to entertain such suspicions of me, and to imagine that I was come with a design of making an unfriendly account of this kingdom; that I knew nothing about surveying or war; that Mr. Hamilton, who was with me, knew as little; that as to the country of Tibet, the Gosain, who

[1] See p. 172.

had been down in Calcutta, could tell him that the Governor had plans of it, and knew the names and situations of the principal places, Lhasa, Chamnamring, Shigatzé, Janglaché, Giansu, Painám, &c.; that although I would own to him that after coming so far, and being within a few days' journey of Lhasa, I would be glad to go to that city, yet it was on a very different account from what Gesub supposed; that my having been at Lhasa would, among my countrymen, tend to my credit and reputation, and I conceived also some hopes that Gesub Rimboché, after seeing and conversing with me, would alter his opinion, and that his jealousy would be removed. He said it was very true, but Gesub's heart was small and suspicious; and, to tell the truth, he could not promise that he would be able to procure his consent, but I might send one of my people. "I will give you an instance," said he, "of the narrowness of Gesub's mind. The Gorkha Rajah has sent some vakils with letters to me and to himself; they are now at Kuti,[1] the frontier town of Nepal: and Gesub, among other reasons, objects to their coming into Tibet lest they should learn the manner of the Kalmuks fighting on horseback, which is practised in this country (describing it at the same time by motions), and should teach it to the Gorkha Rajah's people." I replied that as to my servants going to Lhasa, it would be to their credit, not to mine; and as to giving me an account of the city, it was what I did not wish to know, and that he might himself judge of my indifference on this subject, from my having been so long at Teshu Lumbo, and having never once visited Shigatzé, a town in its neighbourhood. To tell the truth, I had restrained my curiosity merely in order to counteract the idea of my having come to examine and pry into the country; for Shigatzé is commanded by officers subject to Lhasa. The Lama upon this

[1] This place is at the head of the Ni-lam Pass, forming one of the trade routes from Tibet to Nepal, down the valley of the Butia Kosi. It was visited by the native explorer who was sent by Colonel Montgomerie in 1871. He returned from Tibet by this route, which took him to Kathmandu. He describes it as passing through a fearful gorge, where the road crosses the river no less than fifteen times; three by iron suspension bridges, and eleven by wooden bridges 24 to 60 paces long. At one place the sides of the gigantic chasm were so close that a bridge of 24 paces would span it. Along the perpendicular wall of rock a path is supported on iron pegs let into the face of the rock. The path is of stone slabs covered with earth, only 18 inches wide, a third of a mile long, and 1500 feet above the roaring torrent.

offered to give me a map of Tibet from Ladak to the frontier of China, with the names of places and their distances. This was a splendid object, and to obtain it, I was sensible would reflect much lustre on my commission. But I considered the Company could have no interest in this country but that of commerce, and that to know a number of outlandish names or to correct the geography of Tibet, although a matter of great curiosity and extremely interesting to geographers and mapsellers, was of no use to my constituents, or indeed to mankind in general; and that to this I might be sacrificing objects of far greater importance, and exciting that jealousy which had hitherto so cruelly thwarted me in all my negotiations. I replied therefore, in the same style of indifference, after thanking the Lama for his kind offer, that the situation of the country, its strength, forces, &c., were of no concern to my constituents; that the Company considered Tibet as at such a distance from Bengal, and separated by such mountains, the difficulty of which I had but too well experienced, that they never dreamt of any danger to Bengal from that quarter, and the same causes, supposing the Company even had intentions of extending their territories, which their conduct showed they had not, served equally to ensure Tibet from any danger from Bengal; and that in taking a map of this country I would only afford ground for Gesub's suspicions. He replied that Gesub would know nothing of it. I told him that I could not answer for that, and at any rate it was not an object with my constituents; that I would be glad indeed to know the laws and customs of Tibet, because, as every country excelled others in some of these particulars, it was the business of a traveller to inform himself of those, and to adopt such as were good; and I would own to him that the Governor had desired me to inquire about their manners, but at the same time to concern myself in no way about the strength or forces of Tibet. He seemed to be well satisfied with what I said, and told me that he would order his people to write down every particular regarding the laws and customs of the country that I wished to know.

The 19th of January was the first of the holidays at the change of the year. I went to see the ceremonies at church. Before they began the Lama called me into a closet, and told me that the Gorkha Rajah's vakíls, who had been so long stopped on the borders of the country, were arrived; that the principal one was a Gosain, who had formerly resided long in this country; that he had brought a letter from the Gorkha Rajah, in which he said everything was written, but it was in Nagari, and he had given it to be translated, and would afterwards inform me of its contents; that the Gorkha Rajah therein styled himself the King of the Mountains (*Parbat-kai-Padshah*); that formerly he used to send presents of fruit only, but upon this occasion had sent more valuable ones. He said he understood that the Kerant [1] Rajah, upon his country being seized by the Gorkhas, had taken refuge with Demo Jong; but having since, upon the Gorkha Rajah's hostilities with that chief, discovered the insecurity of his situation, had fled towards Purneah. The Lama then asked my opinion of the Gorkha Rajah, and whether he had ever attacked the English or invaded Bengal. I confessed that I knew very little of him till I came into his presence; that from what he had been pleased to tell me, and from what I understood of the number of troops he kept in pay, of his every year entering into some new war and making new conquests, and his late invasion of Demo Jong's territories, I was of opinion that he aimed at making himself master of all the hilly country; that as I was ignorant of his purpose in sending vakils, I could say nothing particular about it; that if at the same time he had withdrawn his forces from Demo Jong's dominions, I should think him in earnest in his professions of friendship and moderation; but I confessed I did not understand a man who made proffers and assurances of friendship with one hand and a sword in the other. "We will see," said the Lama. "In the meantime Gesub Rimboché has sent 18,000 men, under the command of Deb Patza,[2] together with a priest or inferior lama, in order to be prepared either for war or peace." He also told me that the Gorkha Rajah was covered over with blotches and sores, and his health very bad. The service began, and the Lama went to church.

On the 19th I had another audience of the Lama at church, and between the services. He told me that Gorkha had written

[1] Kirats or Kirantis, a tribe of Eastern Nepal, next to the Lepchas, from whom they are divided by the River Arun.

[2] See p. 101.

not only to him, but also to the Dalai Lama, to Gesub Rimboché, and to Gubshay Pundita, who is one of the ministers at Lhasa; that he mentioned in his letters having subdued Kerant, Murung, &c.; that he also wrote that he did not wish to quarrel with this state, but if they had a mind for war, he let them know he was well prepared, and desired them to remember that he was a Rajput; that he wanted to establish factories at Kuti,[1] Kerant, and another place, upon the borders of Tibet and Nepal, where the merchants of Tibet might purchase the commodities of his country and those of Bengal, and desired their concurrence; that he would allow the common articles of commerce to be transported through his kingdom, but no glasses or other curiosities, and desired them to prohibit the importation of them also; that he desired them further to have no connection with Fringies or Moghuls, and not to admit them into the country, but to follow the ancient custom, which he was resolved likewise to do; that a Fringy had come to him upon some business, and was now in his country, but he intended to send him back as soon as possible, and desired them to do the same with us; that he had written also about circulating his coin, and had sent 2000 rupees for that purpose. The Lama then asked me about this Fringy who was with the Gorkha Rajah; but being quite in the dark I could give him no manner of information. The Lama did not at this time desire my opinion upon the Gorkha Rajah's letter, and I made no remarks upon the subject.

On the 26th of January I visited the Lama. It was the first day of the Tibet year. Nothing of business passed.

On the 24th of February I waited upon the Lama to take leave of him for a few days, which I proposed to pass with his nephews at their estate at Rinjaitzay, which is about two days' journey from Teshu Lumbo.

I returned on the 2nd of March, and had an audience of the Lama on the 3rd. After congratulations on my return, and questions about the entertainment his nephews had given me at Rinjaitzay, he told me the messenger he had sent to Lhasa was returned, and had brought him accounts of Gesub being now out of danger; that upon his illness the Chinese officers had consulted

[1] At the head of the Ni-lam Pass from Kathmandu to Shigatzé, following the course of the Butia Kosi. (See note at p. 155.)

some conjurors concerning his fate, who had given an oracular answer; that they had despatched messengers to Peking with the accounts of his being dangerously ill; that extreme unction was performed on him, and he remained several days with his eyes fixed on the ground, and in a manner insensible, but the violence of his disease having abated he was able to walk about the room, though not to apply to business. The Lama further told me that the report of Gorkha Rajah's death was confirmed, and that he had received letters from Lhasa giving an account of it, which was corroborated by the advices of Gosains and Kashmiris; that three wives and six concubines had burnt themselves at his funeral, and that Sing Pertab,[1] his son, had succeeded him in the government. The Lama further informed me that news was received at Lhasa of the Chinese having at length by means of an immense army subdued Ribdyen Gyripo (the rebellious chief who, with a few thousand brave adherents, had defended himself and his hill-bound country against the united power of the Chinese empire); that they had approached almost to the capital of his province, by roads which they made through the mountains with immense labour, when the Kampa chief in despair threw himself from the walls.[2] He told me also that the Dalai Lama was next year to proceed to Peking to wait upon the Emperor. My part of the conversation need not be put down.

On the 18th of March I had a visit from the Nepal vakíl. I told him that I heard from everybody of Gorkha's death, and inquired if he had received any accounts of it. He said he had none, and that he had therefore not ordered the Newars (natives of Nepal) to shave their beards and eyebrows. He spoke of it, however, as a thing there was no doubt of. He said some of the Gorkha Rajah's Sepoys had come to Kuti,[3] and that Gesub Rimboché was offended at it, and had written to the Lama, who had spoken of it to him; that he had told the Lama that it was to teach the Bhutanese troops their exercise; but the Lama replied they wanted to learn no new rules.

[1] The Rajah Pertab Sing Sah deva died in 1775. His son, who reigned from 1775 to 1816, was Girwan Yudh Vikrama Sah deva.

[2] This was a rebellion of some Turpan or Tibetan tribes in the Szechuen province, who, though few in number, defended themselves to the last. The revenge the Emperor took upon the leader was dreadful. (Gutzlaff, 'China Opened,' i. p. 361.)

[3] See note at p. 155.

I had no opportunity of waiting upon the Lama till the 15th of March. He told me that he had been so much engaged with some Kalmuks, and had so much to write on their account, that he had not been able to see me sooner; that several years ago a tribe of Tatars, who were subject to Russia, had gone over to the Chinese, and that the Emperor of China had formerly written to him of this, felicitating himself on his good fortune in it; that the Russians had since sent four ambassadors to China to demand their vassals, whom the Emperor had imprisoned; and, as I understood him, had also confined some other Russian subjects who were afterwards sent upon the same errand, and to request the release of their countrymen. The Russians had not yet begun hostilities, but he imagined they would soon go to war about it. I told him that as the Russians were engaged in a very heavy war with the Turks, which I was uncertain whether they had yet finished, I supposed they would hardly think of entering into another with the Chinese, and encountering two such powerful neighbours at the same time; but as soon as they had made peace with the Sultan of Rum I made no doubt of their resenting the conduct of the Chinese in a very high strain; that the present sovereign of Russia, although a woman, was extremely able and active, going in person to review her forces, receiving all ambassadors, and inspecting every department of government herself; that the Russians were also a very hardy and warlike people, and capable of great efforts, and I doubted whether the Chinese would be able to cope with their troops, who had been so long accustomed to actual and very severe service. He replied that it was very true; that former emperors would have weighed these circumstances, but the present one was too violent and too fond of war to listen to advice, and was besides offended at the Russians for the refuge they had accorded to the Tsungars, a tribe of Tatars whom he had subdued; that things must now take their course, and he was afraid that no representations of his or of his friend, the Lama of Peking, could prevent a war.

On the 27th of March some Kashmiri merchants came to me, and after presenting silk handkerchiefs, according to the custom of the country, informed me that they waited upon me in consequence of the Lama's orders; that he had written to their constituents at

Lhasa (for these at Shigatzé are only agents), acquainting them that the Governor had written to him, and that I had represented to him the Governor's desire of opening the commerce between Tibet and Bengal, so that merchants might freely trade between the one kingdom and the other; that the trade which was formerly carried on through Nepal by the many Kashmiri houses settled there had been greatly obstructed by the oppression of the Gorkha Rajah, and that he, therefore, advised them to send their *gumashtas* into Bengal, through the Deb Rajah's country; that the Governor had engaged to give them every assistance and protection, and that he, on his part, was always ready to encourage merchants and trade. Whether all this was in his letter, or spoken by the Lama himself, I cannot say, for they told me further that they had waited upon the Lama, and he had desired them to come to me. I told them that the Governor had indeed desired me to represent to the Lama how much the trade with Bengal had declined of late years, owing to causes with which they were well acquainted, and to request his assistance in restoring it; and that the Lama had been good enough to promise his best endeavours for that purpose. I then explained to them the steps which had been taken in Bengal for the ease of merchants by abolishing the ancient chokies and exactions upon trade; by fixing the duties at only two rupees in the hundred, and by granting every protection and encouragement to the merchants; that if they choose to send *gumashtas* into Bengal I could venture to assure them of the Governor's readiness to grant them every security and assistance; that the only difficulty was the road by which they were to get to Bengal; that I understood they were all afraid of trusting themselves in Nepal, to which Murung[1] and Bijapúr[2] were now subject; that the Deb Rajah's country only remained, who had granted permission of transporting goods through his territories only to one or two merchants; that I had mentioned the subject to him but very slightly, reserving it till after I had waited upon and received the order of the Lama, to whom I was sent; that, for my part, I should use every argument and every means with the Deb Rajah in order to obtain his consent; that I trusted to the Lama's seconding my applications, and was in hopes they might be crowned with success; but could not

[1] See note at p. 65.

[2] See note at p. 150.

promise with certainty as to the determination of people with whom I was but little acquainted.

They replied, that from the Lama's conversation and assurances they had little doubt of obtaining the Deb Rajah's permission to pass through his kingdom; and that after the unsuccessful war which the Bhutanese had carried on, and having their country restored to them, they imagined the Deb Rajah would be very ready to comply with any demand on the part of the Company, as he would be afraid, in case of refusal, that the English would again invade his territory, and concluded with saying that I might threaten him upon this score. I told them I had no power to use such language to him, and that whatever I did with the Deb Rajah must be by peaceable and friendly means; that the Company, in consequence of the Lama's letter to the Governor, had restored the Deb Rajah's country, and entered into a treaty of peace with him, which, according to the maxims of the English Government, would, on the part of my constituents, remain for ever inviolate. They observed that the Gorkha Rajah was now dead;[1] that they hoped his son would be more favourable to merchants; and in case of the Deb Rajah's refusal, that the Governor's application to the new Rajah of Nepal, Sing Pertab,[2] would certainly procure them a free passage. I said as I was unacquainted with Sing Pertab's character or the measures he intended to pursue, I could say nothing upon this subject; that if he followed the footsteps of his father, made promises and oaths only to break them, and engaged in perpetual wars, it was difficult for my constituents to enter into friendship or negotiations with him; that if he contented himself with the peaceful possession of his own dominions the Governor could then send a vakíl and solicit his protection and encouragement to merchants; but that in this, as well as everything which regarded the hills which separate Bengal from Tibet, I imagined he would be greatly influenced by the opinion of the Lama, whose character and abilities enable him so well to judge of the measures to be pursued with the chiefs to whom they are subject. I then asked them when they proposed to

[1] This was Pertab Sing Sah deva, who died in 1775.

[2] The deceased Rajah was succeeded by a Regent named Bahadur Sah, who was deposed by the nobles in 1800. Then followed Girwan Yudh Vikrama Sah deva, who reigned until 1816.

send their *gumashtas* to Bengal. They told me after the rains, and applied to me for letters to the people on the borders of Bengal, as they were entirely strangers there. I promised them letters to some of my acquaintances, and that if they chose it I would request the Governor to write to the Killadars on the frontier provinces to afford them every necessary assistance; but that in Bengal merchants were always well received, and had nothing to fear. They seemed to wish however for passports. I recollect nothing further of consequence that passed. Before they went away they desired that I would inform the Lama of their having visited me in obedience to his orders.

On the 29th of March about a dozen of the principal Tibetan merchants paid me a visit. They deal principally in tea, some of them to the extent of two or three lakhs a year, though one would not suspect it from their raiment. They also told me they came to me in consequence of the Lama's orders; they mentioned having received a letter from him while at Desheripgay, advising them to send *gumashtas* to Bengal, and that he had likewise spoken to them to the same purpose since his arrival at Teshu Lumbo. They said that being born in a cold country they were afraid of going into a hot one; that their people would die in Bengal; that they had it from tradition that about eight hundred years ago the people of this country used to travel into Bengal, but that eight out of ten died before their return; that the Kashmiris and Gosains travelled into different countries, but that they could not. I replied, that I could only promise them the protection and assistance of the Government of Bengal; that the climate was in the hand of God; and after giving them an account of the climate of Bengal during the cold weather, I told them that if they were afraid of sending their servants thither, the Kashmiris and Gosains would supply them with what they wanted, and it was the same thing to Bengal and to the inhabitants of Tibet. I enlarged on the Lama's desire of preserving peace in the world, and of promoting the trade of merchants and the happiness of mankind, and they in their turn praised the free and equitable government of the English, which they said the Lama had informed them of.

As some of them were very old men, I asked them what proportion they supposed the commodities now imported from

Bengal bore to that of former times. They would not mention any fixed proportion, but said that formerly great quantities of coral, broadcloth, &c., used to come through Nepal, but now what was brought was principally by the fakirs, who smuggled it into the country. They added that as to this country, people imagined from gold being produced in it that it was extremely rich, but this was not the case, and that if extraordinary quantities of gold were sent to Bengal the Emperor of China, who was sovereign of the country, would be displeased at it. I replied that the trade between Tibet and Bengal was no new thing, and had been carried on for many hundred years; that the conquest of Nepal by the Gorkha Rajah had put a stop to it; and that the Governor only wished to see it restored to the same state as formerly. They seemed highly pleased with this, and, after desiring me to report their visit to the Lama, took their leave.

I paid a short visit to the Lama on the 1st of April. He said that Gesub Rimboché's administration was near an end, and that he wished, when the Dalai Lama came of age, that the Governor would send an embassy to him. He said he proposed, if a place on the banks of the Ganges was granted him, to place the Gosain, who was down in Calcutta, there; "and," says he, "if he should stand in need of any small matter, I trust you will supply him." I asked him about what part of the country he wished it to be. He said that he would like it to be near Calcutta, that the people he sent down might have an opportunity of waiting on the Governor, but he would leave it to the Governor and the pundits, only to be near the Ganges. He told me that the troops under the command of Deb Patza had returned, as they were unable to proceed on account of the great quantities of snow, which rendered the road impassable; that Gesub Rimboché was very angry with the commander and had ordered him to return. He said that he had also received a letter from the commander of the Gorkha troops, mentioning that he intended to desist from war on account of his master's death, and proposing a truce for three years. The Lama then gave me a Persian paper containing some memoranda, which he said he wished me to keep in mind. He also gave me some garden seeds and a view of Teshu Lumbo. These last gave rise to a conversation which lasted till the end of my visit.

On the 3rd of April I waited on the Lama to take my public leave of him. He sent first to speak to me in private. I told him I had read the Persian paper he had been pleased to give me. He recapitulated the points which it contained; he mentioned what he had formerly said about the Lama at Peking; that he hoped the Emperor would put the government of the country in the same manner as formerly in the hands of the Dalai Lama, "and then," says he, "I shall have no difficulty in carrying any point that the Governor pleases, and hope to settle it so with the Emperor that the Governor may send his people to Peking, and, if he pleases, establish English factories; but at present, while the administration is in Gesub's hands, he and the Ambas[1] are excessively jealous of foreigners coming into the country, so much so that he stopped the admission of a vakíl from the King of Assam, and you know the difficulty I had about your coming. In regard to the house which I wish to have on the banks of the Ganges," continued the Lama, "I propose that Purungir, who was down in Calcutta, should settle it. I do not wish it to be a large house, and let it be built in the fashion of Bengal." I begged him to give Purungir instructions about it, which he said he would do. "Purungir," says he, "has served me very well, and I have not found him guilty of so many lies as most other fakirs, and I hope the Governor will show him favour. The old Gosain, Suk-Debu, has also asked me leave to go down to Calcutta; he will accompany you; and I have also written to the Governor about him, and I hope he will favour him." I then asked him about Bijapúr, which I had mentioned at a former meeting, and begged to know his opinion as to the answer I should give the Deb Rajah in case he spoke to me on that subject, and also that I might represent it to the Governor. "I have already," says he, "written to Sing Pertab, telling him that his father treacherously and unjustly made himself master of Bijapúr, and as I have heard a favourable character of him, I hope he will restore it to the Deb Rajah, its rightful possessor. I have also advised him to send a vakíl to Calcutta; as yet I am ignorant what answer he will return; but if the Deb applies to you about Bijapúr, I think you should tell him that you understand from me that I had written on the subject, and in case I receive no

[1] Chinese resident officials.

unfavourable answer, then the Governor may, if he pleases, write to Sing Pertab about it."

I repeated his words, to be sure that I understood them right. He then asked me if I had any request to make to him. I said I had before mentioned to him how fond the Governor was of strange animals, and he had been so good as to send some; but there were two wild ones in this country which could not be sent unless they were reared and tamed when young, the one was the musk goat, the other the tús, and I knew how much he would oblige the Governor by giving orders for this purpose, and sending them down to Bengal in the cold weather. Says he, "I will order the musk goats to be caught and given to you on the road." I thanked him, but said it was impossible to keep them alive unless previously tamed. "Well," says he, "I will give orders about the animals, and send some of them down by my people after the rains; and if there are any others or anything in this country which the Governor wishes to have, write to me about it."

My next request was to procure a list of all the comets, with the dates of their appearances, from the earliest period of the Chinese history; which, after some inquiries about comets, and telling me that they expected one in six years, he promised to do, and to write to the great Lama of Peking about it. He told me also that, from the first of the Chinese kings till Hrondzain Cambo,[1] who reigned in Tibet about eight hundred years ago, they reckoned 20,000 years. After this he asked about Russia, and if the King of England had much to say with the Empress. I told him he had more influence at the Court of Russia than any other prince in Europe, although their kingdoms were separated at a great distance from one another. Says he, "I am glad of it, for in the event of a war between Russia and China, I may perhaps be able, through means of the Company, to do something towards bringing about a

[1] This would be *Srong-tsan-gambo* of the list given in the Tibetan grammar of Csoma de Koros, from a work written at Lhasa in 1686 (p. 181); who is said to have been born in 627 A.D. Georgi's list, in the 'Alphabetum Tibetanum' (p. 297), contains a similar name, *Tzhong-tzheng-Chambo*, as of a king who is, however, said to have lived much earlier, in about 60 A.D. He removed the seat of government to the part of Tibet where Lhasa was afterwards founded. He built a palace on the hill where the monastery of Potala now stands, and died after a reign of ninety years. He is the twenty-fourth king of Tibet of Georgi's list.

peace, and that is the business of us Lamas." He then laid before me his presents to the Governor, and showed me his letter before he sealed it. After this he gave them to me in charge. I asked if he did not intend to entrust them to the Gosain; but he desired me to take them, and I accordingly accepted them. "They are very trifling," says he, "but what can I send from this country?" After giving me presents of some silks, purses of gold dust, silver talents, &c., and clothing me in a fine khilat, he took a bit of red silk, and tying a knot upon it himself, he threw it about my neck with his own hands. I then had my public leave, but was to wait upon him again in private.

On the 4th of April I again waited upon the Lama. His room was hung round with festoons of painted paper intermixed with the figures of his deities. It was on account of some religious holiday. He asked me a great deal about our religion. As I am not sent to convert unbelieving nations it is a subject I seldom enter upon, and I gave such answers as turned the conversation. He asked me also particularly about the missionary Padres, who had been in this country, and when expelled had settled in Nepal.[1] I repeated to him what I had formerly mentioned, that I imagined they came from Italy, as there were some of that nation now at Patna; that their religion differed from ours, and in nothing more than in their intolerant spirit and desire of bringing all the world to their own opinions, whereas every religion was allowed in England, and good men of every faith respected. He told me that the missionaries were expelled Tibet about forty years ago, on account of some disputes with the fakirs.

After this he asked me about the English settlement at Canton, and whether any Englishmen had ever gone to Peking. In answer I gave him an account of the trade between England and China. I told him that I believed that no Englishman had ever gone to Peking. "Not one?" says he. I replied that many years since an English physician[2] had gone when very young into the service of Russia, and accompanied an ambassador who was sent about

[1] Whence they were expelled by the Gorkha Rajah. They went from Kathmandu to Betiah, in Champaran, where they now are settled with their flock.

[2] Bell. See 'Travels from St. Petersburg, in Russia, to various parts of Asia, by John Bell, of Antermony,' i. p. 157. This work was published at Glasgow in 1763, and was, no doubt, well known to Mr. Bogle.

fifty years ago to the Emperor, but I never heard of any other. "I will endeavour," says he, "through the means of the Lama at Peking, to get permission for the English to go to the Emperor; whether I shall be able to carry this point or not I cannot say, but I will afterwards write to the Governor how I have succeeded." I expressed my acknowledgments how much it would tend to the Company's satisfaction, and how happy I was convinced it would make the Governor.

"The Russians and Chinese," says he, "are at present on bad terms. If any of the former go to Peking, I am told they are not admitted into the Emperor's presence without being searched, on account of a Chinese man having been some time ago killed by a Russian who concealed a pistol within his sleeve." After this I reported to him a conversation that had passed between me and Chauduri, on which he made no observations, except that the Hindus were fond of appearing of consequence, and scrupled not to tell falsehoods. He then showed me the images and the dress which he intended to send down to Bengal by the Gosain, in order to be put up in the temple which he proposes to build on the banks of the Ganges. He desired me to inquire particularly about the situation of a town called Shambul, about which he said the pundits of Bengal would be able to inform me. I recollect nothing further.

Next day I waited upon the Lama, Dr. Hamilton was with me, and he inquired a great deal about the method of treating the smallpox in England, and described the fatal effects of the disease in Tibet. It is unnecessary to insert what passed on this subject. He showed me about five or six watches which had come overland to him. They had chiefly German or Dutch names upon them, and were all except one out of order. This gave rise to a conversation on watches, which it is also needless to put down. He desired me to speak English, and I repeated some verses of Gray's "Elegy in a Country Churchyard." I mention these things only because they serve to mark his character.

On the 6th of April I again waited upon the Lama. Soon after my entrance his servants who were to accompany me came in to take their leave, and had their heads touched according to the custom of the country and their respective ranks. "These people," said he, "are to accompany you as far as Buxa-Dúar, but the weather is now becoming so hot that everyone is afraid to go to Bengal. As soon as the rains are over, I will send down some gylongs[1] to Calcutta to wait upon the Governor, and to visit the religious places in Bengal, and will write to the Governor by them. I have spoken to you about getting me two lions' skins, a crocodile, and some other things; pray how do you propose to send them?" I said, I thought of transmitting them to the Buxa Subah, who would forward them to him. "The Deb Rajah's people," says he, "will make mistakes, and you had better give them to my people on their return to Bengal." He then asked me how I imagined the Governor intended to send his despatches to him. I said that as to any orders he (the Lama) had given me, or any letters he might have to forward to him, that I would follow his directions as to the manner of transmitting them; but I conceived the Governor could not entrust his letters or presents but to his own servants, who would bring them into his own presence. Says he, "I will be plain with you. I wish the Governor would not at present send an Englishman. You know what difficulties I had about your coming into the country, and how I had to struggle with the jealousy of Gesub Rimboché and the people[2] at Lhasa. Even now they are uneasy at my having kept you with me so long. I could wish, therefore, that the Governor would rather send a Hindu. I am in hopes my letter to the Lama will have a good effect in removing this jealousy, and I expect in a year or two that the Government of this country will be in Dalai Lama's hands, when I will inform the Governor, and he may then send an Englishman to me and to the Dalai Lama. But Gesub is so very suspicious, and looks upon you so much as come to spy the country, that I shall have great difficulty about another Englishman coming." I promised to represent all this to the Governor, for I was sensible of the truth of what he said; but I at the same time used some arguments in order to show how ill-grounded this jealousy was; though I must confess, while I used them, I did it

[1] *Gylong* or *gelung* is equivalent to the Hindustani *bhikshu*, a mendicant; *bhikh*, alms.

[2] That is, the officials. There is not a shadow of reason for supposing that popular jealousy had or has anything to do with the matter.

more to enable him to avail himself of them with others than from any idea that he harboured these unjust suspicions himself. I concluded by telling him that if the Governor had entertained any intentions that were unfriendly, he never would have sent me into this country, and that whatever faults the English might have, all the world knew that treachery was not among them. I promised, however, to represent to the Governor what he had desired me.

Upon this he asked me if I had had any further conversation with the Chauduri. I replied not; that I had told the Chauduri in all matters to apply to the Lama, who was best acquainted with the affairs of Bengal and the state of Hindustan. He seemed pleased with this. "Gesub," says he, "now governs the country, but his administration is, I imagine, near an end. The Governor is a great man, and the Company now are sovereigns of Hindustan. I should like to open a connection between them and the Emperor of China; but Gesub was formerly and will now be again a little man: it would serve no purpose to do it with him." These sentiments are different from what the Lama expressed in a previous conversation; but I imagine the reports of Gesub's endeavours to continue the government in the hands of his own family; his intention, which I am informed of, to put Deb Judhur to death before the Lama should know of it, and perhaps other circumstances of which I am ignorant, had served to render him very cool with regard to Gesub.

The Lama then changed the subject. "I formerly told you," says he, "how the Chinese were engaged in a war in the neighbourhood of Yunnan with a Rajah to the southward of it. The Emperor wrote to me to endeavour to procure intelligence about him, but none of our people are allowed to go into those countries, and I was unable to give him any information. When you return to Bengal I wish you would inquire about this Rajah and write to me." I replied that if it was the King of Pegu I did not despair of procuring him some intelligence, but if it was any of the interior Rajahs who was at war with the Emperor it might not be in my power, but he might depend on my inquiries." Says he, "I wonder you never heard of this war in Bengal." I represented the situation of Pegu with respect to Bengal, and how little interest we had in anything that was passing in that country. He asked me if the Governor had any connection with the King of Pegu. I said that many years ago the King of Pegu had written to the Governor, but I did not know of any correspondence since. Says he, "It is my business to endeavour to settle quarrels and to make peace, and I wish the Governor could put me on a way of doing it in the war I have mentioned. It is not so violent now as it was, but they are still on bad terms." He asked me how many years the Governor would remain in Bengal. It was a question I could not well answer.

I saw the Sopon Chumbo next morning as I went to the Lama's apartment. He told me he had represented what I had said, and the Lama would immediately give orders about the musk goats and tús.

Teshu Lama repeated his concern at my departure; the satisfaction he had received in being informed of the customs of Europe, and concluded with many wishes for my prosperity, and that he would not fail to pray to Heaven in my behalf. He spoke all this in a manner and with a look very different from the studied and formal compliments of Hindustan. I never could reconcile myself to taking a last leave of anybody; and what from the Lama's pleasant and amiable character, what from the many favours and civilities he had shown me, I could not help being particularly affected. He observed it, and in order to cheer me mentioned his hopes of seeing me again. He threw a handkerchief about my neck, put his hand upon my head, and I retired.

After a short visit to Chanzo Cusho I mounted my horse, and bade farewell to Teshu Lumbo.

CHAPTER XVI.

THE EPISODE WITH THE CHAUDURI.

MY connection with the Chauduri forms an episode to the rest of my negotiations at Teshu Lumbo, and I have reserved it for this place. It is needless to enter into long details about an affair that ended in nothing, and I will therefore relate what passed as briefly as possible.

Soon after the Lama's return to his capital a man named the Chauduri[1] came to see me. He was a native of Palpa,[2] or some other of the hilly countries subject to the twenty-four Rajahs. His first visit was merely of ceremony; a few days afterwards he came alone. He told me that he had lately been at Lhasa, and enlarged much on the confidence and favour which Gesub Rimboché had shown him. He said he had been sent by Gesub to wait upon the Lama and to visit me; that Gesub was much pleased with the Company having concluded peace with the Bhutanese, and was desirous of cultivating the Governor's friendship; that he proposed, therefore, to send him (Chauduri) as his vakíl to Calcutta, with a letter and presents, and that he was to accompany me on my return.

As the Lama had never mentioned this man's name to me, and as Gesub's servants, who had visited me the preceding day, had desired me not to attend to what the fakir said, without giving me

[1] A *Chauduri*, or *Desali*, in Nepal, is a subordinate revenue officer under the *Fouzdar*. Next in rank to the Rajah among the Kirantis in Nepal, was an official named the Chautariya (minister), whose title and office were hereditary. This seems to be the same word as Chauduri. (See Hamilton's 'Nepal.') In another place, Hamilton has *Chauduri* as a zemindar, acting as minister to a chief among the Kirantis. In the Gorkha regime *Chautariya* is the title of collaterals of the royal family, who are frequently but not necessarily members of the ministry.

[2] Palpa is a district in Nepal, west of Kathmandu, formerly under a Rajah who formed one of the Chaubisi, or twenty-four Rajahs. The district has long since been subdued by the Gorkhas.

any explanation of this caution, I confess I was suspicious of his exceeding the extent of his commission, but had no doubt of his having some commission. I repeated to him, however, a great many things I had said to the Lama about the Company's friendly intentions towards Tibet, and that if Gesub chose to send a vakíl to Calcutta I was convinced the Governor would show him all respect and attention; that as to myself I would be very glad of his company on the road, but that as I was sent to Teshu Lama, and living under his roof, and as there was no difference between Gesub and the Lama, it was necessary to mention this to the latter. I asked him at the same time whether he had spoken to Teshu Lama about it. He replied that he had had no opportunity, on account of the Lama being so much engaged on his return, and seemed not to like my speaking to him about it, saying it was needless. I told him, however, that it was the custom of the English to deal plainly and openly, and that I could do nothing without mentioning it to the Lama.

I was perhaps wrong in this; and a man more artful than myself, knowing, too, the little cordiality that there was between Gesub and the Lama, might perhaps have carried on his negotiations with the Chauduri without communicating them to the Lama. But I must own, in my small experience through life, I have always found candour and plain dealing to be the best policy, and I had no notion of running the risk of forfeiting the confidence of one who, I had every reason to think, was well disposed towards me and my constituents, in order to take the chance of opening, through an uncertain channel, a connection with a man who I believed entertained no very favourable sentiments of me or my masters.

The Chauduri at length consented to my speaking to the Lama about it, which I did, as mentioned in my conversation of the 4th of April.[1]

After this I had another visit from the Chauduri, who had also spoken to the Lama, on the subject. He repeated the Lama's answers in the style of Hindustan, not of Tibet. He said also that Gesub wished much to gratify the Governor in everything; that if he wanted to establish factories at Lhasa, Gesub was very ready to grant him permission; that Gesub had thought of introducing the

[1] See p. 168.

rupees of Bengal into this country, and hoped the Governor would consent to it.

When I compared in my mind all this account of Gesub's vast benevolence, with his objections to my coming into the country, and recollected what had passed between his servants and me, my suspicions of the Chauduri's veracity increased. After telling him, therefore, how happy I was to hear of Gesub's good dispositions, which I was convinced would be reciprocal on the part of the Governor, I said that I had no order from my constituents for applying about factories; that the Governor had indeed observed with concern the obstacles which the merchants who traded between this country and Bengal were of late years exposed to; and that I had by his order represented them to the Lama, who, I believed, had communicated them to Gesub; and that as the removing of them would be of advantage to this country as well as to Bengal, I had no doubt of his concurrence in so good a work; that, as to the rupees, the Company hindered no person from carrying them out of the country; and if the merchants found their advantage in it they would no doubt bring them into Tibet; but unless the value of a sicca rupee was greatly increased beyond its present price of two *mahendra-mallis*,[1] I did not see how the merchants could find their advantage in it.

The Chauduri said he proposed in about ten or twelve days to go to Lhasa; that he would represent to Gesub what I said about the freedom of trade, and that he would engage, in four days after his arrival, to procure me a favourable answer from him, and would also write to me himself; that after staying some time with Gesub, and receiving his letter and presents for the Governor, he would return to Teshu Lumbo, and accompany me to Calcutta. I recollect nothing further material that passed, either at this or two other conversations, for I was cautious in what I said myself, and an Hindu can say a great deal without saying anything, only that I made him some personal promises in case Gesub should send him as his vakil to Calcutta, and, indeed, at one time I had thoughts of making him some presents.

Meanwhile the Lama had written about the Chauduri to Gesub,

[1] See note at p. 129. The *mahendra-mallis* are now commonly called *mohars*, two of which make a *mohary* rupee, equal to 13¼ sicca annas.

and received an answer, which he sent to me. In this letter Gesub disclaimed having given the Chauduri—who, he said, had gone to Teshu Lumbo on his own business—any commission to me; that he had never spoken about sending him to Calcutta; that he had no connection with him, and only knew his face by having seen him once, at his country seat; and desired the Lama immediately to send him to Lhasa.

I confess I was equally at a loss to reconcile this letter with the intelligence I had received; for although I gave little credit to the Chauduri's vaunting discourses, I had been informed by all the world that Gesub had made him a present of between four and five thousand rupees, and could hardly think he would be so generous to a man he had only seen once, merely for his *beaux yeux*.

The Chauduri was carried away to Lhasa. I did not see him before his departure, but assured him, through one of his people, of my friendly dispositions to him, and of my services, in case he performed what he had promised.

I heard nothing further of the Chauduri till about a week before my departure for Bengal, when he arrived at Teshu Lumbo. For several days he did not come to see me, and I let him know, through a third hand, that I was surprised at it. After this he visited me, when his conversation was to let himself down softly, and to do away with everything he had before said. That Gesub, although well disposed to the Governor, was afraid of giving umbrage to the Chinese, and therefore ordered him, the Chauduri, in case he went to the Ambas, and they should ask about me, to give them an evasive answer, and not to let them know that I was a Fringy; that the Ambas, however, did not ask him; that Gesub had still thoughts of sending him, the Chauduri, to Calcutta after the rain. I said that I had written to Gesub, but he had not thought proper to favour me with an answer; that I could therefore form no judgment of his sentiments or intentions; but if he proposed to send anybody to Calcutta I supposed he would mention it to the Lama; that, as to the Chinese, I thought Gesub's precautions unnecessary; that I was not come into Tibet as a spy, but to wait upon the Lama; that the English were strangers to duplicity and treachery, and I could not help being surprised that he should be so afraid of offending the Chinese by admitting a vakíl from the English, who never had or could have any quarrel with Tibet, while he permitted to go to Lhasa the vakíl of a man who was actually at war with his vassal, and whose ambition and treachery he had so often experienced. He said it was very true, but everybody was afraid of the Fringies. I knew this but too well. Little else passed. I was reserved, and so was he. I had full opportunity to have reproached him for his fruitless promises about procuring me an answer from Gesub; for his confident assurances of being sent with me to Calcutta; and so I might have taken some revenge upon him for deceiving me. But it would have served no good purpose; and as I had not and did not intend to give him anything, what right had I to upbraid him? I therefore took leave of him with fair, but guarded, words.

In endeavouring to account for this strange intrigue, I can only form two hypotheses: either that the Chauduri, according to Gesub's account of the matter, acted entirely from himself, and hoped, upon the strength of his pretended commission, to ingratiate himself with me, to draw from me some presents, and then, by means of this, to ingratiate himself with Gesub; or, which I think the more probable of the two (for I am clear as to Gesub having made him a considerable present), that Gesub, jealous of my visit to the Lama, and desirous to know my errand, had employed the Chauduri to sound me; at the same time, as he could not avow this, that he disclaimed any connection with him, and summoned him to Lhasa on pretence of punishing him; but, in fact, to know what had passed between him and me. Be it as it may, the whole matter ended in smoke.

CHAPTER XVII.

RETURN FROM TIBET TO BENGAL—NEGOTIATIONS IN BHUTAN.

As the time of my departure drew near, I found that I should not be able to bid adieu to the Lama without a heavy heart. The kind and hospitable reception he had given me, and the amiable dispositions which he possesses, I must confess had attached me to him, and I shall feel a hearty regret at parting. In spite of all my journeyings and wanderings over the face of the earth, I have not yet learnt to take leave, and I cannot reconcile myself to the thoughts of a last farewell.

When I look on the time I have spent among these hills it appears like a fairy dream. The novelty of the scenes, and the people I have met with, and the novelty of the life I have led, seem a perfect illusion. Although my days have been spent without business or amusement, they have passed on without care or uneasiness, and I may set this down as the most peaceful period of my life. It is now almost over, and I am about to return to the hurry and bustle of Calcutta.

Farewell, ye honest and simple people! May ye long enjoy that happiness which is denied to more polished nations; and while they are engaged in the endless pursuits of avarice and ambition, defended by your barren mountains, may ye continue to live in peace and contentment, and know no wants but those of nature.[1]

* * * * * *

On the 7th of April, 1775, as soon as I had taken leave of my friends at Teshu Lumbo, I hurried down the hill, got on horseback, and began my journey towards Bengal. There was a large cavalcade of us. For, besides Mr. Hamilton, myself, Mirza Settar, and our Bengal servants, and Purungir, the young Gosain who had

[1] Extract from a letter from Mr. Bogle to his sister, dated March 10, 1775.

formerly been sent to Calcutta by the Lama, and an old Gosain, who, afraid that in passing through Nepal he might be stripped of all the wealth he had been gathering during forty years' trading pilgrimages from the banks of the Indus to the plains of Siberia, had obtained leave to pass in my company through the Bhutan mountains, and Deb Gyloug, a priest of the Lama's household, with Paima, and about ten Bhutanese servants, who were to escort me to the frontier of Bengal, there were all the Kashmiri merchants of Shigatzé, who insisted on paying me the compliment of seeing me fairly on my journey.

After accommodating matters with a large party of clamorous beggars, we rode slowly over the plain which stretches southwards from the palace, and arrived at a large tent, where tea was provided. Having drank two or three dishes, I took leave of my Kashmiri friends, by interchanging handkerchiefs, compliments, and good wishes. The palace and town, the monastery of Teshu Lumbo with its copper-gilt roofs; the castle of Shigatzé, with the town below it, and the high surrounding hills, formed a fine prospect at this distance. But the bleakness and barrenness of the country were a great drawback; for not a single blade of grass had yet sprung, nor a tree budded.

We reached the end of our stage in the afternoon. It is a large village. Our landlord was a priest, and our room set off with an image of a former Lama, as large as life, and small images with lamps burning before them. All our Tibet attendants, Deb Gylong excepted, had well refreshed themselves at parting with their friends at Teshu Lumbo, and I persuaded some of them to deprecate the wrath of the Lama's image by lighting pyes (perfumed torches) before it. However, drunkenness is either not a sin among the laity of Tibet, or, as happens in all cold countries, by being often committed is made light of.

On the road to Painám we met Deb Patza, who was on his way to pay a visit to Teshu Lama, before he went to join his troops. He was preceded by his wife and her female attendants, mounted astride on horseback. She had her face half covered, like the Armenian women. But I was so taken up in getting a handkerchief ready for the General, that I did not observe his lady till she was almost past. We alighted on both sides. The General courteously declined to receive my handkerchief till he had given me his. After some mutual inquiries, he said he had a house in the neighbourhood, where he would have been happy to have received me, and to have played another game at chess;[1] but expecting soon to be again sent towards Nepal, and being obliged to wait on the Teshu Lama before his departure, it was not in his power. This was polite. The rest of the conversation turned upon his late expedition into Demo Jong's country.[2] Soon after parting from him we came in sight of his house. It stands in the plain to the north of Painám, surrounded by willow and other trees. There is a long bridge at Painám, which we passed, and arrived at the house where we had formerly been accommodated.

Our journey from Painám to Bengal was prosecuted nearly by the same road which we had before travelled. Did I intend by these memoranda to enumerate only the names of villages, or the bearings and distances of the several stages, I should have but to put down a list, which might be added to the book of 'Posts of Asia;' for the face of the country had suffered no change by a revolution of six months, and, although the sun was now within twenty degrees of us, continued to exhibit the same inhospitable appearance as in the dead of winter. But I have often thought that trifling incidents, artlessly told, serve to mark the genius and to convey an idea of the manners of a people, better than abstract characters or studied descriptions. The last I will not attempt. If the first is sufficient, I may be able to give them.

A blind man, with a young wife, came into the court and serenaded us. He played on the fiddle underhandwise; she sang; and both, assisted by a young boy, beat time, hoppingly, with their feet. The object of this compliment, I fancy, it is needless to explain.

Our musicians gave way to a parcel of mendicant priests.[3] It may be necessary to state that there are two sets of clergy in Tibet, distinguished by, and classed under the names of, Yellow Caps and Red Caps.[4] The Dalai and Teshu Lamas are at the head of the

[1] See p. 101.

[2] Sikkim. Properly *Deün-jong*.

[3] Gylongs; or *Bhikshu*, in Sanscrit.

[4] The great Tibetan reformer, Tsongkapa, the founder of the Yellow Caps, or Gelukpa sect, was born in about 1355 A.D., near Lake Kokonor. His scholars adopted the yellow head-dress to distinguish them from the prevailing red. Tsongkapa died in 1419, and was buried in the great Galdan Monastery, near Lhasa. He abolished the marriage

Yellow Caps; the Red Caps have their own Lamas and monasteries. In times of old there were violent disputes between them, in which the Yellow Caps got the victory, as well by the assistance of the Tatars as by their superior sanctity. But as I adhere to the tenets of this sect, and have acquired my knowledge of religion from its votaries, I will not here say much upon the subject, lest it should be thought spiteful. I may be allowed, however, just to mention two things, which must convince every unprejudiced person of the wicked lives and false doctrines of the Red Caps. In the first place, many of the clergy marry; and in the next, they persist, in opposition to religion and common sense, in wearing Red Caps. The priests who now visited us were of this last sect. There might be about eight of them. Each held a staff in one hand and a rosary in the other. They formed into a circle, and began to chant their prayers, which, as I understood they were put up for my welfare, I was in no haste to interrupt. At length, to show them that, however hostile to their principles, I bore them no personal grudge, I dismissed them with a few small pieces of silver.

In the night a heavy shower of snow came on, and I was glad to get up to save my dogs from it. I had to pass through the room where all the Lama's servants slept, and I may as well tell how they were lying. Each man was stretched upon one blanket or two, I cannot positively affirm which. He had thrown off all his clothes, and then covered himself with his woollen tunics, of which everyone in the winter time wears at least three. His boots, doublet, belt, and pouch, with the things that were in it, huddled all together, formed a pillow to his chin, for they were all lying on their faces, with their heads over the top of the bed, and in this posture were smoking tobacco and chatting together.

The snow lay upon the road about six fingers deep, and all the hills were whitened with it. It was a good time for beggars to ask charity, and there is no want of them at Painám, no more than

of priests, forbade magic, and introduced the practice of frequent conferences among the Lamas. His sect soon obtained a numerical superiority over the older Red Caps in Tibet. The most important of his reforms was the foundation of the two spiritual successions of the Dalai and Teshu Lamas. The Dalai is an incarnation of Avalokitesvara, a form of Buddha, and the Teshu of Tsongkapa himself. The Red Caps are now in a minority in Tibet, but they retained ascendancy in Bhutan, Nepal, and Sikkim. (See Heeley's article on Tibet, in the 'Calcutta Review,' No. cxvii. pp. 161, 162.)

in all the towns and large villages in Tibet. They are very importunate, and make their petitions in a shrill, plaintive note, following you a great way on the road. A traveller that wishes not to appear uncharitable, and at the same time does not choose to bestow too much money among them, had best make a good many beggars assemble together, and giving a few pieces of small coin, leave it to them to divide the alms. The Tibet folks sometimes give them little bits of handkerchiefs, which is giving nothing; and a *mahendra-malli*[1] rupee, which is worth about a shilling, is the lowest coin in the country.

Next day we arrived at the house of our former hospitable Giansu landlord, Debo Tangu, who received us with much kindness, and insisted upon our passing the following day with him. Mr. Hamilton's medicines had much relieved him from his complaints, and he was in fine spirits; and as we had seen him often at Teshu Lumbo, we were now very intimate. He and I had many long chats together, which we moistened from time to time with tea, and at night we used to get cheery wood fires and sit round them.

A Kashmiri, afflicted with sore eyes, came all the way from Lhasa to Giansu, to apply to Mr. Hamilton.

The same good humour which we had formerly met with prevailed at Dudukpai. The wife, her two husbands, the brother, who is a priest, and all the children came in after supper, and two hours passed in listening to the songs of the men, and in seeing the children dance. A maid-servant of the house also joined in the songs; but it was a difficult thing to get the wife to sing, which often happens with handsome women. As I could now make it out without an interpreter, I had much more satisfaction in these parties, and when one is travelling there is nothing like making amusement out of everything.

A few miles before you arrive at the next stage, there is a hot spring on the top of a pebbly mount. I did not observe it before. It issues out of a piece of rock, which is cut into a small basin to receive it. The water is more than blood heat, and brings up a great deal of air with it. It does not rise equally, but every half minute bursts up in large bubbles, and with a good deal of noise.

[1] See note at p. 129. The coin and weight are so called from the Newar dynasty of the Malls in Nepal.

There are many of these hot springs in Tibet, particularly in the province of Chamnamring,[1] called Chang.[2] I am told coal is sometimes found in the neighbourhood of them, but in no great quantity. Some of these waters are so hot as to boil an egg, or to serve to dress victuals. They are much frequented by sick people, and are considered as a cure for almost every disease. The Lama also and the great people sometimes visit them, though in perfect health. I have brought away a bottle of the water, which anyone that can may analyze.

* * * * *

I arrived at Paro (Rinjipu) in April, and on the 8th of May, 1775, reached Tassisudon.

Besides the Gosain whom the Lama formerly sent to Calcutta, I am accompanied by another, a merchant, who for many years traded between Bengal and Tibet. The danger of returning through Nepal or Bijapúr, where his wealth would be exposed to the Gorkha Rajah's rapacious fingers, has for some time past detained him at Teshu Lumbo; and having procured from the Lama a recommendation to the Deb Rajah, he is glad to embrace the opportunity of proceeding with me to Bengal.

Upon our arrival at Tassisudon we found the Deb Rajah and Lama Rimboché absent at their palace of Punakha. They arrived on the 16th, and next day I paid the Deb Rajah a visit of ceremony.

* * * * *

TASSISUDON, *May* 25, 1775.

I have always considered it as the great object of my mission to remove the obstacles which merchants are at present exposed to

[1] These hot springs are described by Colonel Montgomerie's Tibetan explorer, who set out from Namling (Chamnamring), to travel northwards, on December 26, 1871. On the 28th he reached Chutang Cháká, where there are some fifteen hot springs, whose water was found to be at a temperature of 166° Fahr., boiling water at the same place only rising to 186°. The water has a smell of sulphur. On the 30th they came to Peting Chuja, near which place there is a large stony area from which a dozen columns of hot water issue, and rise to a height of 40 or 50 feet, producing so much steam that the sky is darkened by it, and the noise was so great that the travellers could not hear one another speaking. The water of these jets was 176° Fahr. Similar jets were noticed issuing from the middle of the adjacent river Lakú Chu, to a height of 50 feet.

[2] This should be *Tsang*, or *Dzang*, according to Klaproth (*Tzhang* of Georgi). The provinces of U and Tsang form Tibet proper, Teshu Lumbo being the capital of the former, and Lhasa of the latter.

in travelling between Bengal and Tibet, and by that means revive and increase the commerce between these two countries. If the Deb Rajah allowed freedom of trade through his dominions, and permitted the merchants of Tibet to come and purchase goods in his country, I should have had occasion only to apply for the Deb Rajah's permission for merchants to bring the commodities of Bengal to Rinjipu (Paro), which, being the capital of this country, being situate on the road from Pari-jong, and having a communication with Bengal by Lukhi-Dúar, Dalim-kotta, and Buxa-Dúar, is well adapted to be a central market for the merchandise of Bengal and Tibet. But the whole trade in the more valuable sort of goods is engrossed by the Deb Rajah and his officers, who are, in fact, the merchants of Bhutan.[1] The few Tibetans who come to Rinjipu (Paro) are allowed only to exchange the salt and wool of their country for the rice of Bhutan. Were I, therefore, to apply for permission for merchants to bring their goods only to Rinjipu (Paro), without obtaining leave for those of Tibet to come and trade to that place, the Deb Rajah and his officers, men not wealthy, and who, being engaged in the affairs of government, carry on their commercial concerns but to a small extent, and without that enterprising spirit which merchants possess, would in fact be the only purchasers, and the trade would remain on much the same footing as formerly, only that Rinjipu (Paro), instead of Rangpúr, would become the market for the commodities of Bengal. The consumption of Bengal goods, except tobacco, betel nut, and other bulky articles, is very small in the Deb Rajah's country; and while the people remain poor, and preserve their present simple manners, will probably continue so. It is no object in Bengal; and their only commodities for exportation are musk, horses, munjít,[2] blankets, and some thin twilled cloths. The first three have always been monopolized by the rulers of Bhutan, and they would reluctantly part with them. The importation of the last ought rather to be discouraged, as it interferes with the sale of serge and of coarse broadcloths. In the dread which the administration at Tassisudon

[1] Mr. Brian Hodgson remarks, on this passage, that the engrossing of trade by the officials is probably the real cause of those obstructions to intercourse which are everywhere covered under the allegations of jealousy of the people, or of the Lamas, or of the Chinese.

[2] See note at p. 6.

is at present in of another insurrection in favour of Deb Judhur, supported by the government at Lhasa, it is impossible to apply for the Deb Rajah's consent to allow Tibetans a freedom of trade to Rinjipu (Paro) without awakening their suspicions of treachery. I determined therefore to refer everything in regard to native Tibetan merchants entirely to Teshu Lama, and endeavour to procure leave for Hindus and Mussulmans to go and come through the Deb Rajah's dominions between Bengal and Tibet, leaving it to them either to dispose of their goods at Rinjipu (Paro) or carry them into Tibet.

Having resolved all these things in my mind, and knowing the impracticability of obtaining permission for Europeans to trade into the Deb Rajah's country, I drew up the following paper:

"Whereas the trade between Bengal and Tibet was formerly very considerable, and all Hindu and Mussulman merchants were allowed to trade into Nepal, which was the centre of communication between the two countries;[1] and whereas, from the wars and oppressions in Nepal, the merchants have of late years been unable to travel into that country, the Governor as well as the Deb Rajah, united in friendship, being desirous of removing these obstacles, so that merchants may carry on their trade free and secure as formerly, have agreed upon the following articles:

"That the Bhutanese shall enjoy the privilege of trading to Rangpúr as formerly, and shall also be allowed to proceed, either themselves or by their *gumashtas*,[2] to all places in Bengal, for the purpose of trading and selling their horses, free from duty or hindrance.

"That the duty hitherto exacted at Rangpúr from the Bhutan caravan be from henceforward abolished.

"That the Deb Rajah shall allow all Hindu and Mussulman merchants freely to pass and repass through his country between Bengal and Tibet.

[1] The records of the old Patna commercial agency, and of its subordinate office at Betia, throw light upon this. Mr. Brian Hodgson, in his report, maintains that Nepal is really the proper centre of commercial intercourse between the Cis and Trans-Himalayan regions; but he also lays stress on the advantages of the Sikkim, Bhutan, and Assam lines, and the growth of the tea trade has rendered these lines more and more important.

[2] Agents.

"That no English or European merchants shall enter the Deb Rajah's dominions.

"That the exclusive trade in sandal, indigo, red skins, tobacco, betel nut, and pán, shall remain with the Bhutanese, and that the merchants be prohibited from importing the same into the Deb Rajah's dominions; and that the Governor shall confirm this in regard to indigo by an order to Rangpúr."

The preamble is intended more for the Tibetans than for the Deb Rajah, and I drew it up in this manner with the view of transmitting it to the Lama. The relinquishing the duty upon horses, which I am told is six annas in the rupee, was an offer I had before made, and reckoning it at a much larger sum than I find it yields to government, had laid great stress upon it. The permission for the Bhutanese merchants to trade throughout Bengal is mentioned in a letter to the Deb Rajah from the Governor, of 9th January. I had also proposed it in the course of my conversations at Tassisudon; and the duty upon a trade so beneficial to Bengal may well be given up. I must trust, therefore, to the Governor granting *dustuks*[1] to any *gumashta* whom the Bhutanese may send beyond Rangpúr. At present they seem to have little thoughts of it; but I am convinced that after their people arrive at Calcutta, discover numbers of curiosities which they never saw before, and find the price of broadcloth, coral, spices, &c., much lower than at Rangpúr, they will fall into the practice of purchasing their goods at Calcutta; which will probably have the good consequence of increasing the sale of English broadcloth, and of lessening that of France, of which last great quantities are now purchased by the Bhutanese for the Tibet markets. The *níl*, or indigo, is produced, I believe, only in Rangpúr, and has always been engrossed by the Bhutanese, so that the exclusive right of trading in this article is no more than they have always enjoyed. The other articles of sandal wood, red skins, &c., are too bulky for foreign merchants to trade in them, and I confess I was ready to give them up, in order to secure broadcloth, which I consider as the most important commodity in the trade of Tibet. I have more than once mentioned the impossibility of procuring leave for Europeans to trade into Bhutan, and without quieting their apprehensions on this head, I saw that I should

[1] A passport or permit.

neither carry any point in regard to trade with this government, nor hope to obtain the sanction and concurrence of the administration at Lhasa.

FROM WARREN HASTINGS TO MR. BOGLE, AT TASSISUDON.

May 9, 1775.

I am happy to learn that your visit has proved so acceptable to the Lama, and flatter myself it will be productive of the good consequences proposed from your journey to him. I have given the necessary orders to the Custom masters at Hugli and Murshidabad for passing at those places the boats which you or the Gosain who is accompanying you from the Lama may bring with you.

I recommend it to you to use your utmost endeavours during your stay at Tassisudon to settle conditions with the Rajah for the establishment of an entire freedom of trade between his country and Bengal. The annual caravan may continue its trade to Rangpúr on the customary terms. To effect this purpose you may even consent to relinquish the tribute or duty which is exacted from the Bhutan caravan which comes annually to Rangpúr. To that place all their goods for trade, of whatever kind, may come at all times, free from any duty or impost whatever, and exempt from stoppage; and in like manner all goods shall pass from Bengal into Bhutan free from duty and molestation. The caravan pays to Government about 2000 rupees, but it is probable that the right of levying it may serve as a cover to much greater exactions, and that the surrender of this privilege may therefore be considered by the Rajah as considerable. This is to be the groundwork of your negotiations. You will build such improvements on it as your own judgment and occasion may dictate.[1]

You will probably, in the course of your conversations with the Rajah on this subject, be able to discover how his personal interests may be affected by the proposed scheme; a proper attention to which, and an encouragement of any hopes of advantages he may

[1] By the only commercial treaty with Nepal (March 1, 1792), now obsolete, the duty on imports from both countries was fixed at 2½ per cent. The Nepal duty was reported by Mr. Hodgson to be 6 to 8 per cent. in 1831, and it has lately been stated at 17 to 20 per cent.; while the British Government levies no duty on goods imported from the Himalayan frontier countries.

entertain (provided his particular profits to be derived from it will not interfere with or obstruct the general plan), may greatly facilitate your negotiations; and for this purpose you will be equally solicitous to remove his objections, and calm his apprehensions of detriment to his interests or danger to his country, should any such arise in his mind.

The great object of your mission is, as I have explained it in my letter to the Deb Rajah, to open a communication of trade with Tassisudon, and through that place to Lhasa and the most distant parts of Tibet. The advantages of such a plan to the Deb Rajah himself cannot escape him. His capital will become the centre of a commerce the most extensive and the most lucrative, if properly improved, of any inland trade perhaps in the world, and will derive the greatest benefits from it, by being the medium of communication between the countries of Tibet and Bengal. This country is too poor to be an object of conquest, and the expense and difficulty of maintaining the possession of it, if it were subdued, would be an insuperable objection to the attempt. To these you will add such other arguments as your own experience and recollection may suggest to you to engage the Rajah's acquiescence in your plan, and his steady support of it hereafter. The only obstacle that can oppose your success is the jealousy of this Government. This you will find no difficulty in removing, and in convincing him that it is repugnant to every interest of the Company to look to any other connection with his country, than that of making it a mart or channel for a fair and honourable commerce, which will conduce as much to his interest as ours. Enclosed I send you copies of two letters which I have written to the Rajah since you left him, which you may make use of as arguments of the sincerity and earnestness of my professions.[1]

FROM MR. BOGLE TO WARREN HASTINGS.

KUCH BAHAR, *June* 9, 1775.

I was made very happy by the letter you honoured me with of the 9th ultimo, and would have certainly continued some time longer with the Deb Rajah, who pressed me to it, but the Lama's

[1] See pp. 53 and 54.

Gosain being anxious to get down to Calcutta, and myself out of order, with the rains ready to set in, when I would have found it almost impossible to travel, prevented me, and will, I hope, plead my excuse.

I have settled matters with the Rajah in the best manner I could, though, I am afraid, not according to your wishes. There was, I beg leave to assure you, no possibility of obtaining his consent to allow Englishmen to travel into his country. The account I have given, in a separate address, of his own jealousy, and of his situation with respect to China, will serve to show this, and I know it to be all well founded. The Tassisudon people,[1] who are all very cautious and reserved, among the objections they at first started to my proposals never once mentioned the name of Europeans, but used their apprehensions of its breeding disturbances and misunderstandings; that it had never been the custom; and that it might give offence to the Emperor of China, and such like pretexts, to oppose my arguments and applications about trade. Nay, when I first offered to satisfy them about Europeans, which I knew to be the great bar, they pretended, insincerely, that they had no objections particularly to the English trading into their country; that they would even be glad of it, and accompanied all this with so many professions, that I at first thought I had given up this point without gaining any advantage. My subsequent conferences, however, soon undeceived me. In short, I am convinced, if I had gone strongly upon the article of Europeans, either in Tibet or at Tassisudon, that I should have increased their jealousy, and have been obliged to return without doing anything.

I am afraid, as I have not been able to carry this point, that my commission will gain me but little credit with the world; yet I cannot help flattering myself that it will be attended with not inconsiderable advantages to Bengal. If the Company think that commerce cannot be pushed with spirit, or carried to any extent, without the establishment of factories and the employment of English agents, they have only to consider what the trade of Bengal was before Europeans had anything to do with it; or, which is more to the purpose, to reflect what the trade between Bengal and Tibet

[1] That is, the officials.

was while Nepal[1] continued free and independent. I am sure if your connection with Teshu Lama and the Deb Rajah serves to bring it back to that point, the benefit to Bengal will be very great. But I ask pardon for presuming to trouble you with my ideas on a subject you are so fully master of. As to myself, after having so long had the honour and satisfaction of serving you, I am only anxious that I may not, on this occasion, suffer in your good opinion.

I hope you will be pleased to approve of my reasons for not adhering strictly to the letter of your instructions. I am convinced things will soon come into the channel you seem to wish, and that the merchants, deterred by the length of the journey, and the opposition of climate between Lhasa and Calcutta, will fall into the way of selling and exchanging their commodities either at Rinjipu[2] or at Pari-jong, the frontier town of Tibet. But, without securing to them a freedom of going and coming from Bengal to Tibet, I was afraid that the Bhutanese, having everything in their hands, would be able to fix the prices of goods, and the trade would become trifling and languishing. When the Deb Rajah's fears of another insurrection blow over, I should think permission for the native Tibetan merchants to come to Rinjipu may be easily obtained; but this must be done through the Lama.

I could think of no way so effectual to engage the Rajah's steady support and protection of traders as imposing a small duty upon their goods. I threw out this in my conversations before the receipt of your commands; but it was not taken up, and so I dropped it.

A few days before I left Tassisudon, the Deb Rajah pressed me very much about some indulgence he wants to solicit for the Rajah of Bahar; but as I understood nothing of the matter, and he did not seem to understand it well himself, I would make him no promises, but advised him to represent it to you by his vakíl. He then asked me to represent it also, which I promised to do,

[1] By Nepal, in this work, Nepal proper is always to be understood, or the great valley which was conquered from the peaceful commercial Newars by the martial Gorkhas, who, before the end of the last century, had reduced all the numerous little states between the Mechi and Sutlej, including the Kiranti country, elsewhere adverted to by Bogle.

[2] Paro.

after I shall know what it is; and ventured to assure him of your listening to any *reasonable* application from him; but farther than this I would not do or say.

The Deb Rajah's vakíl accompanied me from Tassisudon to Buxa-Dúar. I have pushed on to Bahar, in order to prepare things for the reception of him and the Lama's Gosains, and I expect their arrival here to-morrow or next day.

I never received the letter you were so good as to write me by the way of Nepal. I saw a vakíl of Gorkha Rajah two or three times at Teshu Lumbo, but he said nothing about it. I was supplied with what money I wanted by the old Gosain who now accompanies me, of which I will afterwards lay the accounts before you.

I gave the Deb Rajah a strong character of the Arab horses, and he is much pleased with your present, which, however, is not yet arrived here. He seems abundantly desirous of cultivating your friendship, but in such a way as may not give umbrage to Lhasa.

I am sorry for the mortality among the cattle, because it occasions the delay of a season. I have given Paima a particular memorandum to get some more goats and cows sent down after the rains; also to put the Lama's people in mind of the tús, which he promised to procure for you; though, being a wild animal, I am afraid it will hardly live. We caught many musk goats, but they all died in a few days.

I am copying out the memoranda about my journey, which I shall have the honour to send you from Sahib Ganj or Dinajpúr; the other papers I beg leave to defer laying before you till my arrival in Calcutta, when I hope to have the pleasure of explaining them to you in person.

CHAPTER XVIII.

GENERAL REPORT BY MR. BOGLE ON HIS RETURN FROM TIBET.

TO THE HON. WARREN HASTINGS, GOVERNOR-GENERAL, &c.

HON. SIR,—The commission for opening a free intercourse between the inhabitants of Bengal and Tibet with which you were pleased to entrust me being now finished, I beg leave to lay before you an account of the course and issue of my negotiations.

But as the state of the countries which I lately visited is little known, it may not be improper to premise some circumstances regarding their situation and government. In doing this, however, I shall endeavour to avoid entering into those minute details which might swell this address to an improper length.

The range of mountains which stretches from the Murung country to the banks of the Brahmaputra and the north-east frontier of Bengal is inhabited by a people known in Bengal by the name of Bhutanese.[1] These mountains are divided by glens or deep valleys, with rapid rivers running through them. They are covered with the loftiest trees, and the snow lies upon the tops of some of them all the year round. The valleys and least steep parts of the mountains are cultivated, producing wheat, barley, and rice, sufficient not only for the support of the people, but even to form a considerable article in their commerce with their northern neighbours.

About two hundred and sixty years ago, this country, which I shall distinguish by the name of Bhutan, is said to have been united under one government by Noanumgay, a disciple of the Lamas of

[1] The Trans-nivean people, whom we call Tibetan and Bhotias, are well known by the latter name in the plains of India. But the Cis-nivean people, or Himálayan tribes, are never so called. They are very numerous both in the mountains and in the *terai*. (See Hodgson's 'Languages and Religion of Nepal and Tibet,' pp. 13–15, 29–44, and 45–65.)

Tibet. Before that time it was parcelled out among a number of petty and independent chieftains, who were engaged in perpetual wars and commanded fierce and barbarous vassals. Noanumgay, by forming laws and introducing religion, in concurrence with other causes, rendered the people obedient to a strict and regular administration. He was reverenced by his subjects during his lifetime as a great Lama, and is still worshipped by his descendants. His fame, however, is confined to Bhutan, and his spirit is considered only as an emanation from the pontiffs of Tibet.

Upon his death his soul was supposed to be divided into equal portions, and to animate three different children, who were regarded as Lamas, and the supreme power was jointly vested in them, assisted by the clergy, to whom they owed their elevation. The same ingenious device furnished them with successors, and this form of government still continues. One of these Lamas, named Lama Giassa-tu, died about twelve years ago, and the person into whom his soul passed is not yet discovered; another, Lama Shabdong, is a boy seven years of age,[1] so that the whole authority of this priestly government at present resides in Lama Rimboché.[2] The executive administration is entrusted to an elective officer, styled Cusho Debo, who is known in Bengal by the name of the Deb Rajah.

The abilities of Deb Judhur, the last person who held this office, enabled him to render himself independent of the Lamas and the clergy, and he ruled Bhutan during five years with an absolute sway; but the oppression of his government, his violent measures in regard to Bahar, and the unfortunate war with the English in which this engaged him, afforded the clergy an opportunity of deposing him, of driving him into exile, and of electing a new chief in his stead. Upon this revolution Lama Rimboché came to be considered as supreme, and regained that authority in the government to which by the ancient constitution he thinks himself entitled.

The kingdom of Bhutan is far from being populous. The natives in the interior part of the country are generally above the middle size, of a robust and muscular make, and of a light copper

[1] See p. 39.

[2] Known in Bengal as the Dharma Rajah. The three Lamas of Bhutan are called by Mr. Davis, the companion of Captain Turner, Lam-Sebdo, Lam-Geysey, and Lam-Rimbochy. (See "Remarks on the Religious Institutions of the Inhabitants of Bhutan," 'Transactions of R. A. S.,' vol. ii. 4to.)

RESIDENCE OF THE LAMA GIASSA-TU, NEAR TASSISUDON.

(FROM A SKETCH BY LIEUT DAVIS IN TURNER'S EMBASSY TO TIBET.)

complexion. They are of a hasty and quarrelsome temper, and addicted to the use of spirituous liquors. Theft and robbery, except in time of public disturbances, are little known. The higher class of people are formal and ceremonious in their manners, fond of long speeches, and although often acute and judicious in the affairs of their own state, yet having almost no intercourse with strangers, are reserved and difficult in business.

The country is defended by the inhabitants, who are all trained to the use of the bow or of the matchlock, and its steep mountains and arduous roads, leading over precipices and covered with thickets, form a barrier which an enemy might find it difficult to surmount.

The revenue of Bhutan is paid chiefly in rice, butter, and other articles, which are consumed by the priests and servants of government, or hoarded up in storehouses. The low countries which they possess on the borders of Bengal yield some money, and the custom by which upon the death of a public officer his estate escheats to the government, opens another source of revenue. But the people, although enjoying all the necessaries of life, are possessed of little wealth, and, indeed, have little occasion for it. The taxes upon the inhabitants are light; their possessions are hereditary; they hold their lands upon military tenures, being bound to fight, to carry burdens, and to perform other services for the government.

The kingdom of Tibet lies to the northward of Bhutan. The frontier town is Pari-jong. Tibet is called by the natives Pu—pronounced as in French. Tibet is full of mountains, inferior in height to those in the Deb Rajah's country, though they take their rise from a more elevated plain, which are intermixed with more extensive valleys. As Bhutan is the most woody country I ever saw, Tibet is the most bare and unsheltered; except in the neighbourhood of villages, a tree is seldom to be seen. The hills are covered with sand, stones, and gravel. The soil of the villages, though poor, is rather better, and produces, with good management, wheat, barley, and some peas, but no rice.

The climate is extremely cold; the lakes and rivers are covered with ice. The thermometer, in the month of December, at Chamnamring, which is in latitude 31° 39′, and about half a degree to the northward of Lhasa, used sometimes to be within 3° of the bottom of the scale, or 29° under freezing point; and even in the middle of April, and in a more southern situation, heavy showers of snow fell, and standing water froze. The great elevation of the country above the sea, and the northerly winds which blow over Tatary, probably occasion this severity in the climate.

The Tibetans are of a smaller size and of a make much less robust than their southern neighbours. Their complexion is naturally as fair as the people in the south of Europe, and many of them have colour, some are quite ruddy: they are of a mild and cheerful temper. The higher rank of people at the Lama's court are polite, and entertaining in conversation, with which they never mix any compliments or flattery.

Tibet was formerly independent, being governed by a succession of hereditary kings. About sixty years ago the ministers, conspiring together, put their king to death, and assumed the administration into their own hands.[1] Mewan Cusho, his cupbearer, escaped towards Ladak, and having spent some years in engaging the interest of the neighbouring chiefs, returned with a powerful army, defeated the ministers, and engaged, in consideration of protection, to hold his crown under the Emperor of China. After a wise and prosperous reign of thirty years he was succeeded by his son Wang Cusho.

The Lamas had long before this established themselves and their religion in Tibet. By the liberality or superstition of its kings, or by their influence with the Tatars, who often invaded the country, they procured grants of lands and villages, where they founded temples and monasteries. They were considered as sovereign pontiffs, and adored as God's vicegerents. Pilgrimages were made to them from different parts of Tatary, offerings of considerable value were presented to them, but they enjoyed not that degree of temporal power which the imprudence of Wang Cusho enabled them to obtain.

The tyranny and oppression of his administration, the murder of his brother, and, above all, his intention of becoming independent of China, were represented by the Dalai Lama in the strongest

[1] This was when an army of Dsungarians invaded Lhasa in 1717, and killed the Gesub Rimboché, or Regent (Nomen-khan), named Latsan.

colours to the Court of Peking, which accordingly issued orders to its officers at Lhasa, and Wang Cusho, betrayed by false promises, suffered death while he expected to be honoured with marks of the Emperor's favour.[1] The tumult raised by his dependents, in which a great number of the Chinese were slain, was soon quelled. Their attempt to place his son in the government was defeated by the timidity and flight of the mother, and, according to the severe policy of the Chinese, every branch of the family was extirpated.

In consequence of this resolution the Lamas acquired fresh power and rose to political consequence. The Emperor, either in consideration of the Dalai Lama's pacific character, or as a reward of his fidelity, committed the administration into his hands, and his mild and popular government continued to the end of his life. Upon this event, which happened about eighteen years ago,[2] Teshu Lama, the next in dignity, came to be considered as the chief man in the country. His character and abilities had secured him the favour of the Emperor, and his representations had great weight at the Court of Peking. About two years after the Dalai Lama's death he discovered the child into whose body, according to their belief, the soul of the departed Lama had passed, and placed him in the chair of Potala, and his influence with the Emperor procured for Gesub Rimboché, the cupbearer of the former Lama, the executive administration during his minority.

Two Chinese viceroys, with a guard of a thousand soldiers, are stationed at Lhasa, and are changed every three years. The Emperor of China is acknowledged as the sovereign of the country; the appointment to the first offices in the state is made by his order, and, in all measures of consequence, reference is first had to the Court of Peking; but the internal government of the country is committed entirely to natives; the Chinese in general are confined to the capital, no tribute is exacted, and the people of Tibet, except at Lhasa, hardly feel the weight of a foreign yoke.

The executive administration is in the hands of Gesub Rimboché and four other ministers, styled Kahlons. The governors of forts and provinces are appointed by them, and the revenue is collected by persons sent annually from Lhasa. But as the Dalai

[1] This was in 1749.

[2] This Dalai Lama's name was Lobsang Kalsang. He died in 1758.

Lama is now nearly of age,[1] it is expected that the Emperor of China will invest him with the supreme authority which his predecessor enjoyed.

The influence of Teshu Lama in the government proceeds chiefly from the veneration that is paid to his character and the weight of his abilities. The Emperors of China being of Tatar extraction, profess the religion of the Lamas, and reverence them as the head of their faith; and the present monarch undertakes no expedition without consulting Teshu Lama, and sending him offerings to engage his prayers for its success. The influence which an able pontiff may derive from this is obvious, and although Gesub Rimboché is jealous of it, yet he is obliged to pay attention to the advice of Teshu Lama.

Any one that would give himself the trouble, might draw a striking parallel between the Lamas and the ancient Roman Pontiffs. The situation of the former, with respect to the monarchs of China, might well be compared to the protection and authority, which the successors of St. Peter derived from the German emperors. Their pretensions to infallibility, the veneration in which they are held by the people, the wide extent of their spiritual dominion, reaching over all Tatary and a great part of China, are perfectly similar. But this influence over the minds of the people, possessed by both, has been exercised by the Lamas, perhaps, in a manner more conducive to the happiness of mankind. The oblations of their followers are voluntary; their government is mild and equitable; they enter into no wars, but, on the contrary, often exert their authority in settling the quarrels among contending states. In their private character they are decent and exemplary, and, if I may judge of others by one under whose roof I lived, they are humane, charitable, and intelligent.

The religion of the Lamas is either derived from that of the Hindus, or improved by it. They retain, therefore, the greatest veneration for the Ganges and the places held holy in Hindustan. Before that country was invaded by the Mussulmans, the Lamas had monasteries and other religious foundations in Bengal, to which the Tibetan clergy used to resort in order to study the doctrines and learning of the Brahmans. But the conquest of the Moghul put an

[1] This was Lobsang Champal, who died in 1805.

end to the intercourse. The Lamas' temples were plundered and destroyed, and their people driven out of the country; since which there has been little connection between the inhabitants of Tibet and Bengal.

The trade, however, which used to be carried on between the two countries was formerly very extensive, and the returns being made in gold dust, musk, cowtails, and other valuable articles, it was highly beneficial to Bengal. I formerly took the liberty to represent to you the causes which of late years have occasioned the decline of the trade, and I now beg leave to lay before you an account of the steps that I took to remove them.

Although Teshu Lama is not entrusted with the actual government of the country, yet his authority and influence appear fully equal to accomplish the views which you entertain in regard to the encouragement of trade. His passports to merchants and travellers are obeyed universally throughout Tibet. He is reverenced by his own people, he is respected by his neighbours, and his mild and pacific character seems peculiarly suited to promote commerce. I found in the Lama, therefore, the readiest disposition to co-operate with you in removing the obstacles to a free trade, and in adopting such measures as might increase the intercourse between the country and Tibet.

The tyrannical and faithless character of the Gorkha Rajah,[1] and his invasion of the territories of Demo Jong,[2] a Rajah subject to Lhasa, left, however, no room for any negotiations with him towards reviving the trade through Nepal. But immediately upon the news of his death, which arrived while I was at Teshu Lumbo, the Lama wrote to his successor, Sing Pertab, advising him, in the strongest manner, to allow merchants to trade through his country. His letter on this occasion was short, and I may be excused perhaps in inserting a translation of it:

"To SING PERTAB,—

"[After a number of titles] I have heard of the death of your father, Prithi Narayan. As this is the will of God you will not let your heart be cast down. You have now succeeded to the throne, and it is proper that you attend to the happiness of your

[1] Prithi Narayan. [2] Sikkim, or Deun-jong.

people, and allow all merchants, as Hindus, Mussulmans, and the four castes, to go and come, and carry on their trade freely, which will tend to your advantage and to your good name. At present they are afraid of you, and no one will enter your country. Whatever has been the ancient custom let it be observed between you and me. It is improper that there should be more on your part, and it is improper that there should be more on mine."

The Lama wrote also to the merchants at Lhasa and Teshu Lumbo, the two principal towns in Tibet. He informed them of the security and protection which merchants enjoy at Bengal, and advised them to send *gumashtas*[1] thither. The Kashmiri and Gosain merchants afterwards assured me, that in consequence of the encouragement and assistance which the Lama had offered them, and the promises which I gave them of freedom and security in Bengal, they proposed, in case they could obtain leave from the Deb Rajah, to pass through his country, to send *gumashtas* to Calcutta to purchase goods, as soon as the rains were over; and a wealthy Gosain merchant, afraid to travel through Nepal, actually embraced the opportunity of accompanying me to Calcutta. The Tibet merchants also came to visit me. But at the same time that they expressed their desire of complying with the Lama's commands, they enlarged upon the heat and unhealthiness of Bengal, and declared their apprehensions of travelling into, what they considered, a distant and unknown country.

Prejudices of this kind are to be cured only by habit, and your compliance with the Teshu Lama's desire of founding a monastery and temple on the banks of the Ganges will probably tend to remove these strong prepossessions against the climate of Bengal, and to produce an intercourse with the northern nations. The safe return of the people whom the Lama proposes to send next winter to visit the holy places in Bengal will serve to inspire their countrymen with confidence; the fondness of the Tibetans for everything strange or curious, strengthened by religion, will probably lead many others to undertake so meritorious a journey; and these pilgrimages, like the Hajj at Mekkah, may in time open a considerable mart for the commodities of Bengal.

Nor is the benefit which Bengal may derive from the resort of

[1] Agents.

Tibetans the only advantage which the Company may obtain by their connection with Teshu Lama. He has written to the Changay Lama, who is the high-priest at the Court of Peking, and in great favour with the Emperor, advising him to send his people to visit the temples in Hindustan. He has also promised to use his best offices with the Emperor of China to procure leave for the Company to send a deputation to Peking. The first, I am convinced, will take place; and although, from the cautious and jealous policy of the Chinese, I am not too sanguine as to the last, yet the advantage of opening even an indirect communication with the Court of Peking is, I humbly apprehend, an object of some importance to the Company.

I could have wished, while I was in Tibet, and within a few days' journey of Lhasa, to have proceeded to that city, in order to have formed a connection with Gesub Rimboché, and the rest of the administration there. But their jealousy rendered them averse from it. I could not have seen them, considering the public character I bore, without a considerable expense for presents; and while the Company's views in a communication with Tibet are only to an extension of commerce, I am inclined to think that Teshu Lama's influence is fully sufficient to accomplish them.

After passing five months in Teshu Lama's palace I returned to Bhutan. The Lama at the same time wrote to the Deb Rajah on the subject of merchants, and sent one of his people to assist me in my negotiations at Tassisudon.

But I had now to prosecute my commission under circumstances very different from what I had experienced in Tibet. Teshu Lama, accustomed to an intercourse with strangers, fond of negotiation, and attentive to everything that can raise his character, entered warmly into views which coincided with his own. He had long wished for an opportunity of forming a connection with some of the powers in Hindustan. The authority of the Company was well known to him, and he had already got great reputation by the peace which his mediation had procured for the Bhutanese. His desire, therefore, of cultivating a friendship which tended to increase his influence, led him zealously to second your application, while his endeavours for the ease and convenience of merchants served to extend his fame. As he speaks the Hindustan language, and possesses a great degree of candour and affability,[1] he conversed with me freely on every subject, and desired me to make my application immediately to him. He communicated to me the opposition which the government at Lhasa had made to my journey; he gave me their correspondence to read; he explained to me the letters which he wrote to them about trade, and told me plainly what could be accomplished and what could not.

The Deb Rajah, on the contrary, secluded from any connection with foreigners,[2] is difficult of access, stiff and ceremonious in his manners, and indecisive in business. He is guided entirely by his officers, who are reserved, suspicious, and evasive; and in every matter of consequence the humour of several hundred priests is to be consulted, and the opinion of Lama Rimboché, who, without experience or abilities, considers himself as supreme in the government, is to be received.

The administration at Tassisudon accordingly made many objections to allowing merchants to pass through Bhutan, insisting that it had never been the custom for strangers to come into their kingdom; that the inhabitants were of a hot and violent temper, and the country woody and mountainous, and, in case of a merchant being robbed, it might occasion disputes and misunderstandings between them and the Company's government. I will not here take up your time with a repetition of the arguments I employed in combating their objections, and in endeavouring to convince them of the benefit which their country would derive from the resort of merchants; for I was sensible, while I used them, that the opposition of the Bhutanese[3] to my proposals proceeded from motives which they industriously concealed. They were apprehensive that the admission of foreign merchants into their

[1] In a similar light the Dalai Lama showed himself to Mr. Hodgson when Resident in Nepal; and Mr. Hodgson remarks that such dispositions might be utilized now that time has demonstrated that we have no purpose to serve, save such an extension of commerce as must benefit the Himálaya and Tibet far more than ourselves, and moreover render the continuance of peace between us more secure, through the inevitable effects of mutually beneficial and kindly personal intercourse.

[2] Yet the Deb was the secular chief. Mr. Hodgson makes the following remark on this: "The Dharma (Lama Rimboché), or spiritual chief, *should* be the secluded one, not the Deb Rajah. Again, the Teshu Lama, though he is also the spiritual chief, is represented by Mr. Bogle as the active and intelligent administrator in regard to international relations. This shows that talent and energy will assert themselves despite theoretical bars."

[3] The officials, not the people.

country would lessen the profits which they at present derive from their trade with Tibet,[1] and they were still more afraid that by allowing strangers to come into Bhutan they would open a door to the introduction of Europeans.

Neither of these reasons, however, were ever avowed, or even mentioned by the Bhutanese, but they were on this account more difficult to overcome. Without quieting their scruples about Europeans, I foresaw that it was impossible to obtain a communication with Tibet through their country, or to procure the aid and concurrence of the ministry at Lhasa in encouraging and extending the trade with Bengal. I therefore gave up a point which it was impossible to carry, and gave them assurances that no European merchants should enter Bhutan.

Some time after my arrival at Tassisudon I received your commands of the 9th of May, in which you direct me to endeavour to render the Deb Rajah's capital the centre of communication between Bengal and Tibet. As I found it necessary to deviate in some measure from the letter of these orders, I hope you will believe that it proceeded only from my desire to accomplish more effectually the purpose of my commission, and that the following reasons will serve to justify my conduct.

If the Deb Rajah allowed freedom of trade through his dominions, and permitted the merchants at Tibet to come and purchase goods in his country, I should only have had occasion to have applied for permission for merchants to bring the commodities of Bengal to Rinjipu,[2] which, being the capital of Bhutan, being situated on the road from Pari-jong, and having a communication with Bengal by Lukhi-Dúar, Dalim-kotta, and Buxa-Dúar, is well adapted for a central market for the merchandise of Bengal and Tibet. But the whole trade in the more valuable sorts of goods is engrossed by the Deb Rajah and his officers, who are in fact the merchants of Bhutan.[3] The few Tibetans who come to Rinjipu (Paro)

[1] This is the real source of the difficulty still, as ever, experienced by us, while trying to open and liberate the Himálayan and trans-Himálayan trade.

[2] Paro.

[3] Mr. Hodgson observes that this is generally the case, and holds true to the present day. But he says that there is no popular jealousy either in Nepal, Tibet, or Bhutan; and the Dalai and Teshu Lamas, could they be got at, may well be supposed not to share the unfriendly sentiments attributed to them, but rather to be ready to promote what is evidently calculated to benefit the people.

are allowed only to exchange the salt and wool of their country for the rice of Bhutan. Had I, therefore, procured permission for merchants to bring their goods only to Rinjipu (Paro) without obtaining leave for those of Tibet to come and trade to that place, the Deb Rajah and his officers—men not wealthy, and who being engaged in the affairs of government carry on their commercial concerns but to a small extent, and without that enterprising spirit which merchants possess—would in fact have been the only purchasers, and the trade would have remained on much the same footing as formerly, only that Rinjipu (Paro) instead of Rangpúr would have become the market for the commodities of Bengal. The consumption of Bengal goods, except tobacco, betel nut, and other bulky articles, is very small in the Deb Rajah's dominions, and while the people remain poor, and preserve their present simple manners, will probably continue so. It is no object to Bengal, and their only commodities for exportation are musk, horses, munjít,[1] blankets, and some thin twilled cloths. The first three have always been monopolized by the rulers of Bhutan, and they would reluctantly part with them; the importation of the last ought rather to be discouraged.

In the dread which the administration at Tassisudon was then in of an insurrection in favour of Deb Judhur, supported by the administration at Lhasa, I could not have applied for permission for Tibetans to trade freely to Rinjipu (Paro) without awakening suspicions of treachery, and I therefore judged it best to refer everything in regard to the merchants of Tibet entirely to Teshu Lama.

After many tiresome conferences and fruitless negotiations, in which I was assisted by Teshu Lama's people, I at length obtained the Deb Rajah's consent to allow Hindu and Mussulman merchants to pass through Bhutan under some restrictions and concessions, which I have now the honour to submit to you, together with the reasons upon which they are grounded.

I transmitted a copy of those articles to the Lama from Tassisudon, requesting him at the same time to give them all advantages with the government at Lhasa, and to write to the Deb Rajah on the subject. I have since received a letter from him, written in answer to the accounts which his people sent him, of the difficulties that the Deb Rajah started to my proposals, of which I

[1] Madder.

beg leave to lay before you a translation, as it strongly marks the earnestness and zeal with which the Lama interests himself in the success of the different objects of my commission.

In regard to procuring permission for Europeans to trade into Tibet, it was a point which I have already mentioned impossible of obtaining. In former times, when Europeans were settled in Hindustan merely as merchants, there would have been no difficulty in establishing factories and freedom of trade; but the power and elevation to which the English have now risen render them the objects of jealousy to all their neighbours. The opposition which was made to my proceeding into Tibet, as well as the many difficulties I had to encounter in the execution of my commission, arose from this source. The government at Lhasa considered me as sent to explore their country, which the ambition of the English might afterwards prompt them to invade, and their superiority in arms render their attempt successful.[1]

I was at much pains during my stay among the inhabitants of Bhutan and Tibet to remove their prejudices; but I am convinced they can be effectually conquered only by the opportunities which a greater intercourse and more intimate acquaintance with the English may afford them of observing their fidelity to engagements, and the moderation of their views, and by an interchange of those good offices which serve to beget confidence between nations as well as between individuals.[2] The increase of influence which Teshu Lama will derive from the government of Tibet being committed to the Dalai Lama, and other circumstances which your connection with him may enable you to improve, will perhaps open the way to a privilege which at present I could not obtain.

I will now beg leave to submit to you my ideas on the nature of the trade between Bengal and Tibet, and on the measures which appear most likely to revive and extend it.

The most important commodity in this traffic is broadcloth;

[1] Mr. Hodgson remarks on this paragraph: "Might not the experience of the long period that has since elapsed be now effectually urged the other way, at Kathmandu, Lhasa, Teshu Lumbo, and Tassisudon? One and all owe much to our good faith and peaceful policy."

[2] On this Mr. Hodgson observes: "The worst of it is that under the present system no room is afforded for the operation of any such interchange, and sooner or later stolid indifference begets spasmodic violence and war."

all the Tibetans of a station elevated above the populace are fond of wearing gowns of it, and it forms also an article of their commerce with the neighbouring tribes of Tatars. The sale of broadcloth, however, from the causes which I have already mentioned, has greatly decreased of late years, and even of what is now consumed a large portion is of French manufacture. I had occasion to buy several pieces in Tibet to give away in presents, and, except once, I never could meet with any English cloth.

The article of next importance is coral beads; great quantities of these are used in Tibet, and from thence also sent into Tatary. The want of supplies, and the consequent enhancement of the price, have affected this commodity in the same manner as the former.

I will not here particularize the different kinds of merchandise which have hitherto been exported from this country to Tibet, but beg leave to refer you to the accompanying list, in which I have put down the prices of the principal articles, together with the expense of transporting them.[1] I must observe, however, that most of them were not to be had. The Bhutan caravan, on its return from Rangpúr, would no doubt carry a supply of goods from Bengal, but in no degree equal to what the consumption of the country used formerly to take off.

But besides the articles hitherto employed in the trade with Tibet, there appears room to introduce or extend the sale of many new ones. The inhabitants are fond of everything that comes from a strange country, and even the lowest class of people possess a curiosity seldom to be met with. This promises a good opening for the sale of cutlery, glassware, and many other European manufactures.

The most eligible and effectual way in my opinion of extending the sale of British broadcloth in opposition to that of France, of increasing the sale of those goods which have usually been exported to Tibet, and of opening a mart for new articles of commerce, is to encourage the resort of Kashmiris, Gosains, Bhutanese, and Tibetans to Calcutta during the winter time;[2] by making a sale

[1] See and compare the lists and remarks in Mr. Hodgson's Report of 1831; and 'Languages, &c., of Nepal and Tibet,' pp. 91-121.

[2] Mr. Hodgson remarks upon this: "Even so. Let the trade be in the accustomed hands, and those hands be rendered more effectually operative by the co-operation at Calcutta of English merchants."

of English broadcloth at that season they will be enabled to procure it at the lowest rate; and by granting them passports and escorts to the northern frontier of Bengal, they will be engaged to purchase the Company's cloth in preference to any other; while the variety of unknown merchandise which they will here find will naturally create a desire of carrying them with them on their return to their own country.

To remove the dread which the natives of Bhutan and Tibet entertain of this climate may, no doubt, require time and use. But when curiosity, religion, and interest conspire to prompt them to visit Bengal, nothing further appears necessary but the encouragement and protection of government.

The Kashmiri and Gosain merchants who propose to come to Calcutta during the next winter will, when furnished with Teshu Lama's passports, find no difficulty in travelling through Tibet; and the Deb Rajah, from the assurances he has given me, will, I am persuaded, readily grant them a passage through his kingdom from Pari-jong to the frontier of Bengal. But as the road has never yet been frequented by merchants, it may be necessary, on their arrival on the borders of Bahar, that they should receive countenance and assistance, and that orders for that purpose should be issued.

The opening of the road through Nepal, and obtaining the abolition of the duties and exactions which have lately been imposed on trade in that country, appears an object of great importance towards establishing a free communication between Bengal and Tibet. The death of Prithi Narayan, the late Rajah of Nepal, seems to afford a favourable opportunity of effecting this point. Teshu Lama is ready to second your endeavours for that purpose; and a proper management of the different interests which prevail among the chiefs[1] on the borders of Nepal will, I am convinced, easily accomplish it. The steps which it may be proper to pursue it becometh not me to point out. But I may be excused, perhaps, in suggesting the advantage which you may derive, in all your negotiations with the people who possess the mountains to the northward of Bengal, by taking your measures jointly with Teshu

[1] All the states between Sikkim and Kumaon have long been merged in the Gorkha kingdom of Nepal.

Lama. His acquaintance with the state of those countries renders his opinion of much weight, and the influence which his holy character gives him among the different chiefs, being employed only to settle disputes and promote harmony, may enable you to accomplish by negotiation and peaceful means what that jealousy of the people and the strength of their situation might otherwise render it difficult to obtain.

When a road is opened through Nepal as well as Bhutan nothing further appears to me necessary towards accomplishing the business upon which I have lately been employed. In matters of commerce I humbly apprehend that freedom and security is all that is required. Merchants, left to themselves, naturally discover the most proper manner of conducting their trade, and, prompted by self-interest, carry it on to the greatest extent.

The disadvantages to which the novelty of my journey and the jealousy of the natives[1] subjected me may, perhaps, entitle me to indulgence. I have executed my commission to the best of my abilities, and I now wait in solicitude for the judgment which may be passed upon my conduct.

[1] Mr. Bogle, here and elsewhere, in speaking of the jealousy of the natives, evidently means the native *officials* only.

CHAPTER XIX.

JOURNEY OF THE TESHU LAMA TO PEKING, AND HIS DEATH. PROJECT OF MR. BOGLE FOR MEETING THE LAMA AT PEKING.

(*Memorandum, written in July*, 1778.)

THE amount of the debts of the Chinese merchants to English individuals is from a million and a half to two millions sterling. Among the creditors are Mr. Bouchier, Sir Robert Harland, Sir John Lindsay, and most of the gentlemen who have gone from Madras, as well as Mr. Boddam and others at Bombay. They can get no redress: have no channel of applying for it. They have sent a Mr. Gordon to England with a representation to endeavour to interest the Government, and perhaps through them the Court of Russia; but have little prospect of success, or at best distant. Besides this, the Company's business is often harassed and oppressed, and its conductors are entirely without any channel of communication or representation to the Court of Peking.

The Emperor of China is now seventy years of age.[1] He is of the Tatar religion, of which the Lamas are the head. The Changay Lama, who is older than him, and resides at Peking, is said to have much influence over him. He has expressed a great desire to see Teshu Lama before his death, and has at length, after repeated applications, prevailed on him to go and meet him. The Emperor has fixed on a place about a month's journey on this side of Peking, and Teshu Lama sets out about two months hence to travel through Tatary. The journey will take up about eight months, so that he may arrive with the Emperor about May next. He will stay at least three or four months; that is to August.[2]

[1] This was the famous Emperor Kien-lung who succeeded in 1736, and reigned until 1796. (See note at p. 134.)

[2] Mr. Bogle's old friend, Purungir Gosain, accompanied the Teshu Lama on his visit to China, and wrote an account of it, a translation of which was published by Mr. A. Dal-

When I was in Tibet, the Lama promised to endeavour to procure for me passports to go to Peking. He has not yet succeeded, but has sent a man to assure me that he will exert himself to procure me at least a passport by the way of Canton. I propose to write him that I shall prepare myself either to go by land over

rymple, in the 'Oriental Repertory' (ii. p. 145). After several most pressing invitations from the old Emperor, the Lama at length resolved to undertake the journey, but not without sad forebodings. He set out from Teshu Lumbo on the 15th of July, 1779, attended by 1500 troops and followers. After forty-six days he reached Duchu, on the banks of a river of the same name. After twenty days more he came to Thuk'thaung, and nineteen days more brought him to Kumbu Giemban, a large city, where he remained four months, owing to the snow. He then set out again, and, after fifteen days, came to the city of Tumdautabe, where he was met by Chi-wang, a son-in-law of the Emperor. Nine days more were occupied in the journey to Nissaur, and two days more brought him to Taubunkaikan, and sixteen days more to Chauraunsuburgan, where he halted two days. Another twelve days were consumed in reaching Khaurambu, and six more brought the Lama to Taigaugumban, where he was met by the Emperor's first son. In thirty-four days more they arrived at Sining, where the Lama was met by another son of the Emperor, who informed him that the Emperor himself had advanced to a country seat called Jiawosekho, about twenty-four miles from Sining. (See and compare the stage route of the Nepalese Embassy to Peking, in No. 27, of the 'Selections from the Records of the Government of India,' p. 83. Siling, or Sining, is the capital of Tangut, or Sokyeul, and is the converging point of all the trade routes.)

During the whole of this long journey sumptuous provision was made for the Lama's comfort, and crowds of devotees thronged to receive his blessing.

At the first interview the Emperor met the Teshu Lama at a distance of at least forty paces from his throne, and seated him on the uppermost cushion with himself, and at the right hand. When the Lama withdrew, he was conducted to a magnificent palace, about a mile from that of the Emperor, which had been specially erected for his abode.

In a subsequent interview the Lama mentioned to the Emperor that there was a great ruler in Hindustan, on the borders of his country, for whom he had the greatest friendship; and that he wished the Emperor to know and regard him also. Purungir Gosain was then called in and interrogated. He said that the ruler's name was Hastings, and described the riches and military resources of India.

After some time the Emperor and Teshu Lama set out for Peking, and the Lama was lodged in a very magnificent house outside the walls of the city, and for several months there were constant interchanges of visits between the Emperor and the Lama. To the inexpressible grief of the Emperor and the whole people of China, the Lama was seized with smallpox, and expired on the evening of November 12, 1780, as he sat at prayer between two large pillows, resting his back against the wall. His death was remarkably tranquil.

The body was placed in a coffin of pure gold, in the form of a temple fixed on poles, and the Emperor ordered it to be conveyed to Tibet in charge of the Lama's brother. The gold temple was placed within a copper temple. The return journey occupied seven months and eight days from Peking to the mausoleum at Teshu Lumbo.

There is an extract from another

THE TOMB OF THE TESHU LAMA.

(FROM A DRAWING IN TURNER'S EMBASSY TO TIBET.)

Tatary, if he thinks it possible to procure me passports, otherwise to go by sea to Canton in the full confidence of his sending me some person from himself to Canton with passports, so that I might get to Peking while the Lama is with the Emperor. I propose also to send back a Gosain who is in great favour with the Lama, and whom he has sent down to Calcutta so as to be with him before he sets out from Tibet; and that this man who is much attached to me, together with one of my servants, should accompany the Lama to China, and come and meet me at Canton. The Changay Lama, who is at Peking, is a native of Tibet, and understands that language, of which I have some knowledge, so as not to be at the mercy of interpreters.

If I succeed in procuring passports, I shall then be in a situation to urge any points at the Court of Peking with the greatest advantage. But even if I should be disappointed, I do not think it is possible for me to fail in procuring a channel of communication with the Court of Peking,[1] and in finding some person stationed at Canton through whom representations can be made.

In order to pave the way, it is necessary that some presents should be got ready that may be acceptable at Peking. Large pearls, large coral, some best birds' nests, some Arabian horses, and some muslins; should be prepared. Most of these articles are the same as make the best remittances to China, so that in case of the negotiation failing they could be sold there without any loss. But

letter, written from Peking by a missionary named Amiot, and dated August 17, 1781. He says that the Pan-tchan Lama, as he calls the Teshu Lama, or Panchen Rimbochê, reached China in very good health, after a journey of extraordinary length; but that on arriving at Peking he was seized with the smallpox and died. M. Amiot gives a translation of the remarkable letter written by the Emperor Kien Lung, then in his seventieth year, to the Dalai, announcing the death of the Teshu Lama. "Although I am well aware," writes the Emperor, "that to come and to go are but as the same thing to the Pan-tchan Lama, yet when I reflect that he made a most long and painful journey for the sole purpose of doing honour to me, and that after having fulfilled that object it was not his fate to return in tranquillity, as I had hoped, to the place of his usual abode, this reflection is distressing to me beyond all expression." ('Oriental Repertory,' ii. p. 273.)

[1] Mr. Hodgson remarks upon this: "What has since been done there as regards the seaboard trade, seems to prove that quiet persistent explanation might succeed in removing the existing obstacles to free social and commercial intercourse between the *Cis* and *Trans* Himálayans, by natives and such of them as have an immemorial prescriptive right to such free intercourse."

the persons interested in the recovery of these debts are so numerous and unconnected that it is difficult to get them to contribute towards this, and still more so to do it with such secrecy as to prevent the scheme from being known, which would put the people at Canton on their mettle to counteract it.

JOURNEY

OF

MR. THOMAS MANNING TO LHASA

(1811–12).

JOURNEY

OF

MR. THOMAS MANNING TO LHASA

(1811–12).

[*The foot-notes with the initials T. M. are by Mr. Manning: the others are editorial.*]

CHAPTER I.

JOURNEY FROM CANTALBARY TO PARI-JONG.

I ARRIVED at Cantalbary[1] on Friday, the 7th of September, 1811, and at Tazigong on Tuesday following; and left Tazigong on Friday morning, on what I call the 14th.[2]

Mr. Roy left me halfway to Cantalbary: Balangham soon after. The magistrate sent out horses and music, and I had a strange entry into Cantalbary, where I spent a good deal of money. All left me but one Chaprasi. Eight miles next day. The Bhutanese lord it over their Hindu subjects; and even my slave was imperious, but it might be because I travelled by authority. One of my Bhutan friends, according to promise, came and met me, not on the frontier, but at Bhitu Bari,[3] on the 10th, and took me with him to a village on a hill about six miles from the mountains, pleasantly situated among orange and lime trees. Thence, next day, I rode to a torrent. The horses, they said, were not to go any farther; an unexpected trouble. The Soubah of the village came to meet me, and salam me on the other side. I walked with him through water and over cruel stones above a mile, which brought me to a wretched

[1] Or Kathal-bari, a town formerly on the frontier of Bhutan, 63 miles north of Rangpúr.

[2] The 7th and 14th of September, in 1811, were on a Saturday, not a Friday. He must, therefore, have reached Tazigong on the 13th.

[3] I cannot find this place on any map.

pigsty of a place, and they said I was to stay there that night. It was still morning, or about noon. I declared I would not, but would go on to Tazigong. I got porters for my things, and set off, I and my Chinaman[1] and my guide, on foot. The road passed over the bed of a torrent with cruel stones, and I was sometimes up to my middle in water. At last it turned out by acknowledgment to be eight good miles; seven on the plain, and one up the hill. I was tired when I arrived at the foot of the hill, and it was steep and stony, and my feet were sore; but we could not stop more than half an hour. I toiled up slowly, and with considerable difficulty, When I got to the top, my servant had palpitation, sweated profusely, eruption broke out, and next day he said his skin peeled away. I told him it would do him good, and prevent fever. Next day I bargained for people to carry us in our chairs.

10th *Sept.*, we reached Tazigong.[2] I saw but one house: stayed two days. Here the Chaprasi left me. On the 15th I reached Dune,[3] and was lodged at the upper end of a large long room. On the 16th, after passing over a swinging bridge, I came to Enji, and was lodged in a large three-storied house. On the 17th and 18th I was at Dumgong,[4] in a very large solid built house, which seemed to be a sort of receptacle for merchandise and travellers. There was a chapel in it, with images.

On the 19th I reached Matakah. I came in thoroughly wet, and dried my clothes on my body. Afterwards, upon walking across the room, I was seized with a violent palpitation. The insects disturbed me all night. I saw a lad gnawing a turnip, and called to him immediately, and, showing it to my conductor, asked the name, and told him to give me plenty of it. I thus got an excellently well-dressed stew with turnips.

Leaving Matakah on the 20th, we walked up a mountain, and

[1] A Chinese servant whom Mr. Manning brought from Canton. Afterwards he usually calls the Chinaman "Munshi." He was detained at Lhasa when Mr. Manning was sent back.

[2] Mr. Manning appears to have entered Bhutan by the Laki Dúar or Tazigong, and to have gone direct to Paro. This is a route never taken by any European before or since, being to the westward of that travelled over by Bogle and Turner. It follows the courses of the rivers Tursa and Dun-chu, and then crosses a ridge to Paro. For details of this route see 'MacGregor,' p. 19.

[3] Duna or Duna-jong, in the valley of the Dun-chu.

[4] Dumgong and Enji are not on the maps.

slept upon it, there being no village or house. Wet, wet; always rain.

On the 21st, we ascended still higher; and after a fearfully long walk up the steep, descended down to Whârai—a toilsome day's work. I find going up hill does not agree with me, perhaps because naturally I am going down hill. Wet above, wet below; hard stones all the way.

At Paro-jong I was lodged in a guardhouse, with no window, and much smoke. I was not permitted to go out, nor to visit the bazaar close by.

In riding over the lofty bridge into Paro,[1] if the horse curvets, it must go slap down thirty feet into the rocky, stony stream; but that danger is imaginary. I could not persuade them to give me any fish.

On the evening of October 16 I left Paro, having been hurried to write six letters in six minutes, though the servants afterwards were not ready for three hours.

At night I found that my Chinese servant had changed our silver spoons into pewter. I told him I would not go on till I got my spoons. Now the Chaprasi I am in charge of is a partner in iniquity. He could procure the spoons in an instant, for we had only gone four miles. But no, he thought to persuade me to go on, and said the spoons would come after. I was obstinate. On the 17th, ten o'clock, twelve o'clock, and nobody went back to Paro. At last my slave went, and returned with one silver and one pewter again. I swore I would have the other, or go back myself and speak to the magistrate. This frightened my rascal: he sent the slave again, and he brought back the other. It was not the value, but the example. I am in bad, bad hands. The Dewan kindly sent yesterday the Chinaman and a lama (who came a child from China by chance of war, and had almost forgotten his tongue) to

[1] The bridge at Paro is a handsome structure, made of large pine beams built into either bank, and projected one over the other till a sufficiently narrow space is obtained to admit of a platform. The entrances to the bridge are paved with large slabs of stone, and at each end is a large, strongly-built stone tower, in which a guard remains at night, under the warder of the bridge. The bridge is very neatly boarded with deal planks. The gates are lined with iron plates and studded with nails. The road from the bridge to the fort is paved throughout. ('Eden,' p. 89.)

see how we were, and whether everything was right. This was a great relief to us, and I sent a civil message back.

18th. This morning I went to salam the petty magistrate of the place, and gave him a rupee and a looking-glass. He was vastly civil. We are now come on about six miles. The Chinaman is as cross as the devil, and will not speak. We are lodged in a loft, open shed-like, but a snuggish place to sleep in. Snow-fall in sight. Charming weather. Strange sensation coming along: warm and comfortable. Horse walking in a lane between two stone walls. The snow! Where am I? How can I be come here? Not a soul to speak to. I wept almost through excess of sensation, not from grief. A spaniel would be better company than my Chinese servant. Plenty of priests and monks like those in Europe.

19th. I found out at night why my servant was cross. He fell off his horse, and thought I took no notice of it. I did not see it. I visited a priest, and he is to pray for my welfare, going and coming. I cannot persuade them to let me taste the fish, though I offer money.

20th. Uphill. In a deserted house at night: could not sleep for the insects and rats. Good-for-nothing horse.

21st. We arrived at Pari-jong. Frost. Frost also two days before. I was lodged in a strange place, but so are the natives.

23rd. I went to visit the religious resident at Pari-jong. I sold cloth, but they cannot reckon. They cheated me of two paranies, even if at their own prices. All cheats. A woman spoke Chinese, and interpreted for us. On 21st, the two magistrates came to look at us, and ask questions. I took them for idle fellows (by mistake), and paid no respect to them.

24th. I visited the magistrate, and took his pipe-boy for a girl. He asked a good many questions, and was very civil. He gave me a sheep and rice, and he invited us to come again after three or four days, and stay longer.

27th. We were obliged to quit our room to make way for Chinese soldiers who are expected. The new room had dirty floors, and was rather cold. We cook for ourselves. Dirt, dirt, grease, smoke. Misery, but good mutton. The Chinaman was cross again. *Note.* Says I, "Was that a bird at the magistrate's that flapped so loud?" —*Ans.* "What signifies whether it was a bird or not?" Where he sat, I thought he might see; and I was curious to know if such large birds frequented the building.[1] These are the answers I get. He is always discontented and grumbling, and takes no trouble off my hands. Being younger and, like all Asiatics, able to stoop and crouch without pain or difficulty, he might assist me in many things without trouble to himself. A younger brother, or any English young gentleman, would in his place of course lay the cloth, and do other little services when I am tired; but he does not seem to have much of the generous about him, nor does he in any way serve me, or behave to me with any show of affection or goodwill: consequently I grow no more attached to him than the first day I saw him. I could not have thought it possible for me to have lived so long with anyone without either disliking him, or caring sixpence for him. He has good qualities, too. The strangeness of his situation may partly excuse him. (I am more attached to my guide, with all his faults, who has been with me but a few days.) My guide has behaved so damnably ill since I wrote that, that I wish it had not come into my mind.

29th. The Chinaman shaved with a razor shaped like a sickle, the edge being where a sickle's back is.

30th. The Chinese mandarin's interpreter arrived.

31st. The mandarin arrived. One of his soldiers, who is also his cook, visited us. He asked me if I was a Mussulman. I answer, "No, I eat pork," which I believe was not interpreted to him. Chinese politeness, even in the common soldiers, forms a great contrast with the barbarians of this place.

Nov. 1st. My Chinese servant visited the mandarin; and afterwards I paid him a visit. Some of his people said I could not sit down before him. In that case I should not have gone. He was very civil, and promised to write immediately to the Lhasa mandarin for permission for me to proceed. I gave him two bottles of cherry brandy, and a wine-glass. He asked me to dinner with my Chinaman, who excused me. The Chinese lord it here like the English in India. The Tibetans stand before them. I was applied to as a physician, to cure soldiers.

[1] The building is immensely large, six or more stories high; a sort of fortress. At a distance it appears to be all Pari-jong; indeed, most of it consists of miserable galleries and holes.—T. M.

2nd. The soldiers described their complaints, but concealed their origin, supposing, perhaps, that I, as a physician, can find that out. True, by dint of questions.[1]

3rd. Things are much pleasanter now the Chinese are here. The magistrate hints at overtures respecting opening a commercial intercourse between the Chinese and English through Bhutan. I cannot help exclaiming, in my mind (as I often do), what fools the Company are to give me no commission, no authority, no instructions. What use are their embassies when their ambassador cannot speak to a soul, and can only make ordinary phrases pass through a stupid interpreter? No *finesse*, no *tournure*, no compliments. Fools, fools, fools, to neglect an opportunity they may never have again![2]

4th. My medicines do wonderfully well, and the patients are very grateful. They have petitioned for me to go with the mandarin to-morrow towards Giansu, and not to have the misery of staying here for an answer from Lhasa. The secretary and others have also asked for us, and the mandarin has consented. Some of our things are gone to-day. We go to-morrow. This is very pleasant. I hear of several patients in Giansu already. *Tout mieux*, though it is a great trouble. The magistrate of the place has neglected lately to supply us with provisions, but the Chinese send us plenty of excellent vegetables.

[1] Mr. Manning then details his treatment for each patient.

[2] One would gather from this that Mr. Manning was given a simple passport by the Government of India, recommending him to the good offices of the authorities, without other official recognition.

CHAPTER II.

FROM PARI-JONG TO GIANSU.

WE left Pari-jong early in the morning of the 5th of November. I expected to have set out after breakfast; but we were called up before four in the morning, as they wanted our things and our beds. Bitter frost. The wine, or rather beer, I had ordered over night arrived just as we were setting off. There was no wine to drink, as it must be heated first. Before daylight I heard the gun go off: the signal that the General had left the place. I went down to the street, and found the head Tibetan interpreter and his second waiting for us. We mounted at dawn of day, and scampered over the plain. Snow all round on the mountains—a strange sight. Sharp frost. About three miles off we passed the mandarin's flag. He had stopped there to settle some cause and take refreshment. Soon after he overtook us. I salamed him as he passed, and we went on in company. We came to a tomb of stones with stakes at top, adorned with hundreds of bits of cloth. A raven sat crouching on the top of one of the stakes. The mandarin alighted and prostrated himself to the ground, as did some of the soldiers, others not—we not. It is the tomb of a holy man. They call it Púsâ. I was surprised to find the ice so strong. The sides of running brooks would bear our horses well; but this was only the first or second day; afterwards, the land lying lower, the frost was much less severe. After riding about 25 miles we found two tents pitched; one for the General and one for me. Here we had boiled mutton. I went up to the General, and thanked him for his kindness in permitting me to go on with him, and stayed about twenty minutes; then on again. Soon afterwards the sun became obscured, and a terrible cutting wind blew upon us. I was not sufficiently clothed against this. I had a thick heavy cloak on, which one of the soldiers had lent me. The aide-de-camp had also lent me a sheepskin under-cloak, which I thought too much, and had packed up with my things. I was so bruised and bit and cut by this wind, that when we came to our resting place I was in a slight fever. I lolled on the cushions before a good fire, but could not recover thoroughly till next day. At night, ten or fifteen of the inhabitants of the village settled themselves in the dirt around our fire, and the scholar of the place made out their shares of expense for provisions for the General and his party, including us. It was a curious scene. A shoe-shaped pan, with a bit of cotton lighted in the bottom, and two or three lumps of tallow laid over, was the lamp. The clerk held the paper in one hand and the pen in the other. One man flared the light as close to him as he could, sloping it, and shoving in the tallow with his finger as the light grew dim. Another put the inkstand in his way when he looked about for a dip. They were eager and noisy. Afterwards they introduced the dice, using their hands for a box, and gambled for their shares and perhaps for money. Afterwards they continued gambling till late in the evening. I saw the *hayta* (*weety-peety*), a strange appearance in the air, strongly resembling the flight of innumerable birds. It is the conflict between the extreme cold and burning heat of the sun. It deceived me at first, and my servant afterwards. I frequently saw the same appearance afterwards, but never so strong. There are very few birds in Tibet. I heard now and then the *weety-peety* cry of a few small birds among the stones and rocks, and on the waters were flocks of wild ducks (very tame) and other wild fowl, but not more than may be seen on all lakes, meres, and broads.[1]

The next day I was still a little unwell, and they told us that the cold and wind would still be severe; which proved untrue, as it was pleasant the whole day, except when the passage between the mountains became narrow, and then it was uncomfortably hot. They gave me a vicious horse. While lengthening the stirrup he kicked, and bit at me. Now I must observe, once for all, that the common horse furniture in these regions is detestable. Shrivelled bits of leather, full of knots, for the stirrup leather; it is almost impossible to untie them, and when done will not take a new bend. Again, if one can be altered, it is a great chance if the other side

[1] A Norfolk word, showing where Mr. Manning hailed from.

admits of it; and as for making the two sides equal lengths, it is a great chance if after half an hour it can be effected. Consequently, setting off at daylight in a hurry, among Tibetan servants, whose language I did not understand, and in the bitter cold, I generally went with one leg long and one short. The bridle was often so short that I could barely reach it; and I managed to hold by the leading rein, which always accompanies the bridle in these parts. Often the bridle broke in the middle of the road; sometimes the stirrup leather; sometimes the saddle, high behind and before, was so short that I sat in pain, unless I twisted myself unequally. After walking the horse ten miles—our pace was generally a walk, and upon the average we did not go three miles an hour, consequently, although our journeys were 12, 14, 20, and, at the most, 30 miles per day, we were from many dawns till evenings' close on our horses—my knees ached so much in consequence of the short stirrups, that I was forced to ride side-saddle fashion.

These and other petty inconveniences I shall in future pass over; they would be as little entertaining to the reader as they were to me. But to return to my vicious horse. He happened to have remarkably bad furniture. In lengthening the stirrups they made them so long that I could scarcely reach them with my toes. I mounted him without his playing any tricks, and thought myself secure; but whether it was the unusual length of legs he felt at his belly, and the unusual mode of riding that made him impatient, or whether it was his natural temper alone, I do not know: he grew headstrong, and would not keep his place, but pressed forward. He fatigued me very much. A soldier offered to change with me, but I thought he would be a good goer after he had had a little run. I put him ahead, and gave him two or three notices with my heels that he might go his own pace. He changed his form instantly; set his head and ears, and at once sprang forward in a full runaway gallop, with the most furious and awkward motion I ever experienced. I could not have imagined he had ever been so fleet. The bridle was of little use. I pulled and sawed at it as hard as I dared; I could easily have broken it. I expected every minute my stirrup leather would break, though I pressed as lightly as I could; but what was worse, the road, which at first was tolerable, grew worse and worse, and I saw we were coming to the fearful bog we had passed the day before, which was full of concealed holes, frozen knobs of earth, flakes of ice; and had proved troublesome to walk our horses over. I reckoned upon a serious fall, but I believe he had had enough. A man driving cattle stood still, in his way, upon my clamorously invoking his assistance, and my horse made that a pretence for falling into a trot. I turned his head towards my companions, who were now nearly a mile off. When they came up they insisted on my changing, which I refused, until I saw they were a little angry, upon which I dismounted and exchanged for a quiet creature, who was as willing to keep behind as the other was to run ahead. What with the violence of the exercise, the weight of my clothes, and the remains of my fever, I felt myself a good deal agitated; by degrees I recovered, and felt no ill consequences after it.

This day we approached the edge of a lake or sea, and here a cushion was spread for the General, and another for me, and tea was served. I had eaten but little, and had preserved some bits of cold meat in my wooden cup, which I drew out of my bosom and ate, and it now proved very acceptable to my stomach. The lake[1] was frozen; at least that part we were next, and would certainly have borne me. My skates were not many miles off, but I was not well enough to regret the losing this opportunity of showing my skill. We stopped but a few minutes and proceeded on to where the lake becomes a river, in a narrow pass between the brown, dry mountains; here it was open in the middle, and running briskly. There were many fine, fat wild ducks on it, which were very tame, and let us come close to them. The people of Tibet never disturb them: they eat no birds, but, on the contrary, let the birds eat them. The sun here was burning hot. There were a few miserable-looking houses scattered about, looking like ruins of villages, as the Tibet houses often do, and a few patches of arable land. We passed on through the defile to a large village, where we two were shown into a strange cavern of a house, and told it was our lodging. It was low, long, dark, narrow, black, windowless, and full of smoke. I sat sometime on the wall beside the house, breathing the pure air and enjoying the sunshine, before I ventured to explore it. At

[1] This is the Calochu of Mr. Bogle. (See p. 73.)

last I crept in, and when I arrived at the farther end found cushions and a good fire, and the good woman of the house preparing the pot. Though it seemed at first so narrow, it was in fact a wide, large room, supported by pillars, leaving an alley in the middle, and against the pillars were a great many packages, which concealed the sides, and left nothing visible but the alley, which I took at first for the whole room. There seemed to be several families belonging to it, and at night several women and girls came in, who undressed themselves in the sides, and spread their beds, long after I was laid down and quiet. I now and then took an impertinent peep, but the smoke was so thick and the light so bad, that I could discern nothing. Every time they opened the door there came a stream of cold air upon me, which prevented my sleeping, and they were not all retired till very late. Getting up and going to the door I found two guards lying before it, in the open air, seemingly very comfortable and composed. I have often seen this since, and learned that it is by no means a miserable situation. A European is not at first aware of the thickness of their clothing and covering. He figures to himself a miserable man in the streets or fields in England, on a bitter, sharp frosty night in January, and shudders.

This night, as well as many others, I slept in my clothes. It was a great trouble to me to undo my bedding, which was but ill contrived; and to get up in the morning before daylight, and arrange it again, and cord it, in a place where I had scarcely room to stir, and where the smoke was so thick that the slightest exertion made me breathe quick and almost suffocated me, and where all was dirt and dust, was painful even to think of, so I often lay in my clothes, as I had done many, many nights at Pari-jong.

The next day the valley opened a little. A stream flowed in the middle. There were stumps of herbs and brown grass, but still not a single tree or shrub to be seen. I saw deer feeding at a distance. We made a very short stage, and put up at a sort of caravanserai which seemed to be destined to receive the mandarins and other public officers. Our room was a little sort of balcony open in the side towards the south. A cloth was stretched against the open side, which moderated the cold in the night. Here a sheep was killed, to be carried along for next day's provisions, as the place we were to lodge at was miserably poor; and Sid in the morning brought me a cup of stewed lights, in order to ingratiate himself, for he wanted to become our servant, and to go with us to Lhasa, which he afterwards did.

We continued along the barren valley, seeing no diversity, but the ever-varying shapes of the still more barren mountains, whose colour, where it was not actually sand, slate, or granite, was a melancholy pale mouldy green, produced no doubt by the scaly covering of dried stems and withered herbage, until we came to two or three houses, one of which was an edifice raised from the ground, and the others were sunk into the ground, having their roofs level with the top of the slight eminence in which they were sunk. The mandarin lodged in the house; we, in one of these cellars, which I found snug and warm enough. A pot of young growing onions at one corner of the room was the greenest thing I had seen for a long time. We had the room to ourselves. The corporal came to see us, as he always did, and asked us if we wanted anything, and sat and chatted for a few minutes.

The next morning the General did not rise so early as usual. The sun was up and lively before we mounted our horses. Lounging about, waiting for the General, I was very near walking against a great dog that lay curled up, and which I took for a sack, until somebody called to me and bid me beware. My horse was so weak, so tottering, and so stumbling, and trembled so whenever he set his foot on a stone, which was about every other step, that I could hardly keep up with the company. With great care I got him on gently three or four miles; after which both he and the road improved. We passed some hot springs;[1] one of which the soldiers called me to look at. I saw the steaming water, but had no time to examine it. I asked whether it was medicinal. They said it was famous. We then passed a strange strait between the mountains, where the water seemed to flow uphill. We went upon masses of stones for a long way; afterwards the road opened into a little area, filled with religious piles of white stones, and with a sort of open temple in it, where was carved a strange gigantic figure.[2] From this we descended down to the river, which was now considerable, and my eyes were refreshed with the sight of a few trees, and some

[1] See p. 181; and Turner, p. 220. [2] See Turner, p. 222.

slight appearance of cultivation. We forded the river, and trotted up to a pleasant sunshiny village, where the people were bustling about, and where we were to lodge. The Munshi and I were shown into a little apartment on the first floor, which opened upon a spacious flat roof or terrace, defended by a parapet wall. I was now so eaten up by little insects, which I shall not name, that I was compelled to set aside shame, and sitting down on a terrace buttress in the sunshine, dismiss as many of my retinue as I could get sight of. Shame prevented me at Pari-jong from performing the operation otherwise than partially and by stealth, for there I was scarcely ever alone for a single minute; and shame still more strongly prevented me, on the road, in the houses where we lodged, before curious strangers, men, women, and children around me. I suffered a good deal from these little insects, whose society I was not used to. I shall say no more of them than that I did not get thoroughly rid of them until some time after my arrival at Lhasa.

CHAPTER III.

RESIDENCE AT GIANSU.

THE next morning we were off early, though we had but a short stage to Giansu. I had a very pleasant-going horse with a handsome countenance. I was tempted to buy him, but was checked by the prudent consideration that he might encumber me at Lhasa, and too much disencumber my lean purse. Half-way towards Giansu we were met by the sub-mandarin and the Tibetan mandarin, with their retinues, come out to meet and honour the General and give him a meat breakfast. From his table the soldiers brought us two or three very palatable viands, which we did justice to. Our room was one extremity of a stable, parted off for us by a cloth, in the Asiatic manner. The word stable might suggest for a moment the idea that we were treated with indignity, but not so. The house was filled with official people; we being but an appendix to the General, could not dine with them. Not to separate me from the rest, consisting of servants and soldiers, would really have been treating me with indignity; besides, our luggage required a separate room; but to settle the matter at once, there really was not any room in the house better than this same corner of a stable. It was the freest from dirt and the smoothest paved I had seen for some time. There were good cushions with the little table before them to hold pans of parched flour; and though we heard the horses kick at the other end, we did not see them, except when curious impertinents lifted up the cloth. After dinner we all rode gallantly forth towards Giansu, where we soon arrived. Upon approaching the town we met several Chinamen, and my companions underwent the troublesome ceremony of dismounting and exchanging salutations with them. My Munshi admitted that this Chinese custom was one that might be advantageously dispensed with.

Giansu is a large town, half situated on a hill and half at the foot. It makes a good appearance until you are close upon it, when the handsome white stone houses are converted into dirty white walls, and the windows into belfry holes. There is an abundance of water flowing about it, which they do not seem to know how to keep off the road. There is not a blade of anything green to be seen; but there are cornfields around and a few trees, and in summer time I should judge it to have a gay appearance. Like every place I have seen in Tibet, it appears a little area surrounded by mountains without any visible outlet. These mountains, both at Giansu and other places, are many of them absolutely barren from foot to summit, as is the greater part of the valley between them. At the time I saw them they had so entirely lost their green livery as to present the same dismal prospect as their neighbours.

We went to the area before the mandarin's house and tribunal, to inquire where we were to lodge. Here I was struck with the appearance of everything being perfectly Chinese. The same neatness, the same folding doors and paved yard, the same figures of mandarins in ancient dresses smugly painted on the folding doors, the same Chinese characters pasted up, the same style of building, and, in short, an exact conformity to the Chinese models.

While standing here there came up a man in a turban, who addressed me in Hindustani. I thought it better to seem to know almost nothing of that language. Indeed, I had not occasion to feign much, for though I know its construction, and can hammer out a few phrases in it, and when speaking with a native of Hindustan above the common class, and who is perfect master of it, can manage to hold a little conversation; yet I do not pretend to know the language, and when asked if I can speak it, I always answer, No. From those who spoke to him in broken Tibetan, and explained to us in Chinese, I learned that he was from Kashmir, which I also heard him say in Hindustani.

The General appointed us a little lodge in the courtyard of the principal house. Here again I seemed to be in China. We took possession of our apartment, which was clean and papered, with a papered window, and door opening to the south. Whatever we required was soon supplied us by the Chinese soldiers who had been under my Munshi, and by others who meant to apply to me. One brought rice, one brought meat, another brought us a table, another brought a little paste and paper and mended a hole in the window, another brought us a present of a pen and candles. There were many inquiries. Every Chinaman in the town came to see us and salute us. Two tomb-like brickwork structures against the wall, with good thick cushions on them, were the places to lay our beds on, and here I slept much more comfortably than I had done for a long time; while the cold was much less. The level of Giansu is much lower than that of Pari-jong, and lower than that of any place between. The rivulet flows the whole way towards Giansu with considerable rapidity.

I had suffered so much from smoke, my breath was so affected by it, and my hands and face were so stained by it, that I determined to live without a fire. We scarcely believe in England that it is possible to be comfortable in sharp frosty weather without a fire, but it is very possible and very practicable: there only needs good warm clothing from head to foot; for how is it that we are comfortable in bed in cold weather? A Chinaman's or Tibetan's cold-weather clothing may be considered as a moving bed; but what makes it more easy in Tibet than it would be in England is the extreme dryness of the air, and the fervent sunshine, which streams forth all day from a cloudless sky. This mode of clothing and being without a fire is inconvenient in some respects.[1] If the hands be employed in writing or otherwise, they become pinched with cold; everything they touch feels like ice. In taking exercise the body becomes too hot, and particularly the feet; many, I believe, on this account use too scanty clothing for their feet. These partial heats and colds occasion frequent rheumatic fevers. Again, the Chinaman, with his smug shaved head, has his ears and part of his head entirely exposed, for of course he wears the same shaped cap here as in China; he can no more change his clothing to adapt himself to Tibet than an Englishman can to adapt himself to India.[2]

[1] The rich have occasionally a large pan of charcoal set in the room. There is no wood in the country, consequently the charcoal, which is brought from a distance, is very dear.—T. M.

[2] Generally speaking, a Chinaman's dress is much better adapted to variety of climate than a European's. When in India I used frequently to rally the absurdity of the English dress, by gravely observing how lucky it was the Russians had no settlement there, for their fur dresses would be an intolerable nuisance to them. The persons to whom I addressed it could not say, "Oh, they would leave them off," because they would be aware that I should say, "No more than you your

This exposure of the ears and head to the cold wind is also, I believe, the cause of rheumatic pains and toothache.

We went out to present ourselves to the General, who was vastly civil and polite. He invited us to dinner for the next day,

neckcloth." The warmth and thickness of a European's cloth coat is not so great an evil, though evil enough in a hot climate, as the tightness of his clothing, which occasions throbbing, and a stifling sensation of heat and sweat, and probably may be very injurious to the health. He will deny, I know by experience, that his clothes are inconvenient, but his natural efforts to relieve himself betray the contrary. When he comes home in the evening, though he be not going to bed for an hour or two, does not he take off his neckcloth and unbutton his breeches' knees, with a pleasing, inarticulate expression, denoting that he is somewhat relieved—that his blood has room to circulate. As I myself have used both kinds of clothing, the European and the Chinese, in hot climates, I can with confidence assert that the difference in comfort, particularly while sitting still, is very great indeed, and in favour of the Chinese dress. And the same is true in very cold weather; but in taking exercise in moderate weather or in cold weather there is an advantage on the side of the European dress.

Women in Europe, if there be a bush or branch in the way, or other mere nothing of an impediment, or if anyone stamps on their robe, or only the foot of a chair, betray a slight uneasiness, and often give vent to some expression of discontent. I have often, when dressed in long slight robes, caught myself in a similar state of mind, and using similar actions and expression, and have observed to my companions that now I understood thoroughly what the evil was that women often seem to make so much of and men make so slight of. This is one of the inconveniences of loose robes that descend to the feet. It seems to me not refining too far to say that this habitual fear of entanglement, and the facility with which the dress can be laid hold of, tend to take off from a man's boldness.

To invent a new dress is a matter of great difficulty: to alter a national dress is perhaps a still greater difficulty. The inconvenience which a European suffers from his dress in India he attributes to the climate; or if he does allow that a cloth coat is hot, yet he says, "for gentlemen to meet in society without cloth coats would be highly improper; that custom cannot be changed." He adds, "The natives would not respect us in any other dress;" as if it was the cut of a European's coat that held the natives in subjection, and not the Europeans.

The natives respect the Europeans, in spite of their dress, for their vigour of body and mind. I am persuaded they would honour them more if their dress was less monstrous; as it is, no doubt respect and fear are associated with that dress; they would soon be associated with any other the Europeans chose to adopt. The military gentlemen I have conversed with in India seem still more certain of the absolute necessity of wearing tight cloth uniforms. They reject with scorn and contempt the idea of making any change, and consider the men that propose a change as very ignorant of the duties of a soldier. The slender-limbed sepoy cannot sit down without unbuttoning his pantaloons. If he wants to pick up anything off the ground he is obliged to convey it to his hand with his foot; he cannot stoop for it as the other natives do; yet he, too, is proud of his dress, and would not willingly change it I suppose.– T. M.

and recommended me what clothes to purchase. He advised me to adopt the Chinese dress completely. Nothing indeed was wanting now but to put on my Chinese boots which I brought from Canton, and purchase a Chinese hat.

Next day, according to appointment, we dined with the General. The sub-mandarin was invited to meet us. I soon found out that the General was no better than an old woman; and it was not long before my Munshi adopted the same opinion. I called him Sai-po-ti, a title which my Munshi afterwards always used when speaking of him; but he was very much of a gentleman, and very civil and polite to me. He was of a good Szechuen family, and by the mother's side a Tatar. The sub-mandarin I perceived to be rather vulgar and awkward, but he seemed a well-disposed man, and I thought him sensible. I afterwards learnt that he had risen from the ranks entirely by his merit. The General gave us a tolerably good dinner, but his cookery was but indifferent. I thought his wine excellent.

He was greatly taken with my beard, and seemed as if he never could sufficiently admire it. He adverted to it both then and afterwards on other occasions. He named such and such a mandarin, such a one he thought had better moustaches; in fact, I had kept mine cut short in India, for convenience of eating soup and drink, and they were not yet full grown. Afterwards, when I had combed my beard and adjusted it properly, and he saw its tapering shape descending in one undivided lock, he again expressed his admiration, and declared he never had seen one nearly so handsome. The General likewise approved of my countenance and manner; he pretended to skill in physiognomy and fortune-telling. He foretold very great things of me. He also foretold good things of my Munshi, but said he was rather hard and unaccommodating. Whether he saw it in his face or in his actions, or knew it by what was told of him by the soldiers, I cannot tell; he certainly hit the mark.

The sub-mandarin, learning I was fond of flour victuals, for I had eaten so little of that food since I left Rangpúr that I had quite a craving for it, politely invited me to a pastry breakfast. He called it a slight pastry breakfast; but besides flour-made viands in meat gravy, there were excellent little sausage dumplings, and other preparations of meat, and good wine. The cooking was better than at the General's; in short, I thought this breakfast very much to the purpose. I made him a present of a little cherry brandy, and he afterwards made me a present of a few candles.

I went to pay my respects to the Tibet mandarin, who lived in a sort of castle on the top of a hill. The Munshi[1] would not go with me; the reason he gave was because there were no horses sent for us. The distance was about a mile! I believe it was that, as a Chinese, he began now to think himself a man of consequence; in fact, he began to display his pride and act with a haughty demeanour towards the Tibet people, which afterwards became doubly conspicuous, and obliged me to counterbalance it by being over civil. The mandarin was evidently puzzled how to return my visit, as he could not visit me without visiting the Munshi. It was ill behaviour in the Munshi not to go with me, as he was professedly my interpreter; but I liked much better to go without him, as I could speak more freely; for if he was present, every question I put or observation I made must pass through him, and if his *sublime crossness* did not approve the question or observation, it was with some peevish word or gesticulation either refused to be passed or else garbled into another thing. I had a Chinaman with me who spoke Tibetan. He was one of my patients and a good-natured fellow. I was ushered into a very large lofty room, with an immense window to the south, full of papers and records, and scribes. The mandarin after a few minutes came in, and tea was brought. We sat together on cushions, and discussed Calcutta and Tibet, for about half an hour, when I took my leave. He intimated that he would call on me the next day, and would send me some eatables. I had made him a trifling present. He sent some rice and a useful piece of cloth, but did not come himself. Another mandarin came in his stead (inferior, I believe), and made some apology; I forget what.

I had great success with my medicines. I had so many patients now, both indoors and outdoors, that my time was fully occupied. My outdoor patients gave me the advantage of having

[1] This is the Chinaman who came with Mr. Manning from Canton; elsewhere called his Chinese servant.

to take daily exercise (either the patient or one of his friends always sent me a horse and guide), and of seeing the internal economy of their houses. I attended one Chinaman who was very ill of a continued fever he had had for several days. I gave him antimony. Whether it was the antimony or whether it was that his fever was come to a crisis I know not; but after two days his head was clear, his fever gone, and he was so persuaded it was the effect of my medicines, that when I saw him again he went down on his knees to me and bowed his head to the ground, in thankfulness. Another Chinaman, very poor and living in a miserable manner, had an intermittent fever, as had also his wife. I cured both of them clearly and satisfactorily. I gave them opium, Fowler's solution of arsenic, and afterwards left them a few papers of bark. The mother-in-law also, who had the complaint of old age, I cheered up with a little comforting physic; and she considered herself under great obligations to me. With various other patients I had more or less success. There were some of the old rheumatic complaints that baffled my skill, and would not yield to the physician of a few days. The water at Giansu is extremely bad, except what is fetched from a considerable distance. I advised all my patients, as well as others, not to spare a few pence or shillings, but always to send for the good water. I was persuaded that the ordinary water drank day after day gave them pains and swellings. They were of the same opinion too; it was the general belief of the place; but the facility with which the water was come at, and the apparent innocence of a cup of tea made with it, beguiled them; and I am afraid my admonition has had but little effect. I several times meditated putting on my skates, but the want of a large sheet of ice, the trouble of going out to seek a place that would at all suit my purpose, and my incessant occupation in seeing patients and making up pills, prevented me from carrying my wishes into effect.

I now made a present of a small rouleau of silver to the secretary, and another to the sergeant or aide-de-camp. They accepted here what they refused at Pari-jong, but I believe would not have been discontented if I had given them nothing. Upon examining my luggage, which had stood unmolested two or three days, I had the misery to find all my clothes and parcels converted into solid lumps of ice. This was owing to the carelessness of the box drivers, who, in passing the river, had neglected to heave up the baskets, and had suffered their bottoms to trail in the water. Nothing had escaped except my Munshi's box. I had in Bhutan given away some of my boxes as they became empty, and had exchanged all the rest for light wicker baskets, which are more convenient for the porters. I had not reserved one box for myself, but had allowed my Munshi to retain his, which was an excellent large Calcutta trunk, light and water-tight, and contained all his things.[1]

I had great trouble in thawing and drying my things; many things were injured and some spoiled.

The General often came to see me; for like many other generals he had nothing to do, and was glad of a morning lounge. I used to receive him in my sunshiny courtyard, rather than in my room, which was somewhat littered. There he sat with me and smoked a pipe or two, and chatted. We sat in my two chairs, and the rest (the soldier and attendants) stood the while. Upon seeing my linen hung out drying, he mightily wondered why I had brought so much light clothing. He called it much, though in fact it was very little; six or eight grass-cloth gowns and two gauze gowns, and a few light drawers, were all that could be deemed useless in Tibet at that season; for shirts I still wore, though perhaps he was not aware of that, and took my eight or ten Madras longcloth shirts, which were flapping on the lines, for so many light summer jackets. He advised me by all means to leave these things at Giansu, and not encumber myself with them to Lhasa. But this was idle advice, even if I had meditated going no farther than to Lhasa and speedily returning again; for though they seemed to occupy much space when spread out drying, when folded up they really made altogether but a very small parcel, and added nothing to the apparent quantity of my luggage. He repeated this advice on other days, but I seemed not much to hear what he said, and turned it off as well as I could; and lucky it was that I did, as afterwards, at Lhasa, when no money came to me from Rangpúr, it was by the

[1] It was also very convenient (with the help of a chair, &c.) for him to spread his bed upon, and sleep on. He never offered it to me for that purpose. —T. M.

sale of these and other things that I managed to keep my pot boiling.

I had now another Chinese servant. I had asked the General at Pari-jong to allow me to have one, and I believe he immediately made up his mind what man to allot me, though he pretended he would consider and look out. He could not keep the secret so close but that I had many intimations what his intentions were. There was a fellow with him in the capacity of cook or cook's helper, who had fixed himself, I know not how, upon the General at Lhasa, and followed him to Giansu. He gave the man no wages, I understood, but suffered him to live with him, and now he was very glad to get rid of him, and pay him out of my pocket. The fellow was a notorious scamp, and two dollars per month would have been very handsome wages for me to give; for as to the pretence that he was an excellent cook, it was nothing to the purpose, as, in the first place, I did not want a servant in such an exalted capacity; and in the second place, the fellow in fact knew nothing at all about cooking. It was intimated to me one morning, that the General had fixed on a servant for me, and if I would step over to his house he would send for the man, that I might see if he suited me. So I found I was to go through the farce of pretending not to know who it was; of saying, "Oh, that is the man, is it, General? And what does he ask for wages?" There certainly was some obligation the General was under to this fellow which induced him to ask me six dollars per month for him. I hesitated, and expressed my surprise at the man's asking so much, saying that it was more than my slender means could afford (the General knew that I was very bare of money at present, and that I hoped for a remittance from Rangpúr). I offered two dollars. The General said that was too little. We split the difference, and settled it at four dollars. I acquiesced with good humour, as I saw the General had made up his mind and had his reasons. I told my Munshi that it was a great deal too much; but whatever the General had determined I should have given without discomposure. The General further stipulated that he should have two months' pay in advance; to which I also agreed with alacrity. My Munshi would not allow that it was high wages for the man, though high for our pockets. He thought him an excellent cook, and was not undeceived for a long time. There was a good body of a Tibetan woman in our kitchen at Giansu, who was accustomed to Chinese cookery, and she and he together certainly made very palatable dishes; but as soon as we left Giansu, I found out that our famous cook did not understand even the elements of his profession. I communicated my discovery to Munshi, but finding he took it crossly, and was inclined to quarrel about it, I dropped the subject and never said another word about it until we parted with the fellow; even when my Munshi had found it out for himself, which seemed to be soon after we arrived at Lhasa, and was partly occasioned, I believe, by excellent dishes we ate at a *mias*, where comedies were acting, and none of which our great cook could imitate. Even then, when Munshi strongly expressed his dissatisfaction with him, I made no observation, except simply and coolly agreeing, with a yawn, that he knew nothing about cookery. I had nothing new to say upon the subject. This fellow, good for nothing as he was, made himself useful. He had a full share of impudence, and claimed things, too, on the road which a more modest man would have let go by. In drying and folding up my linen he saved me infinite trouble. The Chinese are all expert at little domestic offices: folding up clothes, pasting up a hole in the paper, making up parcels, driving a nail where it is wanted, tacking and stitching. They certainly are taught these things in their infancy. For my part, I never could to this day fold up a shirt or other vestment. A handkerchief or sheet I can manage, but nothing further; everything else I roll up, so that if I had to put together my Chinese dresses after I had dried them, I should have made a very clumsy parcel.

One of the soldiers who had been my patient both at Pari-jong and here at Giansu, for pains all over his body, the remains of a former ill-cured complaint, and who now was much relieved, begged hard that I and my Munshi would dine with him. He had a pleasant apartment, and gave us a comfortable dinner, not sparing his wine, and knowing that I was fond of wheat flour had plenty of farinaceous food served up. We were waited upon by his wife—a good-dispositioned tidy body, who was also my patient for a trifling complaint, and to whom the soldier seemed much attached. A Chinaman would think it ill manners, indeed, to permit his wife to sit down with his guests. Nor should a young wife, in strict propriety, appear at all among the guests; but among the lower orders, and particularly here in Tibet, where the women have greater freedom allowed them, and where the Chinamen's wives are in fact but concubines,[1] who, except perhaps in a few rare instances, are left behind when the husband returns to China, they are not so scrupulous. I had made the young dame a present of a looking-glass and other trifling articles upon entering the house, and had given a piece of money to their little boy, by which I had much gratified both them and the husband.

A strange rustic, from the province of Szechuen, lodged for a day or two in the apartment on the opposite side of our courtyard. He was on his way to Hontsong,[2] to see his father, who was a high mandarin there. He was a gross, clumsy, ruddy-faced young man, about twenty, and I should have taken him for some farmer's son. He was silent and seemed uneasy, perhaps from family distresses; and all the observation he communicated to us respecting his travels was, that the country he passed through was detestable. He came over several times, and sat a little while with us, but scarcely spoke. He gave me some very good macaroni, and I upon that made him a little present. Through his stupidity I thought I saw tokens of a good disposition in him, and perhaps he was far from being stupid by nature.

I had heard that the General was fond of music, and no bad performer. I took an opportunity one day, while he was smoking his pipe in my courtyard, of introducing the subject, and paying my court to him by requesting the favour of hearing his music. This brought me an invitation to take an evening repast and wine with him, which was just what I liked. He gave us a very pretty concert; several of his soldiers were performers, and after the concert we all supped sociably together. He himself performed alternately

[1] Although the damsels of Tibet are said to be in general more free of their favours than is consistent with the rules of strict chastity, yet these concubines are universally allowed to be faithful and well behaved. I have heard many of them praised by their Chinese husbands for their good conduct. When their husbands return to China, they look out for an opportunity of making a similar engagement with some other Chinaman, and in the interim keep house by themselves, or with their mother or nearest relations. To judge by their countenance and demeanour, I certainly give full credit to the praises I have heard bestowed on them.—T. M.

[2] Some place to the westward of Giansu occupied by Chinese troops. Probably Jonka-jong, the important position commanding the Kirong Pass into Nepal. See farther on.

on several instruments, and with considerable taste. Two of the soldiers acted a musical scene from a drama, while he accompanied them on the Chinese guitar. The whole was done in a very good style. The Chinese music, though rather meagre to a European, has its beauties, and has, like most other national music, its peculiar expression, of which our musical notation, which we vainly imagine so perfect, conveys no idea whatever. The General insisted on my giving him a specimen of European (or Calcutta) music on the Chinese flute. I was not acquainted with the fingering of that instrument, but I managed to produce something which he politely praised. He made me play several times, always making polite remarks. I constantly hesitated, assuring him the flute with him was in better hands; which was true, and which gave him pleasure to hear. I tried a few country dances, but perceived that that quick kind of music was not very gratifying to their ears. I spent a pleasant evening, and stayed until past my usual bedtime.

The Governor's polite and kind behaviour, and particularly his permitting me to come on with him to Giansu, instead of miserably waiting at Pari-jong, had opened my heart, and I was determined to show my gratitude by making him a handsome present. I had nothing with me that would suit that purpose; therefore, through my Munshi, I ascertained what he would like to have from Calcutta, and determined to write for it. The same opportunity would serve for giving my friends an account of where I was, and requesting a reinforcement of money, and of some trifling articles. I wished much to send a special messenger, and assured the General there was no other way so certain; but he thought it sufficient to forward my letter by way of a despatch to Pari-jong, with special orders to the magistrates to have it expedited through Bhutan. I had great difficulty in persuading the interpreter to give me the General's address in Tibetan language. He could not understand where the difficulty was of addressing a letter from Rangpúr to Giansu; not aware that the word Giansu is utterly unknown in Bengal, as is the Tibet appellation for Chinaman (Gummu). He and his scribe boggled at it above an hour, producing various scraps of paper, some nothing to the purpose, some containing a long story and definition, as it were, of Giansu; and my Munshi began to be cross, and would not familiarly illustrate the matter to them nor willingly suffer me to do so. At length, after various attempts, the eyes of their understandings opened to what I wanted, and they produced a proper address, which I enclosed in my letter. The General's wish was to have fine broadcloth, of a particular (violet) colour, sufficient for the very ample robes for a high mandarin: he meant, he said, to make a present to certain great officers in Szechuen; he also wished for a pound or two of opium.

I had learnt now, to my great sorrow and discomfort, that the chief mandarin at Lhasa was the identical Tatar chieftain who had been disgraced at Canton for his management during the Bengal[1] expedition to Macao. That he was a man of a particular suspicious temper, detested at Lhasa, and that he certainly would give us all the trouble in his power. I slightly alluded to this in a letter to England, but putting a good face upon the matter; for though I was annoyed I was not cast down. The answer from the Lhasa magistrate to my request to be permitted to proceed to Lhasa arrived a few days after we had been at Giansu. It was very favourable, and handsomely worded, ordering me to be provided with everything necessary, and to come on without delay.

The evening of the day the answer arrived, the secretary paid us a visit. He attributed the favourable issue greatly to the excellent words he had inserted in the petition. Being pot-valiant, he let his tongue run on too freely, and boasted of his services rather more than he would have done if he had been sober. My Munshi, instead of laughing it off, began to be spleened, and could hardly keep his temper. He could not bear anyone should repeat the same thing twice, or dwell upon frivolous circumstances. With my patients, for example, he was perpetually in ill humour and crossly checking. I told him it was natural for sick people to indulge in descanting upon their complaints, and to attach im-

[1] If I was to qualify that senseless expedition with the epithets I think it deserves, I might seem harsh.—T. M.

When the projects of Napoleon assumed threatening proportions, the English Government resolved to take under its protection the colonies of its ally Portugal. Madeira and Goa were garrisoned by British troops, and a force was sent from Bengal, by Lord Minto, to garrison Macao. The Portuguese did not oppose, but the Chinese made objections, and the dispute went on until an expedition was fitted out to attack Canton, which was abandoned just at the very moment it ought not. (See Sir John Davis's 'China,' ii. Chap. III.)

portance to trifles very tedious to listen to; that there was no occasion to be very attentive to their repetitions and idle details; but that I as their physician, and he as my interpreter, ought to be attentive, kind, and complacent. Munshi said it was not his nature; he could not bear to hear people talk in that manner. He had been very angry with me once at Pari-jong, upon my saying that Puti, the woman who interpreted for us, and sold us wine, was a great fool. I could not at the time imagine in what I had offended him. I could not suppose he was in love with the lady; for, though she was not old, she was wrinkled, and foolish and dirty. He now informed me that what annoyed him on that occasion was, recollecting that not an hour before I had made the same observation.

The General talked sometimes of his military exploits and toils, and assured my Munshi how much more hardy and active and enduring the soldiers were in his young time than now. I suppose the General told him some anecdotes over twice, or oftener, for I observed towards the end of our stay at Giansu, and afterwards, he spoke more harshly and crossly of the General than I thought there was any occasion for. He was angry with me but once during our stay at Giansu, when upon some trifling occasion he broke out with such bitterness and fury as was scarcely endurable. I begged of him not to eat me up, as I wished to proceed farther on my journey; and then for the first time opened my mind to him on the unfortunate state of his temper, and lamented my ill luck in having a person with me to whom I was so afraid of putting a question, that I was perpetually deterred; it being necessary for me first to go round about, and with civil speech and preface bring him into the humour to listen to it and answer it. That this necessity was a grievous burden to me; that I never used the same precautions with any English gentleman, whatever was his rank. He answered these remarks without much asperity; only observing that he wondered why I brought him with me from Rangpúr; that I should have done better for myself to have left him behind. When these fits were over his behaviour returned to its usual cross level, and I to my usual serenity; never on any occasion taunting him with what had passed, or making any allusion to it whatever.

The General now determined a day for us to depart from Giansu, and mentioned in his despatches to Lhasa what day we might be expected there. It was not to be divulged or known at Lhasa that we had come on with him, but it was to be supposed that we had waited at Pari-jong for the answer from Lhasa; so that the question for the General's sagacity to solve was what day we ought to leave Giansu, so that our arrival at Lhasa, and supposed departure from Pari-jong, might quadrate with the usual equation on these roads between time and space; and I doubt but his solution was perfectly correct, as I never heard of any objection being started as to our arrival at Lhasa being too soon or too late.

The tailor soldiers now brought home our clothes. My robe was prodigiously heavy. It was an ample coarsish red woollen-cloth robe with fur cuffs; it was lined with cotton cloth, and upon the cotton cloth was stitched a dressed sheepskin with all the wool on. I had also bought stockings of the same kind of sheepskin, under which, if I pleased, I could put one or two pairs of common worsted or cotton stockings, and over all draw my Chinese boots, so that I was able to keep my feet cosey whatever weather might ensue. I had a sort of fur tippet, and a quilted cap to defend my face and ears, and which I found very useful at Lhasa, always wearing it in the streets during the very cold weather when I went out to visit the Grand Lama or mandarins early of mornings; although by so doing I perhaps provoked the laughter of the Chinese, among whom it is very unfashionable to wear anything over their ears, except on journeys, that I dare say they would rather have their ears drop off in the streets with cold than cover them. Even the little plush beaver hats they wear in the house, which the common people wear also abroad, are so turned up as to cover only the tops of their heads. I bought one at Lhasa for the house, and wore it turned down comfortably, spite of the remonstrances and smiles of my Munshi and servant, who assured me it was not worn so. I told them my ears were of more consequence to me than the fashion.

CHAPTER IV.

JOURNEY FROM GIANSU TO LHASA.

ON the morning of our departure our friends came about us to assist us and see that all was right and tight. We called on the General, who afterwards had the politeness to come down to our lodging to see that we wanted for nothing, and to give such orders as he thought might be useful to us. After that we chatted half an hour with the soldiers.[1] I made a few jokes to make them laugh. To the soldier I had dined with I gave in charge my large fine light bamboo Cochin China umbrella hat. For the joke's sake he put it on. It was impossible for him, as a Chinaman, to wear such a thing; and I, to increase the hilarity, putting on a serious face, begged of him to take care of it for me, and not wear it out. This joke was so good that, with slight variations, it bore repeating three or four times. At last we took leave, mounted our nags, and trotted off.

Our horses were stout and good, and I expected to have had them for all day. The General had promised that he would take care that the magistrate should give us a passport of the best sort, and such as would make the village we lodged at provide us horses for the day. I have no doubt he intended it to be so, and gave such orders, but he did not look close enough to it. The magistrate merely continued us on the same passport we came with from

[1] The word soldiers may suggest the idea that we were among rough and fierce companions at Giansu, but not so; though their title was military, their appearance, demeanour, and manners were perfectly civil. The soldier tailor had the delicate skin, the indoor gestures and actions, the gentle voice, unwarlike mien of a real tailor; and the rest, if their appearance was not quite so much a contrast to their profession as his was, yet had all of them the civil manners and gentleness and unmilitary carriage of body of so many tradesmen, or tradesmen's clerks. Yet these men ought to be among the best of the Chinese soldiers. They guard the frontiers; they have occasional skirmishes with the Nepalese and Bhutanese. The enemies they have to contend with are still inferior, I believe, and have less military art among them.—T. M.

Pari-jong. Whether it was that this arrangement was really much more convenient to him, or that he was offended at my Munshi's want of respect, and determined to treat us slightingly, I cannot say. We had not gone three miles out of the town before our sturdy horses and bluff cattle were exchanged for sorry jades, lean kine, and half-starved, tottering asses, scarcely able to bear the burdens imposed on them. One of the horses was without a bridle — this, they said, was of no consequence, he was very gentle; the saddle of the other was so small and narrow from head to stern, besides being imperfect and having a great brass bump in the middle, as to cramp me and render my ride uncomfortable. We got on very slowly; the sun was scorching hot, and from the nature of the soil reflected strongly against our faces. One side of mine was completely blistered; and though the stage was short, when we arrived at our resting place I was really indisposed, from fatigue of uneasy posture, heat, and vexation.

Our lodging was at the postmaster's. At every stage, from Szechuen through Lhasa and Shigatzé to Hontsong[1] and the borders of Nepal, is stationed at least one Chinese soldier, to forward the despatches. These post-houses, though from the barrenness of the country they are miserably furnished, yet compared with the ordinary Tibet men's houses, they are elegant and comfortable. The Chinese are really civilized, and do not live like cattle; and it is a comfort, after having lodged in smoke and dirt with the native animals of Tibet, to take shelter in a Chinaman's house, where you are sure of urbanity and cleanliness at least. Our host was a great coxcomb. He was young and rather handsome in his person (and had a handsome Tibet wife), and affected great elegance in his manners and diction. This character amused me; I had never seen it before among the Chinese, though upon inquiring of my Munshi he said it was not uncommon in China.[2]

[1] Clearly Jonka-jong, the important Chinese post, at the head of the Kirong Pass, leading to Nepal.

[2] Almost all the Chinese in Tibet are from the province of Szechuen, and a great many of them are Muhammadans. Our fool of a servant was a Muhammadan. This coxcomb was a Muhammadan. For the most part they are totally ignorant of the doctrines of their religion, and only acquainted with some of its external rites. Our servant knew nothing further of it, I believe, than that Muhammadans circumcise, and abstain, or rather ought to abstain, from pork and wine.—T. M.

The next day our ride was more pleasant and not so hot. Our road seldom lay far from the river, which flowed through the valley towards Giansu, for both this day and the preceding, and part of the next, we gradually ascended to a higher level. We again lodged at the post-house, which was large and, comparatively speaking, magnificent. Our host was quite a different character from the last, being the reverse of a coxcomb, careless in his speech, and not talkative. By something particular in his civility I knew that he wanted my medical assistance: it was for his child, who had an ulcer in an awkward place behind. I left them lotions, and directions. They were very thankful, and his wife or yateu catened[1] me.

We were off very early the next morning, after having taken by candle-light a good meat repast which our host gave us, and which our cook had been busy in helping to prepare for hours before daylight. It was a bitter cold morning. We had now drawn near a set of snowy mountains. One of these mountains we partly wound round. On coming to the side where the streams descend from it, our way lay over masses of ice, which our horses scrambled over with some difficulty. In general, the Tibet horses are very surefooted upon the ice, making but few slides. We afterwards passed at an inconsiderable distance from a small glacier,[2] which descended down to the level of the road we were on. Munshi and our servant now pushed forward, while I continued to jog on with the conductor, who did not seem inclined to leave the cattle drivers. Upon coming to a village where there was a considerable ascent and descent, I found my Munshi waiting for me. He had let the foolish servant trot on by himself. He had done prudently, as it was at this village we were to stop and refresh. Here I found that

[1] Caten means bow down the head to the ground; it is the name for the Chinese prostration before high mandarins. In saluting the Grand Lama I always gave him three catens. The Chinamen in general, I believe, give him only one.—T. M.

[2] The Pundit of 1866 also noticed a glacier between Giansu and the Yamdok-chu Lake. He calls it a very large one. This is the great range of the central Himálayas, from which several of the main tributaries of the Ganges and Brahmaputra, and one branch of the Ganges itself, take their rise. The Indus, Sutlej, and Brahmaputra break through it from north to south; and the Painam, or Penanang, along the valley of which Bogle, Turner, and Manning travelled, from south to north, flowing to the Brahmaputra.

the fame of my medical skill was not promulgated on the road by my servant, but had preceded me, and been conveyed from station to station by couriers or other travellers from Giansu. Almost as soon as I entered the postmaster's house I predicted to my Munshi that he would apply to me as physician. It was for himself and for his pretty wife. I felt both their pulses with due gravity, inspected their eyes and countenances, inquired into particulars, and gave them pills, and directions. Our servant, after proceeding some way alone, found out his error, returned and mounted the hill again, time enough to help in preparing our repast. Pursuing our course, and gradually descending, the valley at length opened into a large stony plain, at the end of which stood a considerable town[1] on the margin of an extensive lake,[2] or little sea, as it is

[1] Probably Piahte-jong of the Pundit of 1866.

[2] The Chinese name for these pieces of water is slaitz. Slai signifies sea, and tz (son) is in this case a sort of diminutive. If the word sealet was current in our language, it would serve to translate slaitz.—T. M.

This was the famous ring-like lake of Palti, which has appeared on all maps since the days of D'Anville. The peculiar lake of Palti, Piate, or Yamdok-chu, with its great central island, like a large ring, first appeared on the map prepared by D'Anville, from the survey of the lamas, under Jesuit instruction, which was published by Du Halde in 1735. It has been repeated on all subsequent general maps. Giorgi, in his 'Alphabetum Tibetanum' (1762) says, that "Palte Lake, otherwise called Jangso or Yamdso, according to native report is of very great size, so that a man could not journey round it under eighteen days. It is three days' journey from Lhasa. From the middle of the lake rises a continuous chain of hills and islands. On the southern side is a monastery, the abode of a great queen, who is born a second time, called Torcepano. She is honoured as a real goddess by the Indians and Nepalese, who worship her under the name of Bovani. The Tibetans believe a certain holy spirit is re-born in its divine essence in this hideous female, just as in the Grand Lama. Whenever she issues from her house, or from the island, or journeys into the city of Lhasa, a procession precedes her," &c., &c.

Mr. Bogle, it will be remembered, made the acquaintance of this female divinity; and Dr. Hamilton cured her of an illness, and visited her constantly. (See pp. 105, 108, and 109.)

Mr. Manning is the only Englishman who ever saw Lake Palti, and it appears from the text that he was not aware that the hills on the opposite shore formed an island.

On the 1st of January, 1866, the Pundit, trained and sent on his travels by Colonel Montgomerie, arrived at the banks of the Palti, or Yamdok-chu Lake, at a small post called Piahte-jong. He describes the breadth of the lake as varying from two to three miles, and says that it is reported to be very deep. In the centre of the lake there is a hill, at the foot of which are situated a number of villages. The circumference of the lake is about 45 miles; it is crossed in wicker boats covered with leather. The Pundit rode along the banks from Piahte-jong to the village of Demalung, from which point the lake stretches to the south-east about 20 miles, and then turns west.

This is the Pundit's account of the lake, extracted from his diary. He

called. From the opposite or farther margin of the lake rose diminutive mountains in a continued chain, which bounded the whole prospect in front.[1] It was near close of day when we reached this town. We had difficulties in procuring a lodging. Our guide had left us to go to the magistrates. Our servant had formerly had some quarrel with or had offended the Chinaman stationed here, and did not choose to apply to him. We rode up one way, and down another, and loitered about, until at last we were shown into a wretched place, where the apartment had walls only on three sides, the fourth being open like a coachhouse, without doors. Moreover, we were told they could give us nothing to eat or drink. As we had money in our pockets, there was no danger of starving in a large town, not to mention that we had provisions in our wallet—mutton and butter, besides a piece of excellent pickled pork that the General had, among other things, given us for prog on the road. So I left them to settle the dispute as they liked, and sat down on the roof of the house to enjoy the view of the lake at sunset.

My Munshi did not seem to have much relish for prospects; he never made a single observation on any one (or indeed, scarcely on any other subject) during our whole journey. I once brought him to acknowledge, coldly acknowledge, the beauty of one. It was the opening to our view of the valley of Paro. The living crystal stream purely flowing and sparkling through the valley as far as the eye could reach; the cornfields and pasturages; the sunbeams checked by the branches of trees; the houses, here collected into villages, there scattered into single farms; the wooded hills, with cattle grazing on their brows; the bold spires and cliffs; blue tops of distant mountains—I made him confess that this was a charming sight after the dreary forests and mountains we had passed enveloped in mist and rain.

further reported to Colonel Montgomerie, that he was informed that the lake encircled a large island, which rises into low, rounded hills, 2000 or 3000 feet high, and covered with grass to the top. Between the hills and the margin of the lake several villages and a white monastery were visible on the island. The Pundit was told that the lake had no outlet, but, he says, its waters were perfectly fresh. Mr. Manning, on the contrary, says, in the text, that the water of the lake is very bad. The Pundit's observations make the lake 13,500 feet above the sea; and the island rises to 16,000 feet above the sea.

[1] These are the hills of the large island in the centre of the lake.

Our conductor afterwards made his appearance, and told us his mission was at an end; he was now to return to Giansu. This surprised us; we expected he was to go with us to Lhasa. I gave him a small gratuity, for which he was very thankful, and went away. But now I found I had been too hasty in my donation; yet it was with the concurrence of my prudent Munshi. I should have deferred it until he had delivered us and our luggage into the hands of some other conductor; for we soon found that we were left destitute; nobody to provide us horses and cattle. My Munshi and I consulted together, and agreed that it was best for him to go to the Chinaman's house, show him our pass, explain our case, and ask his assistance. Upon going into the street, Munshi found our old conductor surrounded by the townspeople, who clamorously pressed upon him, and seemed almost to be coming to blows with him. He was representing our case and trying to serve us; but these townspeople, it seems, had no inclination to forward us on to Lhasa. Whether it was that they thought their cattle better employed for other purposes, or that they wished us to honour their town with our residence, I cannot say. I suspect the former. However, Munshi went to the Chinaman, who came and presently settled the matter for us. He sat down in one of our chairs, and affecting all the decisive gravity and authority of a magistrate, determined what horses we wanted, and provided us a conductor, to whose care we entrusted all our goods and chattels. I had no suitable present at hand to give the Chinaman for his good services, and money might have offended his worship; so we wrapped up two or three pieces of silver in paper, and Munshi went again to his house and presented it to his wife. This was gratefully received as a full recompense for his trouble, and ensured his future services, in case anything further should happen to annoy us. We ate our suppers, hung up an old cloth over part of the room to keep out a little of the wind during the night, spread our beds, and went to sleep.

Our people came very late the next morning, and were a long while in getting our things off; and we had not gone six miles along the lake before we changed horses. We stopped at a respectable farmhouse, where the family had, I thought, very pleasant faces, and great kindness of manner. They were the first Tibet people I had seen that I at all wished to be acquainted with. As the weather was rather cold, the old man of the house ordered a pan of coals into our room, for us to warm our fingers and noses. I was sorry I could not talk with him. As for using the medium of my servant, who spoke bad Tibetan fluently enough, it would have been to no purpose. His impertinent, insolent manner did not at all harmonize with ours. I was vexed and pained to see him encroach upon their kindness, and imperiously demand their services, as it were, keeping the attendants waiting with the broth-pot, after he had enjoyed a plentiful repast, and had as much remaining in his cup as he meant to eat; when with a single word he might have let them go and finish the pot by themselves, while it was warm and good. Though I could not speak, I tried to express by my manners and countenance that their kindness was not thrown away upon me; and as in these cases there is undoubtedly a great sympathy, I trust they partly understood my sentiments.

We now wound round the lake to a village on the other side, where we changed again. Here the people were miserably poor. The scholar of the village read our pass, and found that they were bound to provide us meat; but they pleaded their poverty, and begged us to be contented with che-broth and parched flour. Their plea was not in vain. I knew it to be no fiction; the whole country had been afflicted with bad crops for successive years, and this year a cruel, killing, latter frost, with hail, desolated their fields, and blighted a great portion of their corn. We travelled on, still winding round the lake, in a narrow, stony path between that and the mountains, and in the afternoon I found we were exactly opposite to the town we had set off from in the morning, at no great distance, separated from us only by the width of the lake. I could not help thinking that a ferry-boat might very advantageously be added to this town's appurtenances. But it seems no boats whatever are used on this lake; and though it is stored with fish, which are a great relief to the poor in the summer time, when they come into the shallows and towards the shore, and suffer themselves to be caught, yet they have no nets, I was told, or method of taking them out of the deeps; so that it is only during a few months of the year that they avail themselves of the ample provision Nature had laid before them. The water of this lake is said to be very unwholesome; it is not drank by the inhabitants of the surrounding villages,[1] though I found they permitted their cattle to water at it. I was told they have a custom of throwing their dead into it, which I have no reason to disbelieve. The number of wild fowl in the lake is very inconsiderable. From what I saw and heard of Tibet, from its barrenness, and from the nature of the soil, if soil it may be called, I should judge that it cannot possibly support large flocks of birds. I do not know from what data or what observations Mr. Turner drew a contrary conclusion. Turning my head back towards the west, I had a noble view of a set of snowy mountains collected into a focus, as it were; their summits empurpled with the evening sun, and their majestic, graceful forms ever varying as I advanced into new positions. Though I kept a long, long lingering eye upon them, yet I heartily wished that I might never see them again. My lips almost spontaneously pronounced this wish repeatedly, as I apostrophized them in my mind. Fruitless wish!

Our resting place was a small town[2] on the borders of the lake, embellished and rendered conspicuous by a lofty, massive castle, the residence of the magistrate, who, they said, was a woman, and of whom they complained as capricious and tyrannical.[3] I was amazed for a long time with observing the numerous ravens that were playing about the castle and floating over the lake. I did not know that they were so social, so frolicsome, and so joyous. They wantoned about in a thousand different manners and postures, sometimes pursuing each other, and making a mock fight; sometimes separately; sometimes rising; sometimes falling with closed wings; sometimes floating awhile in the air on their backs; sometimes lying edgewise; sometimes whirling round the building with vast rapidity; and all with an eagerness and joyousness of motions and cries and screams that showed the overflowings of happy sensations too plainly to be mistaken. Many of

[1] If the water is so brackish there is no reason for doubting the report of the Pundit of 1866, that the lake has no outlet.

[2] Probably the Demalung of the Pundit of 1866.

[3] This, doubtless, is the female incarnation of Giorgi, whose acquaintance Mr. Bogle and Dr. Hamilton made. (See pp. 108, 109, and the foregoing note on the Palti Lake.)

the ravens about this lake, and many in Lhasa, emit a peculiar and extraordinary sound, which I call metallic.[1] It is as if their throat was a metal tube, with a stiff metal elastic musical spring fixed in it, which, pulled aside and let go, should give a vibrating note, sounding like the pronunciation of the word *poing*, or *scroong*, with the lips protruded, and with a certain musical accent. The other is similar to that of the ravens in Europe, yet still has something of the metallic sound in it. Whether there be two species of ravens here, or whether it be that the male and female of the same species have each their peculiar note, I cannot say.

Munshi, who had been to the postmaster's to consult and talk with him, came in and informed me that there was no meat to be had in this place; that we must make shift with what we had with us. This gave me no concern; it scarcely made any impression on me; but somehow at supper he fancied I was discontented, and opened with cross speeches, saying we were not great mandarins, he could not command things. I laughed, and assured him (which was really true) that I did not perceive any deficiency in our supper. It was as good as usual, was it not? What had we at other times superior to it? Thus, as I was provoked to it, obliquely hinting my contempt for our servant's cookery. In fact, we this night had some of the General's excellent bacon simply fried; we had eggs, we had flour food, butter, and, if I recollect right, there was a little bit of mutton. A very little satisfies me. I am not at all anxious about my meals, but my palate is very discriminating with respect to the qualities of things, whether wheat, or rice, or meat, and also with respect to the cookery; and I prefer a boiled egg and salt to an ill-dressed ragout.

We had still six or eight miles more along the margin of the lake, after which we were to leave it to the right, and cross over a mountain. We sauntered along to the village at the foot of this mountain. Our servant came slowly after us: he was miserably mounted, and always impatient and brutal with his horse. He had thrown him down and broken our China cups. We found no horses ready for us at the village; they were to seek and fetch up from a considerable distance. The consequence was we were obliged to wait a long time, and set forward a full hour later than we ought. The height

[1] The raven of the Arctic regions (*Corvus corax*) also gives out a bell-like croak.

of the mountain was trifling. After a mile and a half or two miles easy ascent we were at the top; but the level of the valley on the other side was considerably lower than the one we departed from. The descent was long, tedious, and in many places troublesome.[1] It was dark and silent night before we reached the village we were to lodge at.[2] Our conductor was far, far behind, with the baggage. Our servant rode about from house to house vainly endeavouring to find a place for us. After about half an hour the Chinese postmaster came out and escorted us to our destination. Whether it was that my Munshi, tired of the servant's folly, had applied to him, or whether it was that he heard us tramping and talking in the streets, I did not inquire. Being warmly clothed I had a perfect nonchalance on these occasions, and if we had stayed two hours in the street I should not have been impatient or discomposed. We were ushered into a sort of open gallery. The night was fine and calm, though frosty; the house was full of smoke, and I was glad we were not invited into it. The master of the house took our passport in hand, which consisted of about ten lines. Our servant held one of our candles to it. With an audible voice the good man hammered through it again and again, and in the course of about half an hour he seemed to have spelt out and acquired some notion of its general purpose, and gave it back into our hands. At one end of the gallery I found a lofty-walled, square chamber, open at top, in which was piled plenty of clean straw. I made myself a nest and lay down and took a nap while supper was preparing. I intended passing the night there, but after lying about an hour, I found a certain damp and chilliness descending from the sky above, which, together with the remonstrances of my servant, who was more used to the climate than I, dissuaded me from it. We chose a spot under cover, where there was a wall behind, and on one side, and the house in front, which, though not absolutely contiguous, formed a sort of third wall. The fourth side was partly sheltered by beams and rails. I ordered plenty of straw to be brought, pulled my red woollen nightcap over my ears, lay down in my clothes, and slept as usual. Though I felt no immediate ill consequences

[1] The Pundit of 1866 calls this the Khamba-la Mountain, and says it is the boundary between the provinces of U and Tsang.

[2] Probably the Khambá Barchi of the Pundit of 1866.

from thus sleeping exposed to the frosty night air, I believe it to be injurious to a European, who cannot endure to entirely cover up his face and head. I afterwards, at Lhasa, had a pretty severe attack of the acute rheumatism, which—though it might partly be occasioned by frequent alternations from heat to cold, from broiling sunshine to frosty shade, and by the exposure to early morning cold, to which I was subjected during the first part of my residence at Lhasa—I cannot but partly attribute to these partial and imperfect night shelters.

We were now in the valley in which the town of Lhasa stands, distant from it about fifty or sixty miles.[1] No part of Tibet that I have seen is so pleasant as the part we passed through in our next morning's ride. The valley was wide, a lively stream flowed through it, houses and villages were scattered about, and under the shelter of mountains, on the farther side, was a large white town, pleasantly situated, and affording an agreeable prospect. The place was not destitute of trees nor of arable land, and an air of gaiety was spread over the whole, and, I thought, on the faces of the people. We stopped while horses were preparing under a shed in a large, clean, pleasant paved yard, like an inn yard in England. We had good cushions set out for us, and were served with *suchi*, with a cheerfulness and alacrity I had not before witnessed. They also brought us a joint of good mutton to put in our wallet. We trotted on until we came to a town standing on the bank of the river.[2] From this town we descended down to the sandy shore, and found a large and good ferry-boat ready to waft us over the stream,[3] whose width here was considerable. We all went over together, men, cattle, and baggage. The reminiscences occasioned by the motion of the boat brought on a fit of European activity. I could not sit still, but must climb about, seat myself in various postures on the parapet, and lean over. The master of the boat was alarmed, and sent a steady man to hold me tight. I pointed to the ornamented prow of the boat, and assured them that I could sit there with perfect safety, and to prove to them how commodiously I was seated, bent my head and body down the outside of the boat to the water's edge; but finding, by

[1] The valley of the Tsanpu, or Brahmaputra.
[2] Probably Chaksam Chori of the Pundit of 1866.
[3] The great river Tsanpu, or Brahmaputra.

their renewed instances for me to desist, that I made them uneasy, I went back to my place and seated myself quietly. As the boat drew near shore I meditated jumping out, but was pulled back by the immense weight of my clothes and clumsiness of my boots. I was afraid of jumping short and having the laugh against me. Our conductor trotted forward to a village standing at some distance from the road, and ordered out fresh cattle for us. We changed expeditiously; after which I cantered away with the conductor, who did not pull up till we arrived at the end of our day's journey.[1]

The house was occupied by Tibet military going to Lhasa, to be examined for promotion, but there was a vacant upper room for us, from the terrace of which I inspected what was going forward in the yard. I saw the soldiers, their bows and their clumsy muskets. The principal officer had a strong horse, sumptuously furnished, which soon after our arrival was led out for him; and he and his escort set forward. Upon this we went down to a lower room, more convenient, and near the cooking place. The postmaster of this village or town came to visit us, and proved to be of the same province as my Munshi, who, upon that score, invited him to dine with us. He was a grave, well-behaved man, but his company was not very entertaining. At night, after I was in bed, I heard our servant chopping away and preparing things for our next morning's breakfast until a very late hour. To answer the preparations he made he ought to have served us up a sumptuous repast. I could not help laughing, upon seeing provided next morning nothing but one dish of minced meat and some wheat-flour biscuits. He was extraordinarily slow in his operations. I have afterwards, at Lhasa, seen him the whole day in preparing two common dishes for the evening; and when we hired another servant, who was to go on errands and go out with us, and give the cook time to get through his vast operations, he absorbed him, too, into the kitchen, and the day was not long enough for both working conjointly. I am persuaded if we had hired four servants he would have employed them all from morning till night in the kitchen, preparing his two or three nothings.

The following day's journey was rather long. It was divided

[1] Probably Chabonang village of the Pundit of 1866.

into four stages. At the end of the first stage, I was struck with the sight of a child lying neglected and apparently in convulsions. Going up to it, I found that the sunbeams had now entered the shed where it lay, and were shining fiercely upon its face and eyes. I brought my cushion, and placed myself so as to intercept the rays, when the convulsive motion ceased, and the little face assumed a serene smile. At the end of the next stage I do not recollect that anything remarkable occurred. I saw a fat country fellow standing before a magistrate telling his story, or making some complaint: he held his hat in his hand, and was scratching his head as naturally as countrymen do in like situations in England. The third stage was short. My Munshi begged of the conductor to let him proceed on to Litong, the close of a day's journey, without changing his horse. To this the conductor assented; upon which he and the servant trotted off. He was desirous to get in, in time to see after horses for our early departure next morning, as he was particularly anxious to be in Lhasa the next day before noon. Indeed, he seemed to consider that absolutely necessary, and that if we did not appear before the great mandarins before noon, we should be guilty of a fault which they would hardly forgive. I rallied the notion in various ways, but in vain. The Chinese, certainly, have a pernicious dread of their mandarins: it occasionally upsets their senses.

As I was in no hurry, I determined to wait for the conductor, with which he seemed pleased. After Munshi was off, I went into the house, and was served with some excellent *suchi* and parched flour. This seemed to be a sort of religious house. I saw no family, but a great masculine woman made her appearance now and then before the door, whom I took to be a nun. She might be the lady abbess for aught I know. There were whirligigs set up in the house,[1] which the conductor piously twirled as he passed

[1] These whirligigs are cylinders turning freely on an axis, within-side are sentences and prayers. Turning the whirligig is equivalent to reciting the sentence, and is a substitute for it, for the use of those who are so ignorant as not to be able to recite. They are of two kinds: one a hand whirligig, which the pious vulgar perpetually carry about with them, and are almost constantly turning; the other a fixed whirligig, moving on a vertical axis. These are of various sizes, some as big as a clock-case, some about the size of a quarter peck. In the avenues of the temples there are hundreds of them in a row, which good souls twirl one after the other as they pass along. Those

them. I do not know whether it was expected of me to twirl these machines. I certainly never did all the time I was in Tibet; for though I am a great conformist in certain ways, take me in another line and I am a most obstinate non-conformist, and would sooner die than swerve a tittle.

As soon as our horses were ready, and the baggage was adjusted to the cattle, my guide and I set forward briskly. We tinkled[1] over the stony plain, and through the broad and shallow streams of water, until we came to a sort of rocky hill, which we must ascend and descend. Here the guide dismounted, and seemed to expect that I should do the same; but my boots had hurt my heels, and I was determined, if possible, to ride over this hill. Upon coming to bad places, he two or three times looked back, and intimated to me that I had better lead my horse. I still persisted, but at last, in the descending part, we came to an absolute staircase. The guide looked at me, and smiled. I smiled and shook my head, confessed myself foiled, and dismounted. When we had gained the level plain, we again pushed on; but the sun was set, and the shades of night coming on before we could reach Litong. Here I found Munshi in dole and wrath. He had sent out the servant, as soon as they arrived, to seek for the man whose business it was to provide and take care of us. He had been out above an hour, and he was not yet returned. I had none but the old receipt for him—patience. He came back shortly after, and informed us that the said man happened at this time to be so drunk that he could neither stand nor go. This was a great mortification to my Munshi. He feared we should be off late the next morning, and, in truth, the sun was up long before we set off.

We had not gone many miles before we were met by a respectable person on horseback, who dismounted and saluted me; then, mounting again, rode on with our guide. Upon inquiry, I found this was a person sent out by the Grand Lama or his people, or by the Tibet

who use the hand whirligigs acquire the habit of twirling them mechanically. It is the same with the chaplets of beads. I have seen a man with his hands behind him regularly shoving on his beads with his thumb, and all the while talking about other matters, or even disputing. I was advised in Bengal to adopt the rosary, as it would be a means of procuring me respect and good treatment in Bhutan and Tibet. But this was one of the points in which I could not conform.—T. M.

[1] The guide's horse has a bell at his neck, which when he moves keeps up a perpetual tinkling.—T. M.

magistrate of Lhasa, to welcome and honour me, and conduct me to the metropolis. We hurried into the town where we were to change horses, but our haste was fruitless. There we were obliged to wait until our baggage came up long, long after us, and until it was adjusted upon fresh cattle. If we now had galloped all the way to Lhasa the sun would have been in the south before we could have been in the august presence of the Tagin.[1] This was exceeding discomfort to my Munshi, but great comfort to me. I much disliked the idea of hurrying to Lhasa, and without any kind of refreshment going before the mandarins, sweltering and heated, my boots hurting me every step I set; and I could not comprehend what crime it was for travellers like us who could not command prompt attendance, arriving an hour sooner or an hour later.

As there was no use in hurrying now, we proceeded calmly on. As soon as we were clear of the town, the palace of the Grand Lama presented itself to our view. It seemed close at hand, but taking an eye observation upon the change of certain angles as I advanced eighty or one hundred paces, I sagaciously informed my Munshi that it was still four or five miles off. As we approached, I perceived that under the palace on one side lay a considerable extent of marshy land. This brought to my mind the Pope, Rome, and what I had read of the Pontine Marshes. We passed under a large gateway whose gilded ornaments at top were so ill fixed that some leaned one way and some another, and reduced the whole to the rock appearance of castles and turrets in pastry work.[2] The road here, as it winds past the palace, is royally broad; it is level and free from stones, and combined with the

[1] Tagin means great man. It is an appellation given to high mandarins of a certain rank in China. At Lhasa there were at this time actually in office only two Tagins.—T. M.

[2] The least deviation from symmetry and correctness in certain parts of architecture, and where the mass of building is not enormous, soon destroys the effect of the most magnificent plans, and reduces them to mere gingerbread buildings. That severe and correct accuracy which we Europeans inherit from the Greeks is unknown, I believe, in Asia. When the mass is very great and compact, whatever defects there may be in the detail, the effect of the whole is always, I believe, grand and imposing. This is the case with the palace of the Grand Lama, which has no beauties or symmetry in detail, but as a whole has a striking and grand effect. Even the Tuilleries, than which when examined part by part nothing can be more ugly or misshapen, yet viewed as a whole strikes the eye as a majestic mass.—T. M.

view of the lofty towering palace, which forms a majestic mountain of building, has a magnificent effect. The road about the palace swarmed with monks; its nooks and angles with beggars lounging and basking in the sun. This again reminded me of what I have heard of Rome. My eye was almost perpetually fixed on the palace, and roving over its parts, the disposition of which being irregular, eluded my attempts at analysis. As a whole, it seemed

POTALA. THE PALACE OF THE DALAI LAMA.
(*From Kircher's 'China Illustrata.'*)

perfect enough; but I could not comprehend its plan in detail. Fifteen or twenty minutes now brought us to the entrance of the town of Lhasa.

If the palace had exceeded my expectations, the town as far fell short of them. There is nothing striking, nothing pleasing in its appearance. The habitations are begrimed with smut and dirt. The avenues are full of dogs, some growling and gnawing bits of hide which lie about in profusion, and emit a charnel-house smell; others limping and looking livid; others ulcerated; others starved and dying, and pecked at by the ravens; some dead and preyed upon. In short, everything seems mean and gloomy, and excites the idea of something unreal. Even the mirth and laughter of the inhabitants I thought dreamy and ghostly. The dreaminess no doubt was in my mind, but I never could get rid of the idea; it strengthened upon me afterwards. A few turns through the town brought us into a narrow by-lane, and to the gate of a courtyard, where we dismounted, and, passing through that yard, entered another smaller one surrounded by apartments. We mounted a ladder, and were shown into the room provided for us.

CHAPTER V.

LHASA.[1]

Our first care was to provide ourselves with proper hats. The General, indeed, had given us a handsome light one, but his was a small Ciceronian head (in shape, I mean), and neither I nor my Munshi could get his hat on, and the Munshi informed me that if it was enlarged the marks of alteration would render it unfit to wear. I, indeed, as a foreigner might wear it so, but he as a Chinaman among his countrymen would not, except in the house. Notwithstanding this, he afterwards had it altered into an excellent hat for himself, and wore it perpetually. The hatter took our measures and lent us two hats for the interim. We learnt that this was the time of reviewing the Chinese troops. There was a small encampment by the side of the town, where the mandarins daily inspected the exercises. The great men were still in their tents and would not return to their tribunals and be at leisure to see us before the evening. Thus the load of guilt which pressed so heavy on my Munshi's conscience was washed away with a single word.

I was sorely afraid lest the Tatar mandarin should recollect having seen my face at Canton, or should recollect my name, or remember having heard of an Englishman of my description, strangely residing at Canton, and suspected of wanting to get into the country. Besides, he had Canton servants with him, who were still more likely to have seen and heard of me. I put on my China spectacles to disguise my eyes as much as I could, and away we went to the tribunals. It was a long way to walk with a sore heel. I was very much heated. I inwardly grumbled. Coming into their presence I, for the first time in my life, performed the ceremony of *ketese*. My Munshi was afraid I should dislike the

[1] The Pundit of 1866 reached Lhasa on January 12, and remained until April 21. He says that city is two and a half miles in circumference, in a plain, surrounded by mountains. It is in 29° 39′ 17″ N., and 11,700 feet above the sea, according to the Pundit.

ceremony; he knew how averse the Europeans are to bending, but I had no objection whatever, insomuch that, on the contrary, I was always asking when I could *ketese* or kneel; and if there was an option between one *ketese* and three, I generally chose to give three. To the Tibet mandarins I sometimes knelt down, or made as if I knelt, though this was displeasing to my Munshi. He wished this mark of respect to be paid only to Chinamen. In fact, the common Chinese use no ceremony with the Tibet mandarins. They are not to pay them the due reverence, and to offer them an inferior kind would be a sort of insult. I being indifferent towards either side was desirous of treating both as equally as possible.

There was no danger of the Tatar mandarin recognizing my person. The old dog was purblind, and could not see many inches beyond his nose. They asked a few questions, made polite inquiries after my health, and accommodations on the road, and intimated it was they who had provided my lodgings. I wish they had omitted this intimation: it meant nothing, being mere empty words, as they had no concern whatever with my lodging nor with the meat and rice which were offered me upon my arrival. All these things were provided by the people under the Grand Lama or by the Tibet mandarins. But afterwards, when I found our room excessively cold and inconvenient, and was unwell, and wished to change and have some other room, which could have been done without any difficulty, my Munshi thwarted me and absolutely refused. The great mandarins had given us this; to change would offend them; whereas they did not care one farthing where I lodged, provided I paid for what I hired; but such is the superstitious dread the Chinese have of their mandarins. Our room was large; had two small unpapered windows to the north and west; no sunshine entered at them: in the middle of the roof was a very large aperture (four feet square or more) through which the freezing wind came eddying day and night. I was obliged to spread my thin bedding on a rough, stony, uneven floor—ground, for I cannot call it a floor. There were, indeed, two stout cushions given us, but they were of unequal thickness. I did not know how to adjust them. My Munshi, who was expert at these little operations, had not the complaisance to teach me or assist me, but took them on my first rejection for his own bed, though his bedding was much

s 2

thicker than mine; and besides that, he spread it on his large smooth box, helped out and lengthened with a chair or other contrivance. Neither did he quickly comply with my request of having proper cushions made for me, but suffered me to lie in this uneasy manner many, many nights. Every order, every transaction necessarily passed through him. He begged me not to speak much Chinese, or to seem to know the characters; it might bring him into great trouble. I thought this reasonable, and agreed to it. Consequently from the first everybody addressed themselves to me through him; and if at any time I did try to act independently I was referred to my Munshi, and begged to explain to him. I certainly spoke Chinese very imperfectly, nor was it likely I should improve if nobody would converse with me. I was accustomed only to the Peking pronunciation. I very well understood what the mandarins said, but the common vulgar Chinese at Lhasa, speaking the Szechuen dialect, using frequent cant phrases, provincialisms, and idiomatic expressions, pronouncing rapidly and slovenly, how could I possibly understand them readily? A Frenchman or other European will accommodate himself to a foreigner; will repeat a phrase, give an equivalent, or, according to his abilities, explain a word. Not so a Chinaman; if you misunderstand a single word the sentence is lost: he will neither alter it nor explain it. It is not for want of urbanity: he has not that custom: he immediately concludes that there is an invincible bar to your conversing with him. To this unaccommodating way was joined the unfounded prepossession that I was almost entirely ignorant of the Chinese language, so that with respect to speaking Chinese I laboured under great disadvantages at Lhasa.

My Munshi had at first, in a peevish manner, declared that he could not, and would not continue to teach me at Lhasa: he was afraid. I took him at his word, and though afterwards we had good and perfectly safe opportunities, and I believe that he was desirous of using them in order to improve himself in English; yet, as he made no overtures, I made none, and during the whole time we were at Lhasa we scarcely exchanged a single word in Chinese, or conversed on the subject of that language. He was so cross and unaccommodating and ill behaved, that I avoided all conversation with him as much as possible, in order that no quarrel might ensue. When we changed our lodging, and I had a room to myself, as I was at first ill of a rheumatic fever, and ate nothing scarcely, we were separate the whole day, and I afterwards continued the custom of taking our meals separately. We lived on good terms. He used every evening after my supper to come into my room and sit awhile with me, and ask me to explain a few English phrases to him, which I always did with the greatest readiness. I read Chinese by myself. He saw me sometimes turning over one of their inconvenient dictionaries, and labouring hard for what he could have furnished me with in an instant. I could see that he thoroughly understood our relative situation, my reserve and alienation; but how could I subject myself to the humiliation of a refusal or improper answer to a request that I had morally a right to put to him authoritatively? He should have asked me whether I wished to continue my studies with him. The smallest concession on his part would have brought me to amicable terms. I had lent a little Chinese novel to a Chinaman at Giansu, who took care to forget to return it; and though my Munshi wrote to him, and we knew that the letters reached him, he had the incivility to keep it, and not answer the letters. This was a great vexation to me, as it was a book which had been recommended to me. I brought it with me on purpose to read it at Lhasa. It would have amused me, and improved me in the Chinese idiom. I had no other familiar work with me but what I had read over and over again.

We went the following morning to pay our respects to the two head Thalungs[1] in their tents. We sat down on cushions and drank *suchi*. They asked me whether our lodging was convenient. This was a good opportunity of intimating that it was rather cold, and that I wished to hire another. They made some civil answer in words, of course, which neither bound them nor me to anything, saying I had better rest a little while; that they would provide me another, and pay for it. I wished to be explicit on that point, and to let them know that I intended to pay for whatever I had; but somehow my Chinaman was backward in explaining my wishes, and now seemed to be furnished with a new dread of changing without consulting the mandarins and magistrates, though I am

[1] The four principal Tibet magistrates at Lhasa have the title of Thalung. This word is used both by the natives and by the Chinese.—T. M.

sure, from the Thalung's manner, that he would have had no objection to my hiring a lodging; only thought himself bound to make a faint offer of publicly providing everything for me I wanted.

I inquired of the Thalung when it would be proper for me to salute the Grand Lama. He said I had better first rest and refresh myself a few days. This was very agreeable to me. I was muddled and dirty. My face and forehead, having been exposed to the scorching sun during our eight days' journey from Giansu, were fiery red, particularly on the right side, so as greatly to disfigure me. Besides, I wanted a little time to prepare and brush up my presents. We employed part of the interim in presenting ourselves before various mandarins and magistrates.

At two or three miles' distance from the town were stationed soldiers and three military mandarins. The highest of them asked the question whether I had ever been at Canton. I said to my Munshi, "What shall I say?" He answered for me, No; I had never been there. I was inclined to speak the whole truth from the first, and declare myself an Englishman, for I had been guilty of no offence; but Munshi earnestly dissuaded me from it. Perhaps he was right. The second of these said military mandarins was of the same rank as the general at Giansu, and was a relation of his. He was very civil and polite: he invited me to sit down, and ordered tea to be brought me. My Munshi seemed mad as the devil that I should be invited to sit down and he not. The mandarin was inclined to converse and ask questions. Munshi gave such snappish monosyllabic answers as really alarmed me. I could not have thought that his ill temper could so entirely get the better of him. If he had gone there alone he would not have sat down. I was a foreigner, appeared as a respectable character; was his superior in age; was entitled to respect from my beard. I cannot see that he had any plausible grounds of offence and discontent. I only presume that his sudden fit of rustiness and ill humour was occasioned by the circumstance I mention, as it came on the moment I was seated. I took no notice of it to him then nor afterwards, nor he to me. He recovered by degrees while riding home.

CHAPTER VI.

VISIT TO THE GRAND LAMA.

ON the 17th of December, 1811, in the morning, I ascended the mountain, as they phrase it, to salute the Grand Lama and make my offering. I had but a trifle to present him with, not much more than a third part of the fine broadcloth I had destined for him, and that portion I had with the utmost difficulty, and by conveying it secretly into my Munshi's box, saved from the rapaciousness of the Bhutanese. Two pair of china ewers that I meant to decorate with (artificial) flowers, and present him, were unfortunately left behind at Giansu. I had a pair of good brass candlesticks which I had cleaned and furbished up, and into them I put two wax candles to make a show. To speak the truth, these candlesticks belonged to the East India Company. They were what were lent me for my use at Canton, and upon leaving that place I had honestly left them to be returned to the stores. But afterwards my faithful old China servant, taking the opportunity of a parcel that was sent me from Canton to Calcutta, stowed them into the box with other things that he thought might be useful to me, and I, finding they were thus forced upon me, carried them off with me to Lhasa without scruple, and I am persuaded that after this my acknowledgment, the Honourable Company will not only acquit me of fraudulent practices, but will be very well pleased with what has befallen their candlesticks, and with the high and honourable use I made of them. I had intended to offer the Grand Lama a sum of silver in the coin of Tibet, but was told that the small sum I could offer him, unless it was in foreign coin, would not make a handsome appearance. Luckily, I had with me thirty new bright dollars which, with as many pieces of zinc, I carried about with me for the purpose of showing galvanic experiments. Upon showing these at Giansu the Chinamen were eager to buy them as belt ornaments, and I found that a few of them would be considered as a handsome offering to the Grand Lama. Accordingly I allotted twenty for that purpose, and six for the Tí-mu-fu, or Hu-lu-tu, which are names given to the head magistrate, or king, as he is sometimes called, of Tibet.[1] This Tí-mu-fu is a Lama: he ranks above the Tajin or head Chinese mandarins, though they take every opportunity of encroaching upon his dignity, and in fact treat him as an equal. Besides these, I had some genuine Smith's lavender water, with which I filled two large handsome phials for the Grand Lama and one for the Tí-mu-fu. I had also a good store of Nankin tea, which is a rarity and a delicacy at Lhasa, and not to be bought there.

We rode to the foot of the mountain on which the palace[2] is built, or out of which, rather, it seems to grow; but having ascended a few paces to a platform, were obliged to dismount. From here to the hall where the Grand Lama receives is a long and tedious ascent. It consists of about four hundred steps, partly stone steps in the rocky mountain, and the rest ladder steps from story to story in the palace. Besides this, from interval to interval along the mountain, wherever the ascent is easy, there are stretches interspersed, where the path continues for several paces together without steps. At length we arrived at the large platform roof, off which is built the house, or hall of reception. There we rested awhile, arranged the presents, and conferred with the Lama's Chinese interpreter. This interpreter was not an absolute stranger to us; he had been to visit us at our lodging. He was a Chinaman by the father's side and a Tibetan by the mother's. He had resided many years at Peking and in Chinese Tatary. He spoke many languages, but having never learned to read or write in any one, was utterly unlearned. He was a strange, melancholy man, severe in his manner, and extraordinarily sparing in his words, except when he made a narration or continued speech, and then he was equally profuse. Whether it was avarice or poverty I do not know, but notwithstanding he had a

[1] This is the Gesub Rimboché of Bogle and Turner, and the Nomenkhan of Huc. The Pundit of 1866 says that this dignitary was formerly chosen from among the Lamas of four monasteries round Lhasa, called Kontyaling, Tankyaling, Chumuling, and Chuchuling; but that now he is chosen from the Dibong monastery only. (See note at p. 130.)

[2] Potala.

good place, he seemed straitened in his circumstances. They say he lavished his money on women; for though he had the title of Lama and wore the lama dress, he was not bound to celibacy. He had a wife and son.

The Tí-mu-fu was in the hall with the Grand Lama. I was not informed of this until I entered, which occasioned me some confusion. I did not know how much ceremony to go through with one before I began with the other. I made the due obeisance, touching the ground three times with my head to the Grand Lama, and once to the Tí-mu-fu. I presented my gifts, delivering the coin with a handsome silk scarf with my own hands into the hands of the Grand Lama and the Tí-mu-fu. While I was ketesing, the awkward servants contrived to let fall and break the bottle of lavender water intended for the Tí-mu-fu. Of course, I seemed not to observe it, though the odoriferous stream flowed close to me, and I could not help seeing it with the corner of my eye as I bowed down my head. Having delivered the scarf to the Grand Lama, I took off my hat, and humbly gave him my clean-shaved head to lay his hands upon. The ceremony of presentation being over, Munshi and I sat down on two cushions not far from the Lama's throne, and had *suchi* brought us. It was most excellent, and I meant to have mended my draught and emptied the cup, but it was whipped away suddenly, before I was aware of it. The Lama's beautiful and interesting face and manner engrossed almost all my attention. He was at that time about seven years old: had the simple and unaffected manners of a well-educated princely child. His face was, I thought, poetically and affectingly beautiful. He was of a gay and cheerful disposition; his beautiful mouth perpetually unbending into a graceful smile, which illuminated his whole countenance. Sometimes, particularly when he had looked at me, his smile almost approached to a gentle laugh. No doubt my grim beard and spectacles somewhat excited his risibility, though I have afterwards, at the New Year's festival, seen him smile and unbend freely, while sitting myself unobserved in a corner, and watching his reception of various persons, and the notice he took of the strange variety of surrounding objects. We had not been seated long before he put questions to us which we rose to receive and answer. He addressed himself in the Tibet tongue to the Chinese interpreter; the Chinese interpreter to my Munshi; my Munshi to me in Latin. I gave answer in Latin, which was converted and conveyed back in the same manner. I had been long accustomed to speak Latin with my Munshi. There was no sentiment or shade of sentiment we could not exchange. Thus, though the route was circuitous, the communication was quick, and the questions and answers delivered with an accuracy which I have reason to believe seldom happens in Asia when interpreters are employed. The Lama put the usual questions of urbanity. He inquired whether I had not met with molestations and difficulties on the road; to which I promptly returned the proper answer. I said I had had troubles, but now that I had the happiness of being in his presence, they were amply compensated. I thought of them no more. I could see that this answer pleased both the Lama and his household people. They thus found that I was not a mere rustic, but had some tincture of civility in me. A small present of dried fruits was brought and set before me. They motioned to my servant to take it off, and we withdrew. For withdrawing it is not the custom to use any ceremony, other than not turning the back upon the prince until after two or three steps, and even this is not essential, I believe. Upon going out of the hall into the area the interpreter bid us sit down a moment under the gallery while he went back to speak to the Grand Lama. He returned, and asked me if I had anything particular to say to the Lama. I answered, I had a request to make. I begged of the Grand Lama to give me books respecting his religion and ancient history, and to allow one of his learned lamas who understood Chinese to assist and instruct me. Whether my Munshi was not earnest enough, or whether it was the fault of the interpreter, or whether it was that the Lama or his people did not like to comply with this request, I know not; but the Lama afterwards presented me with what he told me was the most essential part of their prayers and meditations. I could get no other books, nor anyone to explain to me and instruct me. The answer the Lama sent me was rather indefinite. At present he had no proper copy of what books he wished to give me. He would have one prepared and delivered to me afterwards. I was extremely affected by this interview with the Lama. I could have wept through strangeness of sensation. I was absorbed in reflections when I got home. I wrote this memorandum (see great book).[1]

I strove to draw the Lama; and though very inexpert with the pencil, I produced a beautiful face, but it did not satisfy me. I drew another which I could not make handsome, yet there was in some respects a likeness in it which the other wanted. From the two together, and instructions from me, a skilful painter might make a good picture of him.

I had now a great many applications made to me as a physician. As I took no fee, people came with the most trifling complaints, and some invented a complaint, perhaps merely to have a lounge and see me. It was great trouble. I was obliged to give every one something, and the making up of so much physic was a heavy burden upon me. There was a great mandarin who had been long unwell, and unable to discharge the duties of his office. He was a little insane, his servants said. They wished me to see him. I found him not a little insane, but good humoured. He was uncombed, unwashed, beslimed with his own spittle and dirt, storming and scolding, and almost intractable. I was very ready to attend him as physician. If I could make a cure of him, my Munshi said, it would be nothing to ask him to get me admitted to Peking: he was of a great and rich family. His servants also said, if I could cure him I might have whatever I asked for, and a grand Chinese title bestowed upon me; but first it was necessary to ask the Tatar mandarin whether he approved of my being called in. Now, the Tatar dog and the crackbrained mandarin were bitter enemies. The Tatar wished for nothing better than the death of the other. He was applied to. He said, as I did not profess myself certain of curing him, it was better not to make the attempt. He neither gave his consent nor refused it, I believe; so the mandarin's servants begged of me to visit their master by night. They would send me a horse and guide. The mad mandarin seemed rather to take a liking to me; he had me sit down, ordered tea for me, told me long unintelligible stories, and when I offered to go was uneasy,

[1] From great book: 1st Dec., 17th of tenth Moon. This day I saluted the Grand Lama! Beautiful youth. Face poetically affecting; could have wept. Very happy to have seen him and his blessed smile. Hope often to see him again.—T. M.

and bid me sit awhile. Sometimes he broke out into exclamations against his servants, and ordered them out of the room. They treated him very ill, I thought; they laughed at him in his hearing, and made various irritating speeches to him for the pleasure, it seemed, of hearing him storm. Sometimes he broke out into invectives and abuse against the Tatar, and ordered his imaginary attendants to take him and kill him. I found he had not a single trusty servant or attendant about him. His nearest friends were foolish young serving men. It was difficult to give him physic; and the ignorance and stupidity of these men made it the more so. If he had had an old woman about him I could have managed better. After I had attended him two or three times, his people thought him better. I thought so too: he was more composed, and his eyes were less wild. I gave him then a few grains of calomel, but I could not make out from his stupid people whether he had taken it or not. They said he had, but as no effect ensued, I did not believe them. I gave him another small dose, and upon that his mouth was affected. To see what might be the cause, I made them give him physic in my presence, and found that they suffered him to retain a part in his mouth and leave the rest at the bottom of the cup. A few grains of calomel rubbed against the palate with the tongue will quickly excite soreness of the gums. His gums swelled and bled a little, and he had a slight salivation. He was cast down, and much quieter than before. His servants were now afraid of giving him more physic. I did not press it. I still continued to visit him—by stealth, if in the daytime—stepping into another near house first, and sending to inquire if any of the Tatar's spies were about the premises, waiting till they were gone, when an accident put an end to my attendance.

A Chinaman under confirmed dropsy had applied to me. I administered calomel, and two or three small doses of digitalis. The swelling somewhat subsided; his health and spirits were better.

One morning his boy came to our lodging, just as we were going out, and said something to our servant, who did not explain it to me. I thought he came to inquire whether there was any physic for his master, as he was an idle lad, frequently moving backwards and forwards between my lodging and his master's. I was that day going out to the military show I have before mentioned, to see plays acted. There was a large temple at the station, dedicated to the God of War; and after the Chinese exercises were over, it was customary to make certain thank-offerings in this temple, and act plays before it. It was also considered as a sort of farewell to that portion of Chinese soldiers whose time of foreign service was expired, and who were in a few days to leave Lhasa in order to return to their native country. Here I stayed all day, some of the minor mandarins inviting me and my Munshi to partake of their dinner, which was excellent. When I came home in the evening I was taken unwell. I was feverish, and had pain in my limbs. I had been too much exposed to the cold, and had sat with my ears uncovered the whole day. I was obliged to go to bed. Presently after comes the sick man's boy again, begging me to go to his master. Now I heard what I ought to have been told in the morning. The sick man had that morning found himself much better, and had indulged himself in eating an enormous quantity of beef. This beef disagreed with him, and he was in great pain and uneasiness. This was the story of the morning. If the case had been stated to me I should have gone to him immediately. Now I was in bed, ill. It was night and cold. The very action of rising and dressing myself in my cold exposed room would be hazardous for me. What to do I did not know. To go to him was impossible; to give him anything strong without first seeing him I dared not. I considered that above twelve hours had elapsed since he had eaten this beef. I thought a moderate dose of calomel was the best thing I could send him. I had no rhubarb by me. The next morning, as the barber was shaving my Munshi, I being still in bed, he informed us the man was dead. I was very much vexed, though I had nothing on my conscience. I did not inquire into particulars. I believe he had risen in the night and the exertion was too great for his strength.

When I got up I went, by appointment, to visit the crazy mandarin, calling first at the house of rendezvous. The master of it, who was one of my patients, said nothing about his complaints. I understood him at once. He did not wish to have any more of my physic. This was very well. He was above sixty, paralytic, growing blind, and, in short, having all the infirmities of age coming on. Such a patient could do me no credit, nor could I do him much service. This man had a beard of about an inch and a half long, consisting of about twenty or thirty hairs. He was never a minute without feeling and adjusting this trifling appendage to his chin. He had a comb perpetually suspended at his breast, which every now and then he applied and drew through the spare hairs without any resistance. These short hairs would no more entangle than the five fingers of his hand; but this was his constant occupation. He must have thought me very neglectful of my long tangling beard. He never saw me touch it, except by accident; and as for comb, I did not carry one about me. After I had sat here a little while, one of the crazy mandarin's servants came, and said I could not see his master that morning; the head servant was out, and the others dared not act without his being present. This again I understood, and was glad to find an opportunity of discontinuing my visits. Though I was afterwards sent for when the effects of the calomel in his mouth were over, and they found he was not hurt, yet I never would go again. He needed physic; but he had no friend, no good attendant. They neither knew what to give him to eat nor drink, nor how to administer the most trifling medicine. About a month after I heard he gradually grew worse and worse, came to the last stage of derangement, and not long after died. His guilty conscience accused him during his illness. In his mad fits he confessed the bribes he had taken, mentioned the sum, and offered to restore it. As the story of these bribes is rather curious, and the events connected with them had considerable influence at Lhasa, I shall relate the whole according to the best information I could obtain.

CHAPTER VII.

STORY OF THE RIOT—EXECUTION OF A GOOD MANDARIN.

THE year before I visited Lhasa, a Chinese soldier had a dispute with a lama about the right to pass the bridge without paying toll. The lama was the bridge-keeper, and refused to let him pass —pushed him back, perhaps. A scuffle ensued. The Chinaman drew his sword and stabbed the lama, so that he died of his wounds. Now, to kill a lama is heinous in Tibet. Murmurs and discontent arose; and one evening a very large body of lamas (who were joined by others) proceeded to a street where lived a number of Chinese shopkeepers, broke down and dismantled about forty shops, and laying hold of one unfortunate Chinaman, who for some cause or another had neglected to get out of the way, stoned him to death. The matter was now serious indeed. The murder of a Chinaman by a Tibetan might call down heavy vengeance from the Chinese government. The Tibet mandarins dreaded having the affair represented to the Emperor. They exerted themselves to bribe the great mandarins to hush it up. They succeeded with the three principal ones—with the Tatar, with the afterwards crazy mandarin, and with another since deposed and degraded—but failed with the fourth. This fourth, according to the Chinamen, had an excellent character; was the only upright mandarin in Lhasa. He was, they say, a really learned man, and was raised to his rank solely by his merit. This mandarín declared that a riot of this nature could not be passed over unrepresented to the Emperor in other than its true colours. The Tibet magistrates had hired or trepanned a poor fellow to have his head shaved and assume the dress of a lama, and to be given up as the culprit who had occasioned the death of the Chinaman. When this supposititious culprit was brought before the upright mandarin, he declared it was a mockery, and refused to go through the business. He would not sign his name to the papers that the other three sent to

Peking, but declared that he would stand alone and himself represent the matter faithfully to the Emperor. What was to be done? This was dangerous to the others. Would they come over to the side of truth? No; the bribes prevailed, and they conspired against the life of this upright magistrate. They suborned some wretched Chinaman to depose that he lent out the public money at interest. He was treasurer. They accused him to the Emperor in the most aggravating manner, as if he was the occasion of discontents at Lhasa, and they stopped and suppressed the letters he sent to Peking. It is said the Tatar was the chief instigator, and persuaded the other two to lend their names. The Emperor in wrath sent an order for his immediate execution. The soldiery and the Chinamen were in consternation. He was beloved, they say, and universally esteemed. They petitioned for him in a body, but in vain: he fell a sacrifice by the hands of the executioner to intrigue and revenge. At Lhasa these scandalous proceedings of the mandarins greatly alienated the reverence of the Tibet people for the Chinese and Chinese government. It is said they were much more humble in presence of the Chinese a year or two ago than now. This humility and reverence may be brought back again, I suppose; no doubt it fluctuates, and depends on the character of the resident mandarin. The Emperor was soon informed of his error. The Szechuen Tsinto delivered in memorials on the subject. The Lhasa mandarins were accused. One was soon deposed and ordered to Peking, where he was utterly disgraced and stripped of his honours and titles, and reduced to the level of a common Chinaman. The Tatar was under continual apprehensions of being served the same. He had other charges against him besides this of disguising the riot and falsifying the character of the beheaded mandarin. He often bewailed his fate, and his apprehensions were not groundless; for the second or third month of my residence at Lhasa came the decree ordering him to give up his seals of office as soon as the mandarin should arrive who was to supersede him, and then to go immediately to Peking. The Chinese did not conceal their satisfaction at this decree; they hope and expect he will be disgraced and degraded as soon as he appears before the Emperor.

The above is the account given by the Chinese and collected by my Munshi. The story was related to me somewhat differently by Tibetans, of whom I afterwards made inquiries. They stated the dispute not to be about a bridge, but about something else that the Chinese soldier demanded, and for which he could show no licence. They said that it was notoriously true that the executed mandarin lent out the public money, and they believed that the after deposition of the second mandarin was not occasioned by the steps they had taken to get him condemned. Both these accounts may be true in the essentials. The executed mandarin very likely lent out the public money at interest, and yet his fault was aggravated to the Emperor, because he would not sign his name to their fictitious account of the riot. The Tibetans speak less unfavourably of the Tatar than the Chinese do. He is impartial, they say, in little causes and disputes between a Chinaman and a Tibetan. This conduct would naturally gain him the ill-will of the Chinese—who, being the master nation, no doubt wish to be on the right side in all appeals—and the good-will of the Tibetans. The Chinese say, he is severe and harsh with them, and favours the Tibetans, and there are stories that justify this accusation of excessive severity, whether Chinese or Tibetan. I never heard anyone speak positively well of him, or deny that he was a bad man. From everything I heard I could safely draw this conclusion: that the great mandarins at Lhasa were generally rogues and scoundrels.

Some say it was these transactions that first unsettled the senses of the mandarin, who afterwards grew crazy. He alluded to them in his illness, and was at bitter enmity with the Tatar. He abused him to his face when officially visited by him, and behind his back also. I have myself heard him more than once. I have mentioned before that he stated the sum he had received in silver: "I had but 300 taels; here, take them back," he frequently exclaimed. His share of the hush money, they say, was 300 taels, and three valuable cap-button jewels. Lhasa being a miserable place to live in, for a great mandarin to be sent there is considered a sort of banishment, and there seldom come any except culprits. The Tatar was a culprit at Canton. His successor, I hear, is likewise from Canton, and has there been guilty of some fault, though the Chinese give him a good general character. The crazy mandarin was a culprit. After he became insane, and grew worse and worse, the others advised the Emperor of it, and asked leave for him to go home. The Emperor answered, it was sham madness: he only was uneasy at being separated so long from his family, and anxious to get home; that he had not yet expiated his offence, and should stay three years longer. The answer arrived a few days after the poor man was dead.

It is very bad policy thus perpetually to send men of bad character to govern Tibet. It no doubt displeases the Grand Lama and Tibetans in general, and tends to prevent their affections from settling in favour of the Chinese government. I cannot help thinking, from what I have seen and heard, that they would view the Chinese influence in Tibet overthrown without many emotions of regret; especially if the rulers under the new influence were to treat the Grand Lama with respect, for this is a point in which these haughty mandarins are somewhat deficient, to the no small dissatisfaction of the good people of Lhasa. I myself have heard Lhasa men inveigh against them for their disrespectful deportment before him.

The Tatar mandarin, hearing that a great many Chinamen came to me for medical advice, signified his displeasure to his people; and though he did not forbid anyone to come, many were thus deterred, to my great relief; for now only such came as had any real complaint sufficient to justify them. My Tibet patients increased, and I was very successful, particularly in coughs, indigestion, and slight disorders of the eyes. Numbers of the monks are afflicted with indigestion and disorders of the alimentary canal, occasioned, as they themselves know, by feeding principally on parched barley flour. This parched barley flour they moisten in their cups with *suchi*, make up into a dough cake, and thus eat it in its crude state. A large quantity of it, I know by experience, is difficult to digest; besides, what the poor people get is often made of bad and blighted barley, and is doubly injurious. Disorders in the eyes are very frequent in Lhasa. Some attribute them to the cold winds, and to remaining too long in the temples. I think there is some other cause: something in the water or in the salt they use.

CHAPTER VIII.

RESIDENCE AT LHASA.

WE were not many days in Lhasa before I found we had spies about us. One day came several Chinamen from the tribunals, and among them a little mandarin. He was vastly civil, vastly inquisitive. One begged me to write a sentence for him in my character, which I willingly did. They made Munshi go over the whole story; where he came from, and what places he had passed through. As soon as they were gone I said they were spies; and the next day the little mandarin came again, and put more questions to Munshi, and confessed he was sent by the Tatar. Afterwards there used to come people, one man at a time, of evenings. Munshi received them in his room, while I sat quiet in mine. They would stay a most unreasonable time, and at coming and going, as if by mistake, open my door, and take a survey, to see if I conspired with anyone of nights. They never found anyone in my room; my patients I always bid come by day, and nobody else at that time visited me. I always knew by the opening of my door what sort of man Munshi had with him. Certainly my bile used to rise when the hounds looked into my room. Sarcastic speeches in English and Latin came to my tongue's end, but I was not sufficiently master of Chinese to turn them, without being gross. It was better for me, perhaps, to say nothing. When I observed to my Munshi, "You have had a spy with you this evening," he generally allowed it was true; but some of them, he said, came with friendly intentions, or simply to chat. I begged of him to beware of all night friends that stayed an unreasonable time. I believe he was very cautious.

The Tatar mandarin detested the Europeans. They were the cause, he said, of all his misfortunes. He frequently betrayed his apprehensions of me. Sometimes he said I was a missionary, and at other times a spy. "These Europeans are very formidable; now one man has come to spy the country he will inform others. Numbers will come, and at last they will be for taking the country from us." Though I passed for a Calcutta man, we could not conceal that Calcutta (in Bengal) was under the English. Ingelikus (English kingdom) was a detestable sound in his ears. The bright comet which had appeared for so many months was connected with my coming, and foreboded something bad, he thought. He inquired of the Lhasa astronomers whether it was visible in my country; they, either from ignorance or designedly, answered it was not. This information, I suppose, took a little weight off his mind. A story got about, and came to our ears more than once, that we were both of us to be examined by torture. Though I never for a moment apprehended being put to the question, yet the word was unpleasant, and it proved with what ill-will and jealousy we were viewed by one, at least, of the great mandarins. The other Tajin, we were told, sometimes joined with the Tatar in his invectives against the Europeans, and his suspicions of us, and sometimes softened his observations. The Tatar would have seen me executed with the greatest pleasure, I be :eve; and the other would have looked on without objection or remorse. The third mandarin (a great rogue) declared his opinion, sometimes, that we were not well treated to be thus examined and cross-examined; for my Munshi had been several times before the Tajin to be interrogated, though always with the appearance of civility; and after some days a paper was brought and shown him for his approval, containing the substance of his answers, his declaration of who he was, and where he had been. This was to be sent to the Emperor.

I being a foreigner the interrogations did not come directly to me, but my name and declaration of myself were included in them. Thus we were announced to the Emperor. Various were the reports as to the wording of this communication; some said it was a simple statement; others without aggravation; others said that Munshi was denounced as having left his country and fled to foreigners, and conspired with them. The fault they could lay hold of was his having left Canton, and gone to a foreign kingdom without leave. This in strictness is an offence, but the magnitude of it depends upon the good or ill-will of the mandarins who take cognizance of it. It is committed by thousands yearly, and the mandarins wink at it; but they have a rod in their hands, which they can use if they think fit. The mandarin at Giansu spoke of this emigration as a thing of course, and that could not be avoided. China was overstocked with men; employment full, and people would go where they could get a livelihood. If the mandarins at Lhasa had been good-natured, this flying the kingdom would not have been brought into question. Munshi might have been suffered to go back with me, with orders to return to Canton, or we might both have had our routes assigned, through Szechuen to Canton, for me to proceed from Canton to Calcutta. The second Tajin mentioned this sometimes in his conversations with Munshi. He said, "You had better not go back by Calcutta, and over the sea." Munshi confessed he had great horror of the sea, and should prefer going immediately to his own country through Tibet; but he had promised the Lama (meaning me) to come and return with him. These were the conditions: how could he leave the Lama to go back alone? The mandarin said, the Lama might go by Canton likewise. "But," says Munshi, "he is a foreigner; I thought it was contrary to *by*[1] (custom) for a foreigner to enter China." "Oh," says the mandarin, "that is nothing; that can easily be got over."[2]

Thus I had hopes of being invited (or ordered) to return by China; their jealousy, I hoped, might lead them to wish me not again to visit the passes of Bhutan, nor return by Nepal. I was asked sometimes by Chinamen whether I should return by Szechuen, and my Munshi had that question often put to him. Some thought I should return that way; others the way I came. I always answered cautiously: "Szechuen! oh, that is a long way about, and I am a foreigner!" For we could not always tell who were spies and who not; nor was it easy to penetrate into what the mandarins' real intentions and wishes were. They might have information from Canton, from the missionaries or others, that I had been there, for the purpose of entering China; and their civil speeches might be a snare laid for me. And here I must observe how unfortunately things turned out for me. To proceed

[1] *By*, approved usage, rites, &c.—T. M.

[2] The Asiatics enter China easily enough. It is only the Europeans that are strictly barred out.—T. M.

to Lhasa with design of getting into China was not altogether a hopeless errand. If there were many chances against me, there were some for me. Good-natured mandarins; success in administering medicine to some great personage; the introduction of the vaccine; favour with the Grand Lama; a douceur to some merchant or petty officer, and permission to travel with the Tibet merchants to Seling[1]—manœuvres, may be imagined, which would have favoured my design, and which, though not very probable, were possible. I was never confident of success. I had sufficient hopes to make the journey seem not unreasonable, and I ventured the trial.

The reports of the manner in which he was mentioned to the Emperor, though uncertain, made my Munshi very uneasy. He tried to get a sight of the recorded copy of the letter, but was unable. If he really was represented as a runaway, associating himself with foreigners, a decree might come ordering, or, at least, authorizing, his execution. Nor did he think it at all impossible that I might have the same fate. It would be strange for a foreigner to come to a place by permission, and afterwards, without having committed any offence, to be punished in that manner. But the Tatar was a strange man; had already at Lhasa done strange things; not only the persecution and execution of the upright mandarin, but many other unreasonable actions. He hated the English and all that were in any way connected with them. If he had the power put into his hands, who could say that he would not use it; and what resource could I have? All this was very true, and very unpleasant.

I never could, even in idea, make up my mind to submit to an execution with firmness and manliness. The sight of the despotic pomp of mandarins at Canton, where I was perfectly secure, has almost turned me sick. What I read of their absolute power, not only in China, but in various Asiatic countries, has always appalled me. I put myself in imagination into the situation of the prisoner accused; I suppose myself innocent; I look round; I have no resource, no refuge; instruments of torture, instruments of execution are brought by florid, high-cheeked, busy, grinning, dull-hearted men; no plea avails; no kind judge to take my part, as in England, but, on the contrary, because I am accused (and

[1] Sining.

perhaps by my judge) I am presumed guilty. They harshly and inequitably examine, not to discover whether I be guilty or not, but in order to force out the conclusion that I am guilty. I am before evil-minded men, void of conscience, who proceed according to the forms, and violate the spirit of justice—no honest jury, who will incline to mercy when the man's character is good, and when the imputed crime is not heinous in its own nature, but only by the accidental regulations of society. If one is before a generous-minded man, who is wantonly exercising his power, one may appeal to what is noble in his nature, and excite a flame that will dissipate his malice and dark suspicions; but these evil-minded men, who outwardly are perfect politeness, and inwardly are perfect selfishness, have no touchwood in their heart; nothing for the spark to catch hold of; one may as well strike fire against the barren sand as appeal to their hearts. This friendlessness, this nothingness of the prisoner is what sickens me to think of.[1] I had rather be eaten up by a tiger than fall into such a situation and be condemned. I own I push this dread too far. Death is death; the form ought not to make so great an impression; but this superstition, to which, perhaps, my mind is by its natural texture prone, has grown upon me by reading and meditation. I have often striven to rectify my sensations, often, often, at Lhasa; but the associations are too strong to be thoroughly disengaged, though I hope and believe I can so far master them as to be able to submit to any fate without acting like a coward. I mention my weakness in order to point out that the occurrences at Lhasa, those which I have already

[1] There are two other ideas which aggravate the uneasiness. First, the idea of possible loopholes to escape at, which, when tried, all fail, and yet cannot be given up, but still present themselves to the mind as possible; as when a child is detained by an ill-natured, grown-up person in order to be terrified, in a place with many outlets; he sees the way to escape and cannot give up the idea. He creeps to a door; the other is looking out of a window, or pretending not to think of the child; but in a moment with his long legs stalks up to him, and bars his exit with his hand against the child's breast. At another time he is absolutely on the threshold, almost free—he is pulled back by the coats. As often as he tries to escape, so often are his hopes dashed, and still the fictitious security and carelessness of the other delude him. Secondly, the idea of the apparent folly of losing his life in this manner may have been no folly. Balancing the object against the probable danger, it may have been a fair venture; but those who regret his loss will never think so. This he knows, and the idea is very painful.—T. M.

mentioned, and others which will hereafter appear in this narrative, were sufficient causes of uneasiness to me. I did not enter upon my journey without some apprehensions of danger. Bhutan was dangerous. Those who ought to know declared they would not, upon any account, trust themselves into the hands of the Bhutanese in the manner I was going to trust myself. These declarations made an impression on me. I balanced, I examined in my mind over and over again what the danger was. I concluded there was some, but not sufficient to justify me in abandoning my object, which was a moral view of China; its manners; the actual degree of happiness the people enjoy; their sentiments and opinions, so far as they influence life; their literature; their history; the causes of their stability and vast population; their minor arts and contrivances; what there might be in China worthy to serve as a model for imitation, and what to serve as a beacon to avoid.

The unpleasant reports and consequent uneasiness I have been describing belong to all that period of our residence at Lhasa, from a few days after our arrival, to the receipt of the Emperor's answer to the mandarins' report of us. I shall now go back and narrate in order such other events as occurred worthy of notice.

I had at my first coming signified that I gave my advice and medicines gratis in all cases except for certain specified diseases; for these I would be paid twenty coins. This I let them suppose was on account of the dearness of the medicines to be used in these cases. I had but my sitting, sleeping, and eating room to receive my patients in, and they came at all times in the morning. Some applied with whom I began a course. They did not pay me the first day. I supposed they had not the money ready in their pockets. But after two or three days, finding nothing forthcoming, upon my explicitly declaring that I had not changed my plan, they dropped off. One man, after three or four days, brought me three coins wrapped up in a piece of paper. This I refused, telling him he knew it was not according to my conditions. He remonstrated, saying he would pay me as his case proceeded; that it was very hard to pay before-hand. I said I did not take money for the cure. I would have twenty coins first; cured or not cured, it was the same. He asked me if I was certain I could cure him. I said I was not. Then he continued his remonstrance in a tone of murmur and dissatisfaction which began to be very disagreeable. I told him I had no ways injured him; if he thought fit to be off he was welcome to the physic he had taken. I should not receive anything for it. I did not at all wish for patients of that sort. He might go to some other physician, and act as if I was not at Lhasa. No: he wished to go on with my medicines; but I was very hard. The more gentle and forbearing I was, the more impertinent he grew. He began to thump the table and push the money towards me, appealing to other Chinamen who were now come in, and who were listening to the dialogue. My Munshi was growing angry. So was I. At last he struck or pushed the table with a violence that endangered the oversetting a box containing phials of medicine, and various pills. I could bear it no longer. I snatched up his dirty paper of money, flung it out of the door, and bid him go after it. He turned pale with anger; he advanced towards me in a menacing manner. I was on my legs in a moment and fronted him firmly. I told him if he came near me with his insolence, by heaven! I would knock him down. I believe I spoke English or Latin in my anger; but he pretty well understood me; he faltered, and was glad, I believe, to have the other Chinamen interfere. One laid hold of him, another fetched him the money. The most respectable among them came to me, begged me to be pacified and to sit down, which I did. The man poured out a torrent of abuse against me and my Munshi, very little of which I understood. They soon had him out of the room. As he passed my window he renewed his abuse, and dropped a word or two about going to the mandarin. But in this my Munshi, who was now completely angry, meant to be beforehand with him.

I afterwards found that my conduct was considered as very bold; to fling a Chinaman's money out of the door: I not being a Chinaman. My Munshi did not blame me: he said it was going too far. I said I had borne him with the greatest patience and good humour, but the more I forbore the more insolen the grew. It was not in a European's nature to forbear further than I did. I do not think that my boldness (if boldness it was, for really I saw none in it) did me any harm. The story was soon known to all the Chinamen in Lhasa, I suppose; and I have heard one tell it to another adverting to me with marks of respect. Those who were eye-witnesses clearly saw that I was not afraid of the man, but should give him as good as he brought, if he had the insolence to touch me; and they certainly did not think the less handsomely of me for that. I never afterwards had any fracas at Lhasa with any man, Chinese or not.

The next morning my Munshi went to complain of him at the tribunal. The sub-mandarin said it was too small an offence to be punished; that he would admonish the man privately, and order him to come and ask our pardons. Whether ordered or not the man never came, nor was I at all desirous that he should. I saw no more of him.

A soldier and his wife occupied two rooms contiguous to ours; his time was expired, and he was one of the party about to return to China. We agreed to take these two rooms as soon as he went, and after some altercation with the woman of the house (who was a cross-patch), and a reference to the Thalung, we hired them at the same easy rent as the soldier lived under, viz. four coins (2*s.* 8*d.*) per month. The whole building, in fact, belonged to the magistrates, only the woman who had the care and management of it had the privilege of taking a small rent. We continued on our great room as hitherto, and which we afterwards exchanged for a smaller one, close to the two others, to the mutual accommodation of the woman of the house and ourselves. My Munshi and I had now each of us a room to ourselves, but I was obliged for a long time still to lie on the hobbly floor, as my bedstead, though boarded in the middle, was now built up with mud, which dried very slowly, and I was afraid to lie in it while any dampness remained. I opened a window to the south, which my predecessor, from some superstitious motive, had blocked up. The sun now for a month or two shone in upon me good part of the day; but afterwards, as the spring advanced, coming into the south higher and higher, his rays fell shorter and shorter on my floor; and before April arrived, as the wall was thick and the window had a small penthouse over it, he entirely ceased to appear for a single moment in my room. I was unwell during the time our new rooms were getting ready. Munshi and the servant were very busy for two or three days, plastering and papering up the rents and bad places. As they prepared the room for me so I took it, never afterwards making any alterations or adorning it, though it was still in a miserable, tattered condition. Not so my Munshi: he embellished his in various ways, until it reminded me of a little milliner's back parlour. A glass here, something suspended by a ribbon there; over all a watch, seal, and ribbon hung gracefully on a little peg. The Chinese are very fond of little decorations, and very dexterous in disposing them nattily. I had a small sextant with me, and an excellent timepiece watch, and I much wished, now the sky remained clear and cloudless, to take a few observations; but the aperture of my window was too small, and I was too subject to interruption. Our lodging had indeed a commodious flat roof, where I could have taken them easily enough; but it would have been madness in me to suffer anyone to see me looking at the heavens through an astronomical instrument. I might perhaps in the night time have observed some of the stars without being observed myself, but it was hazardous, besides I was now very ill with the acute rheumatism, fits of which came on every evening, and lasted until towards morning. There was nothing I could do for geography that would compensate the risk I must run. It was not for the sake of finding the latitude and longitude of Lhasa that I wished to take observations, for they are pretty well ascertained; but for the sake of regulating my watch, and having a point to set off from, in case I should go towards Szechuen, whereby I might determine nearly the situation of some of the principal towns on the road.

In the daytime, when these rheumatic fits had subsided, my general health seemed pretty good, and I trusted for many, many days that my constitution would of itself shake off the complaint; but I was forced at last to have recourse to medicine. Camphor and opium pills seemed greatly to relieve me. Antimony I thought serviceable. I took a dose of Dover's powders, after which I was much better; yet, I do not know whether to attribute my amendment to the medicine, as it operated under circumstances peculiarly unfavourable. It is highly proper after taking Dover's powders to drink plentifully of diluting liquor. I took my dose before the fit came on, and after a short time went to bed. I ordered my half-caste Tibet lad to bring me rice gruel. He brought me two or three small basins full; after which he absolutely and obstinately refused to obey my calls. I repeated these calls twenty or thirty times, raising my voice until I could be heard over all the neighbourhood. I began now to be in a perspiration; partly from anger I believe, and partly from the medicine. My Munshi thrusts his head in at my door with a cross and discontented countenance, and tells me, with a peevish accent, that the servant said I had had enough! I told him I had taken medicine, and judged I had not drank enough; that I was in a perspiration, and loath to get up; but, if I was forced to it, I would give the fellow a good beating. "You can't strike anyone here in Lhasa." "Can't? Oh, we will see."—"You can't," with angry accent. "But I will beat him."—"You can't."[1] These words we bandied about for a minute or two. I sometimes singing or chanting my responses, and he mocking me as closely as his choking anger would permit him. What a kind friend I had in my illness! After he was gone, I continued for some time to call the servant; but finding it in vain, I slipped on my robe, and walked out into the kitchen. There were both the servants cowering over a pan of embers: not gone to bed. I stepped up to the Tibet lad who ought to have answered my call, and fetched him a box on the ear that roused him presently. He started up and ran away. It was too cold, and I too unwell to run after him. I addressed myself to the Chinese, and sharply remonstrated with him for his brutality. I told him if he did not immediately make me something warm I would turn him away the next morning; that I knew what I was saying, and he might depend upon it I would be as good as my word. Then I went back to bed. I heard them afterwards unbar the gate, and go out, so I suppose they were short of water. They soon brought me tea in plenty.

I took no notice to Munshi of his beastly, mulish behaviour. Long, long after I had occasion to say something in praise of the Tibet fellow. I observed that he was not sulky; that after receiving a scolding he was more attentive and well behaved. After I gave him that box on the ear, he was remarkably submissive next day, and ready to serve me. "When did you ever strike him!" exclaimed my Munshi, in great surprise. "Why," said I (affecting great coolness, and speaking in a tone as if I was telling him a story he was unacquainted with), "one night I had

[1] In Latin, he used the words "non potes." He ought to have said, "non licet." My response was, "at verberabo."—T. M.

taken physic, and wanted something to drink. I called him over and over again. He would not come near me. I got up, went to the kitchen, and fetched him a swinging box on the ear." Munshi did not answer a word. The servants, I suppose, had never mentioned the blow to him, and he had thought I had not dared to put in execution the threat I had repeated so often and so positively. Now at once he saw the whole in its true light; his own miserable peevishness no doubt came to his mind—for he was aware his temper was none of the sweetest—and he was ashamed. I turned the discourse to something else.

The season was now come when the Grand Lama annually retires from the world for a month or more, and devotes himself to religious exercises. The interpreter gave me notice, in order that I might see him before he withdrew from the public; but upon my telling him I should stay at Lhasa until the cold weather was over, he said I had better defer it until the Lama came out again. In the meantime I recover my health perfectly, and became rather happy, strong, and well. One of the Thalungs about this time wished me to see his mother, who had an ailment in her eyes. I went with my Munshi. We were received into a handsome room, where I sat *vis-à-vis* with the dame for half an hour. She was still young, plump, and rather handsome, and her face was washed clean. She had a profusion of pearls on her head. Munshi said they were real pearls. I thought from their multitude they must some of them be artificial. Her female attendant stood tittering and giggling about, turning away the pretty faces when I looked at them with a smile, and again looking on giggling when I closely inspected the dame's eyes. She had a slight speck gathering in one of them, and the other was a little clouded. She attributed it to staying too long at her devotions in the temple with the cold wind blowing about her; for she was very devout, and was about to withdraw the very next day, and retire to her chamber for a month's praying, recitation, and mortification. I told her I would send her a pill to take that evening, preparatory to a lotion for the eyes, which she might use during her retirement. She seemed to think it would be a breach of the rules of mortification to use medicine during that time. I tried to persuade her to the contrary. After I had drank my *suchi*, as she had presented me with two or three little baskets of dried fruits, I took my leave. I sent her the pill and the lotion, but I found afterwards that she never took them. I had not promised that I would cure her, and many of Lhasa, both Chinese and Tibetans, are unwilling to take medicine unless they are assured of receiving benefit from it. She satisfied her curiosity, if that was partly her motive for sending for me, and I was very well pleased with my visit. Just before this, I had two handsome, well-dressed, clean-washed lasses come to my lodging with their mother to consult me. I could not find out that there was anything the matter with them, except superabundance of health and spirits. It was so long since I had seen female charms of this order that feeling their pulses rather disordered my own. I asked them many questions—not troublesome ones. They laughed and giggled. What they answered I do not know. My Chinese servant was interpreter, and though he spoke fluently, and never hesitated at explaining anything that was put to him, he in fact understood very little of the Tibet language. I gave them all something very innocent, and after a few days they came again, and brought me a present of some excellent mutton. They were welcome to come as often as they liked, without bringing mutton or anything but their own pretty faces. I understood they were the family of a rich Tibet merchant.

One of the Dalai Lama's physicians requested me to see to him. He had an apartment in the palace. He sent a horse for me and another for my Munshi. We were conducted up the back of the mountain by a road, defended by a parapet wall, which winds up to the palace, and thus were saved the fatigue of ascending the mountain on foot. I found the physician in bed, supported by pillows. He had a stiff neck and back, which he could not straighten, a swelling in his knee, and general debility of body and mind. I found he had used fire for his neck. I gave him a Spanish-fly blister, which he praised, and said was of benefit. I gave him an oily mixture for an inward complaint, which speedily relieved him. But I found afterwards that he had taken only half of it, and that other medicines I sent him he absolutely refused to take, in spite of the remonstrances of his servants. He was childish, they said; he did not like the taste or the smell. I had used mint water: he did not like that. I advised him to drink a small quantity of wine every day. That advice he consented to comply with. I visited him three or four times. I had hopes of relieving him, and afterwards strengthening him with bark, of which I had a good store by me; but it was impossible in his case to make him up medicines that had no taste. I was compelled to leave him to himself. He said, he would try what prayers and recitations of the Lama would do for him, and afterwards send for me again. I saw no more of him. I sometimes inquired how he did, and was told he continued in the same weak, lingering way. Long afterwards, upon seeing one of his acquaintances, he occurred to my mind. "How is that physician?" He held out four fingers, and signified that he had been dead so many days. As it was perfectly well known that he did not take any of my medicines after the first dose, which was of real service to him, not the slightest blame was attached to me: it was lamented that he had been so childish as to see me and not trust himself to my care. I found that my patients often took the liberty of swerving from my directions. If there were two pills, they would take one perhaps, though they were utterly ignorant whether it was a strong or a weak dose. As for a course of alteratives, I scarcely ever could get anyone to continue it above two or three days. Cases of complaints came before me, some of which would no doubt have yielded to vitriolic acid or to mercury, but I could not cure them with a single pill. A few who had the sense to submit themselves entirely to my directions were completely cured, and acknowledged it with gratitude and thanks.

My money now was getting very low. I had written to Rangpúr for a supply, but so long a time had elapsed without an answer that I gave up all hopes from that quarter. I found it necessary to sell such articles of apparel and other things as I could spare. I sold some silk and crape I had brought with me, and which had escaped the hands of the Bhutanese. I sold some sheets, a piece of cotton cloth, gauze gowns, a belt with stone clasp, a large tea box, handkerchiefs, which I at first meant to have kept; a few empty bottles; two or three bottles of cherry brandy, which I had offered to the mandarins on my arrival and again on their birthdays, but which had not been accepted; a handsome opera-glass; a fan; in short, everything I could muster up, except the clothes I should probably want to use, and a few keepsake trinkets[1] that I was unwilling to part with. Thus I raised a reasonable supply of money, and reduced my baggage into a very small compass. I had informed the mandarins and others that I expected money from Calcutta. As it did not come, they knew I was rather straitened in my circumstances, and if at last I should be forced to borrow it would not seem strange. I managed so as to keep up a certain respectability; and though I was not invited anywhere to dinner (I do not know that it is the custom in Lhasa, besides I was considered as a Lama), wherever I went I was treated as a gentleman. I was glad to part with my foolish dawdle of a Chinese servant, who ate up four taels of silver for me per month besides his food, and this without being of any use. As he saw me selling off my things, and knew that my finances were low, he could not be dissatisfied or think that I treated the General's recommendation slightingly. I lent him a small sum of money, and he set up as a butcher, but he had neither sense nor diligence enough to thrive in any line. He spent the money idly and loosely, and soon gave up his new profession. Then he sold cakes and sweetmeats; but that did not answer. When all his money was gone, and his clothes becoming ragged, he took some opportunity of returning to his dear Szechuen, which he extolled as a paradise.

As soon as the Grand Lama came out from his retirement, I went again to salute him. He was pale and worse in health, I thought, for his seclusion. Nothing particular passed at this interview. I took care this time to drink of his excellent *suchi* as nearly to the bottom of the cup as propriety would allow. He made me a little present of rice and dried fruits. From his palace I proceeded to that of the Tí-mu-fu. The Tí-mu-fu received me very kindly, asked me many questions, and bid me come often. He has nothing of the prince in his manner, being I think rather vulgar, and laughing too often and too familiarly. He bears a good character, and I should judge him to be a very good-natured kind-hearted man. He gave me a bag of rice, and excused himself for having nothing better to offer me.

[1] I afterwards gave them to the Grand Lama and Tí-mu-fu as a New Year's offering. I had nothing else. I was loath to go empty handed, and was forced to sacrifice them.—T. M.

I have not yet visited the temples. I was very desirous of doing it, but could find no person to go with me who could properly explain things. My Munshi, too, was desirous that I should go, and obliquely asked me several times whether I intended it. I could not at first understand what his motive was; but upon my declaring my positive intention of going, he told me that the mandarins and one of the Thalungs and their understrappers had several times inquired of him whether I had yet paid my respects to ——.[1] The mandarins, he said, were aware that the Catholics refused to pay these respects; consequently, if I went it would wipe off their suspicions of my being a missionary. He could not go with me; he would not pay reverence to their saints if they were to kill him for refusing. This speech had quite a contrary effect on me to what he intended. I told him I did not know whether I should or should not; if it was expected of me, and if there were ceremonies to go through with the image, I certainly should not go, unless I found that they were considered as matters of course, and practised by the mandarins and others who professedly were non-believers in the religion of Tibet; that the respect I had always professed for their religion was sincere; that I had never by any word or action pledged myself to anything further, neither would I. I was very glad, after inquiring, to find that this reverence to the image was practised by the mandarins as a matter of course and pledged them to nothing.

Accordingly, one day I declared my intention of going next morning, and that I would take my Tibetan servant with me, having nobody better to attend me. No sooner was I ready and had stepped out of my room, but out popped my Munshi from his with a bunch of incense, which he whipped into the servant's hand. I had half a mind to go back, but conquered my disgust, and seemed not to see it. Then he asks me, "Have you got a scarf with you?"—"For what?" "To offer to the saint."—"Pooh!" says I; "I shall give no scarf nor anything else. I know nothing about it. I am a foreigner, and curious to see and learn everything.

[1] This is the name of their great saint, or religious lawgiver. I never could rightly make out his story.—T. M.
The word is not clearly legible in the manuscript. The great religious lawgiver of the Yellow Cap sect, to which the Dalai Lama belongs, was Tsonkhapa.

Any form and ceremony that is required I shall go through, and nothing further." I went to the temple; but it little answered either my purpose or my Munshi's. My servant, who from his childhood had been a neglected orphan, was ignorant as a beast. He was nominally a Muhammadan, but utterly ignorant even of his own religion. He so spleened me with his brutish ignorance and hoggish answers, that I could not help speaking crossly, and this before the images of the saints. There were hundreds of people in the temple; some gathered about me and seemed astounded at my irreverent manner. There were two large figures of women before the principal image. After I had made my salute to him, which consisted of one *kelese*, I asked about these figures. He returned the same general answer as for all the rest: he said they were saint images. I again exclaimed against his ignorance in a manner that did not befit the place. Some idle people laughed, and others stared. I was really angry and vexed to think how fruitless was all the trouble I took, and how impossible it was to get anything explained. I took no notice of the incense; my servant stuck it where he liked. I meant to have told my Munshi that the saint thanked him for his offering and hoped soon to see him in person, as he was better pleased with his attentions than with mine; but Munshi on my return never asked me a single question nor opened his lips on the subject. I heard him questioning the servant. I dare say he was not at all pleased with the account he heard.

In my way home I called in at a little Chinese temple, and also made the shrine a Chinese salute, for I was determined to show myself impartial to the saints. My servant seemed surprised. I asked a few questions of the Chinese sexton, but learned nothing curious. He offered to open other doors and show me all that was to be seen. I said I had no offering with me at present, and that I would defer it till another opportunity.

The next day I visited another large temple, but made no salutes or reverences. This was reported to Munshi by some Chinamen. They said what a strange thing it was that the Lama (meaning me) went to the temple without an offering, and without performing ceremony. No doubt my Munshi made out the best account he could for me to the Mandarin's people, and told them I had worshipped the saint in proper form. How delicate his conscience was! So anxious to damn my soul in order to shelter his own carcass! I had no more objection to bowing to the image than he had to a paper, a roll, or other missive coming from the Emperor. When I entered the temples in Bengal, if there were natives about, I always made a salam. All religions as they are established have a mixture in them of good and evil, and upon the whole they all perhaps tend to civilize and ameliorate mankind: as such I respect them. As for the common idea that the founders of all religions except our own were impostors, I consider it as a vulgar error. I have expressed this opinion long long before I had any thoughts of visiting Lhasa. But my Munshi, being a Roman Catholic, of course was utterly intolerant to all saints not in his own calendar. We are apt to think the Muhammadan religion eminently intolerant; but if it be fairly examined it will be found much less so than the Roman Catholic, both in practice and in principle.

The new year approached: the season of congratulations, pomps, and shows. If there was any little present I could make to the Grand Lama and the Tí-mu-fu on New Year's day I was told it would be acceptable.

Thus far written at Lhasa. The remainder from short notes taken at Lhasa and from memory.

CHAPTER IX.

FRAGMENTARY NOTES—RETURN JOURNEY.

THE Tibetans do not use the Chinese kalends: they have astronomers and a calendar of their own. Their year commences at the same time as the Chinese year, viz. the February new moon. Their astronomical tables and precepts come from Chaking, they say. If this be true, they are very old.[1]

Jan. 8 = 16th of twelfth moon. I visited the Lama and afterwards the Tí-mu-fu. He promised me books.

10th = 29th of twelfth moon. I visited the Lama unexpectedly, and he gave me sacred leaves wrapped up in yellow silk.

Feb. 12 = Chiz. New year.

As I wrote at the time, I have made observations which are incorrect, having been deceived. Example: I say, my servant took an opportunity of returning to Szechuen. He told me he was going, and mentioned some particulars. I afterwards found he had deceived me, and still loitered in Lhasa. Perhaps his coming to take leave of me was for the sake of a farewell present.

New year. I visited the Grand Lama on the last day of the year and on New Year's day, and gave him a telescope.

I determined to ask leave to go back with Munshi and to change our route, hoping to be asked to go by Canton.

[1] The Tibetans have derived their astronomical knowledge both from Indian and Chinese sources. The system formed on the Indian principle is called *Karsis*, and the mode of reckoning years in the Chinese manner is called *Naksis*. The common mode of reckoning time among the people is by the cycle of twelve years, in which each year is denominated from an animal, in the following order:

1. Mouse year.	4. Hare year.	7. Horse year.	10. Bird year.
2. Ox "	5. Dragon "	8. Sheep "	11. Dog "
3. Tiger "	6. Serpent "	9. Ape "	12. Hog "

In books they make use of a cycle of sixty years. The year is a lunar year, with intercalary months for periods of nineteen years, one month being inserted every third year. The year begins in February with the appearance of the full moon. The months are called the first, second, third, &c., months; each of thirty days.—'Csoma de Körös.'

But there are reasons why I must not expect to be asked *that*.

I went to ask leave.

Decree arrived.

Munshi goes again to see whether anything can be done to-day. Comes back in chains. I anxious.[1]

Grand Lama's kindness.

Glad when Munshi goes. Why? Because he writes to me. He comes again to see me. I give him note upon Elphinstone.

Mandarins send for me, and give me letters opened. "Are these yours?" Civil. Promise good news. Advised me to stay awhile.

Dread another decree! Dread missionaries at Peking. Dread something coming to light: that I have been at Canton. I am told the Thalungs say I am to go in a few days.

Visit a magistrate. He thinks I do his eyes good.

Apply again on the 19th. Strangely put off.

Sell my empty bottles.

Get my things in order, to be ready to set off.

Great cold again.

Strange fever and cough: think I am poisoned.

Visited by an Armenian, who wants to go with me. How can I?

12th, or 25th of second month. Ching Tí-mu-fu bids me stay until new Mandarin comes. Why? Uneasy.

2nd of third month. Very cold. Frost. Clear sky.

3rd. Visit the Lama. Ask to go. Go to Tí-mu-fu. Told I shall have good news in a few days. Snow.

4th. Snow remaining in the morning. Fine day.

5th. Go to temple. See three Thalungs, who give me silk and tea.

Munshi bribes the treasurer. Called upon by Chinamen after Munshi is gone.

Bhutan men would have the Pari-jong magistrate brought to Lhasa. Bhutanese at Lhasa show violence. Surrounded by soldiers. Obliged to lay down their knives.

[1] The Munshi was detained as a Chinese subject, while Mr. Manning was dismissed by the route he came. The story of the Abbé Huc about Moorcroft having been at Lhasa (p. 202) can scarcely refer to Manning's visit. It is, I suspect, a pure invention.

April 6. I took leave of the Grand Lama with a sorrowful heart. I said I would tell my king (Governor of Bengal) that I was well treated. His heart rejoices. I thank the Grand Lama, and promise that if afterwards a Lhasa man comes to Bengal it shall not be forgotten. I take leave of Tí-mu-fu. Sorrowful. Receive presents. Go to Tajin and Tay-Ye, but do not see them. Second Tajin gives me a scarf and a piece of stuff for a saddle carpet. Make up things. Rather sorrowful.

7th. Put off by the mandarins until after to-morrow.

Left Lhasa on the 9th of third moon (19th of April). Arrived at Pari-jong the 1st of May.

May 3. Attendants from Pari-jong left me. I then visited the magistrates.

May 22. Conference. Do they think I am a tradesman? How should I know the prices of things at Calcutta, or whether *this* cloth be prime or second?

23rd. My collar to be slipped to-morrow.

24th = fourth moon. Off about sunset, after another foolish conference. Four miles.

25th. Rapasay.

26th. Bída-Balk.

27th. Chazi (two kos).

28th. To Matakah.

29th. Dúmgong.

31st. Tazigong.

June 1. Village. Palm trees.

2nd. Open village.

3rd. Kantalbari.

5th. Linger on. I declare I will positively go to-morrow, even if on foot.

6th. I threatened to walk, and took up my bundle. They gave me a horse.

June 10, 1812. Reached Kuch Bahar.[1]

[1] He seems to have returned by the same way that he came—that of the Lakhi Dúar.

APPENDIX.

I.

Account of Travels of Johann Grueber, Jesuit.[1]

The Missioner set out for China, as we conjecture, in the year 1656. According to the first letter, he went from Venice to Smyrna by sea; from thence to Ormuz by land in five months; from Ormuz by sea in seven months to Makau.[2] There landing, he passed through China partly by water, partly by land, to Peking in three months. He stayed in China three years: in one of which, viz. 1660, he says the fifty-six Jesuits who were then in that empire baptized more than fifty thousand men.

In his return he took a road never perhaps attempted by any European before. Grueber left Peking in the month of June, 1661, in company with Albert Dorville, of the same society. In thirty days he came to Singan-fu,[3] and in thirty more to Sining-fu, crossing the Hoang-ho, or Yellow River, twice in the way.

Sining[4] is a great and populous city, built at the vast Wall of China, through the gate of which the merchants from India enter Katay or China. Here they stay till they have licence from the Emperor to proceed forward. The Wall at this place is so broad that six horsemen may run abreast on it without embarrassing each other. Here the citizens of Sining take the air (which is very healthful, coming from the desert), and recreate themselves with the prospect as well as other diversions. There are stairs to go a-top of the Wall, and many travel on it from the gate at Sining to the next at Sochew, which is eighteen days' journey. This they do by the Governor's licence, out of curiosity, having a delightful prospect all the way from the Wall, as from a high tower, of the innumerable habi-

[1] From Astley's 'Collection of Voyages,' vol. iv.

[2] Macao.

[3] The capital of Shensi, once capital of China.

[4] On the western frontier of Kansuh, towards Kokonor. It is difficult to account for the crossing of the Hoang-ho twice, between Singan and Sining. The maps also place the Great Wall at a distance of 15 geographical miles from Sining, and its continuation to Suchau in Kansuh appears to be broken by palisades. Besides, there is no evidence on the maps that the Wall runs southwards from Sining to Quangsi, Yunnan, and Tibet.

tations on one side, and the various kinds of wild beasts which range the desert on the other side. Besides wild bulls, here are tigers, lions, elephants, rhinoceroses, and monoceroses, which are a kind of horned asses. Thus the merchants view the beasts free from danger, especially from that part of the Wall which, running southward, approaches the more inhabited provinces of Quang-si, Yunnan, and Tibet, for at certain times of the year they betake themselves to the Yellow River and parts near the Wall, which abound with thickets, in order to get pasture and seek their prey.

This desert is partly mountainous and partly level, all over sandy and barren, excepting that in some places you meet with little rivulets whose banks yield good pasture. It begins in the middle part of India, and extends from south to north, but nobody ever yet hath discovered its bounds, which may stretch to the Frozen Ocean. Marco Polo calls this desert Lop, and speaks of its being haunted with spirits. But Grueber says nothing of them. The Tatars formerly called it Beljan, now Samo; the Chinese Kalmuk, others Karakathay. The Tatars, accustomed to deserts, dwell here in tents, removing with their cattle wherever they can find a river or place fit for pasture.[1]

The road from Sining as far as Lhasa is somewhat differently described in different letters. In the first we are told that Grueber, passing out of China, entered the sands of desert Tatary, which he crossed in three days. Afterwards he came to the banks of the Koko-nor, which signifies the Great Sea,[2] being a great lake or sea like the Caspian, where the Yellow River has its source.

Leaving this sea behind him, he entered into the country of Toktokay,[3] which is almost desert and so barren that it need fear no invasion. One meets with nothing but some tents of Tatars. It is watered by the Toktokay, a very fine river, whence it takes the name. It is as large as the Danube, but so shallow that it may be forded everywhere.

Thence, having crossed the country of Tangut,[4] he came to

[1] The beginning of the Desert of Lop, Gobi, or Shamo, *in the middle part of India*, is also unintelligible. The Chinese call this Desert Ko-pih, or Ta Ko-pih; also Sha-moh, and Han-hai, or Sea of Sand. Beljan (so called by Hayton the Armenian, see Yule's 'Cathay,' cxcvi.) may be a Turki name for it. Kalmuk is derived from the Mongol tribe of that name. Kara Kathay is Black Kathay, the old name for Mongolia.

[2] Kokonor does not signify *Great* Sea, but *Blue* Sea, and it is not the source of, nor connected with, the Yellow River, which rises in a distinct system of lakes.

[3] The *Toktonaï oulan mouren* is one of the superior affluents or sources of the Yang tse kiang, or Mouroui oussou ('Mag. Asiatique,' ii. 246, 282).

[4] Tangut is here applied to the high plateau of Tibet, north of Lhasa. (See Yule's 'Marco Polo, i. pp. 184, 186.)

Retink,[1] a very populous province belonging to the kingdom of Barantola,[2] whose capital is Lhasa, where at length he arrived.

According to the fifth letter, or Kircher's abstract, we are told that presently, after they had passed the Great Wall, they found a river stored with fish, on which they supped in an open tent. Then, crossing the Yellow River, they immediately entered that vast and barren desert of Kalmuk, inhabited by the Kalmuk Tatars (the Eluths or Tatars of Koko-nor), who rove up and down it to rob the caravans, and at certain seasons settle with their portable cities on the banks of the rivers. The Jesuits often met with their habitations in the road, and drew their figures, viz. a Kalmuk man, clothed with a leathern garment and yellow cap; a Kalmuk woman in a habit made of a certain skin of a green or red colour, each with a charm about their necks to preserve them from dangers; a Lama, that is one of their Tatar priests or bishops. They wear a white coat or cloak cast backwards, with a red girdle, and a yellow coat, from the girdle of which hangeth down a purse; their cap or hat is painted red. Their habitations are tents made with small sticks twisted or plaited together, and covered with a coarse woollen stuff bound together with cords.

From Sining they, in three months, entered the kingdom of Lhasa, which the Tatars call Barantola. The King is styled Deva,[3] or Teva, descended from an ancient race of the Tangut Tatars, resides at Butala, a castle built on a high mountain, after the European fashion, where he has a numerous court. The great priest of this country is called Lama Konju, and adored as a god. He resides at Barantola, and is the Pope of the Chinese and Tatars, called by them God the Father, whose religion in all essential points tallies with the Romish, although, says the author, no Christian ever was in the country before.

Here they stayed a month, and might have converted many of the natives, but for that devilish God the Father (as the author calls him), who puts to death such as refuse to adore him. However, they

[1] Retink; perhaps the district of the Jang *Railing* Monastery, about 45 miles north of Lhasa. (See map of route to Tengri Nor.)

[2] Barantola. Bourhan is a synonym of Buddha, according to Huc, ii. 115. Hence perhaps the name may mean "country of Buddha." Klaproth, in his notes to 'Della Penna,' asserts that Barontala in Mongolian means the right side, referring to Tibet. (See Yule's 'Marco Polo,' i. 193.) This also is in accord with the Mongolian Dictionary of Kovalensky.

[3] See Klaproth, "Description du Si Dzang ou Tubet," 'Mag. Asiatique,' ii. 212: "On nomme à présent le pays du Dalaï lama, indistinctement Tubet ou Tangut; . . . . le roy du pays est nommé *Diba*. . . . ." The Tepa Lama, who conducts the civil affairs for the Dalai Lama, appears to be the same as the Deva or Diba.

were kindly treated by the people and King, who was the brother of that God the Father.

In the Court of Deva, King of Tangut, they saw a woman, born in Hami,[1] in Northern Tatary, dressed in an unusual habit. She wore hair like knotted cords, her head and girdle adorned with cockle-shells. They saw likewise some women no less strangely dressed, who came from the neighbouring kingdom of Koin.[2] The ladies braid or curl their hair in the manner of hair laces or small bands, and twist it behind them. On their foreheads they wear a red fillet beset with pearls, and on the top of their heads a silver crown, bedecked with turquoises and pearls.

Grueber drew the pictures of the Grand Lama[3] (taken from one hung at the palace gate) and of Han, late King of Tangut. This last, who had fourteen sons, was, for his goodness and justice, reverenced as a god. He was of a dark complexion, his beard of a chestnut colour mixed with grey, and his eyes protuberant.

From Lhasa, or Barantola, they came in four days to the foot of the mountain Langur,[4] which being exceedingly high, travellers can hardly breathe at top, the air is so very thin; neither is it to be crossed in summer without great danger from the exhalations of certain poisonous herbs. Besides, as no waggons or beasts can pass it for the rocks and precipices, they must proceed on foot almost a month till they come to Kuthi,[5] one of the two chief cities of the kingdom of Nekbal.[6] This mountainous tract is plentifully furnished with springs both hot and cold, which issue from all parts of the mountain, affording store of

[1] Hami is one of the Muhammadan cities of Kansuh, beyond the Great Wall, at the eastern end of the Tian Shan mountains. The roads along both sides of the range meet at this point.

[2] This may be Kam, the eastern division of Tibet.

[3] The Dalai Lama in Grueber's time was the fifth since the establishment of the Yellow sect by Tsong-khapa, and bore the name of Ngawang lobdzang ghiamdzo. (See 'Mag. Asiatique,' ii. 214.)

[4] This is the range crossed by the Laghulung-la (pass) and the Dango-la. (See the map of the routes in Eastern Nepal, by explorer No. 9 under Colonel Montgomerie.) According to Brian Hodgson, Langur is a general name for a mountain pass, equivalent to *La* in Tibetan, and *Shan* in Chinese; *Tagh* in Turki, and *Ula* in Mongolian.

[5] This place was visited by No. 9, whose route seems to have been identical with the missionary's. It is also called Nilam.

[6] This form of Nepal is unaccountable. Perhaps it is a misprint for Nehpal. The Chinese name is Palpou (see D'Anville's maps). According to Brian Hodgson, the name is derived from Né, the sender to Paradise, who is Swayambhu Adi-Buddha; and pāla, cherished. It is Naipála in Sanscrit. The Brahmans assert that Né is the proper name of the Saint or Muni who first settled the country.

fish and pasture. From Kuthi, in five days, they came to the city Nesti,[1] still in Nekbal, where provisions are so plentiful that thirty or forty hens are sold for one crown.

From Nesti they came, in five days' journey, to Kadmendu,[2] the metropolis of Nekbal, where reigns a potent king. From Kadmendu, in half a day's time, they came to the city Nekbal,[3] called also Baddan by the natives, the regal city of the whole kingdom.

The first letter relates that Nekbal is a month's journey in extent, and has two capital cities, Katmandir and Patan, separated only by a river. The King, called Partasmal,[4] resides in the first, and his brother, Nevasmal (a young handsome prince), in the latter. He had the command of all the troops in the country, and while Grueber was there had a great army in the field to oppose a petty king, named Varkam, who made frequent incursions into his dominions.

The Jesuit presented this prince with a telescope, wherewith having discovered a place where Varkam had fortified himself, he desired the prince to look that way, which he did, and seeing the enemy so near, cried, "Let us march against them!" not considering that the seeming approach was the effect of the glass. It is not easy to express how pleased he was with this present. He likewise gave the King other curious mathematical instruments, with which he was so taken that he determined not to let them go, but that they promised him faithfully to return. In that case, he promised both to erect a house for their use, endowed with ample revenues, and grant them full power to introduce the Christian law into his kingdom.

In this country, when a man drinks to a woman, the company pour in the liquor *cha* or the wine three times for the parties, and while they are drinking affix three pieces of butter to the brim of the cup, which those who pledge them take off and stick on their foreheads.

They have a most cruel custom in these kingdoms; for when they judge their sick people to be past hopes of recovery, they carry them

[1] This is the Listi of No. 9, at the southern entrance of the remarkable gorge by which the summit of the Southern Himálaya is crossed in coming from Kuti.

[2] Kathmandu.

[3] Nekbal city, or Baddan, "the regal city of the whole kingdom." Although Kathmandu has become the residence of the Gorkha conquerors of Nepal, and Bhatgaon is described by Kirkpatrick as a superior place, the old capital, and the favourite residence of the Brahman priesthood, still the Baddan of the missionary is Lalita Patan, another considerable city in the same valley as Kathmandu.

[4] Pratap malla, king of Kathmandu, and Yoga Narendra malla, king of Patan, 1689. (See Prinsep's Tables of the Rajas of Nepal, p. 116.) There is no account of the petty king Varkam, probably Vikrama.

into the fields, and casting them into deep ditches full of dead corpses, there leave them to perish, and their bodies, when dead, to be devoured by birds and beasts of prey, esteeming it an honour to have living creatures for their tombs.

The women, out of a religious whim, never wash, but daub themselves with a nasty kind of oil, which not only causes them to stink intolerably, but renders them extremely ugly and deformed.

From Nekbal in a journey of five days you meet with the city Hedonda,[1] a colony of the kingdom of Moranga,[2] inclosed in Tibet. From the names of Dominic, Francis, and Antony, still in use with the natives, it appeared that Christianity had been planted there in times past.

In the first letter we are told that in Moranga he saw no towns, but only houses, or rather huts, made of straw, and among them a custom-house. The King pays yearly to the Great Moghul a tribute of 250,000 rix dollars and seven elephants. From Hedonda (crossing the kingdom of Maranga), in eight days they came to Mutgari,[3] the first city of the Moghul's empire. From Mutgari is a journey of ten days to Batana,[4] or Patan, which is a city of Bengal, on the Ganges. From Batana, in eight days they came to Benares, a populous city on the Ganges, famous for an academy of the Brahmans, where persons are instructed in their religion and sciences. From Benares, in eleven days they came to Katampur,[5] and from thence in seven more to Agra. So that from Peking thither was a journey of 214 days, but reckoning the time which the caravans rest, it will come to about fourteen months. Here Dorville, the companion of Grueber in his travels, died. The author's travels from Moranga are related, with some variation, in the first letter. It is there said that from thence he entered India and came to Minapor,[6] the metropolis of the country, where he crossed the Ganges, twice as broad as the Danube. Thence

[1] Hitounda of Brian Hodgson, a town at the foot of the mountains, 44 kos from Kesriah, a port on the Gandak, and 19½ kos from Kathmandu. Merchandise is conveyed by bullocks from the river to Hitounda, whence it is carried over the mountains by athletic porters ('Bengal Selections,' No. xxvii. p. 22. 1857).

[2] Probably the Murung or Terai, the swampy region between the mountains and the plains. If there is no discrepancy in connection with Radok, which is said to be the capital of Moranga, the reference may be to Rohtut, a district of the Nepalese government of the Terai, the principal place of which now appears to be Kuttioul. (See 'Kirkpatrick's Nepal,' 40, 41, and the map of Nepaul, 1855.)

[3] Mutgari, "the first city of the Moghul's empire" (reached by the missionaries). This is Motihari, in the district of Sarun.

[4] The city of Patna, on the Ganges.

[5] No place more likely than Cawnpore.

[6] Dinapúr.

he travelled to the city Patna, and from Patna in twenty-five days to Agra, the chief royal seat of the Moghul's empire, eleven months after he had left China.

This first letter furnishes us also with an account of his travels from Agra to Europe, and several other particulars not to be met with in Kircher's Memoirs. From Agra he got in six days to Delhi, and from Delhi in fourteen to Lahore, on the Ravi, which is as broad as the Danube, and falls into the Indus, near Multan. At this last place he embarked on the Indus, and in forty days journeyed down to Tata, the last city of Hindustan, and residence of a Viceroy called Laskarkan. Here he found many English and Dutch merchants. From thence, sailing to Ormuz, he landed, and passing through Persia, Armenia, and Asia Minor, came to Smyrna, where, putting again to sea, he arrived first at Messina, and then at Rome, fourteen months after he had left Agra.

He had not been long at Rome before he received orders to return to China. Accordingly he went into Germany, and from thence to Poland, with a design to cut out another new road through Russia, having, by the Emperor's means, obtained passports from the Dukes of Curland and Muscovy. But when he arrived on the borders of Russia, news came that the King of Poland, in conjunction with the Tatars, had invaded the Grand Duke's dominions. Fearing, therefore, that it would be difficult to get to Moscow, called by the Tatars Stoliza, he thought it best to return to Venice, which he did just at the time the Emperor was sending Count Lesly on an embassy to the Porte. In the train of this lord he travelled to Constantinople, designing to take his way through Natolia, Persia, and the Indies; but on his arrival he was seized with a violent flux and pains in the stomach, so that, being unable to proceed, he returned by sea to Leghorn, and thence to Florence. Here his disorder abating, he repaired to Venice, in order to pass through Friuli to Vienna, and so to Constantinople, once more to attempt getting to China by that road. But how he succeeded we do not find.

The author, in 1665, when he set out on his return to China, was about forty-five years of age, of an affable temper and extremely civil, joining to other good qualities the German sincerity, which rendered his conversation perfectly agreeable. The variations found in the letters seem to be owing to the defects of the author's memory, and mistakes of those who took the relation from his mouth. With regard to the Chinese and Tatars, he has explained some things more fully than other authors have done, as well as related others in a different manner.

TABLE OF LATITUDES OBSERVED ON THE JOURNEY.[1]

	°	′	″
Sining	36	10	0
Lhasa, or Barantola	29	6	0
Khatmandu	27	5	0
Hedonda	26	36	0
Batana, on Ganges	24	44	0
Benares, on Ganges	24	50	0

II.

A Letter from Father Ippolito Desideri, Missionary of the Society of Jesus, to Father Ildebrando Grassi, a Missionary of the same Society, in the Kingdom of Mysore. (Translated from a French translation by Du Halde in the 'Lettres Edifiantes,' vol. xv. *p.* 184.)

LHASA, *April* 10, 1716.

REVEREND FATHER,—The peace of our Lord be with you. Having been appointed to the Tibetan mission, I left Goa on the 20th of November, 1713, and arrived at Surat on the 4th of January, 1714. Being compelled to sojourn here awhile, I took advantage of my leisure to learn Persian. On the 26th of March I set out for Delhi, whither I arrived on the 11th of May, and where I joined company with Father Manuel Freyre, who had been appointed to the same mission as myself. On the 23rd of September we together began our journey towards Tibet. We went by way of Lahore, which we reached on the 10th of October, and where we had the pious satisfaction of administering the sacraments of repentance and the Eucharist to some Christians, who were bereft of any spiritual pastor. We left Lahore on the 19th of October, and in the course of a few days reached the foot of the Caucasus.

The Caucasus is a long range, consisting of remarkably steep and lofty mountains. After crossing one mountain you encounter a second still higher; this is in turn succeeded by a third, higher than either of the two former ones; and the farther you go the higher you climb, till you reach the highest of all, named Per-Pangial.[2]

[1] These latitudes, according to the latest authorities, should be as follows:—

°	′	″		°	′	″	
36	39	20	Jesuit surveys.	27	26	0	Pundit.
29	39	17	Pundit.	25	35	0	Indian survey.
27	41	28	„	25	17	0	„

[2] Pír Punjal, a pass on the first range of the Himálaya, which is crossed in going to Kashmir.

The Gentiles hold this mountain in great awe; they bring offerings to it, and in their superstition worship a venerable old man, whom they believe to be guardian of the region. Herein is doubtless contained a reminiscence of the fable of Prometheus, who, according to the poets, was bound in chains to the Caucasus.

The summits of the highest mountains are always covered with snow and ice. We took twelve days to traverse these mountains on foot, crossing at times, with incredible difficulty, impetuous torrents, which, formed by the melting of the snow, dash down with extreme violence amid rocks and boulders. The torrents which we had ever and anon to stem, and the rocks, made it an extremely difficult business to get across, and often was I compelled to hang on by the tail of a bullock to avoid being carried away by the force of the stream. I do not speak of the extreme cold I had to suffer, through not having taken the precaution to obtain clothing suitable for so rude a climate.

This country of mountains, though in other respects so inhospitable, is pleasing through the number and variety of its trees, the fertility of the soil, and the different races which inhabit it. Some petty States here are dependent on the Moghul. The roads are nowhere impracticable for a horseman or for a *jampan*, a sort of palanquin.

On the 10th of March[1] we arrived at Kashmir. The enormous quantity of snow which falls during winter, and which absolutely closes up the passes, obliged us to remain there for six months. An illness, apparently caused by the first hardships I had undergone, reduced me to the last extremity. I did not fail in continuing my study of Persian, and in making inquiries respecting Tibet; but though I took every pains, I could only learn about two Tibets. One extends from the north to the west, and is called Little Tibet, or Baltistan. It is a few days' journey from Kashmir, and its inhabitants and its princes are Muhammadans and tributaries of the Moghul. However fertile this country may be in other respects, it is sure to be barren as far as preachers of the Gospel are concerned; for a long experience has taught us only too surely to expect but little fruit in countries where rules the impious Muhammadan race.

The other Tibet, which is called Great Tibet, or Bhutan, extends from the north to the east, and is rather more distant from Kashmir. The route thither is pretty well frequented by caravans, which go every year in quest of wool, and as a rule runs through defiles. The first six or seven days' journey are not very trying; but as one goes on travelling becomes very difficult, through the wind, the snow, and the excessive rigour of the biting frosts, to which must be added

[1] March appears to be written in mistake for November.

having to rest at night on the bare ground, and at times on snow and ice.

Great Tibet begins at the summit of an enormous snow-clad mountain, called Kantel.[1] One side of the mountain belongs to Kashmir, and the other to Tibet. We had left Kashmir on the 17th of May, 1715, and on the 30th, the festival of our Lord's Ascension, we crossed the mountain and entered Tibet. Much snow had fallen on the path, which winds between mountains as far as Leh, or Ladak, the fortress where the King resides, which are the very picture of desolation, horror, and death itself. They are piled one atop of another, and so close as scarcely to leave room for the torrents which course impetuously from their heights, and dash with such deafening noise against the rocks as to appal the stoutest traveller. Above and at their foot the mountains are equally impassable; you are therefore forced to make your way about half way down the slope, and the path, as a rule, is so narrow as barely to leave room for you to set down your feet; this obliges you to pick your way with extreme care. A false step, and you are precipitated down the abyss with the loss of your life, or at the least with broken limbs, as befel some of our fellow-travellers. Were there bushes you might cling by them, but these mountains are so barren that neither plants nor even a blade of grass grows thereon. Would you wish to cross from one mountain to another, you must pass over the foaming torrents between, and there is no bridge, save some narrow, unsteady planks, or some ropes stretched across and interwoven with green branches. Often you are obliged to take off your shoes in order to get a better foothold. I assure you that I shudder now at the bare remembrance of these dreadful episodes in our journey.

Trying as the climate is, there is no food save the flour made from *battu*,[2] which is a kind of barley. The people of the country eat it unprepared; but we generally made a broth of it, and it was no small thing for us to get enough wood to cook it.

One's eyes are terribly tired with the reflection of the sun's rays from the snow, which dazzles and nearly blinds them. I was obliged to bandage mine, and admit only just enough light to see my way. Then, every other day or so, we encountered customs officers, who,

[1] According to Vigne, the summit of Bultul (Zoji la pass) is the Mount Kantul of the old maps. It is north-east of Srinagar (Kashmir), on the road to Baltistan (Little Tibet).

[2] A *chenopodium*, something like the *quinua* of Peru. It is cultivated at heights of more than 5000 feet, chiefly for its grain, but the leaves are also used as a pot-herb. (See 'Punjab Plants,' by J. L. Stewart, M.D., Lahore, 1869, p. 179.)

not content with demanding the usual dues, exacted all they pleased by any right they fancied.

In these mountainous regions there are no large towns. There is no particular coinage, that of the Moghul being chiefly used; each piece of money is worth five Roman Giuglii. Trading is usually carried on by exchange of goods. The journey from Kashmir to Ladak we made on foot, and it lasted forty days, so that we reached the last-named place on the 25th of June. The kingdom of the second Tibet begins, as I have already remarked, at Mount Kantel,[1] and extends north-eastwards. There is only one Gyampo, or sovereign ruler; the present one is called Nima Nangial, and he has a tributary king below him. The first races one meets are Muhammadans; afterwards they are Gentiles, but less superstitious than idolatrous nations usually are.

Here is what I learnt of the Tibetan religion. They call God Konciok; and they appear to have some notion of the Holy Trinity, for at times they call him Konchok-chik (one God), and at other times Konchok-sum (three Gods). They use a kind of chaplet, over which they repeat these words: *Om, ha, hum.* This they explain by saying that *Om* signifies knowledge or an arm, that is, power; *ha* is the word, and *hum* is the heart or love, and that these three words mean God.[2] They also worship a being called Urghien, who, so they say, was born seven hundred years ago. When asked if he be God or man, some reply that he is both God and man, that he has neither father nor mother, but that he was born of a flower. Nevertheless they have statues representing a woman with a flower in her hand, and her they call the mother of Urghien. Many other personages do they worship and treat as saints. In their churches you may see an altar covered with a cloth and ornaments; in the middle of the altar is a kind of tabernacle, wherein, as they say, Urghien dwells, though there are some who assert he is in heaven.

The Tibetans have priests, called lamas. They are clad in a uniform different from laymen; they neither plait their hair nor carry earrings, as other men, but wear a tonsure like our ecclesiastics, and have to observe perpetual celibacy. Their occupation is to study the books of the law, which are written in a tongue and in characters differing from those ordinarily in use. They recite certain prayers in chorus; and theirs it is to celebrate rites, to present offerings in the temple, and to light the sacred lamps there. They offer up wheat, barley, paste and water, in little vessels of scrupulous cleanliness. Where an offering has been made, the remainder of the

[1] See *ante*, p. 304. [2] Om mani padmi hum. (See pp. 1, 29, 32, 337.)

food is eaten as if it were consecrated. The lamas are greatly respected; as a rule, they live together, shut out from all profane intercourse; they have local superiors, and also a general superior, whom the King himself treats with great veneration.

The King and many of his court look upon us as lamas of the faith of Jesus Christ, who have come from Europe. When he saw us reciting our prayers, he was curious to see what books we were reading, and he eagerly inquired the meaning of the various figures therein depicted. After having carefully examined them, some of them said among themselves, "*Nuru*," that is, very good. They remarked two things: firstly, that their book was very like ours. This similarity I failed to perceive; but one thing I am certain of is, that though many may know how to read their mysterious books, not one can explain them. The second observation they made was: "Oh! if you knew our language, or if we understood yours, what pleasure it would give us to hear you expound your religion." This proves that this people is well disposed to taste of Christian truths.

The Tibetans are naturally gentle, but uncultivated and coarse. There are neither arts nor sciences among them, though they are not wanting in intelligence. They have no communications with other nations; no sort of meat is forbidden to them; they do not hold the doctrine of the transmigration of souls, and do not practise polygamy; three points in which they differ widely from the idolatrous natives of India.

As you may have learnt from what I have said, the climate is very severe, and winter prevails nearly all the year round. The mountain tops are always covered with snow; the soil yields only wheat and barley; trees, fruits, and vegetables being rarely seen. The houses are small, narrow, and built of stones piled in rude fashion one above the other. They use nothing but woollen stuffs for their clothes. While we were at Ladak we had no other lodging but the hut of a poor Kashmirian who lived on charity.

Two days after our arrival we went to call on the Lompo, who is next in rank to the King, and commonly called his right arm. On the 2nd of July we had our first audience of the King himself, who received us seated on his throne. On the 4th and 8th we were again summoned to his presence, and he then treated us more familiarly. On the 6th we paid our respects to the Grand Lama. He was accompanied by several other Lamas, one of whom was a son of Lompo, and another a near relative of the King. They received us most honourably, and presented us with some refreshments, as is the custom of the country.

These honours and tokens of friendship did not, however, drive all anxiety from us. The wool trade serves to draw many Muhammadans from Kashmir to Ladak. Some of these, prompted either by jealousy or hatred of the very name of Christians, told the King and his ministers that we were in reality rich merchants, with pearls, diamonds, rubies, jewels of various sorts, and other valuable commodities in our possession. An officer of the court came to our lodgings; everything was opened before him, and the report he made thereon excited the King's curiosity. His Majesty ordered to be brought unto him a basket and a leather bag, in which we carried our smaller effects, such as linen, books, writings, some instruments for self-mortification, chaplets, and medals. The King examined everything, and then openly declared that it gave him greater pleasure to inspect goods of this sort than to see pearls and rubies.

Affairs were in this state, and I was thinking of tarrying in a country where I had resolved to suffer whatever it might please Providence to inflict upon me; I was in the highest degree overjoyed at having found a settled State, where I could labour towards the salvation of men's souls; I was already beginning to learn the language, with the hope of seeing some of my teaching bring forth, even among these barren rocks, fruit acceptable in the sight of Him, when we learnt that there was a third Tibet. After several consultations, it was decided, against my wish, that we should go thither and discover it. The journey takes usually from about six to seven months, and the route lies through countries of deserted aspect, and scantily peopled. This third Tibet is more exposed to the incursions of the border Tatars than the other two Tibets.

We left Ladak on the 17th of August, 1715, and we arrived at Lhasa, whence I have the honour to address you, on the 18th of March, 1716. I leave you to imagine what I had to suffer during this journey, what with snow, ice, and the excessive cold of these mountains. Shortly after our arrival, certain tribunals of the country occasioned us a good deal of annoyance. Thanks to God, this storm was appeased in the following manner. I was passing by the palace to attend one of the tribunals, when the King, who was seated in a balcony with one of his ministers, happened to be informed who I was. Our case had been made known to this minister, who is a thoroughly just and equitable man, and he took occasion to represent to the prince the wrong that was being done to us. The King immediately summoned me to his presence, and gave orders that we should be no more troubled.

A few days after I called upon the minister referred to, and he good-naturedly rebuked me for not having yet presented myself to the King. I excused myself on the ground that the custom of the country did not allow people to approach those in authority without making them some present, and that I had nothing worthy of so great a monarch's acceptance. My excuse, though genuine, was not listened to. I was obliged to obey, and repaired to the palace. More than a hundred people of consequence were awaiting audience in the hall. Two officers took down their names, according to custom, and carried the paper in to the King, who immediately gave orders for my admittance together with a Grand Lama. The Lama's present was a handsome one, while mine was quite insignificant; but nevertheless that of the Lama was deposited at the entrance, according to custom, while the King ordered mine to be brought to him, and to show how pleased he was with it, kept it by him. This in the court is considered an exceptional mark of favour. He made me sit down opposite to him and quite close, and for the space of two hours plied me with innumerable questions, without speaking a word to the others present. At last, having made my final compliments, he bade me good-bye. On several occasions after my first visit I strove to take advantage of the King's kindly disposition and to discourse of our holy religion, and of the mission I wished to undertake in his kingdom, but unfortunately I had no opportunity of doing this. This monarch is of Tatar race, and some years ago he conquered this country, which is not very far from China, for it takes only four months to travel hence to Peking. Not long since an envoy came thence, and he has since returned to Peking.

Having given you, Reverend Father, this brief account of my travels, and of what has happened since my arrival in the capital of the third (province of) Tibet, it only remains for me to entreat the aid of your prayers. After undergoing so much suffering, I need them sorely to sustain me in the labours of the ministration to which by Divine favour I have been called, all unworthy though I be. In the hope of sharing the blessings of your holy offices, I subscribe myself, &c.,

IPPOLITO DESIDERI.

III.

BRIEF ACCOUNT OF THE KINGDOM OF TIBET,

BY

FRA FRANCESCO ORAZIO DELLA PENNA DI BILLI,[1]

1730.[2]

THE word Tibet is a Tatar corruption, the proper term being Thobot, or Tangut katzar. Tangut means dwellers in houses, and katzar country or kingdom; so the whole expression signifies "the kingdom of dwellers in houses," the Tatars dwelling in tents of felt, or of a coarse material woven from the hair of the yak or hairy ox, and the Tibetans in houses. Tibet, in the language of the country, is called Poôt, and the inhabitants Poôt ba, while in the language of Nekpal it is called Seen, and a Tibetan, Seena. In Hindustani, Tibet is called Butant, and a Tibetan Butia. The capital of Tibet is called Baronthala in the Tatar tongue. *Baron* signifies right, *tha* towards, and *la* south; so the whole means, on the right hand, southward. In the Tibetan tongue it is called Lha-sà, which means Land of God.

According to the royal ministers, who are expressly charged with the duty of keeping count of the numbers of the population of the whole kingdom, the total amounts to thirty-three millions,[3] of whom 690,000 are soldiers. The families of those provinces which have to furnish youths to be monks are exempt from supplying soldiers. The provinces of U and Tzang together contribute 130,000 soldiers, at the rate of one for every three families. The state of Kham contributes 360,000 soldiers at the same rate, while those of Ngari and Chang maintain 100,000 each, at the rate of one for each family. From the states of Hor and Amdoa no soldiers are taken, from motives of mistrust, as the first are adherents of the Tatar rather than the Tibetan cause, and usually speak the Tatar language, while the second dwell on the confines of China beyond the Great Wall, and speak more Tibetan than Tatar and Chinese. The provinces of

[1] Francis Horace were the author's baptismal names. Penna di Billi is the name of the district where he was born. It is situated in the march of Ancona, about twenty miles from Macerata. Keith Johnston's 'Gazetteer' places it in a different position, twenty miles W.N.W. of Urbino.

[2] Published by Klaproth, from the autograph manuscript of the author.

[3] Klaproth thinks this an exaggeration, and would fix it at five millions only.

Kombo and Takpo furnish soldiers in the same way as the other states. The figures I have omitted to notice, and must give them conjecturally. I think that together they may supply 140,000 soldiers, one from every three families. The kingdoms of Brukpa[1] (in Hindustani, Laltopivala), Lata or Ladak, and Nekpal are now subject to and have voluntarily made themselves tributary to Tibet, after the Emperor of China had made himself master of it.

The following are the kingdoms and provinces of Tibet: the kingdom of Lata or Ladak, which to the west abuts on Kashmir, to the south the Mogol, to the east Ngari, and to the north Tatary and (I believe) the Usbek Tartars.

Ngari is divided into three provinces, Ngari Sankar, Ngari Purang, and Ngari Tamo. Ngari Sankar is bounded on the west by Lata, on the north by Tatary, and (I believe) by Gaskar or Kaskar, on the east by Ngari Purang, and on the south by the Mogol. Ngari Purang is bounded by Ngari Sankar on the north, and for two points on the west, on the north by Tatary, on the east by Ngari Tamo, and on the south by the Mogol. Ngari Tamo is bounded on the west by Ngari Purang, on the north by Tatary, on the east by the province of Tzang, and on the south by the Mogol. The province of Tzang is bounded by Nekpal on the west, on the north by Ngari Tamo, on the south by Lho ten ke and Bregion,[2] and on the east by the province of U. Towards the west the furthermost town of Tzang is called in Hindustani Kuti or bitch, and in Tibetan Gnialam and Tzongtu, which means the place whither the merchants resort to bargain with one another. The easternmost place is called Kambala, which is the name of a great mountain, on the slopes of which are many (inhabited) places, and in the plain at the foot to the south is a great lake called Iandro,[3] which is eighteen days' journey round, according to those who have made the circuit, but within are some hilly islands. The same lake has no outlet that I know of, and during a day and half's march round it, I can vouch that I saw none; while as regards the remaining portion, I have the authority of those who have made its circuit. To pass

[1] Bhutan. (C. R. M.)

[2] Sikkim. (Klaproth.)

[3] Probably the correct spelling is Yang dhro, warm and extensive. The Tibet name is Phal dhi yu mthso, or the lake of the turquoises of Phal-dhi, a town or village to the north of the lake. In the middle of the lake are three mountainous islands, named Minaba, Sangri, and Yabotu, which are inhabited by some men who pasture herds of yaks. Many fishermen also live there: their boats are of leather. The lake is very full of fish, but its waters are salt and bitter. See the "Description of Tibet," in the second vol. of my 'Magasin Asiatique' (Paris, 1826, 8vo.), p. 285, and 'Nouveau Journal Asiatique,' vol. iv. p. 295. (Kl.)

Mount Kambala one has to ascend certainly for half a mile, and then to descend for five good miles, after which one comes upon a very large river called Chasum, Tzampo, or Tzangchu,[1] which rises in Ngari. It passes three days' journey distant from Lhasa, and continues its course under the fortress of Sgikakungar,[2] and before arriving at Takpo Cini it loses itself, during a whole day's journey, in Lhoga;[3] they say also that it flows under a mountain, because after passing this mountain one comes upon the river again; from Takpo it passes by Kombo, and they say that it joins the Ganges towards Ragmati or Shategang. The capital of this province (Tzang) is called Sgigatze.[4] The kingdom of Bregion, or Bramashon,[5] is bounded on the north by the province of Tzang, to the south by Mon Altibari and Brukpa, or Laltopivala, to the east and south by Lhoba, to the east by Kako and Kombo, and to the west by Maronga and Nekpal.

The province of U is bounded on the west by Tzang, on the east by Sharbigonti, on the south by Ialba and Takpo, on the north by Chang, while its extreme points are Kambala, Sharbigonti, Talung, and Ratren, in the west, east, and north respectively. The capital of U is Lhasa, and near this city flows the river Tsangchu, which rises in Sharbigonti, and joins the river Chasum, near Chuchur, three days' journey from Lhasa. U signifies "middle," as this province is in the middle of Tibet; and Lhasa, which is situated in the middle of the province, is called the navel of the wealthy kingdom of Tibet.

The province of Chang is bounded on the west by Ngari, on the north by Kokonor, on the east by Kham, on the south by U. In the province of Chang is situated the duchy of Dam, which is eight days distant from Lhasa, and in Dam there is nothing else but the palace belonging to the King and his court, the remainder of the inhabitants (which are mostly Tatars and the other Tibetans) dwelling in tents of felt and of cloth woven out of hair. Two days distant from Dam is Nak chu ka, where is the last fortress of Tibet, but no other dwellings except tents, as before mentioned. In this place there flows a large

[1] This river is generally called Tsang po tsin, or the pure water. (Kl.)

[2] A fortress on the right of the Tsangchu and to the north-east of Lake Yang mtso. Robbers are generally drowned in the river, but sometimes as an act of favour they are sent to Sgikakungar, or Ji-ka-ghong-kar, where the unhealthiness of the spot usually kills them within a year. (Kl.)

[3] L'ho ka, or L'ho k'ha pha, is the name of some cannibal mountain tribes north and north-east of Assam. (Kl.)

[4] One of the largest towns of Tibet, situated about one *kos* north-east of Tashi-lumbo. The river Churerku, which is very deep and about three hundred paces wide, flows two or three hundred yards distant. It is crossed by an iron bridge on eight arches, called Sambachur, or the eastern bridge. (Kl.)

[5] Sikkim. (C. R. M.)

river called Nak chu,[1] which means black water, and has given the name to the place. For about forty days' journey there are no more houses to be seen, but only tents and numerous herds of yaks or hairy oxen, flocks, and horses; travellers can buy nothing to eat but meat and butter, and are obliged to carry everything else with them. After tràversing this country one reaches a very large river called Bichu,[2] which, as Signor Samuel Van der,[3] a native of Fleshingh, in the province of Zeland, in Holland, has written of it, is so large, that to cross it in boats of skins he embarked in the morning, and landed on an island in the evening, and could not complete the passage across till the middle of the following day. In the vicinity of the river there is a large population, which live in tents. At the distance of about a month's journey hence one comes to Zoloma,[4] the people of which also live in tents, and after five days' journey more one reaches Kokonor, which is the northernmost limit of Tibet in this direction.

The province of Takpo is pretty extensive, and is divided into seven districts, among which are Takpo Chini, where the Capuchin missionaries have a hospice, and Takpo Chara, which is bounded on the north by U, on the south by Kombo, on the east by Kham, and on the west by Tzang.

The province of Kombo is bounded on the north by Takpo, on the east by Kham, on the west by Bregion and Lhobei, and on the south by Lhò k'haptrà, *Lhò* meaning south, *k'hà* mouth, and *ptrà* cut, because in infancy the lips of the children are cut and coloured red, yellow, blue, and otherwise in the incisions.

Kham is bounded on the west by Bikum, Takpo, and Kombo, on the north by Kokonor and Chang, on the east by Tarchenton, China, and Amdoa, and towards the south by Bengal, Siam, or Pegu and Tonquin. The state of Kham is divided into the following twelve provinces: (1) Tzava Kham, which is bounded on the west by Bikum and Takpo, on the east by Pombor Kham, and on the south by Lhò k'haptrà. (2) Pombor Kham, which is bounded on the west by Tzava Kham, on the east by Mingara Kham, on the south by Bengal, and on the north by Bichu. (3) Mingara Kham, which is bounded on the west by Pombor Kham, on the east by China, and, it is believed, by the province of Chentofu and Amdoa, on the south, as far as it is believed, by Pegu, and on the north by Kokonor. (4) Ketong Kham, which is bounded on the west by Kombo, on the east by Tzava Kham, to the south, as far as is known, by Pegu or

[1] The upper Lu-kiang. (Kl.)

[2] The Murui-ussu, or Upper Yang-tse-kiang. (Kl.)

[3] Van de Putte. See p. lxii of Introduction.

[4] "The junction of three rivers," where the road from Sining to Lhasa crosses the upper Hoang-ho. (Kl.)

Siam, and on the north by Kokonor. (5) Chungbu Kham, which on the west is bounded by Talung, on the east by Chamto, on the south by Shopado, and on the north by Chang. (6) Konchuduru Kham, which on the east is bounded by Kemorang, on the west by Chang, in the direction of Dam, on the north by Kokonor, on the south by Bha,[1] which, whether it belong to Pegu or Tonquin, is unknown. (7) Chamto Kham, (8) Kemorong Kham are provinces, of which not only the boundaries, as in the case of the other four provinces, but even the names of places are uncertain, as information could not be procured from those who knew, and, through the jealousy of the Tibetans, it has been found impossible to copy a map in the palace of Varanga (?) or Lhaprang.

The King of Tibet is also ruler over the state of Amdoa, mentioned above, which is bounded on the east by China, on the north by Kokonor and Chang, on the west by Kham, and on the south by Tonquin, Pegu, or Siam, as far as is known; but this is not known for certain, as the Tibetans have very little knowledge of those countries and the states neighbouring them. Amdoa is divided into the following provinces, Chenisgungba, Iarba, Ara, Margniu, Tzator, Tariong, Tebo, Ngaba, Sunggiu, Korlung, Chusang, Samblo, Tongor, Kungbung, and they say that there are others, but there was no opportunity afforded us of ascertaining these matters, owing to the necessity for not awakening suspicions.

In all these provinces there are cities, estates, castles built of stone and other durable materials. The native tongue is Tibetan, but they speak also Tatar and Chinese, and possess a high class of intellect. In my time nearly all the lecturers and lamas of the university, masters of the Supreme Lama, and the Grand Lamas who have been born again, came from Amdoa, a province from which they do not draft soldiers, as mentioned above.

Between Tatary and the provinces of Chang and Ngari are the people of Hor,[2] who are of mean intellect, wear their hair in tresses and dress in the Tatar fashion; they live in tents, and speak both Tatar and Tibetan, but the former with greater facility. In the province of Tzang there are two large and several small rivers. One rises in the Langur mountain and flows as far as Sekia, and then turning south traverses the state of Bregion or Bramashon, and Bengal, where it joins the Ganges under the name of Ponchu.[3] The other river, called Sanchu, comes from the north, it is believed from

[1] Bha is the country of Bha, or Bhatang (plain of cows). (Kl.)

[2] Hor, according to M. Csoma de Körös, is the name applied by the Tibetans to the people of the Turk race in Central Asia. (Kl.)

[3] The Tísta, which however does not rise in Mount Langur, but in some mountains to the north. (Kl.)

Chang larzi, flows to the south of Sgigatze, passes Giantze and Pari, leaving Bregion on the west, and joins the Ganges in Bengal.[1]

The boundaries of Tibet on the east meet those of China and Tarchenton.[2] This state or province, I believe, joins China beyond the Great Wall. In ancient times, when the Grand Lama was both the spiritual and temporal ruler in Tibet, the Emperor of China always gave him supreme authority over it, but when the Emperor gained possession of Tibet, in 1720, he reserved the chief power for himself. This country produces abundantly several species of tea, with which it supplies the whole of Tibet, which on the south is bounded by Bengal, Lho ten ke, Altibari, Mon, Brukpa, Lhoba, Lhò k'haptrà, Shapado, Bha (to whom this belongs is not known), and, as far as can be told, with Pegu, Siam, and Tonquin; on the west by Kashmir, a part of the Mogol, Nekpal, and Moronga; on the north by Usbek, Gaskar,[3] and Giongar[4] Tatary, and it is believed by Yarkand and Kokonor. Giongar is derived from *Gion*, left, and *kar*, hand; and Kokonor from *Koko*, blue, and *nor*, lake; these being Tatar words. In the Tibetan tongue Kokonor is called Tzoka, which is derived from *Tzo*, lake, and *ka*, dwellers. Kokonor is also called Tzo ngonbo, which means blue lake, the water being blue. The Tibetans pretend that this lake belongs to them, and that the limits of Tibet adjoin those of the town of Shilin or Shilingh. From this lake there issues no river. The five rivers which the old maps show as issuing from a lake, whether it be the above-named Iandro or Iantzo, which is three days' journey west of Lhasa, or Kokonor lake, which is about one day's journey from Shilin, on the confines of Tibet, these being the only two lakes in that country, are absolutely imaginary, as no river at all issues from those lakes; but there are other large rivers, as mentioned above, viz. Tzangchu, in the province of Tzang, and Nakchu and Bichu, in the state of Chang, as well as two others which I have forgotten. These facts are derived from well-informed persons, who also state that the Ganges rises in Ngari towards Tatary.

It appears fitting here to record what has been told to me by those who have travelled through and beyond Tibet.

The river Erchis divides Muscovy from the whole of Tatary. Towards the confines of the latter, between the west and south, dwell the Turkut[5] Tatars, who voluntarily became subjects of Mus-

[1] Klaproth says there is some confusion here.

[2] A large fortified town not in the maps.

[3] Kaskar or Kashgar. (Kl.)

[4] Dzungar. (Kl.)

[5] These are the Torgod Kalmaks who left Russian territory to place themselves in subjection to China. (Kl.)

covy, on condition of being provided with the means of sustenance, their own country being barren. They profess the same religion as the Tibetans, a fact which I know from this, that in 1730 their king died, and his queen and son sent some nobles with an escort of 300 men and plenty of money and other gifts to Lhasa, to make prayers and offerings to the Grand Lamas and convents for the benefit of the late king's soul. They went by sea, landed in China,[1] and from thence journeyed to Lhasa, which they reached in October, 1731, and where I had several conversations with their chiefs, carried on by means of Tibetan interpreters, their own language being Tatar and a little Muscovite, while they are not entirely ignorant of Christianity.

In the map Kabul is inserted, but the name is called Kamul. About a month's journey from it is Turfan. Kaskar is a kingdom, the capital of which is called Kaskar, and is distant three days' journey on horseback south from Yarkand. Andigen is a city and kingdom, distant from Kaskar a month's journey southward. Yarkand is the name of the kingdom, and the capital is called Yarkand. The people of Yarkand, Kaskar, and Usbek are for the most part of the Muhammadan religion, and speak Turki. Samarkand, Bokara, and Balak are nearly wholly Muhammadan, and speak Persian, while the people of Turfan, between Yarkand and Kamul, are mostly Muhammadans, and speak Turki. Turfan belongs to Giongari, and Kamul to China. The people of Andigen, Turfan, and Kamul profess Muhammadanism, but those of Andigen speak Tatar, and the other two, Turfan and Kamul, Turki and Tatar. From Shilin or Shilingh to Kamul, the merchants with their caravans take forty days on the road, and twelve from Kamul to Turfan, whence their route runs in a north-west direction. Tarsy, a district of Amdoa, is a good day's journey from Shilin.

Regarding the situation of our five religious houses, I may mention that the first is at Chandernagor, in Bengal, in latitude 22° 20′ north, where the sun is in the zenith on the 3rd June and 9th July. The second is that of Patna, in the kingdom of Behar, twenty days distant from Chandernagor, and in latitude 26° 30′ north. The third is in Nekpal, at Kadmandu or Batgao, in latitude 27° 30′. The fourth in the capital of Tibet, in Lhasa, in latitude 30° 20′. The fifth at Trongnge, in Takpo, about 30° north latitude.

[1] Evidently an error. The Embassy traversed Mongolia. The Kalmak king, who was called Ayuka Khan, died in 1731. (Kl.)

A Short Account of the Great Kingdom of Tibet, as far as regards the Position of the Country and its Products; the Food and Drink of its People; its Commerce; the Manners, Politics, and Temporal Rule of the People; the Administration of Justice; and a Succinct Abstract of the Great Chaos of Tibetan Laws.

The Kingdom of Tibet and its Products.—The kingdom of Tibet is mountainous throughout, and between the mountains there are plains, where are built cities and castles in the southern parts, and groves of willows and stunted trees have been planted, the mountains being destitute of everything except shrubs.

Towards the south, in the provinces of Takpo, Kombo, and Kham, there are forests, but in all the mountains in the provinces of Ngari, Tzang, U, and Chang, there are no shrubs, but only a few trees, too few indeed to supply beams for building houses, so that they only take the branches of the trees for fuel, and sell them at an extremely high price, as their usual practice is to burn the dung of horses, oxen, and other animals. The climate is extremely cold, and the summits of the mountains are covered with snow all through the year. Owing to the great altitude and the rudeness of the bleak winds which there prevail, the ground for six months is hard as rock, and the climate and soil being alike inhospitable, no poisonous animal is to be found.

Sowing takes place in the beginning of May; they gather little wheat, little being sown, much barley, and some peas which they bruise (as they do not cook them), and give to horses and cattle, the latter crop being gathered in September. These harvests, as well as that of rape (from the seeds of which oil is made), yield sixty-fold, and in good seasons eightyfold. The people sow nothing else, except some small red turnips, radishes, garlic in large quantity, and a few very small onions. In the southern parts nothing else is found, with the exception of a few nuts, some small peaches, and wild apples (in Trongnge there are some wild vines which yield a few grapes), and a few different sorts of flowers, make up the total of the fruits of the earth.

For clothing purposes they have only cloth of wool, serge, or yarn, blankets, which are at the most a palm and a half wide, and skins with the hair on. There are many gold mines in the provinces of U, Tzang, Chang, Takpo, Kombo, and Kham, and silver (as far as is known) in the province of Kham. There are also mines of iron, copper, and another mineral, of a white colour, like tin, which is called *tikzà*, and is worked into a sort of brass by being mixed with copper; of sulphur, vitriol, cinnabar, cobalt, turquoise stones, a yellow substance called *paula*, borax, rock-salt, a white mineral earth, used in the houses instead of lime; another species of earth, bright and corrosive, used instead of soap, to eradicate stains and cook food quickly; square stones of three kinds, the colour of iron; of silver and of gold; mountain crystals, which are used for flints, and alabaster; rhubarb and other medicines are to be found. There are numerous mineral springs, and medicinal springs, both hot and cold, which, however, are not good for drinking purposes, owing to their being mixed with the aforesaid minerals.

There are horses, a few oxen like ours, but extremely small, oxen peculiar to the country with long hair, which are used as beasts of labour, mules, sheep in abundance, goats, cows, which yield plenty of milk, from which butter is obtained in large quantities, but not cheese, which they know not how to make, small pigs, whose flesh is not unlike the other flesh they eat, a great number of very large dogs, and a few fowls. As regards wild animals, there are a few hares, a large quantity of musk rats, marmots, a few stags and goats, and hairy oxen. The birds comprise sparrows, a few larks, ravens, falcons, eagles and other birds of prey, wild ducks and geese in abundance. There is also plenty of fish, but from the first day of the year to the end of the seventh month all fishing is prohibited, while the killing of birds is always prohibited.

Food.—The Tibetans drink a quantity of tea, made with milk, butter, and salt, and leave a little tea in the cup, in which they make a paste with barley meal, and afterwards eat it. For dinner and supper they make the barley-meal paste with tea or water, and eat it with meat or fish, which they eat raw, or with dried meat without salt. Well-to-do people, however, live rather better.

Commerce.—The above-mentioned minerals, woollen cloth, yarn, woollen blankets, musk, and the foregoing animals, paper made in Takpo and Pari, in the south of the province of Tzang, are all, as far as Tibet is concerned. From other kingdoms, as well as from China, come porcelain, glass in small quantities, fabrics of raw and prepared silk, brocades, white and coloured cotton fabrics, sewing silk and thread, tea in small quantities (the greater part coming from the state of Tarchenton), and other things. From Nekpal come cotton cloths, wrought brass, and copper. From Mogol come white and figured cloths, silk, and embroidered stuffs, brocades, scarlet, corals and amber (these last three articles from Europe), small diamonds, and other things. From other kingdoms come other goods; and I believe that the merchants must make great gains, as they will borrow money at interest from 120 to 140 per cent., and give a pledge in addition, in order to secure their loan.

Morality.—The Tibetans, speaking as a rule, are inclined to vindictiveness; but they know well how to dissemble, and when opportunity offers, will not fail to revenge themselves. They are timid, and greatly fear justice; so that when they commit some crime, through timidity and dread of justice they know neither how to apply a remedy nor to take to flight, and if taken before a judge, at the first or second examination they confess; and if they do not make open confession, they nevertheless betray their guilt by the confusion in which they involve themselves. If, however, they are protected by some great lord, they lay aside all fear, and become arrogant and proud. They are greedy of money; and yet they show admiration for those who are independent thereof and disinterested. They are also somewhat given to lust; but this is more owing to their atrocious laws than to any real inclination thereto. They are addicted to habits of intoxication and to drinking barley beer, and a kind of brandy (mixed with the beer referred to), which does not differ greatly from the beer which the Tatars make from the milk of mares, and which is like water in appearance and taste, but is of considerable strength. They are but slightly loyal to their chiefs, and are fond of new forms of government and revolutions, as it would appear from the Tibetan histories; but the causes of the most recent disturbances were the monks. They are also dirty and nasty, and without refinement; but from their intercourse with the Chinese in 1720 they have begun to be a little more cleanly and civilized.

Notwithstanding the above-mentioned objectionable qualities and blameable habits of the Tibetans, they have some good points, among which, being generally intelligent (although not equal to the people of the state of Amdoa, who are extremely quick), they are gentle and humane and amenable to reason, the laymen submitting to the precepts of the land more readily than the monks, who are most obstinate in defence of their sect, but who, when convinced, abandon their opposition and even their former tenets; as, when convinced by the arguments brought by the Capuchin missionaries against magic, they ceased to practise it any further. They (more especially the laymen) are much given to piety and devotion and to almsgiving, and in these pious works they take no count of money or riches, more especially when they wish to pray for the souls of the dead; while in almsgiving they are not less generous, but even institute solemn prayers and many sacrifices, calling together many monks for those spiritual duties, and they consider it a great crime to keep back the smallest coin belonging to the deceased. The monks also do not fail to give alms and do other works of charity to the deceased.

As far as I have seen and heard, and judging from my knowledge of the country, there is great modesty observed in the dress and behaviour of women, in their appearance in public, and in their own houses in private throughout the kingdom, Lhasa and some other commercial towns being excepted, as the variety of the nations which there meet has brought about rather more liberty. At dances women dance with women, and men with men, and it would be considered a great scandal were a man and a woman to dance together.

The Political and Temporal Government.—Before 1706 the Grand and Supreme Lama[1] was master of all Tibet, but in order that he might be able better to attend to the spiritual rule, he kept as protector of the kingdom a Tatar, of the family of the chief of the thirty-two petty rulers of Kokonor, Talakuchy,[2] to whom he gave the name of King, a dignity which descended from father to son, while in

[1] Lama means that there is no one higher, and it is applied to the superior of a convent. These lamas are of various kinds. Some are called lamas born anew, and these are supposed at death to pass from one body into another. The Grand Lamas belong to this category, and are many in number, each of them having several monasteries under him, the superiors of which are elected by the Grand Lama, either for their virtues or as a mark of favour; and from this post they are not removed during lifetime, except for very grave offences, albeit sometimes they are transferred from an inferior convent to a higher one, from which cause they are called elected lamas, and not lamas born anew. The Supreme Grand Lama cannot exercise authority over the monks of the convents, who depend on the other Grand Lamas to create them lamas of the university. The Grand Lamas, however, are not subject to the supreme one, although he and (at the present time) his deputy take precedence of them, and in differences between them the Supreme Lama or his deputy is he who decides. These people hold and believe that the bodies of these lamas are instructed by the soul of one of the Chanchub, which are numerous, as mentioned above. (Della Penna.)

Lama, or *bLama* as it is written in Tibetan, signifies priest or superior priest. In the term *Talai lama*, *talai* is a Mongol word meaning sea or ocean, and is a translation of the Tibetan *rGhia mtso* of the same meaning, a title which has long been adopted by the upper members of the Buddhist hierarchy. (Kl.)

[2] The celebrated Guchi Khan turu baikhu. He was the first of all the Dzungarian chiefs who received a title at the hands of the Manchu dynasty of China. Under the Dalai Lama of the fifth generation, great troubles arose in Tibet. Tsang-pa Khan, chief of the nomad tribes in the country, endeavoured to do away with Buddhism. The *diba* or viceroy of the kingdom invoked the aid of Guchi Khan, who came, and having beaten Tsang-pa Khan, placed his own son Dayan Khan on the throne of Tibet. (Kl.)

default of male issue, the Supreme Grand Lama elected some other member of the same family, giving him as appanage the whole of the province of Chang both for revenue and rule. This king resided during the summer at Dam, and the winter at Lhasa, in the palace of Kaden khang sar, and it was his duty to defend the kingdom, with his own Tatar and the Tibetan soldiery of the kingdom, from the invasion of foes, extending his political rule only over the above-named Tatars, but for military purposes and in times of war over the Tibetan soldiers as well.

The Supreme Grand Lama had also another Tibetan of great rank, chosen for his ability, nobility, intelligence, and wisdom, to whom he gave the name of *Tisri*; and the authority conferred on him by the same Supreme Grand Lama in the political rule of the whole kingdom was so great, that the same Tatar king had to give way and place in public meetings to the *Tisri*, without, however, being subject to him. This Tisri, in public meetings and on the occasion of visits from the Supreme Grand Lama, had to dress in the garb of a monk. The Tisri alone had the right of electing the four *Khalongs*, or ministers of state, on whom he conferred the power of electing the governors subordinate to the governors-general of provinces, and of chief towns throughout the kingdom, these being elected by the Tisri alone, similarly with all the other principal ministers and upper officers of the whole kingdom, while he reserved to himself the power of life and death, and other matters of great import, which he could not entrust to the authority of the ministers of state or governors-general, or other chief officers. By this organization of the ministry and temporal offices, the Supreme Grand Lama managed to avoid being burthened with any political matters, except appeals to him against the decision of the Tisri, and to devote increased attention to spiritual matters and laws.

The last Supreme Grand Lama, absolute ruler of Tibet, by name, *Loszang-rincen-tzang-yang-ghiamtzho*, which means "great and best heart and sea of the musical or concerted song of Tzang" (which is a place of the Lha[1] or gods), although he was possessed of great and conspicuous abilities, was liberal almost to prodigality, and a lover of

[1] *Lha*, gods, those who receive the reward of their good deeds by transmigration into other bodies in places of delight, which number in all thirty-two, and to one of which (according to the amount of their good deeds) the passage is effected. The books of their laws say that they can sin, but not perform meritorious actions, and in proportion to their sins, past or present, they then transmigrate into beasts, or into Tantali, or into hell: and if they have no sin they become men again. The *Lha* in places of delight, are invoked and revered. (Della Penna.)

magnificence, nevertheless lived in very dissolute fashion, and neither the Tisri, whose name was Sangkie Ghiamtzho, nor the Tatar king, Ginkir Khan, nor the Emperor of China, nor the King of Gionkar, nor the Chiefs of Kokonor, through their ambassadors, could prevail on him to abandon his wicked ways. In this year 1706 there were great dissensions between the king, Ginkir Khan, and the Tisri Sangkie Ghiamtzho, which finally resulted in the king, Ginkir Khan, causing the Tisri to be assassinated. After the event the above-named Supreme Grand Lama still continued his dissolute life, and the king, Ginkir Khan, being unable to endure it any longer, determined, with the consent of the Emperor of China, to depose him. Wherefore, pretending that the Emperor of China had summoned him to his presence, for the sake of honouring him, from the convent of Brepung or Brebon, whither the monks, being all armed and numbering above 60,000, had forcibly conducted him for safety, the valour of the King's arms tore him from the hands of the priests and led him to Dam, where (as is commonly reported) the King caused him to be decapitated. But the historical work, called *Naue c'iu len i k'hyk' hun ka sgiuso*, in referring to it says that in order to attend very carefully and hear with joyful heart the registration of events (that is in this book), he was sent to China, and on the road died of dropsy, and this happened towards the end of the year 1707, in which year, on the 12th June, our first Capuchin missionaries from the march of Ancona, forming the Tibetan mission, arrived.

After these events the king, Ginkir Khan, made as Supreme Grand Lama the lama of the monastery of Chapohri,[1] named *Ngawang yi shie ghiamtzo*, into whom, as the Chokhiongs pretended, not the soul but the breath of the former one had passed.

In the year 1709 there arrived five ambassadors from the Emperor of China, who bore his commands to all the Tibetans to recognize the above-named lama as the true Supreme Lama, and the King Ginkir Khan as the true and lawful King of Tibet, which was done by all.

It must be mentioned that the soul of the deceased Supreme Lama, according to the foolish notion of the Tibetans, had passed into the body of a child, son of a Tibetan monk who had been driven out of the monastery of Brepung or Brebon, in the city of Lithang, province of Kham, and who, they say, was thus born again. He was born in 1706, and the report then spread that the Grand Lama was born again, so that a great number of monks and scholars came to recognize him; but as the Emperor of China wished the one nomi-

[1] Id est, "iron mountain." (Kl.)

nated by the Tatar king, and whose appointment had been confirmed by him, to hold the spiritual power, he caused the child and all his family to be taken and guarded, and this was done with the aid of 5000 soldiers. He was placed in the fortress of Shilin or Shilingh, and kept there till 1720, in which year the Chinese army, composed of 107,000 Chinese soldiers and 30,000 Tatars, retook the metropolis of Lhasa, and made themselves masters of the whole of the kingdom of Tibet, on the 20th September, and overthrew completely the Gionkar Tatars, who had treacherously invaded Tibet, and with the connivance of a great part of its people, had plundered the country, and taken Lhasa, in November and December, 1717. The Chinese having thus retaken Tibet and Lhasa from the Gionkar Tatars, replaced in possession on the 6th of October, 1720, the said newly-born Lama, in whom alone the Emperor of China vested the spiritual rule, and appointed to the temporal and political rule, as subordinate to the Grand Lama, the king, Telchin bathur, in place of Ginkir Khan, who had been slain in the defeat of all the family of Gionkars.

In 1727, by order of the Grand Lama, of his father, of the three ministers of state, and of many nobles of the kingdom, the king, Telchin bathur, was assassinated in the royal hall on the 5th of August. In 1728 the Emperor of China sent another army of over 40,000 soldiers, ordered all those implicated in the crime to be arrested, and on the 1st of November caused seventeen of the ringleaders to be executed most cruelly, and many others who could not fly, and were concerned in the murder, were sent into China. On the 23rd of December in the same year, 1728, the Grand Lama and his father were led away, with their respective retinues, and placed in a fortress near Chen-to-fu; and the same Emperor selected as spiritual ruler instead the much-respected and powerful Lama of the monastery of Chotin, in the same province of U, four days' journey from Lhasa. His name was Kiesri-riboche, and he resided in the palace of Putala,[1] or at Brepung, as all the other Grand Lamas used to do. In 1729 the Emperor of China appointed as king of the said Tibet, and

[1] Putala is the name of the palatial residence of the Grand Lama, an extremely high edifice. Putala is built on a little hill, on the slopes of, and around which, there are monasteries. The Grand Lama never sits *on* the altar, but close to it, whether in church or in the palace, where there is a chapel with an altar. The Grand Lama rises to his feet and touches heads when the King, Grand Lamas who have been born again, ambassadors from other kings, and similar personages visit him. The late Grand Lama had 400 monks, elected by himself; this one has 200, but they are monks, not lamas, and from these are chosen the lamas of monasteries. (Della P.)

tributary to him, the present ruler Mi-vang, whom God prosper and render happy, so that he may embrace the holy Catholic faith, to which he, as well as all his family and subjects, are well disposed.

The same Emperor of China, in appointing king the above-mentioned Mi-vang, entrusted to him also the temporal, judicial, and political authority, as he had done with his predecessor Telchin bathur, thus depriving the Grand Lama entirely of all the temporal sway, so that at the present time the king *auctoritate propria* elects the four *Khalongs*, or ministers of state, the *Teba*, or *Deba chinbo*, which is the title given to the governors-general of the provinces and chief towns, as well as all the other ministers and upper officers and chiefs, giving them all authority in political and criminal matters, and in all military causes which are neither capital nor grave. In the selection of these governors-general, ministers, and upper officials, he consults the said four ministers of state, with whom and the other ministers the king holds counsel three times a week. In the absence of the king the first minister of state presides, but he takes no action on the deliberations without the approval of the king. The latter does not decide any case of importance or involving life and death without taking the advice and counsel of these ministers of state, the nobles of his court, and a secret council. The ministers, too, with the other councillors meet together every other day to discuss other causes of an ordinary character. It devolves on the ministers of state to choose the other governors, ministers, and subordinate officers, the subalterns and dependents of the governors of provinces, and of the chief ministers and officers, so that at the present day the Supreme Grand Lama has nothing left to him but the spiritual rule. As regards the monks, if they are professed monks, and for grave offences are expelled their monasteries, they are punished by the same tribunal which punishes those who are not professed; if however they are not guilty of a grave offence, the priests are punished by the chief lama of the monastery, or the Deputy Supreme Grand Lama, who at the present day rules instead of the Supreme Grand Lama, who is confined in the fortress near Chen-fu, as mentioned elsewhere.

Administration of Justice.—The Tibetan judges, who are three, award the punishments prescribed in their books, which may be called law books, and which assign penalties for misdemeanors in criminal matters as well as in civil disputes. There are besides other books which treat of similar matters, in the shape of glosses upon them, but the commentators have taken no heed of others which treat of religion.

There is a right of appeal from the chiefs,[1] who are ordinary judges, to other officials who review causes, from the reviewers of causes to the ministers of state, and from these (at the present day) to the king; and when the Supreme Lama was absolute in temporal matters, and appointed the Tisri to discharge these duties, they had recourse to him, and then in case of need to the Grand Lama himself; but with this caution from the ministers or chamberlains, not to refer the criminal cases of those condemned to bodily punishment, whether by flogging, cutting off the hand, or death, unless they wished the culprits to be pardoned, as they were sure of receiving pardon. They accordingly brought them before him only when they wished to pardon them, the Grand Lama being the fountain of mercy. The above-named three judges meet together in their courts at fixed hours, both in the morning and evening. In the morning neither merchant nor tradesman can sell anything until the said judges open the greater bar of their palace, which remains open by the market-place; towards midday they shut it up, and all shopmen must shut up their goods and return after dinner, in the same manner as in the morning, provided only that there is at least one judge in the palace.

I have not read many books of justice, and will only mention what little I have read and seen practised.

In civil causes it is necessary to produce writings, proofs, or testimonies, and according to these sentence is given; thus, if they deposit their writings, proofs, and testimonies to-day (unless the writings be long and require much deliberation) to-morrow they give judgment, and they first decide the case which is first brought before them, there being no need of feeing the judges or other officials, as they are all salaried by the royal chamber; and if a pecuniary fine be adjudged, they set it apart to be handed over to the ministers of state at the end of the year, as shall be told hereafter; if, however, there be neither writings nor proofs nor testimonies, in small cases, such as, for instance, in the case of a disputed loan, the judges cause dice to be produced in their presence, and he who scores highest is considered to have the right on his side. In matters of importance they give judgment in two ways: one is by placing two stones, one white and the other black, in a vessel of boiling oil, and, without seeing, by causing one of the stones to be taken out by the hand. If the stone be white and the hand uninjured, that man is in the right, without the other party having to dip his hand; if on the other hand he first encounters

[1] Chiefs, who are the judges of the common men, and who dispense justice in cases that come before them. In Lhasa there are three, who meet in their own residence, as mentioned in the other paper on the administration of justice. (Della P.)

the black stone, even if he does not injure his hand (for this ordeal they make use of a certain secret or magical art), he is adjudged liar, and the other must insert his hand likewise. The other method of giving judgment is to heat a long round bar of iron, and when red hot to cause the hand to be drawn along the whole of the bar, and if the hand be not injured the right is on his side.

In criminal cases of a different character, abuse, blows, and the like, a fine and a beating are inflicted; and if the culprits have no money, they double the number of blows, the same practice being observed in the case of the women. The practice in flogging the men and women is to place them on their faces on the ground, and to inflict the requisite number of blows with long sticks on the bare buttocks. But if the accused was drunk at the time, there is no penalty. If he has struck a blow and the blow be not fatal, imprisonment and a certain number of blows are adjudged, the penalty being lessened if the accused was intoxicated; if the blow proves mortal and the injured party dies after a certain number of days, the accused is shot to death with arrows, or thrown into the river with a great stone round his neck. If the death is immediate on the quarrel, they preserve the corpse and take and bind the murderer to it, and after twenty-four hours bury both the dead and the living together. In quarrels where spectators see weapons of offence drawn, they are bound to interfere, and should they fail in doing so, they are liable to fine as well as those who take part in the same. If masters, either in their senses or when intoxicated, strike their subordinates or servants, even if they should kill them, there is no penalty attached thereto; they are merely held in bad repute and lose their good name, so that they cannot be promoted to any dignities.

At the end of the year the three judges of Lhasa present the account and proceeds of all fines, and by order of the king those for civil cases are placed in the royal chamber, and those derived from criminal cases are set apart as presents to the monks for the sacrifices and prayers offered up by them. The judges under the governors-general observe the same practice, and submit their account to the king direct.

In cases of rape, if one be a monk and the other a nun employed outside of a convent as servant to those within and to beg alms for them, or if it be a nun of a convent which has not a *clausura*, such nun is expelled the service of the convent and sent home, which is reckoned a great dishonour. If she be a professed nun, the dishonour is very great, and she cannot marry even though she might find a suitable match. If the monk has taken the vows, he is expelled his cloth, and for some years he is sent into the mountains among wild animals; if neither he nor the nun be professed, and if they are willing to marry, there is no penalty; but if they do not marry, the monk is expelled, and bastinadoed in public, and banished from that part; and if the ravisher of a nun be a layman, he is branded on the forehead and banished from the kingdom.

Regarding adultery, the same penalty is awarded to the adulterer that the husband exacts from the adultress; and if he should refuse to take her back she returns to her home dishonoured, but if he consents, she returns to live with him. And concerning divorce, if they go before the judge, the judge examines both sides, and if the woman be in the right, the husband is bound to restore to her all her dowry, and to give her besides four *analy* of barley (every *analy* weighs about two Roman pounds, 24 ounces French weight) for every day of their married life up to the date of divorce; if the man be in the right, the woman forfeits all her dowry and returns to her former home. As regards other offences against the Sixth Commandment, there are penalties attached to them, but I have neither read nor have I been informed concerning them.

With regard to theft, when the thief is caught he is cast into prison, and when he has confessed his crime, if the property be recovered it is handed over to the owner; if the goods have been sold, the receiver thereof forfeits both the goods and the money, the property being handed over to the rightful owner; if the money be recovered from the thief, the judge claims it for the royal chamber; if he has spent it, he who has received it is bound to restore it and hand it back in the same way for the royal chamber; if the thief has stolen money in coin, it is restored to its owner, and the judge inflicts a fine on the thief for the chamber, and if he be poor the corporal punishment is doubled. If the thief has stolen but little, and it is his first offence, they imprison him and give him a flogging; if he has stolen much, and from private individuals, the flogging and imprisonment are doubled. If on the occasion of his first offence he has stolen much or little from the royal chamber, or in the royal palace, or in the monasteries or temples, he is thrown into the river, but often as an act of mercy they cut off both his hands; if he has stolen for the second time they cut off his left hand, if for the third time both the hands, and then cast him into the river; and if they do not cast him into the river, as an act of mercy they send him alive to the fortress of Sgikakungar, four days south of Lhasa, where, through bad treatment and fatigue, they do not often live beyond a year at the most, while there are few that even reach the place.

If the thief be a monk and the theft be committed in his own monastery, for small thefts the superior of the monastery inflicts punishment, and for great thefts, the Supreme Grand Lama, or in his absence the Deputy; but at the present time for a theft of consequence, or for other crimes committed by monks, the king tries the cause. If a monk steals from laymen, from temples, or from other people of consequence, and to a considerable amount, he is first expelled the monastery, and then the judges cast him into prison, and when the property is recovered they send him to tend wild cattle on the mountains, either for life or for a period, or else he is flogged and sent into banishment. It is, however, wrong that the buyer of the stolen property, although he may not know that it is stolen, and may have paid a proper price for it according as the thief may ask, from whom it is impossible to ascertain whether it be stolen or not, should lose all the money he has paid; and still worse that they should believe the thief, who may say that he has sold the property to such an one, although it may be untrue, and (as has happened several times to my knowledge) an innocent man is compelled to give up the property or its money's worth.

There are many other penalties for divers other crimes, but I do not recollect them, and I have not brought with me the book which treats of the administration of justice and the penalties awarded to criminals. In the case of strangers they considerably diminish the penalties. The tortures they inflict as a mark of disgrace or otherwise are flogging, dipping them naked up to the head in cold water, and then drawing them out and beating them with thongs of leather, and then plunging them in again and repeating the process several times; wounding them slightly with knives, and smearing the wounds with salt; binding them naked to a post in the public square, and leaving them there all day; or else fixing them naked in a frame or gibbet of wood. They also inflict other tortures which I do not remember, until they extort a confession of their crimes from the criminals.

It is also the custom, if as a special favour the corporal punishment is commuted into a fine, and the culprit through his poverty be unable to discharge it, for five or six principal folk who are charged with the duty of begging alms, to collect all sorts of goods, till the desired amount is reached, and the judges take the same goods until they are sufficient to satisfy them completely, and set free the culprit.

Another custom is for twelve other people of consequence, who are appointed for the purpose, and charged with the duty, to go to the king, and beg off as a favour some criminal condemned to die or to suffer some severe bodily punishment, and if the king be disposed to show mercy he grants an audience to these gentlemen, and when he is unwilling to show mercy, he refuses them audience, on some pretext or other. The above-named gentlemen of rank, when anyone is condemned to death, go with many persons of consequence and many people to make the circuit of the temple many times, and also when the condemned man is led to suffer punishment, the ministers of justice, together with the culprit, make the circuit of the temple, followed by many people.

Tibetan Laws.—The books of Tibetan laws, which they look upon as gospel, consist of eight hundred large volumes, called *K'hagiur*, which means translated precepts, that is, precepts translated from the Hindustani into the Tibetan tongue. This *K'hagiur* has its commentaries, which consist of more than four hundred books, and they have many other books of history and philosophy, in which are many things which the teachers of religion and the people hold as articles of faith. In this very voluminous law of the *K'hagiur* they are told that there are eight millions of worlds actually existing besides our own visible and palpable one. This last and another world only owe their creation to the agency of the inhabitants of the other invisible worlds; but the manner in which these two worlds were created being a lengthy matter, and it being desirable to follow the same brevity as previously observed, I omit recording it. All the other worlds are *ab æterno a parte ante*, and one *a parte post*, as shall be mentioned. The souls of all living beings are eternal *a parte ante et a parte post*, the law is *ab æterno* and *a parte ante*, but not *a parte post*, because when all transmigrations are at an end, and the living conveyed into paradise, as shall be told presently, all law is at an end.

This law teaches that in some of the fabled worlds there is no law, and in all the other worlds, where there is law there is also paradise, which they believe to be *etiam a parte ante, et a parte post*, as they believe all the souls of the living beings to be, excepting, however, this visible world of ours, where they do not admit of a paradise, but instead, thirty-two places of bliss, to some of which are conveyed those who have attained the position of saints in this world, where there are *Lha*, who are like gods. They imagine these places to be in the air above that great mountain about 160,000 leagues high (the Tibetan league consists of five miles), and 32,000 leagues in circuit, which is made up of four parts, being of crystal to the east, of the red precious stone called *peimaraca* [1] (which I believe is ruby)

[1] Sanscrit, *padmarâga*, ruby. (Kl.)

to the west, of gold to the north, and of the green precious stone called *bendruie*[1] to the south. In these abodes of bliss they remain as long as they please, and then pass to the paradise of other worlds.

According to their law, in the west of this world there is an eternal world, *a parte ante* and *a parte post*, where there is a paradise, and in it a saint called *Ho pahme*, which means saint of splendour and infinite light. This saint has many disciples, who are all *Chang chub*.[2] These *Chang chub* have not yet become saints, but they possess in the highest degree five virtues, called Chinba, Tzultrim, Szopa, Tzontru, and Samden, which mean great charity, both temporal and spiritual, perfect observance of laws, great patience in whatever event may occur, great diligence in working to perfection, and the most sublime contemplation. These *Chang chub* have finished their course, and are exempt from further transmigrations, passing only from the body of one Lama to that of another; but the Lama is always endowed with the soul of the same *Chang chub*, although he may be in other bodies for the benefit of the living to teach them the law, which is the object of their not wishing to become saints, because then they would not be able to instruct them. Being moved by compassion and pity they wish to remain *Chang chub* to instruct the living in the law, so as to make them finish quickly the laborious course of their transmigrations. Moreover, if these *Chang chub* wish, they are at liberty to transmigrate into this or other worlds, and at the same time they transmigrate into other places with the same object.

The transmigration of the soul of any living being from one body to another, as remarked already, is a point of primary importance in the Tibetan laws, and for these transmigrations there are six places assigned.

Firstly, those of the *Lha* or of gods. These places are almost innumerable, although they only assign them here thirty-two; just as they forget the shape of the Tibetan world in the description of the great mountain in the middle of the said world. Besides these places, the same law says that there are places of transmigration for the *Lha* in

[1] Sanscrit, *vaidûryya*, or lapis lazuli. (Kl.)

[2] *Chang chub* means the spirit of those who, on account of their perfection, do not care to become saints, and train and instruct the bodies of the reborn lamas, as for instance, the Chenretzi, Sembachenbo, Isetrung rimboche, &c., so that they may help the living and put an end to their numerous transmigrations, as can better be seen in the other written abstract of their law. (Della P.)

The word is written, in Tibetan, *Byang tsiub*, and means "accomplished." It is the name given to those beings who have attained the highest degree of perfection next to Buddha. (Kl.)

the seven planets, and in all the stars, where the souls transmigrated into the *Lha* will receive the reward of their good works for a fixed time, in proportion to their good deeds; after which happy existence the *Lha* go to receive the punishment due to them for their sins, committed either before passing into the places of the *Lha* or during their sojourn in those places, for they admit the possibility of sinning in the place of bliss of the *Lha*, just as these same *Lha* can sin and not do meritorious actions. To receive their punishment they pass in the shape of other bodies into places of punishment, as shall be told anon; but if they have not sinned since enjoying their reward, they transmigrate into bodies of men.

The second place is that of the *Lha ma in*, or of demigods, and it is the only one where the souls pass with other bodies to receive the reward of their good works. They do not, however, have here as many pleasures as in the other places of the *Lha*, which have been described, but much fewer.

The third place is *Tudro*, which is the place of all sorts of animals and beasts, where souls are transmigrated for venial sins and mortal offences.

The fourth place is that of the *Ita* or Tantalus, whither they migrate with other bodies to receive the punishment of sins of a less venial character, and of graver mortal offences.

The fifth place is that of *Gnielva*, or hell, whither the souls with other bodies go to receive the punishment for mortal sins which have not been expiated by pain. There, in proportion to the greatness of the men, they receive torments; in process of time, which is of exceeding length, though not infinite, on completing their punishment, they transmigrate, if they have committed no crime, into men, and if they have committed fresh sins, they either increase their punishment in hell or pass into beasts and Tantali.

In all the above-mentioned places every soul must take a fresh body, because, as they say, the soul separated from the body can receive neither reward nor punishment.

The sixth place, *Gikthen*, is this world, or rather mankind in it, and this is the best transmigration of all, since here they can do good and work deserving actions, and cancel sins by pain and resolutions; while in the other places they cannot do this. The blind, deaf, lame, and crippled, are thus afflicted on account of some small mortal sin of other transmigrations unexpiated by pain, while the poor, menials, labourers, peasants, and others who are occupied in manual labour, servants, and slaves, are thus transmigrated for the same reason. Property, riches, nobility, the authority of great people, of princes, of the king, as taught in their law, is due to the good works done in other transmigrations for the good of others. They wish to be saints, as said above, and even the *Chang chub*, according to their legends, change many times into kings.

It is an article of their faith that anyone observing all laws during the period of five hundred transmigrations, without committing any sin, becomes a saint; but if he commits sins they increase proportionately the transmigrations until, by good works, they become saints. But before becoming a saint, a man must become *Chang chub*, and in order to become *Chang chub* it is necessary that in the last transmigration he at least be a monk, because scholars of whatever condition, rank, and eminence, although they may live correctly, cannot become *Chang chub* without first becoming monks in their last transmigration, as mentioned above. In order that the *Chang chub* may become saint, it is necessary that first he should have been a monk either in this world or in some other world, where law exists; and to know those who have become saints since the restoration of law, it is not necessary that it should be declared by some action, but he is recognized as such, when, in the last transmigration he has thirty-two signs in his own body and eighty qualities, and by these he is recognized as saint and adored. The signs are as follows: The mark of a wheel in the palms of the hands and feet, a soft skin of gold colour, a small twisted mark like a ring in the forehead, the fingers and toes webbed as in ducks, &c.[1] The qualities comprise walking like an elephant, flying like a bird, walking as upright as a pole, and walking always with the right foot first.

From all these saints united there proceeds one being, and this is the god which the Tibetans worship; by increasing the saints the being becomes greater, and when all mankind have become saints, the being will not be able to grow any greater. Its name is Sankia K'honchoa,[2] which signifies "the best of all," or, "god proceeding from saints," and it comes to be considered as the first person by them, distinguishing as they do the people who are really distinct one from the other, and all three constitute one being, or best and perfect substance.

The second person they call Cho K'honchoa,[3] God of Law, because these saints had restored the law to its pristine state; and as they had given the law, and it came from god, it has thus become god.

The third person is called Kedun-K'honchoa,[4] which signifies the

[1] In the Mongol history of Sanang setsen the same thing is said of the hands and feet of the first king of Tibet, who came from Hindustan. (Kl.)

[2] "The very precious Buddha." (Kl.)

[3] "The very precious law." (Kl.)

[4] "The very precious assemblage of the virtuous," i. e. the clergy. (Kl.)

assemblage of all the monks, which is god, because the saints, having restored the law, have consequently restored the laws and rules of the monks, and as all these saints were monks, and have as it were the very essence of the same monks, they call it Kedun-K'honchoa.

The law teaches that all these three persons are really distinct, but that the essence is one. The essence of this, their god, is united to a body, and this body is made of a precious stone like crystal or diamond, and they add this body because, as said above, the mind alone can neither enjoy nor suffer.

To this god of theirs alone they attribute pity, sympathy, and all other perfections joined to the highest degree of piety, but not justice or punishment, because they consider those to be opposed to pity. These acts of compassion on the part of their god do not operate *extra se* upon human beings, but only within him, because, although they do not believe him to be a punisher of evil, they do not look upon him as a rewarder of good, holding as they do that good and evil proceed from the good and bad actions of human beings, and in consequence that this power is the cause of all actions which really proceed from men's hearts, and not from god, who has within himself compassion only for the troublous and lengthy course of the transmigrations referred to.

The Tibetan law admits the presence of god, but through *multiplicationem corporum et animarum*, so that when one invokes him, or prays to him, or offers sacrifices, he is immediately present, though invisible, and seen only of those who have become *Chang chub*, and if he reveals himself to anyone else, it is because of the goodness of that man's heart, being, as he is, omniscient and knowing the hearts of all. All the good which this god can do is to impart good inspirations to the heart, through which men can do good if they will, unless they be hindered by the force of evil done in other transmigrations.

This law teaches that the essential part of the beatitude of paradise (and paradise they call *Teva chenbo*,[1] or, *Teva tzeme*, which would mean, place of greatest or immeasurable peace) consists in being free from the slightest trouble, and in having all imaginable joys, and in being ever *in amplexibus et illecebris absque consumatione.*

To the place of purgatory (to call it by our own term), the law consigns those animals and Tantali into which men have been transformed, and who are suffering punishment, by which, so they say, they purge their venial sins and mortal offences, believing, however, that during that period they can sin, but do no good. If they do not

[1] "The highest beatitude." (Kl.)

commit fresh sins in this purgatory the punishment is at an end, and they return again into men.

They believe also in a hell, reserved for mortal sins, for the expiation of which they assign eight places of torment by fire, and eight other places of cold and other torments. The judge of hell is a *Chang chub*, called Chenrezi, but as judge of hell he is called Shinche chio kiel, which means most upright and just king of law. This judge of their hell holds in his hands a very smooth mirror, in which he sees all the works and sins, according to which he judges. Each man has a *Lha* as guardian and as his advocate to represent to the judge the good actions of the culprit. The Lha at such times places in the balance the white balls, while on the other side there is a *Dre* (which is a sort of demon), who shows the wicked actions, and according to the number of the mortal sins he places in the other scale of the balance black balls; and according as the sins or the good works prevail he is judged. Of these kinds of demons there are two sorts.

The first are called Dre, who are no other than men and women, who from too great love of this world, or of riches, or corruptible beauty, or the like, do not on death experience any transmigration, but remain in *Parto*, which is the separation of the soul from the body for seven days, this being also an article of their faith; as, according to their law, when men and women die, the soul remains separated from the body for seven days before transmigration, and on the conclusion of those seven days the soul transmigrates according to its good or bad actions.

The above-named souls of the men and women remain in Parto, or are separated from the body, on account of the worldly lusts referred to above, not for seven days, but for a long series of years, wandering through the air enraged and disconsolate, and happy only when they can injure men, after which their satisfaction is turned into madness at not having inflicted greater injury, and on all mankind. When their term is expired they migrate to the hell called *Narme*,[1] and become a sort of demon called Dre, as has been said, being appointed ministers of justice in hell, and as they torment the condemned souls, so the more are they tormented by the others.

The other sort of demon is called *Tu*, which are also men and women who migrate to the place of the Lha, called Dokham or Dope kham, and who have no other object than perpetually to injure others. When these return to transmigrate into men they become very wicked, and always work mischief to others. The chief of this place, Dok-

[1] "The fire of suffering." (Kl.)

ham, is called Karob vang chu, and every day he shoots five arrows throughout the world, which are *Ngarkiel*, pride; *Dochia*, luxury; *Shetang*, wrath; *Pratoa*, envy; and *Thimu*, sloth; and those who are struck by these weapons are enrolled under his rule, and become wicked men. If this chief should transmigrate into the world or into others in the person of some king, in that time the kingdom will always be troubled, whether by war, or famine, or pestilence, and such a king will always oppress greatly his subjects. This kind of demon called Tu, as well as its children, is a tempting demon, and tempts men in the world to sin.

The last saint that restored the Tibetan law is called *Shakia Thupba*, which means the powerful one of the Shakias, which is the name of his family. In Hindustani he is called Shakia Muni, son of King Sezang Shakia, of the city of Serkiasgy, in the kingdom of Bengal, born through an enormous aperture in the right side of his mother Lha mo tzu prul,[1] a prodigious goddess, and brought up by a *Lha* called Kiachin.[2] He was washed in tepid water from heaven, and soon became a gold colour; and according to a story told to me in 1730, he first came into the world 959 years before Christ, or 2696 years ago. This Shakia Thupba restored the laws, which they say had then decayed, and which consist now, as said elsewhere, of 106 volumes, in which volumes the disciples of Shakia Thupba wrote all the contents of these books after the death of their master, just as they had heard it from his mouth. They say that there were first 300 volumes, but that the heretics (who were the Bracmans and their followers, of whom they say they converted many to their laws) burned 192.

In this kingdom of Bengal and its confines, and some other places, Shakia Thupba propagated his law. These volumes divide themselves into two kinds of laws, one of which comprises 60 books, which are called laws of Dote, and the other, which consists of 38 volumes, are called Khiute.

In the first 60 volumes, called Dote, the life of Shakia Thupba is recorded, with all his titles, and the deeds and miracles done throughout his life, which lasted 161 years, how his death occurred, and all that is here briefly referred to is told, as well as what the rule of the monk is, together with the different grades of dignity, the offices and functions of the monk. For novices, a stage which is of some years' duration, there are five commandments; and for those who have finished their novitiate, and up to the time of their profession, which every monk is at liberty to take or not, there are ten commandments; and

[1] The goddess of illusion. (Kl.)

[2] The Indra of the Hindus. (Kl.)

for those who have made their profession there are 254 commandments, beside three vows of chastity, obedience, and poverty; but poverty as among the monks, whose possessions, if any, go to the monastery on their death. The rule is the same for the nuns; and it is recorded in the said books that Shakia Thupba did not wish to lay them down, as he said that these nuns had prejudiced greatly the pure rites of the monks, as afterwards happened, as their writers say, which they extol as a truthful prophecy of this saint of theirs, who, however, to please his disciples, who were importuned by the women, instituted the rule as mentioned. Of the monks there are some who have no *clausura*, and can go out, but into whose monasteries no woman may enter. These monks have also monasteries with a *clausura*, so that women cannot enter without the licence of the superiors; and the monasteries of the nuns have also a *clausura*, so that neither scholars nor monks may enter, excepting he who has the special care of the monastery by order of the superior to whom the care of it properly belongs.

There are also the three ways of perfection of the beginners, the proficients, and the perfected, which comprise as it were methods of purging oneself, repentance for sins, because they recognize contrition and a resolve to correct one's ways, and a kind of confession almost like that of St. Augustine. All the monks, and nearly all the scholars, choose for themselves a lama or monk for spiritual father, and the penitent acknowledges having sinned before his spiritual father, and his spiritual father offers up a prayer for the remission of the sin which he has confessed. The spiritual father is called *Shiakpabo* at that time, which means one who pardons; he who confesses is called *Shiakiul*, which means penitent; and the act is called *Tholshia*, or confession. The second grade after this is to attend to the acquisition of the moral virtues; and third, to take part in the contemplation of the delights of a future life, free from all the affairs of this present life, pitying the innumerable miseries of men, and being subject to a laborious course of transmigrations.

There are also common commandments for all monks as well as scholars, but for a monk to transgress them is a much more serious affair than for a scholar. They are, firstly, not to kill (that is, either man or any sort of animal); secondly, not to commit fornication; thirdly, not to steal; fourthly, not to complain; fifthly, not to lie; sixthly, to love one's father and mother; and besides these six precepts, one is enjoined to watch the three doors, of the heart, the tongue, and the body, which would mean thoughts, words, and works. To husbands there is enjoined another obligatory precept, which is, that they shall not approach their wives in the daytime, but only at night, and only as often as the law allows, and not more. Having fixed the duties of married folk, it is fit to explain the rest. The law of the Dote ordains that those about to marry shall not take blood relations or connections unless the seventh degree be passed, and yet it is true that these great lords and nobles do not observe this; and in the marriage tie among people of no great means there is a very bad abuse not ordained by the law, but introduced by the abuse of it, that as many brothers as live in one house take one wife for all, and attribute the offspring to him by whom the woman says she was with child; but this seldom occurs with noble folk or those in easy circumstances, who take one wife alone, and sometimes, but rarely, more. The nuptials are celebrated thus: after having made the matrimonial contract, and arranged a day for the wedding, the bridegroom goes with his own relations to the house of the bride, where he will find the relations of the bride, and the father or the nearest relation of the bridegroom asks her whether she will take his son or relation for husband, and if she says yes, he places a piece of butter on the head of the bride; the father or nearest relation of the bride asks the same question of the bridegroom, and having both their consents he places a piece of butter on his forehead, as in the case of the bride. These rites having been performed the marriage is completed, after which they all go to visit the temple and go round it, and return to the bride's house, where, for fifteen days, they remain feasting, go about the city in company with the relations and friends, engage in conversation, and congratulate each other. At the end of the fifteen days the bridegroom conducts the bride to his home.

In this law of Dote there are prayers and methods of praying which the monks use, and modes of sacrificing, which consist in making pyramids of barley paste and rosettes of butter, white, yellow, red, blue, green, or other colours, and fastening them to that part of the pyramid which is seen. They then place them on the altars, if held in the temple, or on the little altars, which, as well as chapels, all the scholars and monks have in their own houses and rooms with their idols. These sacrifices are offered up every day with some prayers, both in the temples and houses, but only by monks appointed to the office of sacrificial duties. On other solemn occasions they sacrifice with songs and music, and the instruments are of several kinds. Some are like a sort of large flute, others like trumpets, being twisted and excessively long. There are also great conch shells, rattles, drums, tambourines, &c. The songs are figured and with notes, and the above-named instruments harmonise with them. There is also the sacrifice done by fire, and many things are thrown into it.

This is a long rite, and it is celebrated with songs and music and much solemnity, but not often. They also make many other offerings every day, both in the temples and houses of monks and laymen, such as plain water and water coloured with flowers, beer, and other things (beer they always place on the heads of men), all the first fruits, and, before meals, a little of what is served up. The pyramids, when offered up, are given to the poor, the beer to the monks and scholars, and the water, flowers, &c., are thrown away on the following day, and renewed if it is desired. There are many prayers, but the commonest among monks and scholars is this: *Hom mani peh me hum*,[1] which is a summary of magic prayer, having a great meaning attached to each letter. The meaning would take too long to explain, and is therefore omitted.

The monks and laymen have, if they please, two sorts of fasts, called Niunne and Nienne, meaning a rigorous and a plain fast respectively. The first they observe rigorously for four-and-twenty hours, neither allowing themselves to spit nor to smoke; and if any-one wishes to observe it for three days consecutively (as many do), they take every four-and-twenty hours, in the morning, only three cups of plain tea, in the Tibetan fashion. The other sort of fast, Nienne, is not so strict, as in the evening, if they do not eat, they may drink. But these fasts are held more for the scholars than the monks. The professed monks are enjoined during their lives to eat nothing after dinner, though they may drink, beer alone being excepted, and even this is forbidden to all monks to drink unless it be offered up or sacrificed. They are advised by their law, the monks more especially, to observe every year a period of spiritual seclusion, for ten or fifteen days, one month, or more, according to their wish. The well-to-do scholars and the great lords keep it in the monks' monasteries, and the King sometimes in the monasteries and sometimes in the principal palace; and at the time of seclusion no one does business with them, except when absolutely necessary. Another monk has the duty of supplying the wants of those in seclusion, without, however, speaking to them, except by signs; and if they are in their rooms, except for such brief time as they confer, they attend to the reading of their books, to prayers, and meditations on the miseries of human existence; and whoever wishes to confer with them must first obtain permission.

In the processions which they make during the year the priests carry a sort of surplice, little differing from ours, and the Supreme Lama, as well as all the Grand Lamas and re-born Lamas, and all the

[1] "*Om mani padmi hum.*" (See pp. 1, 29, 32, 305.)

superior Lamas of the monasteries, carry priests' capes, just like ours, worn simply over the religious dress. They have a sort of cross which they hold in veneration.

This is a very brief account of the law called Dote, by observing which they think they proceed more surely, though more slowly, on account of the number of transmigrations which they have to experience before becoming saint.

The other part of the thirty-six volumes of the law Khiute gives precepts for practising magic, and other foul matters of luxury and lust; and the monks and followers of this Khiute have monasteries and a temple, and rooms for the Lama or superior of the convent, but the monks eat and drink in common in the said temple. I have not read this infamous and filthy law of Khiute, so as not to stain my mind, and because it is unnecessary. For to confute it one must know in the abstract of what it treats, and there is little good or indifferent that is not mixed up with much more witchcraft, magic incantations, and obscenity. For the monks of this unworthy law it is enough that they learn by heart twenty-five papers to attain the doctor's degree; but for the other monks of the Dote to become doctors they must study philosophy for twelve years, and for six months in every year they have daily discussions. After the twelve years have passed they are examined and attain their doctorship. This law of Khiute is the shortest road to holiness, but it is uncertain and rough, because those who observe well the precepts of this law, and practice that which it teaches, can become saint in one life without any other transmigrations, but if they do not observe them well they increase their transmigrations, and very often go to the hell *Narme*, where they must remain longer than all the others, or are tormented more than all the others.

There is also in Tibet another law, called Urkien, which is worse than wicked, and consists entirely of magic and obscenities. Its lawgiver has also instituted monks and nuns, but different from those of Shakia Thupba, as the nuns of this Urkien are the wives of the monks, who have more than one. In this law of Urkien, as well as in the other two of Shakia Thupba, they teach you to make crowns of human bones, to use human skulls for magic goblets, as also out of the shin and arm bones to make pipes, or trifles with which to carry on incantations, sorceries, and every sort of magic.

If the monks are asked they visit the sick, being treated and fed with great liberality by the laymen. If the sick man is expiring or has breathed his last, one of the monks appointed to the task is called to extract the soul from the body by the top, by removing some hairs from the summit of the head, as it is an article of their faith that the soul does not issue from the top of the head for a good transmigration unless it be extracted by one of the appointed monks, in the manner described, because if it were not extracted so it would issue from the lower part of the body, and would take an evil transmigration.

This rite being performed, and divers prayers having been recited by the said monk, with the assistance of the friends and relations of the deceased, they consult the Chokhiong[1] as to what hour the dead man must be carried to one of the places set apart for the remaining rites, and take him thither with the above-mentioned people accompanying, and many others reciting divers things; and when they have arrived they celebrate other rites, placing the naked corpse on a great stone. Then a professed scholar, taking for himself all the clothes, breaks the corpse to pieces with a great bar of iron, and distributes it among the dogs in presence of all the company. After the mastiffs are satisfied, the relations of the deceased gather up the most clean-picked and the largest bones, and make a bundle of them, throwing all that is left by the dogs into the neighbouring river, near which are the places set apart for this inhuman rite. The men during the time of mourning never dress in silk, but only in wool; and the women take from their hats, and from every other part of their dress, the pearls and other precious ornaments, which according to the fashion of the country they are accustomed to carry at other times. They let down their hair and bind it upon their hats for six months, and for another six months they wear it dishevelled below the hat. If the deceased is of the first degree, for a year, and if of an inferior rank, for less. The relations carry the above-mentioned bundles of bones home. They

[1] *i.e.* defender of the law. This official is elected by the people by order of the Supreme Grand Lama, whom he assists, with the concurrence of the King, ministers of state, great lords, and many people, in the temple, on the occasion of a festival. He is chosen for his great experience in art magic. After being elected by the above-mentioned personages, and acknowledged by the people, he is consulted by the people in all private matters, and for his oracular replies in questions relating to the future. At the four seasons of the moon he goes out in public to make the *Kora*, or circuit of the great temple, being dressed in a costume peculiar to himself, with a retinue of servants, who carry standards, knives, and arrows; and walking proudly, poising himself on the tips of his toes, while from time to time he hurls knives and arrows, according as he is more or less possessed, and he who is struck goes and throws himself at his feet and places them on his own head. The said *Kora* having been made, he returns to his house and puts on the dress of a monk, if he be a churchman, and that of a layman if he be such. They elect many of these *Chang chub* in other cities and inhabited places. (Della P.)

hang them up in the room where the deceased was, and there for many days they employ monks to pray and sacrifice for the departed, that he may not suffer in his transmigration, distributing largely according to their means to the monks and the poor such goods and money as the deceased possessed.

On the anniversary of the death, the relations and friends, with the monks who were invited, grind to powder the above-mentioned bones, and carry them to the river, and for some days afterwards the monks offer up prayers and sacrifices as before, in the house of the deceased.

The corpses of some nobles, with the permission of the Supreme, or Vice-Grand Lama, are burned.

Those of the Kings, the Supreme or Vice-Grand Lamas, are burned with sandal wood, as well as the other Grand Lamas. Those of the monks and nuns are carried to the mountain tops as food for the birds of prey. The giving of the corpses to the dogs is done as an act of charity, so that after death they may be useful to the living. Those of the monks are given to birds, because they believe that the monks transmigrate into birds and other flying creatures, on whom they confer acts of charity by giving them the flesh of their own bodies. And this is all that can be told briefly respecting so prolix and intricate a subject as that contained in the confused chaos of Tibetan law.

FRA FRANCESCO ORAZIO DELLA PENNA DI BILLI,
Capuchin Missionary of the March of Ancona, now Prefect of the Mission of Tibet.

INDEX.